AHRC Research Centre for Textile Conservation and Textile Studies

THIRD ANNUAL CONFERENCE

Textiles and Text: Re-establishing the Links between Archival and Object-based Research

POSTPRINTS

AHRC Research Centre for Textile Conservation and Textile Studies

THIRD ANNUAL CONFERENCE *26–28 July 2005*

Textiles and Text: Re-establishing the Links between Archival and Object-based Research

POSTPRINTS

Edited by Maria Hayward and Elizabeth Kramer

First published 2007 by Archetype Publications Ltd.

Archetype Publications Ltd.
6 Fitzroy Square
London W1T 5HJ

www.archetype.co.uk

Tel: 44(207) 380 0800
Fax: 44(207) 380 0500

© Copyright is held jointly among the authors and Archetype Publications 2007

ISBN: 978-1-904982-26-5

British Library Cataloguing in Publication Data
A catalogue record for this book is available from the British Library.

The views and practices expressed by individual authors are not necessarily those of the editors or the publisher.

All rights reserved. No part of this publication may be reproduced, stored in a retrieval system, or transmitted, in any form or by any means, electronic, mechanical, photocopying, recording or otherwise, without the prior permission of the publishers.

Melinex, Perspex, Skala, Spectralon, Stabiltex and Tyvek are registered trademarks

Typeset by Kate Williams, Swansea
Printed and bound in Malta by Gutenberg Press Limited

Contents

Foreword
Maria Hayward
ix

Introduction
Elizabeth Kramer
xi

Into the archive

Researching the domestic interior: the example of the 'Chintz Lady', Elsie de Wolfe
Penny Sparke
3

'I have bought cloth for you and will deliver it myself': using documentary sources in the analysis of the archaeological textile finds from Quseir al-Qadim, Egypt
Fiona J.L. Handley
10

What Essex man wore: an investigation into Elizabethan dress recorded in wills 1558 to 1603
Ninya Mikhaila and Jane Malcolm-Davies
18

Abundant images and scant text: reading textile pattern books
Philip A. Sykas
23

Recovering identity: the role of textual evidence in identifying forgotten azlon fibres from the mid-20th century
Mary Brooks
29

Adopting other strategies, using other sources

'Wherein Taylors may finde out new fashions': constructing the Costume Research Image Library (CRIL)
Jane Malcolm-Davies
37

Unlocking one facet of Henry VIII's wardrobe: an investigation of the base
Maria Hayward
45

A portrait, two dresses, two samplers and a burning steamship
Edward F. Maeder
52

(Ad)Dressing the century: fashionability and floral frocks 58
Jo Turney

Sound recording and text creation: oral history and the Deliberately Concealed Garments Project 65
Dinah Eastop

Uncovering institutions

Late medieval Ladies of the Garter, 1348–1509: fact or fiction? 73
Shelagh Mitchell

Lace and documents: the Istituzioni di Ricovero e Educazione (IRE) collections in Venice 76
Isabella Campagnol Fabretti

Undated, unattributable and unfinished: forgotten samplers and their re-evaluation through archival research 82
Joyce A. Taylor Dawson

Tracing textiles in trade: from account books to patents

Fashioning the Tudor court 93
Cinzia Maria Sicca

Costume at the court of Cosimo and Eleonora de Medici: on fashion and Florentine textile production 105
Bruna Niccoli

Bought, stolen, bequeathed, preserved: sources for the study of 18th-century petticoats 114
Clare Rose

Analysing patents and objects: a preliminary investigation into the crinolines of W.S. Thomson 122
Katy May

Patents as a source of information about synthetic textile dyes 128
Rosemary M. Baker

The interaction between East and West

A paradise of pretty girls: the kimono and perceptions of Japan 135
Elizabeth Kramer

Dragon robes and prairie ladies: the incongruity between archives and artefacts 143
Julia Petrov

Chasing the dragon: researching Chinese textiles in early 20th-century domestic interiors 149
Sarah Cheang

Domesticity and gender explored and challenged

'A Linnen Pockett a prayer Book and five keys': approaches to a history of women's tie-on pockets 157
Barbara Burman

The antimacassar in fact and fiction: how textual resources reveal a domestic textile 164
Alice McEwan

'Inoffensively feminine': First World War military concert parties, female impersonators and their costumes 173
Sarah Norris

Inspiring textile collections: textiles and text combined in Winchester School of Art Library and
in the Special Collections, Hartley Library, University of Southampton Libraries 182
Linda Newington

Collaborative approaches: curators, conservators and dress historians

Thistles and Thrissels: Scottish Covenanting flags of the 17th and early 18th century 189
George Dalgleish and Lynn McClean

Dye analysis, textiles and text: unravelling the puzzle of Queen Charlotte's state bed 197
Maria Jordan and Mika Takami

Joining forces: the intersection of two replica garments 204
Hilary Davidson and Anna Hodson

Information uncovered by conservation

Understanding the full story: acknowledging intimate interactions of textiles and text as both
help and hindrance for preservation 213
Cordelia Rogerson

The interaction of textile and text: the conservation of a mid-16th-century chemise binding 221
Maria Hayward

The investigation and documentation of a communion table carpet in Corpus Christi College, Oxford 225
Florence Maskell

Who put the text in textiles? Deciphering text hidden within a 1718 coverlet: documentation of
papers hidden within an early 18th-century coverlet using transmitted light photography 237
Karen N. Thompson and Michael Halliwell

Jewish ceremonial textiles and the Torah: exploring conservation practices in relation to ritual
textiles associated with holy texts 244
Bernice Morris and Mary M. Brooks

A flag's life in New York: The New York State Battle Flag Preservation Project 249
Sarah C. Stevens

Objects without documentation: the role of conservation science in revealing more about these artefacts

Collecting a near infrared spectral database of modern textiles for use of on-site characterisation 257
Emma Richardson, Graham Martin and Paul Wyeth

Photodegradation of *Phormium tenax* fibres: the role of naturally occurring coumarins 264
*Gerald J. Smith, Raukura Chadwick, Ngaire Konese, Sue Scheele, Stephen E. Tauwhare
and Roderick J. Weston*

Foreword

The primary focus of this conference was on the interrelationship between archival or bibliographic research and the study of extant objects. For some researchers this multifaceted approach is their usual way of working, while for other contributors to the conference this style of research represented a change or a return to a previous practice. It was this diversity of approach that caused us to select the title, *Textiles and Text: Re-establishing the Links between Archival and Object-Based Research*. This theme allowed researchers working within the Textiles and Text and Worldly Goods research strands of the AHRC Research Centre for Textile Conservation and Textile Studies (2002–2007) to present elements of their research alongside an international panel of speakers.

Papers covering a wide geographical remit and a broad chronological span – prehistory to the present day – were actively encouraged. The aim was that this diversity should stimulate debate about the similarities of approach in spite of differences in terms of time and place, and also to highlight points of divergence and suggest reasons why this might occur. Consequently, sessions were devised that allowed the speakers to consider how archival and bibliographic research combined with the study of extant objects can inform our knowledge of textiles and dress in terms of their production, consumption, dissemination and deterioration. Equally, sessions were also to be devoted to considering what tools, including oral history, can be used to investigate textiles produced by cultures that are not predominantly text-based and how scientific and photographic analytical techniques can provide clues which cannot readily be gleaned either from the objects or written sources. The result was a rich selection of essays that took a wide variety of approaches and presented a broad spectrum of research.

This interdisciplinary, object-based approach was one that was very familiar to the late Janet Arnold, a highly esteemed historian of textiles and dress. While she is best known for her seminal book, *Queen Elizabeth's Wardrobe Unlock'd* (Maney Publishing, 1988), Janet's interests were very wide ranging in terms of period and her publications, including the *Patterns of Fashion* (Macmillan) series, ensured an international reputation for her scholarship. Much of her research was predicated on a detailed understanding of dress gained by the close examination of surviving garments and she recorded this process with sketches, photographs and copious notes. She generously bequeathed this material, along with her library, to the Textile Conservation Centre (TCC). The books, research papers and slides are housed in the Winchester School of Art Library, while her personal papers and drawings are kept in the Special Collections at the Hartley Library on the main University of Southampton campus. This conference was dedicated to the memory of Janet Arnold and her study of textiles and dress and it was an honour for the Research Centre and University of Southampton to act as host.

The selection of essays published here represents the vast majority of the papers and posters presented at the conference. All of the contributions were refereed and I would like to thank all of the anonymous referees for their invaluable contribution to this volume. Their comments and insight have made this book much richer and I am most grateful to all of the contributors for responding so positively to the refereeing and editorial process. The grouping of the papers follows the order of the conference sessions quite closely and the posters have been integrated into the relevant sections to make the organisation of the material more coherent. Some poster authors expanded their text, while others have presented material closer to their original submission and this is the reason for the varying length of these papers.

The smooth running of this conference was a credit to the hard work and careful planning of the conference team and grateful thanks go to Chris Bennett, Nell Hoare and Elizabeth Kramer. A special vote of thanks goes to Mike Halliwell for his invaluable AV/IT support before, during and after the conference, the latter reflected in the quality of the images within this publication. Our student volunteers, Ruth Gilbert, Konstantinos Hatziantoniou, Wendy Hickson and Vicky Leong played an important role, as did the session chairs, Mary

FOREWORD

Brooks, Barbara Burman, Sarah Cheang, Dinah Eastop, Paul Garside, Edward Maeder, Cordelia Rogerson and Philip Sykas. The conference was funded by the AHRC Research Centre grant and the conference and postprints represent the successful completion of two of the Centre's milestones. Finally, I owe a huge debt of gratitude to Chris Bennett and Elizabeth Kramer, my co-organiser and co-editor, for all their invaluable contribution to this publication.

Maria Hayward
April 2007

Introduction

Elizabeth Kramer

Textile and dress history has become a particularly exciting area of enquiry over the past few decades. The object-based study of dress and textiles was once viewed as betraying amateurish, feminine concerns tied to the fleeting and unpredictable realm of fashion rather than primary source enquiry into 'issues of production, technological determinism, work and trade organisation and on issues of entrepreneurship' (Taylor 2002: 64).

However feminist, and more recently cultural, studies have criticised and shown the latter investigations to be both narrow and exclusive. Material culture studies have further demonstrated that we all live within, act through and are shaped by the material world. Consumption studies argue that consumption is not a by-product or the wasteful end point of production, but a stimulus to it and a creative act in its own right.

Textile and dress historians have pointed out that textiles compose the largest imaginable body of material culture (Schneider 2006: 203; Schoeser and Boydell 2002: 1) and indeed, the wide-reaching significance of textiles can hardly be overemphasised, as they pervade every imaginable setting – domestic, personal, public, social and ceremonial – and transcend historical and geographic boundaries as well as national, economic, ethnic, gender and age barriers. With regard to dress history, Lou Taylor has written that, 'because of the multi-faceted "levels" at which clothing functions within any society and any culture, clothing provides a powerful analytical tool across many disciplines' (Taylor 2002: 1). Indeed, because of the prevalence of textiles and dress in every aspect of human life, a multiplicity of disciplines has taken notice of these objects, including art and design history, history, media and cultural studies, gender studies, material culture studies, studies in consumption, museology, sociology, and anthropology, to name a few.

Organisation of the papers

This interdisciplinarity is demonstrated in a number of the papers presented in this volume through the various approaches they take in discussing the production, consumption, dissemination and deterioration of textiles and dress. These conference proceedings provide the opportunity to meditate on research methodologies applicable to object-based and archival research, not as separate but inclusive entities. As such, the papers and posters presented were grouped thematically rather than by chronology or typology to promote a dialogue transcending specific disciplines and methodological approaches. This organisation provides researchers of textile and dress history with an opportunity to evaluate critically the successes, challenges and disappointments that a multiplicity of techniques allow.

Into the archive

This section considers both the insights and challenges offered by a variety of archival sources in exploring textile and dress history. By drawing upon these sources, research into the social, cultural, political and economic contexts in which textiles and dress are produced and used is widely explored. In the case of the limited survival or absence of extant objects, papers by Penny Sparke and Mary Brooks demonstrate how researchers can analytically and innovatively draw from archival and visual sources to reconstruct a material picture of the past. To construct her case study of the work of interior decorator Elsie de Wolfe**,** which she uses to explore issues surrounding feminine taste, Sparke calls upon texts written by and about Wolfe, letters, and photographs. Mary Brooks uses fashion and technical magazines, trade literature, business archives, patents and garment labels as well as personal records and interviews to explore azlon. These fibres, developed in the mid-20th century from organic proteins, played an important sociopolitical role as they were produced under the fear that wool supplies would be devastated by the onset of war and with the desire for nations to be self-sufficient.

Ninya Mikhaila and Jane Malcolm-Davies are the first of a number of authors to show ways in which archival and object-based research can be used to widen our understanding of the textile and dress history across social strata. Through their close investigation of wills and inventories they move beyond the evidence offered by pictorial, archaeological and documentary sources of the elite dress worn in Tudor society to identify that which was worn by the middling and lower classes.

While the above authors demonstrate largely how textual sources can provide new insights into understanding the production and use of textiles and dress in their social, cultural, political or economic contexts, Philip Sykas provides archival examples that blur the distinction between textile and text and reveal how the analysis of artefacts can provide compelling new information unobtainable by other means. His discussion of textile pattern books, typically composed of numerous textile samples sometimes accompanied by limited written text, demonstrates not only how these objects can be used to support text-based study but also to critique it.

Finally, the difficulties encountered in relating information gathered from archival sources with extant objects is explored in Fiona Handley's paper. In her discussion of textual sources from antiquity and the Middle Ages in relationship to archaeological textile finds from Quseir al-Qadim, Egypt, a port dedicated to a long-distance trade in luxury goods from the East, Handley identifies the difficulty of correlating written descriptions of textiles to the material record.

Adopting other strategies, using other sources

The authors in this section enhance their archival and textile-based research by considering additional sources and employing innovative approaches to the material at hand. In addition to the pictorial, documentary and archaeological sources most often called upon in investigating 16th-century English dress, Jane Malcolm-Davies suggests the use of a fourth source: church effigies. Her paper discusses a pilot project which attempted to link the dead, their dress and their documents to create a visual research resource for 16th-century costume. Likewise, in addition to consulting primary sources such as the Great Wardrobe accounts, inventories and narrative sources as well as visual material from Henry VIII's reign, Maria Hayward's investigation of a base from the king's wardrobe includes a consideration of armour. She further uses details gathered from these diverse sources to construct a replica in order to get an idea of what a base might have looked like, how it was made, what it was made from and how it might have been worn.

Just as replicas offer insight into the creation and use of historical dress, museum professionals and dress historians have employed a variety of methods to reinvigorate the exhibition of dress. The display of dress in museums and galleries has often been criticised as frustrating in terms of lifeless displays far removed from everyday, ceremonial or special occasion use and its attached social and cultural significance in these settings. The exhibition of dress has also been criticised as presenting a tendency toward the display of designer objects. Edward Maeder removes clothing and related ephemera from the confines of the storeroom and sterility of the exhibition space by looking at them in relationship to each other and through considering further textual sources. He examines a watercolour portrait of Sophia Smead (1813) alongside her wedding dress, a christening robe and cap and two samplers, and further contextualises these objects through the examination of family records, letters, account books, grave markers and newspaper sources, bringing to life the educational, cultural and fashionable world of early 19th-century New England. Similarly, in recounting the research project behind an exhibition of 20th-century floral frocks, Jo Turney invigorates the floral frocks under investigation through the use of oral history testimonies. This method was called upon to determine the implications of pattern and fashionable clothing within everyday life as the exhibition organisers wished not only to establish a dialogue between fashion and textile design but also to move away from designer-led display to that which focused on lived experience. In common with other papers presented in this volume, questions regarding feminine taste are explored through the discussion of the relationship between floral motifs and the creation of femininity. Dinah Eastop also demonstrates the value of oral history testimony as an approach in her discussion of the Deliberately Concealed Garments Project (DCGP), which was set up to document dress and other things found deliberately concealed within buildings. This approach was used to help tease out the connection between the people who hide, discover, report, curate, conserve and study the concealments, the concealments themselves and the language used to describe the practice.

Uncovering institutions

The papers presented in this section demonstrate how archival and object-based research can provide fresh insights into the educational, social, political and economic history of institutional life. These essays further offer insights into women's neglected histories from a variety of historical periods and geographical locations. Shelagh Mitchell argues against the longstanding belief that royal ladies had only an informal affiliation to the medieval Order of the Garter, asserting instead that they were indeed members of this order of chivalry. She calls upon the Great Wardrobe accounts and the alms and oblation accounts, the Issue Rolls of the Duchy of Lancaster and the Registers of the Black Prince to argue her case, which presents a picture of the livery issued to these women and its wider significance in court politics and social etiquette at this time.

The final two papers in this section focus particularly on textile production in convents. Isabella Campagnol Fabretti discusses the economic importance of lace production at Venetian charitable institutions from the end of the 15th century as well as the educational and moral role that lacemaking played in these *hospitali* through a discussion of surviving lace and documents relating to the production and sale of these laces. Similarly, through her case study of undated and unattributed embroidered samplers produced at the Ursuline Convent School for Girls in Québec City in the 18th and 19th centuries, and related documents such as a needlework curriculum, timetables, registers and account books, Joyce Taylor Dawson moves away from a traditional formal, stylistic and iconographic discussion of embroideries to examine these objects and their embroideresses in light of their role in educational and social history. She further presents a historiography of embroidery, which demonstrates how the treatment of this subject has changed over the past two centuries and discusses the link between this artistic medium and ideas of femininity.

Tracing textiles in trade: from account books to patents

The way in which the close examination of textiles and related text-based and visual sources such as account ledgers, letters, merchant cards, patents and portraiture can further enrich our understanding of political, social and economic history is discussed in this section of the book. Cinzia Maria Sicca closely examines diverse visual, material and archival sources, including portraits and surviving textiles and fragments, sumptuary laws, ledgers and letters, to trace luxury textile consumption in Tudor England to production in Florence via Italian merchants. Her investigation provides not only a revealing look at international textile trade during this time, but also the underpinning political, social and economic issues informing it. Bruna Niccoli's investigation of the significance of court dress in Florence in the mid-16th century also demonstrates the political symbolic overtures made by dress. Her research calls upon literary sources and archival sources, such as the Medici documents and private papers of Florentine aristocratic families, and connects court fashion back to Florentine production.

Clare Rose also offers a paper towards an understanding of the ways in which clothing expresses social distinctions and how retail advertising can be understood in relationship to these distinctions. She moves away from the consideration of dress associated exclusively with the elite and ruling classes in her investigation of the sale and consumption of women's 18th-century petticoats. Through the use of wills, inventories and accounts of thefts she examines the ways in which consumers understood and valued petticoats and further discusses how this information can be used to elucidate a reading of retailers' documents and merchants' cards, a reading informed by consideration of the work of Pierre Bourdieu and Colin Campbell relating to consumption and taste.

Patents are also discussed as a useful source material in considering textiles and trade. Katy May looks at the relationship between a range of crinolines by the manufacturer W.S. Thomson & Co. and the patents applied for by this company to demonstrate how these sources offer a better understanding of the company with regard to both the process of manufacturing and its business practices. Rosie Baker explores how patents serve as a lucrative source of information on the development of dyes in the 19th century, providing information not only useful for dating, identifying place of manufacture and recommending conservation treatment, but also in investigating commercial activity in the field of textile dyeing.

The interaction between East and West

The papers in this section demonstrate the difficulties presented in examining textiles that have moved across cultures, in particular from Japan or China to Britain or Canada. By drawing upon object-based and archival sources, the authors illuminate the social, cultural, political and economic contexts in which these textiles were produced, consumed and displayed as well as the imperial narrative informing them. The papers by Elizabeth Kramer and Julia Petrov further demonstrate the sometimes contradictory messages presented in examining both textiles and textual sources. Kramer's paper uses both archives and objects from the collection of Scottish painter E.A. Hornel to demonstrate the cultural biases not only presented in written texts but also in informing object acquisition. To facilitate these considerations, the paper looks specifically at Hornel's special interest in Japanese kimono, which is discussed in relationship to his travels in Japan, his paintings of the country, and perceptions of Japan widely held in Britain. His paintings of brightly costumed women as well as the kimono in his collection reinforce ideas of Japan as a timeless and exotic land, rather than indicate the rapid modernisation and social changes taking place in the country. These changes are noted with some degree of despair in the travel literature of the time, however, including Hornel's own writing. Julia Petrov also notes the disparity between textiles and texts in museum collections and archives through her examination of Chinese dress and textual sources located at the museum of the Calgary Chinese Cultural Centre. These include an early 20th-century correspondence between a landlady and the mayor of Calgary; the former is concerned that the manner of dress of her Chinese neighbours might impact negatively on her business. Petrov argues that despite the obvious significance of culture attitudes expressed in these letters, the objects exhibited in the museum present instead an accepted, even stereotyped, view of 'Chineseness'. She further asserts that the gap between such sources needs to be bridged by the museum, allowing it to better present narratives of immigration, integration, assimilation and cross-cultural communication.

Sarah Cheang also puts forward a case that demonstrates how the combined study of textiles and text can enrich our understanding of cultural, political and social interaction between the East and West, in particular China and Britain. She focuses on the meaning of Chinese textiles within the British domestic interior by calling upon two examples: 25 panels of Chinese embroidery that are fixed to the walls of an Oriental drawing room at Quex House, Kent and the diaries that shed light on their installation, and the use of Chinese textiles by Queen Mary between 1911 and 1925 in the interior and in her dress, for which Cheang gathers evidence from printed sources, such as royal memorabilia, biographies, magazines and newspapers. She uses these examples to analyse the articulation of class, gender and empire.

Domesticity and gender explored and challenged

In this section the authors use textiles and text to bring to light domestic objects and dress often ignored in social history despite their widespread use and social and cultural significance. These papers further detail how these objects and examples of dress have been gendered as feminine. Barbara Burman outlines the AHRC-funded Pockets of History project, which looked the production and consumption of women's tie-on pockets in Britain from *c.*1690–1914 by describing the range of material, visual and textual sources used in the study and detailing some of its findings to demonstrate the social significance of these obscure yet formerly commonplace domestic objects as well as to explore the subjective experiences of their female users. She calls upon 18th-century criminal court proceedings to ascertain what women carried in their pockets and also looks at 19th-century stitched and inked marks on surviving pockets to situate them within the practices of household economy and management. Through these examples Burman describes not only their everyday relevance but also reveals them to be an important social and symbolic interstice between the body, or private, and public spaces. Alice McEwan also closely examines a ubiquitous domestic object, the antimacassar, through texts and images. Through her investigation of textual sources including inventories, autobiographies, advice literature, ladies' periodicals, newspapers and novels, McEwan demonstrates not only how this object, intended originally to protect furniture from the macassar oil that men used in their hair, came to be viewed as purely decorative and feminine over the course of the 19th century, but also reveals how it came to serve as a trope for the feminised, cluttered Victorian domestic interior and has been viewed with suspicion as disingenuous into the 20th century. Despite its negative connotations, she further shows how this textile continued to be used by individuals to express their identity, challenging widespread assumptions about its use that were reliant upon gendered distinctions.

Sarah Norris analyses dress that although ubiquitous in the military during the First World War has now fallen into relative obscurity in its material form, not to be found in any British military museums or dress collections: the military concert party costumes of the female impersonators. She uses archival evidence including photographs, programmes, articles and reviews, to show the styles, means of procuring or producing costumes as well as to discuss the modes of femininity and fashionability embraced by these female impersonators and their significant role in the military. The relationship of these costumes to contemporary fashions, modernity and conceptions of gender are also explored.

While the previous papers demonstrated the ways in which examples of gendered textiles and dress can illuminate a variety of sociocultural values and ideological positions, Linda Newington's paper can be read as drawing attention to a group of collections that can be used in future research exploring issues related to domesticity and gender. She provides an overview of the collections that belonged to Janet Arnold, Montse Stanley and Richard Rutt, now part of the Winchester School of Art and the Special Collections, Hartley Library, University of Southampton, in which she discusses how these collections might be used for research and teaching related to the history of textiles, dress and knitting as well as to inspire current textile practice.

Collaborative approaches: curators, conservators and dress historians

These papers demonstrate how dress historians, curators and conservators collaborating on a project can create a dialogue that stimulates new questions and possibilities for further research.

George Dalgleish and Lynn McClean explore how the conservation of an important collection of flags relating to the 17th-century Scottish Covenanting movement aided curatorial investigation and interpretation. Using the scientific analysis of dyes to puzzle out the colour changes of the bed hangings of Queen Charlotte's state bed (1772–78) described in various textual sources, Maria Jordan and Mika Takami demonstrate how this object-based, scientific research yields evidence bridging a 100-year gap in the archival material, allowing for new research opportunities. This paper further demonstrates how current trends in conservation and curatorial thinking are concerned not only with preserving the integrity of the object but also with embracing alterations made by previous generations and acknowledging each of these changes as important. Hilary Davidson and Anna Hodson's paper describes the collaboration of a textile conservator and a dress historian who made a toile of an early 17th-century jacket and a late 16th-century underbodice respectively and brought these two independently created 'replicas' together. This collaboration allowed for new understandings of the function and shape of the original garments. Their research further demonstrates the value of using replicas as a tool in relationship to the study of extant objects and use of bibliographic resources in the fields of dress history and textile conservation.

Information uncovered by conservation

The papers included in this section illustrate the ways in which scientific analytical techniques can provide information that enriches or challenges archival and bibliographical research. Cordelia Rogerson cautions that while textiles and texts are intimately linked and the study of each may enrich each other, they can also act as a hindrance in preservation by limiting interventive conservation treatment options or preventing full interpretation of either the textile or texts. She urges for the application of adaptable ethics as well as an acknowledgement of the role of judgement in treatment decisions. The potentially problematic relationship between textiles and text is demonstrated in Maria Hayward's discussion of the conservation treatment of a velvet chemise binding on a mid-16th-century royal indenture. She demonstrates that although the text and any accompanying illustrations are widely viewed as giving a manuscript its particular importance, the binding of a book can also provide clues as to its social or economic importance. In the case of the luxurious chemise binding, Hayward shows how conservation treatment was carried out to stabilise the binding, while at the same time allowing continued access to the text. A sumptuous textile, a cloth of gold table carpet at Corpus Christi College, Oxford, also discussed by Cinzia Maria Sicca, forms the focus of the paper by Florence Maskell. A combination of instrumental analysis, archival work, photographic techniques and careful examination of the object allowed Maskell to draw some pertinent conclusions about the use and reuse of the cloth of gold and how the textile can be linked to references in inventories and trade accounts. In the case of text actually concealed within a textile, in this case an 18th-century coverlet, Karen Thompson and Michael Halliwell describe how transmitted light photography has been used to record hidden papers without damaging the coverlet. Photography revealed that these papers included bills, receipts, letters and extracts from political tracts, which all provide hints about the interests and status of the people who made or owned the coverlet.

Conservators have been increasingly concerned with respecting the needs of particular religious or ethnic communities when treating their ritual and sacred objects and have begun to tailor conservation treatments accordingly. Bernice Morris and Mary Brooks explain why and how the rules put forward in the Torah and rabbinical writings may impact on the actual conservation treatment, handling, storage, display and disposal of Jewish ritual textiles. Issues concerning the care of objects imbued with nationalistic importance and the research leading to an increased understanding of their history are debated in Sarah Stevens' paper, which discusses the New York State Battle Flag Preservation Project. In this paper Stevens further details how archival sources, including documents kept by the Bureau of Military Statistics, annual reports to the New York State Legislature, donation ledgers and federal and local government records, as well as bibliographic sources including published regimental histories, newspaper articles and booklets, are paired with the analysis of the extant flags to gather information about them as well as identify whether damage occurred during use and/or in storage.

Objects without documentation: the role of conservation science in revealing more about these artefacts

The papers presented in this section demonstrate how the scientific analysis of textile material can offer new insights into their composition, selection and use in lieu of the absence of textual sources. Emma Richardson, Graham Martin and Paul Wyeth discuss the non-evasive role that near infrared spectroscopy (NIR) can play in the identification of modern textile material, recognising this method as particularly useful in identifying manmade and synthetic textile materials that would greatly assist in the long-term preservation of these materials in contemporary collections. Gerald Smith, Sue Scheele, Stephen Tauwhare and Roderick Weston discuss their examination of the photostabilities of New Zealand flax or harakeke, used by the Maori to make mats, cordage, containers and garments, to determine whether this factor may have influenced their cultivation and selection.

References

Schneider, J. (2006) 'Cloth and clothing', in *Handbook of Material Culture*, C. Tilley *et al.* (eds). London: Sage.

Schoeser, M. and Boydell, C. (2002) *Disentangling Textiles: Techniques for the Study of Designed Objects.* London: Middlesex University Press.

Taylor, L. (2002) *The Study of Dress History.* Manchester: Manchester University Press.

Into the archive

Researching the domestic interior: the example of the 'Chintz Lady', Elsie de Wolfe

Penny Sparke

ABSTRACT Researching the historical material culture of interiors, their textiles included, is notoriously hard. Unlike buildings and objects, interiors – comprising spatially arranged ensembles of furniture, furnishings, decorations and personal knick-knacks for the most part – are almost always temporary, in transition and ephemeral. We can usually only access them through representations, and then they have an air of being 'unreal' and frozen in time.

This paper describes the methods I used for researching the work of the pioneer American interior decorator, Elsie de Wolfe, whose interiors and their contents have almost completely vanished from view. As a result of her pioneering use of the fabric as curtains, wall coverings and furniture upholstery in the urban context of turn-of-19th-to-20th-century New York, de Wolfe is often referred to as the 'Chintz Lady'. She also employed a wide range of other textiles, from muslin as a translucent window covering to rich brocades in her more sumptuous settings to historic Oriental and French rugs as floor coverings.

The sources used for my research included photographs, visual and textual archive material, texts written by the decorator herself, contemporary magazine articles, memoirs, an autobiography, a biography and handful of journal articles. Access to these sources, in combination with each other, allowed me to reconstruct and analyse – albeit, arguably, given the absence of any extant interiors or their contents, to a limited extent – her extensive oeuvre to which, in this paper, I offer an introduction.

Keywords: household textiles, chintz, interior decorator, advice books, domesticity, femininity

As a historian of 20th-century design I approach the study of the produced and consumed material culture of the past from a particular perspective. Inasmuch as my work seeks to describe and analyse its subject from a cultural perspective, to use manifestations of visual, material and spatial culture, that is, as forms of evidence that enhance our understanding of social and cultural historical phenomena, events and values beyond that provided by the written text, it differs from that of the conservator or the curator whose efforts are usually more directly focused on the detail of the materiality of objects in and for themselves. Although there is a considerable amount of overlap between our approaches – in cases where material objects are no longer in existence I am compelled to use the same 'detective' methods as the conservator to discover what existed in the past, and conservators and curators also take a huge interest in the social and cultural contexts of their objects in order to be able to understand them better – the ends to which we are working towards are significantly different. This paper aims to show my working methods in action, to provide one example of how I have researched and used material artefacts in conjunction with texts and archives, and to show where my methods both converge with, and diverge from, those of the conservator and the museum curator. While many of the practical methods are shared, and the same sources frequently used, the difference in the final goal affects, I would suggest, the emphases, the directional decisions and the priorities that occur along the way.

For the last decade or so I have been researching the work of the pioneer American interior decorator, Elsie de Wolfe, known from 1926, after her marriage to a minor British aristocrat Lord Mendl, as Lady Mendl (Fig. 1). My reason for researching her stems from my longstanding intellectual interest in the relationship between gendered values (especially 'femininity') and taste in the 19th and 20th centuries and the emergence of a concept of 'feminine modernity'.

In 1995 I published a book entitled *As Long as It's Pink: The Sexual Politics of Taste* in which I outlined what I believed could be demonstrated as the marginalisation of 'feminine' taste by architectural and design modernism (Sparke 1995). Like a conservator or a curator researching this subject I needed to have an accurate as possible knowledge of the materiality of de Wolfe's creative work – in her case domestic and non-domestic interior spaces for which she selected the textiles and furniture and manipulated the internal space. She also articulated her decorating principles in a number of texts and, of course, there was a body, albeit small, of secondary literature describing her work, both of which were important sources. Although, as it constituted the subject of my cultural analysis, I needed to know as much about her work as possible, my ultimate aim was to shed new light on the cultural questions that I have been addressing for some time. For me, therefore, de Wolfe offered an interesting case study rather than a subject in and for itself. In the following account of de Wolfe and her work, it is important for the reader to remember my reasons for undertaking this project as it sheds lights on the ways in which I used my sources and the roles played by material objects, archives and written texts in my research.

De Wolfe was one of a number of female interior decorators who emerged in the late 19th and early 20th century. Inasmuch as she was not educated as an architect like many of her contemporaries, she had worked as an actress on the Broadway stage before becoming a decorator, and she understood her role as a very broad one which involved acquiring antiques, facilitating the production of new items and assembling them into a 'tasteful' ensemble for her clients, she had a unique entrée into the profession. Her clients were, for the most part, wealthy, nouveau-riche Americans for whom the acquisition of taste was crucial. They were also nearly all women who had taken on the responsibility of the decoration of the home and who were expected, through that activity, to express their social status and aspirations. Between 1905 and her death in 1950, the decorator worked for hundreds of private clients, as well as on a number of interiors in her own homes in both New York and Paris. De Wolfe's New York office opened in 1907 and closed in 1938, but in 1916 she made Paris her personal base, only to return temporarily to the USA with the outbreak of the Second World War. She worked predominantly in the USA, but also in France and, albeit to a limited extent, in the UK.

My initial awareness of de Wolfe's existence came through reading her 1913 publication, *The House in Good Taste* (Fig. 2). One in a long line of advice books written from the 1880s onwards to help women in their new roles as beautifiers of the home, it became one of the most popular books of its kind in its time and it appeared in several editions up to 1920. It contained 50 illustrations, some of them identified, others not. I first came across the book in the early 1990s and I was curious to see where this woman fitted into the picture that was emerging for me at that time about the relationship between femininity, taste and the interior and the marginalisation of 'feminine taste' by avant-garde modernism.

In addition my curiosity was aroused by the images in her book. They all manifested the same aesthetic – that of the interior styles of 18th-century France for the most part – and seemed to have come from the same hand, even though only a few were identified and most were included as anonymous exempla of good decorating practice. I subsequently began investigating de Wolfe and her work, a task which turned into a major piece of work that absorbed my energies for over a decade, culminating in the publication in 2005 of a book that described and analysed 29 of her projects in some depth and placed them within a broader account of her creative life (Sparke 2005).

In this paper I outline some of the methods I used to research this work and the combination of sources I ended up using. It did not prove to be a straightforward research task as there was very little material to work with initially and what existed was highly fragmented. All I had to work from at the beginning was a book containing some acknowledgement of decorative authorship and some strong ideas about decorating. There was no information in it concerning de Wolfe's life, her business practices or about the ways in which she went about the job of decorating, of sourcing her materials, or of working collaboratively with others. I defined my task as one of attempting to fill those gaps as far as possible, of documenting

Figure 1 Elsie de Wolfe, in the frontispiece to her book *The House in Good Taste*, 1913.

Figure 2 The front cover of de Wolfe's 1913 book, *The House in Good Taste*.

what she achieved, and of understanding, above all, how she constructed and defined her role as a professional creative practitioner. For me the decorative work itself represented the material 'trace' of her working practices and evidence relating to her self-definition as a female decorator.

Textiles played a key role within de Wolfe's work – as indeed they did more broadly in the early 20th-century interior. This was not a new phenomenon, however – the role of textiles in the interior goes back centuries. It was reinforced when, from the 18th century onwards, home decorating was put into the hands of 'upholders' (upholsterers), tradesmen who brought together all the elements of the interior, including its furnishing textiles. By the mid-19th century, at the high end of the market, firms such as Waring and Gillows were performing a similar function (Girling-Budd 2004: 27–47). For example, describing a house created by that firm for the family of James Clarke, Amanda Girling-Budd has written, 'Crimson moreen curtains from Swarthdale House were altered to fit the dining room windows and the new seat furniture was covered in crimson morocco leather … The drawing room had a new suite of curtains of "green twilled chintz lined and fringed"' (2004: 35). Their approach to the interior stressed its 'soft' components. The role played by textiles in the bourgeois Victorian interior was highly significant as they helped create the idea of the comforting sanctuary which enclosed its inhabitants within its softness and protected them from the harsh world of commerce outside the domestic sphere. Describing their ubiquitous presence in these spaces, Thad Logan has explained that while, 'some, such as lamp mats and antimacassars served a purpose … various other kinds of covering, such as crocheted lampshades, seem to have been purely ornamental' (Logan 2001: 132–3). Even when Victorian clutter, which was enhanced by the covering of any and every surface with a protective fabric, was being rejected by the design reformers later in the century, textiles continued to play a significant role within the interior, although in a more controlled manner. This was evident in the work of the Arts and Crafts architects and designers from William Morris onwards, and in that of their continental followers, the members of the Viennese Werkstatte among them. Describing the work of the latter, and the continuing gendering of roles within the construction of the domestic interior, for example, Rebecca Houze has explained, 'while the men composed the rooms and designed furniture, the women produced the majority of the decorations including rugs, linens, porcelain and silver' (Houze 2002: 15).

Although she was not part of the Arts and Crafts reforming movement, and did not align herself with avant-garde taste, nonetheless, like them, through the introduction of the pastel colours, light painted furniture, wood-panelled walls, the use of a single surface pattern in one space, and of the elegant, integrated aesthetic of 18th-century French interior styles into the early 20th-century interior, de Wolfe also set her primary goal as moving away from the excesses of the Victorian interior. Although historicist in origin, the lightness and simplicity of her interiors in relation to their Victorian predecessors marked them out, in their time, like those of the European avant-garde, as 'modern'. Like them, as well, de Wolfe continued to depend upon the role of textiles in her ensembles while rejecting what she saw as their excessive presence in the Victorian household.

'How often', she wrote in 1913, 'do we see masses of draperies lopped back and arranged with elaborate dust-catching tassels and fringes that mean nothing?' (De Wolfe 1913: 84). In the form of curtains, upholstery, tapestry chair coverings and rugs, nonetheless, household textiles constituted a very important decorative element within her spaces. They provided colour, pattern and texture but, above all, they softened her rooms' otherwise hard architectural features and aligned the interior with the body of its inhabitant, usually female. De Wolfe was deeply committed to the importance of women in the domestic interior, even going as far as to claim that, 'It is the personality of the mistress that the home expresses. Men are forever guests in our homes, no matter how much happiness they may find there' (De Wolfe 1913).

One of de Wolfe's most noted uses of textiles was the transference of chintz – seen by late 19th-century sophisticated urban American eyes as an unpretentious rural fabric – into a chic 'city' fabric used in stylish New York homes. Chintz had been widely used before the mid-19th century in European middle and upper class homes, especially in the 18th-century English country house, but in the USA in the late 19th century, it was not much seen in sophisticated settings. De Wolfe transformed its image dramatically and, from 1905 onwards, she used it extensively in her interiors to replace the heavier, more sumptuous fabrics of the 'Victorian' interior. The title of the 'Chintz Lady' was given to her after she had exploited the effects of that fabric in the interiors of the Colony Club, New York's first all-women's club. The commission – her first as a 'true' professional – came to her through the club's architect, Stanford White of the New York firm, McKim, Mead and White, and her close female companion, Bessie Marbury, who was on the club's board.

Both of them had seen her use of chintz in the women's home on Irving Place and 17th Street where de Wolfe had 'modernised' the interior, exchanging a Victorian 'cozy corner' and heavy velvets for lighter, 18th-century French furnishings. A bird of paradise chintz featured in Marbury's bedroom, for example, where the decorator used the same pattern on a tight bedcover, the cushion of a small chair, a screen and a sofa, creating a strong visual unity in that small room. The decorator described the chintz as 'so subdued in tone that one never tires of it' (De Wolfe 1913: 38). She also hung sheer white muslin against the windows (de Wolfe hated lace curtains) to create an effect of lightness and airiness.

At the Colony Club, de Wolfe developed this use of chintz but on a much larger scale. On the sofas in the entrance hall she used a green and white striped glazed chintz which was, she said, 'as much at home in the New York drawing room as in the country cottage' (Sparke 2005: 41). Modern side chairs in the reading room were covered in a bird and vine chintz, while a grapevine-patterned chintz was used to cover the sofas and armchairs on the roof terrace. The overall effect was one of lightness and freshness and critics were quick to notice the novelty of de Wolfe's work. Her aesthetic became fashionable overnight and was soon much in demand from ladies across the USA.

Later in 1907 de Wolfe received a commission to decorate Brooks Hall, a girls' dormitory at Barnard College in New York. Each room contained 'chintz curtains of varied light patterns and a cover for couch and chair of the same' (Sparke

2005: 63). The linings of all the curtains in the building were cream-coloured to create a unified effect from outside. In the communal parlour, sofas with glazed striped chintz, probably English, sat alongside lamps with silk shades. Interestingly, as this project was not a domestic interior and it focused on the creation of appropriate settings for young girls, de Wolfe did not use the French style but relied, instead, upon simple furnishings such as Windsor chairs and items of furniture in the Mission style. Chintz was, however, still the ideal textile to soften the highly 'feminine' interiors she created there.

Probably de Wolfe's most dramatic use of chintz was in the show house on East 71st Street, which she created with the architect, Ogden Codman. She approached this project as if she was designing a home for herself and Marbury but she undoubtedly knew from the outset that the couple would never inhabit it. Probably because she wanted to use it as a showpiece she used dramatically coloured chintzes. In 1912 she wrote that, 'The strongest, the most intense thought I have about decoration is my love of color,' and her work at East 71st Street, especially in the bedroom suites on the third and fourth floors, bore witness to this commitment (De Wolfe 1912: 132). In the large front bedroom on the third floor, for example, she took her colour cues from a set of Chinese ceramic jars positioned on the mantelpiece which combined turquoise blue-green, mauve, mulberry and black. To match these she chose a mauve chintz patterned with roses and peacocks for the curtains, chair covers, mattress and boxspring. Writing about her use of chintz at this time she explained, 'Many of the newer chintzes have dark grounds of blue, mauve, maroon or gray and a still more recent chintz has a black ground with fantastic designs of the most delightful colourings' (De Wolfe 1913: 96). She used such a chintz, patterned with colourful parrots and green foliage, to dramatic effect in a dressing room in East 71st Street. The dark colours in the chintzes were offset, however, by the pastel colours used in the decorating scheme, the light panelled walls and the light colours of the furniture's painted wood and the overall effect was one of airiness.

While chintz played a crucial role in her interiors it was not the only fabric to which de Wolfe was committed. She also frequently utilised linen, often backed with muslin, for curtains, for example, and she made extensive use of damask, silk and toile de jouy. For her bedding in Irving Place, for example, she employed a soft carnation pink silk that could only be acquired in the Bon Marche in Paris (Sparke 2005: 33). This was a rare instance of de Wolfe revealing where she acquired her textiles. One of her projects however is documented in an existing archive that describes how she sourced her material for interiors. We know from her letters to her client, Henry Clay Frick, for whom she created a series of rooms around 1914, and from his to her, that she travelled to London and Paris in search of materials for the new family home on East 70th Street (now the Frick Museum). The letters tell us, for example, that she went to Charles of London to buy six Chippendale chairs and stayed at the Ritz during her visit.[1] She also bought a number of silver sauce boats and four candlesticks at Phillips and some furniture from Partridges. Other London sources of the fine furniture she bought for the Frick mansion were Mallett, Daniell and Sir Sydney Greville. Altogether she spent £4,669 in London, £609 over her budget. She provided no indication of where she acquired her textiles, however, although it is extremely likely that she obtained many of her chintzes from the English company, Warners, which had an American outlet in those years.[2] In Paris she shopped at Doucet and Jansen.[3]

Archive material relating to de Wolfe's commissions is extremely revealing but unfortunately limited in its availability. In addition to the Frick archive, one of the few other available archives is located in the Hyde Collection in Glen Falls, New York. It relates to the work the de Wolfe studio undertook for the home of Nell Pruyn Cunningham in 1918–19 and through the 1920s. For the Hyde family (Charlotte Hyde was Nell Pruyn Cunningham's sister) – we learn from letters in the Hyde Collection archive – de Wolfe Inc. purchased two small, 18th-century, 'Jacob' tapestry-covered chairs in 1920.[4] The letters to the client are mostly signed by Blanche Judge, who described herself as the manager of the de Wolfe Studio, Elena Bachman and H. Joan Hofford – both de Wolfe employees – which suggests that this project was undertaken in the decorator's absence. A letter from the studio to Pruyn Cunningham of 13 December 1920, for example, itemises the purchase of a 'footstool covered in old green damask'.[5] In 1921 Bachman wrote to Nell Pruyn Cunningham asking about fabric requirements for her Lake George cottage.[6] A 17 December 1920 invoice to 'Miss N.K. Pruyne' lists the purchase, from the studio, of '13 yards of Green Herring Bone Linen and 2 and a half yards of Persian Chintz'.[7] Yet more chintz, velvet and damask were bought in 1921. A letter Bachman wrote to Miss Pruyn in April that year provides some detail of the fabrics in the commission. 'It seems impossible', Bachman wrote, 'to get any linen to match the chintz so I have decided to buy white and have it dyed ... the taffeta curtains are going to be ready in about a week and they are indeed going to make the room look much prettier ... I sent you the Ritz chair in muslin ... and would you please let me know when it will be convenient for you to have me send you samples of glazed chintzes with black grounds.'[8]

A small number of letters between de Wolfe and her client also form part of Barnard College's archive in New York which provides an insight into the scope of the work she undertook for Brooks Hall. De Wolfe wrote to the college's director, Dean Laura Drake Gill, for example, explaining that, 'I can have $35,000 to cover all the furnishings, electric lights, kitchen utensils, china, glass, linen &c. This does not include anything of the kitchen fitments, ranges, plumbing, tubs &c., with which I prefer to have nothing to do.'[9]

The level of detail provided about de Wolfe's use of textiles in her interiors available in the Hyde Collection gives a sense of the way in which she and her studio operated in executing commissions. It suggests that, as indeed is still the case today in the world of interior decoration, the studio would make suggestions to clients about possible fabrics through the use of swatches and then work together with them until the desired colour and texture combinations were achieved. Letters and invoices are invaluable sources in this context, providing access to the actual materials used and to an understanding of the decorating principles that underpinned their selection and deployment. Together with de Wolfe's own published words – in her two books and in her articles in magazines – they are extremely useful sources of information for someone researching de Wolfe's work. In the case of de Wolfe, however, such archives are unfortunately few and far between; there are no extant business records for the studio; no fabrics themselves remain; and we are left, for the most part, with black and white photographs – themselves located in a number of different locations – as the only means of understanding how she used textiles in her interiors.

There are, inevitably, many difficulties in relying on black and white photographs when undertaking textile history research. There is no substitute for the real thing. In the case of items made of silver, for example, historians more often than not can refer to the 'real thing' which has lasted up to the present because of the durability of the material and its monetary value. Textiles – especially those intended as interior furnishings – do not fall into either of these categories. In addition interiors, like garments, are changed according to the whims of fashion and are notoriously transient. They are spatial and material arrangements rather than tangible 'things' and they are usually lost to history as complete entities. Very little material evidence of de Wolfe's work survives. Where her textiles are concerned, a few fabric swatches she used in the 1940s in the decoration of her Los Angeles home, After All, appeared in a 1999 Christies sale in Los Angeles, but this was exceptional. In addition, de Wolfe's company archives were destroyed when the company went bankrupt in the 1930s.

Given the paucity of archive material, the few publications that relate to de Wolfe's work are important sources in this context. As well as *The House in Good Taste*, a number of other publications exist including her own autobiography written in 1934 (not to be believed wholly); a very good biography of 1982 by Jane S. Smith, which mentions many of her projects but not in enough detail for the historian of decorative arts or material culture; and an account of her work written in 1992 by Nina Campbell and Caroline Seebohm, which contains some useful photographic material but the text of which is rather lightweight and unanalytical (De Wolfe 1935; Smith 1982; Campbell and Seebohm 1992).

As a result of the fragmentary nature of surviving de Wolfe material and evidence, I had to work very intuitively and rather unsystematically at first. My aim was to try to create whole 'stories' around her most significant and influential commissions. I was not just interested in 'reconstructing' the interiors, although inevitably this was part of it, but rather in understanding who the clients were, why they were working with de Wolfe, how the collaboration worked and what resulted from it. Each project was seen as a process which had a beginning, middle and an end and I wanted to understand as much about them as I could. This involved a great deal of detective work consulting obituaries, local press material, local historical societies etc. Each project had a local specificity and research into the buildings in which the interiors were located proved highly productive. Accounts of the projects in contemporary architectural and fashion journals also needed investigation.

My first piece of detective work, identifying the 50 illustrations in *The House in Good Taste*, involved comparing the book's text with its mostly unidentified images. By matching the author's verbal descriptions with the images provided, I eventually worked out where the illustrated interiors were located and of which commissions they were a part. It turned out that all the illustrations showed de Wolfe-designed interiors undertaken between the years 1907 and 1911. This method of analysis allowed me to distinguish the designs for her own houses – Irving Place, Villa Trianon in Versailles and her East 55th Street home – from the commissions from private clients whose names were either embedded in the text of the book or included in the captions to the illustrations. I also discovered that the individual chapters of *The House in Good Taste* had been published prior to 1913, as articles in both *The Delineator* magazine and *Good Housekeeping* magazine between 1911 and 1912, and that different images had been used to illustrate some of these.

From analysing these texts I began to construct a list of de Wolfe designs and to date them, at least roughly. My knowledge of clients' names allowed me to undertake a new level of research, mostly online, which focused on finding out more about them and their houses. Where had they lived? Who had built their houses? What had their interiors looked like? I undertook this work through local historical societies in the USA and the archives of architects who had collaborated with de Wolfe. New sources of archival material – including that of the architectural firm, McKim, Mead and White (located in the New York Historical Society), of the architect/decorator, Ogden Codman, and of Everett Shinn (in the Archives of American Art, Smithsonian Institution) – both broadened and deepened my knowledge of de Wolfe's work. I also looked at archives of architects' drawings of buildings (such as the Ogden Codman Drawings in the Avery Architectural Drawings Collection in the Library of Columbia University in New York) in which de Wolfe had designed interiors, in order to gain a sense of the room layouts. Given the (im)practicalities of working with material in the USA much of this work was undertaken online, but some was undertaken on field trips. I undertook visits, for example, to Mellody Farm, the Ogden Armours home in Lake Forest, Chicago (now a private boys' school), as well as to Barnard College, among other places.

The evidence I depended upon most for my research was historical journal articles and photographs. Through discovering a number of photographic archives in, among other places, the New York Historical Society and the Museum of the History of New York (interestingly some of them were listed as collections of images taken by well-known photographers of interiors, such as Mattie E. Hewitt who worked for a number of prestigious magazines), I gradually began to acquire a strong visual knowledge of de Wolfe's decorating strategies. Through a combination of her own words, and the discovery and close analysis of an ever increasing number of photographic representations of her interiors, I began to recognise details that she used over and over again and which came to characterise what I began to see as her unique 'language of the interior'. I discovered that she reused her prized possessions in new ways when she moved house and that she worked with a particular range of craftsmen who provided her with reproduction furniture items and painted new pieces to make them look old. I noticed, for example, the inclusion of a small, kidney-shaped side table in Isabella Stewart Gardner's home in Boston which was credited to de Wolfe and then discovered different versions of it executed in different woods in many other of her interiors. Ram's head sconces were also used repeatedly.

Much of the research I undertook was with the kind assistance of local historians/curators who looked after specific historic properties to which de Wolfe had contributed interiors

Figure 3 Anne Morgan's dressing room in her New York house, designed by Elsie de Wolfe, c.1910.

when they had been private houses. They included the Nell Pruyn Cunningham residence and the Mai and William Coe residence – Planting Fields in Oyster Bay, Long Island. I recently discovered another de Wolfe interior in a Greene and Greene house in Pasadena when I met the curator of their famous Gamble House. I suspect more de Wolfe interiors will keep turning up.

In conclusion, my design historical research into de Wolfe's work, both in general and, more specifically, in terms of her use of textiles, was very archive dependent, especially on those (albeit limited in number) which contained records of her communications with clients, and of the work of her collaborators. My work was not at all dependent upon extant 'objects', other than those which were available to me through black and white photographic representations and textual descriptions. While I would have loved to have found extant de Wolfe interiors full to the brim with original furniture and textiles – and of course on one level we are the poorer for not having this material at our disposal – I came to the conclusion that absences of this kind should not discourage historians of the interior, and of interior textiles, from pushing their analytical skills to the limit with the material they *do* have, and from using their imaginations to reconstruct a material picture of the past which would otherwise be completely lost to us.

In the end I felt that I had undertaken work of an archaeological nature, resulting in the discovery of many de Wolfe interiors which had hitherto been lost; that I had developed an expertise in recognising her work through the visual languages she employed and the clues she included; and that new knowledge about her decorating strategies and her place in interior decorating history had been acquired. Above all, though, I felt that I had accessed the life and mind of a female creative practitioner of the first half of the 20th century and, through so doing, learnt more about the ways in which modernity became meaningful for women at this time.

Notes

1. Letter from Gerald A. Letts to Elsie de Wolfe, dated 1 May 1914 (Helen Clay Frick Foundation Archives).
2. Several have been identified by the former Warner's archivist, Sue Kerry.
3. Letter of 26 May from de Wolfe to Frick (Frick Foundation Archives).
4. Letter from the Elsie de Wolfe studio to Mrs L.F. Hyde, dated 16 December 1920 (Hyde Collection Archives, Glen Falls, New York).
5. Letter of 13 December 1920 from de Wolfe studio to Miss N.K. Pruyn (Hyde Collection Archives, Glen Falls, New York).
6. Letter from Bachman to Pruyn, 29 April 1921 (Hyde Collection Archives, Glen Falls, New York).
7. Invoice from de Wolfe studio to Miss N.K. Pruyne, dated 17 December 1920 (Hyde Collection Archives, Glen Falls, New York).

8. Letter from Elena Bachman to Miss N.K. Pruyn, dated 29 April 1921 (Hyde Collection Archives, Glen Falls, New York).
9. Letter from de Wolfe to Gill, 25 May 1907 (Barnard College Archives).

References

Campbell, N. and Seebohm, C. (1992) *Elsie de Wolfe: A Decorative Life*. New York: Panache Press.
De Wolfe, E. (1912) 'Transforming a small city house', *The Delineator* (February): 132.
De Wolfe, E. (1913) *The House in Good Taste*. New York: The Century Company.
De Wolfe, E. (1935) *After All*. New York: Harper and Brothers.
Girling-Budd, A. (2004) 'Comfort and gentility: furnishings by Gillows, Lancaster, 1840–55', in *Interior Design and Identity*, S. Mckellar and P. Sparke (eds), 27–47. Manchester: Manchester University Press.
Houze, R. (2002) 'From Wiener Kunst im Hause to the Wiener Werkstatte: marketing domesticity with fashionable interior design', *Design Issues* 18(1): 15.
Logan, T. (2001) *The Victorian Parlour: A Cultural Study*. Cambridge: Cambridge University Press.
Smith, J.S. (1982) *Elsie de Wolfe, A Life in the High Style: The Elegant Life and Remarkable Career of Elsie de Wolfe, Lady Mendl*. New York: Atheneum.
Sparke, P. (1995) *As Long as It's Pink: The Sexual Politics of Taste*. London: Pandora.
Sparke, P. (2005) *Elsie de Wolfe: The Birth of Modern Decoration*. New York: Acanthus Press.

The author

Penny Sparke is Pro Vice-Chancellor (Arts) and Professor of Design History at Kingston University, London. She taught the history of design from 1972 to 1982 at Brighton Polytechnic and at the Royal College of Art in London from 1982 to 1999. She has published over a dozen books and numerous articles in the field of design history over the last 25 years with an emphasis, since the mid-1990s, on the relationship between design and gender, and is currently writing a book entitled *The Modern Interior* (Reaktion Press).

Address

Penny Sparke, Galveston Lodge, Galveston Road, Putney, London SW15 2SA, UK (p.sparke@kingston.ac.uk)

'I have bought cloth for you and will deliver it myself':[1] using documentary sources in the analysis of the archaeological textile finds from Quseir al-Qadim, Egypt

Fiona J.L. Handley

ABSTRACT The analysis of textiles discovered in the archaeological excavations at the port of Quseir-al-Qadim on Egypt's Red Sea coast from the Roman (1st–3rd century AD) and Islamic (11th–14th century) periods offers an exciting opportunity to compare rare material culture with documentary sources. The written records found at the site in both periods, and important regional documents such as the 1st-century merchant's guide *The Periplus of the Erythraean Sea*, aid the interpretation of the textiles found, but also raise many issues. Documents can provide much more information than a straightforward list of items that can be 'checked off' against archaeological finds. While the texts must be deconstructed as social documents created through the concerns and priorities of the merchants and officials who wrote them, close reading reveals multiple ways that they aid the interpretation of the Quseir textiles in transport, and as dress, trade goods and furnishings.

Keywords: Quseir al-Qadim, Myos Hormos, textiles, *tiraz*, *thawb*, trade

Introduction

The analysis of textiles discovered in the archaeological excavations at the port of Quseir al-Qadim on Egypt's Red Sea coast offers an exciting opportunity to compare rare material culture with documentary sources. Abandoned since the 15th century when the port relocated south to the current town of Quseir, it had two periods of occupation: the 1st–3rd century AD when it was the Roman port of Myos Hormos, and the 12th–15th century when it was a late Ayyubid and Mamluk port. The port existed to serve the long-distance trade in luxury goods such as spices, gems and silks coming from the East. In the later period of occupation it also served as a pilgrim and supply port to Jedda, the port of Mecca (Makka). It is located at the farthest point north a sailing ship could travel against the prevailing southerly winds and is just three days travel overland to the most easterly bend of the Nile and to the towns of Koptos in the Roman period, and Qus in the Islamic. The site is referred to in texts from both antiquity and the Middle Ages, and knowledge of the site has been expanded through two archaeological expeditions, first by a team from the Oriental Institute, Chicago from 1978 to 1982 (Whitcomb and Johnson 1979, 1982), and then by a team from the University of Southampton from 1999 to 2003 (Peacock and Blue 2006), of which I was the textile specialist.[2]

The Roman period

Myos Hormos along with its sister port Berenike to the south were the two key ports that connected the Roman Empire with the East, exporting Roman fine wares, gold and wine, and importing luxury goods such as spices and textiles (Peacock 1993). The balance of this trade was certainly in India's favour, with huge amounts of money being sent from Rome to be spent on these luxuries. Notoriously Tiberius grumbles that 'the ladies and their baubles are transferring our money to foreigners' (Tac., Ann. 3.53 cited in Casson 1989), and a similar complaint is made by Pliny. Myos Hormos seemed to be more favoured in the 1st and 2nd centuries, and was then eclipsed by Berenike, which had the advantage of being farther south and therefore less of an effort to sail to, especially given the increasing size of ocean-going ships. Its distance to the safety of the Nile, however, meant that in times of insecurity in the Eastern desert merchants favoured Myos Hormos with its much shorter and therefore safer journey to the Nile at Koptos.[3]

There are unfortunately no references to textiles in the written material actually excavated at Myos Hormos; however there are a few references on *ostraka* and papyri[4] found at the military way stations on the roads that linked Koptos to Myos Hormos and Berenike. These texts mainly concern day-to-day supplies to the stations (wood, straw, wheat and barley) which were carefully noted, threats and attacks from barbarians in the area, and the routine administrative tasks of the Roman army. Personal correspondence concentrates

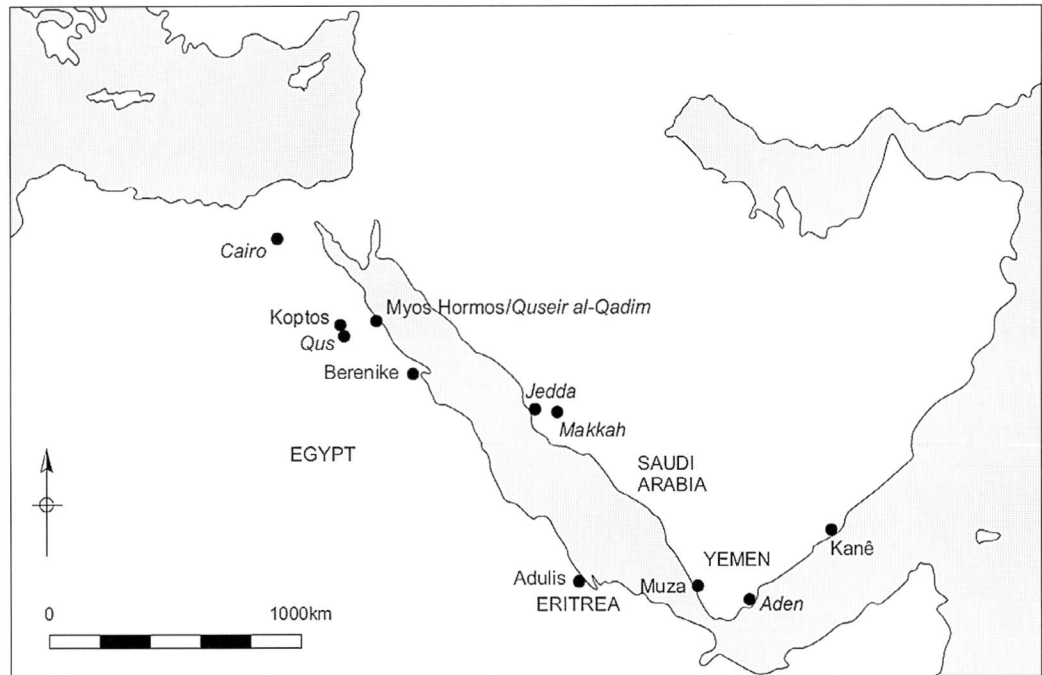

Figure 1 Map of the region (italics indicate Islamic towns).

on passing on information such as arranging meetings, while referring to the procurement of necessities such as bunches of vegetables. Other goods were only mentioned if they were in urgent demand or had to be ordered, and here we find a few references to clothing and textiles. There is one mention of the slave Ioulas requesting his master to provide him with leather to make a pair of sandals (Cuvigny 2005: 121), while Serapias tried to find linen at Myos Hormos to send to her 'father' at one of the desert stations (Bulow-Jacobsen 2003a: 58). Other more passing references state, for example, that the prostitute Procla should be supplied with a cloak and a tunic (Bulow-Jacobsen 2003b: 402). These references relate to the needs of people living in the desert; almost no mention is made of the commercial trade which passed along these roads, and nothing is written of the valuable cargoes of textiles and spices from the East. The 'Nikanor' archive of Koptos, which relates to the activities of merchants dealing with trade out of Myos Hormos (rather than military records) is of more interest. It mentions eight packages of purple-dyed cloth (Cuvigny 2003: 275), which were surely for export, as discussed below, cloaks or garments, which may have been exported, and rush mats, which were probably for local consumption (Wild 2004a).

Thus from excavated written material there is little evidence for either the trade in exotic and high-quality textiles or their more ordinary uses at Myos Hormos, or indeed in the Eastern desert. That clothes were not mentioned as items that needed to be sourced suggests that people contented themselves with the clothes with which they travelled and 'made do and mended' rather than ordering in new garments when the old wore out, a system of use and reuse which is supported by the archaeological evidence from sites across the Eastern desert. In contrast, there is plenty of documentary evidence for textile production and use across the Roman Empire as a whole, for example the writings of Pliny, and the Edict of Diocletian. These sources have been closely studied and provide a wealth of information on textile production, trade and use across the Roman Empire (Forbes 1956; Wild 2004b). Given the generality of these texts, however, they will not be explored here. At a regional level there is one text of profound importance for understanding the trade in textiles (and indeed all goods) through Myos Hormos: *The Periplus of the Erythraean Sea*, an anonymous 1st-century mariners' guide which gives a comprehensive description of the products the various ports along the coast of East Africa, Arabia and India would buy and sell. This is the most important source of written information on the textile trade with the East from this period, and describes both the exports from Egypt and the textiles imported from the East, giving an insight into both Egyptian textile production and the type of cloth in demand at various places along the route to India.

As the starting point of the sea trip, Myos Hormos appears as the first entry in the book. It reads 'Of the designated harbors of the Erythraean Sea and the ports of trade on it, first comes Egypt's port of Myos Hormos, and, beyond it, after a sail of 1800 stades to the right, Berenice [Berenike]. The ports of both are bays of the Red Sea on the edge of Egypt' (Casson 1989: 51).[5] No clues are given as to the goods that passed through Myos Hormos, but information about them can be extrapolated from the records at their final destinations. For example, the imports to Adulis, the port of the Aksumite kingdom in present-day Eritrea, include 'articles of clothing for the Barbaroi, unused, the kind produced in Egypt; wraps from Arsinoe; coloured *abollai* (cloaks) of printed fabric; linens' (Casson 1989: 53). Roman fabrics tended to be standardised and fell into distinct types, some of which we can identify today and which presumably the manufacturers and consumers in the past were also aware. Some of these types of cloth can be identified in the archaeological assemblage at Myos Hormos. The Arsinoitic wraps are probably medium and high-quality wool fabrics typical of Roman dress in the Eastern Empire, while cloak fabrics seem to be more specifically associated with the Roman army. These are often heavier than tunic fabrics, and are sometimes in twill weaves or decorated with distinctive *clavus* patterns, which may explain their description as 'printed'. At least some of the twill weaves (2/2 even twills) are probably European imports, so it seems likely that it was the cloaks decorated with clavus that were exported. By the 1st century AD, Egypt already had a long tradition of linen cloth manufacture, almost all of which must have been products of the Nile Valley and Lower Egypt, and it is probable that Egypt exported a range of qualities of linen textile.

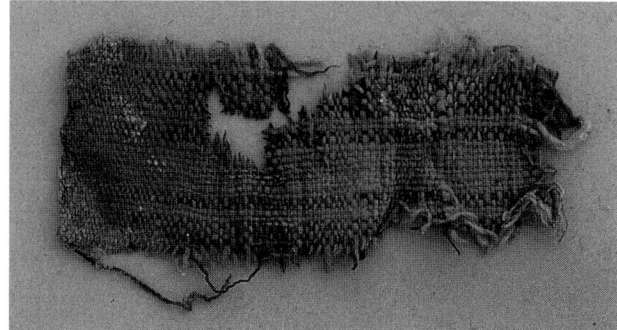

Figure 2 Roman blue and white cotton check
(Plate 1 in the colour plate section).

Similarly if we look at imports to places around the Arabian peninsula the same Egyptian woollen and linen textiles can be identified, with tunics, cloaks and blankets being sold. The large port of Muza, whose lucrative exports were myrrh and frankincense, lay at the entrance to the Red Sea and is described as teeming with 'shipowners or charterers and sailors – and is astir with commercial activity' (Casson 1989: 63). As well as the familiar Egyptian fabrics, it also imported what appear to be garments made specifically for its market. These are described as Arab sleeved clothing, either with 'the common adornment or with checks or interwoven with gold thread' (Casson 1989: 65). Arab clothing was also sold in Kanê, farther east along that coast. Muza also imported cottons from India, and while it cannot be ruled out that this Arab sleeved clothing was made there, Casson considers that the Arabian clothing was an Egyptian export. This type of fabric can be identified through its description as being checked. Woollen checks were not a product of the eastern Roman Empire and are more associated with central and western Europe, however fabric in both linen and cotton in blue and white checks is found at many sites in the Near East and Egypt, and it would seem probable that this type of blue and white checked linen or cotton fabric travelled on the backs of Arab sailors and merchants throughout the wider region. Two examples are found at Quseir (Figs 2 and 3), many more at Berenike (Wild and Wild 1998, 2000), and others at Palmyra. Blue and white stripes and checks were found at Kellis (3rd–4th century) (Bowen 1999), and the At-tar caves in Mesopotamia (Fuji *et al.* 1997). These connections are also supported by growing ceramic evidence connecting the Roman world and South Arabia (Tomber 2004). It may be that archaeological finds from Myos Hormos and Berenike were from fabric that passed through these ports, were sold in Arabia and returned to Egypt on the backs of sailors and merchants.

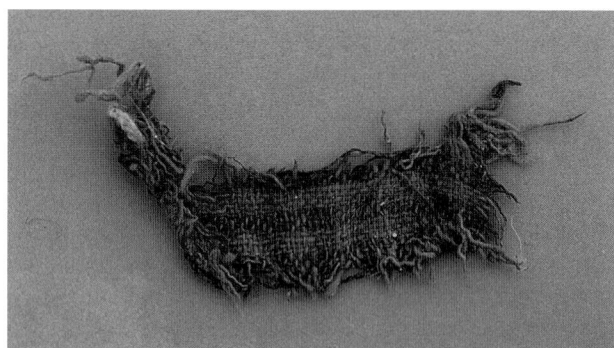

Figure 3 Roman blue and white cotton check
(Plate 2 in the colour plate section).

Figure 4 Roman 'shaded band' wool textile
(Plate 3 in the colour plate section).

Also imported into Muza was purple cloth of 'both fine and ordinary quality', which relates to the purple cloth described in the ostrakon in Koptos, and 'girdles with shaded stripes' (Casson 1989: 65), described by other authors as shaded bands and identified as a type of woven woollen stripe found at sites across the Eastern desert (Fig. 4). While the examples being imported into Muza (and the ones imported into Barygaza in India itself and described as 18 inches wide) were to be worn as a garment, it is not clear how shaded stripes were used in the Roman Empire. They do not appear in mummy portraits as the stripes on tunics or cloaks, and it seems more likely that along with other multicoloured stripes they were a type of furnishing fabric. If they were just 18 inches wide this suggests they were used to make cushions and bolsters, although it remains a possibility that these widths were made specifically for the export market.

However, while the trade down the east coast of Africa and around the Arabian peninsula was important, especially for merchants who could not afford or did not want to run the risk of a long and perilous journey to India, the reason for Myos Hormos' existence was to tap into the spice and textile markets of the western coast of India. Here, spices and gems from all over Asia and the Far East, and Chinese silks and yarns from the overland Silk Road were traded. These silks dominated the textile trade, but the other key textile export was Indian cotton cloth of varying qualities including muslins, 'cotton garments of the very finest quality, the so-called Gangetic' (Casson 1989: 55). Many of these cottons, presumably of medium quality, were traded on the route back to Egypt. In return, the markets of India imported many different items, most importantly of course money, but also metals, wine and cosmetics. Two of the most important markets, Barbarikon and Barygoza, both imported a wide range of Egyptian clothing and textiles, however it is presumed that these were of modest commercial value and may have been supplies for settled Roman communities in these places.

Unfortunately, as the luxurious textiles to be purchased here were the obvious reason for the journey, little was said about the nature of them, and all the descriptions simply refer to Chinese cloth and yarn. This seems typical of communications which are aimed at organising the trade, whether in the Periplus or at the outposts across the Egyptian desert: as the trade in luxury items was the purpose of the whole exercise it was not necessary to describe them. This is not a handicap in interpreting the textiles excavated at Myos Hormos, however, as there is as much a lacuna in the material evidence as there is in the documents. No fragments of any high-quality textiles from the East have been found, with the possible exception of tie-dyed silk found during the Chicago excavations. The one example of a possible Chinese textile is a patterned double-weave cloth, however, its wool fabric places its origin in central Asia rather than China, suggesting that it arrived in Myos Hormos via the Near East and through Egypt. The textile evidence for the trade actually comes from the much less glamorous remains of three sails, and the 63 fragments of the webbing that were used in their construction.

The Islamic period

In contrast, the Islamic period offers a much richer textual resource with which to work, and luckily for the textile specialist, much of this has been translated and published with a focus on textiles (Lamm 1937; Serjeant 1972). The original sources include manuscripts, books published at the time such as travelogues and biographies, and the discarded official and personal documents found in the Cairo Geniza. The latter were thoroughly researched by Goitein, the results of which were published in four volumes (Goitein 1983a). This extensive publication covers every area of 10th–12th-century life in Cairo, which although based on documents kept by the Jewish community, historians have understood the resource as being broadly applicable to the whole society. Goitein's work has been invaluable in its examination of the trade and use of textiles as clothes and furnishings, and has the advantage of looking at the way textiles were used in society and creating a context for them through discussing other types of material culture. For example, it played a key role in validating that the brightly coloured cotton prints and resist dyes found across Egypt, including at Quseir, do indeed come from India (Barnes 1997).

Both texts and textiles were very important types of material culture in economic and social terms in Ayyubid and Mamluk society. Writing was considered the word of God as revealed to the Prophet Muhammad at the beginning of the 7th century, and this special association made it a suitable decoration across all forms of Islamic art from architecture, ceramics and metalwork, to calligraphy itself. In terms of textiles, words most famously decorated the *tiraz* fabrics created from the 8th century up until the mid-14th century in state-supported workshops. *Tiraz* fabrics were distributed through society as markers of goodwill, thanks and of patronage, their writing variously covering names and dates of commissioning or ownership, or religious or secular messages. The production and consumption of *tiraz* fabric demonstrates the central role of textiles in Islamic economy and society; more generally, wealth was reflected in the use of luxurious fabrics imported from everywhere between the Mediterranean and the Far East. Textiles were a key way of storing wealth and appeared prominently in trousseaus and wills; they were also used as a method of payment (Stillman 1979). This conspicuous demonstration of wealth through textiles was also apparent in clothing (Goitein 1983b: 151), and all sectors of society placed much emphasis on dressing well.

Figure 5 Fragment of Ayyubid period *tiraz* textile (Plate 4 in the colour plate section).

At Quseir however, the material record reveals only a glimpse of this world of luxury. Out of the many thousands of pieces of textiles uncovered, only a handful can be related to the textiles mentioned in texts, or indeed compared to textiles preserved in other collections. This can be explained by several factors. Unlike sites in Egypt with rich finds of high-quality fabrics, the material at Quseir comes from rubbish deposits rather than burials, meaning that no complete fragments of textiles are found. At Quseir, just two fragments of *tiraz* fabric have been found, and two others which are fragments of cloth that were probably decorated with *tiraz* (Fig. 5).[6] While the texts such as those translated by Serjeant and Goitein discuss the trade and wearing of silks, just 12 fragments of silk from Quseir have been found, excluding tapestry weave fabrics embroidered in silks. While this is of course because these precious textiles were worn until only the tiniest fragments remained, it must also be a reflection of the limited role that these textiles played in everyday life of towns such as Quseir, despite their prominent role in the literature and perhaps in cities such as Cairo. As in the Roman period, Islamic Quseir was a place that exotic textiles passed through rather than being traded,[7] and most of the high-quality fabrics found there were produced in Egypt. Only one silk fabric, a *mulham* (silk on a cotton warp) can be definitely identified as not being made in

Egypt and this was made in Persia or central Asia, rather than in lands farther east. This suggests that high-quality fabrics passed through in bales, or arrived on the backs of visitors, and left the same way. The few fragments which remained were the exception. In contrast, although the residents of Goitein's Cairo were not necessarily well off, they were the end recipients of the trade in cloth that Goitein describes.

Many references from the key works that draw together selections from various writings on textiles could be cited as explaining or inspiring new interpretations of the archaeologically excavated material from Quseir. There are too many to be fully explored here, however a few examples do stand out. Seven small bags were found at Quseir which on first inspection seem a slightly impractical shape, being rather long and thin, with generally no evidence for a method of holding them closed. They are all about twice as long as they are wide (Figs 6 and 7). All except one have an opening at the short end, and only one, which has a neatly folded hem at the mouth with a drawstring running through, appears to have been expressly made as a bag. The others are slightly irregularly shaped, three are clearly reused, and of these at least one was once a sleeve with one end sewn up. One very clearly has an imprint of whatever was once pushed into it (Fig. 7), and another has ink marks suggesting a pen was carried in it. Due to their shape and overall size, these bags seemed to form a group, however it was only on reading Goitein that a suggestion for their use became apparent: 'the wide sleeves served as receptacles ... Men and women kept there a *mandil kumm*, a sleeve kerchief, in which money and a wide variety of other objects could be stored. Such a *mandil* could cost up to a dinar; its color was white, it was sometimes embroidered' (Goitein 1983b: 161).

While these bags were not kerchiefs, nor were they white or embroidered, they would be exactly the right shape to be carried along the length of the lower arm in a sleeve. And interestingly at least one was itself originally a sleeve. The question of the open neck would be solved by being folded to keep the contents in, or the simple pressure of sleeve against arm keeping the bag closed. These were definitely bags, however Goitein's passage states that in fact money and objects were kept not in bags, but kerchiefs, which would presumably be square pieces of fabric, perhaps hemmed.

Identifying a kerchief, which could simply be a fragment of cloth cut into a square or rectangular shape, is a difficult task at Quseir. Many hundreds of fragments are cut into roughly square shapes and of course a square piece of fabric has many dozens of potential uses. It is hard to decipher why apparently new cloth was cut into fragments – was it a piece of a pattern book, used to show the range of fabrics available? Could it have been used as cheap and disposable packaging material for small items? Among the more hypothetical explanations we must include the idea of kerchiefs, as they at least have some evidential support from texts. If they were, they must have been folded up several times to have held something in them. Out of the group identified as 'resist dyes' at Quseir, about a dozen have been clearly cut into a rectangular shape (Fig. 8). Two of them are hemmed, but most have raw edges, also suggesting that they were fairly disposable. This is perhaps just one possible explanation for them, and realistically this may be because they served more than one function.

Figure 6 Bag (Plate 5 in the colour plate section).

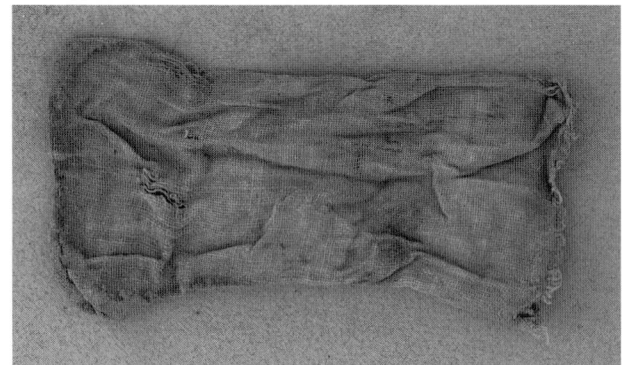

Figure 7 Bag showing where an oval object was pushed into the bottom (Plate 6 in the colour plate section).

Figure 8 Resist-dyed cotton fabric, possibly an example of Goitein's 'kerchief' (Plate 7 in the colour plate section).

The kind of textiles and clothes that Goitein considers to be at the bottom of the quality pile – those in blue (considered inauspicious – 1983b: 174) or in cotton (1983b: 165) – make up the majority of garments found at Quseir. From this we can deduce that these clothes belonged to people at the bottom end of the social ladder, not unsurprisingly as most of the residents of Quseir would have been the sailors and harbour workers who ran the port and its ships. And it seems very unlikely that as people involved in hard physical labour they would have been following the fashions described as typically

Ayyubid or Mamluk – layering of clothes would be impractical working in the heat,[8] or even dangerous as scarves and loose layers could get caught in the ropes and blocks of the ships. In all the fragments of cuffs found, there is no evidence for the loose baggy sleeves associated with Islamic clothing; the surviving sleeves, even ones in fancy fabrics, are tailored as tubes. Likewise there is at least one hat found – a red, yellow and blue striped woollen hat, covered in yellow tassels – which was certainly not worn under a turban.

Depictions of sailors in, for example, some versions of al-Hariri's Maqamat, show them wearing nothing but loincloths; this may have been suitable on board ship in the Tropics, but on land sailors (especially Muslim sailors) would be expected to cover up. Goitein points out that even the poorest people recorded in the Cairo Geniza documents had multiple sets of clothes, but it remains probable that some had even less, particularly if they were only temporary residents. What we can say however is that dressing well was something that most people in Quseir would aspire to and that in reality this would mean that there would be a spectrum of qualities of dress apparent. At the very bottom end, perhaps a simple *thawb* (a basic shift-like garment worn by men and women), belt and a cap may have sufficed for a man, and a *thawb* and some kind of veil for a woman in public, while those with the means would be increasingly covered in layers of clothes, including turbans, outer dresses, mantles and scarves, in more expensive fabrics as wealth and occasion allowed. Given that Guo describes the town's most prominent family, that of Shaykh Abu Mufarrij, who ran a shipping company and who fulfilled most of the important administrative roles in the town, as only 'modestly prosperous' (Guo 2004: 90), it would seem that there were no permanent residents at Quseir who would be dressed in top of the range, high-quality textiles. The wealthiest people in Quseir would probably only be passing through, perhaps on the Hajj, perhaps visiting as merchants, and would take their clothes with them.

The lives of Shaykh Abu Mufarrij, his son Shaykh Ibrahim and their family have been revealed through hundreds of fragments of documents excavated at Quseir (Guo 2004). Many of these relate to the business activities of the family's warehouse in the centre of the town, which dealt with the shipping of merchandise, mainly to Arabia and the Yemen. Trade was dominated by the export of grain, although textiles were also an important trade item. The main textile-related commodity was linen fibre (Guo 2004: 40), which from antiquity had been an important item of export from Egypt. In 13th-century Quseir, substantial quantities of it were stored in the Shaykh's house and exported in bales made of canvas. One delivery note informs Shaykh Ibrahim about the arrival of one camel load of flax (*himl kattan*). The note makes it clear that the Shaykh's warehouse was used as storage, or for brokerage services, as the sender explains that the goods were for a third party, and instructed Shaykh Ibrahim to 'put it in a good place' (Guo 2004: 40). Interestingly, despite the large quantities of cotton fabric found at Quseir, it is only mentioned in a text once, and probably as part of a revenue payment rather than a trade item (Guo 2004: 41).

The documents from Quseir do mention the trade in *tiraz* and fine silks (*harir zakhir*). One letter deals with fine pure silk robes, fine shawls (*ashyal*) and fine galabiya clothes (*jalalib*). The noting of two camel loads (*himlayn*) of women's wraps with inlaid gold and gem ornaments (*milayat haram murassa'a*) suggests that even high-quality clothing was traded in large quantities, however it seems probable that none of these garments were actually worn by the people at Quseir. Indeed it seems there was a vigorous trade in new and second-hand clothing. At Quseir, one merchant wrote: 'Now o master make sure that you sell the turbans on my behalf. Nu'man has sold long coats for twenty-six dirhams; and he still has eight [long coats?] left by God Almighty! As for me, all [the items] in [my storage] are sold out, and we need [more] children's clothes. We have pure gold, which we will use [to pay for them] by God's blessing' (Guo 2004: 194).

The mention of children's clothing being imported into Quseir is interesting, as we have three almost complete children's garments, and previous excavations have found two complete and two fragmentary examples (Vogelsang-Eastwood 1987). At least one of these garments found at Quseir was made from the cut-down remains of an adult garment, and while the above quote does not make it clear whether these are newly made or second-hand clothes being sold, it would seem probable that old or worn-out clothes would be sold or discarded to be repaired and reused, a cycle which would continue until the garment was no more than a rag. Many textile fragments at Quseir show evidence for repairs and re-tailoring, and other fragments show how worn cuffs and hems were cut off, presumably so that garments could then be re-hemmed with neater edges. Even at the higher end of society, selling clothes, which were such a major investment, was a way of raising money, and the giving of second-hand high-quality clothes as gifts is attested to in travel accounts such as that of Ibn Battutah (Mackintosh-Smith 2002). There was actually a relatively long-distance trade in second-hand clothes, with many being exported from Sicily and worn in Cairo (Goitein 1983b: 184). Again we know little about the quality of such garments, however the distance they travelled would suggest that they would be reasonably high quality to justify the trade. More ordinary repairs and re-tailoring would surely take place locally.

Other ordinary clothes mentioned in the Quseir documents are a cloak-blanket cover (*shamla*), a cloak-like woollen wrap, an item which Guo translates as all-season wear, and waist wrappers popular with Yemeni men (*futa*). Textiles more generally (*qumash*) are also referred to, many of which are not clearly identified, such as the cloth mentioned in the title of the paper ('I have bought cloth for you and will deliver it myself'). The Quseir documents have also suggested a use for a class of textile found at Quseir whose use was a mystery. Three examples of a very open weave textile, woven in horsehair, in a plaid pattern were found. Intriguingly, one had faded leaving a clearly defined edge that suggested it was held in a round frame. My initial thoughts were that this could have been some kind of window screen, as it didn't seem open weave enough to act as a kind of sieve. The documents shed light on this however, as Guo identifies oil strainers (*gharbalat zayt*) as an item in demand in Quseir (Goitein 1983b: 38).

The importance of the *thawb* is reflected in the number of times it is mentioned in many fragmentary texts at Quseir, with the buying and selling of up to 18 garments at a time being mentioned. Rather confusingly, however, the word also refers to a length of cloth. There are plenty of textile fragments at Quseir that fit the description of this garment, having well-tailored seams but in medium-quality relatively lightweight fabric, often in white, or a variety of blue stripe or check. The more complete children's garments from Quseir mentioned above suggest that these were relatively well fitted to the body, based on vertical panels and a vertical slit neck opening. On adult examples, the neck opening is elaborated through a series of different collar designs, presumably this being the area that would still be apparent when extra shifts, wraps or mantles were placed over the top.

Identifying the garment *thawb* in the material record is relatively straightforward, but it would seem a much more challenging task for the material record to contribute something to the understanding of the length of material *thawb*, as no complete lengths of cloth survive. In reality, their presence can be identified, albeit by a process of negative evidence. The relevant fragments look like bundles of tangled cut warps. When stretched out, there are a few centimetres of weft, followed by an approximate 12-cm stretch of exposed warp that had never been woven, and then some tightly woven fabric, which is the 'true' cloth (Fig. 9). They are in appearance the same as the 'empty weft' decorative technique found on many types of fabric in Egypt; however these were disposed of when new. Three of these were found and there are five examples of similar warp fringes. Initially they appeared to be the very beginning of the warp just before the spacer weft which organised the warps before the true weaving commenced. This seemed unlikely, however, as the long length of warp left after the spacer would allow the warps to wander, making the spacer irrelevant. If they weren't at the beginning of the weave, it would then seem logical that they must have been embedded in the length of fabric, perhaps to mark a certain length of cloth, possibly a *thawb* length. This may explain why *thawb* had two meanings and the length of cloth could be exactly that which was needed to make the garment. The excessively long lengths of warp on either side of the spacer, however, needed explaining. The slight over-spinning of the warp caused them to tangle (again suggesting that these were not decorative 'empty wefts'), and on fragmentary examples the warps piled themselves spontaneously into a fringe. If these were systematically plied the result would be a fringed wrap or shawl. Could the word *thawb* then have a third meaning, as a wrap or shawl that functions in itself as a garment, but also a length of cloth that could be cut up to make a shirt? Perhaps it could serve as a wrap until stained or worn, then made into a *thawb* which would be disguised under layers of clothes.

Conclusion

The relationship between texts and archaeological textiles is a complex one. The most basic problem is being able to identify the written word for a textile with its material correlate; this is compounded by these words then having to be translated into a European language to be understood. The research involved in identifying and translating textile terminology is in itself a huge task, and it is easy to appreciate why this has been the goal of much past research. This should be an initial stage, however, to the more important task of finding out how the textiles were used and understood in the past.

This paper has tried to draw out the relationships between texts and textiles at Quseir. It has highlighted the benefits of both resources in inspiring interpretation in the other, but has also pointed out some of the ways the textual record has not aided archaeological interpretation. During the Roman period there is very little documentary evidence beyond passing references from texts found in the region; our information is more general and reflects the economic importance of the textile trade through Myos Hormos. We have some information on the textiles that left Egypt, but surprisingly little about those that came in. The texts from the Islamic period are very different in nature; many have been found at the site and therefore refer much more directly to the material record. The main issue is the over-emphasis on high-quality textiles in the Islamic documents. This leaves a gap in the written evidence about huge sections of textile use in the past, but this is something that textiles share with most of the material culture excavated at the site. What can be stated is that even if the textiles found were not the ones written about, the written record serves as a useful gauge by which to understand their production, use and status. But the opposite is also true – the excavated textiles reveal much more about the kinds of textiles that were used on an everyday basis, for example, construction and patterns of use and disposal, than the written records. It is perhaps rather simplistic to conclude by stating that to fully understand how textiles were used in the past we must use all available historic resources; the challenge is to fully appreciate the strengths and weakness of all sources in terms of disciplinary methods, the type of information they provide, and the kind of statements that can be made about the past using them. This is a complex business, but one which all archaeologists working in historic periods grapple with, and all historians looking at material culture face. Exploiting the dynamics of these relationships is one way of exploring how material and textual evidence contributed to social practice in the past.

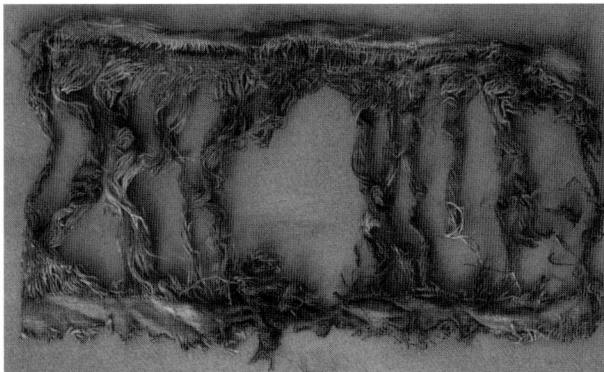

Figure 9 Length of cotton fabric with empty warps (Plate 8 in the colour plate section).

Notes

1. From letter RN1064 (Guo 2001: 91).
2. I would like to thank the AHRC Research Centre for Textile Conservation and Textile Studies for funding a one-year Fellow-

ship which has allowed the detailed study and writing up of this material.
3. A similar relationship existed between Quseir and the port of Aydhab in the Islamic period.
4. *Ostraka* are texts written on fragments of ceramic, papyri on paper made from papyrus leaves.
5. Berenike (modern Berenice), farther down the coast, is also subject to archaeological excavation, the textiles from which are being processed and published by John Peter and Felicity Wild.
6. Textiles from Quseir decorated or marked with either *tiraz*, resist-dyed or written texts are the subject of a separate study.
7. However, in both periods foodstuffs from India were consumed at the site (Van der Veen 2004).
8. Quseir is substantially hotter than Cairo, where Goitein reports that no one complained of the heat, only cold (Goitein 1983b: 171). Summer temperatures are regularly over 50 °C.

References

Barnes, R. (1997) *Indian Block Printed Textiles in Egypt: The Newberry Collection in the Ashmolean Museum, Volume 1*. Oxford: Clarendon Press.

Bowen, G.E. (1999) 'Textiles, basketry and leather goods from Ismant el-Kharab', in *Dakhleh Oasis Project: Preliminary Reports on the 1994–1995 to 1998–1999 Field Seasons*, C.A. Hope and G.E. Bowen (eds), 87–103. Oxford: Oxbow Press.

Bulow-Jacobsen, A. (2003a) 'Poponyms and proskynemata', in *La Route de Myos Hormos. L'armée romaine dans le désert Oriental d'Egypte*, vol. 1, H. Cuvigny (ed.), 51–60. Cairo: Institut français d'archéologie orientale.

Bulow-Jacobsen, A. (2003b) 'The traffic on the road and the provisioning of stations', in *La Route de Myos Hormos. L'armée romaine dans le désert Oriental d'Egypte*, vol. 2, H. Cuyigny (ed.), 399–426. Cairo: Institut français d'archéologie orientale.

Casson, L. (1989) *The Periplus Maris Erythraei*. Princeton, NJ: Princeton University Press.

Cuvigny, H. (2003) 'Les Documents ecrits de la route de Myos Hormos à l'epoque Gréco-Romaine', in *La Route de Myos Hormos. L'armée romaine dans le désert Oriental d'Egypte*, vol. 2, H. Cuyigny (ed.), 265–94. Cairo: Institut français d'archéologie orientale.

Cuvigny, H. (2005) *Ostraca de Krokodilô: La correspondence militaire et sa circulation*. Cairo: Institut français d'archéologie orientale.

Forbes, R.J. (1956) *Studies in Ancient Technology*, vol. IV. Leiden: Brill.

Fuji, H., Sakamoto, K. and Ichihashi, M. (1997) 'Textiles from At-Tar Caves – Cave 17, Hill C', *Al-Rafidan* XVIII: 311–60.

Goitein, S.D. (1983a) *Mediterranean Society*, vols I–IV. London: University of California Press.

Goitein, S.D. (1983b) *Mediterranean Society*. Volume IV: *Daily Life*. London: University of California Press.

Guo, L. (2001) 'Arabic documents from the Red Sea port of Quseir in the seventh/thirteenth century, Part 2: Shipping notes and account records', *Journal of Near Eastern Studies* 60: 81–116.

Guo, L. (2004) *Commerce, Culture and Community in a Red Sea Port in the Thirteenth Century: The Arabic Documents from Quseir*. Leiden: Brill.

Lamm, C.J. (1937) *Cotton in Medieval Textiles of the Near East*. Paris: Librarie Orientaliste.

Mackintosh-Smith, T. (ed.) (2002) *The Travels of Ibn-Battutah*. London: Picador.

Peacock, D. (1993) 'The site of Myos Hormos; a view from space', *Journal of Roman Archaeology* 6: 226–32.

Peacock, D. and Blue, L. (eds) (2006) *Myos Hormos – Quseir al-Qadim. Roman and Islamic Ports on the Red Sea. Survey and Excavations 1999–2003*. Oxford: Oxbow Press.

Serjeant, R.B. (1972) *Islamic Textiles: Material for a History up to the Mongol Conquest*. Beirut: Librairie du Liban.

Stillman, Y.K. (1979) 'New data on Islamic textiles from the Geniza', *Textile History* 10: 184–95.

Tomber, R. (2004) 'Rome and South Arabia: new artefactual evidence from the Red Sea', *Proceedings of the Seminar for Arabian Studies* 34: 351–60.

Van der Veen, M. (2004) 'The merchants' diet: food remains from Roman and medieval Quseir al-Qadim', in *Trade and Travel in the Red Sea Region. Proceedings of the Red Sea Project 1*, P. Lunde and A. Porter (eds), 123–30. Oxford: Archaeopress.

Vogelsang-Eastwood, G.M. (1987) 'Two children's galabiyehs from Quseir al-Qadim, Egypt', *Textile History* 18: 133–42.

Whitcomb, D. and Johnson, J. (eds) (1979) *Quseir al-Qadim 1978 Preliminary Report*. Cairo: American Research Centre in Egypt.

Whitcomb, D. and Johnson, J. (eds) (1982) *Qusier al-Qadim 1980*. Malibu: Undena Publications.

Wild, F.C. (2004a) 'Sails, sacking and packing: textiles from the first century rubbish dump at Berenike, Egypt', in *Purpureae Vestes*, C. Alfaro, J.P. Wild and B. Costa (eds), 61–7. Valencia: Consell Insular d'Eivissa I Formentera, Universitat de Valencia.

Wild, J.P. (2004b) 'The Roman textile industry: problems, but progress', in *Purpureae Vestes*, C. Alfaro, J.P. Wild and B. Costa (eds), 23–7. Valencia: Consell Insular d'Eivissa I Formentera, Universitat de Valencia.

Wild, J.P. and Wild, F.C. (1998) 'The textiles'. Berenike 1998 First Interim Report (unpublished).

Wild, J.P. and Wild, F.C. (2000) 'Berenike 2000', *Archaeological Textiles Newsletter* 31: 18–20.

The author

Fiona Handley is a postdoctoral Research Fellow at the AHRC Research Centre for Textile Conservation and Textile Studies. During her years as an archaeology student at the University of Southampton and the Institute of Archaeology, London she worked in Egypt at the Roman and Islamic site of Quseir-al-Qadim. As the textile finds supervisor, she recorded in detail over 3000 pieces of textile uncovered during the archaeological excavations. Fiona has also acted as an independent researcher for heritage and arts consultancy companies.

Address

Fiona Handley, AHRC Research Centre for Textile Conservation and Textile Studies, Textile Conservation Centre, University of Southampton, Park Avenue, Winchester SO23 8DL, UK (fjlh@soton.ac.uk)

What Essex man wore: an investigation into Elizabethan dress recorded in wills 1558 to 1603

Ninya Mikhaila and Jane Malcolm-Davies

ABSTRACT This paper reports findings from an extraordinary series of volumes of Essex wills compiled and edited by F.G. Emmison and published by the Essex Record Office between 1983 and 2000. They were examined specifically for references to clothing and textiles in order to find evidence for the dress of the ordinary people. There are several revealing sources of evidence for 16th-century dress: pictorial, object-based including archaeological material and documentary, although these have considerable limitations. Much of this evidence relates to the elite in Tudor society, with relatively little material which gives a clear insight into the wardrobes of the middling and lower classes. The research problem tackled in this paper was the lack of reliable evidence for the dress of the ordinary man. A good number of the Essex wills were left by labourers, sailors, servants and the lower status craftsmen and tradesmen, such as carpenters, blacksmiths, bakers and butchers. This study systematically examined a vast number of documents, enabling conclusions to be drawn on the conventional use of certain garments, fabrics and colours by Tudor men of relatively modest means. This research offers valuable insights into the wardrobes of ordinary Elizabethan men.

Keywords: Essex, Elizabethan, wills, middling classes, russet, men, costume

Introduction

There are several revealing sources of evidence for 16th-century dress: pictorial, object-based including archaeological material and documentary, although these have considerable limitations (Mikhaila and Malcolm-Davies 2006: 7–9). Much of this evidence relates to the elite in Tudor society, with relatively little material which gives a clear insight into the wardrobes of the middling and lower classes. The research problem tackled in this paper was the lack of reliable evidence for the dress of the ordinary man.

Research methodology

A few surviving items, such as the leather and knitted fragments retrieved from the *Mary Rose* and the fragile remains of a woollen miner's coat at Leicester Museums Service provide tantalising glimpses into the dress of ordinary Tudor men. They offer the advantage of being real textiles of the era but the disadvantage is that there is no way of knowing whether they are typical dress of the day. Evidence from wills and inventories has been used in studies of ordinary dress but without a systematic interrogation of the data (for example, Cunnington 1967; Huggett 1999). Details of labourers' dress have also been drawn from inventories but these rarely provide a large body of data (for example, Burnett 1969; Hovinden 1965). In contrast, this study systematically examined a vast number of documents, enabling conclusions to be drawn on the conventional use of certain garments, fabrics and colours by Tudor men of relatively modest means.

The Essex Record Office has published an extraordinary series of volumes compiled and edited by F.G. Emmison between 1983 and 2000. Although wills were rarely made by the very poor and the majority of the testators are described as husbandmen or yeomen, a good number of the Essex wills were left by labourers, sailors, servants and the lower status craftsmen and tradesmen, such as carpenters, blacksmiths, bakers and butchers.

Each of the ten published volumes of Essex wills was examined for references to clothing and textiles. These were categorised by garment or accessory type and by colour and fabric where specified by the testator. The volumes contain 10,630 documents of which 2230 contain references to clothing, with a total of 3707 men's garments mentioned. The findings were mapped across garment types in order to reveal patterns of use for fabrics and colours. The key men's garments under investigation included breeches, coats, doublets, gowns, hats and hose. At this stage, the social status or occupation of the garments' owners was not mapped, although this is planned and findings will be reported in the future.

There were some identifiable limitations to the data. Some garments appeared infrequently and did not present an adequate sample from which to extrapolate findings. For example, only 1% of wills mention shoes compared to 21% which include clothing. Hats, although numerous in the wills with 200 items recorded, were rarely described. Just nine were listed by colour and seven by fabric. Nevertheless, some analysis of these small data sets was desirable. Hat linings, for example, were described as silk, velvet and taffeta.

One interesting observation was the lack of clothing detail supplied by male testators in comparison to female testators. Fewer specified garments were bequeathed by men (3707) than women (5995) even though there were far more men's wills in the archive. In addition, considerably less detail was recorded in the descriptions of men's clothing than those of women's clothing. A typical entry for many male testators was to refer to 'all my wearing apparel'. This would seem to confirm the stereotype that women are more concerned with their appearance than men and consequently take a greater interest in their clothes. Equally, women sometimes stated where their clothes were stored as in the case of a single woman's will of 1588 which recorded '1 upperbody in my hutch', while men tended not to do so.

Social pressure undoubtedly played a role in how men and women viewed and valued clothes and religious convention exhorted women to dress in appropriate ways for their rank and responsibilities. They were also castigated for vanity if they paid too much attention to their clothes, as illustrated by Lady Grace Mildmay's attitude to female propriety in dress (Pollack 1993: 7 and 44–5). In contrast, men were under fewer strictures as to how to dress, although the general principles of propriety and sobriety were regularly invoked. Even so, a few male testators took sufficient care in the disposal of their garments to suggest pride in their personal appearance: in 1587 a yeoman bequeathed 'to Thomas Nutbrowne of London barber surgeon my doublet of violet-coloured cloth cut', while in 1590 a gentleman made specific reference to 'a fustian doublet lined with silver lace'.

Certain terms presented specific difficulties in data analysis. Russet is a 16th-century term, which, by the later part of the Tudor era, was used to describe both a fabric and a colour. There are several other examples of fabrics giving names to colours in this way, the best known being scarlet (Munro 1983: 52–7). Russet does not describe one colour but rather the various hues of natural, undyed sheep's wool. All 69 references to russet were examined in order to determine whether it was more likely to indicate the colour or the fabric. Only five references mentioned russet in conjunction with a fabric ('a silk russet coat' for example), suggesting that it was describing the colour. There were an equal number of instances of it being used with a colour, such as '1 pair of white russet breeches', and as a single descriptor ('my pair of russet short hose' for example). For this research, unless classified to make the meaning clear, russet was taken to refer to the fabric rather than the colour. Russet is worthy of study in its own right since it was what contemporaries perceived as the standard wear of the countryman, and acquired a symbolic significance which endured through subsequent centuries (Cunnington and Cunnington 1970: 196–7; Buck 1992: 24).

Where garments were described, colour was stated far less frequently than fabric. For 29% of garments a fabric was given whereas only 16% of garments were described by colour. Doublets are described by fabric (284 times) almost five times more often than by colour (61 instances); breeches are described by fabric twice as many times (53 times) as by colour (25 instances), as are hose (106 by fabric and 51 by colour). Descriptions of coats and gowns by fabric or colour are, however, roughly equal. There were clear patterns in the data which reveal the conventional use of colours and fabrics for specific garments and not others.

Findings

Colours

For the most regularly mentioned male garments – gowns, doublets and coats – black was the most popular colour choice, while white predominated for two types of leg wear, namely hose and breeches. The black and white referred to here are likely to be 'sheep's colour', i.e. the natural colour of the wool, or a 'poor black' which was made with fugitive dyes rather than an expensive 'true black', which was favoured by the Tudor elite. A more detailed analysis of the colour preferences within the whole male wardrobe in Essex emphasises the preponderance of black, white, blue and russet (see Table 1).

Table 1 Summary of the colour of men's garments in Essex wills, 1558–1603.

Garment type and number of items	Top three colours in descending order		
Breeches (25)	White (28%)	Black (24%)	Blue (20%)
Coats (157)	Black (45%)	Blue (32%)	White (9%)
Doublets (61)	Black (57%)	White (31%)	Red (5%)
Gowns (24)	Black (67%)	Russet (23%)	Marble (8%)/blue (8%)
Hose (51)	White (37%)	Black (31%)	Blue (18%)

Of these colours, blue is an interesting case. Coats, breeches and hose were often blue but gowns were rarely so and doublets never. This is in keeping with the prevalence of blue as a colour for servants' livery during the 16th century and the fact that the coat was the principal garment of a livery (Cunnington 1974: 196–7; The National Archive (hereafter TNA) E101/418/1; TNA E101/420/1; TNA E315/456).

Although red is thought of as a typically Tudor colour, it is notably absent from Table 1. Where it does appear, it accounts for just 5% (or three) of doublets. Two of these doublets are described as being of red satin, one of which belonged to a yeoman. In contrast, red garments do appear in great quantities in the wills of female testators. Here it is used almost exclusively for petticoats, 87% of which, where the colour is identified, are described as red. The evidence points towards a convention in the use of 'everyday red' for female undergarments, that is the shades achieved by dying with madder, rather than the more costly and restricted kermes.

Violet is found in greater quantities than might be expected. Shades of violet could be produced with mixes of madder and woad or with a lichen called orchil which allowed humble people to own garments in this colour even though true violet, dyed with kermes 'in grain', was restricted by sumptuary law to the immediate royal family (TNA E315/456 f9v). There are 29 examples of violet garments listed in the Essex wills. More than half are men's garments including three pairs of breeches, two coats, two cloaks, one pair of hose, one pair of gaskins, a pair of venetians, a doublet and a hat.

Fabrics

The five most popular choices of fabric for the principal male garments can be broken down as follows: leather for 40% of breeches and doublets; frieze for 75% of coats and 50% of gowns, while russet was the most popular choice for hose (47%) (see Table 2).

Table 2 Summary of the fabrics used to make men's garments in Essex wills, 1558–1603.

Garment type and number of items	Top three fabrics in descending order		
Breeches (53)	Leather (40%)	Russet (38%)	Frieze (8%)/canvas (8%)
Coats (163)	Frieze (75%)	Russet (12%)	Cloth (7%)
Doublets (284)	Leather (40%)	Canvas (24%)	Fustian (21%)
Gowns (64)	Frieze (50%)	Fur (18%)	Cloth (14%)
Hose (106)	Russet (47%)	Leather (29%)	Cloth (7%)

The Essex man's wardrobe shows a preponderance of leather, frieze and russet together with good quantities of canvas, fustian and cloth (wool). This does not necessarily mean, however, that these were very humble garments. For example, in 1588, a glazier left his 'white canvas doublet with the silver buttons' and another testator left 'a white fustian doublet with silver buttons'. Gowns were the only male garments bearing fur.

The most popular material for doublets was leather (40% of 284 items), with canvas (24%) and fustian (21%) offering less frequent alternatives. There is a surprising lack of wool used for doublets. Sumptuary law, however, forbade the use of imported wool to certain classes who are well represented in these data. Much of the reissued sumptuary law of the 16th century was based on an act of Henry VIII (Records Commission 1820–1828) against 'excesse in apparayle'. Journeymen, servants and husbandmen, who were listed below those able to spend £5 a year, were not permitted to wear non-woollen doublet cloth except leather, fustian or canvas. Nearly all the doublets of these three fabrics which are listed with the status or trade of their owners are bequeathed by yeomen or husbandmen. This would seem to suggest that some sumptuary law was effective as people who could afford better and were allowed it avoided these lower status fabrics. The wills also hint at fabrics which are found elsewhere in documentary sources but are rarely pictured such as striped cloth. A striped canvas doublet is mentioned in the will of an Essex gentleman in 1584.

The ease with which linen can be washed was crucial to the Tudor concept of personal hygiene. Given that most garments were made from fabrics which are professionally cleaned today, it is not surprising that linen formed an indispensable barrier between the body and the more expensive fabrics which were not so easily cleaned. Even the poorest testators in Essex who left shirts owned at least two or three. This point is made most clearly by citing several examples. John Day of Braintree, in his will dated 2 August 1564 left 'To John Daye my brother … [a] lockram shirt. To Richard Daye my brother my best holland shirt. To Anthony Becwt my 2 canvas shirts.' Separate bands

Figure 1 A doctor wearing a fur-lined gown. (Drawing by Michael Perry based on a woodcut of William Bullien from *Bullien's Bulworke of defence againste all sickness*, British Museum, 1562.)

Figure 2 A musician wearing a cassock and venetian hose. (Drawing by Michael Perry based on a woodcut in *Orchesographie* by Thoinot Arbeau, British Library, 1588.)

Figure 3 A mat seller wearing a jerkin over doublet and venetian hose. (Drawing by Michael Perry based on *Cryes of the City of London*, Pepys Library, Cambridge, c.1600.)

and cuffs were used to decorate shirts, as indicated by the will of John Price of Walthamstow, schoolmaster (1586) which included '15 shirt bands, 12 pairs of cuffs [and] 9 shirts'. The varying quality of a man's shirts can be seen in the 1597 will of Robert Marley of Waltham Abbey which left 'To James Proddlam my countryman 2 of my best shirts excepting my best of all'.

The social context of clothes

The social context of some garments was also revealed by the wills. The wills confirm that clothes were a form of stored wealth (Stallybrass and Jones 2000: 29), not least because so many items of clothing are bequeathed. Linen garments were often made in the home while all others were made by professionals. For example, garments were described as being made by tailors even for those at the lower echelons of society: the will of Anthony Bret of Langforn, yeoman, from 1588 referred to 'A doublet and a pair of hose ... [and] paid to Thomas the tailor for making the doublet 4s ... [and] for making the hose 2s'.

Twenty-nine of the testators were described as sailors, mariners and seafaring men. A garment that is notably absent in the wills of these men is the doublet. Several of the sailors owned a number of petticoats or waistcoats however. In addition, numerous loose outer garments, such as coats and cassocks, were also listed, which suggests that they were worn directly over the petticoats to protect the body from severe cold and damp while still allowing easy movement of the limbs. By the same token, the will of Thomas Searle, citizen and mercer, dating from 1584, demonstrates the various functions and social roles of the gown: 'To Thomas late son of Valetye Lucas my best puke gown faced with satin and welted with velvet ... To 4 poor men that shall carry my [body?] to church each a cloth gown and to four other poor men of South Weald each against next winter a frieze gown of 10d a yard'.

Testators recorded clothes in a clearly defined hierarchy. Searle identified his 'best puke gown' as a bequest. Even the worst item in an individual's wardrobe was worth leaving to a grateful relative or neighbour. Nicholas Cooch, a husbandman (1572/3), left his 'worst black coat' to one beneficiary while another received his 'best black coat'. Searle had a gown which was 'faced with satin and welted with velvet'. In addition, Essex wills show considerable evidence of people aspiring to wear better quality cloth and silk in small details of their dress: for example, a coat 'which is lined with velvet in the collar' (1585). Several wills refer to best versus workaday wear and to summer and winter clothes. 'Against next winter' was the phrase Searle used to indicate the appropriateness of items of dress to the seasons. In addition, he, like Manuel Chamberlyn, made provision for the poor. The latter left his best clothes to his fellow servants and 'all my other old raiment to the poor people of Magdalen Laver'. Searle even indicated a price for frieze at '10d a yard' in line with several other testators who give the value of their clothes or clothes to be provided for others: 'to his fellow John Linsey 10s to buy him a pair of garters'. Some testators stipulated the value of the clothes to be made for their funerals, for example 'a mourning gown of 16s the yard at least' (1589).

The data also confirm the symbolic role played by gloves in the second half of 16th-century society (Cumming 1982: 21). An Essex servant left money for gloves in 1592 in the hope that he was respectable enough to be worthy of remembrance: 'I will that special gloves be provided for my good master, good mistress, Mr Walter Myldmay, and my good friend Mr Pickering if it please them to wear gloves for my sake'. Likewise, wedding clothes were bequeathed by men and women which suggests that, long after they had married, these were still valuable outfits. Without exception, it is women who owned and left wedding rings in the Essex wills, confirming that men did not wear them.

Conclusion

A study of ten Oxfordshire inventories dating from between 1550 and 1596 has suggested that the average labouring man owned clothes that were worth from a couple of shillings to a pound (Hovinden 1965). His wardrobe was likely to comprise a pair of leather breeches, a coat, a waistcoat, a couple of shirts, stockings, shoes and a hat. This study has permitted some robust conclusions to be drawn from 10,630 wills from Elizabethan Essex and the data compare well with Hovinden's findings. The wills indicate that Elizabethan Essex man wore leather or russet breeches or hose, a leather, or black or white canvas doublet, black freize coat or gown, and a hat.

References

Buck, A. (1992) 'Pamela's clothes', *Costume* 26: 21–31.
Burnett, J. (1969) *A History of the Cost of Living*. London: Penguin.
Cumming, V. (1982) *Gloves*. London: Batsford.
Cunnington, C. and Cunnington, P. (1970) *A Handbook of English Costume in the 16th Century*, 2nd edn. Boston: Plays Inc.
Cunnington, P. (1967) *Occupational Costume in England from the 11th Century to 1914*. London: A & C Black.
Cunnington, P. (1974) *The Costume of Household Servants from the Middle Ages to 1900*. London: A & C Black.
Emmison, F. (1983) *Elizabethan Wills of South-West Essex*. Waddesdon: Kylin Press.
Emmison, F. (1987) *Essex Wills: The Archdeaconry Courts 1577–1584*, 4. Chelmsford: Essex Record Office.
Emmison, F. (1989) *Essex Wills: The Archdeaconry Courts 1583–1592*, 5. Chelmsford: Essex Record Office.
Emmison, F. (1990) *Essex Wills, The Archdeaconry Courts 1591–1597*, 6. Chelmsford: Essex Record Office.
Emmison, F. (1991) *Essex Wills, The Archdeaconry Courts 1597–1603*, 7. Chelmsford: Essex Record Office
Emmison, F. (1993) *Essex Wills, The Commissary Court 1558–1569*, 8. Chelmsford: Essex Record Office.
Emmison, F. (1994) *Essex Wills, The Commissary Court 1569–1578*, 9. Chelmsford: Essex Record Office.
Emmison, F. (1995) *Essex Wills, The Commissary Court 1578–1588*, 10. Chelmsford: Essex Record Office.
Emmison, F. (1998) *Essex Wills, The Commissary Court 1587–1599*, 11. Chelmsford: Essex Record Office.
Emmison, F. (2000) *Essex Wills, The Commissary Court 1596–1603*, 12. Chelmsford: Essex Record Office.
Hovinden, M. (ed.) (1965) *Household and Farm Inventories in Oxfordshire, 1550–90*. Historical Manuscripts Commission, JP10.

Huggett, J. (1999) 'Rural costume in Elizabethan Essex: a study based on the evidence from wills', *Costume* 33: 74–88.

Huggett, J. (2001) *Clothes of the Common Woman 1580–1660*. Bristol: Stuart Press.

Huggett, J. (2002) *Clothes of the Common Man 1580–1660*. Bristol: Stuart Press.

Huggett, J. (2005a) *Clothes of the Common Man 1480–1580*. Bristol: Stuart Press.

Huggett, J. (2005a) *Clothes of the Common Woman 1480–1580*. Bristol: Stuart Press.

Mikhaila, N. and Malcolm-Davies, J. (2006) *The Tudor Tailor: Reconstructing 16th Century Dress*. London: Batsford.

Munro, J. (1983) 'The medieval scarlet and the economics of sartorial splendour', in *Cloth and Clothing in Medieval Europe: Essays in Memory of Professor E.M. Carus-Wilson*, Pasold Studies in Textile History, no. 2, N. Harte and K. Ponting (eds), 13–70. London: Heinemann.

Pollack, L. (1993) *'With faith and physi': The Life of a Tudor Gentlewoman 1552–1620*. London: Collins & Brown.

Records Commission (1820–1828) '24 Henry VIIIc13: "An acte for reformacyon of excesse in apparayle"' in *Statutes of the Realm*.

Stallybrass, P. and Jones, A. (2000) *Renaissance Clothing and the Materials of Memory*. Cambridge: Cambridge University Press.

The authors

- Ninya Mikhaila studied costume interpretation at the London College of Fashion where she graduated in 1994. She established her business in the same year, making accurate reconstructions of period dress for heritage sites around the UK. Her clients include Historic Royal Palaces, the National Trust, Royal Armouries and the National Archives. Ninya was the principal supplier of costumes to JMD&Co at Hampton Court Palace from 1995 to 2003. The Tudor Tailor, the company Ninya runs in partnership with Jane Malcolm-Davies, provides consultancy on setting up costumed interpretation and educational sessions as well as lectures, practical workshops and costume-making. She is a part-time lecturer on the social history of 16th-century dress at Nottingham University.
- Jane Malcolm-Davies is director of JMD&Co, the company responsible for managing costumed interpretation at Hampton Court Palace from July 1992 to March 2004. She was lecturer in leisure management at the University of Surrey, where she specialised in heritage issues until March 2005. Jane now advises Historic Scotland on the use of costumed interpretation, runs evaluation programmes for the National Trust's education service and trains front-of-house staff for the Royal Collection and English Heritage. She is currently researching Tudor dress in effigies as a postdoctoral Research Fellow at the AHRC Research Centre for Textile Conservation and Textile Studies.

Addresses

- Ninya Mikhaila, 1b Hamilton Drive, The Park, Nottingham NG7 1DF, UK (ninya@ninyamikhaila.com)
- Jane Malcolm-Davies, Millstones, Tilthams Green, Godalming GU7 3BT, UK (jane@jmdandco.com)

Abundant images and scant text: reading textile pattern books

Philip A. Sykas

ABSTRACT Textile pattern books originating from business archives normally present numerous textile samples alongside some written text. Thus they form a natural subject for the theme of 'textiles and text'. This paper uses examples drawn from recent research on pattern book archives to illustrate how object-based study can be used to support or to critique related text-based study. Examples show how artefactual data analysed on visual terms can generate new information unobtainable by other means, and suggest that such information can subsequently be used to evaluate other written texts or object evidence. Techniques discussed include pattern matching and stylistic sequencing.

Keywords: archives, artefactual evidence, calico prints, Lancashire silks, matching, pattern books

Introduction

In the early 1850s, textile pattern books from local manufacturers were solicited for a proposed history of calico printing by the secretaries of the Manchester Literary and Philosophical Society. The signatories to this appeal, chemists Robert Angus Smith and Edward Schunck, wrote of such pattern books 'These will tell to those who can read them nearly the whole history of their manufacture' (Smith and Schunck c.1850: 2). Such is the potential of textile pattern books: offering nearly the whole history of calico printing. But the proviso 'to those who can read them' speaks of a meaning accessible only to those with specialist knowledge. This meaning, that was then available to only a few, has been further obscured by the intervening 150 years. There is undoubtedly a steep learning curve for those who wish to 'read' historical textile pattern books today.

Typically, pattern books present a dense body of visual evidence in the form of pattern samples, sometimes with no written information at all, but more usually accompanied by text-based clues such as headings, numbering systems and inscribed notes. As objects, they also hold rich layers of artefactual content in the form of binding styles, materials and their associated technologies. Careful and persistent study of several pattern book archives in north-west England has uncovered internal and external links between textiles and texts that suggest ways of penetrating the rich historical meaning indicated by Smith and Schunck. This paper highlights a few examples taken from the context of textile pattern books that show how textiles and text can be read together.

Pattern matching as an indicator of shared origin

Perhaps the most instinctual activity of the pattern book researcher is a search for visual matches. When a chronological sequence is presented by a pattern book, a pattern match can confirm dating; when the book's compiler is known, a match can indicate provenance. It is also possible, since so many textile company archives have been split apart, to find good matches between pattern books as whole entities. An illustration of such a match is that between two shipment record books now held in separate institutions, one at Manchester Archives and the other at the Museum of Science and Industry in Manchester.[1] The earlier book details the cargoes of printed chintzes and woven muslins shipped from England to India between May 1822 and August 1823.[2] Each entry is headed by the name of the ship and date of sail, followed by a list of the contents case by case, identified by their bale mark and number. Each different pattern is represented by a sample, beside which the number of pieces of cloth is written. The second book (Fig. 1) begins at the month the first book finishes.[3] Although the earlier book has lost its original binding and the text block differs somewhat in size and paper stock, the entries follow the same layout and recording format. There are also further matches between individual fabric samples to indicate the books stem from the same source and are consecutive volumes.

The originating company of the earlier book is not identified, but the later volume notes a sailing from Liverpool in July 1824 carrying a consignment on account of the Bombay merchant house Ritchie Steuart & Co.[4] From 1825, shipments employ the company initials RS as the bale mark, and some of the ships have eponymous links with the company, for example the *Thomas Ritchie* and *Mount Steuart Elphinstone*.[5] These are sufficient to identify the source of the later book as Ritchie Steuart & Co., and because of the multiple visual and textual

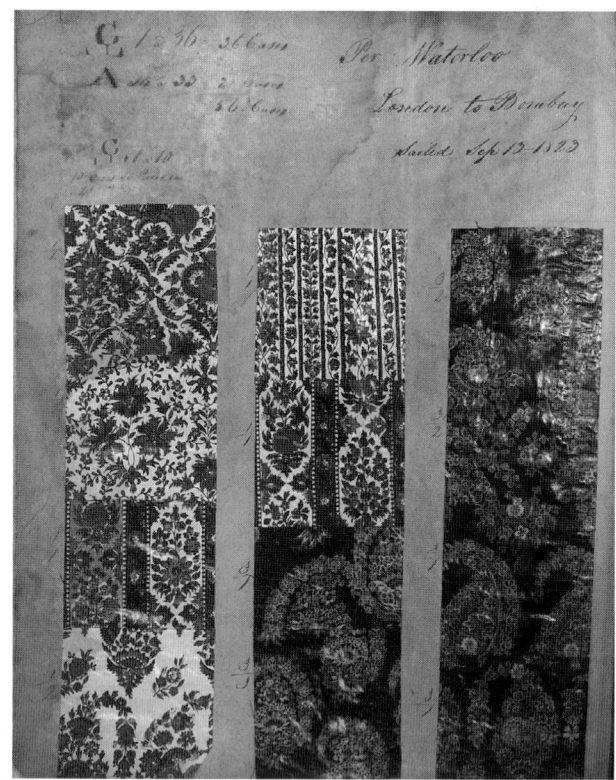

Figure 1 Page from Ritchie Steuart & Co. shipment record
(© Museum of Science and Industry in Manchester)
(Plate 9 in the colour plate section).

Figure 2 Sample from the Lyon 'show book' with two contiguous patterns (© by permission of Special Collections and Archives, Aldham Robarts Centre, Liverpool John Moores University) (Plate 10 in the colour plate section).

matches found with the earlier pattern book, to confidently attribute this unidentified volume to the same source.

Straightforward visual matching, simple as it seems, is labour intensive and requires both perseverance and good fortune. For example, a fabric match between one of the Ritchie Steuart chintzes and a quilt of Indian provenance in the collection of the Musée de l'Impression sur Etoffes was recently identified as a result of the chance publication of a particular image from the Manchester Archives pattern book.[6] Although precise matches such as this are a relative rarity, the rich contextual connections that they provide are still sufficient cause for the researcher to optimise chances for encountering them. Nevertheless, even with matching patterns, the researcher cannot automatically conclude a straightforward commonality of origin. For instance, there is evidence that engraved copperplates were purchased and reused by different printers. Patterns engraved for Moore Johnston and Mason of Wandsworth turn up later in the books of another London printer.[7] Alternatively, these might be a few of the numerous instances of copied textile patterns that must be contended with, always leaving to visual matching an element of doubt where it cannot be supported by further evidence.

Written evidence providing a context for artefactual evidence

Sometimes it is only alongside written evidence that the significance of object-based evidence is fully understood. A pattern book made to present a range of silks for sale to potential customers illustrates such a case. In a book format, the full range available from a manufacturer can easily be viewed and selections made for purchase. This type of textile pattern book is still used today and was historically known as a 'show book'. Show books are usually characterised by neat presentation, with samples cut to standard sizes and often arranged in colourway groups. The pattern book we are concerned with here is from an unknown Lyon silk weaver of the 1860s.[8] Neatly arranged on numerous pages are 755 samples representing nearly 250 different patterns, often in three or more colourways. These are small-figured silks intended for a middle market, rather than high fashion novelties. Just one of the many samples happens to include parts of two patterns within the same swatch (Fig. 2). This small, unintentional error signals that the patterns in the book have been sampled only, rather than woven as complete pieces in a production run. In other words, the book did not present to the buyer goods already made and held in stock, but goods that could potentially be made if orders were forthcoming. Although considerable sums would have been invested by the manufacturer at that point in cutting jacquard cards to produce the pattern samples, money was not tied up in patterned stock, and there remained an opportunity to change colourings or weaving yarns to suit the customer.

Thus this pattern book illustrates the sales practice of offering customers the opportunity to select patterns 'in the cloth', a practice probably originating in France. In the 1830s, it had been noted as an advantage of French over English manufacturers who sold their designs painted on paper only. A silk mercer from the flourishing Regent Street firm Howell & James[9] explained to the 1835 Select Committee on Art and Manufactures how their patterns were chosen:

> It is usual for Lyons [sic] manufacturers to come twice a year to England, that is, in the spring for the autumn, and the autumn for the spring, and they produce perhaps 200 or 300 patterns, not paper patterns, but [woven] silk patterns or gauze patterns, or whatever it may be, and from these patterns we make our selection; and it sometimes happens that we have so good an opinion of certain patterns, that we say, 'Now you must withdraw that, it must be made for us only,' and for [an order of] 20 or 30 pieces they will do that. Now the English manufacturers never give us that advantage, they think

it very expensive to put to work a pattern to show us the effect of it, whether we shall have it or not, and we often urge them to bring us a little piece ready, to see the effect of it; sometimes we want colour, sometimes we want a little change in the disposition; but there has always been an objection to the expense incurred, and therefore we are obliged to bear the expense if we are content to order from a paper pattern.[10]

By the 1860s, English silk manufacturers were able to produce similar patterns to those in the Lyon show book. In fact, samples in the archive of Charles Hilton & Son of Leigh show similar styles and colourings,[11] but they do not reveal if the English had yet adopted the French marketing strategy. The Lyon show book demonstrates how one small piece of artefactual evidence – just one sample among over 700 – is able to indicate the original function of the book, in this case a book assembled to solicit advance orders, rather than a record of production. It is the written evidence, however, that places this information in the context of the continuing French practice of sales by cloth pattern described three decades earlier as one of their marketing advantages.

Artefactual evidence as a support for otherwise questionable written evidence

Sometimes artefactual evidence is required in order to back up written evidence made doubtful by the author's partisan views. For example, in 1826, the *Manchester Guardian* reported that a petition was in preparation by a deputation of calico printers,

the prayer of which is for the removal of the duty on printed calicoes, which at present is pressing on the trade with more severity than at any former period. On many descriptions of prints – on almost all those which are worn by the labouring classes – it adds from 60 to 100 per cent to the value of the cloth, thus inflicting a very heavy tax on those who are least able to bear it.[12]

A pattern notebook assembled at Birkacre printworks and dating from the mid-1820s confirms the claims of the calico printers[13] (Fig. 3). This notebook holds some 40 costings for printed cottons. Some are arranged in pairs that differ in one or two features, so that the relative cost of such features can be compared. The duty is shown at the head of each column with the sum below, so that the proportion of the value added by the duty is easy to calculate. The duty averages around 44% of the total costs, or an addition of 79% on the value of the cloth – exactly in the middle of the range submitted by the calico printers to parliament. This evidence is particularly pertinent because the figures were recorded during the period of agitation for repeal of the taxation when manufacturers' public claims could have been exaggerated for political effect.[14] In the printer's notebook, where a breakdown of printing charges, dyeing charges and colouring matters is set out alongside actual pattern samples, there can be little opportunity to massage the figures. In fact, the addition of two shillings for 'wear and tear' (W&T) actually reduces the overall effect of the duty, and might have been omitted if it was the intention to exaggerate. Therefore, the pattern book evidence can be seen as a reliable confirmation of the journalistic account.

New object-based evidence casting doubt on previous historical interpretation

In another example, artefactual evidence can be seen to cast doubt on written historical interpretation. This case concerns James Thomson, who was considered by his contemporaries as

Figure 3 Page from the Birkacre notebook showing costings including duty
(© Bolton Metropolitan Borough Council) (Plate 11 in the colour plate section).

the leading calico printer in the north-west region during most of the first half of the 19th century. Thomson vigorously promoted printed textile design not only from the perspective of copyright protection and design education, but in the furtherance of quality hand-block printing to realise his own patterns. Thomson expanded his use of hand-block printing at a time when the technique was generally in decline and was accused by the historian Agusti Nieto-Galan of 'aesthetic Luddism' in his attitude toward design. Evoking the machine-breakers of the early 19th century, the term 'Luddism' is applied here to anyone opposed to the introduction of new technology. Nieto-Galan writes:

> Thomson's 'Luddism' was more 'refined'. He proclaimed the priority of artistic designs over the constraints imposed by mechanisation …Thomson did not use only aesthetic arguments in the defence of quality printed cloth; he also mentioned rates of employment [that is, average output per employee], a factor which a Luddite would also consider important. In general he aimed to show that quality printed goods were a better strategy in terms of both labour and markets (Nieto-Galan 2001: 159 and 161).

Nieto-Galan's assumption is that Thomson was evading the inevitable triumph of mechanised mass production over hand craftsmanship. It is odd, however, that Thomson of all manufacturers should be accused of Luddism when he was praised by his contemporaries for being 'the first to encourage any mechanical or chemical improvement in calico printing … at once trying what it was worth. This speculative tendency, whilst costing money, gave him immense advantages, and to this cause may be ascribed his success' (Anon. 1850: 66). So, it is fortunate that a pattern book survives from Thomson's printworks[15] that can shed further light on his managerial legacy.[16] This is a notebook of 1853 that compares costings for printing related styles of work (Fig. 4). These are styles on wool *delaines* that combine machine printing with hand-block work, thus from the start showing no nostalgic clinging to tradition. Analysis of several costings shows that labour and colouring matter for adding one further hand-blocked colour to a *delaine* pattern could amount to an increase of 12–20% on the total costs of printing. Another sample, however, demonstrates that use of a tobying sieve to hand-block three colours at once could reduce the added cost to only 7%. Thus the pattern book provides evidence not only for the level of understanding of their expenses that managers of the firm possessed, but their awareness of the technological means for making savings without depreciating the design qualities of their work.

While it is true that Thomson pursued the high-end home trade entailing labour-intensive hand-block printing, registered designs show the company did not neglect more widely saleable roller-printed work. The Thomson costings notebook reveals that the firm did not shrink from using new technology to increase the efficiency of traditional techniques even while endeavouring to maintain quality production. Nieto-Galan's charge of Luddism cannot be upheld.

Artefactual evidence for a stylistic sequence potentially useful for dating

Perhaps the most effective use of object-based evidence is where the new information ascertained can be used in turn to evaluate other surviving objects. An example is provided by the pattern books of Charles Hilton & Son, a silk manufacturing firm with its weaving mill in the Lancashire town of Leigh. Founded as a partnership in 1837, Charles Hilton continued the firm on his own from 1844 until joined by his son in 1869. Typical of Lancashire silk manufacturers, the bulk of Hilton's business was in plain silks and in simple striped

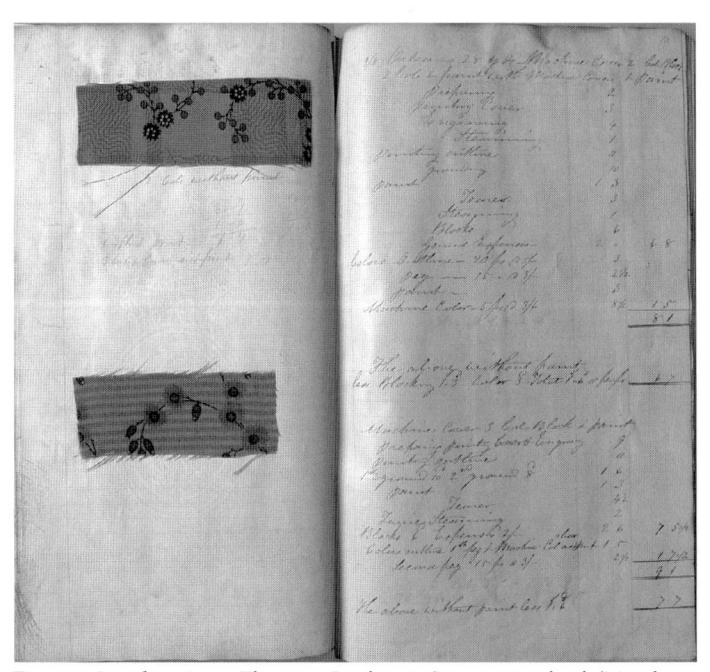

Figure 4 Page from James Thomson, Brothers & Sons costings book (Manchester Archives and Local Studies: BRf 667.2 T4 © Coats plc) (Plate 12 in the colour plate section).

and checked patterns. Such silks were probably a mainstay of the British home market and would have found much use in the day dresses of middle-class women. Lacking the strong visual appeal of expensive figured silks, this type of production generally has been neglected by the historian.

One of the first tasks I undertook in cataloguing the Hilton & Son archive[17] was to put the surviving pattern books into chronological order. The category 'checks and stripes' was the largest of three strands of patterned silk production pursued by Hilton. Thirty pattern books survive to cover the period from 1847 to 1875, practically year by year, often season by season. In the close and repeated observation of the patterns required to return the books to date order, it became apparent not only that striped patterns were always attuned to checks in technique and coloration, but that together checks and stripes followed their own stylistic sequence conforming to dress fashions. The Hilton pattern books not only document this sequence in detail, but if the fashions they describe are as general as those found in figured silks, they could be used to date other check and stripe patterns found on surviving silk dresses in museum collections.

There is insufficient space here to run through the full sequence of fashion changes. Instead, a few examples from one decade are used to illustrate the type of pattern features observable. The Hilton books begin with autumn 1847 when bold tartans woven in shot colours were predominant. Textural contrast was also apparent, created by 'raised bar' effects using an extra weft. Such raised textures became more prominent during the next couple of years, and in spring 1849, a form of extra-warp patterning known as 'stitch' patterns came into use. By autumn 1852, alternating barring in the ground became the prominent feature, with or without 'stitch' patterns. From 1853 to 1855, finely barred grounds were much used, often specifically alternating four wefts of one shade and four wefts of another (Fig. 5). The overall colour effect was more unitary than the checks of the late 1840s. The year 1857 saw an increased emphasis on the horizontal in keeping with the expanding crinoline shape, and check fashions began to pursue broad, banded effects. Even when square checks returned to fashion in 1858, these were altered by fine two-and-two barring to give a tonal emphasis in the horizontal direction. This much-abridged sequence of patterns hopefully serves to indicate the distinctiveness of checked silk styles and how stylistic changes can be followed.

The Hilton pattern sequence appears to compare favourably with the photographic evidence of the era. For example, a photographic portrait of around 1854 (Scourse 1983: 78) depicting Thereza Mary Dillwyn Llewelyn, a relative of the photographer Fox Talbot, shows a silk very much in keeping with the Hilton pattern books with the fine barred grounds of the mid 1850s. A dress worn by Mrs Fisher of Aberdeen around 1857 (Gernsheim 1981: pl. 39) illustrates the new wide banded style. The Hilton books suggest a profitable line of research, charting check and stripe patterns against the photographic evidence in order to test and refine the stylistic sequence, which could then be applied to the dating of surviving Victorian dresses.

Conclusion

Textile pattern books present an interesting hybrid of textiles and text within the spectrum of documentary evidence on offer to textile historians. It has been noted that pattern matching is an important methodology for establishing the wider context of pattern book evidence, but it is not free from problems of interpretation due to the transfer of pattern matrices from company to company, and also to widespread copying of designs. Applying internal evidence to the interpretation of a pattern book places the historian on firmer ground, especially where this is supported by written historical evidence, as in the case of French silk manufacturers selling patterns 'in the cloth'. On

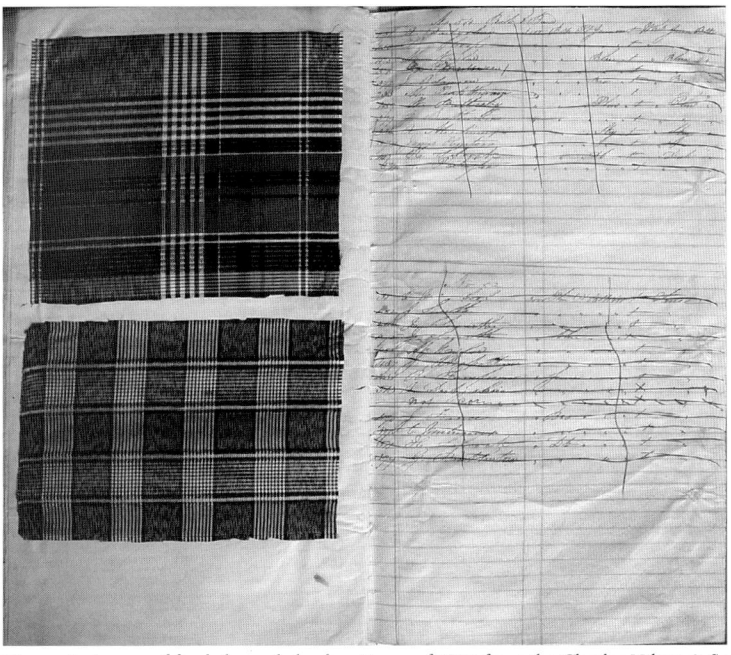

Figure 5 A page of finely barred check patterns of 1854 from the Charles Hilton & Son archive (© Wigan Heritage Service: The History Shop) (Plate 13 in the colour plate section).

the other hand, pattern book data can provide crucial support for written evidence in cases where political bias is inherent in published texts, as has been seen with the calico printers' campaign for the repeal of duty in the 1820s. It has also been seen that pattern books can provide compelling new evidence that questions previous historical interpretations, as with James Thomson's support for new technology. Finally, the artefactual evidence can be analysed on visual terms for its stylistic values as with the Hilton check and stripe patterns. Here, the stylistic analysis must be validated by comparison with other forms of visual or artefactual evidence before it can be applied as a dating parameter. It is hoped that the range of examples drawn from the specialist subject area of textile pattern books has served to demonstrate that object-based study is not simply an instrument to give added depth to information available through the study of texts, but rather a source of new information unobtainable by other means – information that can be explored on its own visual or artefactual terms – and can subsequently be used to evaluate other written texts or 'readings' of objects.

Acknowledgements

The research on which this paper is based was undertaken as part of the North West Pattern Book Project supported by the Heritage Lottery Fund. The author is indebted to the project partners for giving access to their archives.

Notes

1. I am indebted to Tina Fenwick Smith for first alerting me to the possibility of this match.
2. Manchester Archives; M/75/ Design Department 3. Warehouseman's shipment record for Ritchie Steuart & Co., Bombay, 1822–23.
3. Museum of Science and Industry in Manchester, MS 0488. Warehouseman's shipment record for Ritchie Steuart & Co., Bombay, 1823–27.
4. Ritchie Steuart & Co. began trading in Bombay by 1817 and had connections with warehousing firms in Manchester and London through their head company James Finlay & Co. of Glasgow (Brogan 1951). The archives of James Finlay & Co. are held by Glasgow University Archive Services; GB 0248 UGD 091.
5. The convincing match between the two pattern books is further supported by the inclusion of later sailings of some of the same ships in the second volume: the *Bombay Merchant*, the *Theodosia* and the *Dorothy*.
6. Letter from Jacqueline Jacqué, 14 November 2005. Musée de l'Impression sur Etoffes; 956-37-1. Quilted 'prayer rug'.
7. G.P. & J. Baker Archives; inv. 61: Plate patterns. Downing Collection at Manchester Metropolitan University; Moore Johnstone & Mason pattern book, 1825–31.
8. Aldham Robarts Learning Resource Centre, Liverpool John Moores University; 746/FAB. Lyon show book, *c.*1867–70 (Sykas 2005: 142).
9. George Augustus Sala recalled Howell and James as 'flourishing as silk mercers and jewellers' around 1836 to 1837 (Sala 1894).
10. Evidence of John Howell, a partner in Howell & James, 3 August 1835, para. 415 (House of Commons 1836: 30).
11. Wigan Heritage Service; B78/508. Charles Hilton figured weave pattern book, 1863–70.
12. *The Times* 8 August 1826, 'Memorial for the removal of the duty on printed calicoes', 3. Extracted from the *Manchester Guardian*.
13. Bolton Museums, Art Gallery and Aquarium; A.1-1967. John Mellor notebook, 1824–27.
14. For an account of the 1826–30 campaign concerning the print duty, see Hurst 1948: 7–10.
15. Manchester Archives; BR f667.2/ T4. James Thomson, Brothers & Sons pricing book, 1853. For an account of how close this book came to destruction, see Sykas 2005: 136–7.
16. James Thomson died in 1850, and his firm was then run by his sons and nephews. Thomson's strength of character was such, even directing operations from his deathbed, that it is probable his successors ran the firm along similar lines in the few years it remained viable after his death (Anon. 1850: 65–6).
17. Wigan Heritage Service; B78/ L441-L548 and additional numbers. Charles Hilton & Son Archive.

References

Anon. (1850) 'Obituaries of eminent manufacturers: memoir of the late James Thomson, Esq, FRS, of Clitheroe', *Journal of Design and Manufactures* 4: 65–72.

Brogan, C. (comp.) (1951) *James Finlay & Company Limited: Manufacturers and East India Merchants 1750–1950*. Glasgow: Jackson Son & Co.

Gernsheim, A. (1981) *Victorian and Edwardian Fashion: A Photographic Survey*. New York: Dover Publications.

House of Commons (1836) (568) ix, 1. *Minutes of Evidence before the Select Committee on Arts and Manufactures*.

Hurst, J.G. (1948) *Edmund Potter and Dinting Vale*. Manchester: E. Potter & Co.

Nieto-Galan, A. (2001) *Colouring Textiles: A History of Natural Dyestuffs in Industrial Europe*. Boston Studies in the Philosophy of Science vol. 217. Dordrecht: Kluwer Academic Publishers.

Sala, G.A. (1894) *London Up to Date*. London: A. & C. Black.

Scourse, N. 1983. *The Victorians and their Flowers*. London: Croom Helm.

Smith, R.A. and Schunck, E. *c.*1850. *Proposed History and Museum of Calico Printing*. Manchester: Manchester Literary and Philosophical Society.

Sykas, P.A. (2005) *Secret Life of Textiles: Six Pattern Book Archives in North-west England*. Bolton: Bolton Museums.

The author

Philip Sykas pursued an active career as a textile conservator and a costume curator before beginning a research degree at Manchester Metropolitan University in 1995. Since completing a doctoral thesis on calico printers' pattern books in 2000, he has continued to focus on the history of calico printing in England. Through analysing visual evidence from manufacturers' pattern books alongside contemporaneously written texts, a richly illustrated documentary history is emerging from the research. This is demonstrated in his book, *Secret Life of Textiles*, a 2005 publication disseminating the results of two years of research in regional archives.

Address

Philip A. Sykas, Textiles/Fashion Department, Manchester Metropolitan University, Cavendish Building, Manchester M15 6BG, UK (p.sykas@mmu.ac.uk)

Recovering identity: the role of textual evidence in identifying forgotten azlon fibres from the mid-20th century

Mary Brooks

ABSTRACT Text has been critical in establishing the identity of a group of largely forgotten mid-20th-century textiles, the azlons. These fibres were developed from proteins in milk, eggs, peanuts, soya beans and corn by researchers in America, Europe and Asia who were seeking substitutes for wool. This technological innovation was driven by concern that imminent war meant normal supplies of wool would become unavailable. This paper describes two of the main types of textual evidence used in developing an understanding of these fibres. The first derives from the very names of the fibres themselves and is evident in the text which is closest to the textile – the label giving the name of the fibre. Given that so few surviving examples of these fibres have been identified in museum collections, the second source of textual and contextual evidence is fashion and technical magazines, trade literature, business archives and patents as well as personal records and interviews. The huge potential of these sources will be discussed. It is hoped that this review of the benefits and limitations of textual sources will help curators and conservators identify such fibres in their collections.

Keywords: azlon, regenerated protein fibres, wool, labels, branding, Ardil

Introduction

Identifying unfamiliar textile fibres is always a challenge but one that becomes even more difficult when the fibres in question are largely not represented and identified in museum collections. This paper explores the role that text played in recovering the identity of a group of largely forgotten mid-20th-century textiles known as azlon.

Regenerated protein fibres

Azlon fibres are regenerated protein fibres made by processing proteins from a range of animal and vegetable sources such as milk, animal and fish flesh, egg white, peanuts, soya beans and corn. They were largely developed by researchers in America, Europe and Japan who were seeking substitutes for wool during the middle years of the 20th century[1] (see Table 1).

Table 1 Azlon fibres produced commercially in the mid-20th century.

Date	Country	Manufacturer (where known)	Fibre name	Protein source
	Great Britain	Courtaulds	Fibrolane	Milk
1934	USA	Drackett Co.	Drackett's Soybean	Soya beans
1936	Italy	Snia Viscosa	Lanital Merinova	Milk
1938	Japan		Silkool	Soya beans
1938	USA	Henry Ford, Ford Motor Co.	Soylon (?)	Soya beans
1939	USA	National Dairy Atlantic Research Associates	Aralac	Milk
1940–50s	Great Britain	Imperial Chemical Industries	Ardil	Peanuts
1940s	Germany		Carnofil	Animal flesh
1940s	Germany		Marena	Gelatine, horns & hooves
1940s	USA		Sarelon	Peanuts (ground nuts)
1941	Japan			Whale or shark protein
1948–57/8	USA	Virginia-Carolina Chemical Co.	Vicara Zycon	Corn (maize)
*c.*1952	Japan		Cetalon	Whale blubber

This search for technological innovation was driven by fears that the onset of war would mean a catastrophic reduction in wool supplies for both military requirements and the civilian market. Although some regenerated protein fibres were marketed intensively to both the textile industry and consumer and were clearly produced in some quantity, their poor wet strength remained a persistent problem and the more technically effective synthetic fibres quickly surpassed them. After the war, azlon fibres quickly disappeared from both the marketplace and cultural memory.

Text and textile

The primary clue to identifying these fibres lies in the text which is closest to the textile – the label physically attached to it. Two of the examples shown here are literally woven text with the name created using a supplementary yarn in a colour that contrasts with the ground weave (Figs 1, 2 and 3). Labels function to identify the maker – designer or manufacturer – sometimes of the garment, sometimes of the textile fibres themselves. In Saussurean terms, labels are both the 'signifier' and the 'signified' (Saussure 1974: 67). They provide information about sizing, fibres and aftercare. This may influence the purchasing decision as well as being a constant reminder when the garment is being worn or hanging in the wardrobe of its origins, source, fibre and cleaning requirements.[2] They are thus important, albeit miniature, opportunities for establishing identity through branding and marketing. It is also important to apply the same critical evaluation to the data on these labels that is applied to any other object-based or textual evidence. Contemporary consumer legislation has accustomed us to the idea that labels tell the truth but this was not always the case and exceptions can be found today.[3]

Identifying regenerated protein fibres

A handful of garments and accessories have been identified as containing azlon fibres (see Table 2).

The labels bore tantalising names but did not provide much in the way of clues towards an initial identification. What were Ardil (Fig. 1), Ardingle (Fig. 2) or Aralac (Fig. 3)? Microscopic analysis of fibres from the few available samples showed they were relatively smooth and featureless with circular cross-sections, and that they were proteinaceous. Microstructural and microchemical analysis using conventional and polarised Fourier-transform infrared spectroscopy (FTIR) provided further data (Brooks and Garside 2005). Without comparative data to contextualise this information, neither the label nor greater understanding of the fibre could help identify the fibres.

In order to understand what lay behind this woven text, it was necessary to turn to contemporary documentation including fashion and technical magazines, trade literature, business archives and patents as well as personal records and interviews. The clues hidden in the names slowly became clear through this textual evidence. Standard textile histories such as Cook's *Handbook of Textile Fibres* (1959: 225-226) established that Ardil was made from peanuts (*Arachis hypogae* L.) by Imperial Chemical Industries (ICI). Evidence from promotional literature, internal documents and advertisements provided further insights into the naming of the fibre (Brooks 1993). The checked scarf is labelled Ardil. Written evidence from the manufacturer's literature and from secondary texts suggests that this name may be derived from ardein, the source protein in peanuts or that it comes from the name of the Scottish town Adeer where the fibre was initially made in ICI's Nobel factories. This knowledge illuminates the statement on the scarf's label 'A Nobel Division'. Information on this label also indicates another reason why these fibres are hard to identify: 'An Ardil blend'. Azlon fibres were often blended with other natural or manmade fibres to compensate for the lack of wet strength. Interestingly, the label on the nightdress states that 'This fabric contains Ardil'. Together with the information that the nightdress should be washed like wool, this strongly suggests the fabric is an Ardil/wool blend which was borne out by analysis. As well as naming the manufacturer, the label contains the suggestive information that this is 'Potter's Ardingle', implying that manufacturers or textile converters were producing their own blends of Ardil.

The American milk fibre Aralac contains similar coded information within its name. The stamped label in a small black hat provides the name of the manufacturer 'Merrimac Hat Corp.' and the country of manufacture as well as details of the fibre blend '94% wool 6% "Aralac" fiber'. The letters 'ara' are the clue here. These combined the Latin for milk, *lac lactis*, with the initials of the company which produced the fibre: Atlantic Research Associates (ARA). This was the research arm of the National Dairy Corporation which marketed its new fibre extensively. Numerous advertisements appeared in American fashion magazines in the 1940s containing a variety of Aralac logos (Fig. 4). Textile converters in California and elsewhere built on this naming formula. The use of 'ARA' in any fibre name mentioned in these advertisements – such as Duvalara, Sutara or Lacara – becomes an instant alert to the

Table 2 Azlon fibre garments and accessories.

Fibre name	Source	Garment & accessories	Collection
Aralac	Milk	Hat, Merrimac Hat Co., USA	Private collection, UK
		Petticoat	Private collection, UK
Ardil	Peanuts	Nightdress, Potter's Ardingle	York Castle Museum, York, UK
		Scarf	Karen Finch Reference Collection, Textile Conservation Centre, University of Southampton, UK
		Scarf	Nottingham Castle Museum, Nottingham, UK

Figure 1 Ardil blend scarf made by Imperial Chemical Industries (a) and label detail (b) (Plate 14 in the colour plate section). (Karen Finch Reference Collection. Reproduced by permission of the Textile Conservation Centre, University of Southampton.)

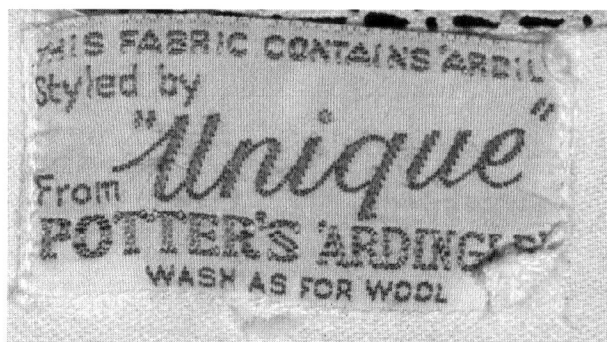

Figure 2 Ardil blend nightdress styled by 'Unique' using Potter's Ardingle (a) and label detail (b) (Plate 15 in the colour plate section). (York Castle Museum. Reproduced by permission of the York Museums Trust.)

Figure 3 Aralac blend hat made by Merrimac Hat Corp. (a) and label detail (b). (Private Collection. Reproduced by permission of the owner.)

presence of Aralac, probably as a blend with either natural or other manmade fibres.

A similar principle seems to have informed the naming of the milk fibres produced by the Italian textile manufacturer Snia Viscosa. Lanital integrates the Italian/Latin word for wool, *lana*, while Merinova combines echoes of luxury merino wool fibres with the Latin for sheep, *ovis*. The licensed versions of these fibres followed suit. The Dutch fibre Lactofil clearly links the fibre to its source protein while the British textile firm Courtaulds named their milk fibre Fibrolane, implicitly linking the synthetic fibre with the natural fibre wool by echoing the Latin word.

Conclusion

This brief exploration of labels on garments made from forgotten fibres demonstrates how the text on the textile was vital in uncovering their actual identity. It enabled links to be made with contemporaneous written and visual evidence, so re-contextualising these unusual garments and their value. Such name recognition may also enable further examples of a period of exciting mid-20th century technological innovation to be rediscovered.

Acknowledgements

Thanks are due to the Getty Conservation Institute, Los Angeles; University of California Los Angeles Library; the Doris Stein Research Centre, Los Angeles County Museum of Art; Katherine Dirks, Smithsonian Institution; Jennifer Harris and Ann Tullo, Whitworth Art Gallery, Manchester; Dr Susan Mossman, Science Museum, London. The author would like to thank Dr Maria Hayward, Director and Dinah Eastop, Associate Director, of the AHRC Research Centre for Textile Studies and Textile Research for their support and Nell Hoare, MBE, Director of the Textile Conservation Centre, University of Southampton, for permission to publish.

Notes

1. Regenerated protein fibres from gelatine and milk fibres had been developed earlier but were not commercial successes (Brooks 2006a). A new generation of regenerated protein fibres from soya bean and milk proteins is now being developed and is commercially available (Brooks 2006b).
2. Anecdotal evidence suggests that many women cut the size tag out of their clothes to avoid reminding themselves of a possi-

Figure 4 Atlantic Research Associates logo for Aralac.

bly unpalatable fact – and, of course, preventing friends and colleagues seeing this tell-tale information in garments which are removed in public such as jackets and coats.
3. Analysis by Dr Paul Garside of the AHRC Research Centre of a face cloth labelled as 'Made using fibres derived from milk protein' and sold at Body Shop (purchased in 2004) revealed it to be synthetic.

References

Brooks, M.M. (1993) 'Ardil: the disappearing fibre?', in *Saving the Twentieth Century: The Conservation of Modern Materials*, D.W. Grattan (ed.), 81–93. Ottawa: Canadian Conservation Institute.

Brooks, M.M. (2006a) 'Forgotten fibres? Issues in the collecting and conservation of regenerated protein fibres', in *The Future of the Twentieth Century: Collecting, Interpreting and Conserving Modern Materials. AHRC Research Centre for Textile Conservation & Textile Studies, 2nd Annual Conference, Textile Conservation Centre, 26–28 July 2005*, C. Rogerson and P. Garside (eds), 33–40. London: Archetype Publications.

Brooks, M.M. (2006b) 'Fibres from soyabeans: their past, present and future', in *Biodegradable and Sustainable Fibres*, R. Blackburn and E. Starr (eds), 369–440. Cambridge: Woodhead Publishing.

Brooks, M.M. and Garside, P. (2005) 'Investigating the significance and characteristics of modern regenerated protein fibres', in *Art '05. Proceedings of the 8th International Conference on Non-Destructive Investigations and Microanalysis for the Diagnostics and Conservation of the Cultural and Environmental Heritage. Lecce (Italy), 15–19 May 200*, C. Parisi, G. Buzzanca and A. Paradisi (eds), 1–14. Lecce: Italian Society for Non-Destructive Testing Monitoring Diagnostics, Ministry of Cultural Heritage and Activities, Central Institute of Restoration & Department of Materials Science, University of Lecce.

Cook, J.G. (1959) *Handbook of Textile Fibres*. Watford: Merrow Publishing.

Saussure, F. (1974)[1916] *Course in General Linguistics*, Wade Baskin (trans.). London: Fontana/Collins.

The author

Mary Brooks trained at the Textile Conservation Centre after working in the book world and management consultancy. She has worked as a conservator and curator in Europe and America. At York Castle Museum, she jointly curated 'Stop the Rot', which won the 1994 IIC Keck Award for promoting public understanding of conservation and is a member of the ICOM Conservation Committee's Task Force for raising awareness of heritage conservation. She has a special interest in the contribution that object-based research and conservation approaches can make to the wider interpretation of cultural artefacts.

Address

Mary M. Brooks, Textile Conservation Centre, University of Southampton, Park Avenue, Winchester SO23 8DL, UK (mmb1@soton.ac.uk)

Adopting other strategies, using other sources

'Wherein Taylors may finde out new fashions':[1] constructing the Costume Research Image Library (CRIL)

Jane Malcolm-Davies

ABSTRACT This paper reports a pilot project which attempted to link the dead, their dress and their documents to create a visual research resource for 16th-century costume. The precise construction of 16th-century dress in the British Isles remains something of a conundrum although there are clues to be found in contemporary evidence. Primary sources for the period fall into three main categories: pictorial, documentary and archaeological. Each has their limitations. Sources that shed new light on the construction of historic dress and provide a comparison or contrast with extant research are invaluable.

There is a fourth primary source of information that has considerable potential but as yet has been largely overlooked by costume historians. Church effigies are frequently life-size, detailed and dressed in contemporary clothes. The greatest barrier to the use of effigies for costume research is the lack of a detailed inventory of examples with accurate descriptions and their locations. The project reported here was an investigation into the practicality and usefulness of a database of images of effigies as source material for costume historians, costumiers and educators.

Keywords: Tudor, costume, 16th century, effigies, monuments, church

Introduction

The precise construction of 16th-century dress in the British Isles remains something of a conundrum although there are clues to be found in contemporary evidence. Primary sources for the period fall into three main categories: pictorial (artworks of the appropriate period), documentary (written works of the period such as wardrobe warrants, inventories, personal letters and financial accounts), and archaeological (extant garments in museum collections). Each has their limitations. These three sources provide a fragmentary picture of the garments worn by men and women in the 16th century. Further sources of evidence are required to add to the partial record of dress currently available to scholars and, increasingly, those who wish to reconstruct dress for display or wear, particularly for educational purposes. The need for accessible and accurate information on Tudor dress is therefore urgent. Sources that shed new light on the construction of historic dress and provide a comparison or contrast with extant research are invaluable. This paper reports a pilot project that attempted to link the dead, their dress and their documents to create a visual research resource for 16th-century costume.

The research problem

There is a fourth primary source of information that has considerable potential but as yet has been largely overlooked by costume historians. Church effigies are frequently life-size, detailed and dressed in contemporary clothes. They offer a further advantage in the portrayal of the middle classes who do not appear in pictorial sources in as great a number as aristocrats.

Effigies have been the subject of long and distinguished work by scholars of the Church Monuments Society. Their studies, however, have been admirably focused on sculpture and sculptors (Gunnis 1968; Markus 1996), the subjects depicted (Wilson 1995) and art and architecture (Ward-Jackson 1993) rather than the clothing and accessories of the deceased. A notable exception is a discussion of an actual garment preserved as part of a memorial in Canterbury Cathedral (Arnold 1993).

Effigies have been used as sources for the illumination of armour (Capwell 2004) and academic dress (Beaumont 1928). Nevertheless, they have limitations in line with the other primary sources discussed above. Funeral monuments can be misleading, some being commissioned by the deceased well before his or her death, and others by a sorrowing but impoverished spouse, many years afterwards. Effigies are sometimes portrayed in a stylised form of dress (for example, children and weepers may be dressed as exact miniatures of the main figures). Funerary and memorial sculpture tends to show an idealised representation of the person who has died and there is no guarantee that the sculptor was representing dress exactly as he saw it in life. These challenges are not limited to the Tudor era; effigies through the centuries suffer similar confusions.

Table 1 Monuments in 38 English counties in rank order of density (number of monuments over square miles) (based on Llewellyn 2000: 8).

County	Number	Square miles	Density	Corrections
Kent	308	1524	4.95	
Oxfordshire	150	755	5.03	
Middlesex/London	105	693	6.60	2.86 not 6.6
Buckinghamshire	112	749	6.69	
Northamptonshire	131	914	6.98	
Bedfordshire	67	473	7.06	
Berkshire	94	726	7.72	
Worcestershire	90	700	7.78	
Gloucestershire	159	1257	7.91	
Leicestershire/Rutland	105	832	7.92	
Cambridgeshire	61	492	8.07	
Warwickshire	111	982	8.85	7.13
Hertfordshire	68	632	9.29	
Essex	154	1528	9.92	
Somersetshire	144	1622	11.26	
Huntingdonshire	32	366	11.44	
Derbyshire	81	1021	12.60	
Surrey	56	722	12.89	
Norfolk	153	2055	13.43	
Suffolk	110	1499	13.63	
Staffordshire	83	1154	13.90	
Wiltshire	93	1345	14.46	
Devon	179	2600	14.53	
Herefordshire	55	842	15.31	
Dorset	63	973	15.44	12.93
Sussex	88	1457	16.56	
Hampshire	99	1649	16.66	
Nottinghamshire	50	844	16.88	
Cornwall	77	1355	17.60	
Shropshire	71	1347	18.97	
Cheshire	47	1015	21.60	
Lincolnshire	103	2662	25.84	
Yorkshire	145	6089	41.99	
Westmorland	7	739	105.57	
Lancashire	17	1869	109.94	
Cumberland	10	1520	152.00	1000 not 10
Northumberland	10	2019	201.90	
Durham	5	1014	202.80	72.95
Average			31.63	

The greatest barrier to the use of effigies for costume research is the lack of a detailed inventory of examples with accurate descriptions and their locations. The project reported here was an investigation into the practicality and usefulness of a database of images of effigies as source material for costume historians, costumiers and educators. It focused on Hampshire, partly because it was convenient for travel from Winchester School of Art and because the density of monuments (at 17 monuments per square mile) is typical of the most challenging counties in terms of travelling time (Table 1). In contrast, Kent, which is in the least challenging third, has five monuments per square mile, while Surrey is in the middle third with 13 monuments per square mile.

Definitions and literature review

This project had two clear lines of enquiry: (a) the feasibility of locating, photographing and describing 16th-century effigies in Hampshire and (b) a method of creating a storage and retrieval system (a visual database) which would make those images readily available to researchers via the Internet.

Tudor effigies and dress

For the purposes of this project, Tudor was defined as 1485 to 1603 – from the date of Henry VII's accession to the death of Queen Elizabeth I – in order to cover as wide a range of dress as possible. A definition of 'monument' was taken from previous work in the field: 'A monument is … a permanent memorial whose primary function was to record the death of one or more persons, and which was originally intended to be placed within a church' (Finch 2000: 7). The *Oxford English Dictionary* definition of an effigy is 'a likeness, portrait or image – now chiefly applied to a sculptured representation'. Studies of monuments often include memorial brasses. This project, however, concentrated on three-dimensional representations of people in stone (which also excluded wooden effigies, a decision which may be reviewed). It specifically excludes representations of armour and focuses on civilian dress for both men and women.

Much of the art history literature on church monuments makes depressing reading, for example: 'The history of English sculpture in the 16th century is a sorry tale' (Whinney 1988: 27). An emphasis on extraordinary examples and their treatment as a marginal branch of gallery sculpture has done the genre a disservice (Finch 2000: 1). Though effigies may not demonstrate renaissance refinement to the cognoscenti of the art world, they do offer a rich resource to the dress historian. A few authors mention monumental costume where it is interesting to them (Whinney 1988; Llewellyn 2000) or praise detailed depictions (Esdaile 1946: 55; Whinney 1988: 49). These cursory remarks belie the wealth of information stored in church monuments.

There are a few examples of scholarly research which use effigies as evidence for dress (Bagnell-Oakley 1893–94). Others (Scott 1987) tend to describe monuments when the individual families represented are the focus of the research rather than as part of a broad survey of dress. The Cunningtons' series of volumes, including the one on the 16th century (1970), makes frequent references to church monuments, often through textual description and re-drawings, to provide contrasting or supporting information about extant garments or documentary sources. An example is a brass memorial which provides a useful representation of a woman of 1511 at Worlingham Church in Suffolk (Cunnington and Cunington 1970: 54). Likewise, Arnold cites monuments to compare and contrast these three-dimensional references with extant garments, such as the tombs of Richard Alington and his wife Joan *c.*1561 at the Rolls Chapel in London (Arnold 1988: 134) and Sir Rowland and Lady Cotton dated 1610–15 at the church of St Chad in Norton-in-Hales, Shropshire (Arnold 1985: 29).

The first question, which is answered to a limited extent by the literature, is whether the representations of people in effigy are realistic and reliable. There is some evidence to suggest that this was the case even if monuments did not present perfect portraits. Trends in monument design have been interpreted against a backdrop of rising individualism – a theory expounded by two eminent historians (Aries 1983; Stone 1977, 1987). It has been argued that the gradual realisation of the individual is exemplified in the increasing naturalism of tomb sculpture, among other changes (Gittings 1984; Finch 2000: 3). This realisation, however, occurs over 500 years – from the 14th to the 18th century – and Tudor effigies lie toward the early end of this spectrum, when 'individualism' is still in its infancy. Royalty and other notables were often modelled from death masks, which resulted in an exact portrait (Esdaile 1946: 47) but this is not the case with the majority according to one commentator who asserts that 'none of the contracts [for monuments] specify a portrait, only a counterfeit of an esquire or lady' (Crossley 1933: 7).

A closer examination of these contracts (between monument builders and their patrons) shows that some do specify a portrait, although the term may not mean an exact likeness (Llewellyn 2000: 233), that London craftsmen such as Gerard Johnson were offering 'exact portraitures' of the dead in the 1590s (Esdaile 1946: 48), and the monuments themselves show evidence of characterisation, as in, for example, a monument to Blanche Parry (died 1590) in St Margaret's Church, Westminster (Whinney 1988: 65–6). However, 'the early documentation is inconclusive on whether or not effigies were assumed to be portraits' and it is not until the 1620s and 1630s that effigies are clearly intended to be 'to the life' (Llewellyn 2000: 230, 233).

Extant contracts do describe the details of dress required. An agreement between George Shirley and the Roileys for a tomb at Somerton (Oxfordshire) to Thomas Fermor and his wife of 27 October 1582 specifies 'a decent and p'fect picture of a faire gentlewoman wth a Frenchood, edge and abilliment, with all other apparel furniture jewels, ornaments and things in all respects usuall, decent and seemly, for a gentlewoman' (Crossley 1933: 32). There was quite a flurry of correspondence between John Gage of Firle Place and his Southwark-based builder in 1591. This features an initial design drawing and Gage's subsequent revisions which stripped his two wives of their fashionable wired hair and farthingales and resulted in a model of part of the required headwear – a French hood with 'cornetts' – being sent to London in a box (Llewellyn 2000: 176, 233).

A second question partly answered by the literature is whether the monuments of today accurately reflect what their contemporaries intended. Again, recourse to the original documents suggests that the monuments were coloured with oil paint, certain parts also being gilded (Whinney 1988: 46). An example is the monument to Sir Richard Kingsmill (1600) at Highclere, Hampshire (TNA PRO, SP Supp, 46/23, f137 quoted in Whinney 1988: 430). Most have lost their Tudor colours and some have suffered damage and neglect: 'Whitewashed in Puritan times, they have suffered even a worse indignity at the hands of the "restorers", who when not actually destroying or turning out the tombs, have scrubbed and reworked the surfaces of many of the effigies, and removed not only the whitewash but the coloured decoration as well, giving them a dull, mechanical appearance, to the detriment of their value

and the loss of their beauty' (Crossley 1933: 38). Damage has been caused by 'Cromwellian brutality … [and] … partial disfigurement often due to choir-boys, careless visitors and … careless clergy and churchwardens' (Esdaile 1946: 61). Despite the approximation in personal appearance and the vagaries of time and neglect, what remains of effigies and their dress today is well worth observing.

Visual databases

A review of relevant texts revealed that the critical issue in image archives is not the demands of storage but the need to relieve the bottleneck presented by largely inadequate access and retrieval systems (Bamidele *et al.* 2004: 151). Most systems rely on manual description of images to produce text which is searched using keywords. There is a general recognition, however, that this method of retrieval is inadequate because it is costly, slow and prone to error (Bamidele *et al.* 2004: 151). In addition, textual labels cannot fully capture the visual nature of data (Del Bimbo 1996: 353). Images are no longer considered as pure communication objects or appendices of a textual document; they have become self-describing entities so that related information can be extracted directly from them (De Marsicoi *et al.* 1997: 119). The future for visual databases is the development of content-based image retrieval (CBIR) which does not rely on descriptive text attached to images (Idris and Panchanathan 1997).

The Technical Advisory Service for Images (TASI) provides advice on standards, guidance and good practice in creating an archive of images. It is advisable to use a file format that retains all the information that was created by the capture device. Further, a master archive should be set up to retain a copy of each image in a form as close as possible to the original captured data. This enables the project to go back to the archive knowing that there is an exact copy of everything that was originally created by the capture device for the project. Another consideration is the appropriate file format for delivery. Since it was intended that the images be accessed via the Internet, a file format which works well with a web browser is required. The JPEG format is recommended by TASI for this purpose.

Tudor effigy research methodology

Stage 1: Identifying churches with relevant effigies

An electronic search of descriptions of church architecture and furnishings taken from Pevsner's survey of England was undertaken using keywords such as 'monument' and 'effigy' (Good 2004). The reliability of these keywords was tested by reference to two thesauri – one national and one international: English Heritage's National Monuments Record Thesauri (NMRT)[2] within which there is a broad term 'commemorative monument' and a class listing 'commemorative' which includes 'effigy' with the definition: 'A sculptured likeness, portrait or image, often found on a tomb or other memorial'; and the Art and Architecture Thesaurus (AAT)[3] created by the J. Paul Getty Trust, which defines effigies as a subset of funerary sculpture: 'sculptured representations of the deceased on a tomb'.

The only difficulty in consulting this database is that the Tudor era is not easily isolated. The results for Hampshire span three eras: c.15th and 16th centuries and c.1550–1630. The search produced a list of about 90 monuments worthy of further investigation. This figure is close to the 99 monuments identified in a survey of post-reformation (1530–1660) monuments in Hampshire, representing 2.7% of the national total (Llewellyn 2000: 9).

An important caveat to this first stage is that Pevsner's county guides were intended as a *vade-mecum* for visitors, and, as a secondary source, 'cannot be construed as sound evidence' (Finch 2000: 5). It was intended that a series of spot checks would be conducted at churches not listed in Pevsner but time and resources precluded this. By way of an alternative, the National Monuments Record's (NMR) photographic database was consulted. There are 402 churches listed in this *Images of England* database for Hampshire. A careful keyword search showed that Pevsner was not infallible but generally reliable. There were 22 churches which featured figures, 16 with effigies, and 10 included the word 'recumbent', which is usually associated with the representation of a person lying on a monument. Those not listed in Pevsner but identified on the NMR's database were not of the Tudor period as defined for this project.

A selection of guides and gazetteers to churches and monuments was also consulted (for example, Cox and Ford 1935) to see if there were effigies not included in Pevsner's survey. These did not, however, produce any further examples. The sources mentioned above permitted some checks to be made on the dates when monuments were built. There were many for which the specific date and the presence of effigies was unclear, necessitating a comprehensive survey of the monuments *in situ*.

Stage 2a: Locating the effigies and photography

Churches were located with the aid of the *Ordnance Survey Touring Map of Hampshire and the Isle of Wight*, which is a convenient scale for visiting several churches in one day by road. Despite having places of interest and tourist attractions marked, however, it does not feature churches. The precise location of each church was pinpointed with the aid of the *A–Z Street Atlas of Hampshire*. This has the disadvantage of not including the Isle of Wight. A satellite navigation system might have proved useful but it is very difficult to discover a church's postcode, which is what most electronic systems rely on to identify destinations. The Royal Mail's database of postcodes does not include churches.

Most churches in Hampshire were open and the monuments freely accessible. The Open Churches Trust[4] has contributed to this by helping with security measures and funding. In those cases where the church is locked, the telephone numbers of the clergy and churchwardens are often available. One of these people is usually able to assist or make an appointment for a return visit. Additionally, some churches display notices showing the opening hours.

On examination, many of the churches with monuments of the appropriate date do not have effigies. Of the 82 monuments identified, 17 had effigies of the right era. In total, there were 43 individual figures and ten groups of people (where each figure was incompletely shown or it was difficult to photograph them individually) in 16 churches. A total of 13 of these figures were men in armour and not relevant to this study. Nevertheless, the representation of men's civilian dress is not much less than that of women: 19 to 23 figures (or groups of figures) reflecting the changing fashion away from depiction as knights. A study of monuments in Norfolk has shown that armour was appropriated by esquires at the beginning of the century and that this may signal a renegotiation of social roles and status among the rural elite (Finch 2000: 51). There were 44 figures or groups of figures photographed during fieldwork for this project.

An Olympus Camedia c-50 Zoom digital camera was used to take most of the photographs. A drawback to this camera, however, is that it does not capture raw data files which are of a sufficiently high resolution for publication. It delivers the photographs as JPEGs which can be archived and manipulated with relative ease. In order to offer some comparison for similar work in the future, all the photographs of effigies in the Isle of Wight were taken using a Canon 20D with two additional lenses (28–135mm and 10–22mm). In most cases, the Canon 20D provided better results than the Olympus mainly because of the higher resolution images it produced. It was possible to zoom in on a photograph of a whole monument and focus on details without losing any quality in the image. This was not possible with the images taken on the Olympus. In addition, the Canon's wide angle lens was invaluable for achieving a complete photograph of monuments with recumbent effigies – another task which was impossible with the Olympus.

A standard portfolio of images for each effigy was constructed. This consisted of 16 views (plus accessories or other items of interest, as necessary) (Table 2).

It soon became apparent that photographing effigies presents a number of logistical challenges. Lighting is often poor or garish; monuments are high on a wall or very tall; furniture may be piled against a monument obscuring it from view. A stepladder is an essential piece of equipment in this context. It was necessary on occasions to stand in precarious positions to achieve specific shots, which suggested that lone researchers might do well to inform others of their movements in advance in case of accidents. This was particularly important when visiting remote churches. Many of the effigies were dusty and dirty, which produced rather depressing images.

Table 2 Standard photographic shots of monumental effigies.

Monument	Full					
Front	Full	Head	Torso	Neck	Sleeve	Hem
Back	Full	Head				
Side	Full	Head			Sleeve	Feet
Top		Head				Feet
Bottom						Feet
(Other)			(Girdle)	(Chain)	(Ring)	

Stage 2b: Commissioning the database

A number of alternative database systems were considered. Filemaker Pro is an off-the-shelf database that permits the storage and retrieval of images, although a weakness is that the images are stored outside the database, which uses specified locations to retrieve them. Although Filemaker can be configured for web browser access, this is not its primary purpose. Vernon[5] is another off-the-shelf database for cataloguing museum collections. It is currently used for recording one project at the Textile Conservation Centre and another within the Winchester School of Art, both of which are drawing heavily on objects in museums. It is beyond the remit of the current project to catalogue the effigies in the way a collection of museum objects is recorded. End users are as likely to be enthusiastic amateurs as serious scholars of dress history. A more user-friendly interface, such as those used by Internet shopping sites, was considered appropriate.

The database was built by a freelance IT consultant on an SQL platform, which is compatible with most servers. This was an important consideration as it was envisaged that the pilot database would be made available to users via the University of Southampton's website. Its format is similar to that used by photographic agencies to showcase and sell their images.

Stage 3: Uploading the images and configuring the database

The front full-length view became the main image for the effigy's database entry with all the other views filed as details. Each of the main images was also made available as a thumbnail image. The photographs were converted to 500-pixel width (main images) and 160-pixel width (thumbnails) and saved in a 'for web' format using Adobe Creative Suite software. TASI advises, however, that all digital image archives make the original image available to end users. The original images are not yet in the database but are available to upload at a future stage.

Each figure (or group of small figures) on a monument was treated as a separate effigy. Each element of dress was captured in a separate image and uploaded to the database. A management area is accessed by a password-protected entry system. This allows new images to be added, text to be edited and entries to be deleted as necessary.

A home page welcomes visitors to the site and explains how its three features are used: browse, search, contact us. The search function checks all the text associated with each effigy and presents the results in chronological order (earliest to latest). Feedback is invited on the home page and the menu bar of each page offers an automatic email message form to encourage users to respond.

Testing the database and feedback

A selection of potential users was invited to visit the database and provide feedback on an email message form. These were drawn from Internet news groups for costume and theatre designers, re-enactors and from informal networks of academics and costume enthusiasts (for example, the Costume Society of America and the Costume Society of Great Britain). A selection of comments (all received February 2006) illustrates the variety of users and the usefulness of the images:

> Great website and really excellent introduction ... Effigies have been a longstanding subject of antiquarian research but their wider interest and educational potential have been undervalued. This study illustrates how they can be made relevant to a wider audience as well as demonstrating the unique resource churches represent for the study of the past at local and national levels.
> Roy Porter, Advisory Board for Redundant Churches, UK

> The fact that the database is online makes it invaluable to those of us in other parts of the world who cannot take a weekend and visit the effigies in person.
> Melanie Schuessler, Assistant Professor of Costume Design, Eastern Michigan University

> This is marvellous! Thank you so much for making this available. It is a great resource, and I look forward to seeing it grow.
> Shelley Monson, Librarian and Costume Director, Guild of St George, US

> Congratulations on a very interesting project and website. I was going to write with some practical suggestions having hit a number of the difficulties of taking photos of monuments – and then I found you had most of them documented in your report. The one suggestion I would make is to use an external lighting source. The natural lighting in churches is not usually good, and camera mounted flash tends to wash out the details you are trying to capture. I hope you get the funding to extend this nationwide – this will be a very useful tool for research.
> Trevor Williams, Renaissance Footnotes Dance, UK

> Having them available for viewing, and with various details shot close up, really helps me to understand the garment they wore better than I did just viewing portraits and sketches of the time.
> Kimiko Small, Student, Fresno, California

Findings

The 24-day project (over three months) proved manageable and the budget of £5,100 adequate. In Hampshire churches, a base of 90 monuments yielded 44 useful effigies or groups of effigies. The technical demands of loading photographs into the database, however, took much of the time originally intended for describing dress. A model for the storage and retrieval system was developed using a framework of standard shots and an SQL platform for the visual database which can now be expanded easily in the future.

JANE MALCOLM-DAVIES

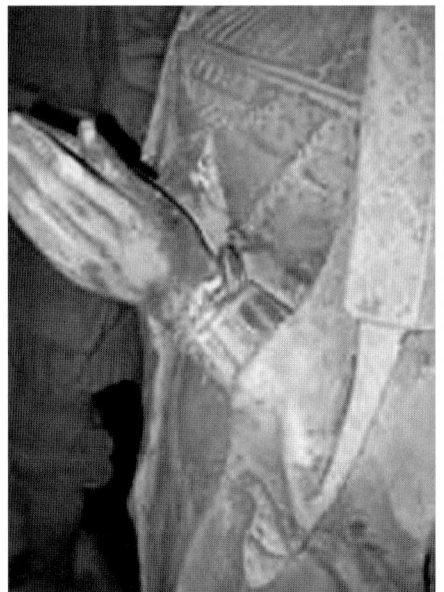

Figure 1 Lady Joan Lisle, *c.*1510, Church of St Peter and St Paul, Thruxton, Hampshire.

Figure 2 Unknown woman, *c.*1520, St Leonard's Church, Oakley, Hampshire.

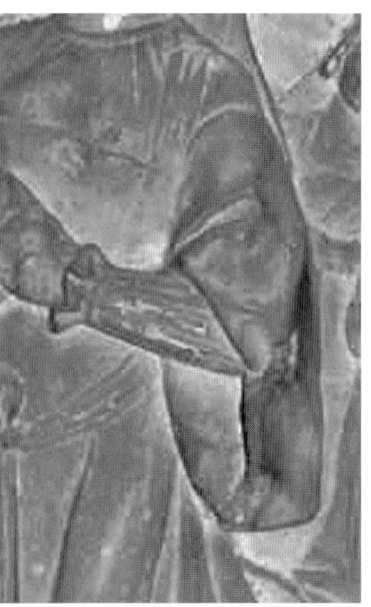

Figure 3 Elizabeth Norton, *c.*1530, Church of St James, East Tisted, Hampshire.

In addition, three approaches to studying dress emerged when the photographic data were uploaded into the pilot database. Three examples are given below using the limited data currently available. A much greater body of evidence is desirable for firm conclusions to be drawn using these methods. In addition, it should be noted that dating effigies is a considerable challenge if no date is inscribed on the monument and textual evidence is unavailable (Blair 1992). The problem is exacerbated by the fact that church guidebooks infrequently cite their sources for dates and sometimes refer to the costume worn as the rationale for the date given. Researchers must take care not to fall foul of circular logic in these cases. Where dating is uncertain, 'circa' or a question mark is used in the database to indicate doubt.

Tracking changes in dress through the 16th century

Seven examples of sleeve arrangements are provided by the database. The three shown above are dated *c.*1510, *c.*1520 and *c.*1530. Lady Joan Lisle's smock cuff (Fig. 1) is visible at the wrist underneath a pleated foresleeve, which is mostly covered by a mantle (cloak) with a revere. The Oakley woman (Fig. 2) has a similar arrangement of sleeves and mantle. Elizabeth Norton's smock cuff and pleated foresleeve (Fig. 3) are very similar to the earlier examples but she wears a French gown characterised by a sleeve with a generous cuff turned back and pinned high on the arm. This arrangement is also visible on Edith Pexall's effigy in St Andrew's Church, Sherborne St John, which is dated *c.*1535.

Comparing features of 16th-century dress

In the effigies shown right, both women wear hoods (which later came to be known as 'English', 'gable' or 'kennel' hoods). Lady Wadham's hood (Fig. 4) is noticeably pointed at the top

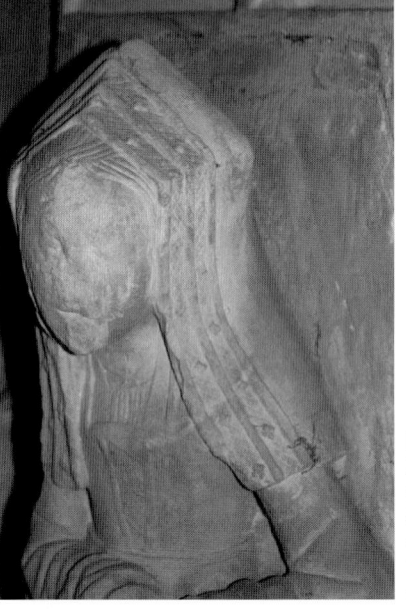

Figure 4 Lady Margaret Wadham, *c.*1520, Church of St Mary the Virgin, Carisbrooke, Isle of Wight (Plate 16 in the colour plate section).

Figure 5 Unknown woman, *c.*1520, St Leonard's Church, Oakley, Hampshire (Plate 17 in the colour plate section).

Figure 6 Lady Oglander, 1536, St Mary the Virgin, Brading, Isle of Wight (Plate 18 in the colour plate section).

Figure 7 Johan Fantleroy, 1538, Church of St Mary, Michelmersh, Hampshire (Plate 19 in the colour plate section).

while the other has a softer line. The Oakley woman (Fig. 5) is wearing what has been termed a later style with the lappets pinned back on themselves rather than hanging loose.

Contrasting features of 16th-century dress

Figures 6 and 7 are dated to within two years and yet show very different styles of formal dress. Lady Oglander's clothes (Fig. 6) are reminiscent of medieval style with her long mantle, loose gown and flat hood with a veil. Johan Fantleroy (Fig. 7) wears a French gown and an English hood with assymetrical lappets. One is pinned in a similar way to Jane Seymour's 'whelkshell' headdress in her 1537 portrait by Holbein.

Conclusions and recommendations for further work

The main conclusions drawn from this project were that identifying likely churches with relevant effigies is easily achieved with desk research. The resources taken to locate, photograph and upload images of effigies produced considerable useful data which would otherwise be relatively inaccessible. In Hampshire churches, a base of 90 monuments yielded 44 useful effigies or groups of effigies, most of which offered detailed, three-dimensional depictions of items or features of dress. Providing textual descriptions of the effigies' dress proved to be beyond the scope of this project. The time allocated for labelling the effigy details was taken up by the technical demands of uploading the images to the database. Future projects will need to allocate at least one day per monument for annotating the photographs with a minimum number of keywords. The set-up costs associated with designing and refining the database were covered by this pilot project. Adding to the image archive will not incur IT costs in the future. Although refinements to the user interface (see below) may need further funding, these will not be as costly as the set-up fees.

A number of potential improvements to data quality were identified: using a high-resolution camera with a range of lenses, giving users access to the high-resolution original images via a downloadable file, facilitating rich text description in the main effigy descriptions for bold, italic, underlining and the possibility of inserting hyperlinks to other web resources and investigating what appropriate, sensitive cleaning might be undertaken without causing undue wear and tear to the effigies before photographing them.

Further development of the database could be achieved through an investigation into the accuracy of the dress represented in effigies. Are the garments and accessories shown accurate renderings of real garments, as is the case with representations of armour (Capwell 2004)? Equally, it would be useful to analyse what the dress represented in effigies demonstrates and to assess whether they support or contradict theories about Tudor dress reported elsewhere. Case studies based on specific effigies or a range of effigies could provide a detailed analysis of the dress represented. These would document findings which result through comparison or tracking a feature of dress through the century. Finally, the creation of a user group would allow for exchanges of observations and queries, and a regular html newsletter could link the often disparate groups of dress historians and amateur enthusiasts.

The Costume Research Image Library (CRIL)[6] for Hampshire was constructed within its time and budget constraints. It has provided some useful images for dress researchers to examine, although detailed feedback is currently being submitted by users and, when analysed, will offer useful insights into future improvements. Work elsewhere has linked economic information from tax assessments of 1522 and 1524 to the geographical distribution of monuments in Norfolk (Finch 2000: 54). Similarly, wills and corporation records have helped to identify trades among those commemorated in monuments (Finch 2000: 59). There is clearly a great deal more to be learned from reuniting the dead, their dress and their documents.

Notes

1. J. Weever, 1631, *Ancient funerall monuments*, original text in the British Library. Facsimile version published by Theatrum Orbis Terrarum in Amsterdam, 1979.
2. National Monuments Record Thesauri (NMRT) – effigy entry http://thesaurus.english-heritage.org.uk/thesaurus.asp?thes_no=1 [last accessed 27 January 2006].
3. Art and Architecture Thesaurus (AAT) – effigy entry http://www.getty.edu/vow/AATFullDisplay?find=effigy&logic=AND&note=&page=1&subjectid=300047108 [last accessed 27 January 2006].
4. The Open Churches Trust – http://www.openchurchestrust.org.uk/ [last accessed 30 January 2006]
   Technical Advisory Service for Images (TASI) – http://www.tasi.ac.uk [last accessed 30 January 2006].
5. Vernon Systems – http://www.vernonsystems.com [last accessed 30 January 2006].
6. The CRIL is available at www.tudoreffigies.co.uk.

References

- Bodleian MS Top. Norfolk B/3: contract between Sir William Paston and the tombmakers William Wright and John Key (1608).
- The National Archive (TNA) PRO Ancient deed C.8873: contract between Bartholemew Atye, Isaac James and Sir Edward Denny (1600).
- TNA PRO MS Special suppl 46/23 ff145r-v: contract between Sir Thomas Lucy, Isaac James and Bartholemew Atye (1601).

References

Aries, P. (1983) *The Hour of our Death: From the Middle Ages to the Present*. London: Penguin.

Arnold, J. (1985) *Patterns of Fashion: The Cut and Construction of Clothes for Men and Women c1560–1620*. London: Macmillan.

Arnold, J. (1988) *Queen Elizabeth's Wardrobe Unlock'd*. Leeds: Maney.

Arnold, J. (1993) 'The jupon or coat-armour of the Black Prince in Canterbury Cathedral', *Church Monuments* 8: 12–24.

Bagnell-Oakley, M. (1893–94) 'The dress of civilians in the Middle Ages from monumental effigies', *Bristol and Gloucester Archaeological Society* 18: 252–70.

Bamidele, A., Stentiford, F. and Morphett, J. (2004) 'An attention-based retrieval approach to content-based image retrieval', *BT Technology Journal* 22(3): 151–60.

Beaumont, E. (1928) *Academic Costume Illustrated by Ancient Monumental Brasses*. London (privately printed).

Blair, C. (1992) 'The date of the early alabaster knight at Hanbury, Staffordshire', *Church Monuments* 7: 3–18.

Capwell, T. (2004) *The English Style: Armour Design in England 1400–1500*. PhD dissertation, Institute for Medieval Studies, University of Leeds.

Cox, J. and Ford, C. (1935) *The Parish Churches of England*. London: Batsford.

Crossley, F. (1933) *English Church Monuments 1150–1550*. London: Batsford.

Cunnington, C. and Cunnington, P. (1970) *Handbook of English Costume in the 16th Century*, 2nd edn. Boston: Plays Inc.

De Marsicoi, M., Cinque, L. and Levialdi, S. (1997) 'Indexing pictorial documents by their content: a survey of current techniques', *Image and Vision Computing* 15: 119–41.

Del Bimbo, A. (1996) 'Image and video databases: visual browsing, querying and retrieval', *Journal of Visual Languages and Computing* 7: 353–9.

Esdaile, K. (1946) *English Church Monuments 1510 to 1840*. London: Batsford.

Finch, J. (2000) *Church Monuments in Norfolk before 1850: An Archaeology of Commemoration*. BAR British Series 317. Oxford: Archaeopress.

Gittings, C. (1984) *Death, Burial and the Individual in Early Modern England*. London: Routledge.

Good, M. (2004) *The Buildings of England Database*. Oxford: Oxford University Press (http://www.pevsner.co.uk).

Gunnis, R. (1968) *Dictionary of British Sculpture: 1660–1851*. London: Abbey Library.

Idris, F. and Panchanathan, S. (1997) 'Review of image and video indexing techniques', *Journal of Visual Communication and Image Representation* 8(2): 146–66.

Llewellyn, N. (2000) *Funeral Monuments in Post-Reformation England*. Cambridge: Cambridge University Press.

Markus, M. (1996) '"An attempt to discriminate the styles" – the sculptors of the Harrington Tomb, Cartmel', *Church Monuments* 11: 5–24.

Scott, M. (1987) 'A Burgundian visit to Scotland in 1449', *Costume* 21: 16–25.

Stone, L. (1977) *The Family, Sex and Marriage in England, 1500–1800*. London: HarperCollins.

Stone, L. (1987) *The Past and Present Revisited*. London: Routledge.

Ward-Jackson, P. (1993) 'The French background of Royal Monuments at Windsor and Frogmore', *Church Monuments* 8: 63–8.

Whinney, M. (1988) *Sculpture in Britain 1530 to 1830*. London: Penguin.

Wilson, J. (1995) '"Two names of friendship, but one starre" – memorials to single-sex couples in the early modern period', *Church Monuments* 10: 70–83.

The author

Jane Malcolm-Davies is director of JMD&Co, the company responsible for managing costumed interpretation at Hampton Court Palace from July 1992 to March 2004. She was lecturer in leisure management at the University of Surrey, where she specialised in heritage issues until March 2005. Jane now advises Historic Scotland on the use of costumed interpretation, runs evaluation programmes for the National Trust's education service and trains front-of-house staff for the Royal Collection and English Heritage. She is currently researching Tudor dress in effigies as a postdoctoral Research Fellow at the AHRC Research Centre for Textile Conservation and Textile Studies.

Address

Jane Malcolm-Davies, Millstones, Tilthams Green, Godalming GU7 3BT, UK (jane@jmdandco.com)

Unlocking one facet of Henry VIII's wardrobe: an investigation of the base

Maria Hayward

ABSTRACT The lack of surviving garments poses one of the major difficulties when studying the dress of Henry VIII. In part this lack can be addressed by consulting primary sources such as the Great Wardrobe accounts, inventories and narrative sources alongside visual material from Henry's reign. A passing comment made by an armour specialist, however, provided the inspiration for this paper. When jousting, Henry VIII often wore a base or base coat over his armour. These bases were made from expensive silk textiles and were often very richly decorated. But, in some instances the base was made in metal rather than textile. Is the steel base, as suggested, an exact copy of its textile counterpart and if so, will it provide insights into how bases were made, decorated and worn? Or does the steel base just echo the visual appearance of the base, while having a distinctly different role and construction? This paper considers the question of whether a study of the armour when considered in conjunction with material derived from written and visual sources can provide reliable evidence about one small facet of Henry VIII's wardrobe.

Keywords: base, Henry VIII, Great Wardrobe account, James Worsley, wardrobe of the Robes, the Revels

Introduction

The records of the Great Wardrobe, the section of the royal household that was responsible for making clothes for the monarch, his family and household, make it quite clear that Henry VIII dressed in a manner suited to his station. While the documents provide detailed insights into his preferences for colour, cloth and cut, which can be partially corroborated by reference to the visual impression provided by Holbein's portraits, none of the king's clothes have survived. This poor survival rate was caused by a tendency to recycle garments combined with a conscious policy of giving the king's clothes away as perquisites; this is in direct contrast to the wish to preserve and catalogue royal clothes, which can be seen in Sweden and a number of German princely states. All that can be linked somewhat tenuously to Henry VIII are a deerskin hawking glove and a hawk hood covered with cloth of tissue.[1] While these small accessories reinforce ideas about the high quality of materials and workmanship associated with the king's clothes, they do not provide a tangible sense of Henry VIII's wardrobe.

Although no examples of the principal garments in the king's wardrobe are known to survive, the metal base or skirt associated with the silver and engraved armour for man and horse which was made for Henry VIII in *c.*1515 provides the essence of an ephemeral garment captured in a more durable material (Fig. 1).[2] Taking this steel base as a starting point for an investigation of one of the less well-known facets of the early 16th-century elite male's wardrobe, it raises the question of whether it conveys only the visual suggestion of its textile counterpart or if it replicates the exact form. In turn,

Figure 1 The silver and engraved armour for horse and man (Royal Armouries, Tower of London © courtesy of the Board of Trustees of the Armouries) (Plate 20 in the colour plate section).

this relates to how closely the king's armourers worked with his tailor and the other royal artificers. In order to follow these lines of enquiry further it is necessary to consider what a base was, what evidence can be extracted from the armour in tandem with the visual and written sources and then to evaluate the resulting data.

The base: what was it?

The base was a knee-length pleated skirt that was fashionable for men from 1490 to 1540 and it was particularly associated with the military pageantry popular at Henry VIII's court (Cunnington and Cunnington 1954: 25; Hayward 2007). Examples were included in the inventory of the 'Stuffe of Thomas Culpepper Esquire' kept within his office in the tilt yard at Greenwich on 16 November 1541. He had a harness for the tilt, a coffer to store it in and two bases, one of purple velvet lined with white sarsenet and the other of russet velvet lined with the same.[3] As this list indicates, the base was often worn over armour for jousting. The king's bases were frequently very sumptuous, as in the case of 'a Base with a placard of white cloth of gold of tissewe to were opon harnes with a riche trapper of the same lyned with grene saten frenged with white silke & gold & laces of silke & gold' that was 'delyuerd by the kinges commaundement to Sir Henry Guylford knight to be kept for the kinges vse' [A264].[4] The bases worn for jousting echoed the form of the knee-length skirts on doublets and jerkins of this period, being flexible yet with a degree of rigidity so the fabric fell in distinct pleats or folds. Bases were often highly decorative and made en suite with the horse harness and trapper. A base could also be worn with, or form an integral part of, other pieces of sporting dress such as riding coats and on occasion, with items of fashionable dress, as in the case of 'a di cote with a Base of Russet veluet with iij weltis of Russett Satten lyned with Sarcenet' [B310]. The wardrobe book and inventory kept by James Worsley, who was yeoman of the Robes between 1516 and 1528, recorded several items including a satin doublet with a base, an arming coat with a base, half, demi or short coats with bases (for example B310) and 'a Base with a placard of grene cloth of gold of tissewe lyned with white saten and frynged with silke and golde' [A265].[5]

The social significance of the base at Henry VIII's court

Along with a suitable suit of armour, the base was a key part of a knight's attire, both for ceremonial occasions, such as the royal coronation, and for jousts. When the king's champion challenged anyone who disputed the monarch's claim to the throne during the coronation banquet held in Westminster Hall, his base and trapper were integral to his overall appearance. In 1509 the chronicler Edmund Hall described how Robert Dymoke 'entered the hall riding on a huge horse decorated in tissue-cloth and embroidered with the arms of England and France. The knight himself wore a skirt to his armour made of richly embroidered tissue and a great plume of ostrich feathers stood out from his helmet' (Hall 1809: 509). The ritual role of the royal champion was highly significant but it was only fulfilled once in a monarch's reign. In contrast, bases were made regularly for the series of royal jousts that were held in the first half of Henry VIII's reign. As such, the base formed a very small but significant part of the male court culture which was predicated upon military skill and overt displays of strength and bravery. Being invited to participate in one of the king's jousts was a clear sign of standing at court and influence with the king. Those who took part, either jousting with the king or against him, were provided with cloth with which to make their base and trapper.

Bases and trappers were usually provided by the office of the Revels but James Worsley's wardrobe book reveals that officers of the Robes played an important part in selecting and supplying the fabric. This emphasises how important these events were politically; this is reinforced by the quality of the cloth used and the expense. Worsley supplied 346 yards of cloth of gold and velvet to 30 named individuals for bases and trappers. Of these, 18 men including Nicholas Carew received six yards of blue cloth of gold on 10 August 1518 'to prepare themself for the kinges justes at Grenewyche agenste the commyng of the inbassadors of Fraunce' [A400] with further deliveries being made in September.[6] The event in question was the joust held on 6–7 October 1518 to celebrate the Treaty of Universal Peace with France. In addition to this provision made for the main protagonists, Richard Gibson received a further 439 yards of cloth to make bases for the attendants at this event including footmen, armourers and grooms.

Evidence from armour

Sixteenth-century armourers often made allusions to contemporary male dress in their work. This could be restricted to one element, as in the case of the helmet accompanying the armour made in Flanders, c.1500, for Philip I of Spain, which was modelled on the ecclesiastical biretta (Ortiz *et al.* 1991: 114–17).[7] Or it could be more all-encompassing as demonstrated by the so-called Maximilian armours that were made in the early 16th century. The metal of the breast and back plates, as well as the arm and leg defences, was fluted to echo the pleating fashionable in male dress, while the costume armour or *pfeifenharnisch* imitated slashing (Rangström *et al.* 2002: 30–31, 297).[8] Armour could also be decorated with bands of applied textile, with passementerie or with textile accessories. To take an example, the jousting armour of Philip I of Spain was intended to be worn at the *justa real* or royal jousts. It is displayed with a pleated base decorated with appliqué and braid which is in very poor condition. The top fabric has degraded in places to reveal the heavyweight cellulosic interlining (Ortiz *et al.* 1991: 110–13).[9] It is possible, however, that the base is a later addition as it is not included in the armour's entry in the *Inventario Illuminado*, an illustrated inventory drawn up during the reign of Philip II.

The examples cited so far indicate that armour could replicate features or decorative techniques used on clothing. Two suits of armour, however, made by different armourers, provide evidence of a very specific type of garment: the base. The first is a parade armour made in 1512–14 for Archduke Charles, the future Charles V of Spain, by Conrad Seusenhofer of Innsbruck (Pfaffenbichler 1992: 19).[10] The second was made for Henry VIII, probably by the Italian or Flemish armourers at Greenwich, and decorated by Paul van Vrelant in c.1515.[11] In both cases the base is presented as a knee-length, pleated skirt decorated with guards or applied borders around the hem, and in the case of the armour made for Archduke Charles, running down some of the pleats too. Focusing on Henry VIII's base, it was made in two sections: the collar or upper section and the skirt. The base was also made in two halves, opening at the front and hinged at the back. It was cut away at the front and back to allow the base to be worn while riding. The base was originally decorated with a fringe of red silk and gold-wrapped metal thread which would have been stitched in place via a series of small holes made in the cut-away edge at the front and back.[12] The king's silk woman, Mistress Elizabeth Philip, who supplied passementerie to decorate the king's clothes, was paid 'for the fringe of Crymsyn on the gollde for the steel base, and for the gyllt barde' (Blair 1965: 3, 30).[13] There was a second type of metal skirt that could be worn with armour: the tonlet. The tonlet was a hooped metal skirt worn with armour designed for foot combat. Henry VIII owned a tonlet made for him by Martin van Rone in the Greenwich workshop. Unlike the base, however, the tonlet did not have a textile counterpart.

Looking at extant objects

Extant items of dress from the 16th century are rare and this is especially true of objects that were essentially ephemeral in nature. Richard Gibson, the tailor responsible for the Revels costumes, often recycled garments as in the case of a half coat made into a trapper and base [A239] or bases being unpicked to make other Revels costumes. An article published in 1922 described a recently purchased base in the Metropolitan Museum of Art in New York which was thought to have come from the *waffenkammer* of the dukes of Saxony (Dean 1922). The base is made of crimson velvet and the original lining and fastenings were lost at the time of its sale. Even so, some evidence of its construction remains: it is heavily pleated at the front, padded with flax, lined with blue linen and it weighs 4½ pounds. The skirt is 21 inches long and the lower edge or circumference measures 4 yards. Twenty pleats are stitched in place at the front of the base, while the side panels are quilted and the garment fastens at the back (Norris 1938: 36–7). Current thinking, however, indicates that this base is possibly Russian and dates from the 18th century.

Dean's article also referred to four bases in the collection in Dresden. None of these are padded, although a winter riding coat dating from 1601 does have padding and pleats that are reminiscent of those on the base in the Metropolitan.[14] The pleats are secured with a narrow ribbon or stay-tape. In addition, there are several examples in the Swedish royal collection. Two of these, with matching bards, were made for Gustav Adolphus II in 1620 and although he wore them 73 years after Henry VIII's death and closer to 90 years after Henry's youth, they are still very similar in style to those listed in the Tudor king's wardrobe. Both knee-length bases are made from black velvet heavily worked with silver gilt, silver and pearl embroidery. They are front opening and form a flared skirt with little or no pleating. While one has a straight hem, the lower edge of the other is cut in points. In addition there are examples dating from the later 17th and 18th centuries which include the carousel costume 'a la Romaine' from 1672 made for Charles XI (Rangström *et al.* 2002: 187–9, 367–8) and the blue satin base decorated with crowns and gold fringe worn on 29–31 August 1776 by Gustav III (Rangström 1997: 138–43). The base made for Charles XI is reminiscent in style of those listed in the accounts of Philip Henslowe, discussed below.

Perhaps the most promising example belongs to the Stibbert Museum, Florence. The leading figure in the Sala della Cavalcata, or Hall of the Cavalcade, wears a base similar in style to the contemporary visual sources.[15] While the base may be a 19th-century copy, there is evidence to suggest that it is not. First, the materials are in keeping with the period. It is made from paned red and green velvet and appears to be lined with a heavyweight material like felt. A Spanish/English dictionary of 1599 defined felt as 'whereof ... bases are made' (Alçega 1979: 64) and while its use was quite unusual in Henry VIII's wardrobe, felt was listed as a lining material in Worsley's book for three cloaks and a frock [B111, 128–30]. Secondly, it fastens at the front and the centre-front opening is closed using points, a typical manner of fastening such a garment at this time.

The documentary evidence

Payments for bases appear in the Great Wardrobe accounts for 1510–11, 1523–25 and 1526–27, which coincides with the period when the king was an active participant in the jousts.[16] In addition, these entries reveal that the king's bases were often made by his tailor and as such they were made to the same high standards as the rest of his clothes. Worsley recorded 22 matching bases and trappers, made from a range of fabrics including tilsent [A268], cloth of gold [A271], cloth of gold tissue [A264-5], velvet [A200; B150, 310] and satin [B309].[17] A further six examples of matching bases, trappers, saddles and harness were recorded made from cloth of silver damask, tilsent and velvet.[18] Worsley's wardrobe book also included references to bases decorated with cut work [B150] and trimmed with fur [B309]. They were usually lined with a lightweight silk such as sarsenet or a slightly heavier weight silk such as a satin. On occasion the bases had an interlining too.

The accounts record the quantities of cloth used to make bases. For example, a base of green Kendal was made from seven yards of green Kendal, with three yards of green velvet for the six borders and two yards of green sarsenet for a partial lining, while another base required six yards of green sarsenet for lining. Bases were also made for members of the king's household including a base for riding of frisado for Master Carey bordered with six borders of black velvet costing 10s. The accounts also reveal the cost of these bases: making a base for riding of russet cloth bordered with six borders of russet velvet, lined with cotton and sarsenet cost 13s 4d, while the materials cost £4 8s 10d, making a total of £5 2s 2d.[19]

Figure 2 Henry VIII jousting before Catherine of Aragon in 1511 (Westminster Tournament Roll, College of Arms) (Plate 21 in the colour plate section).

The four bases listed in the accounts for 1510–11 were quite plain with no decoration, while the nine listed in 1523–25 were consistently decorated with applied borders as in the case of a base of russet cloth bordered with six borders of russet velvet and lined with cotton and sarsenet. This change in level of decoration may well reflect the increase in price for making bases. Stephen Jasper, the king's first royal tailor, was paid 6s 8d to make a base, while his successor, William Hilton received 13s 4d. To set this in context, Jasper also received 6s 8d to make a glaudekin, a doublet or a riding coat. Bases were made by tailors, either the tailor working for the Revels or the king's tailor. The Great Wardrobe accounts only record one example of the king's tailor being engaged in making padded armour for Henry VIII (Blair 2005). Yet Gibson and the armourers were both present at the royal jousts and would have been well aware of each other's work.

By the time the 1547 inventory was taken, Henry VIII's days of wearing a base were long gone but a selection of his bases was still stored with the Revels costumes, possibly as a symbol of his youthful military prowess. The entries indicate a few additional points about bases: that they came in a range of sizes as indicated by 'twoo large Bases' (8609) and 'a di base' (8617) and that they were often highly ornate, for example 'ij bases of clothe of golde blew Tilsent Crimsen and purple velet in Clockes' (8613). The designs often had symbolic or heraldic significance such as 'one Base of Cloth of golde Clothe of Siluer and Russet vellet enbrdered with Sisars fawcon feter locke and Rooses of Crymsen Satten' (8616) or another 'enbrodered with flowers of golde bearing the white hinde' (8617). As such, the base and matching trappers often acted as a vehicle for presenting the knights as individuals and as members of a team.

The visual sources

There are only a handful of depictions of Henry VIII wearing a base including several images in the Westminster Tournament Roll of 1511 (Fig. 2) and the narrative painting by an anonymous artist of the meeting of Henry VIII and the Emperor Maximilian at Thérouanne (Anglo 1968). In both cases, the king and the other chief protagonists were dressed in armour and a base. This style of dress was also adopted by Francis I in his equestrian portraits and in *The Conquest of Tunis* tapestries which were woven for Charles V. He was depicted in *The Review of the Troops at Barcelona* wearing a basecoat. In a similar vein, a young man who is often identified as Dom Louis, the infante of Portugal, but now thought to be his page, also wears a base over his armour (Ortiz *et al.* 1991: 74–8).[20]

When Sir Nicholas Carew was painted by Holbein (or a member of his studio) in 1528, he chose to be depicted in his jousting armour as a visual reminder of his prowess in the tilt. More importantly for this study, he wears a base over his armour (Fig. 3). Now discoloured to brown, the base was originally purple and yellow (Foister 2006: 122). Bases continued to be worn by the participants in Elizabeth I's Accession Day tilts, as indicated by Nicholas Hilliard's miniature of George Clifford, Third Earl of Cumberland. Clifford was made the Queen's Champion in 1590 and in this miniature he wears a blue silk basecoat with half-length sleeves embroidered with gold (Hearn 1995: 126).[21]

By this date, the base symbolised military prowess and as such formed part of the collection of costumes belonging to

Figure 3 Sir Nicholas Carew, by the workshop of Hans Holbein, *c.* 528, SNPG O NO 18 (by kind permission of the Duke of Buccleuch and Queensbury, KT).

Philip Henslowe, owner of the Rose Theatre in London during the 1590s. The implication of the term 'base' in a theatrical context, however, was the military skirt worn as part of classical Roman dress. While there are no extant illustrations of Henslowe's actors on stage, a list of his costumes has survived, which includes 'ij leather anteckes cottes with bases, for Fayeton' or Phaeton (Foakes 2002: 319). An inventory of playing apparel held by Edward Alleyn included several examples listed under the heading 'Antik sutes': 'i cloth of gould cote with grene bases', 'i cloth of gould cote with oraingtawny bases' and 'embroyderde bases' in blue and in white (Foakes 2002: 292).

The impression gained from the visual sources is that the base fitted at the waist and then came out over the hips and hung in folds to the knees. It appears to be front fastening because the codpiece, attached either to the hose or the armour, shows through the opening, just as it did between the long skirts of the contemporary doublet. Bases often had defined pleats yet the fabric was still flexible enough to flare over the wearer's thighs when on horseback. The written records indicate that while some bases were plain, others were heavily decorated with guards, borders and fringe or with more complex figurative and heraldic designs, an impression that is corroborated by visual sources.

Piecing together the base from the evidence

Janet Arnold was a leading proponent of object-based research and she was well aware of the value of replicas to help understand the construction of 16th- and 17th-century dress. She used both approaches to good effect when working with fragmentary items such as the Medici burial clothes (Arnold and Westerman Bulgarella 1996) or items of which there are almost no extant examples such as ruffs, which were known as the devil's fashion, and the farthingale (Arnold 1988: 197). With this thought in mind, the final aim of this investigation was to see if it was possible to recreate a plausible base by drawing on the evidence from all the available sources (Fig. 4).

Starting with the steel base, it was possible to collect some basic but essential working measurements such as the waist measurement (97.5 cm), the length of the base (61 cm), the depth of the border (5.5 cm) and the size of the monogram (3.5 cm deep and 7.5 cm long). There were 12 pleats on each side, measuring 140 cm at the top of the main section and 172 cm along the lower edge. The visual sources, such as the Westminster Tournament Roll, often suggest a smaller number of wider pleats, but the number of panes visible in Carew's portrait suggest a total number similar to that on the armour. The likelihood is that the number varied from that indicated by the armour to none at all, according to the maker and the visual effect being sought. Equally, it is worth noting that metal and textile behave in very different ways and so pose different constraints on any object made from them: textiles are soft, flexible and drape, while metal is hard, fixed and holds a shape. Consequently, the steel base has to have a collar and a skirt to create the width needed to accommodate the wearer's hips, while the necessary fullness can be provided more simply when working with textiles. This caveat apart, it is clear that the armourers understood how a textile base was made and echoed its key characteristics in steel.

The Great Wardrobe accounts reveal that bases were usually made from expensive silks including those which incorporated metal thread such as tilsent and tissue; the extant examples in the Stibbert Collection (Florence) and the Livrustkammern (Royal Armoury, Stockholm) reflect this. While the base in the Metropolitan had a heavy padded layer and a linen lining and the example in the Stibbert appears to be lined with felt; the accounts suggest that the bases worn at the English court only had a canvas, linen or buckram interlining and a lightweight linen or silk lining. Scale size replicas demonstrated the difference in drape for bases with a thick or padded interlining and one with a linen interlining.

The next consideration was the question of how the base might have been cut to achieve the sort of shape created by the armourers and illustrated in the visual sources. There are at least two possibilities: either a separate section cut for each pleat or fold, as adopted by the armourers, which were then stitched together or a full or partial circle. In the case of the latter, if the base was multicoloured, the sections would be pieced and then applied as one section to the interlining and lining. An example of the former is presented by the base in the Stibbert Collection, mentioned above. Each section or pleat is cut as a separate section. In the same way, each 'pleat' of the silver and engraved armour was cut from a separate section of metal. Piecing panels of fabric would certainly create a pleated effect and it would be a logical approach for paned and parti-coloured bases, or bases of the type worn by Sir Nicholas Carew. It is also hinted at in the 1547 inventory which included 'ij Bases of clothe of golde reised with redde silke

Figure 4 A base made drawing on the evidence collected for this paper (Plate 22 in the colour plate section).

Tinsell Satten and blacke vellet paned clocke wise' (8612). An example of the latter is provided by the skirts of a late 15th-century red satin coat which were cut in four sections and they make a full circle (Christie 2004: 88). Although there are two patterns for a saddle trapping for jousts in Juan de Alçega's book of 1589, there are no patterns for bases. There is a pattern for a felt cloak with skirts, however, which are shown as being cut from semicircular pieces of fabric. A Spanish/English dictionary of 1599 defines skirts as 'skirts or quarters of a coat, skirts such as those that run at tilt use below their armour' (Alçega 1979: 64).

It is likely that both methods of construction were used. It is possible that the sense of pleats would have been reinforced in the first method and created in the second using a range of techniques including cartridge pleating, plain pleating, simple gathering or the drape from the flat curve. Where distinct pleats or folds were desirable, they may have been held in place using a stay-tape of the sort that was used to help form the short puffed sleeves of men's gowns. An excellent example of this is provided by a predella panel from Lotto's Martinengo Colleoni Altarpiece formerly in the church of San Stefano, Bergamo dated 1516. The altarpiece depicts *St Dominic reviving Napoleone Orsini nephew of the Cardinal of Fossanova*. The young Napoleone is lying flat on his back with the bodice of his *saione* (jerkin) open at the front and the skirts (bases) spread out on either side. The pleats are clearly shown as kept in place on the inside by tapes horizontal to the hem.[22]

Neither the evidence from extant textiles nor the available texts is sufficient to get a definitive sense of what the bases worn by Henry VIII were like. Indeed, it is most likely that they were made using at least two different methods of cutting the fabric, supplemented by a range of ways to create the pleated appearance and to apply the surface decoration. By combining details gleaned from the Great Wardrobe accounts, visual sources and the king's armour, however, it is possible to piece together an idea of how a base would have looked, how and from what material it was made. In fact it is possible to take it one step further and make a working model of a base to get an understanding of how they were made and how they might have been worn. While the replica raises many new questions, it has demonstrated the validity of Claude Blair's assertion that Henry's steel base has preserved vital evidence of its textile counterparts.

Acknowledgements

The author is most grateful to Jenny Tiramani who has greatly enriched this paper with her comments. She would also like to thank Philip Abbott, Claude Blair, Jutta von Bloh, Jane Bridgemen, Bridget Clifford, Karen Christie, Mike Halliwell, Anne Kvitvang, Stuart Pyhrr and Karen Watts for their help with this research. Finally, she would also like to acknowledge Nell Hoare for her support and encouragement and the support of the AHRC Research Centre for Textile Conservation and Textile Studies (2002–07) under whose auspices this research was undertaken.

Notes

1. For example, the red thrummed hat attributed to have been worn by Henry VIII in 1544 and given by him to Nicholas Bristow. I would like to thank Susan North for bringing this hat to my attention.
2. I am most grateful to Claude Blair, former Keeper of Metalwork at the Victoria and Albert Museum and a specialist on early modern arms and armour, for pointing this out to me.
3. The National Archive (TNA) E314/79, not numbered.
4. British Library (BL) Harley MS 2284; transcribed and published in Hayward 2007. Entries are cited by their number preceded by A and given in square brackets. Items cited from BL Harley MS 4217 have a B before the entry number.
5. Also see A1229, B150, B309-10, A268.
6. Carew, along with the duke of Suffolk, the Lord Admiral and Sir Henry Gilford, also received 10 yards of white cloth of gold damask for this occasion.
7. Inv. no. A 11, Real Armeria, Madrid.
8. Inv. no. 2613 and 2614 Livrustkammaren, Stockholm.
9. Inv. no. A 16, Real Armeria, Madrid.
10. Inv. no. A109, Hofjagd-und Rüstkammer des Kunsthistorisches Museum, Vienna.
11. Inv. no. 11.5 and VI.1-5, Royal Armouries, HM Tower of London.
12. H.R. Robinson drew a series of drawings of the base which were published in Blair 1965.
13. TNA E36/217, f. 241.
14. I would like to thank Jutta von Bloh for sending me information about the winter coat, inventory number 12.
15. Grateful thanks are accorded to Jenny Tiramani for discussing the base with me.
16. TNA E101/417/4, E36/224.
17. See also A375, 400-1, 417, 425, 427, 491-6, 1200-9.
18. See also A376, 505, A725, A925-7.
19. It was made from 2¾ yards of russet cloth (27s 6d), 3 yards of russet velvet (40s), 6 yards of cotton (4s) and 4 yards of russet sarsenet (17s 4d).
20. Inv. no. PN. S.13/2.
21. National Maritime Museum, Greenwich.
22. I am most grateful to Jane Bridgemen for providing me with this reference. The panel is now in the Accademia Carrara di Belle Arti, Bergamo; see Brown *et al.* 1997: 108–12.

References

Alçega, J., de (1979) *Tailor's Pattern Book 1589*, introduction by J.L. Nevinson. Carlton: Ruth Bean Publishers.

Anglo, S. (1968) *The Great Tournament Roll of Westminster*. Oxford: Oxford University Press.

Arnold, J. (1988) *Queen Elizabeth's Wardrobe Unlock'd*. Leeds: Maney.

Arnold, J. and Westerman Bulgarella, M. (1996) 'An innovative method for mounting the sixteenth-century doublet and trunk-hose worn by Don Garzia de'Medici', *Costume* 30: 47–55.

Blair, C. (1965) 'The Emperor Maximilian's gift of armour to King Henry VIII and the silver and engraved armour at the Tower of London', *Archaeologia* 99: 1–52.

Blair, C. (2005) 'A 16th-century reference to the making of a coat of mail', *Arms and Armour Society* 18(3): 105–6.

Brown, D.A., Humfrey, P. and Lucco, M. (eds) (1997) *Lorenzo Lotto: Rediscovered Master of the Renaissance* (exhibition catalogue, The National Gallery of Art Washington, Accademia Carrara di Belle Arti, Bergamo & Grand Palais, Paris). New Haven and London: National Gallery of Art Washington and Yale University Press.

Christie, K. (2004) 'Neuentdeckungen im Bernischen Historischen Museum: Der sogenannte Burgunderrock (BHM Inv. 20)', *Waffen- und Kostümkunde*: 83–92.

Cunnington, C.W. and Cunnington, P. (1954) *Handbook of English Costume in the Sixteenth Century.* London: Faber and Faber.

Dean, B. (1922) 'A sixteenth-century military skirt', *Bulletin of the Metropolitan Museum of Art* 17(2): 29–31.

Foakes, R.A. (ed.) (2002) *Henslowe's Diary*, 2nd edn. Cambridge: Cambridge University Press.

Foister, S. (2006) *Holbein in England.* London: Tate Publishing.

Hall, E. (1809) *The Union of the Two Noble and Illustre Families of Lancaster and York.* London: J. Johnson.

Hayward, M.A. (2007) *Dress at the Court of Henry VIII.* Leeds: Maney.

Hearn, K. (1995) *Dynasties: Painting in Tudor and Jacobean England 1530–1630.* London: Tate Publishing.

Norris, H. (1938) *Tudor Costume and Fashion.* New York: Dover.

Ortiz, A.D., Carretero, C.H. and Godoy, J.A. (1991) *Resplendence of the Spanish Monarchy.* New York: Metropolitan Museum of Art.

Pfaffenbichler, M. (1992) *Medieval Craftsmen: Armourers.* London: British Museum Press.

Rangström, L. (1997) *Kläder för tid och evighet.* Stockholm: Livrustkammaren.

Rangström, L. et al. (2002) *Lions of Fashion: Male Fashion of the 16th, 17th and 18th Centuries/Modelejon Manligt Mode 1500-tal 1600-tal 1700-tal.* Stockholm: Livrustkammaren.

The author

Having graduated with a history degree, Maria Hayward completed the postgraduate diploma in textile conservation at the Textile Conservation Centre, Hampton Court Palace (TCC). After working as a conservator and completing a PhD, she is currently a Reader and Head of Studies and Research at the TCC, University of Southampton and the Director of the AHRC Research Centre for Textile Conservation and Textile Studies (2004–07). In 2004 she was elected as a Fellow of the Society of Antiquaries and joined the editorial board of *Studies in Conservation*. She is also Assistant Editor of *Costume*.

Address

Maria Hayward, AHRC Research Centre for Textile Conservation and Textile Studies, Winchester School of Art, University of Southampton, Park Avenue, Winchester SO23 8DL, UK (mh11@soton.ac.uk)

A portrait, two dresses, two samplers and a burning steamship

Edward F. Maeder

ABSTRACT Early on the morning of 13 January 1840 the steamship *Lexington* burst into flames and all but four of the 142 passengers were lost. This modern and efficient ship had been purchased by Cornelius Vanderbilt two years before and it was taking a newly engaged young lady and her fiancé to Connecticut to be married. Her failure to reach her family was only explained a number of days later when the letter she sent from New Jersey, where she had been teaching, reached them. The young woman was Sophia Wheeler (1821–1840), the daughter of Sophia Smead (1784–1843) of Greenfield, Massachusetts and Robert Wheeler (1772–1863) of Stonington, Connecticut. Historic Deerfield, Inc. owns a watercolour portrait of Sophia Smead dated 1813, her wedding dress from 1815 of woven and embroidered Indian cotton, Sophia Wheeler's embroidered christening robe and cap of 1823, and two silk and linen samplers, the mother's (*c.*1794) and the daughter's unfinished work, worked when she was eight (1829). Put into context with family records, letters, account books, grave markers and newspaper sources, these textiles illuminate the educational, cultural and fashionable world of New England in the first decades of the 19th century. This paper explores an extended family's relationship to the textiles that were part of their lives.

Keywords: embroidery, New England, cotton, birth, marriage, death, Historic Deerfield

Introduction

On a spring Monday morning in 2000, Donald R. Friary, the Executive-Director at Historic Deerfield announced he had some interesting news. He had just returned from a trip to California where he visited a family long connected with Deerfield, the remote community that was settled in the mid-1660s and incorporated in 1673 on the western frontier of the British colonies in the Commonwealth of Massachusetts. He had brought back from his trip what he considered to be two important needlework samplers from a prominent family in Greenfield, a community just a few miles north of Deerfield, which had become a separate town in 1753.

Sophia Smead and her sampler

For many years, schoolgirl needlework – and in particular samplers – has been considered to be one of the most uninteresting and, frankly, dull forms of embroidery and at first glance it was clear that these particular pieces were most uninspiring. The smaller one, stitched in silk on a linen ground, 10¾ × 10 in. and quite faded, was based on a simple symmetrical design with baskets of flowers, both block and cursive alphabets surrounded by a traditional border (Fig. 1). The maker's name, 'sophia smead', was barely legible and it was in a cartouche, just below the centre of the design. The piece was also undated. This device of the name being set into a cartouche within a

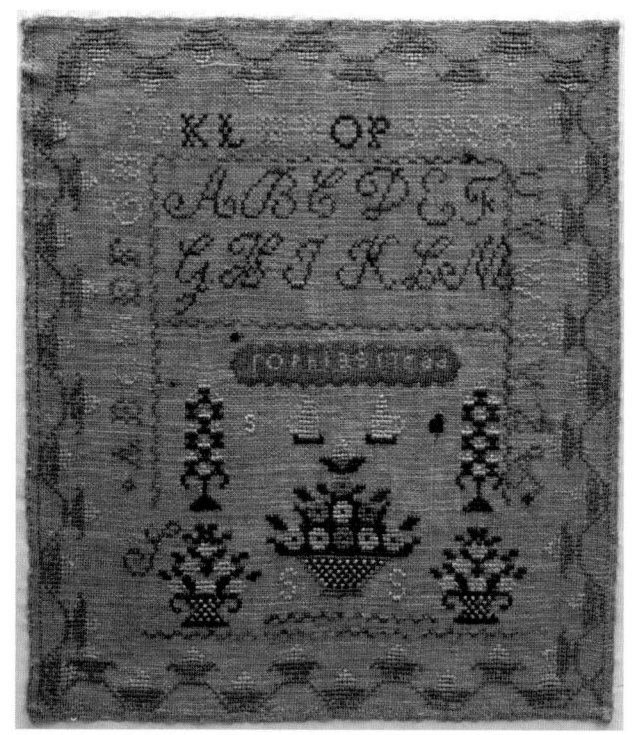

Figure 1 Embroidery sampler by Sophia Smead about 1794, silk on linen (Historic Deerfield 2000.4.1, Gift of Karen Dunn) (Plate 23 in the colour plate section).

completely stitched ground was a defining characteristic of this type of needlework local to the area from about 1790 until nearly 1840.

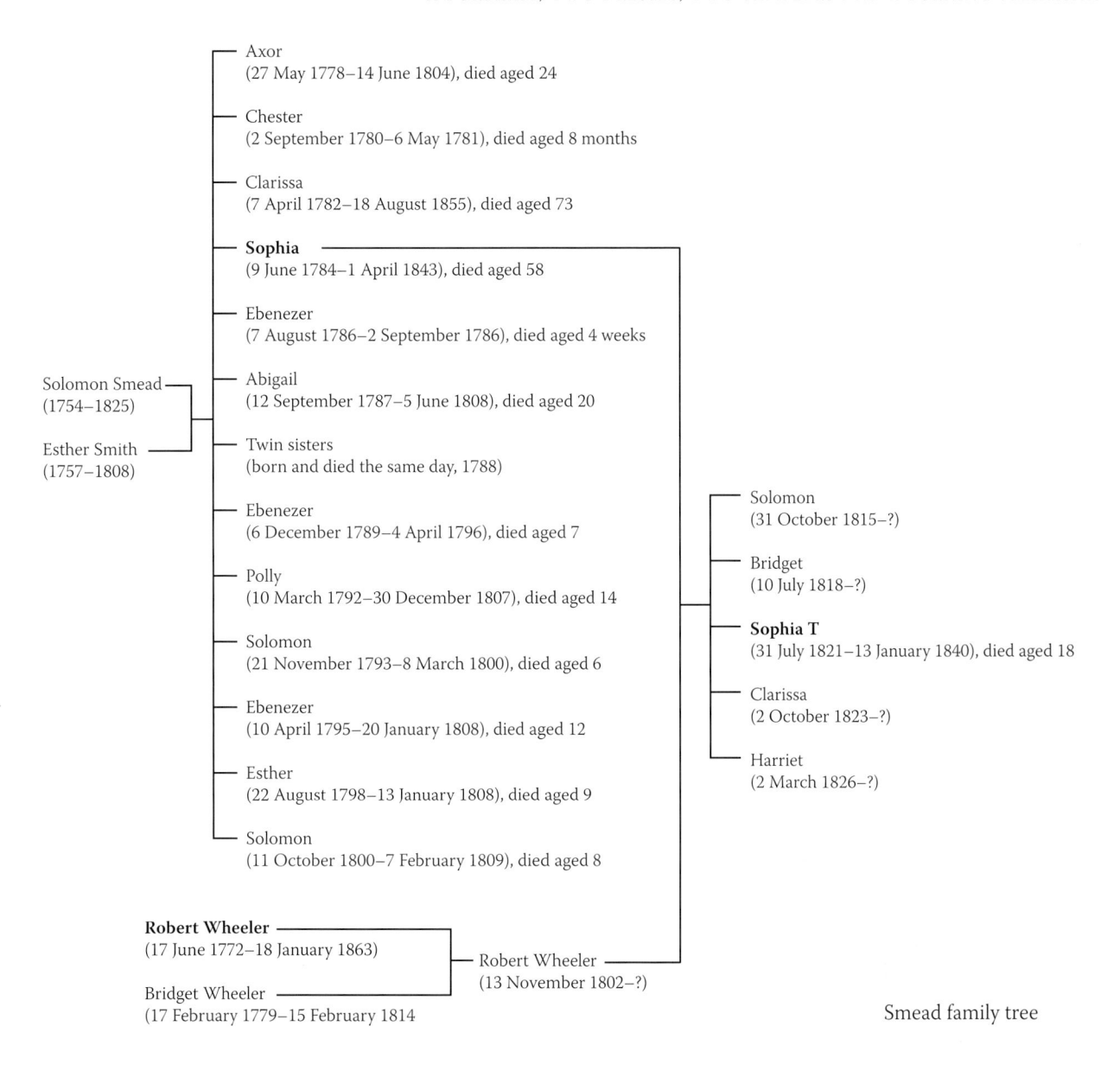

A PORTRAIT, TWO DRESSES, TWO SAMPLERS AND A BURNING STEAMSHIP

```
Solomon Smead ─┐
(1754–1825)    │
               ├─┬─ Axor
Esther Smith ──┘ │  (27 May 1778–14 June 1804), died aged 24
(1757–1808)      │
                 ├─ Chester
                 │  (2 September 1780–6 May 1781), died aged 8 months
                 │
                 ├─ Clarissa
                 │  (7 April 1782–18 August 1855), died aged 73
                 │
                 ├─ Sophia ────────────────────────────────┐
                 │  (9 June 1784–1 April 1843), died aged 58│
                 │                                          │
                 ├─ Ebenezer                                │
                 │  (7 August 1786–2 September 1786), died aged 4 weeks
                 │                                          │
                 ├─ Abigail                                 │
                 │  (12 September 1787–5 June 1808), died aged 20
                 │                                          │
                 ├─ Twin sisters                            │
                 │  (born and died the same day, 1788)      │
                 │                                          │
                 ├─ Ebenezer                                │
                 │  (6 December 1789–4 April 1796), died aged 7
                 │                                          │
                 ├─ Polly                                   │
                 │  (10 March 1792–30 December 1807), died aged 14
                 │                                          │
                 ├─ Solomon                                 │
                 │  (21 November 1793–8 March 1800), died aged 6
                 │                                          │
                 ├─ Ebenezer                                │
                 │  (10 April 1795–20 January 1808), died aged 12
                 │                                          │
                 ├─ Esther                                  │
                 │  (22 August 1798–13 January 1808), died aged 9
                 │                                          │
                 └─ Solomon                                 │
                    (11 October 1800–7 February 1809), died aged 8
                                                            │
Robert Wheeler ─┐                                           │
(17 June 1772–18 January 1863)                              │
                ├─ Robert Wheeler ───────────────────────────┤
Bridget Wheeler ┘  (13 November 1802–?)                     │
(17 February 1779–15 February 1814                          │
                                                            ├─ Solomon
                                                            │  (31 October 1815–?)
                                                            │
                                                            ├─ Bridget
                                                            │  (10 July 1818–?)
                                                            │
                                                            ├─ Sophia T
                                                            │  (31 July 1821–13 January 1840), died aged 18
                                                            │
                                                            ├─ Clarissa
                                                            │  (2 October 1823–?)
                                                            │
                                                            └─ Harriet
                                                               (2 March 1826–?)
```

Smead family tree

The sampler was accompanied by documentation including material from the published Vital Records of Greenfield, Massachusetts.[1] It included details of the birth, marriage and death of Sophia who was born on 9 June 1784 to Solomon Smead (1754–1825) and Esther Smith (1757–1808), of Greenfield. She was the fourth of 14 children and her life was saturated with death. An older brother died three years before she was born and she lost four brothers and twin sisters before she was 20 years old (Smead 1928: 39–40). She was 24 when spotted fever took her mother, two brothers and a sister within three weeks. By the time she was 25, she had lost her mother and 12 siblings. Only her father and her sister Clarissa, two years her senior, remained. It is interesting to speculate if fear caused her to wait until she was nearly 30 to marry.

Her modest sampler opened a door to an investigation that has proved to be both challenging and rewarding. Sophia was christened at the age of ten and although there is no date stitched into the embroidery, it is probable that her sampler was worked at about this time (1794). In the majority of surviving examples, the girl's age at the time the work was undertaken was included. A large proportion of these schoolgirl embroideries in the Historic Deerfield collection were worked by girls between the ages of eight and 12.

An investigation into the collection produced some fascinating results. A small watercolour and pencil silhouette portrait of Sophia was donated to the museum in 1970 by a descendant[2] and according to family tradition it was painted in 1813, when she was 29 years old[3] (Fig. 2). The artist has not been identified but portraits of this type were often made by relatives or neighbours who had been trained in the technique in one of the many private schools for young women that were popular in rural New England since the early days of the republic.[4]

The Flint family and Historic Deerfield

Helen Geier Flynt and her husband Henry N. Flynt established Historic Deerfield, Inc. in 1952. Their son Henry[5] attended the prestigious Deerfield Academy from 1936 to 1940 and they purchased Allen House, on Old Main Street in

Figure 2 Profile portrait, Sophia Smead (1784–1843), watercolour and pencil on paper (Historic Deerfield 70.132, Gift of Mrs. Robert Stebbins Lipp) (Plate 24 in the colour plate section).

Figure 3 Dress worn by Sophia Smead about 1815, cotton (Historic Deerfield V.053B, Gift of Mrs. Robert Stebbins Lipp) (Plate 25 in the colour plate section).

Deerfield in 1945 (McGowan and Miller 1996: 178). Many of the original 18th-century houses became available at this time and the Flynts began to purchase additional houses. They started collecting furnishings including textiles and in 1948 Ashley House opened for public viewing at the north end of the street. From the beginning, Mrs Flynt's primary area of interest was textiles and costumes. Although she made a few purchases in 1946, 1947 and 1948, it was only in 1949 that she began to systematically catalogue the collection. The system was F (for fabric) followed by a sequential number. This system was used off and on until 1985 and ended with F-1022. Like many private collectors of her generation, the process of cataloguing was often a creative endeavour. Mrs Flynt decided that everything made after the year 1800 would be classified with a letter 'V' for Victorian, and this broad category included a white cotton dress that had belonged to Sophia Smead of Greenfield.

Sophia Smead's married life

Purported to have been her wedding dress, it is a stylish gown of fine cotton muslin with narrow vertical bands of leno weave upon which small floral and leaf patterns have been embroidered in chain stitch[6] (Fig. 3) According to family tradition, the embroidery had been done by Sophia herself but there is no evidence to support this. The cotton is very fine and in widths of 28 in. In my opinion the cotton originated in India, even though large quantities were imported from Lancashire and other cities in north-west England and there was an important cotton industry in Connecticut at this time. It was this very local cotton industry that was the cause of further tragedy in Sophia's personal life and this will be discussed below. She was married in Stonington, Connecticut, on 8 January 1815 (Smead 1928: 40), only four months before her 31st birthday and it is unlikely that this cotton dress was worn on this occasion.

Her husband, Robert Wheeler, was from a prominent family in this shipping community, a widower, 12 years her senior and with a 13-year-old son from his first marriage (Anson Wheeler 1966: 642). His first wife, Bridget Wheeler, who he had married in 1796, had been a cousin.[7] She died 15 February 1814. Her father Hosea was a successful merchant in Stonington and an entry in his father-in-law's store records notes that on the following day, Robert purchased two black silk handkerchiefs, which were later returned.[8] Tax assessment records for North Stonington indicate that just eight years after his first marriage, Robert Wheeler had a two-year-old horse, four oxen, six cows and sheep, five acres of plowed land, 24 of cleared land, 51 acres of bush pasture and three chimneys.[9] So it is evident that he was engaged in farming. How he happened to meet Sophia Smead, living over 120 miles away, has not yet been discovered but further research may provide an answer.

Their first child, Solomon, named for Sophia's father, was born just short of ten months after the marriage and in the next 11 years she had four more children. The second child, a daughter, was named after her father's first wife Bridget. Sophia was born 31 July 1821, Clarissa two years later in 1823 and the last child was born in 1826 just three months before Sophia Smead Wheeler's 42nd birthday.

A dress purporting to be the family christening dress with a matching embroidered cap was also given to the collection at Historic Deerfield and it was always believed to have been stitched by Sophia Smead for her daughter Sophia Wheeler (Fig. 4). From the style and design of the embroidery, it is likely that this white-on-white cotton dress with a very high waistline and short, slightly puffed sleeves, could easily have been worked in this fashionable form. The details of the cap show a meandering design of grapes and leaves, a popular motif of the time. Patterns, carefully executed in ink on paper, were often copied by ladies, sometimes from publications but just as frequently from an actual piece of embroidery on a piece of clothing worn by a much admired friend or relative. A number of these patterns, drawn in India ink on laid, are in the collection at Historic Deerfield. They are typical of the type of meandering vines and leaves with interspersed cornucopia with a variety of leaves and flowers.

The details seen on the christening robe indicate that whoever was responsible for this work was an accomplished needlewoman. If these were a christening dress and cap, they would have been suitable for a child of about two or three years of age. It was not unusual for a family in western Massachusetts to wait until they had a number of children and then to have them christened at the same time. This appealed to the well-known Yankee frugality, as the minister had to be paid only once for the act of christening, no matter how many children were involved. The exception to this rule, of course, was a child who was born ill or who did not seem likely to survive childhood.

The collection and publication of the Vital Records of Massachusetts was an enormous project undertaken in the wake of the Colonial Revival movement of the late 19th century. Compiled primarily from church records and gravestones, these useful books have been the basis for much of the genealogical research that is still being done today. Sophia Smead Wheeler died at the age of 58 on 1 April 1843 having seen three of her five children married and experiencing the tragic death of her middle child Sophia. On her tombstone is written 'Her end was peace'.[10]

The second stitched sampler was an equally dull, faded and even unfinished example made by her daughter, Sophia Wheeler when she was eight years of age[11] (Fig. 5). Based on a much larger format that was popular in the 1820s in New England, it is immediately apparent that the border is nearly identical to that worked by her mother. There is little evidence to support the idea that mothers taught their daughters embroidery but it is possible to speculate that the teacher may have adapted the border from the mother's surviving embroidery.

Figure 4 Christening robe worn by Sophia Wheeler about 1823, cotton, white-on-white embroidery (Historic Deerfield. Gift of Mrs. Robert Stebbins Lipp) (Plate 26 in the colour plate section).

Figure 5 Embroidered sampler by Sophia Wheeler at age 8 in 1829, silk on linen (Historic Deerfield 2000.4.2, Gift of Karen Dunn) (Plate 27 in the colour plate section).

The sinking of the *Lexington*

The steamship *Lexington*, built in 1834, was an engineering marvel. Every consideration for safety as well as luxury was carefully considered and there was a fully functional fire engine with hoses and pumps. Based in Stonington, Connecticut, this wonder of the modern transport era was purchased in 1838 by the New Jersey Steamship Navigation and Transport Company, owned by Cornelius Vanderbilt (1794–1877), for the sum of $60,000. The boilers were converted to coal for additional heat that would turn the 34-ft paddlewheels even faster. According to court records, there had been several

55

Figure 6 'The Steamboat *Lexington* on fire on Long Island Sound, January 13 1840' Nathaniel Currier, for the *New York Sun* (newspaper) coloured lithograph (Plate 28 in the colour plate section).

small fires after the conversion and corrective measures had not been taken. The inspector was ultimately charged with negligence and fined.

At daybreak on 13 January 1840 the *Lexington* was tied up in New York. It was more than 30 degrees below freezing and ice was forming on the water surrounding the ship. One hundred and fifty huge bales of cotton were loaded under the promenade deck and some were placed within just a few feet of the smokestack casing. There had been a minor fire just a few days before but some temporary repairs had been made and no one seemed concerned. Passengers began to arrive in the early afternoon and they paid $1.00 for the trip to Stonington.

The captain was George Child (the regular captain was Jacob Vanderbilt, the brother of Cornelius, who was at home with a cold). One hundred and fifteen passengers were on board along with 28 crewmen. The boat departed at 3:00 in the afternoon. By 7:30 a fire was reported and it was later discovered to have been caused by the bales of cotton that had been stored too close to the boiler's smokestack. Unfortunately, only three lifeboats were on board. In the midst of shouts and chaos, the lifeboats were quickly filled with hysterical passengers; vastly overcrowded and hastily launched, they immediately sank. Panic ensued and many passengers plunged into the water, quickly succumbed to hypothermia and died.

By midnight the ship was completely engulfed in flames and by 3:00 in the morning, it slowly sank into the Long Island Sound in 120 ft of water (Fig. 6). Only four people survived, three by floating to shore on cotton bales.[12] David Crowley, the second mate, was able to dig his way into the bale of cotton and he drifted ashore 48 hours later, nearly 50 miles east of the disaster. He kept the bale of cotton in his Providence, Rhode Island home for many years until he 'sacrificed it in the cause of patriotism. It was worked into cotton cloth, appropriately named the Lexington brand' (Williams McAdam 1939: 52).

According to the *Gazette and Mercury*, Greenfield, published on Tuesday 28 January 1840:

It becomes our melancholy duty to add another name to the list of victims on board the *Lexington*, the night she was burnt – Miss Sophia T. Wheeler, of this town, aged 18. She had been absent from home about six months in Middletown, New Jersey, where she had been engaged in teaching. She had closed her school and was on her way home for the purpose of being married. She left Middletown on Monday morning in company with Mr. Jonathan G. Davenport, formerly of Coleraine, intending to take the *Lexington*, on their arrival in New York. On hearing of the catastrophe, their friends in M.[Middletown] made inquiries and traced them to the wharf, at which the *Lexington* was lying, since which, no intelligence has been received of either.—Fears had been entertained from the first, by her friends here, that Miss Wheeler was on board the *Lexington*, as she was expected to return about that time, but as her name had not been given among the list of those on board, it was hoped that she might have escaped, til a letter was received in town stating that she started 'in company with Mr. D. intending to take the *Lexington*'. This woeful calamity will long be remembered in the community. Surely when the judgments of the Lord are abroad in the earth, the people will learn righteousness.

The image of the burning steamship *Lexington* was the first 'extra' illustrated section in any American newspaper. It was the work of a relatively unknown artist by the name of Nathaniel Currier (1813–1888) who joined James Merritt Ives (1824–1895) 12 years later and formed the important print firm of Currier & Ives at 33 Spruce Street, New York City.[13] From evidence on the family tombstone it was apparent that Sophia was the child made famous by her death aboard a steamship in what was one of the most celebrated non-military tragedies in American history to that date.

Figure 7 Part of the exhibition: *Embroidered History – Stitched Lives: Needlework & Samplers from the Historic Deerfield Collection 1670–1850* (Plate 29 in the colour plate section).

Conclusion

The textiles and texts discussed in this paper formed the centrepiece of an exhibition at Historic Deerfield until December 2006. The exhibition, called *Embroidered History – Stitched Lives: Needlework & Samplers from the Historic Deerfield Collection 1670–1850*, included an important section on Deerfield samplers and explored the teachers who produced the designs and how local schoolgirls worked closely related designs over a period of more than 30 years (Fig. 7).

How two uninspiring, faded and even unfinished samplers opened a window into the lives of a local family and their connection with a nationally prominent maritime disaster has been the topic of this paper. Cotton played a crucial role in the lives of so many people and its impact is clearly seen in this brief history of a New England family. The survival of the garments and needlework associated with this family has been the inspiration for this paper. Some questions remain unanswered but the foundation has been laid for further research and investigation.

Notes

1. Vital records of Greenfield, Massachusetts to the year 1850, New England Historic Genealogical Society, Boston, 1915.
2. Mrs Robert Stebbins Lipp.
3. Historic Deerfield, 70.132 (5⅜ × 4½ in.).
4. Deerfield Academy was established in 1797 and opened in 1799 as a co-educational school where needlework and drawing were taught by a number of talented preceptresses. The first so employed was Eunice Woodbridge (1763–1832) in 1802 (Sheldon 1983: 283).
5. Henry N. Flynt, Jr. (1922–).
6. Historic Deerfield, V. 053B (cb 50 in.).
7. Stonington Court Records, vol. 3, 1730– , p. 198, vol. 4, p. 66.
8. Stonington Historical Society, Woollworth Library, Hosea Wheeler General Store Ledger, p. 30.
9. North Society/Stonington Records, Assessments, 1804.
10. Greenfield Cemetery Records, South Meadows Cemetery.
11. *Ibid.* p. 645.
12. Captain Chester Hilliard was the only passenger rescued: he shared a 3 × 4 ft cotton bale with Benjamin Cox of New York. Stephen Manchester, the *Lexington's* pilot, Charles B. Smith, a fireman and David Crowley, mate of the *Lexington*, were the only survivors.
13. 'Awful Conflagration of the Steamboat Lexington in Long Island Sound on Monday Evening, January 18, 1840 by which melancholy occurrence over One Hundred Persons Perished.' The *New York Sun* newspaper approached Currier to print a single-sheet addition for their paper. This single-page sheet was the first colour extra in any American newspaper. Between 1835 and 1907 the firm produced more than a million prints with 7,500 titles. It was the most successful print company in American history to that date.

References

Anson Wheeler, R. (1966) *History of the Town of Stonington, County of New London, Connecticut, From Its First Settlement in 1649 to 1900, with a Genealogical Register of Stonington Families*. Mystic, CT: Lawrence Verry Incorporated.

McGowan, S. and Miller, A. (1996) *Family and Landscape: Deerfield Homelots from 1671*. Deerfield, MA: Pocumtuck Valley Memorial Association.

Sheldon, G. (1983) *A History of Deerfield Massachusetts*, facsimile of 1895–96 edition. Deerfield, MA: Pocumtuck Valley Memorial Association.

Smead, E. (1928) *A Smead Geneology*. Greenfield, MA: E.A. Hall and Company.

Williams McAdam, R. (1939) *Salts of the Sound: A Story of Steamboating on Long Island Sound from 1815 to the Present*. Brattleboro, VT: Stephen Daye Press.

The author

Edward F. Maeder, Director of Exhibitions and Curator of Textiles at Historic Deerfield, was Curator of Costumes and Textiles, Los Angeles County Museum of Art for 15 years. He curated more than 30 exhibitions and published several books and catalogues on 18th-century costumes, textiles and embroideries and Hollywood costumes, and was involved with the Sistine Chapel restoration, completed in 1990. He lectures widely in the US and abroad and is currently organising exhibitions, international symposia and writing projects.

Address

Edward F. Maeder, P.O. Box 127, Deerfield, Massachusetts 01342 USA (maeder@historic-deerfield.org)

(Ad)Dressing the Century: fashionability and floral frocks

Jo Turney

ABSTRACT This paper stems from a research project and exhibition entitled *Pick of the Bunch: The Floral Printed Dress in the 20th Century*.[1] The project aimed to address and investigate the relationship between fashion and textiles from a material culture perspective in order to question traditional methods of display and established discourses in fashion and textile history. This approach intended to move away from designer-led display, which frequently discounts the significance of textile design in the construction of garments as well as the experience of wearing floral printed dresses. This paper explores the ways in which a more inclusive or interdisciplinary approach is necessary in the study of textiles and fashionable dress, and how this might be achieved.

Assessing the meanings of floral printed dresses in relation to an established hierarchy of fashion was anticipated to highlight the ways in which messages surrounding what it was to be fashionable, and indeed how the formation of the fashionable self, was communicated. This paper focuses on oral testimony and the ways in which responses to artefacts offer the potential for reappraising established notions of what it is to be fashionable, as well as highlighting the disparities inherent in the dissemination of styles, motifs, techniques and fabrics. The argument here demonstrates the difficulties arising from attempts to establish absolutes in relation to contemporary dress.

Keywords: floral prints, femininity, oral history, fashionability, display, everyday life

Introduction

In the introduction to *Adorned in Dreams*, Elizabeth Wilson romantically discusses the display of dress in a museum context. She noted that:

> These clothes are congealed memories of the daily life of times past. Once they inhabited the noisy streets, the crowded theatres, the glittering soirees of the social scene. Now, like souls in limbo, they wait poignantly for the music to begin again. Or perhaps theirs is a silence patient with vengefulness towards the living (Wilson 1985: 1).

The emphasis on the experience of clothing existing through their wearing, as outlined by Wilson, highlights the need to investigate, discuss and perhaps catalogue the ways in which fashionable clothing informs and is performed in daily life and vice versa. This is particularly evident with regard to the display of fashionable dress in the museum and gallery setting which frequently manifests as disembodied garments, hanging lifelessly in cases, devoid of movement, prohibiting reverse views and close-up detail. Such display tactics appear not only to negate the significance of fashion per se, but also the experience of what it might be like to actually wear these garments.

Clothing is what people wear, and derives from 'cloth', or fabric that is suitable for wearing. Fashion, however, is culturally constructed and refers to process and changes in styles – it is dynamic, about change, movement and aesthetics. Fashion also connotes issues surrounding the contemporary, taste, style and indeed, temporary popularity (Kawamura 2005: 3–4). One might suggest therefore, that fashionable clothing is the demonstration of 'being part of things' by its wearers (Kawamura 2005: 5; Polhemus 1994). With this in mind, the experience of wearing specific items of clothing is central to the formation of an understanding of the self within the wider world, yet this more subjective appraisal of fashion is rarely evidenced in exhibitions.

This investigation draws from oral history testimonies that have been central to a collaborative research project between Bath Spa University and the Museum of Costume, Bath, which aimed to address the significance of the floral printed dress in the 20th century, culminating in an exhibition, *Pick of the Bunch*, a website and publication. The juxtaposition between objects from the museum's collection, fashion spreads and advertisements in women's magazines and the fashion media, and the recorded experience of consuming (buying/wearing) floral dresses in everyday life, centralises the praxis at which official designer-led histories merge with the unofficial oral testimony and experience of wearing specific clothes.

Pick of the Bunch project rationale

The premise underlying *Pick of the Bunch* was primarily to initiate a dialogue between fashion and textile design, focusing on floral printed dresses. An emphasis was placed on the ways in which printed design enhanced the garment and how shape and cut exhibited pattern and technique intended to move away from hierarchical forms of display which privilege fashion above textile design. A focus on fashion rather than textile design is largely the result of the reliance of design history on a modernist approach to the classification of 'good design', which charts the progression of design through the work of named designers (the 'designer as hero'). Fashion designers and fashion design are frequently understood and promoted in this way, i.e. a dress by Dior and so on, with labels in garments associating other fashion designers with products. Yet textile design and textile designers, although integral in the creation of the garment as a whole, remain largely anonymous. The aim of the project was therefore to attempt to level the playing field and address both fashion and textiles as a unified whole, moving away from a focus on named designers towards the experience of design.

One way of achieving this aim was to outline the implications of pattern and fashionable clothing within everyday life. This approach encompassed the selection of garments demonstrating the diffusion and dissemination of fashion, and consequently the exhibition consisted of floral printed dresses from museum collections (designer and non-designer objects) alongside those worn in everyday life, donated or loaned by members of the public. Oral testimony regarding the consumption of such garments, including purchase and the actual experience of wearing, became a fundamental aspect of uncovering why certain garments were deemed fashionable, or were valorised outside of a traditional design history methodology.

Such a seemingly disparate approach aimed to be inclusive, but also aimed to exemplify a material culture approach to the display and understanding of specific items of fashionable dress. This meant that it was essential to employ an interdisciplinary methodology, including design history, fashion and textiles history and theory, oral history and discourses arising from anthropology, and cultural theory. Interdisciplinarity was intended to widen the sphere of reference, bridging gaps of knowledge marginalised or trivialised by single methodologies. For example, a traditional design historical approach would prioritise innovation and notions of taste emerging as a response to the European modernist avant-garde, but the aims of a design history methodology might be overlooked or negated within an oral history methodology, which privileges the spoken word above all else, and so on.

The emphasis on first-hand experience, particularly in relation to tactile and emotive objects such as clothing, adds an extra dimension to the study of fashion and textiles that goes beyond designer intent and notions of the avant-garde. Similarly, this added dimension, which involves sentiment, recollection and interaction with personal objects, offers the potential to redress notions of established hierarchies of taste and systems of valorisation. This means that oral history offers the potential for participation, levels the playing field and challenges the writing of history in general. We might conclude that oral history creates a postmodern approach to history and the historical process in which talking about the social enables a multiplicity of histories to exist simultaneously, with no one gaining privilege over another (Rowe 1995: 1–2).

Oral history projects and anthropological studies are all very different as there is no single set group of activities, collective environment or one social or ethnic group that the subject focuses on, e.g. an ethnographic approach would, according to the anthropologist Hortense Powdermaker, entail a method which:

> was forged in the study of small, homogenous societies in which the anthropologist lived for an extended period of time, participated in them, learned the language and constantly observed (Powdermaker 1996; Taylor 2002: 193–4).

But in 20th- and 21st-century Britain, the potential study of 'small homogeneous communities' is distinctly limited. Anthropological studies within contemporary Britain exist, however, examples of which include the research projects undertaken by Daniel Miller and Alison J. Clarke on a north London council estate (Miller 1990) addressing issues of taste, the use and decoration of space within the home, personal identity and shopping, combining anthropology with consumption theory, while their more recent work addresses issues surrounding clothing consumption (Clarke and Miller 2002: 191–214). Although participants in these studies cannot literally be described as 'homogeneous', they exist in a particular location at a particular moment in time, and can therefore be seen as a group (Miller 1998: 9–11).

With regard to *Pick of the Bunch*, oral history respondents were selected from replies to an advert placed in the local daily newspaper, *The Bath Chronicle*. The Bath respondents were all over 50 years old and offered a valuable insight into growing up in the 1950s and 1960s. It was deemed necessary, however, to seek younger respondents with whom to compare experiences and to demonstrate if concepts of fashionability and floral dresses differed in terms of time and location, so a group of friends aged 25–35 years old, working in professional occupations in London, formed a contrast group.[2] It is important to note that these were merely sample groups, and responses may well have differed should other groups have been sought or the sample widened. Therefore the potential for interpretation and reinterpretation of responses to floral printed dresses is multifarious.

The possibility of creating a multiplicity of meanings and interpretations that are largely based on subjective information is not without its problems, and it is particularly pertinent to draw attention to them. First, it is quite difficult to establish and formulate a clear and representative sample group. Respondents tend to have professional backgrounds and have either an interest in history or the project's themes. In other words, they think they have something to contribute. Secondly, memory is notoriously sketchy, and often recollection is neither exact nor detailed. This means that respondents are liable to elaborate or embroider their recollections. And finally, the past can never be understood with the benefit of hindsight, therefore memories are recontextualised to suit contemporary needs (Lomas 2000: 363–70).

Nonetheless, the potential for oral history research has been outlined as threefold according to the oral historian Paul Thompson. These are first, to 'introduce unknown voices' into the discourse of fashion otherwise not remembered (Thompson 1997: 44). Secondly, oral history offers the potential for the 'exploration of hidden spheres' of history such as the conflict between work and home or the domestic or everyday as a sphere for the consumption and performance of fashionable dress, specifically floral printed dresses which are synonymous with women and discourses surrounding women's taste. Finally, oral history can track transitional life phases, including education, family, work, leisure and so on (Thompson 1997: 45). The aim of this paper is to address the significance and experience of wearing floral printed dresses through oral testimony while outlining its contribution to exhibition display.

Case study: 'Talking' frocks – femininity, fashionability and floral printed dresses

The relationship between floral designs and the creation of femininity has been the subject of much feminist discourse within the visual arts (Parker and Pollock 1981; Sparke 1995). Much of this discourse refers to 19th-century concepts of the construction of the feminine through biological determinism (Brown and Jordanova 1995: 485–90; Nead 1998) and binary opposites arising through analyses of gender distinction (Kirkham 1996). With this in mind, it is possible to suggest that floral design exists outside of the remit of modernist 'good taste', which essentially forms the basis of good design and the Good Design Movement in the 20th century, and is distinctly linked to the 'frippery' of women's taste (Sparke 1995) and therefore defies the avant-garde and in turn, fashion.

In her recent discussion of the popularity of floral printed textiles in *Print in Fashion*, Marnie Fogg opined that:

> The appreciation of flowers is part of that universal yearning for a pastoral idyll that evokes the simplicity of a sun-filled childhood spent running through meadows. In the frenetic pace of modern urban life, city dwellers tend to feel progressively more alienated from nature, and so seek solace in a romanticised rural idyll (Fogg 2006: 27).

Fogg's appraisal of the significance of floral design highlights a sense of the timeless, of the lost and the nostalgic, and, one could argue, says nothing about the contemporary world that is not retrogressive. This implies also that floral design and fashion are contradictory as floral design embraces the past while fashion is fuelled by innovation and newness. Yet floral printed dresses do change in terms of style, shape and motif, embrace new print technology, and have continuously remained in fashion and popular with consumers throughout the period of study regardless of the efforts of the Good Design Movement (Jackson 2002).

The relationship between femininity and floral designs has been addressed by feminist art and design historians, and this relationship was fundamental to many of the interviewees.

One respondent discussed shopping with her mother during her teenage years in the 1950s:

> I would shop with my mother in department stores in London. She was a fashionable woman who had impeccable taste. She always chose my clothes, which were watered-down versions of her own; not quite so grown-up, girlish and floral (DS 2004).

The testimony outlines the significant influence of one's mother on performing femininity during a transitional life phase. Clothing was selected on terms of suitability, which reflected age and experience, and the interviewee appeared happy to emulate her mother in terms of dress (she was 'fashionable' with good taste) and by aping her dress, albeit in a modest and understated way, the transition was seen to be eased. Access to the dynamic world of fashion presupposed a dynamic self. So, clothing and the performance of femininity appeared pivotal in the development of the female self to the interviewees.

Similarly, the theme of life transition, in relation to the wearing of floral printed dresses and the construction of 'femininity', recurred in testimonies. It seems pertinent therefore to start a discussion surrounding florals in fashion with notions of youth and youthfulness, of that which is doomed to be lost, but which formulates and develops an understanding of the adult self.

The older interviewees often expressed little sentiment when discussing photographs of their early adult lives. Instead, these times and the garments they wore seemed to represent a naivety and almost impossible romanticism that was lost; representative of a transitional life stage that was now gone (Attfield 2000). The cynicism outlined in the testimonies bear witness to another age in terms of time, but also in relation to personal development, speaking of the unfulfilled expectation of romance and relationships, of broken hopes, aspirations and the desire to conform to unattainable ideals (Church-Gibson 2000: 79–89). On speaking of her teenage years in the 1950s, a respondent commented on photographs of an earlier self:

> I look at myself there and think of how silly I was … These days girls don't feel the need to get married, catch a husband. Everything was so formal, so fussy. People don't realise how many clothes that you had to wear or the dress codes that needed to be observed. We always wore a hat and gloves when we went out … even if it was only for afternoon tea. Even in the height of summer (DW 2004).

The sentiment expressed encapsulates the distance between the here and now and the there and then. Both society and the respondent had moved on; time had changed sociocultural conventions and life expectations. Loss in this testimony exists not as nostalgia but as a symptom of 'being born too early', having missed out on freedoms afforded to a younger generation. As Rebecca Arnold suggests, this emotional response to the past in relation to dress and a sense of self is not uncommon:

> Fashion has a great resonance, acting as a collective memory; nostalgic styles are traces of the past, mapping

Figure 1 A floral frock, c.1940s.

Figure 2 John Bates (designer), Jamaica, 1970s (BATMC 2004.198) (reproduced with permission from the Museum of Costume, Bath) (Plate 30 in the colour plate section).

individual and group experiences, recalling both reassuringly familiar and yet ... upsettingly clear evocations of earlier histories (Arnold 2001: 7).

Similarly, younger respondents were keen to link recollections of floral dresses with romance, its potential, and loss:

> The last floral dress I wore was one I bought for a ball I went to at Uni. It was black with white outline flowers printed all over it and had a ribbon wrapped around just under the boobs with a tiny bow. It was tight fitting at the top and then floated out at the hips and came down to the knees, zipping up at the back. I loved wearing it because my boyfriend at the time loved it. We actually got back together the night of the ball after being split up for 3 months! I felt very feminine. Can't really wear it now though because it reminds me of him too much (NJ 2004).

A drive for romantic love proved a poignant reminder of specific garments, linking the clothes with emotive, rather than special occasions. This suggests that the wearing of the garments recollected acted as markers of sociability, of the attractiveness of the wearer to others, specifically with the possibility of interacting with members of the opposite sex and acquiring meaningful relationships. Of equal significance, it could be stated, was the tone of the testimonies; the expression of a more simplistic and idealistic approach to relationships that had subsequently been tainted by experience. This exemplifies a transitional process that had been painful but necessary in order to achieve the present self, which can be understood as a life narrative, or a learning curve, punctuated by the association with the visible and emotional self (as demonstrated through clothing worn) and the experiences and expectations of particular times.

Frequently, the older interviewees referenced the significance of floral pattern in the creation of a sense of their early selves. They all mentioned the ways in which floral motifs appeared to be representative of a specific kind of respectability, which could be understood as the acknowledgement and display of the moral (Ribeiro 1986: 12). Indeed, the significance of specific motifs as communicators of morality are essential to an understanding of either the acceptance or rejection of the group mentality in addition to a key component inherent in the language of clothes; the ability or possibility to both reveal and conceal.

> The dress took me through my early teaching career in the 1960s. It was quite fashionable and I was young, but it was professional and quite modest. I remember receiving lots of flattering comments about it (MB 2004).

For the women interviewed, the social display of femininity through their fashion choices was distinctly limited by their understandings of social norms (Roach and Eicher 1973: 28–31). The significance of a belief system dictated and mediated by a general understanding of clothing and modesty belied their ability to wholeheartedly embrace fashion. One respondent noted:

The dresses I had were either plain or had very small prints. The floral prints were natural and quite innocent. They were clean and crisp. Larger prints or brighter coloured designs were worn by girls who were loud, easy, if you like. I would never have worn them (DW 2004).

The intimation that boldness in design was synonymous with character seems rather far-fetched, yet morality and motif was alluded to in all the testimonies of the older women. The centrality of respectability appeared to pervade a sense of femininity, while also reinforcing class distinction and stereotypes. The separation between them and us can be paralleled with good and bad taste, and to studies such as Clement Greenberg's essay on kitsch, which highlights the degenerative and subversive potential of popular culture (Greenberg 1968: 116–26).

For the younger women (speaking of the 1990s), floral print dresses were indeed subversive, exemplifying the opportunity to express an anti-respectability, which was both mainstream and individual. They represented the potential for reappropriation, manipulation through customisation and accessorisation and the potential to emulate their media and fashion role models.

I do remember one floral dress. I bought it when grunge was fashionable and I was madly in love with Kurt Cobain in an attempt to be cool. It was a long strappy summer dress with a floral print of red and pink roses featuring specs of light green foliage. It had side ties that I tied at the back which gave it a nipped in waist and the skirt was kind of A-line. I wore it teamed with a rather lovely army (sludge coloured) green vest and DM boots – what an ensemble! I bought it in Top Shop and I think it cost between £20 and £30. I absolutely loved that dress and when I wore it I felt incredibly cool – the bees knees – when in fact, on reflection, I probably looked a right idiot! I was trying to emulate the style of Alicia Silverstone in the Aerosmith videos of the time (I believe 'Crazy' was one of them). I think she wore a short floral dress in one of the videos with a pair of scuffed DMs. I remember my mum commented that she liked the dress but wished I would wear it with a nice pair of sandals rather than 'those unflattering boots' (ZK 2004).

The rejection of the respondent's mother as a role model in favour of the then teen celebrity Alicia Silverstone, combined with a quest for coolness, highlights a transition from familial to collective role models based on age and peer group (Lurie 1982: 52–9; Klepp and Storm-Mathisen 2005: 323–42). Indeed, the creation of cool was not a response to the dictates of the fashion industry, but a personal manipulation and interpretation of existing styles to create an individual whole (Davis 1992: 183–8; McRobbie 1989: 23–49).

The distinction between what was considered fashionable and what was 'cool' recurred in the testimonies. Cool it appeared, was a personal response to fashionable mass market clothing, available to the teenagers on small budgets. It was about making something everyone else had your own.

I had a great brown floral dress, which is a bit of a contradiction I suppose, you don't normally buy a pretty floral dress in BROWN, but it was fake 60s style flower power print that I bought when I was about 14 and wore (constantly) until I was about 18, it was stretchy lycra type fabric but not tight, not too short. Just right. It probably only cost a tenner and I altered it on a sewing machine myself. I suppose it was bought from the only local clothes shop in our town when I was younger, that's now closed. It made me feel summery, not fashionable but that was fine by me. I felt cool and it said a lot about how I was at the time. It was a familiar old thing that I would still wear now if I wasn't two stone heavier and a foot taller (JS 2004).

The floral, modified dress became a symbol of the individual self, rather than a sign of the mass fashionable self. The notion of individuality, however, was extended to include the respondent's peer group through the sharing of clothes, which demonstrates the potential of clothing as a social mediator.

Me and my friends would all wear it, in fact it did the rounds so much I still have photos of old mates wearing my lovely little dress, including a big group photo of us all on my 18th birthday, with me sporting my old faithful flowery brown dress. I remember one occasion and the embarrassment of having it pulled up around my ears by my best friend when we were out in a busy pub. The next day I got her back when she wore the same dress and I pulled it up around her ears when we were out shopping on a busy high street. Why we always wore the dress I don't know (SJ 2004).

The dress here represented a bond between individuals that aided a sense of inclusion. Similarly, it represented both good and embarrassing times, of modesty and display, of group and individual identity, of fitting in and (in a somewhat shameful way in this case) of standing out. The emphasis appeared to evoke a sense of fun, femininity on one's own terms, and therefore can be seen as the expression of newfound freedom.

Freedom was also expressed as anti-fashion in relation to an understanding of other, older women. One younger respondent remembered her grandmother's fondness for floral printed dresses:

My grandma was a rather large woman with a big round belly. The dress I'm thinking of stretched tightly across her belly and was in spring colours, actually quite citrus – pink, white and yellow flowers. The print was quite a big design. It came with a matching jacket and finished at her knees. I remember it being that viscose material – maybe a cotton mix – it wasn't a nice material to cuddle her in as it was a bit scratchy. I think she used to buy them from the catalogue. This memory is quite vague but it reminds me of Sunday lunchtimes in the garden waiting for the BBQ food and stuffing myself with crisps and dips when I was about 11 (NJ 2004).

The testimony reflects an understanding not only of family, but also of lineage, of times past and the distance between the here and now and the there and then. References to the fabric and colours of the large design as well as the mode of purchase situate the memory in time, but also demonstrate a common recollection of what grannies wore. Tinged with nostalgia, the comments paid testimony to an understanding of not just family times and the youthful recklessness of stuffing oneself with party food, but of how grandma felt when embraced, and intimates her position within the family, how she was perhaps larger than life, so much so that her clothes couldn't contain her. The recollection is also indicative of the relationship between floral motifs, generation and shopping habits; granny and her floral frocks are representative of an older generation, one that buys clothes from catalogues, made from unpleasant fabrics and, by association, exists outside of the remits of the world of fashion.

Conclusion

Ethnographic and oral history approaches to fashion are not without their critics. Elizabeth Wilson notes:

> Those fashion commentators, therefore, who still feel able to discuss fashion in terms largely of social psychology – as primarily a form of behaviour – miss its significance for the twentieth century. An investigator of the psychology of clothes might interview individuals to discover their feelings about their clothes and might observe the sartorial behaviour of various social groupings ... This is often done, but misses the crucial historical dimension of fashion ... To reduce fashion to a psychology also excludes, or at best minimises, the vital aesthetic element of fashion. Fashion's changing styles owe far less to psychological quirks than to the evolution of aesthetic styles generally (Wilson 1985: 8–9).

Wilson's observation accentuates the significance of fashion as a process, the articulation of zeitgeist and the fashion system per se. Yet it appears vital to combine ethnographic elements with the dynamism of fashion in order to uncover an understanding of individual and group sartorial appropriation. Similarly, the ways in which styles are adopted as a means of conformity, subversion or as a vehicle for expressing social change, in addition to personal responses as to how one fits into wider cultural discourse through recollection and memory, add alternative and lived histories to the study of textiles and dress. Indeed, it seems necessary to use such a methodology to avoid Wilson's description of dress in museums as appearing as 'empty ghosts or shadows of a lost and untold past' (1985: 1).

The intention of this paper has been to uncover experiences of wearing floral printed dresses otherwise unheard of and excluded from fashion history. The aim therefore has been to see garments as object and artefact as well as a symbol or memento of life journeys undertaken in the construction of the self.

There is nothing new in using oral history in the construction of an understanding of dress. Nor is there anything revolutionary in suggesting that clothing plays a significant role in everyday life. From feminist and Marxist design histories of ordinary dress developed in the 1980s (Ash and Wilson 1992; Attfield and Kirkham 1995; Burman 1999; Guy 2001; Gregson and Crewe 2003) through to more recent autobiographical accounts of a life in clothes (Elms 2005; Picardie 2005), the expression of the personal in the establishment of collective memory of clothing extols and perpetuates alternative fashion histories. Indeed, these approaches encourage personal recollection in the reader, for example, 'I had one like that ...' and so on, which simultaneously add to and appear to confirm their validity.

Clothing is inherently close to the wearer and therefore oral testimony and garment recollection is highly significant, but highly personalised. The memory of clothing is emotive, often sentimental and frequently representative of a linear life narrative as demonstrated in family photographs and so on. Revisiting the clothes that we have worn either through photographic evidence or through the garment itself is a link with the past and our position within it (Taylor 2002; Kuchler and Miller 2005).

This paper has aimed to address one aspect of the meaning of floral dresses in the construction of femininity, which mirrors changing attitudes of the performance of the feminine self within society per se. The fondness with which floral dresses have been recollected by interviewees have all highlighted the cultural significance of floral motifs, for example nostalgia, youthfulness (delicate and in bud or wild and untamed), femininity, romance, subversion and freedom. It has also demonstrated that fashion is more to do with social conventions and either their acceptance or rejection, than specific garments, emphasising that the fashionable self really is less about what you wear and more about how you wear it.

In relation to the *Pick of the Bunch* exhibition, oral history enabled an assessment and appreciation of garments outside of design and fashion history methodologies. Personal recollection about what was worn by whom and when, as well as evocative experiences of the actual wearing of garments informed the selection of objects for display. In this respect, oral history proved to be a tool which allowed visitors to the exhibition with no prior knowledge of fashion and its histories to engage with the display on a personal level, while simultaneously addressing examples of floral printed dresses designed by key names in fashion. The removal of a hierarchy of garments made the exhibition accessible, and by association, the ordinary extraordinary.

Fashion is ephemeral by nature, but for interviewees and visitors to the exhibition, it became less so, marking not merely the zeitgeist but evidencing snapshots of life narratives, of times remembered. Floral frocks are essentially feminine garments which have been worn by grannies, mothers, wives, daughters and sisters. While floral patterns may well have been at the cutting edge of fashion, the meanings they convey and the memories they evoke burst into life through the testimonies of their wearers.

Notes

1. Exhibition, *Pick of the Bunch: The Floral Printed Dress in the Twentieth Century*, at the Museum of Costume, Bath, UK, 18 July–27 August 2007.
2. Interviewee testimonies are referenced in the text and are cited

using the initials of the respondents. All interviews were conducted between September and December 2004.

References

Arnold, R. (2001) *Fashion, Desire and Anxiety*. London: I.B. Tauris.
Ash, J. and Wilson, E. (eds) (1992) *Chic Thrills: A Fashion Reader*. London: Pandora.
Attfield, J. (2000) *Wild Things: The Material Culture of Everyday Life*. Oxford: Berg.
Attfield, J. and Kirkham, P. (eds) (1995) *A View from the Interior*. London: Women's Press.
Brown, P. and Jordanova, L. (1995) 'Oppressive dichotomies: is female to male as nature is to culture?', in *A Cultural Studies Reader*, J. Munns and G. Rajan (eds), 509–18. London: Longman.
Burman, B. (ed.) (1999) *The Culture of Sewing*. Oxford: Berg.
Church-Gibson, P. (2000) '"No-one expects me anywhere": invisible women, ageing and the fashion industry', in *Fashion Cultures: Theories, Explorations and Analysis*, S. Bruzzi and P. Church-Gibson (eds), 79–89. London: Routledge.
Clarke, A. and Miller, D. (2002) 'Fashion and anxiety', *Fashion Theory* 6(2): 191–214.
Davis, F. (1992) *Fashion, Culture and Identity*. Chicago: University of Chicago Press.
Elms, R. (2005) *What We Wore*. London: Picador.
Fogg, M. (2006) *Print in Fashion*. London: Batsford.
Greenberg, C. (1968) 'The avant-garde and kitsch', in *Kitsch: The World of Bad Taste*, G. Dorfles, G. (ed.), 116–26. London: Studio Vista.
Gregson, N. and Crewe, L. (2003) *Second-hand Cultures*. Oxford: Berg.
Guy, A. (ed.) (2001) *Through the Wardrobe*. Oxford: Berg.
Jackson, L. (2002) 'Who's afraid of pattern design?', *Crafts* 177: 28–31.
Kawamura, Y. (2005) *Fashion-ology*. Oxford: Berg.
Kirkham, P. (ed.) (1996) *The Gendered Object*. Manchester: Manchester University Press.
Klepp, I.G. and Storm-Mathisen, A. (2005) 'Reading fashion as age: teenage girls' and grown women's accounts of clothing as body and social status', *Fashion Theory* 9(3): 323–42.
Kuchler, S. and Miller, D. (eds) (2005) *Clothing as Material Culture*. Oxford: Berg.
Lomas, C. (2000) '"I know nothing about fashion. There's no point in interviewing me": the use and value of oral history to the fashion historian', in *Fashion Cultures: Theories, Explorations and Analysis*, S. Bruzzi and P. Church-Gibson (eds), 363–70. London: Routledge.
Lurie, A. (1982) *The Language of Clothes*. New York: Hamlyn.
McRobbie, A. (1989) 'Second-hand dresses and the role of the rag-market', in *Zoot Suits and Second-hand Dresses*, A. McRobbie (ed.), 23–49. London: Macmillan.
Miller, D. (1990) 'Reappropriating the state on the council estate', in *Household Choices*, T. Putnam and C. Newton (eds), 43–55. London: Futures Publishing.
Miller, D. (1998) *A Theory of Shopping*. London: Polity.
Nead, L. (1988) *Myths of Sexuality*. Oxford: Blackwell.
Parker, R. and Pollock, G. (1981) *Old Mistresses: Women, Art and Ideology*. London: Pandora.
Picardie, J. (2005) *My Mother's Wedding Dress: The Fabric of our Lives*. London: Picador.
Polhemus, T. (1994) *Street Style*. London: Thames and Hudson.
Powdermaker, H. (1966) *Stranger and Friend: The Way of an Anthropologist*. New York: Norton.
Ribeiro, A. (1986) *Dress and Morality*. London: Batsford.
Roach, M.E. and Eicher, J.B. (1973) *The Visible Self: Perspectives on Dress*. New York: Prentice Hall.
Rowe, D. (1995) *Popular Cultures*. London: Sage.
Sparke, P. (1995) *As Long as It's Pink: The Sexual Politics of Taste*. London: Pandora.
Taylor, L. (2002) *The Study of Dress History*. Manchester: Manchester University Press.
Thompson, P. (1997) 'The potential for oral history and life story research on the crafts movement', in *Obscure Objects of Desire: Reviewing the Crafts in the Twentieth Century*, T. Harrod (ed.), 44–5. London: Crafts Council.
Wilson, E. (1985) *Adorned in Dreams: Fashion and Modernity*. London: I.B. Tauris.

The author

Jo Turney is a Senior Lecturer in Historical and Critical Studies in the School of Art and Design at Bath Spa University. She has a PhD from the University of Southampton (2003), which investigated amateur needlecrafts in contemporary Britain. Her publications include *Floral Frocks*, written with Rosemary Harden (2007). She is currently writing a book entitled *The Culture of Knitting*, to be published by Berg in 2008.

Address

Jo Turney, Jubilee Hall, 1 Longdown Road, Little Sandhurst, Berkshire GU47 8QG, UK (jo@jubilee-hall.co.uk)

Plate 1 Roman blue and white cotton check (Fig. 2, p. 12).

Plate 2 Roman blue and white cotton check (Fig. 3, p. 12).

Plate 3 Roman 'shaded band' wool textile (Fig. 4, p. 12).

Plate 4 Fragment of Ayyubid period *tiraz* textile (Fig. 5, p. 13).

Plate 5 Bag (Fig. 6, p. 14).

Plate 6 Bag showing where an oval object was pushed into the bottom (Fig. 7, p. 14).

Plate 7 Resist-dyed cotton fabric, possibly an example of Goitein's 'kerchief' (Fig. 8, p. 14).

Plate 8 Length of cotton fabric with empty warps (Fig. 9, p. 16).

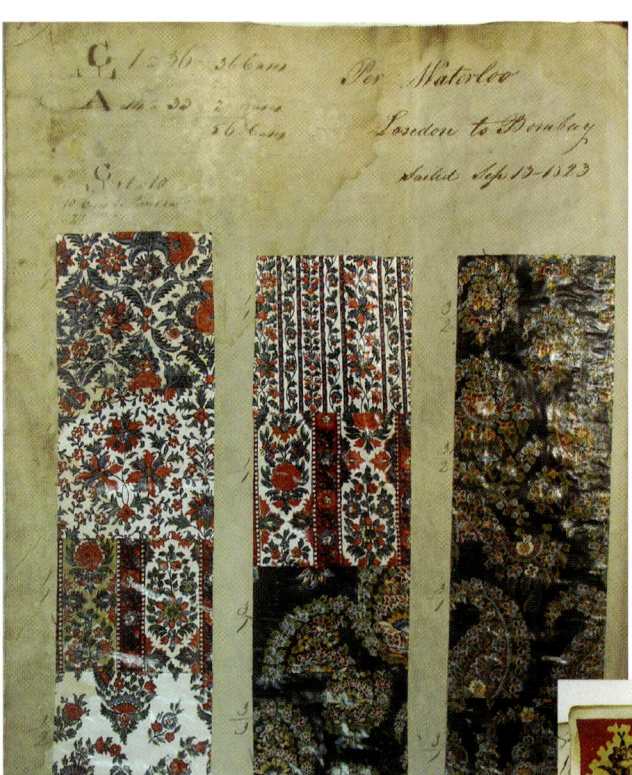

Plate 9 Page from Ritchie Steuart & Co. shipment record (© Museum of Science and Industry in Manchester) (Fig. 1, p. 24).

Plate 10 Sample from the Lyon 'show book' with two contiguous patterns (© by permission of Special Collections and Archives, Aldham Robarts Centre, Liverpool John Moores University) (Fig. 2, p. 24).

Plate 11 Page from the Birkacre notebook showing costings including duty. (© Bolton Museums, Art Gallery and Aquarium) (Fig. 3, p. 25).

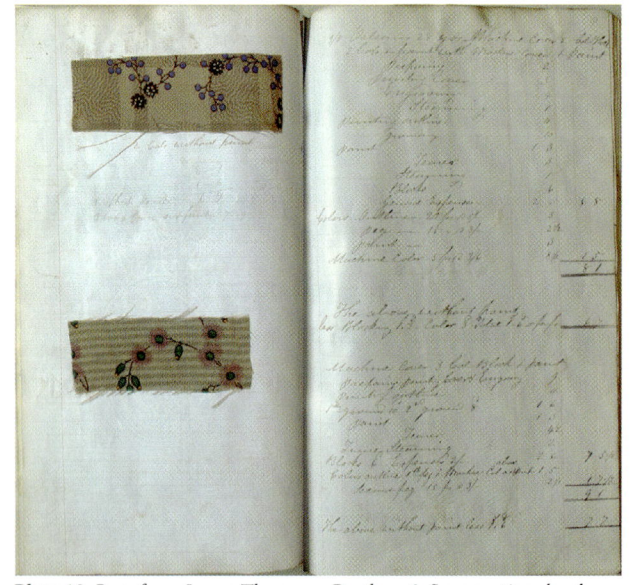

Plate 12 Page from James Thomson, Brothers & Sons costings book (© Manchester Archives and Local Studies: BRf 667.2 T4) (Fig. 4, p. 26).

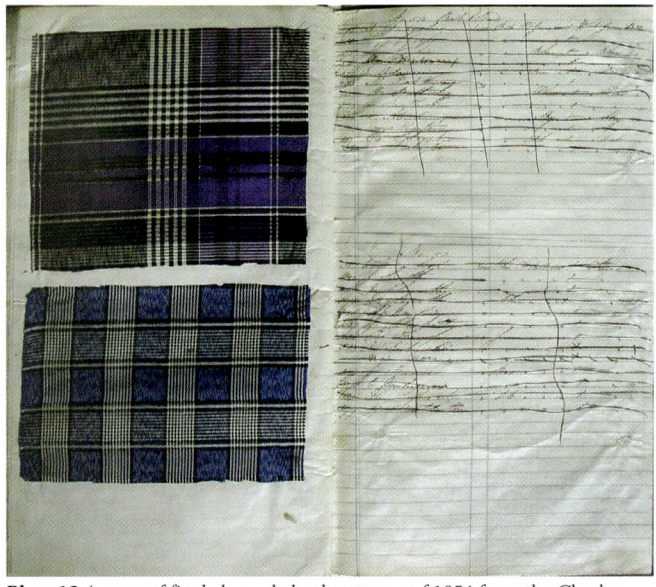

Plate 13 A page of finely barred check patterns of 1854 from the Charles Hilton & Son archive (© Wigan Heritage Service B78.511) (Fig. 5, p. 27).

Plate 14 Ardil blend scarf made by Imperial Chemical Industries (a) and label detail (b) (Fig. 1, p. 31). (Karen Finch Reference Collection. Reproduced by permission of the Textile Conservation Centre, University of Southampton.)

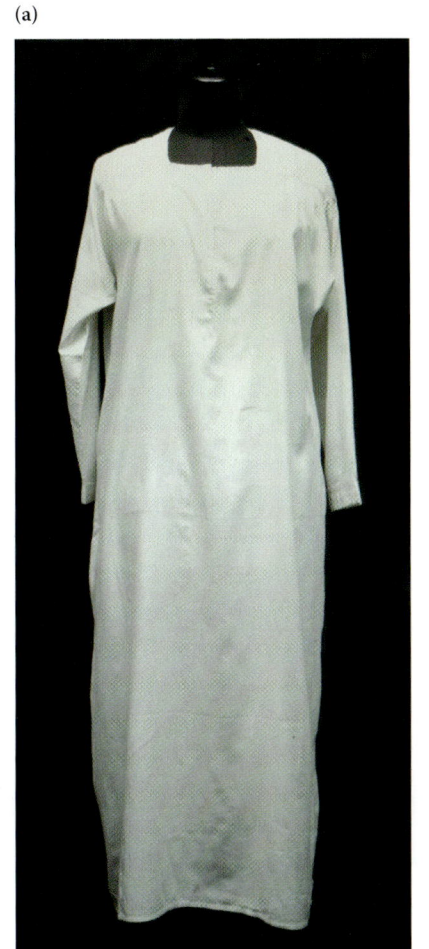

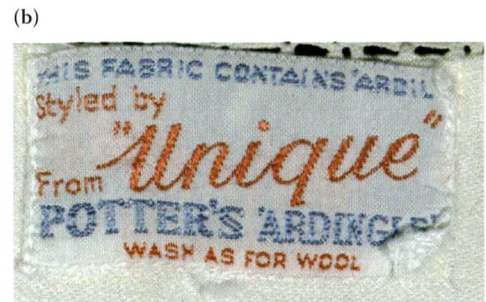

Plate 15 Ardil blend nightdress styled by 'Unique' using Potter's Ardingle (a) and label detail (b) (Fig. 2, p. 31). (York Castle Museum. Reproduced by permission of the York Museums Trust.)

Plate 16 Lady Margaret Wadham, c.1520, Church of St Mary the Virgin, Carisbrooke, Isle of Wight (Fig. 4, p. 42).

Plate 17 Unknown woman, c.1520, St Leonard's Church, Oakley, Hampshire (Fig. 5, p. 42).

Plate 18 Lady Oglander, 1536, St Mary the Virgin, Brading, Isle of Wight (Fig. 6, p. 43).

Plate 19 Johan Fantleroy, 1538, Church of St Mary, Michelmersh, Hampshire (Fig. 7, p. 43).

Plate 20 The silver and engraved armour for horse and man (Royal Armouries, Tower of London © courtesy of the Board of Trustees of the Armouries) (Fig. 1, p. 45).

Plate 21 Henry VIII jousting before Catherine of Aragon in 1511 (Westminster Tournament Roll, College of Arms) (Fig. 2, p. 48).

Plate 22 A base made drawing on the evidence collected for this paper (Fig. 4, p. 49).

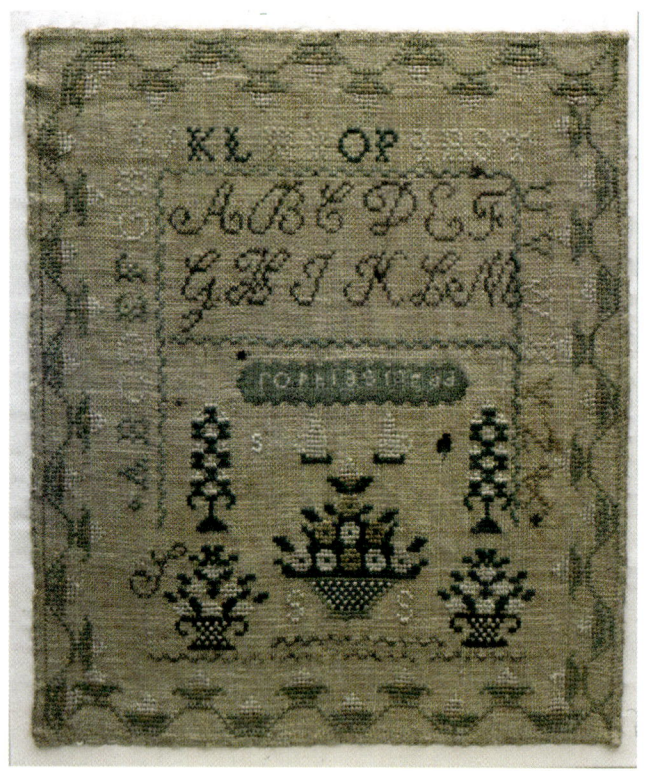

Plate 23 Embroidery sampler by Sophia Smead about 1794, silk on linen (Historic Deerfield 2000.4.1, Gift of Karen Dunn) (Fig.1, p. 52).

Plate 24 Profile portrait, Sophia Smead (1784–1843), watercolour and pencil on paper (Historic Deerfield 70.132, Gift of Mrs. Robert Stebbins Lipp) (Fig. 2, p. 54).

Plate 25 Dress worn by Sophia Smead about 1815, cotton (Historic Deerfield V.053B, Gift of Mrs. Robert Stebbins Lipp) (Fig. 3, p. 54).

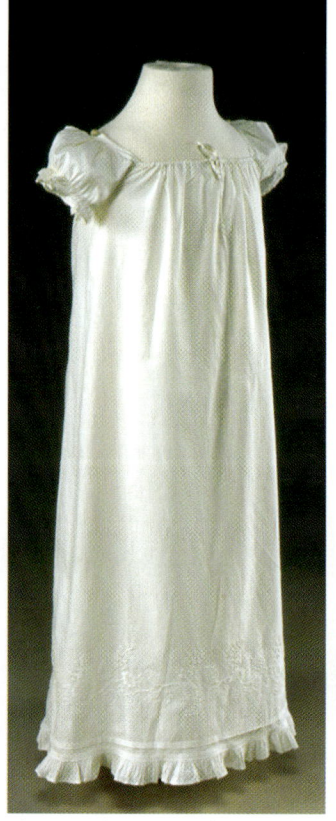

Plate 26 Christening robe worn by Sophia Wheeler about 1823, cotton, white-on-white embroidery (Historic Deerfield. Gift of Mrs. Robert Stebbins Lipp) (Fig. 4, p. 55).

Plate 27 Embroidered sampler by Sophia Wheeler at age 8 in 1829, silk on linen (Historic Deerfield 2000.4.2, Gift of Karen Dunn) (Fig. 5, p. 55).

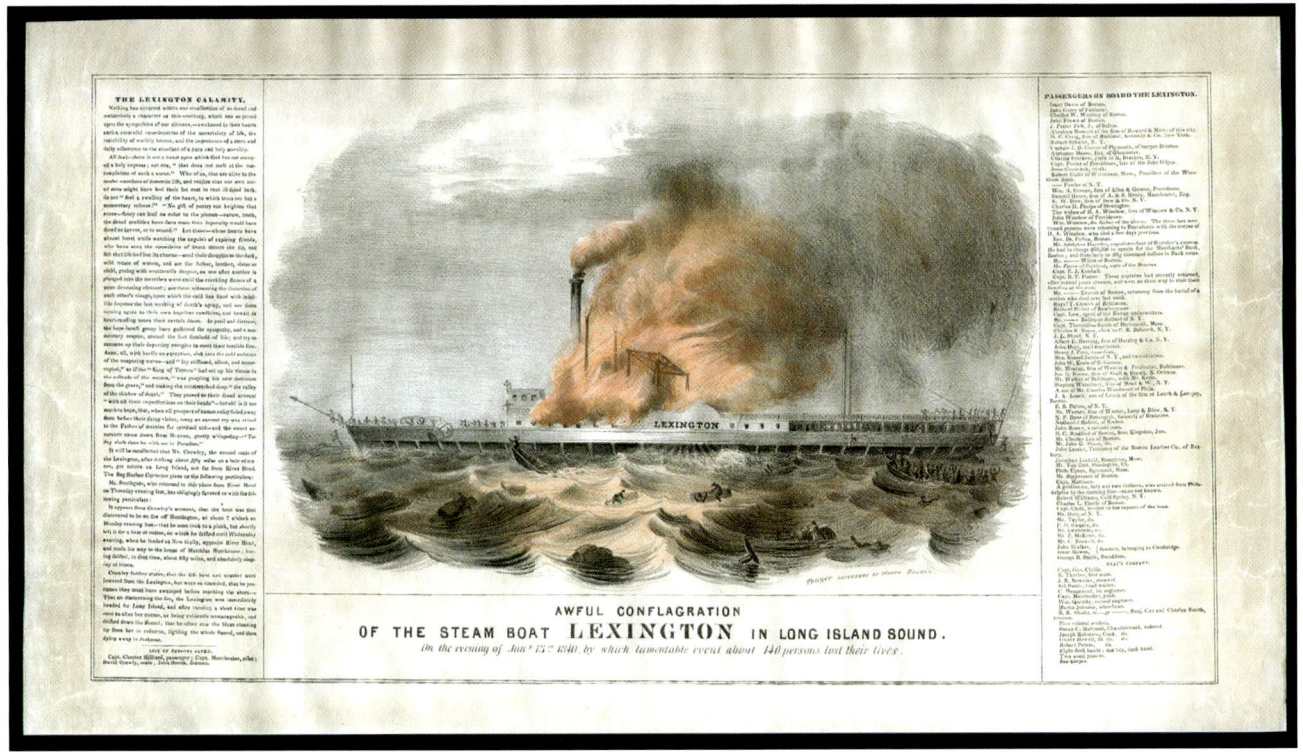

Plate 28 'The Steamboat *Lexington* on fire on Long Island Sound, January 13 1840' Nathaniel Currier, for the *New York Sun* (newspaper) coloured lithograph (Fig. 6, p. 56).

Plate 29 Part of the exhibition: *Embroidered History – Stitched Lives: Needlework & Samplers from the Historic Deerfield Collection 1670–1850* (Fig. 7, p. 57).

Plate 30 John Bates (designer), Jamaica, 1970s (BATMC 2004.198) (reproduced with permission from the Museum of Costume, Bath) (Fig. 2, p. 61).

Plate 31 Pair of stays (corset), dated *c.* 1620/1630, found (with the garment pictured in Fig. 3) under floorboards in an old public house in Sittingbourne (image courtesy Textile Conservation Centre) (Fig. 1, p. 65).

Plate 32 Display case made for the exhibition *Hidden House History* to show where many items from the Sittingbourne Cache were found (image courtesy Textile Conservation Centre) (Fig. 2, p. 66).

Plate 33 Lining of a pair of breeches found (with the stays pictured in Fig. 1) under floorboards in an old public house in Sittingbourne (image courtesy Textile Conservation Centre) (Fig. 3, p. 67).

Plate 34 Phil Talbot and Alan Abbey as shown in the *Hidden House History* exhibition, with a 'speech bubble' featuring an extract of the oral history recording of Alan's account of the discovery of the Sittingbourne Cache (image courtesy Textile Conservation Centre) (Fig. 4, p. 67).

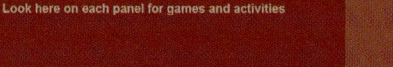

Plate 35 Portrait of Elizabeth Woodville (d. 1492), wife of King Edward IV, and a Garter Lady. She was the daughter of Sir Richard Woodville, only recently created Lord Rivers, and the widow of a knight, Sir John Grey, heir to Lord and Lady Ferrers de Groby (© The President and Fellows, Queens College, Cambridge) (Fig. 1, p. 73).

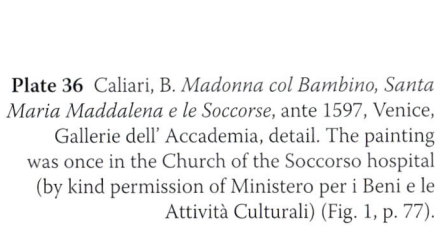

Plate 36 Caliari, B. *Madonna col Bambino, Santa Maria Maddalena e le Soccorse*, ante 1597, Venice, Gallerie dell' Accademia, detail. The painting was once in the Church of the Soccorso hospital (by kind permission of Ministero per i Beni e le Attività Culturali) (Fig. 1, p. 77).

Plate 37 Detail from the Chasuble 'St Augustine', first half of the 18th century (Musée des Ursulines de Québec, Collection du Monastère des Ursulines) (Fig. 2, p. 85).

Plate 38 Sampler, Marguerite Falardaux, 1780, worked in green wool on coarse linen ground, 12.5 × 16.0 cm. Sampler fragment, undated, unattributed, possibly *c.* 1780, worked in red wools on coarse linen ground, 24.09 × 10.0 cm (Musée des Ursulines de Québec, Collection du Monastère des Ursulines) (Fig. 3, p. 86).

Plate 39 Spot or motif sampler, unattributed, undated, probably mid-19th century, worked in wools and silks on fine linen canvas ground, 32.20 × 41.70 cm (Musée des Ursulines de Québec, Collection du Monastère des Ursulines) (Fig. 4, p. 87).

Plate 40 Samplette 'Pray Make the Kettle Boil'. Polychrome Berlin-type wools on linen ground, 18.00 × 16.30 cm (Musée des Ursulines de Québec, Collection du Monastère des Ursulines) (Fig. 5, p. 87).

Plate 41 Twenty-four scraps and samplettes worked in cross stitch and running stitches on a variety of linen and cotton grounds in wools (Musée des Ursulines de Québec, Collection du Monastère des Ursulines) (Fig. 6, p. 87).

Plate 42 Raphael, *Guidobaldo da Montefeltro*, Florence, Uffizi (Soprintendenza Speciale per il Polo Museale Fiorentino, Gabinetto Fotografico) (Fig. 1, p. 93).

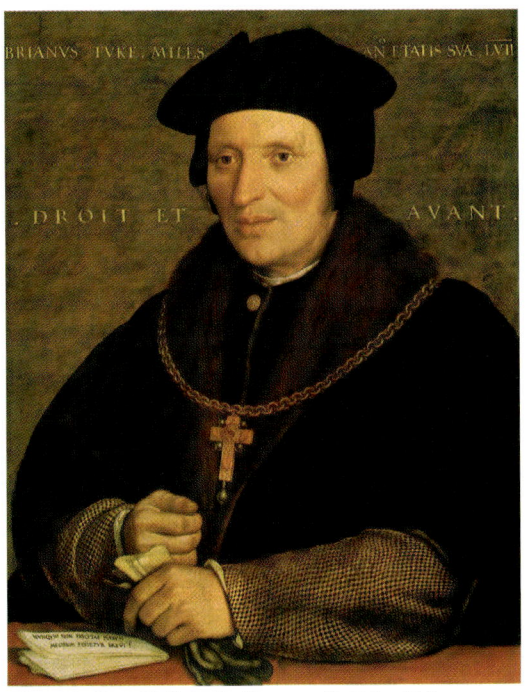

Plate 43 Hans Holbein the Younger, *Sir Brian Tuke*, National Gallery of Art, Washington, Andrew W. Mellon Collection (© Board of Trustees, National Gallery of Art, Washington. National Gallery of Art, Washington, Department of Visual Services) (Fig. 2, p. 94).

Plate 44 Raphael, *Francesco Maria della Rovere*, Florence, Uffizi (Soprintendenza Speciale per il Polo Museale Fiorentino, Gabinetto Fotografico) (Fig. 3, p. 94).

Plate 45 Remnants of a cope commissioned by Richard Fox, Bishop of Winchester (Oxford, Corpus Christi College) (Fig. 4, p. 95).

Plate 46 Cope belonging to Cardinal Silvio Passerini, Cortona (Museo Diocesano. Dipartimento di Storia delle Arti, Pisa, Gabinetto Fotografico) (Fig. 5, p. 95).

Plate 47 Hans Holbein the Younger, *Sir Henry Guildford*, The Royal Collection (© 2007, HM Queen Elizabeth II. A.C. Cooper Ltd) (Fig. 6, p. 99).

Plate 48 Hans Holbein the Younger, *Edward, Prince of Wales*, National Gallery of Art, Washington, Andrew W. Mellon Collection (© Board of Trustees, National Gallery of Art, Washington. National Gallery of Art, Washington, Department of Visual Services) (Fig. 7, p. 99).

Plate 49 A sketch of one of the stage costumes used in the *Mammalucchi*, Niccolò Tribolo, Gabinetto Disegni e Stampe, Uffizi Gallery, Florence (Fig. 1, p. 107).

Plate 50 Agnolo Bronzino, *Eleonora of Toledo with her son Giovanni*, c. 545, Uffizi Gallery, Florence (Fig. 2, p. 107).

Plate 60 Detailed analysis of 'Empress A' crinoline belonging to Barbara Burman (Fig. 1, p. 124).

Plate 61 Image showing the back of eyelet holding hoops in place (Paris Prize No. 375. 1964/536. Worthing Museum and Art Gallery) (Fig. 5, p. 125).

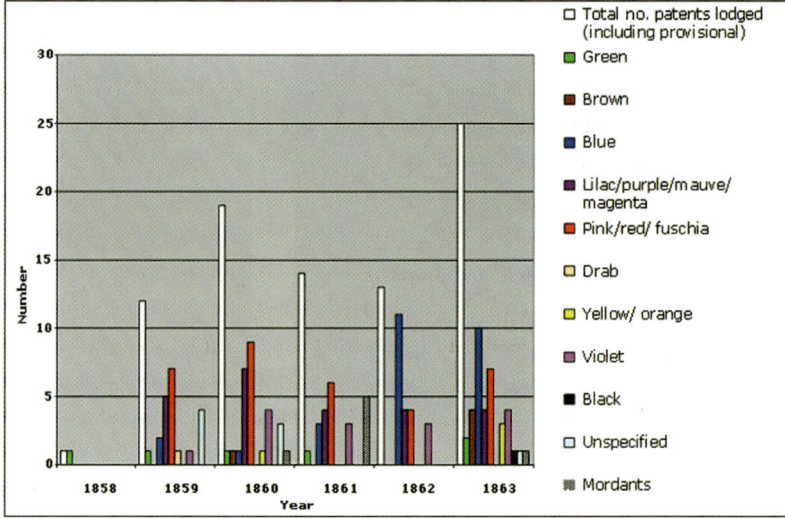

Plate 62 Analysis of patents lodged by date (see p. 129).

Plate 47 Hans Holbein the Younger, *Sir Henry Guildford*, The Royal Collection (© 2007, HM Queen Elizabeth II. A.C. Cooper Ltd) (Fig. 6, p. 99).

Plate 48 Hans Holbein the Younger, *Edward, Prince of Wales*, National Gallery of Art, Washington, Andrew W. Mellon Collection (© Board of Trustees, National Gallery of Art, Washington. National Gallery of Art, Washington, Department of Visual Services) (Fig. 7, p. 99).

Plate 49 A sketch of one of the stage costumes used in the *Mammalucchi*, Niccolò Tribolo, Gabinetto Disegni e Stampe, Uffizi Gallery, Florence (Fig. 1, p. 107).

Plate 50 Agnolo Bronzino, *Eleonora of Toledo with her son Giovanni*, c. 545, Uffizi Gallery, Florence (Fig. 2, p. 107).

Plate 51 Agnolo Bronzino workshop/Florentine school, *Eleonora of Toledo*, second half of the 16th century, private gallery, Rome (Fig. 3, p. 107).

Plate 52 *Cosimo de'Medici together his Court Artists*, Palazzo Vecchio, Florence (Fig. 4, p. 107).

Plate 53 Agnolo Bronzino, *Eleanora of Toledo with her son Francesco*, 1549, Museo Nazionale di Palazzo Reale, Pisa (Fig. 5, p. 108).

Plate 54 Titian, *Felipe II*, 1550, Palatina Gallery, Florence (Fig. 6, p. 109).

Plate 55 Agnolo Bronzino, *Lodovico Capponi*, Frick Collection, New York (Fig. 7, p. 109).

Plate 56 Agnolo Bronzino, *Cosimo de'Medici*, Palazzo Vecchio, Florence (Fig. 8, p. 110).

Plate 57 Petticoat with sleeves, *c.* 1560, Museo Nazionale di Palazzo Reale, Pisa (Fig. 9, p. 110).

Plate 58 A quilted petticoat in green shot silk, with plain diamond quilting, *c.*1740–50, to be worn with a contrasting gown or jacket. This represents the mid-range of commercial quilting (Victoria and Albert Museum T.306-1982) (Fig. 2, p. 117).

Plate 59 A cotton pocket woven in an imitation of quilting known as 'marcella', *c.*1760–80. The woven motifs imitate those on stitched versions (Victoria and Albert Museum T.150-1970) (Fig. 3, p. 117).

Plate 60 Detailed analysis of 'Empress A' crinoline belonging to Barbara Burman (Fig. 1, p. 124).

Plate 61 Image showing the back of eyelet holding hoops in place (Paris Prize No. 375. 1964/536. Worthing Museum and Art Gallery) (Fig. 5, p. 125).

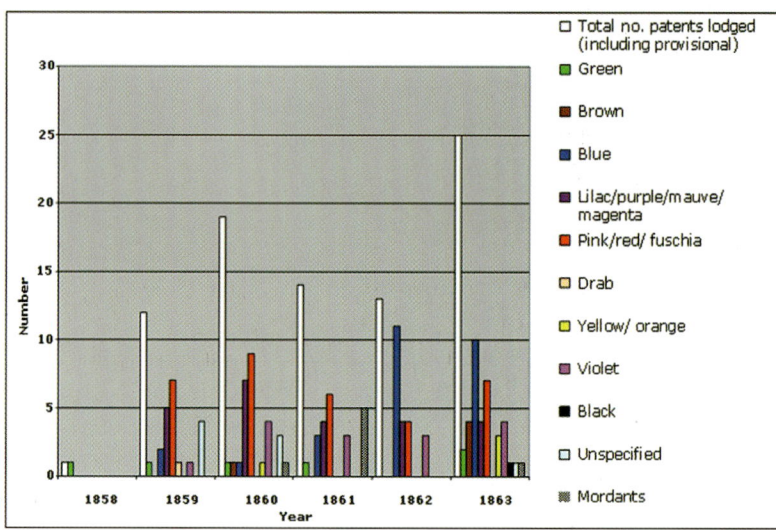

Plate 62 Analysis of patents lodged by date (see p. 129).

Sound recording and text creation: oral history and the Deliberately Concealed Garments Project

Dinah Eastop

ABSTRACT Oral history accounts (sound recordings and their transcriptions) are important sources for the study of textiles and dress. This paper demonstrates the value of such accounts for the Deliberately Concealed Garments Project (DCGP), set up to document garments and other things found deliberately concealed within buildings. This paper focuses on one oral history account of the Sittingbourne Cache, the collective name for over 500 items found within an old public house in Sittingbourne, Kent, UK. The account provides information about the location of the cache sites within the building and the circumstances of the 'excavation' of the finds. It also provides a vivid record of the finder's excitement at the discovery. Understanding the views and attitudes of finders was important for developing the conservation strategy of the DCGP and led to a focus on measures to raise public awareness of the practice of concealment and the evidential significance of finds and cache sites. The DCGP provides a useful model of 'material culture', not as a new term for artefacts, but as the interconnection of persons, artefacts and language. In the case of the DCGP the interconnections are shown to be between: the persons who hide, discover, report, curate, conserve and study caches; the artefacts that are involved in the concealments (e.g. buildings and garments); and, the language used to describe the practice. The oral history accounts of the DCGP provide a rich illustration of material culture as linking persons to language (in both speech and text) with textiles.

Keywords: Deliberately Concealed Garments Project, Sittingbourne Cache, Wessex Film and Sound Archive, cache, material culture, oral history

Introduction

Oral history accounts are recognised as important sources for the study of textiles and dress (e.g. Biddle-Perry 2005; Burman 1999; Guy *et al.* 2001; Lomas 2000). Sound recordings and their transcriptions may be viewed as research tools and as a means of archive creation (Samuel 1998: 391–2). This paper demonstrates the value of oral accounts for the Deliberately Concealed Garments Project (DCGP). The paper starts by introducing the DCGP and then focuses on one of the oral history recordings relating to over 500 items discovered within an old public house in Sittingbourne, Kent, UK. The paper draws attention to the benefits of integrating evidence from a variety of historical and contemporary sources, material, oral and textual, in order to enhance the understanding and conservation of garments (and other objects and materials) found hidden within buildings.

The Deliberately Concealed Garments Project

This project was set up by the author in 1998 at the Textile Conservation Centre (TCC), Winchester School of Art, University of Southampton, with the aim of locating, documenting and researching garments and associated objects found concealed within buildings (Eastop 2001). The project builds on and complements the pioneering work of June Swann (1969, 1996) at Northampton Museums and Gardens, where an index records hundreds of boots and shoes found concealed within buildings. The DCGP encourages the recording and preservation of garment and other finds by raising awareness of concealment practices and providing conservation advice. The project website[1] presents an online database of garment and associated finds, a guided tour of garment caches from

Figure 1 Pair of stays (corset), dated *c.* 1620/1630, found (with the garment pictured in Fig. 3) under floorboards in an old public house in Sittingbourne (image courtesy Textile Conservation Centre) (Plate 31 in the colour plate section).

across the UK, interviews from the oral history programme, case studies and bibliography (Eastop and Dew 2003). Another outcome of the project was the exhibition *Hidden House History*, which toured Hampshire and Dorset between July 2005 and September 2006. Several very rare garments were displayed for the first time including the fragmentary remains of an 18th-century stomacher (Barbieri 2003) and a pair of stays (corset) dated to *c.*1620/1630 (Fig. 1) (Eastop and Dew 2006). Some caches were displayed in cases replicating three cache sites: under floorboards, within a wall and alongside a chimney flue (Fig. 2).

The deliberate concealment of garments and other objects within the structure of buildings has a long history but is seldom reported. These concealments (known as caches from the French word 'to hide') are usually uncovered during building work, rather than during planned architectural or archaeological investigations. Finds are sometimes viewed as rubbish or as too damaged to be of interest and are thrown away. A cache found in Saltville, Virginia, USA, which included a shoe and a 'corset type thing', was burned by the house owner 'thinking there was no significance to them'.[2] Some finds may be recognised as rare examples of dress, while others may be viewed as evil-averting agents and be re-concealed (Brooks 2000).

The DCGP was established in 1998 to help preserve these finds and information about them. It has resulted in a new resource for the study of textiles and dress through the creation of a virtual collection of once concealed garments (available via the project's website) by fostering awareness of the significance of garment and other finds, by providing a mechanism for reporting and recording finds, and by recording information about cache sites. The project provides a vivid example of the benefits of integrating the study of textiles and text, where the latter includes the recorded accounts and views of finders. The DCGP offers a model of conservation as material culture, where people (notably finders), objects (for example, the early 17th-century stays found in the Sittingbourne Cache) and language (for example, oral testimonies) inform current understanding of concealed garments and concealment practices (Eastop 2006a, 2006b).

Oral testimony

One of the distinctive features of past concealment practices is the lack of contemporaneous written explanation or commentary. It is possible that many of the people who assembled caches were unable to read or write or they felt no need to write down this aspect of their lives, or that no written records have survived or yet been identified. This means that, as in archaeology, the significance of the finds has to be deduced from the finds themselves (from their location, distribution and contents) and by comparison with other finds. This has led to intensive investigation of the materials and construction of garment finds. It has also led to special attention being focused on the circumstances of their discovery and on the views of finders and custodians (Eastop and Dew 2006).

An oral history programme was initiated as part of the DCGP as a means of understanding more about the circumstances of discovery and concealment, and learning more about the views of finders, custodians and conservators. Recordings relating to the following UK caches have been recorded: the Brixham Cache (Eastop and Dew 2006), the Nether Wallop Cache, the Reigate Cache (Eastop 2000) and the Sittingbourne Cache (see below). The recordings are held by the Wessex Film and Sound Archive, Winchester, UK, where they are publicly accessible.

The Sittingbourne Cache

The Sittingbourne Cache is the collective name given to a large group of artefacts found within the fabric of an old public house in Sittingbourne, Kent, in the south-east of the UK, shortly before the building's demolition. The garment finds were discovered in three main locations in the building: in the voids on either side of a stepped, brick chimney flue; under floorboards in a first-floor room at the front of the building; and under floorboards in another part of the building. Most of the finds were found alongside the chimney flue; examples include shoes, a felt hat, fabric scraps, scraps of leather harness, rope, the remains of clay pipes and lots of paper scraps. The under floorboard finds include two garments found in the same location: a pair of stays (corset), dated *c.*1620/1630 (Fig.

Figure 2 Display case made for the exhibition *Hidden House History* to show where many items from the Sittingbourne Cache were found (image courtesy Textile Conservation Centre) (Plate 32 in the colour plate section).

SOUND RECORDING AND TEXT CREATION

Figure 3 Lining of a pair of breeches found (with the stays pictured in Fig. 1) under floorboards in an old public house in Sittingbourne (image courtesy Textile Conservation Centre) (Plate 33 in the colour plate section).

Figure 4 Phil Talbot and Alan Abbey as shown in the *Hidden House History* exhibition, with a 'speech bubble' featuring an extract of the oral history recording of Alan's account of the discovery of the Sittingbourne Cache (image courtesy Textile Conservation Centre) (Plate 34 in the colour plate section).

1), and what may be the lining from a pair of breeches of similar date (Fig. 3). The stays may be the second oldest pair in the UK.

What follows are extracts from one account of the discovery of the Sittingbourne Cache. The quoted extracts come from the (annotated) transcription of the oral account given by Phil Talbot, a local historian, who helped to uncover the Sittingbourne Cache (Fig. 4). Mr Talbot was interviewed by the author at Rochester Museum, Kent, on 5 August 2005 (Wessex Film and Sound Archive, *Deliberately Concealed Garments Oral History Project, Phil Talbot*).

We [a group of local historians] became aware of the pub when it closed because it's (or was) almost diagonally opposite the museum [Sittingbourne Museum]... we became very interested in the building opposite knowing that it was closed down; it was decaying; the 'squatters' had been in there and we wanted to get in there to have a look round, just to see what historical features were still left in the building ...

'This is the time we were allowed a weekend to photograph and subsequently search the building.'[3]

Alan [Abbey, another local historian] wanted to do a photograph of the stepped chimney; we knew there was a hole in the lath and plaster work in a cupboard, like a 'walk in' cupboard at the side of the fireplace, and it was while Alan was just easing a little bit more of the lath and plaster off the wall so that you could get a decent photograph that he noticed the heel of one of the shoes sticking out of the back of this chimney void which would have fronted the room behind us ... pulled the shoe out ... or realised it was a shoe as he pulled it out, and the height it was obviously sitting at, we realised there must be a helluva lot of other stuff underneath it ... we started breaking the lath and plaster, the laths were pinned to just half-round pieces of wood – they'd just cut the pieces of wood down the middle.

'At this point we ceased our search for the day and rapidly reconvened with our "squad" on the following day.'[4]

[Dinah Eastop] like trees ... tree trunks?
Yes, still had the bark on at the back and they'd just put the lath across and then plastered over the top of that. So it was quite easy to break through the laths which are very, very thin and feeble and quite dry obviously being there that length of time and above a fireplace and we did have the vision originally, thinking that it was a deposit that had been made over time, we thought we could excavate it layer by layer. But the rats had made a nest in it as well, so things had been pulled diagonally through layers and so we might have part of a garment at the top of the layer but we were having to move other parts of the layer away before we could get to the bottom part of it, so we realised it was all sort of intermingled and then at that time everything just started turning up. We were working by torchlight; it was very difficult to see; we did have visions originally of trying to collate the stuff

67

as we found it but it ended up being so much we were just putting what we found into carrier bags...

... it was just so amazing. I mean we started finding the shoe and then something else would come up and the shout would go out. This voice would just be heard in the darkness by everybody else saying that 'we've got another shoe, a hat, or we've got a pair of gloves' or something.

... the actual deposit started from sort of waist level and then almost up to eye level so it was good two to two and a half feet, I suppose, of deposit which went probably three feet across the chimney breast and where the chimney is stepped in on the side there was a small amount that had gone round the side as well, so it was quite a large area in total. But as I say, we didn't notice the environment or the problems you know, the dust, we were just so enthralled with what we were finding that nobody complained of being cold or dirty or wet or hungry; we just had a job to do and we were just focused on getting on with it, you know, because obviously we realised that time was running out [because demolition of the building was planned].

Phil Talbot goes on to describe how a second investigation was made of the public house about two to three weeks after the discovery of the fireplace cache. Access was granted to the building for one morning and help was provided in lifting some of the floorboards in the front room. 'At this stage by the time I arrived on site the pub had been demolished down to second floor level with the walls removed and I was allowed to access the floorboard area of the first floor as they prized them up. Immediately following this the demolition continued and I watched as the remains of the building was demolished into the cellar area and the excess rubble removed.'[5]

that was very lucky because obviously that's where we found the stays, the gentleman's undergarment [lining of breeches] and, I think, I'm sure it was the lace[-edged] hat although we've found so much on the day it was very difficult to keep a track of what was [where]...

[Dinah Eastop] Were they laid out flat or rolled up? *They [the stays] were folded. They'd been flattened sort of front to back so you had the whole of the front in one piece and then they'd just been folded in half down the middle rather than across. And they were just laid under the floorboards.*

Phil Talbot's account provides valuable information about the circumstances and conditions of the discovery, the subsequent 'excavation' of the material, and the locations of the finds. The excitement of discovery is also very clear from the oral recording.

You know, I mean, excitement doesn't really cover it; it was just a ... that feeling of, you know, well I suppose a mixture of excitement, euphoria ...

Methodology

The advice of the Wessex Film and Sound Archive was sought about the methodology, ethics and permissions required for making oral history recordings (Lee nd) as each of the sound recordings made for the DCGP was made by novices of oral history. A list of questions was developed to facilitate the recordings with a view to helping to structure the interviews and to record comparable data about each cache. As can be gauged from the extracts above, Phil Talbot gave a very lucid, chronological account, which addressed the questions without any need to ask them. The only listed question put to him was about what he thought should happen to the Sittingbourne Cache.

The sound recording was transcribed by the interviewer (the author) who determined the spelling, punctuation and spacing, and who also selected the extracts given above. In transcribing the text, every effort was made to reflect the rhythm and sense of the speaker, as well as his enthusiasm for the subject. As recommended by Samuel (1998), sentences that are incomplete or which trail off have been transcribed and have not been altered to meet the conventions of written prose. It must be noted, however, that transcription remains an act of interpretation (Perks and Thomson 1998; Samuel 1998) and transcriber bias is inevitable and should be acknowledged. The handwritten transcription was later typed and then checked by the interviewer/transcriber, who also annotated the above extracts. The transcript and the annotated parts quoted above were sent to the interviewee (Phil Talbot) prior to publication. He gave permission for the transcript to be published and added that 'Some of the summations are slightly incorrect and I have added extra text ... to explain and correct where necessary.'[6]

Discussion

The quoted extracts of Phil Talbot's spoken account (in italic text above) focus attention on the circumstances of the discovery. The later part of his account concentrates on media interest in the finds and the future of the collection. The selected extracts show his pride and deep interest in local history, and his familiarity with museum practice arising from his long association with metal detecting and local museums. A sense of awe, hard work and teamwork characterise his account of the discovery. The sense of revelation in a site of neglect, darkness and imminent destruction is highlighted in this use of oral history. It is important to point out, however, that the written transcript does not do full justice to the original spoken account, which is much more evocative of Phil's experience of discovering the cache. The sound recording of the interview is a more reliable and accurate account than the transcription because the many qualities of oral communication cannot be captured in transcription, e.g. nuances of accent, timing and the tentative quality of speech (Thompson 2000:126).

This brief analysis focuses on just one interpretation of one part of one account. Other accounts exist of the discovery of the Sittingbourne Cache, for example Phil Talbot's additions,[7] Alan Abbey's oral testimony (Wessex Film and Sound Archive,

Deliberately Concealed Garments Oral History Project, Alan Abbey) and his published account (2005). The accounts of these finders, and others involved in the discovery, preservation and display of the cache, form a network of narratives. Each account, as well as the narrative network they create, could be understood in different ways, for example, in terms of gender, community and group identity.

As shown by the extracts above, the oral recordings made as part of the DCGP have proved to be a valuable part of the project in providing useful information about the cache sites and the circumstances of discovery. They also provide information about finders' attitudes to what they have found, and how they went about seeking advice and information about the finds. This has informed the preservation strategy of the DCGP, for example, we focused on 'outreach activities' which draw public attention to the evidential potential of what may, at first glance, look like rubbish. We stressed the importance of finders' reports and views in the display panels of the touring exhibition *Hidden House History*. For example, one of the display panels included a photograph of Phil Talbot and Alan Abbey with a speech bubble containing an extract from the transcription of Alan Abbey's account of the discovery of the Sittingbourne Cache (Fig. 4). Without the interest and commitment of finders like Phil Talbot and Alan Abbey, it is likely that the Sittingbourne Cache would have been destroyed when the building was demolished. This would have been a loss to the study of textiles and dress. Their spoken accounts of the discovery provide a new source for the study of concealment practices and establish a new link between textiles and what people say about them.

The Deliberately Concealed Garments Project provides a vivid model of 'material culture', not as a new term for artefacts, but as the interconnection of persons, artefacts and language (Eastop 2006a). In the case of the DCGP the interconnections are shown to be between: the persons who hide, discover, report, curate, conserve and study caches; the artefacts that are involved in the concealments (e.g. buildings and garments); and, the language used to describe the practice. The oral history recordings and transcriptions of the Deliberately Concealed Garments Project provide a rich illustration of material culture as linking persons to language (in both speech and text) with textiles.

Acknowledgements

The Deliberately Concealed Garments Project has been funded by the L.J. Skaggs and Mary C. Skaggs Foundation and the Arts and Humanities Research Council, and forms an important project of the AHRC Research Centre for Textile Conservation and Textile Studies. The exhibition *Hidden House History* was made possible thanks to the support of Hampshire County Council Museums and Archives Service, the Esmée Fairbairn Foundation and Hampshire County Council. The oral history recording has been facilitated by David Lee of the Wessex Sound and Film Archive, where the recordings are now held; the staff of the Guildhall Museum, Rochester, where the oral history accounts were recorded; and, Rosie Baker and Helen Welford, who helped with the transcription of Phil Talbot's account. Special thanks go to Alan Abbey, Phil Talbot and to the South East England Development Agency (SEEDA) for their help and support. The author would also like to thank: Alison Carter, Ian Chipperfield, Susan North and Jenny Tiramani, who advised on the dating of the Sittingbourne stays; Liz Linthicum for editorial advice; and Charlotte Dew, who facilitated the development of the DCGP and its oral history programme when she worked as the DCGP Development Officer. Last but not least Barbara Burman and the anonymous referee are thanked for extremely helpful comments on the history and practice of oral history.

Notes

1. www.concealedgarments.org.
2. C. Schwartz, pers. comm., 26 June 2005.
3. P. Talbot, pers. comm., 23 February 2007.
4. P. Talbot, pers. comm., 23 February 2007.
5. P. Talbot, pers. comm., 23 February 2007.
6. P. Talbot, email dated 23 February 2007. These additions are indicated by notes 3, 4 and 5.
7. Of 23 February 2007.

References

Abbey, A. (2005) 'Concealed garments', *Kent Archaeological Society Newsletter* 64: 14–15.

Barbieri, G. (2003) *Memoirs of an 18th-century Stomacher: A Strategy for Documenting the Multiple Object Biographies of a Once-concealed Garment*, MA dissertation, Textile Conservation Centre, University of Southampton.

Biddle-Perry, G. (2005) 'Bury me in purple lurex: promoting a new dynamic between fashion and oral history', *Oral History* 33(1): 88–92.

Brooks, E. (2000) 'Watch your step: a tale of "builders' sacrifice" and lost soles', *National Trust Magazine* 91: 67–8.

Burman, B. (ed.) (1999) *The Culture of Sewing: Gender, Consumption and Home Dressmaking*. London: Berg.

Eastop, D. (2000) 'Textiles as multiple and competing histories', in *Textiles Revealed: Object Lessons in Historic Textile and Costume Research*, M.M. Brooks (ed.), 17–28. London: Archetype Publications.

Eastop, D. (2001) 'Garments deliberately concealed in buildings', in *A Permeability of Boundaries? New Approaches to the Archaeology of Art, Religion and Folklore*, R. Wallis and K. Lymer (eds), 79–83. BAR International Series S936. Oxford: British Archaeological Reports.

Eastop, D. (2006a) 'Conservation as material culture', in *Handbook of Material Culture*, C. Tilley, W. Keane, S. Küchler, M. Rowlands and P. Spyer (eds), 516–33. London: Sage.

Eastop, D. (2006b) 'Outside in: making sense of the deliberate concealment of garments within buildings', *Textile: Journal of Cloth and Culture* 4(3): 238–55 [special issue: 'Shaping Space: Textiles as Architecture and Archaeology' edited by J. Jefferies and D. Wood Conroy].

Eastop, D. and Dew, C. (2003) 'Secret agents: deliberately concealed garments as symbolic textiles', in *Tales in the Textile: The Conservation of Flags and other Symbolic Textiles. Preprints of the North American Textile Conservation Conference*, J. Vuori (ed.), 5–15. Albany: NATCC.

Eastop, D. and Dew, C. (2006) 'Context and meaning: the conservation of garments deliberately concealed within buildings', in *The Object in Context: Crossing Conservation Boundaries. Preprints of the 2006 Biennial Congress of IIC, Munich, 28 August–1 September 2006*, D. Saunders, J.H. Townsend and S. Woodcock (eds), 17–22. London: International Institute for Conservation of Historic and Artistic Works.

Guy, A., Green, E. and Banim, M. (eds) (2001) *Through the Wardrobe: Women's Relationship with their Clothes*. Oxford and New York: Berg.

Lee, D. (nd) *Oral History Guidelines*. Winchester: Wessex Film and Sound Archive.

Lomas, C. (2000) '"I know nothing about fashion. There's no point in interviewing me": the use and value of oral history to the fashion historian', in *Fashion Cultures: Theories, Explorations and Analysis*, S. Bruzzi and P. Church-Gibson (eds), 363–70. London: Routledge.

Perks, R. and Thomson, A. (1998) *The Oral History Reader*. London: Routledge.

Samuel, R. (1998) 'Perils of the transcript', in *The Oral History Reader*, R. Perks and A. Thomson (eds), 389–92. London: Routledge.

Swann, J. (1969) 'Shoes concealed in buildings', *Northampton County Borough Museums and Art Gallery Journal* 6: 8–21.

Swann, J. (1996) 'Shoes concealed in buildings', *Costume: Journal of the Costume Society* 30: 56–69.

Thompson, P. (2000) [1978] *The Voice of the Past: Oral History*. Oxford: OUP.

Wessex Film and Sound Archive, *Deliberately Concealed Garments Oral History Project, Alan Abbey, 05.08.05* (sound recording).

Wessex Film and Sound Archive, *Deliberately Concealed Garments Oral History Project, Phil Talbot, 05.08.05* (sound recording).

The author

Dinah Eastop is a Senior Lecturer at the Textile Conservation Centre (TCC), University of Southampton, UK. She initiated the Deliberately Concealed Garments Project (DCGP) (www.concealedgarments.org) and is the lead applicant, award holder, and founding Director of the AHRC Research Centre for Textile Conservation and Textile Studies, an interdisciplinary research partnership between the universities of Southampton, Bradford and Manchester, UK (2002–07). Her research focuses on broadening the academic base of textile conservation to include the social as well as physical sciences. She is interested in the changing roles of artefacts and the effect this has on conservation and curatorial decisions.

Address

Dinah Eastop, The Textile Conservation Centre, University of Southampton, Park Avenue, Winchester SO23 8DL, UK (D.D.Eastop@soton.ac.uk)

Uncovering institutions

Late medieval Ladies of the Garter, 1348–1509: fact or fiction?

Shelagh Mitchell

ABSTRACT This paper re-examines the question of whether women were members of the Order of the Garter in their own right and argues strongly for this being the case. The author draws on evidence from a range of sources including the Great Wardrobe accounts and the alms and oblation accounts, the Issue Rolls the Duchy of Lancaster and the Registers of the Black Prince. Evidence has been gathered to present a picture of the livery issued to these women and its wider significance in court politics and social etiquette.

Keywords: Garter ladies, livery, order of chivalry, Great Wardrobe, Edward III, Isabel

Introduction

Printed sources variously claim that the period between the 1350s and *c.*1494 saw certain royal ladies and their kin designated as Ladies of the Garter. It has also been asserted, however, that these Ladies did not have actual membership of the most Noble Order of the Garter, England's foremost order of chivalry. The works of Elias Ashmole (1672) and John Anstis (1724) provide the basis for this claim and although it was challenged by Sir Nicholas Harris Nicolas (1842), he found no supporters. Indeed the picture of the Garter Ladies, as presented by Anstis and Ashmole, has remained largely unchallenged in the 20th century by James Gillespie (1985), Peter Begent (1989) or even Hugh Collins's doctoral research (Collins 2000).

The present research was initiated by an investigation into the identity, social status and dates of the late medieval Ladies of the Garter and the means for identifying them. Equally important was the need to address issues such as the nature of their role, the political and social implications of their nomination and the lack of any mention of women in the extant statutes of the Order. The question of paramount importance, however, was whether these ladies were members of the Order of the Garter in their own right or whether they only had an informal affiliation as is currently claimed (Fig. 1).

Aims

The year 1348, the accepted foundation date of Edward III's Order of the Garter, was chosen as the starting date for this research project (Boulton 1987). The documentation for Edward III's reign proved very rich and the line of enquiry dictated that the research should be continued into the beginning of Richard II's reign. Thus the present research has focused on the years 1348–79. The aim, however, is to continue the research up to 1509 because the Order of the Garter nominated women from *c.*1376 to 1509 and disbursed robes to them via the Great Wardrobe. Women, except sovereigns, were then excluded until the 20th century.

Figure 1 Portrait of Elizabeth Woodville (d. 1492), wife of King Edward IV, and a Garter Lady. She was the daughter of Sir Richard Woodville, only recently created Lord Rivers, and the widow of a knight, Sir John Grey, heir to Lord and Lady Ferrers de Groby (© The President and Fellows, Queens College, Cambridge) (Plate 35 in the colour plate section).

Results to date

The work completed so far centres on the accounts of the Great Wardrobe, chiefly on the documents pertaining to the accounting and distribution functions of the Great Wardrobe. This is because these documents include the specific identification of 'Knight' or 'Lady' of the Order of the Garter. The means of identifying the Knights and Ladies of the Garter and so making chronological lists of both groups has been established. Even so, from a close scrutiny of the documents, it is very clear that not all of the Garter Ladies were recorded and, on a few rare occasions, neither were all of the Knights.

Research to provide fuller lists of Knights and Ladies has been completed in the 'documents subsidiary' to the Great Wardrobe. These documents comprise warrants under the privy seal by which the king authorised the Great Wardrobe keeper to release specified articles to named persons. Since these warrants are usually filed by month and year and are not indexed, a search for the Garter Ladies has involved detailed examination of 300 or more warrants in any given year, in addition to the stock accounts. These searches have not always proved successful but have sometimes provided a few names and dates from sources which have not previously been used.

Another previously untapped source was the 'Brevia directa baronibus' section of the documents of the King's Remembrancer. While this proved singularly unproductive for the reign of Edward III, it has highlighted material that will be very productive indeed for 1377–99. The records of the Wardrobe of the Household were also analysed, especially those in undated and/or damaged documents from the reign of Edward III, and in household itineraries. Other previously unused sources researched during the project include the alms and oblation accounts, the enrolled accounts of the Great Wardrobe, the Issue Rolls the Duchy of Lancaster, the Registers of the Black Prince and the Wardrobe Books in various British Library categories.

The close study of the documents from the period 1348–79 has acted as a corrective to several aspects of current thinking on the role, timing and significance of the Garter Ladies. Preliminary findings have covered a range of areas and have shed light on a number of small details as well as some larger trends. The identity of the first Garter Lady has been established. To date, it has been stated that the first Garter Lady was either Edward III's wife, Philippa, in the 1350s or his eldest daughter, Isabel, who was appointed in 1376. The documents studied for this research, however, clarify this point and reveal that Isabel was the first Garter Lady and that she was appointed in 1375. A range of sources has been used to locate the Garter Ladies. The Ladies were identified in the accounts by the very specific wording used in the Great Wardrobe accounts to denote their receipt of robes – *de secta militum de garterio*. The same wording was also used for the Knights of the Garter and it has long been accepted that it only related to male membership of the Order. As a consequence of working on the Garter Ladies, it has also been possible to provide correct dates for some of the Garter Knights.

Focusing on Isabel, although she was Edward III's eldest daughter, she was unusual in that she was an unmarried, lay woman, living in her own household. Her father had endowed her with lands to maintain this position in an age when marriage or the cloister was the more usual option. For three years, Isabel was the sole Garter Lady and the significance of her robes was especially important at a time of potential political unrest in Edward's Gascon territories. This in turn links to the political uses to which the Order of the Garter was put and the role women played within it, for example during the king of France's captivity in England.

Moving on to consider the livery worn by the Garter Ladies, prior to 1375 women sometimes received robes to celebrate the feast day of St George, the patron saint of the Order, but they were not described as receiving a Garter robe. In 1379, however, the women who received robes *de secta militum de garterio* were described as having been received into 'the Society of the Garter'. This status is denied or argued against in some current literature. In addition, the documents make clear that both the Knights and Ladies of the Garter received the same type of robes, but this had not always been the case. The evolution of the Garter robes for the Knights and Ladies can now be stated, along with the first date of their standardisation. Equally, a more accurate assessment of the significance of the furs given to Garter Knights and Ladies can be made and this can be compared with the furs given to Edward III's Chamber Knights and to the Knights Bachelor of the Order of the Garter. This brief paper presents a summary of the findings to date (a fuller examination of the evidence and results is planned).

References

Anstis, J. (1724) *The Register of the Most Noble Order of the Garter... Called the Black Book*, 2 vols. London.

Ashmole, E. (1672) [1971] *The Institutions, Laws and Ceremonies of the Most Noble Order of the Garter*. London: Frederick Muller.

Begent, P.J. (1989) 'Ladies of the Garter', *Coat of Arms*, n.s. 8(145): 16–22.

Boulton, D'A. J. D. (1987) *The Knights of the Crown: The Monarchical Orders of Knighthood in Later Medieval Europe, 1325–1520*. Woodbridge: Boydell.

Collins, H.E.L. (2000) *The Order of the Garter 1348–1461: Chivalry and Politics in Late Medieval England*, Oxford Historical Monographs. Oxford: Clarendon Press.

Gillespie, J.L. (1985) 'Ladies of the Fraternity of Saint George and of the Society of the Garter', *Albion* 17: 259–78.

Nicolas, Sir N.H. (1842) *History of the Orders of Knighthood of the British Empire*, 4 vols. London: William Pickering and John Rodwell.

Acknowledgements

The author would like to thank Philip for his on-going support and interest in her work and she acknowledges the support of the AHRC Research Centre for Textile Conservation and Textile Studies which made this research possible.

The author

Since completing her PhD in 1998, Shelagh Mitchell has taught at the LSE and Royal Holloway. She held a postdoctoral Research Fellowship within the AHRC Research Centre for Textile Conservation and Textile Studies from January to August 2004 during which time she undertook her research on the Garter Ladies. She has presented papers on her research at the Centre for Medieval Studies seminar series in 2004 and at the Fourteenth Century Court Symposium, CMS, University of York in July 2005.

Address

Shelagh Mitchell, c\o AHRC Research Centre for Textile Conservation and Textile Studies, Winchester School of Art, University of Southampton, Park Avenue, Winchester SO23 8DL, UK (tccuk@soton.ac.uk)

Lace and documents: the Istituzioni di Ricovero e Educazione (IRE) collections in Venice

Isabella Campagnol Fabretti

ABSTRACT A document dated 1576 originating from the Pia Casa delle Cittelle records the purchase of a large quantity of linen thread for a total sum of 350 lire. This apparently mundane and secondary detail opens a window inside this, and other similar, Venetian charitable institutions created in the Serenissima from the end of the 15th century, safe havens where abandoned girls and young women without family protection were housed in order to safeguard them from any sort of physical or moral danger. Inside the institutions, the everyday life of the 'daughters' of the *hospitali*, as they were called, was equally divided and organised between prayer, work, rest and recreation. The girls were, in fact, supposed to contribute to the economic life of these *hospitali* through their artistic skills, by performing[1] or by making, among other things, needlework and laces. Part of the income derived from the sales of these needle (and bobbin) crafts was put aside for a dowry, therefore ensuring a marriage and a socially secure future.

A relatively large number of these laces survived the centuries and these are now preserved in the collections of the Istituti di Ricovero e Educazione (IRE) along with a surprisingly rich number of archival records. These favourable circumstances allow new research opportunities, making it possible to reconstruct the daily routines and tasks of these young women and examine their specific lacemaking skills inside these almost cloistral walls. At the same time, the archives and objects offer an opportunity to study the correspondence between the *hospitali* sales records of laces to Venetian shops and the amount of laces sold by the shops themselves. Finally, it is also possible to study actual laces similar to those described in the records or ancient samples of the linen thread used in needlework.

These documents can, therefore, reveal connections between the objects and their archival history and deepen the knowledge of institutional lacemaking and its sale and retail, 're-establishing the links between archival and object-based research' and offering fresh starting points for new research.

Keywords: Venetian lace, Istituzioni di Ricovero e Educazione (IRE), archival research, Derelitti, Venice; Zitelle, Venice; Mendicanti, Venice

A document dated 16 October 1576 from the archives of the Pia Casa delle Cittelle in Venice records the purchase of a large quantity of linen thread: 'La Magnifica Madonna Marina Bernardo et Madonna Soprana Cornera Governatrice ale Cittele die dar per ace lire 114 soldi 60 monta lire 342; 16 novembre die dar lire 81 soldi 30 monta 243 lire soldi 15.'[2] This apparently mundane document represents the key that will allow us a glimpse inside the daily routine of this, and other similar Venetian institutions, charitable refuges or *hospitali* (Savio and Savio 1977: 39–40) created in the Serenissima[3] from the end of the 15th century as safe havens where abandoned girls and young women without family protection were housed in order to safeguard them from any sort of physical or moral danger.

One of the characteristics of Renaissance Venice was, in fact, the presence of numerous such institutions (Aikema and Meijers 1989: 19–33) dedicated to the aid and relief of the socially forgotten. Each *hospitale* aimed to help a specific group of the needy: the Incurabili was founded in 1521 to care for the terminally ill, followed in 1528 by the Derelitti, a refuge for the destitute and hospital for the sick. The Convertite was founded in 1530, providing basic medical care for women affected by venereal diseases and cloistral refuge for repentant prostitutes.[4] The Soccorso (Fig. 1) was founded in 1577 and provided a temporary home for women in serious family trouble, while the Pia Casa delle Cittelle (also known as Zitelle) was founded in 1559 to house beautiful and poor young girls and women without the protection of their families.[5] Although some institutions, such as the Incurabili (Aikema and Meijers 1989: 131–48), the Catecumeni (Aikema and Meijers 1989: 215–24) and others, also accepted boys and men, the vast majority of the 'guests' of the hospitals (considering the specific mission of some of the institutions) were female, from very young girls to more mature women, the lives of whom were equally and strictly organised between prayers, meals, work and sleep, with little time for recreation.

The main purpose of these charitable enterprises was to transform endangered young women or helpless children into women of worth who could legitimately aspire to a decent marriage or to enter a convent. The *hospitali* relied on needlework to teach to the *figlie* or *putte* (daughters) a 'morally proper' craft, the profits of which were used both to support the missions of the hospitals themselves and to earn enough money for a dowry to enter a convent or get married and to supplement a family income once married.[6]

Figure 1 Caliari, B. *Madonna col Bambino, Santa Maria Maddalena e le Soccorse*, ante 1597, Venice, Gallerie dell' Accademia, detail. The painting was once in the Church of the Soccorso hospital (by kind permission of Ministero per i Beni e le Attività Culturali) (Plate 36 in the colour plate section).

Lace, particularly needlelace, was a craft indigenous to the city on the lagoon, and its patterns were deeply influenced and characterised by references to the original Venetian architectural details (Davanzo Poli 2001: 21–4). These ethereal products of needle and thread were worked by the vast majority of Venetian women: in the luxurious halls of palaces, middle-class homes, convents and charitable hospitals, women of every age could be found occupied by some form of needlework. Lacemaking was not only regarded as a socially acceptable and creative outlet, but it was also propagandised as an ennobling occupation. This connection clearly emerges from the titles and dedications of the numerous lace and embroidery pattern books published in Venice from the early 16th century, where words such as 'honesty', 'virtue' and 'nobility' regularly appear in connection with the practice of needlecrafts.[7] Patronesses and lacemakers themselves could be the Venetian noblewomen, and no less than three *dogaresse*[8] have been associated with the sponsorship of lace. Giovanna Malipiero Dandolo in 1457 supported a protective law in favour of lace, as did, a century later, Lidia Priuli Dandolo, while Morosina Morosini Grimani, according to tradition, created a lace workshop in her palace in the Santa Fosca area (Davanzo Poli and Lunardon 2001: 23).

Because of the level of concentration that they required, needlecrafts were also the work of choice in *hospitali* and monasteries. Benedetto Palmio, founder of the Zitelle, stated in the rules of the Pia Casa that:

> ... l'occupazioni continue che hanno nei lavorieri, che fanno li uffizj dell'obedienza, alli quali sollecitamente e con molta carità attendono per sovvenire a i bisogni e alle necessità della presente vita, fanno che diventino donne di valore, e da questa Casa bandiscano l'ozio fomento di tutti i mali.[9]

Likewise, Francesco Sansovino described the monastery of the Convertite as the place for the 'peccatrici pentite che si essercitano con ordine mirabile in diversi artificij'.[10]

These 'educational'[11] laces and embroideries offered another advantage to the *hospitali:* the sale of the needlework contributed to the financing of the charitable institutions themselves, while a small part of the profit was set aside for the dowry of the daughters, therefore ensuring a marriage, either secular or divine, and a socially secure future. The preservation of the *Registri Capitolari dell' Ospedaletto dei Derelitti* has given us the opportunity to understand how the work inside this Venetian hospital was organised and, it seems, throughout all the hospitals. The pay system revolved around the so-called *tascha*, a term that indicated a slit in the dress worn by the girls and women housed in the hospital inside which could be found a little hanging fabric pouch, the *tascha*, where the thread and tools necessary for the daily work were kept. To every woman and girl, in fact, even to the very young, the overseer assigned a specific amount of daily work, and if she did not complete her task without a justifiable explanation, a fine and penalty would be imposed. It was the duty of the overseer to give a detailed account of all the *tasche* worked by the women of the Ospedaletto and of the money, also called, by association of ideas, *tascha*, that was paid for their work (Fig. 2).[12] It is interesting to read in the original document

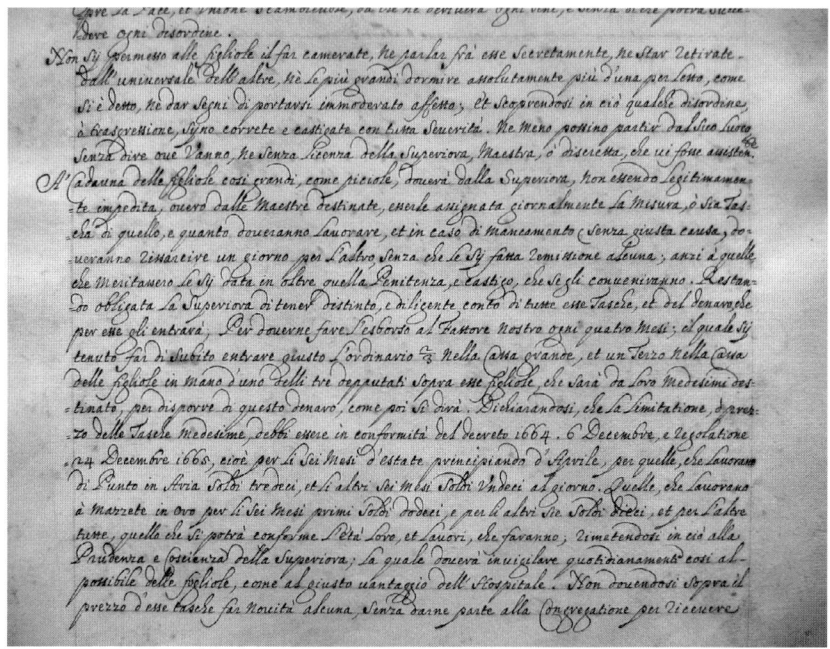

Figure 2 *Capitolare* of the *hospitale* of the Derelitti, 1668, Venice, Archivio IRE, DER A 5, c. 15 r (by kind permission of the IRE). (Reproduction or duplication of this image is forbidden.)

describing the '*tasche* system' that the amount of daily work requested by the hospital changed significantly over the different seasons of the year. More work was assigned during the warmer months, given the increased hours of natural light, and less was requested in the winter.[13]

The prices of the completed needlework were set directly by the governors of the hospitals and it was strictly prohibited for the girls to directly negotiate the prices of the laces or to contact merchants:

> restando sempre assolutamente vietato alle figliole, niuna eccettuata, di trattare e concludere li prezi o mercati delli lavoreri. Ma questi sijno maneggiati dalla Superiora, e discrete loro unitamente, facendone fare (in quanto fosse solito e necessario) nota distinta in un libro per mano del Mastro, o mercante che farà lavorare.[14]

One of the most important benefactors of the Ospedaletto was Bartolomeo Cargnoni, a merchant who owned several haberdashery shops in the Mercerie area, between St Mark's and Rialto.[15] In the account books of his *Bottega all'insegna dello Struzzo d'Oro*[16] we can verify the economic importance of his commerce of different kinds of lace, those made with linen, silk or gold and silver thread:[17] this shop had a turnover of 176,835 ducats with a net profit of 8,908 ducats. Among his clients, specifically his debtors, were important foreigners such as the duke of Modena and Alessandro di Parma, who, in 1662 owed the shop 209 ducats.[18]

Lacemaking and sewing played an important part also in the life of the women and in the economy of the Pio Hospitale di San Lazzaro dei Mendicanti. Its *Capitolare*[19] lists the *incombenze,* or duties, of every member of the hospital, including the prioress, governors, farm workers,[20] choir teacher and the *maestre de' lavorieri*, the teachers of needlecrafts.[21] The duties of the latter *maestre* included the careful supervision of the work of all the girls, depending on their skills;[22] it was also her job to make sure that every girl fulfilled her daily work. The teacher who was appointed, needless to say, would have to teach on the premises. Much attention and scrutiny was given to the choice of this key figure and, when in 1673 an Anzola Gozata was accepted as Maestra di Ponto in Aria (Fig. 4), it was clearly specified that she was a woman of singular 'virtù et ottimi costumi'. Her salary amounted to 24 *grossi* per year and the hospital provided her with food and lodging.[23]

The interest in the sponsorship of charitable enterprises and lacemaking by Venetian noblewomen was confirmed by the decision, taken on 3 September 1617, that the commerce of the laces made by the daughters and women of this institution be supported by noblewoman Cilia Pisani: 'il negozio sopra li Lavorieri delle figliolule, et Donne de loco sij appoggiato alla ND [*Nobil Donna*] Cilia Pisani'.[24] The Mendicanti also shared the same policy of the Ospedaletto that forbade the daughters to directly contact the merchants to sell their laces. An interesting document recalls the role played by one of the governors of the hospital, merchant Agostino Coreggio, who suggested selling the works of the hospital to two of his colleagues and offered 300 lire in advance as some sort of guaranty for the business.[25]

The charitable institution that has been regarded as the most famous for its lacemaking activities is the Pia Casa delle Cittelle.[26] On 29 March 1800, a report compiled by Luigi Nordio to the Regia Deputazione ai Luoghi Pii mentions the 'merletti per i quali questo luogo era un tempo celebre' (Savio and Savio 1977: 39–40).[27] At the Zitelle, young and beautiful girls under the maternal care of four noble *protettrici* and six *magnifiche governatrici* created amazing masterpieces with their needles so renowned that Louis XIV commissioned from them the famous lace collar made with white hair that he wore for his coronation ceremony. Two sisters, Lucrezia and Vittoria Torre, worked for over two years to create this incredible piece for which '250 pieces d'or' was paid (Ceresole 1878: 8). These two lacemakers had certainly been chosen from among the most skilled artisans, those who were expected to make lace

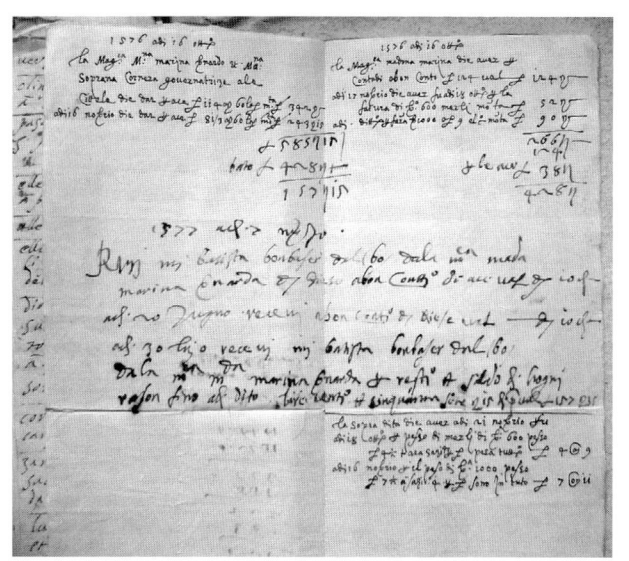

Figure 3 Bill of purchase of thread and bill of sale of laces, 1576, Archivio IRE, ZIT G 1 c. 4 (by kind permission of the IRE). (Reproduction or duplication of this image is forbidden.)

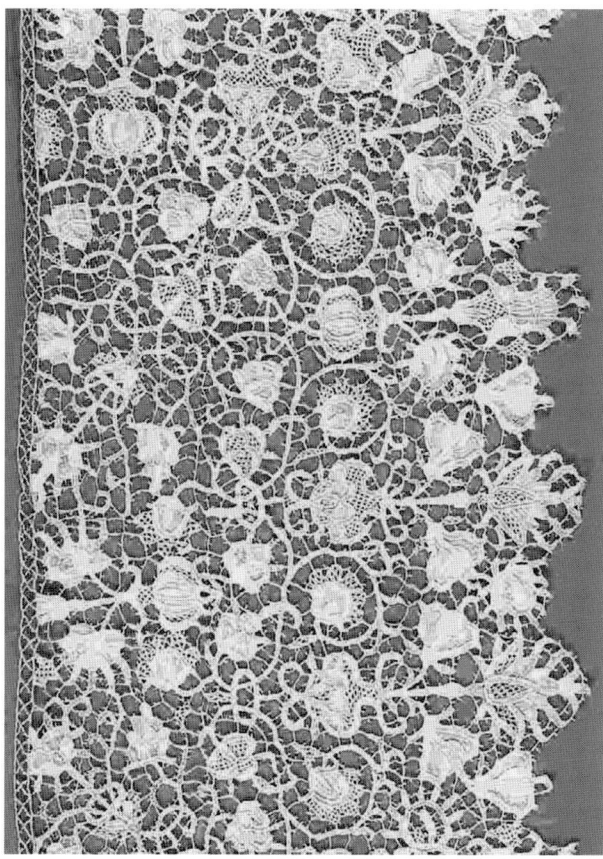

Figure 4 Needle lace, Venice last quarter of the 19th century, Zitelle, IRE, 798 (by kind permission of the IRE). (Reproduction or duplication of this image is forbidden.)

for a total of ten *soldi* per day. Younger and less experienced girls were required to produce half this amount, five *soldi* per day.[28] Records recalling or connected to the lace production at the Zitelle appear frequently in the documents still preserved in the archives of this institution,[29] the most ancient being the previously mentioned bill of purchase of linen thread and a corresponding bill of sale of laces that demonstrates the profitability of such a commerce. While 350 lire was spent to buy linen thread to make laces, a bill of sale documents that laces were sold by carats (as diamonds) for a value of 1,314 lire, bringing the total profit for the Zitelle to 1,236 lire,[30] a clear demonstration of the profitability of such commerce (Fig. 3). Another financial document dated 1686 bearing a long list of payments received by the treasurer of the Zitelle from the governesses confirms the success and the popularity of the laces made there well into the 17th century and beyond.[31] The Zitelle continued its centuries-long charitable work until the first half of the 20th century, producing artistic embroideries right up to the end.[32]

This journey through the documents detailing the production and sale of the laces made in the ancient Venetian charitable institutions, now preserved in the IRE artistic collections[33] and archives, has deepened our knowledge about the relationship between lace production and its sale and retail, 're-establishing the links between archival and object-based research' and offering fresh starting points for new archival investigations about, for instance, the subsequent marriages of the daughters, their continuing relationships with the institutions in which they were raised and the use of their lacemaking skills to support their families.

Acknowledgements

The author wishes to acknowledge the financial support of the Pasold Research Fund that permitted her to present her paper at the Third Annual Conference of the AHRC Research Centre for Textile Conservation and Textile Studies and the helpfulness of the Conservatori of IRE, Giuseppe Ellero and Silvia Lunardon, who allowed her to explore the many 'secrets' of the IRE archives.

Notes

1. Many of these girls were renowned musicians and *figlie da coro* (choir daughters); particularly famous were those of the Ospedaletto as well as the Hospitale della Pietà. Their music teachers were also widely known and appreciated; for instance, Vivaldi was the music and choir teacher at the Pietà.
2. 'The Magnifica Madonna Marina Bernardo and Madonna Soprana Cornera Governess at the Zitelle must pay 114 *lire* and 60 *soldi* and 342 *lire* for linen thread; on 16 November 81 *lire* and 30 *soldi* and 24 *lire* and 15 *soldi*.' Archivio IRE, Zit G 1, c. 4. One *lira* was divided into 20 *soldi*.
3. Serenissima Repubblica di Venezia was the official name of the city-state until 1797, when Venice fell into the hands of the Napoleonic army and ceased to be a political entity.
4. In Renaissance Venice, the moral and social status of prostitutes was extremely low and in the rules of the Convertite it was written very clearly that these women were 'donne peccatrici a Dio convertite' or 'sinners converted to God' (Aikema and Meijers 1989: 191–5).
5. 'accogliere fanciulle che dotate di bellezza, dagli anni 12 fino li 18 di loro età, mancanti di mezzi ad una onesta sussistenza, o che per la perdita, poca cura o sceleratàggine de' propri genitori o parenti fossero in procinto di perdersi per sempre.' Archivio IRE, *Capitolare Zitelle*, ZIT A 1.
6. From the second half of the 16th century it is documented that married women of the middle/lower classes sold their needleworks in order to help support their families. Just to mention one source, on 2 June 1609 Pietro Lippomano wrote in his report about the city of Chioggia (on the southern border of the Venetian lagoon) that the women of the island 'support their families with their bobbin laces' (Davanzo Poli and Lunardon 2001).

7. Some examples of these titles are: N. D'Aristotele detto Zoppino, *Esemplario di lavori dove le tenere fanciulle et altre donne nobile potranno facilmente imparare il modo et ordine di lavorare, cucire, ricamare* (1529); M. Pagan, *L'honnesto esempio del vetroso desiderio che hanno le donne di nobil ingegno ...* (1550); J. Calepino, *Splendore delle virtuose giovani, dove si contengono molte et varie mostre a' fogliami, cioè ponti in aere et punti tagliati* (1563); C. Vecellio, *Corona delle nobili et virtuose donne ...* (1591); G.A.Vavassore, *Opera nuova universal intitolata Corona di racammi: dove le venerande donne et fanciulle troveranno di varie opere per fare colari di camiciola et torniamenti di letti ...* (1525–30).
8. Dogaressa was the official title of the wife of the doge, the elected chief magistrate of the Serenissima Republic of Venice.
9. '... the continuous and diligent practice of obedience and needleworks at which they work in order to provide for themselves, makes them women of worth, and banishes from this House idleness, root of every evil.' Archivio IRE, *Notatorio*, ZIT B 1, p. 73. The daily work also helped in making the days seem much shorter: 'siccome l'ozio fa parere i giorni troppo lunghi, così l'occupazioni scuoprono la gran brevità loro', ZIT A 1, p. 109.
10. '... repenting sinners that with admirable skill practice needlework', F. Sansovino, 1591. '*Venezia città nobilissima et singolare...*', 92, Venetia: appresso Iacomo Sansovino, 1581. Centuries later Pompeo Molmenti also wrote about the conventual workshop of the Convertite in which repented prostitutes worked day and night at their needlework (Molmenti 1973: 50).
11. Other educational activities commonly practised by the *putte* of the hospitals beside needlework, music and singing included plain sewing and weaving. The Derelitti employed two weaving instructors, a man and a woman, to teach the boys and girls. In 'male' institutions the music and needlework were commonly replaced by instruction on woodwork, tailoring and shoemaking.
12. 'A cadauna delle figliuole, così grande, come piccola, doverà dalla Superiora, non essendo legittimamente impedita, overo dale Maestre destinate, esserle assegnata giornalmente la Misura, o sia Tascha di quello, e quanto doveranno lavorare, et in caso di mancamento senza giusta causa, doveranno risarcire un giorno per l'altro senza che le sij fatta remissione alcuna, anzi a quelle che meritassero le sij data in oltre quella Penitenza, e castigo, che se gli convenivano. Restando obligata la Superiora di tener distinto e diligente conto di tutte esse Tasche, et del denaro, che per esse gli entrerà.' Archivio IRE, *Capitolare Derelitti*, DER A 5, c. 15. See also Savio and Savio (1987) in which there is a probable connection between this *tascha* and the English word 'task', both meaning a specific assignment.
13. 'Dichiarandosi, che la limitazione, o prezzo delle Tasche medesime, debbi essere in conformità del decreto 1664, 6 dicembre, e relatione 24 decembre 1665, cioè per li sei mesi d'estate, principiando d'Aprile, per quelle che lavorano di Punto in aria soldi tredici , et li altri soldi undeci al giorno. Quelle che lavorano a mazzette in oro, per li sie mesi primi sodi dodici e per gli altri sie soldi Dieci, et per l'altre tutte, quello che si potrà conforme l'età loro, et lavori che faranno, rimettendosi in ciò alla Prudenza et Coscienza della Superiora; la quale dovrà invigilare quotidianamente così al possibile delle figliole, come al giusto vantaggio dell'Hospitale.' Archivio IRE, *Capitolare Derelitti*, DER A 5, c. 15.
14. '... it is always forbidden to the daughters, without exceptions, to negotiate and close the prices or sales of the needleworks. These have to be negotiated by the Superiora and her assistants, and need to be transcribed in different books according to the merchant who commissioned the laces.' Archivio IRE, *Capitolare Derelitti*, DER A 5, c. 16.
15. His portrait, sculpted by Bernardo Falcone, can be found in the church of the Ospedaletto, while another portrait, painted by Daniel van den Dyck, is preserved in the IRE artistic collections. In his will dated 1662, Bartolomeo Cargnoni stated that part of the money left by him to the Derelitti had to be spent to finance the restoration of the *hospitale* and the construction of an internal court in order to give the daughters a place '... to breathe a little'. Archivio IRE, DER E 63-67, 12 August 1662.
16. Archivio IRE, DER E 64, b. 5, Balance of the shop at the sign of the Golden Ostrich in Merceria San Salvador, 1662.
17. Between the *maestranze in merli de oro* (lacemakers who worked with gold thread) can be found the Casa delle Cittele (Archivio IRE, DER E 64, b. 5, p. 27) and other women from the populace who worked independently as lacemakers. One of them, Elena, is qualified as the wife of a *barcariol*, a boatman; others are only identified by their vague addresses. According to Cargnoni, a Cornelia lived nearby Santa Maria Zobenigo or Santa Maria del Giglio, a parish not far from St Mark's Square, Archivio IRE, DER E 64, b. 5, p. 27.
18. Archivio IRE, DER E 64, b. 5, p. 29.
19. Archivio IRE, MEN C 2.
20. Every hospital could count on some possessions on the mainland outside Venice or in the islands of the Lagoon, possessions acquired either with donations or legacies left to the hospitals from which they received payments or tributes.
21. Archivio IRE, MEN C 2, c.147 r.
22. *Ibid*.
23. '... singular virtue and very high morality'. Archivio IRE, MEN C 2, c.147 r. and 22 December 1673, Catastico in Archivio IRE, MEN, B 2, c. 156 v., resolution 2372.
24. '... the commerce of the needleworks of the daughters and Women of this place is sponsored by Noblewoman Cilia Pisani.' Archivio IRE, MEN C 2, c. 148 r. The sponsorship of these institutions by numerous Venetian noblewomen highlights the significant role played by these ladies in the management of the institutions themselves and, by extension, in Venetian society.
25. See note 24 above.
26. 'lavori ... di merlature e pizzi, ne' quali era una volta questo luogo celebre, e singolare' or 'the laces for which this place was once upon a time famous' (Lunardon 1992: 27).
27. Even before, in 1792, according to the *Gazzetta Urbana Veneta*, the laces of the Zitelle were used as a term of comparison with the laces made by the women of the island (Ceresole 1878: 7).
28. Archivio IRE, ZIT G 2, b. 3, 18 September 1686.
29. Mentions of the lace trade also appear in other economic records of the Pia Casa, for instance in the monthly balances of October 1591, February 1609, August, September and October 1629 and February 1630.
30. 'A ricevuta di Tomaso Baglioni, Cassier della Pia Casa e Isabella Casotti Coadiutrice Lire 475 e soldi 10.' Archivio IRE, Zit B 18, cc.73-75.
31. See note 30 above.
32. See, for instance, an embroidery made at the Zitelle around the last quarter of the 19th century that represents a view of the Fondamenta delle Zitelle. Inv. IRE 798 (Fig. 4).
33. In the IRE artistic collections are preserved paintings by such artists as Jacopo Palma il Giovane, Sebastiano Ricci, Francesco Fontebasso, the Tiepolo workshop, Francesco Guardi and many others. The IRE also preserves many historic sites in Venice such as the church of the Ospedaletto, the Zitelle and the Oratorio dei Crociferi (Lunardon 2001: 7-19).

References

Aikema, B. and Meijers, D. (ed.) (1989) *Nel Regno dei Poveri. Arte e storia dei grandi ospedali veneziani in età moderna 1474–1797*. Venice: IRE.

Ceresole, V. (1878) *Origines de la dentelle de Venise*. Venice: Antonelli.

Davanzo Poli, D. (ed.) (1997) *Tessuti, merletti ricami degli antichi ospedali veneziani*. Vicenza: Ente Fiera di Vicenza and IRE.

Davanzo Poli, D. and Lunardon, S. (eds) (2001) *Merletti. Esposizione di una selezione di antichi merletti veneziani dalle collezioni IRE*. Venice: IRE.

Lunardon, S. (1992) 'Le Zitelle alla Giudecca', in *Le Zitelle, Architettura, Arte e Storia di un'Istituzione Veneziana*, L. Puppi (ed.), 27. Venice: Albrizzi.

Lunardon, S. (2001) 'Le eredità d'arte delle istituzioni caritative veneziane', in *Merletti. Esposizione di una selezione di antichi merletti veneziani dalle collezioni IRE*, D. Davanzo Poli and S. Lunardon (eds), 23. Venice: IRE.

Molmenti, P. (1973) *La storia di Venezia nella vita privata*, vol. 2. Trieste: Lint.

Savio, L. and Savio, R. (1977) 'L'organizzazione del lavoro femminile nelle antiche istituzioni di ricovero ed educazione', in *I pizzi: moda e simbolo* (exhibition catalogue), A. Mottola Molfino and M.T. Binaghi Olivari (curators). Milan: Electa.

Savio, R. and Savio L. (1987) 'L'organizzazione del lavoro femminile a Venezia nelle antiche istituzioni di Ricovero e di Educazione', in *I pizzi: moda e simbolo*, A. Mottola Molfino and M.T. Binaghi Olivari (eds), 39–42. Milan: Electa.

IRE Archives

- Archivio IRE, *Capitolare Derelitti*, DER A 5, c. 15.
- Archivio IRE, DER E 63-67, 12 agosto 1662.
- Archivio IRE, DER E 64, b. 5
- Archivio IRE, MEN B 1 c. 163
- Archivio IRE, MEN B 2 c. 156 v, resolution 2372.
- Archivio IRE, MEN C 2
- Archivio IRE, *Capitolare* Zitelle, ZIT A 1.
- Archivio IRE, *Notatorio*, ZIT B 1
- Archivio IRE, ZIT B 18, cc.73-75.
- Archivio IRE, ZIT G 1, c. 4.
- Archivio IRE, ZIT G 2, b. 3.

The author

In 2006 Isabella Campagnol Fabretti obtained the *laurea specialistica* (summa cum laude) in art history at the Ca' Foscari University, Venice with her thesis entitled *Tra il sacro e il mondano. Vesti secolari in dipinti a soggetto religioso nella Venezia del Cinquecento* [*Between Sacred and Fashionable: Secular Dresses in Religious Paintings in Sixteenth-Century Venice*]. She is Editor of *Filoforme*, a textile and dress history magazine, teaches history of dress at the University of Udine and was recently appointed Curator of the Rubelli Textile Collection in Venice.

Address

Isabella Campagnol Fabretti, Cannaregio 3456/C, 30121 Venice, Italy (i.campagnol@rubelli.it)

Undated, unattributable and unfinished: forgotten samplers and their re-evaluation through archival research[1]

Joyce A. Taylor Dawson

ABSTRACT Neglected and ignored scraps of samplers are the subject of this paper. A case for their recognition is argued through the examination of a collection of such works held in the Musée des Ursulines in Québec City. These compete ineffectually with complete and better-designed and executed examples in the collection. Each has a *raison d'être*, however, and collectively these offer much in terms of the insights they provide into the social and the textile history of the Ursuline Convent School for Girls where they were produced. This paper reviews the historiography of embroidered samplers and the myths that surround them as stitched embodiments of femininity. It then focuses on a collection of samplers produced between 1780 and 1900 by *pensionnaires* at the Ursuline Convent School, which ranges from accomplished examples to those that are the subject of this enquiry. In a shift away from traditional approaches to the study of embroidery through the examination of materials and iconography, this paper examines how documents preserved in the Archives des Ursulines provide text-based tools for an analysis from a social/historical and contextual perspective. These documents illuminate the practices surrounding the production of these samplers, the teachers who taught, the pupils who stitched and the curriculum and traditions of needlework at the Convent School. The objects are also examined as a collection to evaluate how their 'group value' is enhanced through archival documentation.

Keywords: Ursuline nuns, needlework and embroidery, womens' history – Canada, samplers, textile history – Canada

Introduction

Often neglected and more often ignored or discarded, samplers and scraps of embroidery that have been deemed unworthy of interest are the subject of this paper. The reason for their survival and the justification for their recognition are argued through a case study of just such a group of embroidered samplers and scraps held in the collection of the Musée des Ursulines in Québec City. These objects all suffer in varying degrees from being plain, in disrepair, incomplete and in some cases, simply incompetent examples of stitchery. In most cases, though not all, neither the author nor the date of production is known, nor is the reason for their survival within the set of textiles held by the museum. When compared with more complete and stylistically interesting examples in the collection, these run a poor second in terms of quality and interest. Individually, however, each of these embroideries has a *raison d'être* and collectively these works have much to offer in terms of the insights into the field of textile history that they can provide.

This paper briefly reviews the historiography of the embroidered samplers that are often seen (particularly from the perspective of collectors) as stitched embodiments of femininity, skill, piety and perseverance, which every young 'lady' produced. They were an indicator that she had acquired what Mirra Bank has referred to as 'needle wisdom' (1979: 10). It will then focus on the collection of samplers produced by the pupils of the Ursuline Convent School in Québec from 1780 to 1900.[2] This collection, stitched by the pupils of the Ursulines, demonstrates a range of skills from more highly accomplished examples through to those that are the subject of this enquiry. In a shift away from traditional approaches to the study of embroidery, such as the scientific analysis of fibres and dyes or the consideration of design and iconography, this paper examines how the wide range of documents available in the archives of the Ursuline Sisters of Quebec provides text-based tools for analysis from a different perspective. This is not intended to imply that scientific and art-historical methodology is not useful, or indeed necessary, but that archival documentation is another avenue of enquiry that may be pursued. By supplementing the analysis available through physical examination, these archival documents serve to illuminate the practices surrounding the production and consumption of the samplers, via the teachers who taught and the pupils who stitched, the curriculum they followed and the strong traditions of needlework that have been in place at the Convent School since its inception. The paper also examines these objects in their collective form and discusses how the individual object compares to the collection in terms of the types of text-based materials used in their analysis.

Figure 1 Engraving, 'The Ursuline Ladies Boarding School – Lower Canada'. Illustration from the cover of the Ursuline Prospectus, 1847 (Musée des Ursulines de Québec, Collection du Monastère des Ursulines).

Historiography of the sampler

A wealth of information on the subject of embroidered samplers is available. From Bolton and Coe (1921), pioneers in the United States, and more recently through Krueger (1984) and Ring (1993) to Huish (1913), Christie (1920), King (1960), Browne and Wearden (1999), and Quinton (2005) in Britain, through to Young (1985) and Salahub (1994) in Canada, samplers have always been among the most researched topics in the field of embroidered textile history.[3] This is not surprising when one considers the wealth of information they can provide and the enormous appeal samplers have for embroiderers, collectors and historians alike.[4] What should be noted is that for the most part these writings fall into two separate categories: (1) histories, descriptions of collections, catalogues from exhibitions and (2) 'how to' books.

In the first of these, authors have provided details plus illustrations of the history of the sampler in its many forms, with social history and context taking on an increasing importance in more recent years. Here the emphasis has tended to be placed on those samplers in collections that contain obvious data such as names and dates. In exhibition catalogues too, there is, as a general rule, a privileging of the named and the dated since curators and exhibit designers would naturally feel that this type of sampler adds interest to the display by allowing the viewer an enhanced insight into the context of the work as well as the specifics of its production. Identification and association with towns, regions and families gives any exhibition an added dimension, especially for those who visit. Exhibition catalogues also provide an accurate record of the variety of samplers gathered together at one particular time and place. An added feature of these catalogues is that they provide avid private collectors as well as historians with a sound basis for comparison and evaluation. In the second category, that of 'how to' books, much less emphasis has been placed on history, as might be expected, but these have played a valuable role by always providing brief historical notes and references which allow the embroidery enthusiast to use stitching designs and methods of the past as a springboard to the future.

From an academic perspective, the historiography of samplers in the past 25 years has moved from the descriptive to the analytical and from a single discipline to a multidisciplinary approach. This movement can be traced back to the interest in women's arts by feminist historians such as Mirra Bank (1979) and Rosika Parker (1984). Textile historians have become increasingly aware of the value of linking cloth to its context and the sampler to its social and cultural history. One of the principal methods of achieving that connection has been through the consultation of archives and documents, that is, linking textiles to text.

There exists within this historiography a parallel that is worthy of note: a parallel with dress and costume history, a significant part of the field of textile history. In recent years, dress historians have been faulted for their concentration on the dress of the elite, on those garments that were grand and sumptuous and belonged to the aristocracy and highest echelons of society. The counter-argument to this position was that those were the garments that had survived, along with the documents (text), which supported their history. This criticism can also be levelled at embroidery historians who studied and wrote about the works of the great and the good for precisely the same reasons (Swain 1973). In essence, the exquisite and highly skilled samplers, the ones whose artistic merit shines forth and whose makers were undoubtedly 'ladies' have been the focus of most histories. Such works may clearly be seen as the elite of the sampler world. They are the ones that have survived and can be linked to genealogy and social history. It is little wonder that they are the samplers that are sought after, collected, conserved, displayed and written about. They have, as Schoeser and Boydell would argue (2002: 2–9), locational, archival, iconographical, aesthetic and transferral value, which greatly increases their appeal to historians and collectors alike.

More recent trends in dress and textile history have moved from analysis of production and consumption of clothing and fabrics of the elite to an examination of the middle and working classes, utilising analytical techniques previously associated with other disciplines such as economics, sociology and social history. In a similar way, this paper has turned away from the examination of elite samplers to look at those that have achieved lesser heights via a more multidisciplinary approach. What value they have in relation to those named by Schoeser and Boydell needs to be carefully drawn out, and given the nature of these objects, little information can be ascertained through the simple visual examination formerly utilised by textile historians.[5] The value of these forgotten scraps can, however, be teased out in large measure from text associated with them.

Text and the case study

Among the many documents in the Archives des Ursulines de Québec pertinent to the undated, unattributable and unfinished samplers to be discussed in this paper, one in particular holds striking relevance. Tables 1 and 2 show the original French version of a transcription found in the archives of a document entitled *Ouvrage Manuel* and its translation. This document details the curriculum for needlework taught at the Convent School. Unfortunately, at present there is no way of ascertaining the date of its original version.[6] Only a typed transcript was found in the file and it is notable that this edition refers, in the First Division, to the use of a sewing machine, first produced en masse in the 1850s. Therefore, this copy must postdate the general availability of that invention. Further investigation and linkage to embroideries in the collection, however, underpins an argument that some version of this type of curriculum dates back at least as far as 1780, and research indicates that it is not unreasonable to conclude that it may predate that time.[7]

Within the Ursuline archive there exist additional documents related to the samplers that form the focus of this study. These include timetables that offer some idea of the amount of time spent by the pupils on their sewing and needlework lessons. For example, one document of 1844 shows that boarding pupils spent approximately two hours on weekdays and four hours on Saturday afternoons on these activities.[8] Another document, the *Programmes de la Joureire*, as yet undated, outlines the daily activities of boarders and half-boarders and

Table 1 *Ouvrage Manuel* (original text).

4ème Division
Canevas: point de marque.
Points de couture: point devant ou coulé, point piqué ou arrière-point, point pour ourlet simple.
Couture rabattue.
Applications sur lingerie de poupées ou d'enfants.
Bien montrer à commencer une couture à la bien arrêter.

3ème Division
Ajouter au programme précédent le point de surjet: pose de dentelle, point d'ourlet ornementé, les fronces. Montrer à regulariser les fronces, montages des fronce (poser une bande, une ceinture) le point roulé pour tissus fuis, ourlet à festons, attache des rubans ou des galons à la lingerie, attache des boutons, point de boutonniere, bordage d'une fente par un ourlet, par un biais arête d'une fente par un gousset
Application sur vêtements de coton, de flanelle, de mousseline.
Tricot à l'aiguille, montage de mailes, confection de bas, de mittaines &. &.
Reprise: ravaudage de mailes, reprise sur toile à fils droits, à fils biaisés selon les tissus.

2de Division
Ajouter aux programmes précédents:
Couture: lingerie complète avec les points d'ornements: point croisé, point d'arête simple ou double, dentelle á l'aiguille. Crochet: mailles serrée points de rose, oint russe, point á côtes, brides simples ou double ou triple, maille au point de minute, au point ananas, au point d'écailles, picots.
Application sur bas, chaussettes, bonnets, gilets de bébé.

1ère Division
Ajouter aux programmes des autres divisions: Couple des vêtements d'après patrons ou dessins faits sur tableau – usage de la machine à coudre avec tous les instruments, jours sur toile, dentelles tricots, confections de boules, de glands, rous les genres de raccommodate.
Spécialités: les broderies et ouvrage de luxe.

Table 2 *Ouvrage Manuel* (author's translation).

Fourth Division
Canvas: marking stitch.
Sewing stitches: running and back stitches, piqué stitch, hem-stitch.
Finishing stitch.
Applications on doll's or children's clothes.
Demonstrate how to begin and to end a seam.

Third Division
Add overstitching to the preceding programme: insertion of lace, ornamental hemstitching, gathers. Show how to make even gathers, mounting a gather (inserting a band, a waistband, a belt), rolling stitch for fine fabrics which fray easily, scalloped hems, attachment of ribbons and braids to clothing, attaching buttons, buttonhole stitch, edging a vent (slit) with a hem, with a bias – finishing a vent by a gusset
Application on cotton garments, flannel, mousseline.
Knitting with needles, learning the stitches, making stockings, mittens, &. &.
Mending: mending/darning of dropped stitches (holes, tears, ladders?), repeated on the straight threads of linen or on the bias according to the fabrics.

Second Division
In addition to the preceding programmes:
Sewing: Lingerie (clothing?) complete with ornamental stitches: cross stitch, single and double herringbone stitches, satin stitch. Fitting pieces with a flat seam, with overstitching. Mend a sheet with hair or invisible mending.
Knitting: In addition to the programme of the third division, single and double knitting, needle lace. Crochet: dense stitches, rose stitch, Russian stitch, edging stitches, single, double and triple brides, point de minute (? – see original text, Table 1), pineapple stitch, shell stitch, picots.
Application on stockings, socks, bonnets and baby jackets.

First Division
Added to programmes of the other divisions: Cutting of garments after patterns or designs made from a picture – use of the sewing machine with all its attachments, openwork on cloth, laces, knitting, confections of beads, tassels, all types of repairs (mending, darning?).
Specialties: luxurious embroideries and handworks.

indicates additional non-instructional times such as recreation when embroidery or sewing could have been taken in hand.[9] The archives further hold a register of pupils, a register of nuns and account books, all of which relate to the school.[10] Cross-checking these documents uncovered countless details about pupils, their families and the nuns who taught them as well as when they attended the school.[11] How this information can be linked to the unattributed and undated samplers is discussed below.

Textiles

Within the remit of my doctoral research at the Ursuline Convent has been the examination of a collection of embroidered textiles held both within the monastery and within a museum which was founded by the Sisters in 1939, a full 300 years after the foundation of the convent. Primary among the issues that have emerged from this study is that of survival: how and why the undated and unattributed samplers survived to the present day. My thesis further addressed the question of what significance their survival holds in relationship to the history of these embroideries and the institution itself, not to mention the history of the lives of the women who actually stitched these objects.

As this research progressed, three key reasons for survival emerged: choice, chance and location. The first of these, choice, becomes apparent primarily in the consideration of the larger, more significant embroideries contained in the collection.[12] These are objects which form part of the liturgical patrimony of the monastery: altar ornaments and sacerdotal vestments whose religious significance and continued use in the celebration of that liturgy have assured their survival (Fig. 2). While actual use today is limited to very few of these objects, they have survived because of their use until the mid-20th century when they were retired in favour of more 'modern' examples.[13]

These were fashioned in the nuns' workshop and although their specific attribution is uncertain as nuns rarely signed their work, the high value attributed to them by those who cared for them as an integral part of the liturgy ensured their survival (Dawson 1999; Turgeon 2002).[14] Other items have survived perhaps because of their relationship by virtue of authorship to a skilful pupil who then went on to enter the noviciate and to become an Ursuline, and indeed, several of the named samplers in the Ursuline collection are attributed to pupils who became Ursuline nuns.

The second factor, chance, seems the most likely explanation of why the undated and unattributed embroideries have survived in the collection. Examination of the accession records and catalogue of objects at the museum, however, reveals no details as to how, why or when these objects became part of the collection.[15]

The third factor involved in the survival of these objects, location, is self-explanatory: the embroideries simply remained where they were produced. There may have been a number of reasons for this to have occurred, but the research carried out so far suggests that an attribution of an object to a pupil who moved directly from the school to the Ursuline noviciate and then to the Order on profession of her vows may be chief among them. Where unattributable samplers and scraps are concerned, however, this remains a speculative though likely explanation. It is also possible that the samplers under investigation were left behind at the school, having been deemed of little or no value to the pupil. Such an action, or inaction, relates back to chance, in that they were then retained rather than discarded.

Figure 2 Detail from the Chasuble 'St Augustine', first half of the 18th century (Musée des Ursulines de Québec, Collection du Monastère des Ursulines) (Plate 37 in the colour plate section).

Description of objects

In all, the samplers and scraps examined in this section of my research total 33 embroidered pieces. Of these, four contain features considered typical of 19th-century samplers, although they were never completed. While variations of this format are numerous, these features include an embroidered alphabet and numbers, possibly a meaningful verse and perhaps small pictorial elements, all enclosed by a border of some description.

Three of the objects scrutinised are spot or motif samplers, unfinished in that they have never been finished around the edges. A spot sampler was fashioned as a simple record of designs, which were kept to be used in other embroideries at a later time. Of these spot or motif samplers whose designs were quite sophisticated, two are related by virtue of the similarity of materials (an identical ground and similar types and colours of wool threads) and contained motifs including garlands of flowers, monograms, a memorial tablet and even a parrot. The third showed a variety of borders and two monograms (IHS and MR, both relating to the Catholic faith) worked on a much finer ground than the previous pair and executed in silks rather than wool. None of these were properly hemmed around the edges to 'finish' them. Two additional works were more or less complete samplers, although one does not include a signature and the other either lacks or has lost its signature due to damage or thread loss. Twenty-six of the embroideries sampled are scraps or samplettes. Of these (see Fig. 6), only one can be deemed a completed work; the rest are incomplete and were probably only intended as exercises.

Figure 3 shows the sampler of Marguerite Falardaux, dated 1780. It is the earliest dated sampler in the Ursuline Collection and while it is almost miniature in size (12.5 × 16.0 cm), its significance is considerable. The reader might be forgiven for assuming that Marguerite Falardaux was one of the younger pupils, so basic is her work even in its rather time-worn condition. In fact, according to archival documentation, she was in her early 20s when she came to the Convent School as a pupil, engaging in this same course of handwork as girls less than half her age. Marguerite was born in Québec City in 1759 amid the turmoil of the British Conquest of New France. Although she wished to become a nun, she could only enter the Convent School as a boarder since new British laws forbade the entry of girls into the noviciate until they had reached their 30th birthday.[16] Eventually she became Soeur de St. Laurent (Converse).[17] Marguerite's sampler strongly supports the hypothesis attributing the survival of the embroideries considered in this study to their makers becoming Ursulines.

Paired with the sampler in Figure 3 is one of the 'scraps' in the collection, whose maker and date are both unknown. This small scrap bears some resemblance to Marguerite's sampler in terms of the alphabet embroidered upon it, the use of the Greek cross-fourchee immediately preceding the letters and the striking similarities in the type of wool used. Without any reference to the sampler or archival information regarding Marguerite, the viewer would be hard pressed to attach much significance to this small and incomplete work. But taken together with the archival information and considering the visual similarities between the two works, however, the scrap takes on as much significance as the sampler in that it was probably embroidered at about the same time. The relationship of both of these rather plain objects to the marking stitch requirement in the Fourth Division of the *Ouvrage Manuel* is evident, lending credence to the assumption that such a programme was in place as early as 1780.[18] The relationship between these two embroidered pieces requires further research both by closer examination of the two objects and further scrutiny of archival documents such as the Convent's Annals. While these documents reveal who was in the same class as Marguerite for example, they have so far yielded little more data on the embroideries of the period.

In terms of sophistication, at the other end of the spectrum is the spot sampler shown in Figure 4. Complex and skilful in its design and execution, this undated and unattributed work fully expresses progress well beyond the Fourth Division's rudimentary elements. Without the archival information linking this work to the *Ouvrage Manuel* however, little would be known of the training that led to its creation. That said, it does not take much imagination to visualise these designs 'at home' in a lady's boudoir or drawing room, precisely where most of these pupils would likely have displayed their later fancy work endeavours.

Figure 5 shows a tiny samplette where the text on the object itself becomes significant in an unexpected way. It is testament to the bilingual nature of the Convent School in the 19th century and the cultural influences brought to the school by its English pupils. The Ursulines began to accept English girls into the school immediately following the Conquest in 1759 but it was not until the early 19th century that classes for these girls were taught in the English language. Archival documents and published materials leave no doubt as to the bilingual and bicultural nature of the school and the good relationship

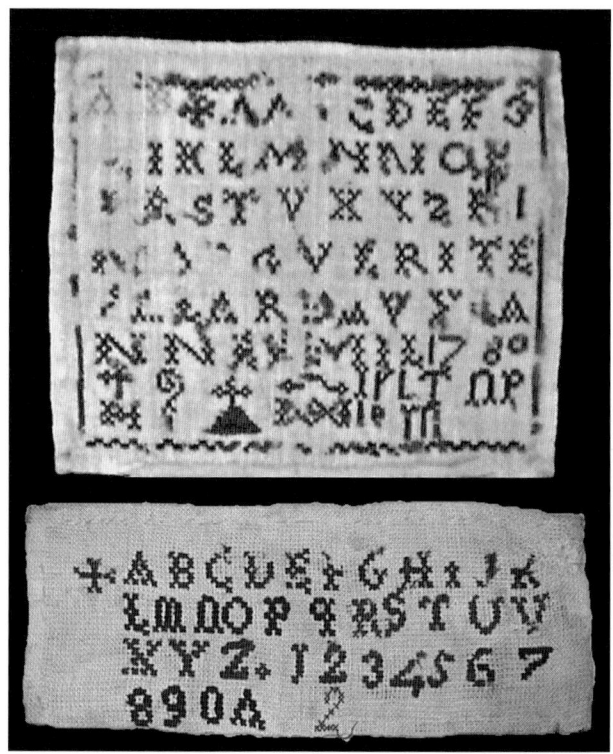

Figure 3 Sampler, Marguerite Falardaux, 1780, worked in green wool on coarse linen ground, 12.5 × 16.0 cm. Sampler fragment, undated, unattributed, possibly *c.* 1780, worked in red wools on coarse linen ground, 24.09 × 10.0 cm (Musée des Ursulines de Québec, Collection du Monastère des Ursulines) (Plate 38 in the colour plate section).

Figure 4 Spot or motif sampler, unattributed, undated, probably mid-19th century, worked in wools and silks on fine linen canvas ground, 32.20 × 41.70 cm (Musée des Ursulines de Québec, Collection du Monastère des Ursulines) (Plate 39 in the colour plate section).

Figure 5 Samplette 'Pray Make the Kettle Boil'. Polychrome Berlin-type wools on linen ground, 18.00 × 16.30 cm (Musée des Ursulines de Québec, Collection du Monastère des Ursulines) (Plate 40 in the colour plate section).

that developed between the Ursulines and the British Colonial government as well as with members of the new elite society (Mere St. Croix 1897: 271). Worked in Berlin-type wools, its design, materials and technique are typical of the time during which it was produced, i.e. the mid-to-late 19th century. The authorship of this samplette is unknown, however it most certainly contains elements from the traditional sampler as described above and includes marking stitches as per the *Ouvrage Manuel* in its design.

Figure 6 shows 24 of the scraps and samplettes which first prompted this research. Between them they display a wide range of skill levels, the use of many different materials, the use of some religiously purposeful motifs as part of the exercise, and a shared (with the possible exception of three which appear to be name plates) didactic purpose. The designs in many cases are simply repetitions of the same stitch, including running stitch and cross stitch, with variations of these line after line. Some are competently worked while others are not as convincing in terms of the skill of the stitcher. Overall, they demonstrate that the range of embroidery skills achieved by young ladies was not always of the high quality that the traditional history of samplers might lead us to believe was commonplace by offering this detailed look into embroidery skill acquisition.

Figure 6 Twenty-four scraps and samplettes worked in cross stitch and running stitches on a variety of linen and cotton grounds in wools (Musée des Ursulines de Québec, Collection du Monastère des Ursulines) (Plate 41 in the colour plate section).

The individual and the collective

Taken individually, many of these objects seem hardly worthy of consideration and yet their shared traits establish them as objects of interest: they are part of a collection of works found within the walls of the Ursuline Monastery and for some reason, by choice or by accident, have been saved as part of a museum collection; they were probably worked by pupils or teachers at the school; and they are all related in one way or another to the curriculum known as the *Ouvrage Manuel*.[19] Each of these objects provides an example of a young girl's progress through a curriculum of embroidery that would otherwise be unrecognised but for a document contained in the archives. It may be the case that the scraps or samplettes are all from one class, despite the variation in ground fabrics and threads. It may also be the case that they were collected and saved by one particular teacher of sewing and embroidery who considered that they might be useful in some way.[20] It is unlikely that the young stitchers who toiled over them would have deemed them worthy to take home for Mother and Father to admire. Nonetheless, when viewed in combination with the aforementioned texts and documents, they take on a new meaning and the collection is indebted to whoever it was who saved them for posterity.

The distinct nature of this small collection lies in the fact that each item was stitched at this one school, by one group of pupils following a programme that has been in place for centuries within the walls of the cloister.[21] By virtue of this collection of seemingly insignificant embroideries, the full range of level of skills achieved at the point they were made can be better understood. The social identity of the girls who made them is known; not by name of course, but by the information found in archival documentation describing these pupils as a group, how they were being educated in the Convent School, their status in life and what status they might they eventually attain in their mature lives.[22] My research has also shown that most of the girls did not attend school as boarders until they were at least eight years old and that many did not stay for an extended period of time: some as little as three months while they prepared for their first communion. For these little ones these tiny scraps were perhaps all that they achieved. There is evidence, however, that many young girls stayed longer, some as long as eight to ten years, and achieved much more. Of these most reached the First Division of sewing and needlework and proudly took their samplers and other decorative embroideries home with them. Still others stayed on to become novices and then choir nuns and consequently some of their work has remained in the cloister. Paradoxically, while these unfinished and unattributable works might be considered the 'lower classes' of this textile collection, their survival has come about precisely because of the upper echelon social status of their makers.[23]

Conclusion

In this research the juxtaposing of objects and texts has teased out the value of both. Where there is little to say about the iconographic value of these unfinished pieces, most can be related to the techniques, stitches and patterns dictated by the *Ouvrage Manuel*. Being extant in the convent/museum adds locational value to these objects – they are examples of everyday work from 19th-century Québec and as such provide a base against which other works of this type may be compared. They can also be viewed as having archival value, for they too are documents of a kind, as much a part of the archives of the Ursuline Monastery as the paper documents that underpin that value. Schoeser and Boydell (2002: 7) suggest that 'aesthetic or taste value is the level of appreciation associated with the pattern or general appearance of an object' and is a factor in its worth. It is fair to argue that these objects are somewhat lacking in that aesthetic value but from an embroidery history perspective, they are not diminished by that shortcoming.

To summarise the interplay between text and textile in this research, the documents have become more important because of the objects and these seemingly unimportant objects have taken on a new and significant meaning because of the documents. This is the common thread that runs through so many of the papers presented at this conference. This is not to say that this tiny collection is unique in the world – there are undoubtedly many other collections like this of undated, unattributed and unfinished bits of embroidered cloth. Many of them may be sitting alongside the documents that explain and illuminate them awaiting discovery and valuation. How fortunate that the Ursulines of Québec saved these scraps and that I was privileged to discover them.

Notes

1. This paper has its basis in my doctoral dissertation, *Ursuline Nuns, Pensionnaires and Needlework: Elite Women and Social and Cultural Convergence in British Colonial Québec City, 1760–1867*, scheduled for completion in 2007.
2. The Ursuline School for Girls at Québec was founded in 1639 and took in its first *pensionnaires* in 1642. It has served these boarders, the daughters of Québec's elite inhabitants, ever since that time. The convent also began a free school for *externes* (children from less affluent, mostly Irish immigrant families) in the 19th century but these are a topic for future research. Because of the sheer numbers involved, my doctoral research has had to be confined to the elite boarders and half-boarders who attended the school as fee-paying students.
3. These are only a small sample of the many books published on the subject.
4. This interest has increased in recent decades as general interest in genealogy has grown given the clues that samplers can provide to family history.
5. This comment must not be misconstrued as a dismissal of the valuable techniques for physical analysis described, for example in Elliot 1994: 562 and Prown 1994: 333.
6. The paper on which this manuscript is typed is undated.
7. This research and the conclusions reached are part of my doctoral research. It should be noted that the *Ouvrage Manuel* begins with the Fourth Division (as does the academic class ranking system within the school, where the Fourth Division refers to the little ones) and progresses to the First Division.
8. Archives des Ursulines de Québec, Vol. 1K/2.2 Education.
9. Archives des Ursulines de Québec, Vol. 1K/2.2 – *Cours secondaire, Reglements, Horaires, Programmes de la Joureire*. Once again, the paper on which the information is transcribed offers no clue as to the date of the original document.
10. My current research has involved the preparation of a database taken from the register of pupils which includes nearly 2800

boarders and half-boarders who attended the school from 1760 to 1867 as well as a database of 100 choir nuns from the same period. The *Registre des Élèves* held in the Archives des Ursulines covers the entire period of the school's history.
11. It should be noted here that such information is only available on written application to the Archives des Ursulines de Québec.
12. For an examination of these works see Turgeon 2002 and Dawson 1999.
13. The majority of these liturgical embroideries are now in the collection of the Musée des Ursulines de Québec.
14. For example, through the judicious scrutiny of many archival documents a number of these early works have been attributed with a fair degree of certainty to Mère Marie LeMaire des Anges and the workshop which she directed in the late 17th and early 18th century.
15. Later in this paper a speculative opinion will be offered.
16. In 1763 the British passed a law that required that young girls must reach their 30th birthday before they were allowed to enter the noviciate of any order. Under these circumstances it was felt that most would abandon the idea and marry thus progressively reducing their numbers. This law was repealed in 1770 by Governor Sir Guy Carleton (later Lord Dorchester).
17. This information is contained in the *Registre des Soeurs* held in the Archives des Ursulines de Québec, no page available.
18. The marking stitch referred to here is today more commonly referred to as cross stitch. A survey of the many published sources for patterns and designs available to young ladies in Canada in the 19th century may be found in Salahub 1998.
19. There is always the possibility that some of these may have been worked by teachers as examples for their pupils to copy but if that were the case with these samplers, one suspects they would be more neatly done and finished.
20. Both these options must be considered as speculation on my part.
21. It is very possible that other such collections exist within other institutions, however research on samplers in Québec has focused primarily on individual objects from a variety of institutions. See Salahub 1994.
22. For example, preliminary information taken from the register of pupils indicates that a large proportion of the boarders were destined to marry members of the elite and professional classes in Québec.
23. The 'eliteness' of the *pensionnaires* at the Ursuline Convent School is firmly established in my doctoral research (see note 1).

References

Bank, M. (1979) *Anonymous was a Woman*. New York: St Martin's Press.
Bolton, E.S. and Coe, E.J. (1921) *American Samplers*. Facsimile reproduction (1987). New York: Dover Publications.
Browne, C.W. and Wearden, J.M. (1999) *Samplers: From the Victoria and Albert Museum*. London: V&A.
Christie, G. (1920) *Samplers and Stitches: A Handbook of the Embroiderer's Art*. London: Batsford.
Dawson, J.T. (1999) *For the Monastery to the Museum: History, Tradition and Invention. Issues Surrounding Mère Marie LeMaire des Anges and her Embroidery Atelier at the Ursuline Monastery in Québec 1671–1760*. MA dissertation, Winchester School of Art, University of Southampton.
Elliot, R.E.A. (1994) 'Towards a material history methodology', in *Interpreting Objects and Collections*, S. Pearce (ed.), 109–24. London and New York: Routledge.
Huish, M.B. (1913) *Samplers & Tapestry Embroideries*. Facsimile reproduction (1970). New York: Dover Publications.
King, D. (1960) *Samplers*. London: HMSO.
Krueger, G. F. (1984) *A Gallery of American Samplers: The Theodore H. Kapnek Collection*. New York: Bonanza Books.
Mere St. Croix, O.S.U. (1897) *Glimpses of the Monastery: Scenes from the History of the Ursulines of Québec during Two Hundred Years 1639–1839*. Second Edition Revised, Augmented and Completed by Reminiscences of the Last Fifty Years: 1839–1889. Québec: L.J. Demers et frére.
Parker, R. (1984) *The Subversive Stitch: Embroidery and the Making of the Feminine*. London/New York: Routledge.
Prown, J. (1994) 'Mind in matter: an introduction to material culture theory and method', in *Interpreting Objects and Collections*, S. Pearce (ed.), 133–8. London and New York: Routledge.
Quinton, R. (2005) *Patterns of Childhood: Samplers from Glasgow Museums*. London: A & C Black.
Ring, B. (1993) *Girlhood Embroidery: American Samplers and Pictorial Needlework, 1650–1850*. New York: A. A. Knopf.
Salahub, J.E. (1994) *Québec Samplers: ABC's of Embroidery*. Montreal: McCord Museum of Canadian History.
Salahub, J.E. (1998) *Dutiful Daughter: Fashionable Domestic Embroidery in Canada and the British Model 1764–1911*. PhD dissertation, Royal College of Art, London.
Schoeser, J. and Boydell, C. (2002) *Disentangling Textiles: Techniques for the Study of Designed Objects*. London: Middlesex University Press.
Swain, M.H. (1973) *The Needlework of Mary, Queen of Scots*. New York: Van Nostrand Reinhold.
Turgeon, C. (2002) *Le fil d'art: les broderies des Ursulines de Québec*. Québec: Musée de Québec.
Young, D.A. (1985) *A Record for Time: An Exhibition of Decorated Family and Individual Records, Memorials, Tokens of Friendship and Embroidered Memorials and Samplers Produced in Nova Scotia Prior to 1900*. Halifax, NS: Art Gallery of Nova Scotia.

The author

Joyce Taylor Dawson is a doctoral student at the Winchester School of Art, University of Southampton. Her thesis, entitled *Ursuline Nuns, Pensionnaires and Needlework: Elite Women and Social and Cultural Convergence in British Colonial Québec City, 1760–1867* is scheduled for completion in 2007. She has carried out research on early Canadian needlework in general and Ursuline embroideries in particular since the early 1970s. She was also in private practice as a textile conservator until her retirement in 1997. She received her MA (History of Textiles and Dress) from the Winchester School of Art in 1999.

Address

Joyce A. Taylor Dawson, 5 Short Road, Greensville, Ontario, Canada L9H 5L8 (joyceTdawson@cogeco.ca)

Tracing textiles in trade:
from account books to patents

Fashioning the Tudor court

Cinzia Maria Sicca

ABSTRACT Present in London since 1509, the Cavalcanti and Bardi company was granted in 1522 permission 'to import cloths of gold, silver and damask, gold cloths of "tynsyn saten"'. The company ledgers provide detailed descriptions of the dyes, colours and patterns of the textiles imported, as well as the names of their buyers. Most of these customers were portrayed by Hans Holbein the Younger, thus specific entries in the ledgers can be associated with the clothes they wear in the paintings. Select portraits by Holbein are compared with those of continental sitters wearing the same textiles or colour variants of the same patterns. While the courtiers' clothes are only preserved in portraits, the remnant of Bishop Fox's cope, surviving at Corpus Christi College, Oxford, can be associated with a payment in the account books and shown to be closely allied to the Passerini cope in Cortona. The discussion focuses on textile patterns, retailing practices, concepts of identity through clothing in 16th-century Europe and how these were combined to fashion a modern image of the English court.

Keywords: Henry VIII, Holbein, Florentine textiles, silk, velvet, tissues

Textiles and portraits

'I send you this book as a portrait of the court of Urbino, not by the hand of Raphael or Michelangelo, but by that of a lowly painter and one that only knows how to draw the main lines, without adorning the truth with pretty colours or making, by perspective art, that which it not seem to be.'[1] The analogy used by Baldassar Castiglione in the dedicatory letter of his book to Don Miguel De Silva is more than a rhetorical figure, for the *Book of the Courtier* is a group portrait, conjuring up the image of a society described in all its complexity and contradictions. Like Raphael had portrayed Guidobaldo da Montefeltro, so Castiglione, by different yet analogous means, produced a group portrait of the court under that duke. At about the same time Hans Holbein had embarked on a similar enterprise, becoming to the English court what Castiglione was to that of Urbino. In Holbein's hands, portraiture substitutes itself for life and becomes our best tool to evoke what is absent and lost.

Raphael's gracious and poised portrait of Guidobaldo in the Uffizi (Fig. 1) and that of Sir Brian Tuke by Hans Holbein, in the National Gallery of Art, Washington (Fig. 2) show the two painters' identical aims.

Though light and airy, Raphael's portrait of the duke exudes a sense of sadness and doom largely achieved by setting the figure in a rigidly frontal view against a background in which the usual breadth of the landscape behind is compressed and fractioned by the architectural frame, and by the window ledge placed at shoulder height behind the sitter. In a premonition of death, the duke, whose health was exceedingly fragile, is shown with expressionless eyes and chiselled features. Indeed of Raphael's many portraits this comes closest to sculpture, and achieves its mood precisely by exploiting the funerary associations of the portrait bust, which he subtly combines with the allusive windowsill, almost shorthand for a funer-

Figure 1 Raphael, *Guidobaldo da Montefeltro*, Florence, Uffizi (Soprintendenza Speciale per il Polo Museale Fiorentino, Gabinetto Fotografico) (Plate 42 in the colour plate section).

ary *stelae* (Rosand 1983). Painted in *c.*1532, Tuke's portrait is equally sombre. The sitter is identified by the inscription at the top of the panel – BRIANVS TVKE, MILES, AN.º AETATIS SUAE LVII[2] – and by his personal motto recorded immedi-

Figure 2 Hans Holbein the Younger, *Sir Brian Tuke*, National Gallery of Art, Washington, Andrew W. Mellon Collection (© Board of Trustees, National Gallery of Art, Washington. National Gallery of Art, Washington, Department of Visual Services) (Plate 43 in the colour plate section).

Figure 3 Raphael, *Francesco Maria della Rovere*, Florence, Uffizi (Soprintendenza Speciale per il Polo Museale Fiorentino, Gabinetto Fotografico) (Plate 44 in the colour plate section).

ately below: DROIT ET AVANT (upright and forward). The inscription recording the sitter's age refers to the passing of time and thereby directly confronts the fact of death. In his hands, attracting the viewer's gaze, Tuke holds a folded piece of paper bearing a Latin inscription from the Book of Job – NVNQVID NON PAVCITAS DIERVM MEORVM FINIETVR BREVI?[3] – adumbrating the idea of death. This latter concept is further reinforced by the prominent cross hanging from the garter chain on his chest and adorned with the symbols of the five wounds of Christ. By the time Tuke was portrayed by Holbein he was treasurer of Henry VIII's household. Prior to this appointment he had been knight of the king's body, and subsequently governor of the king's posts.[4] He was a courtier, depicted at a time when the court in which he lived was entering its darkest days.

The commemorative mood is not the only common feature of the two portraits. Guidobaldo and Tuke are in fact shown wearing different garments made of the same material: the duke's overcoat, worn over a jet black top, is of the same gold chequered fabric as the sleeves of the king's treasurer. The latter emerge from underneath a black coat lined with brown fur. The colour scheme as well as the material of the clothes worn by the two sitters is the same, though in Raphael's portrait, perhaps due to the state of conservation, the gold cloth is less shiny than Tuke's.

There are no extant samples of this textile, which Raphael depicted in a red velvet variant in the Uffizi portrait of the young Francesco Maria della Rovere (Fig. 3). The fabric is also represented around 1515 by the Maestro della Morte di Maria as the cloth of the Virgin's mantle in his *Holy Family* in the Kunsthistorisches Museum, Vienna (Buss *et al.* 1983: 130–31). The letters of Ginevra de' Fanti to Isabella d'Este reveal that in 1488 the duke had ordered brocades for his wife in Florence, wherefrom presumably also came the material for his own garments.[5]

Most viewers would no doubt think this an extraordinary coincidence of textiles either manufactured by the same weaver or supplied by the same merchants, but there is no case of serendipity here as another instance of uncannily similar textiles demonstrates. The 14 fragments from two copes, now sewn to form an altar carpet (Fig. 4) – bequeathed by Richard Fox, Bishop of Winchester, to Corpus Christi College, Oxford, and described in 1566 as made of 'purple velvet with branches having the pellicanes of golde' (Fowler 1893) – are closely allied to the design pattern of a set of vestments donated in 1526 to Cortona Cathedral by Margherita Passerini on behalf of her son Silvio (1469–1529), appointed in 1513 cardinal-bishop of Cortona.

The distinctive feature of this fabric is represented by a bull – Passerini's emblem – sitting on a stylised chunk of green silk turf contained within the motif of the *broncone* with acanthus leaves and pomegranates. A further device is used in the pattern repeat, namely the diamond from which the intertwined branches depart. The diamond, alone or set within a ring, is a well-known Medici emblem which here serves the purpose of advertising the source of Passerini's fortune (Ames-Lewis 1979)[6] (Fig. 5).

The Passerini set – which consists of a cope with hood and orphrey band, chasuble, dalmatic, tunic, corporal case, chalice veil, lectern cover and altar frontal – was made in Florence at some point between 1522 and 1526.[7] Though the details of the design differ to some extent, the notion of the heraldic animal – the bull in Passerini's case and the pelican in Fox's – standing on a grassy bank is absolutely identical. The 14 fragments of cut crimson velvet cloth of gold are juxtaposed together without reproducing the original pattern repeat. The motif of the branch forming garlands at the centre of which is placed a bouclè pomegranate, with bouclè bunches of grapes at the four corners, alternates with lozenges framing a brocaded and bouclè silver-gilt pelican standing on a stylised chunk of green silk turf set against a blue sky. The pelican's neck is twisted in a mannerist spiral as the bird wounds its breast causing it to bleed. The awkward movement is further stressed by the banderole with the motto EST DEO GRATIA (grace be to God) uncoiling to the left. The inclusion of motto and emblem presupposes that the textile was woven to order in Florence and that, like the fabric worn by Tuke in Holbein's portrait, it was imported into England by merchants trading in luxury textiles that could be personalised if necessary.[8]

Like Brian Tuke, the bishop of Winchester – or his men on his behalf – furnished himself with precious fabrics from the London *drapperia* of the Florentine business partnership of Cavalcanti and Bardi in Throgmorton Street (Sicca 2002). The company's ledgers and letterbooks preserved in the Florence State Archive contain explicit references to the bishop of Winchester in 1523 and 1526 when he is mentioned in connection respectively with a ready-made chasuble and with the material for a second one of crimson damask with gold pattern,[9] as well as with significant quantities of 'telette d'oro tirato e filato a braccia 18 fino a braccia 20 alta' and

Figure 4 Remnants of a cope commissioned by Richard Fox, Bishop of Winchester (Oxford, Corpus Christi College) (Plate 45 in the colour plate section).

Figure 5 Cope belonging to Cardinal Silvio Passerini, Cortona (Museo Diocesano. Dipartimento di Storia delle Arti, Pisa, Gabinetto Fotografico) (Plate 46 in the colour plate section).

'arricciati a n.° 7 fino a n.° 8 braccia'.[10] A bill of 10 November 1527 in one of the company's ledgers[11] records the cost of textiles handed over to the men of 'Monsignore di Uyncestry', that is Bishop Richard Fox.

There is no way of knowing whether the 'broccato alexandrino da chiesa' frequently listed among the textiles provided by the Mannelli of Florence, or the 'broccati di pelo rosso da chiesa' produced by the Carnesecchi[12] were acquired on Fox's behalf. What is certain is that the *Schedule of Church Goods* found in the chapel of Corpus Christi College during the visitation of 1566 records fabrics of remarkable similarity: hangings of cloth of tissue for the high altar, purple velvet for priest, deacon and subdeacon vestments, and a 'canopy for the sepulchre of red silk braunched with golde'.[13] The affinity in the design patterns of Passerini's and Fox's vestments is so extraordinary as to suggest that only very special merchants could have obtained permission to elaborate on such an exclusive design and use it in England in what was tantamount to a sign of the pope's special favour towards the bishop.

The London company of Cavalcanti and Bardi

Giovanni Cavalcanti and Pier Francesco de Bardi were no ordinary merchants: not only did they sell and distribute in England the fabrics produced by the best weavers for the great firms of *setaioli* and *battilori*, but they also acted on behalf of the papacy as collectors of both Peter's pence and of the duties on alum. Endowed with powerful connections to the Medici,[14] business acumen, sophisticated manners, exquisite artistic judgement and courtly skills, Giovanni Cavalcanti (1480–1544) strategically positioned the company to provide financial services and ordnance.[15] In October 1512, a month after the Medici restoration in Florence, the king granted Cavalcanti 'safeconduct and protection to trade in England for ten years'. It must have been at this point that Giovanni expanded his trade to include luxury fabrics; in fact the first royal payments to Cavalcanti for cloths of gold and silks are dated February 1513.[16] In March 1513, after the election of Cardinal de' Medici to the papacy as Leo X, Cavalcanti's long-standing allegiance to the cardinal while in exile was immediately rewarded with a post as gentleman of the chamber, under the control of his relative Giovanni degli Albizzi. Just a month after Leo's election, Henry VIII granted Cavalcanti denization for life, thus acknowledging his very special status and the role he was increasingly called to play as a linchpin between the papacy and London. The new company formed with Pierfrancesco di Piero Bardi, and entirely devoted to a more diversified trade in luxury goods, appears to have been set up around this time.[17] It was only in 1519, however, that the luxury textile side of the company's trade took off in its own right and the volume of this type of merchandise began to exceed that in armoury.[18] This trend followed the success of the French campaign and not surprisingly coincided with four years of unprecedented public spectacles which took place at home and abroad to mark the new power England had acquired on the international political stage. The marriage of Princess Mary to the dauphin at Greenwich on 5 October 1518 was followed by Emperor Charles V's visit to England on 26 May 1520. By 31 May, Henry VIII was leaving for Calais and then Guines, where he took up lodgings in an ephemeral palace which provided his base during the whole month of June 1520, when he and François I met and jousted at the so-called Field of Cloth of Gold, the greatest of Tudor pageants (Giustiniani 1854; Nichols 1846; Anglo 1997: 124–206).

On Tuesday 10 July 1520, the English retinue set out toward Gravelines for another Anglo-imperial interview followed by dances and revels. In January 1521, the visit of the papal nuncio, Matteo Ghinucci, provided a new occasion for conspicuous display followed in March 1522 by an imperial embassy to negotiate the emperor's visit to England which took place between 28 May, when Charles landed in Dover, and 6 July, when he sailed for Santander. The date of the new trading licence granted to Cavalcanti – 20 April 1522 – is intimately bound to this chronology and appears to have served two purposes: it renewed and extended for an unlimited period of time the 1512 licence, while at the same time it sanctioned the changed nature of the goods imported, over which the king claimed the prerogative of first choice.[19]

On 10 July 1518, reporting to Isabella d'Este the arrival of the Flemish embassy in London, Francesco Chiericati described the attire of the king and his courtiers: 'His Majesty that day was clad in bouclè brocade according to the Hungarian fashion and wore round his neck a collar of inestimable value. The Queens, Duke, Marquesses and other earls were all wearing cloth of gold and collars. Such was the pomp and splendour that everything sparkled with gold.'[20] Chiericati remarked also on the munificence of the king: 'He [the King] gave Monsieur de Luxembourg, his relative, a splendid horse richly apparelled, together with a coat of cloth of gold lined with furs of martens and worth seven hundred ducats.'[21] The Mantuan ambassador's comments to his own sovereign are proof of the crucial role dress played even in international politics. If clothes were – all over Europe – powerful indicators of status, royal clothes fulfilled an even more important role as they provided outward illustration of the moral and philosophical quality of magnificence, befitting of a king (Gunn 1993; Hayward 1996; Hayward 2004: 165–78). International embassies, entries into foreign cities and the associated pageantries and revels required the king of England to be 'marvelous to behold' (Hall 1809), a mirror of the new greatness of his realm. On the occasion of such international gatherings – the first to be systematically attended by an English monarch – king and courtiers needed to appear exquisitely dressed, which meant lavishly as well as fashionably. This type of effect could only be achieved using predominantly foreign fabrics: the Italian silks and metal cloths offered an unchallenged range of design patterns and colours.

Styles of dress as well as types of textiles could be constructed as symbols of social mobility, potentially holding the power to undermine the hierarchical structure of society. This is reflected in the sumptuary legislation on dress which was concerned not so much with the extravagance commonly associated with women, but rather with men and their social status (Hooper 1915; Baldwin 1926; Harte 1976). Under Henry VIII, sumptuary legislation became a tool which, used in combination with the emanation of the Eltham Ordnances (1526), identified the members of the privy chamber and the court favourites (Starkey 1973, 1987). The first of the five major

Tudor 'Acts of Apparel', or 'Acts for Reformation of Excess in Apparel' was passed the year after the king's accession to the throne, and restricted both cloth of gold of purple and silk of purple to members of the royal family. Discriminations were introduced among the nobility since only dukes could use cloth of gold for their attire or that of their horses, and no one under the rank of an earl could wear sable. Dukes and earls alone were allowed satin, silk or anything mixed with silk. Only Knights of the Garter could wear velvet in crimson or blue, and 'furs of martron'. Imported fur was prohibited to all below the rank of the gentry, except for the graduates of the universities and certain royal servants.

Two further Acts were issued in 1515. The first added little to that of 1510, except for tightening up the connection between yearly income and restriction in the use of certain colours and textiles. The second Act of 1515 was much more detailed: the social hierarchy was expanded, the wearing of velvet was extended to a large number of the king's servants; and the privileges of the fathers were now accorded to the sons and heirs of barons and knights. Differentiation within the royal household was more precisely specified, while two provisions stated that the king could 'grant and give licence and authority to such of his subjects as his grace shall think convenient to wear all and such apparell on his body or his horses as shall stand with the pleasure of the king's grace', and that the regulations were not to apply to anyone wearing apparel given by the king or queen (Harte 1993). Thus the second Act of 1515 allowed the king to promote his close friends – the *minions* (Richardson 1999) – and contradict the normal social order. Clothing thus served to define an individual's attachment to the king's most intimate circle, not simply because magnificent textiles were often donated by the monarch as evidence of his favour, but also because permission granted by him to wear certain fabrics and colours disguised in fact the enormous disparity in social standing separating the old aristocracy – men such as John Bourchier, Second Baron Berners, George Hastings, First Earl of Huntingdon and Third Baron Hastings, or Sir Thomas Knyvet[22] – from younger men on the make such as Henry Guildford[23] or Charles Brandon (Gunn 1988).

Cavalcanti and Bardi were among the principal suppliers of textiles to the monarchy; they did so both by direct sales to the Wardrobe and through sales to mercers, silkwomen and taylors employed by the royal household. Courtiers too were supplied by the company whose account books, maintained with the sophisticated discipline of bilateral format *alla Veneziana*, use of double entry with cross-references to subsidiary books,[24] provide us with a veritable who's who of the Henrician court as well as with the equivalent of a 'written sampler', a rare and accurate catalogue of the most luxurious Italian manufactured wares. The king, styled as 'Arrigo nostro re d'Inghilterra', heads the list of illustrious customers, followed by the queen, and later by 'Miladj Anna'. Sir Henry Guildford's name[25] is meticulously recorded together with those of many other customers, often identified by their title and office: Henry Wyatt, Treasurer of the King's Bedchamber;[26] William Blount, 4th Lord Mountjoy;[27] George Talbot, Earl of Shrewsbury;[28] Thomas Fettiplace;[29] Sir John Daunce;[30] William Carey;[31] Charles Brandon, Duke of Suffolk;[32] Walter Devereux, Lord Ferrers;[33] Sir Rhys ap Thomas;[34] William Fitzwilliam, Earl of Southampton;[35] Edward Stafford, Duke of Buckingham;[36] Charles Somerset, Lord Herbert, Earl of Worcester;[37] Charles Knyvet, one of the minions;[38] William Compton, Groom of the Stool, closest friend and body-servant of the king;[39] Bryan Tuke;[40] Thomas Wolsey, Cardinal of York;[41] Catharine Aldwin;[42] Nicholas Vaux, Lord Vaux of Harrowden[43] and Richard Lister, the Attorney General.[44] We even catch glimpses of some of the courtiers' servants, such as Richard Shadwell, Somerset's servant;[45] Camillo Sabinello, Charles Brandon's falconer;[46] John Gostewyck, a servant of Wolsey[47] and John Draper, one of Compton's men.[48]

The bulk of the fabrics acquired by these fashionable customers consisted of the exclusive metal cloths produced in Florence and were referred to in the accounts by their established name of *teletta* (tissue or cloth of tissue). This was a silk fabric (velvet and brocatelle) incorporating gold or silver loops forming floral or geometrical motifs against a light or dark base (Morelli 1976: 85; Monnas 1998).[49] As Lisa Monnas has shown, the word 'tissue' (*teletta*) was used to describe fabrics which were still velvets, while it seems that the truly metallic fabrics, made of silk woven with gold and/or silver threads, were referred to as 'plain cloth of gold' (or silver). The distinction is clearly made in an entry from the *Quadernaccio* (the wastebook) covering the years 1522–1525.[50] The accountant recorded the trip made to the court by Antonio Carsidoni,[51] the company's factor, on 14 June 1525 to deliver and show to the king a range of fabrics: woollen cloth (*drappo*), cloth of tissue (*teletta bianca arricciata d'argento, teletta bigia arricciata doro*), plain cloth of silver and gold (*teletta dargento tirata, teletta doro tirato tane*), and tinsel satin (*tinselo nero a solchi duccellinj*).[52] The entry is interesting also as it shows what is even more evident in other similar documents, namely the fact that the fabrics sold were by no means only the products of a parent company in Florence as one might be led to think. As well as being established bankers,[53] the Cavalcanti were in fact wool and silk manufacturers with various branches of the family enrolled in the Florentine Silk Guild.[54] In Florence, Giovanni Cavalcanti was the junior partner in a silk company (operating under the name 'Francesco Mannelli e Giovanni Cavalcanti e compagni di Firenze') with Francesco Mannelli, the scion of one of the most famous families of *setaioli* and bankers.[55] In London, Cavalcanti and Bardi, acting as merchants in their own right or on commission, sold the wares produced by firms belonging to the Mannelli and Cavalcanti families[56] as well as those produced by other celebrated silk manufacturers, such as Zanobi Bartolini, Niccolò Capponi, Giuliano e Pierfrancesco Da Galliano, Marco Del Nero, Federico and Giuliano Gondi, and Francesco Pitti.[57] The 1525 document mentioned above also contains the name of Bartolomeo Carnesecchi,[58] the senior partner in a company of *battilori* (gold beaters), which together with the companies of Tommaso Minerbetti & Vincenzio Taddei, Roberto Nasi & compagni battilori, and of Gherardo Taddei & compagni battilori – all from Florence – supplied the best tinsels and tissues. These gold beaters were members of leading merchant families who in the previous century had invested in this type of workshop as a way of enhancing their textile trade (Dini 2000; Tognetti 2002: 11–42). Due to the obvious frailty and delicacy of these *telette* and *tinseli* very few samples have survived, but their comparison with the documentary descriptive evidence suggests that truly the most refined fabrics were shipped to London, remarkable for both their design patterns and colours.[59] The *battilori* and *setaioli* did not simply dispose through Cavalcanti and Bardi of stock already produced, they also wove to order (*su misura*) as shown by the copy of a statement of account sent to Francesco Pitti.[60]

A sizeable proportion of the trade consisted also of cut and uncut velvet, two-pile velvet, figured, highlighted with little loops of gold or silver (*allucciolato*), or decorated with embroidery (Orsi Landini 1993; Leclerq 2001: 186–95). The exclusive black velvet (*velluto negro*), sold in the two variants of cut and figured velvet, was produced in Genova by the companies of Francesco Salvago, Uberto Centurioni and Antonio de' Vivaldi. When Cavalcanti and Bardi did not receive sufficient material from these suppliers they turned to the stocks of the London company of Agostino Pinello & Paolo Spinola.[61] The classic Italian damask, which enjoyed wide international dissemination, was successfully produced in Florence in even more plentiful and varied types of patterns and colours. The Cavalcanti and Bardi ledgers testify to the availability of damasks *in un cammino* or *in due o tre cammini*;[62] this specification, always present when damask is being described, does not refer to a type of decorative pattern but rather to the particular mounting of the loom which in turn determines whether the decorative motif will consist of two or three patterns (Schorta 1991; Orsi Landini 1997, 1999). The typical design employed for this textile consisted, in the words of the anonymous author of the *Trattato dell'Arte della Seta* (Anon. 1868: 90, 141), of *pigne, fogliame e foglie*, that is pine cones, palmettes and heart-shaped leaves branching from a vertical stem.

Purveyance for the royal household

Selling cloth to the king and the Wardrobe required patience and a great deal of work. The king and the court were rarely in the same place and winter was, as much as the summer, a time of continual changes in scene. The company was thus forced to adapt and follow the itinerant court with their bulky wares. The period 1523 to 1525 provides good evidence for this. On 16 December 1523 the queen was at Guildford where two cases wrapped in oilskin and cloth were brought[63] and consigned to Richard Justis, *guardarobiere della Regina d'Inghilterra*,[64] to show to the queen; overall 35 yards of metal cloth had been delivered but only eight were actually sold, and two days later it was necessary to deliver eight more yards of silver metal cloth with a different design pattern. On 18 December 1523 the king was at Chertsey where the company's factor reached him by barge, bringing an impressive range of tissues and tinsel satins.[65] Something in the course of the interview, however, must have determined Carsidoni to go back to London and return the following day with a long case containing a ready-to-wear (prêt-à-porter) doublet of gold tissue. It looks as if this time he remained at court, following it to Hampton Court where, on the 21st, he was reached by a company servant delivering more metal cloth, some of which was for William Compton in whose presence it was measured.[66] By the end of the month the court had removed to Windsor with Carsidoni still in tow, peddling even more precious goods brought by the faithful servant Stewart by barge in *uno baschetto grande quadro* (a square basket).[67] Inside there were pearl, coral and cornelia necklaces, as well as diamonds in different cuts and sizes. The following year fabrics were sent to the court on 15 and 16 December, leaving them in the care first of Ralph Worsley, then page of the Wardrobe,[68] and subsequently of Sir James Worsley, the actual keeper of the Wardrobe.[69] On 16 December, Antonio Carsidoni went in person to the court bringing with him cloth of gold and precious tissues.[70] He appears to have remained at court for he was reached there on the 19th by the company's bursar bringing 33 *braccia* of black damask.[71] In 1525 there was more frantic travelling: the king and the court were at Eltham where Carsidoni went first on 20 December with jewels as well as loose gems.[72] On 23 December he went back with a wide range of tinsel satins and tissues which he left with the Wardrobe for some months; only in the following March was the company able to record the income from that sale.[73] Another entry, this time dated 1529, vividly illustrates the whims of the king. This time Carsidoni had been summoned to Greenwich. He then went back to the City, to be called again several times to Westminster, but the king decided to move to Hampton Court where the fabrics had to be taken by barge accompanied by Niccolò Pandolfini and a servant. They had to wait five days before they could collect the money and whatever had not been acquired. On this particular occasion, the king did not allow the bargees to enter his privy chamber so the servants of Sir Henry Norris, the then groom of the stool, were called to assist in the transport of the cases which moved between the Wardrobe and the king's chamber, and back again.[74]

This costly to and fro was not burdensome so long as the factor succeeded in showing the fabrics to the king in person and in praising to him their quality, colour and design. These presentations appear to have taken place in the king's privy lodgings and were followed by a session in the Wardrobe where, once a decision had been reached, the fabrics were measured.[75] Whenever a personal interview with either the king or queen could not take place it was necessary to enlist the support of the keeper of the Wardrobe or of other courtiers.[76] All these shenanigans were recorded in the wastebook for two reasons: the costs of porterage, transport, victuals and lodging involved were ultimately charged to the manufacturers of the goods,[77] and the favours of the groom of the stool or of John Parker, yeoman of the king's robes, had to be rewarded.[78] The extraordinary antennae and courtly skills of these Florentine merchants are unveiled by an entry of 1529 when the recipient of one of these gifts in return for support was none other than Anne Boleyn, daughter of Viscount Rochford.[79]

It was not unusual, however, for Parker or for the royal tailors[80] to supply their master and mistresses directly from the London *drapperia*, which was also attended by other tailors, mercers and embroiderers, all of whom furnished themselves with fabrics and threads.[81] As mentioned earlier, the quality of gold thread produced by the Florentine *battilori* enjoyed a high reputation and the conspicuous consumption of gold and silver threads documented by the accounts is therefore not altogether surprising.[82] The yarns were used in the technically complex and highly refined embroideries which had been peculiar to the decoration of English aristocratic dress since the early 16th century (Ashelford 1983: 12–17). Indeed they

Figure 6 Hans Holbein the Younger, *Sir Henry Guildford*, The Royal Collection (© 2007, HM Queen Elizabeth II. A.C. Cooper Ltd) (Plate 47 in the colour plate section).

Figure 7 Hans Holbein the Younger, *Edward, Prince of Wales*, National Gallery of Art, Washington, Andrew W. Mellon Collection (© Board of Trustees, National Gallery of Art, Washington. National Gallery of Art, Washington, Department of Visual Services) (Plate 48 in the colour plate section).

were deemed so precious as to be offered on New Year's Day, which was the great gift-giving day when every member of the court, from the lord chancellor to the humblest servants, gave the king a present, and in return received from the king a gift of plate, whose weight was precisely graded in accordance with the rank of the recipient. On New Year's Day 1532, Giovanni Cavalcanti presented the king with 'a gilt chest with 44 alabaster pots, and a box full of fine thread'.[83]

The king acquired textiles for his own wardrobe and for the royal family throughout the year, but peaks are recorded in the Cavalcanti and Bardi accounts every year during the month of December. There might be a number of explanations for this seasonal trend. The first is that it reflects the arrival of the last shipments from Italy before the onset of the winter storms. It could also be that this was the time when the king's personal wardrobe was renewed and items given away as gifts of clothing to the nobility. Maria Hayward (2004) notes that such gifts occurred in December with a certain regularity; she also remarks that small pieces of high-quality cloth were given away to the group of young men at court known as the minions. It seems reasonable to assume some correlation between these sets of events.

Cavalcanti and Bardi provided Henry VIII with ready-to-wear garments too. The king's hawking gloves and hawk's hood, part of the collection of the Ashmolean Museum, Oxford,[84] are likely survivors from the many orders and payments for such items, all of which carried the royal arms.[85] Prêt-à-porter doublets, as we have seen earlier, were also brought to the court but they could be very tricky garments to sell as Pierfrancesco de' Bardi explained in a somewhat irritated letter written to Giovanni Cavalcanti in Florence on 31 May 1527.[86] One such rich piece of clothing had been delivered to the Wardrobe where it had been left for quite some time in the hope that eventually Henry would be convinced to buy it. This ploy still had to bear fruit, but certainly this was not due to lack of effort on either the factor's or partner's part. Two reasons were given by Bardi for the failure to sell the doublet; the first, but by no means the principal one, was that buyers valued the uncut length of cloth more than the convenience of a ready-made garment on account of the loss of material, and the fact that the pattern repeat was not visible. Then, in what was tantamount to a lesson in etiquette, Bardi reminded Cavalcanti of the most important reason: a king is always unwilling to wear clothes made of fabrics woven with his badges and arms. The implication being that the king could grant his purveyors permission to manufacture such fabrics but could not tolerate that they were not turned into garments cut and sewn by the royal tailors under the strict control of the Wardrobe. What the letter adumbrates is the latent conflict between exclusive royal couture and the rationale of market enterprise guiding the Florentine industry. Cavalcanti is depicted by Bardi as the epitome of such creative entrepreneurship;[87] '*voi auete ghrande fantasia in fare questi giubboni e queste opere noue*', he wrote, suggesting that his partner's novel ideas affected the design patterns of textiles as well. The king could not countenance the uncontrolled and unlicensed use of textiles decorated with his marked livery; this would have undermined the whole financial and symbolic value of cloth and clothes-giving at the Henrician court.

The fact that, in his 1527 portrait by Holbein (Fig. 6), Sir Henry Guildford wore cloth of gold with the same Tudor knots on the sleeves and double knots emerging from a *broncone* on the front, exactly like the baby Edward, Prince of Wales in 1539 (Fig. 7), was a sign of the exceptional favour he enjoyed and of his standing in a society ruled by sumptuary laws.

Florentine merchants and manufacturers had to tread carefully and be mindful of not overstepping their role; they set trends and disseminated through their fabrics the allure of the Italian Renaissance; they could not however attempt to establish intercultural identities that challenged the underpinning social structure or, as Thomas Dekker was to claim in 1606, clothes would turn into the epitome of treason.[88]

Acknowledgements

Research for this essay was made possible by a MIUR grant in 1999–2001 for Progetti di Rilevante Interesse Nazionale (9910247288-002) and by a Freese Senior Fellowship at the National Gallery of Art Center for Advanced Studies in the Visual Arts, Washington DC in 2002–2003. The author is also grateful to Marchese Lorenzo Ginori for permission to consult and quote from his archives.

Notes

1. Castiglione 1987: 50.
2. 'Brian Tuke, Knight, in the fiftyseventh year of his life.'
3. 'Shall not my few days be ended shortly?'
4. It is not known when Tuke (d.1545) was introduced at court but by 1509 he was clerk of the signet, in 1516 he was made a knight of the king's body, and in 1517 he became 'governor of the king's posts'. After some time as secretary to Cardinal Wolsey, in 1522 he was promoted to the post of French secretary to the king, and in 1528 he was made treasurer of the household; it was in this capacity that he came into contact with Holbein, whose salary it was his business to pay. There are six portraits of Tuke ascribed to Holbein, all variants of the original in the National Gallery of Art, Washington DC (Hand 1980; Rowlands 1985: 144–5).
5. Letter dated 20 March 1488 (Luzio and Renier 1893: 29).
6. Passerini had been raised and educated at the court of Lorenzo the Magnificent and became very close to Lorenzo's son Giovanni. As papal commissioner and envoy for Perugia and Umbria, Passerini amassed a considerable fortune. The true measure of the Medici reliance on Passerini is provided by his being made regent of Alessandro de' Medici as lord of Florence; on 17 May 1527, when the Medici were chased from Florence for the second time, it was Passerini who secured the safe escape of his young charges, Ippolito and Alessandro de' Medici.
7. The dating, which has been discussed by Ragghianti (1949), Freedberg (1963, 2: 136–9) and Shearman (1965, 2: 249–50), and more recently by Devoti (1987: 56–83) and Natali (1998: 171–3) hinges in particular on the scene of the *Transfiguration* embroidered on the hood. This is so evidently dependent upon Raphael's *Transfiguration* in the Vatican that the date of that painting must be taken as *terminus post quem* for the Passerini hood. Responsibility for the overall design of the Cortona fabric and embroideries has been attributed on stylistic grounds to Raffaellino del Garbo and to Andrea del Sarto, who presumably took over after the latter's death in 1524.
8. The use of a similar design pattern for the fabrics of bishops' vestments in different corners of the papacy's sphere of influence raises some questions concerning the overall commissioning process. These will form the subject of a forthcoming article by the author.
9. Archivio di Stato di Firenze (henceforth ASF), Venturi Ginori Lisci (henceforth VGL) 469, f. 100 v : '[28 May 1523] una pianeta di raxo roxo con andj doro che a pier fran.co/ braccia 5 di raxo roxo per unaltra pianeta'.
10. ASF, VGL 475, f. 145.
11. Archivio Ginori, MSS 217, f. 44 v.
12. ASF, VGL 470, f. 5 v.
13. '... two hangings of cloth of tissue for the higher Aulter; Item, the best red of purple velvet for Priest, Decon and Subdecon, lacking a stole, ... Item, ii best white hangings for the high aulter called bodkin; ... Item, one canapye for the sepulchre of red silke braunched with golde; ... Item, ii other copes of purple velvet with braunches having the pellicanes of golde; Three corporas cases, viz., ii of clothe of golde ...' (Fowler 1893: 114).
14. Giovanni Cavalcanti, the son of Lorenzo di Filippo Cavalcanti and Contessina di Ugo Peruzzi, was related through his father's family to the collateral branch of the Medici family as well as to the Albizzi, while his matrilineage provided close links to the Peruzzi historical web of business connections with the Bardi and the Frescobaldi (Sicca 2006).
15. On 1 March 1508 Giovanni Cavalcanti and Pierfrancesco de' Bardi, had received from Migiotto and Rinaldo de' Bardi £1,150 to deposit and invest in London, with the freedom to trade in all kinds of goods they deemed profitable. This *accomandita*, in which the two young men acted as the travelling partners, was due to last only until 13 January 1509 (ASF, Mercanzia 10831, *Accomandite 1435–1531*, f. 136 v). Subsequently, on 9 June 1509, Migiotto de' Bardi in partnership with Cavalcanti obtained a royal licence to trade in Cotswold wools for five years (Brewer 1864, Ii, n. 34: 1509, henceforth referred to as *LP*). On 6 September 1512 Cavalcanti signed an indenture 'for the delivery to the King's use by Lady Day next of complete harnesses for 4,000 footmen (backs, breasts, saletts, gorjettes and pairs of splynts)' (*LP*, Iii: 1553). By 13 October 1512 he was granted 'safeconduct and protection to trade in England for ten years' (*LP*, Ii, n. 16: 668); up until this date his name had appeared in the king's *Book of Payments* only in relation to financial services provided either in London or in the Flanders (*LP*, IIii: 1448, 1449, 1451, 1452, 1453, 1456, 1458). Throughout November and December 1512 the same document shows Cavalcanti acting as supplier of 'harnesses for the ordnance' (*LP*, IIiii: 1458), an activity further documented by the set of payments for the war where the goods mentioned range from 'guns great and small' to 'sulphur and saltpetre' shipped from Naples (*LP*, I: 575, 640, 651, 671; on the Ordnance Office see Davies 1963: 119–36 and Davies 1964). The accounts of Sir John Daunce, then treasurer of wars (Grummitt 1999), reveal that at this time Cavalcanti was working in partnership with two exchange bankers from Lucca, Antonio Cavallari and Antonio Buonvisi; the choice of partners for this particular company was predicated upon the Buonvisi's established presence on the Antwerp and Hanseatic markets (Boyer-Xambeau *et al*. 1994), as well as on Antonio Cavallari's partnership with Buonvisi and Girolamo and Leonardo Frescobaldi in the salpetre and alum trade (*LP*, Iii: 1503). To secure the assistance of a banking house in Antwerp, such as the Buonvisi's, was of crucial importance when all the traffic of new military equipment passed from that port; significant in this respect is a letter, dated Antwerp 22 September 1512, sent to the king by Young, Boleyn and Wingfield concerning the swift delivery to England of 13 great guns which Cavalcanti had had cast in Germany (*LP*, I: 640).
16. *LP*, IIii: 1469, the sum paid was £316 5s.
17. *LP*, Ii: 758, grant dated 20 February 1513. This company existed alongside other *accomandite* and partnerships in which either Cavalcanti or Bardi continued to take part; this explains why, in a letter from Mechlin of 2 May 1514 to the king in London, Sir Richard Wingfield could refer to Cavalcanti as 'Philip Gualterotti's factor in London' (*LP*, Iii: 1249), and why similarly, on 27 February

17. ...1513, Pierfrancesco would be granted 'protection and defence to trade with England for 10 years' in partnership with Pietro Corsi and Francesco de' Bardi (*LP*, Ii: 758).
18. Prior to 1519, payments for £495 were registered to Cavalcanti for tapestries delivered to Lord Berners for the use of the queen of France, including 'seven pieces of the story of Arcules', bought in the Flanders by Philip Calthorpe (24 September 1514, *LP*, Iii: 1517), and in September and December 1516 for diamonds and pearls (respectively for two diamonds and 21 pearls worth £270, and for an unspecified amount of gems worth £596; *LP*, IIii: 1472 and 1473).
19. 'John Cavalcanti, merchant of Florence, gentleman-usher of the Chamber. Licence to import cloths of gold, silver and damask, gold cloths of tynsyn saten with gold, and all other cloths wrought with gold. The King to have the first choice. A copy of this licence, signed by the Duke of Norfolk, treasurer, to be a sufficient warrant'; *LP*, IIIii: 941.
20. Morsolin 1873: 25–6. The Hungarian fashion of the king's clothes had been the topic of an earlier letter (12 November 1511) written from London by Lorenzo Pasqualigo to his brother Francesco in Venice. He reported the recent issue of a proclamation forbidding under penalty any native, save lords and knights, to wear silk, their apparel likewise to be restricted, no doublets of any other material than camlet to be worn. To set a good example to the others, the king and the whole House of Lords had dressed themselves in long grey cloth gowns in the Hungarian fashion. Pasqualigo added that this law was very damaging to the Genoese and the Tuscans, who had gone to London with cloths of silk; should it remain in force, he noted, they would assuredly be unable to remain (*Calendar of State Papers and Manuscripts...* 1871: 54).
21. *Ibid*.
22. Sir Thomas Knyvet (d.1512), eldest son of Edmund Knyvet of Buckenham in Norfolk, was knighted in 1509 and held the office of master of the horse from 1509 to 1510. In 1512 Knyvet was captain of the *Regent*, the largest ship in the royal navy which was sunk off Brest. He married the daughter of Thomas Howard, Second Duke of Norfolk, and widow of John Grey, Second Viscount Lisle.
23. Guildford (1489–1532) was the nephew of Sir Nicholas Vaux. Knighted in 1512, the year also of his marriage to Margaret Bryan, in 1513 he was appointed the king's standard bearer. From 1515 to 1522 he held the office of master of the horse, and in 1525 is recorded to have been one of the officers called 'chamberlains of the receipt of the exchequer'. By 1528 he was controller of the royal household and remained in favour until 1531, when it became increasingly difficult for him to disguise his views on the matter of the royal divorce.
24. In total 27 registers survive in the Florence State Archive and three in the Ginori Archive. They include one *quadernaccio* (the wastebook, or book of primary entry in double-entry bookkeeping), one *quadernuccio di cassa* and several *quaderni di cassa* (all cash books), several *giornali* (account books to which entries are posted from the wastebook to the ledgers), two *libri mastri* (ledgers), several *libri di ricordanze* (memorandum books in which business matters of all kinds were entered roughly), four *copia lettere* (letter books), and one *giornale di drappi* (the register of textiles sold by the company, which does not, however, contain cloth samples). In one of the two ledgers (ASF, VGL 472), the debits and credits are split and placed on separate facing pages instead of horizontally; in 15th-century Florentine bookkeeping, this style was called *alla Veneziana*. This articulated account, which recorded payments for textiles, yarns of silk, gold and silver, cotton and wool, as well as for fashionable accessories such as silk gloves, jewels, belts or stockings, was provided with an index at the front listing the names of all debtors and creditors.
25. 'Messer Arrigo Guldfort' (ASF, VGL 472 f. 14).
26. 'Arrigo Wyat, cavaliere inglese e tesoriere della Camera del re d'Inghilterra' (ASF, VGL 472, f. 248); his portrait by Holbein is in the Louvre, Paris (1347) while copies are in the National Gallery, Dublin (370) and in the Spiridon Collection (Rowlands 1985: 134).
27. 'Guglielmo Blont, signore di ...' (ASF, VGL 472 , f. 14). Lieutenant of the castle of Hammes, in Picardy, and of the marches of Calais since 1509, Mountjoy (d. 1534) became chamberlain to Queen Catherine in 1512. In 1523 he was made master of the Mint. Mountjoy, who had studied in Paris under Erasmus, was responsible for the scholar's first visit to England in 1498 and maintained with him a continuous relationship and correspondence.
28. 'Giorgio Talbot, conte di Sherisbery e Stuardo del re d'Inghilterra' (ASF, VGL 472, f. 14).
29. 'Thomas Fetiplas, cavaliere inglese' (ASF, VGL 472, f. 14); Sir Thomas Fettiplace (1458–1523), of Lancastrian descent, married first Elizabeth Norris and subsequently Elizabeth Carew.
30. 'Messer Gianni Dans, cavaliere inglese' (ASF, VGL 472, f. 15). John Daunce (d.1545) was probably introduced to royal service by Sir Thomas Lovell, Henry VII's first treasurer of the chamber. In 1505 he was made one of the four tellers of the receipt. In the reign of Henry VIII he became treasurer at war during the 1513 campaign, when he was knighted. He progressed to receiver-general of wards (1509–40), one of the principal surveyors of land (1514–15; 1517–42); chief butler of England (1515–17), and finally, in 1542, he became the head of the new court of general surveyors. His son William married Elizabeth More.
31. 'Guglielmo Caro, gentiluomo inglese' (ASF, VGL 472, f. 15). William Cary (d.1528), gentleman of the privy chamber, had married Mary Boleyn in 1520. His portrait by an unknown artist is in a private collection.
32. 'Carlo Brandon, duca di Soffolk' (ASF, VGL 472, f. 16). In the early years of Henry VIII's reign Charles Brandon (c.1484–1545) shared the king's favour with a small circle of his friends: Edward Howard, Thomas Knyvet, and Edward and Henry Guildford. In 1511 he was appointed marshal of the household, and in October 1512 he became master of the horse. His creation dates to 1514 and was a reward for his role in the English victory over the French at the battle of the Spurs. In 1515 he married Mary Tudor, the widow of Louis XII and Henry's sister. A portrait of Brandon by a follower of Holbein is in the National Portrait Gallery, London (NPG 516) (Strong 1969, 2: 305–6).
33. 'Walter de Vereux, signore di Feris' (ASF, VGL 472, f. 16) succeeded his father in 1501. In 1525 he was appointed steward of the household of Mary, Princess of Wales, and in 1526 chamberlain of South Wales. Edward VI created him First Viscount Hereford in February 1550.
34. 'Messer Risap Thomas, cavaliere di Uallia' (ASF, VGL 472, f. 17); Sir Rhys (d.1525) served as chamberlain and chief justice of the principality of South Wales (Griffiths 1993).
35. 'Messer Guglielmo Figuglielmo, cavaliere inglese' (ASF, VGL 472, f. 17); his portrait in the Fitzwilliam Museum, Cambridge (inv. 164), is attributed to Holbein but rejected by Rowlands (1985: 235).
36. ASF, VGL 471, f. viii r: 'Il ducha di bochingam'. Edward Stafford, Third Duke of Buckingham, played a conspicuous part in court festivities such as royal weddings and the reception of ambassadors and foreign princes, dazzling observers by his sartorial splendour. At the wedding of Prince Arthur and Katherine of Aragon in 1501 he wore a gown said to be worth £1500 (Harris 1986).
37. 'Carlo Somestry, conte di Worcester e Gran Ciambellano d'Inghilterra' (ASF, VGL 472, f. 490), created earl of Worcester in 1514; no authentic painted portrait is known (Strong 1969, 2: 336–7).
38. 'Carlo Kenevet, gentiluomo inglese' (ASF, VGL 472, f. 18).
39. 'Guglielmo Conton, cavaliere inglese' (ASF, VGL 472, ff. 279, 334). Compton's ascent dates from shortly after the funeral of Henry VII when he was a groom of the king's chamber; in 1510 he was first described as a groom of the stool, a title he held until 1526 (Bernard 1981).
40. 'Brian Tuke, maestro delle poste del re d'Inghilterra' (ASF, VGL 472, ff. 19, 543).
41. 'Thomaso, cardinale di York' (ASF, VGL 472, f. 121).
42. 'Catarina Alwin, donna di Guglielmo Alwin, uno degli auditori del re d'Inghilterra' (ASF, VGL 472, f. 21).
43. 'Nicholas Vas [Vaux], cavaliere inglese' (ASF, VGL 472, f. 17),

was knighted in June 1487 after Henry VII's victory at Stoke, near Newark. In 1502 he became lieutenant of Guisnes, an office he held until after 1520 when he was in fact busy organising the meeting at the Field of Cloth of Gold where, together with Sir William Parr, he represented the knighthood of Northamptonshire.

44. 'Ricciardo Lister, sollecitatore del re' (ASF, VGL 472, f. 371). Sir Richard Lyster came to public prominence in 1521 when he was appointed solicitor-general, from which position he was promoted to attorney-general on 4 September 1525.
45. 'Ricciardo Shadwell, servitore di monsignor il ciamberlano' (ASF, VGL 472, f. 12).
46. 'Camillo Sabinello, falconiere del duca di Soffolk' (ASF, VGL 472, f. 131).
47. 'Gianni Gostuyke, gentiluomo del cardinale di York' (ASF, VGL 472, f. 19); in 1523, together with John and Thomas Russell, John Gostewyk was appointed supervisor of the lands of the bishopric of Worcester (*LP*, IIIii: 1193); he was also treasurer of first fruits and tenths.
48. 'Gianni Drapper, homo di messer Guglielmo Compton' (ASF, VGL 472, f. 279).
49. *Teletta* was translated into English as tissue, although during the 15th and 16th centuries this word referred to rather different textiles.
50. ASF, VGL 477, f. 133.
51. On 25 July 1540 Carsidoni – described as a native of Florence – was granted the prebend of Netherbury in Salisbury Cathedral. Cf. *LP*, XV: 479.
52. I am grateful to Lisa Monnas for her assistance in finding the English equivalent of the word *tinselo*; she believes that tinsel may be 'silk woven (plain or figured) with a flat silver or silver-gilt thread' and points to only one extant example from the 16th century excavated in the 1980s from Hunsden House, Hertfordshire (pers. comm., 21 November 2006).
53. ASF, Manoscritti 545, *passim* and more specifically f. 1131 for Giovanni di Lorenzo di Filippo's own enrolment ('Ioannes Laurentij Filippi de Caualcantibus Bene. Francisci Rainaldi 7 feb 1519').
54. ASF, Libri di commercio 33, *passim* and ASF, Arte della Seta 11, *passim* (De Roover 1999: 97).
55. Francesco di Leonardo Mannelli enrolled in the banker's guild in 1483 (ASF, Manoscritti 545, f. 1110: 'Franciscus Leonardi Nicholai de Mannellij 12 abrij 1483'). At the beginning of the 16th century, wool manufacturers and merchant bankers started to invest massively in the silk industry (Goldthwaite 1968: 86–7; Dini 1995: 195–7).
56. The ledgers document trade with Francesco Mannelli's old firm, with the Lyon firm of Giovanni Mannelli as well as with the latter's company in Florence ('Giovanni Mannelli e compagni di Firenze', respectively ASF, VGL 472, ff. 30 and 34). 'Mainardo Cavalcanti e compagni di Firenze' also appears in the principal ledger of the London company, without however the specification of their being *battilori* (ASF, VGL 472, f. 29); this information is provided instead by his company's account books in Florence (ASF, Libri di Commercio di Famiglia 33, *Quaderno di Mandate di Drappi, Mainardo Cavalcanti Battiloro, 1510–1514*; Libri di Commercio e di Famiglia 34, Maestri d'ori, *Mainardo di Bartolomeo Cavalcanti Battilori, 1531–1534*).
57. A list of still unsold fabrics, addressed to Pierfrancesco de' Bardi then in Florence, indicates precisely the different manufacturers and is explicative of the way the operation was run (ASF, VGL 471, *Ricordanze N. 229*, f. vi).
58. In 1526 the debtors of Bartolomeo Carnesecchi included Lord Mountjoy, the earl of Shrewsbury and the mercer Raph Warren who was twice appointed mayor of the city of London (1536–37 and 1543–44); ASF, VGL 470, f. 5v.
59. A receipt of 1522 records the arrival in London of 7 *pezze* of gold *teletta* provided by Bartolomeo Carnesecchi; all except one were black and with varying patterns: *con opera a mandorle, con opera a ochi d'uccellini, con opera a mandorline, con opera a stuoia, con opera a ruote* and *con opera piana* (ASF, VGL 468, f. 204r). The *pezza* was the regulation length of woollen cloth in Florence, and therefore the measurement found in cloth transactions on the wholesale market. The variety of colours offered by Carnesecchi is shown, for instance, by a 1526 inventory of items jointly owned (ASF, VGL 469, f. 490 verso).
60. ASF, VGL 469, f. 489.
61. Examples are provided by the velvet account of Charles Somerset, First Earl of Worcester (ASF, VGL 472, f. 496 [left]), and by the Wardrobe account of December 1524 (ASF, VGL 477, f. 98v).
62. A sample entry is contained in the *quadernaccio* (ASF, VGL 477, f. 1v) under the date of 3 November 1522, documenting acquisitions by the mercer 'Giannj Guggie'.
63. ASF, VGL 477, f. 34 v.
64. His position is identified in ASF, VGL 472, f. 71v, f. 375r, f. 399 r.
65. ASF, VGL 477, f. 35 v.
66. ASF, VGL 477, f. 36 v.
67. ASF, VGL 477, f. 37 .
68. ASF, VGL 477, f. 98.
69. ASF, VGL 477, f. 98 v.
70. ASF, VGL 477, f. 99 v.
71. ASF, VGL 477, f. 100.
72. ASF, VGL 477, f. 162 v.
73. ASF, VGL 477, f. 163v.
74. ASF, VGL 471, f. v.
75. When the accounts mention the Wardrobe they presumably refer to the king's and queen's wardrobe of the robes. All the greater houses were provided with this as well as with the king's and queen's jewel-houses, the wardrobe of the beds and a standing wardrobe (Thurley 1993: 74–5).
76. ASF, VGL 477, f. 173 v.
77. ASF, VGL 469, f. 486 r.
78. ASF, VGL 477, f. 174, 'To the above named master Compton, because he favoured us in the sale of these cloths as well as in that of a teletta belonging to Giovanni Cavalcanti, we have promised to wave the price of a casket of wine he received from us some time ago'; ASF, VGL 472, f. 297 [left].
79. ASF, VGL 471, f. v: '... to a pot of olive oil given to master Amsor from Wales who measured the fabrics £- 1.- / to a length of cloth of gold promised to Lady Anne Rocheford who helped us in selling those fabrics'.
80. See for instance ASF, VGL 463, f. 20 recording the accounts with John Malte, the king's tailor, and with John Parker, *ibid.*, f. 22 r: 'To Mylady Anne on our account £8.7.6 which is the cost of 6 ¼ braccia of plain cloth of gold with silk tane pattern given to her on New Year's day so that the King's majesty may be made to assist in the matter of the Cardinal's debts and all the other business recently occurred to Bernardo.'
81. 'Tomaso Atkinson, abardassiere inglese' (Thomas Atkynson, habardasher, VGL 469, ff. 24r, 25r; VGL 472, ff. 11, 377), 'Ricciardo Giustis, guardarobiere della Regina d'Inghilterra' (Richard Justis, VGL 472, ff. 71, 399, 564), 'Ricciardo Gressam, merciere inglese' (Richard Gresham, agent for the crown with the trading interest, or, as it was called, king's merchant, an office of the highest importance and trust inasmuch as it united the duty of raising money for royal occasions by private loans with that of protecting and cherishing the sources from which they were derived. He was knighted and became mayor of London in 1537, and died in 1548. VGL 472, f. 170; Nicolas 1827: 116, 261), 'Guglielmo Lok, merciere di Londra' (William Lock, merchant, VGL 472, f. 348, Nicolas 1827: 14, 45, 74, 78, 87, 128, 144, 163, 261, 276), 'Gianny Malt, sarto del re d'Inghilterra' (John Malte, taylor, VGL 472, f. 118; Nicolas 1827: 222, 223), 'Ricciardo Robinson, broderiere di Londra' (Richard Robinson, embroiderer, VGL 469, ff. 24r, 25r; VGL 472, f. 264).
82. ASF, VGL 468, *passim*; ASF, VGL 472, *passim*; ASF, VGL 477, *passim*.
83. Cf. *LP*, Vii: 328, he received in return a 'gilt cup with cover 26oz.'; on this same occasion Carsidoni, who used to attend on the king and extol the qualities of the wares to him, offered 'treacle and a cheese of Parmasan', obtaining in return a 'gilt salt with a cover, 14½ oz.'. Parmesan cheeses were provided by the Venetian merchant Gerolamo Molini (cf. ASF, VGL 471, f. 73 v, 1530). In 1534 Cavalcanti gave the king 'a brooch of gold and a cameo' (Hayward

2005: 173) and received in return 'two gilt cruses with covers, 23 oz.' (*ibid.*, p. 160), his name does not appear in the 1539 gift roll. In 1534 Carsidoni presented the king with a diamond ring and was rewarded with a 'gilt cruse with a cover 14½ oz.' (*ibid.*, pp. 161, 173); in 1539 he offered a 'broche of gold' and was given by the king 'a gilte cruse with a couer Cornelis 13¾ oz' (*ibid.*, pp. 150, 161).

84. The collection was given to the University of Oxford in 1683 by Elias Ashmole but derived largely from the museum of the Tradescants, father and son, at Lambeth (MacGregor 1983: 226–7; 1989: 406–7; Glanville 1991; Hayward 1996: 38; Monnas 1998: 73–4).
85. ASF, VGL 469, f. 95 v (1522); *ibid.*, f. 192 v contains a damaged and almost erased order dated 3 April 1526 for 'cappelli da falcone per il re'; ASF, VGL 477, f. 51 (April 1523).
86. ASF, VGL 475, f. 189: '1527 to Giovanni Cavalcanti in Florence, written until the last day of May ... As to the rich doublet we left it at court in the wardrobe for quite a long time, in the hope that there would be an opportunity to make the king buy it; but this has not happened yet and we have been unable to do better. You have a great fancy in commissioning these doublets and these new design patterns, and think that these people here would believe it took more than ten lengths of cloth. But you are mistaken, they do not value it more and the first thing they do is to estimate the actual amount of cloth of gold employed, the amount of pattern which has been discarded and the fact that the doublet comes ready-made increases its cost. Furthermore, in case you are not aware, a king is never happy to wear fabrics woven with his badges and devices as you have done in several instances. Anyway, we shall do our best with anything of yours which is left and you will be kept informed.'
87. The desire to experiment and put on the market new products is shown also by an earlier letter dated 15 December 1526; this time Pierfrancesco was taken aback by the shape and decoration of beer tankards of Montelupo slipware which had recently reached him in London, and which he was convinced would not gain the approval of the market on account of their shape (ASF, VGL, f. 88 v: '15 December 1526 to our senior partner Giovanni Cavalcanti in Florence. Francesco Lapo Ducati has sent us by your order three cases of beer tankards manufactured in Montelupo. We received them a few days ago and found that about half the shipment was intact, the remainder was damaged. Please instruct us as to what should be done. We believe we can make no big profit since most are of a weird shape that narrows from the middle down and has some holes, this leads us to believe it will not please').
88. 'An English-mans suit is like a traitors bodie that hath been hanged, drawne, and quartered, and set up in severall places: the collar of his doublet and the belly in France; the wing and narrow sleeve in Italy; the shorte waist hangs over a Dutch botchers stall in Utricht; his huge sloppes speakes Spanish; Polonia gives him his bootes; the blocke for his head alters faster than the feltmaker can fit him' (Dekker 1606; Jones and Stallybrass 2000; Ginzburg 2000).

References

Ames-Lewis, F. (1979) 'Early Medicean devices', *Journal of the Warburg and Courtauld Institutes* XLII: 122–43.
Anglo, S. (1997) *Spectacle, Pageantry, and Early Tudor Policy*. Oxford: Clarendon Press.
Anon. (1868) *L'Arte della seta in Firenze. Trattato del XV secolo*, G. Gargiolli (ed.). Florence: G. Barbèra.
Ashelford, J. (1983) *A Visual History of Costume: The Sixteenth Century*. London: Batsford.
Baldwin, F.E. (1926) *Sumptuary Legislation and Personal Regulation in England*. Baltimore.
Bernard, G.W. (1981) 'The rise of Sir William Compton, early Tudor courtier', *English Historical Review* XCVI: 754–77.
Boyer-Xambeau, M.-T., Deleplace, G. and Gillard, L. (1994) *Private Money and Public Currencies: The 16th Century Challenge*. Armonk, NY and London: M.E. Sharpe.
Brewer, J.S. (1864) *Letters and Papers, Foreign and Domestic of the Reign of Henry VII*. London: Longman, Green, Longman & Roberts.
Buss, C., Molinelli, M. and Butazzi, G. (1983) *Tessuti Serici Italiani 1450–1530*. Exhibition catalogue, Milan Castello Sforzesco, 9 March–15 May 1983. Milan: Electa.
Calendar of State Papers 1871. *Calendar of State Papers and Manuscripts Relating to English Affairs, Existing in the Archives and Collections of Venice, and in other Libraries of Northern Italy. Volume I, 1509–1519*, R.D. Brown (ed.). London: Longman, Green, Longman, Roberts and Green.
Castiglione, B. (1987) *Il Libro del Cortigiano*, a cura di G. Carnazzi, introduzione di S. Battaglia. Milan: Rizzoli.
Davies, C.S.L. (1963) *Supply Services of English Armed Forces, 1509–1550*. D.Phil dissertation, University of Oxford.
Davies, C.S.L. (1964) 'Provisions for armies, 1509–1550: a study in the effectiveness of early Tudor government', *Economic History Review* n.s. XVII(2): 234–48.
Dekker, T. (1606) *The Seven Deadly Sinnes of London*. London: Printed by E.A. for Nathaniel Butter.
De Roover, F.E. (1999) *L'Arte della seta a Firenze nei secoli XIV e XV*. Florence: Leo S. Olschki Editore.
Devoti, D. 1987. *Parato Passerini*, in *Arte aurea aretina. Tesori dalle Chiese di Cortona* a cura di M. Collareta e D. Devoti, exhibition catalogue. Florence: SPES.
Dini, B. (1995) *Saggi su un'economia-mondo. Firenze e l'Italia fra Mediterraneo ed Europa (secc. XIII–XVI)*. Pisa: Pacini.
Dini, B. (2000) 'I battilori fiorentini nel Quattrocento', in *Medioevo Mezzogiorno Mediterraneo. Studi in onore di Mario del Treppo*, G. Rossetti and G. Vitolo (eds), vol. 2, 139–62. Naples: Liguori.
Fowler, T. (1893) *The History of Corpus Christi College with Lists of its Members* (tr.) Oxford: Oxford Historical Society.
Freedberg, S.J. (1963) *Andrea del Sarto*, 2 vols. Cambridge, MA: Belknapp Press of Harvard University Press.
Ginzburg, C. (2000) 'Selfhood as otherness: constructing English identity in the Elizabethan age', *Historein: A Review of the Past and Other Stories* II: 31–46.
Giustiniani, S. (1854) *Four Years at the Court of Henry VIII: Selection of Despatches Written by the Venetian Ambassador, Sebastian Giustinian, and Addressed to the Signory of Venice*, R. Brown (trans.), 2 vols. London: Smith Elder.
Glanville, P. (1991) 'Plate and gift-giving at court', in *Henry VIII: A European Court in England*, D. Starkey (ed.), 164–7. London: Collins and Brown.
Goldthwaite, R. (1968) *Private Wealth in Renaissance Florence: A Study of Four Families*. Princeton, NJ: Princeton University Press.
Griffiths, R.A. (1993) *Sir Rhys ap Thomas and his Family: A Study in the Wars of the Roses and Early Tudor Politics*. Cardiff: University of Wales Press.
Grummitt, D. (1999) 'Henry VII, chamber finance and the 'New Monarchy': some new evidence', *Historical Research* LXXII, n.s. 179: 229–43.
Gunn, S.J. (1988) *Charles Brandon, Duke of Suffolk c. 1484–1545*. Oxford: Blackwell.
Gunn, S.J. (1993) 'The courtiers of Henry VII', *English Historical Review* CVIII: 23–49.
Hall, E. (1809) *The Union of the Two Noble and Illustre Families of Lancastre and Yorke*. London: Printed for J. Johnson.
Hand, J.O. (1980) 'The *Portrait of Sir Brian Tuke* by Hans Holbein the Younger', in *Studies in the History of Art*, vol. 9, 33–49. Washington, DC: National Gallery of Art.
Harris, B.J. (1986) *Edward Stafford, Third Duke of Buckingham, 1478–1521*. Stanford, CA: Stanford University Press.
Harte, N.B. (1976) 'State control of dress and social change in pre-industrial England', in *Trade, Government and Economy in Pre-*

Industrial England, D. Coleman and A.H. John (eds), 132–65. London: Weidenfeld and Nicolson.

Harte, N.B. (1993) 'Silk and sumptuary legislation in England', in *La Seta in Europa Sec. XIII–XX*, S. Cavaciocchi (ed.), 801. Florence: Le Monnier.

Hayward, M. (1996) 'Luxury or magnificence? Dress at the court of Henry VIII', *Costume* XXX: 37–46.

Hayward, M. (2004) 'Fashion, finance, foreign politics and the wardrobe of Henry VIII', in *Clothing Culture, 1350–1650*, C. Richardson (ed.), 174–5. Aldershot and Burlington, VT: Ashgate.

Hayward, M. (2005) 'Gift giving at the court of Henry VIII: the 1539 New Year's Gift Roll in context', *Antiquaries Journal* 85: 125–75.

Hooper, W. (1915) 'The Tudor sumptuary laws', *English Historical Review* XXX: 443–9.

Jones, A.R. and Stallybrass, P. (2000) *Renaissance Clothing and the Materials of Memory*. Cambridge: Cambridge University Press.

Leclerq, J.-P. (2001) *Jouer la lumière*, catalogue of an exhibition at the Musèe de la Mode et du Textile 2001–2002. Paris: UCAD.

Luzio, A. and Renier, R. (1893) *Mantova e Urbino. Isabella d'Este ed Elisabetta Gonzaga nelle relazioni famigliari e nelle vicende politiche*. Turin/Rome: L. Roux.

MacGregor, A. (1983) *Tradescants' Rarities: Essays on the Foundation of the Ashmolean Museum 1683 with a Catalogue of the Surviving Early Collections*. Oxford: Clarendon Press.

MacGregor, A. (1989) *The Late King's Goods: Collections, Possessions and Patronage of Charles I in the Light of the Commonwealth Sale Inventories*. London and Oxford: A. McAlpine in association with Oxford University Press.

Monnas, L. (1998) 'Tissues in England during the fifteenth and sixteenth centuries', *Bulletin du CIETA* 75: 63–80.

Morelli, R. (1976) *La seta fiorentina del Cinquecento*. Milan: Giuffrè.

Morsolin, B. (1873) *Francesco Chiericati, vescovo e diplomatico nel secolo XVI*. Vicenza.

Natali, A. (1998) *Andrea del Sarto*. Milan: Leonardo arte.

Nichols, J.G. (1846) *Chronicle of Calais*. London: Camden Society.

Nicolas, N.H. (1827) *The Privy Purse Expences of King Henry VIII from November 1529 to December 1532*. London: W. Pickering.

Orsi Landini, R. (1993) 'Il Trionfo del velluto. La produzione italiana rinascimentale', in *VELLUTO. Fortune. Tecniche. Mode*, F. De Marinis (ed.), 19–28. Milan: Idea Books.

Orsi Landini, R. (1997) 'Alcune considerazioni sul significato simbolico dei velluti quattrocenteschi', *Jacquard* 33: 5.

Orsi Landini, R. (1999) 'The origin of modern production: the differences in velvet produced for clothing and for furnishing in the sixteenth and seventeenth centuries', in *Velluti e moda tra XVI e XVII secolo*, A. Zanni (ed.), 159. Catalogue of an exhibition at the Museo Poldi Pezzoli, Milan, 7 May–15 September 1999. Milan: Skira.

Ragghianti, L. (1949) 'Andrea del Sarto a Cortona', *Critica d'Arte* VIII(2): 113–24.

Richardson, G. (1999) '"Most highly to be regarded": the privy chamber of Henry VIII and Anglo-French relations, 1515–1520', *Court Historian* IV(2): 119–40.

Rosand, D. (1983) 'The portrait, the courtier and death', in *Castiglione: The Ideal and Real in Renaissance Culture*, R.W. Hanning and D. Rosand (eds), 91–129. New Haven and London: Yale University Press.

Rowlands, J. (1985) *The Paintings of Hans Holbein the Younger*. Oxford: Phaidon.

Schorta, R. (1991) '*Il Trattato dell'Arte della Seta*: a Florentine 15th-century treatise on silk manufacturing', *Bulletin du CIETA* 69: 57–83.

Shearman, J. (1965) *Andrea del Sarto*, 2 vols. Oxford: Phaidon.

Sicca, C.M. (2002) 'Consumption and trade of art between Italy and England in the first half of the sixteenth century: the London house of the Bardi and Cavalcanti company', *Renaissance Studies* XVI(2): 163–200.

Sicca, C.M. (2006) 'Pawns of international finance and politics: Florentine sculptors at the court of Henry VIII', *Renaissance Studies* XX(1): 1–34.

Starkey, D.R. (1973) *The King's Privy Chamber 1483–1547*. Unpublished PhD thesis, University of Cambridge.

Starkey, D.R. (1987) 'Intimacy and innovation: the rise of the privy chamber', in *The English Court from the Wars of the Roses to the Civil War*, D.R. Starkey (ed.), 71–118. London: Longman.

Strong, R. (1969) *Tudor and Jacobean Portraits*, 2 vols. London: HMSO.

Thurley, S. (1993) *The Royal Palaces of Tudor England: Architecture and Court Life 1460–1547*. New Haven and London: Yale University Press.

Tognetti, S. (2002) *Un'industria di lusso al servizio del grande commercio. Il mercato dei drappi serici e della seta nella Firenze del Quattrocento*. Florence: Leo S. Olschki Editore.

The author

Cinzia Maria Sicca currently holds the post of Associate Professor, European Art History, University of Pisa, Italy (since 1993). In June 2002 she was team leader of a two-year Getty Collaborative Research Grant on John Talman's Collection of Drawings as a History of Art from Antiquity to Christianity and from 2002 to 2003 she was Frese Senior Fellow, CASVA, National Gallery of Art, Washington DC. She has published widely on the work of William Kent and Lord Burlington. Her recent work has focused on the early modern period and she has written several articles on the Bardi and Cavalcanti and their close links with the court of Henry VIII.

Address

Cinzia Maria Sicca, Università di Pisa, Dipartimento di Storia delle Arti, Piazza San Matteo in Soarta 2, I-56127 Pisa, Italy (sicca@arte.unipi.it)

Costume at the court of Cosimo and Eleonora de Medici: on fashion and Florentine textile production

Bruna Niccoli

ABSTRACT This paper investigates the significance of dress in Florence, one of the oldest Italian states, from the marriage of Duke Cosimo I to Eleonora da Toledo in 1539 to the end of their marriage in 1562. Much of this research is original and is based on an analysis of literary sources and archives in Florence and Pisa. Fashion played a new role as a political symbol for Cosimo's idea of government and it became part of the court's display of pomp and power. Eleonora introduced a new taste and foreign influences on Florentine dress by imposing her official style of attire on the court and the ruling classes. The daily records of the *Guardaroba* document fabrics needed for the fashion and life at court and they provide a complete panorama of Florentine production, revealing types of fabric of which there was very little record until now. The parallel reading of Medici documents and of the private papers of Florentine aristocratic families allows a detailed reconstruction of the wardrobes of these courtiers.

Keywords: costume, sources, textile, production, Florence, Renaissance, Medici

Introduction

In the mid-16th century, Florence was under the rule of Duke Cosimo I (1519–1574), a descendant of the younger branch of the Medici who had just consolidated his political power in 1537. His marriage to Eleonora of Toledo (1522–1562), daughter of the Emperor Charles V's viceroy in Naples, contributed considerably to transforming Florence into a modern court (Niccoli 2005a; Baia 1907). Of course, the marriage festivities (1539), organised with theatrical magnificence throughout Tuscany including events at Pisa, Villa Poggio a Caiano and Florence, served to demonstrate to all – for the first time – the power of the duchy and Cosimo himself as political leader.

Between the lines of Cosimo's letters, it is evident that 'sumptuous decorations were prepared at the explicit request of the duke in the Medici palazzo in Pisa' (Niccoli 2005b: 47).[1] When Eleonora arrived in Pisa, she dressed in the Spanish style: black satin or violet cut velvet with rich gold brocades. The choice of black, for this young lady, was justified by the death of the Empress Isabella of Portugal. It was the duke and duchess's first public appearance as a couple. For her triumphal entry into Florence, the Spanish princess chose to appear before the people in an elegant crimson satin *toilette* with fine gold lamella embroidery. To underscore her noble standing: 'she was surrounded by Pages in livery, on horses adorned with ornate trappings in gold and silver' (Giambullari 1539: 4).

The marriage festivities carried on for many days, among banquets, plays and theatrical performances, as described in Giambullari's account. Private Medici documents reveal that many of the costumes were created for these celebrations by none other than Niccolò Tribolo. The occasion was made all the more memorable by the fantastic costumes, traditionally created in the finest fabrics by Italian artists since the early Renaissance (Kaufmann 1970). An unpublished drawing attributed to Tribolo (part of the collection at the Uffizi's Gabinetto Disegni e Stampe in Florence)[2] may represent a sketch of one of the stage costumes used in the *Mammalucchi*, which was a public play like a hunt with horses held in the square of Piazza Santa Croce (Fig. 1). The drawing depicts a fantastic costume following in the tradition of Florentine festival costumes for plays and masquerades, probably worn by a player dressed as a Turkish character such as the 'caftan of green taffeta' (*casache di taffeta verde alla turchesca*) and the 'caftan of white taffeta' (*casache di tafeta bianco alla turchesca*) as described in Cosimo's marriage documents.[3]

Many kinds of costumes are recorded in the Medici inventory of 1539. The most interesting typologies of masquerade costumes are 'antique', 'German', 'oriental', 'Moorish', ' Indian' and 'mammalucchi' or 'Turkish', all of which were made in costly silk fabrics such as velvet, satin or taffeta.[4] Agnolo Bronzino also worked on the team of artists and assistants directed by Tribolo and Aristotile da Sangallo for the wedding *apparato* – a pompous display of dynastic opulence – thereby beginning what was to become a lifelong relationship with the duke (Brock 2002).

The importance in Italian art history of the patronage of the Medici family and court is legendary, and Cosimo, the future first grand duke of Tuscany, brilliantly secured his own place in this history. During his reign many writers, humanists and artists, such as Baccio Bandinelli and Benvenuto Cellini, as well as numerous highly skilled artisans were to turn their art to the service of Medici propaganda. The artist chosen as court painter was Bronzino (1503–1572), who decorated Eleonora's private chapel at Palazzo Vecchio, which represents an extraordinary essay in the Mannerist style. Bronzino's portraits were to immortalise the ducal family, their personalities and their fine, elegant clothing as symbols of nobility and the power of the state.

The duchess's most famous suit – one of the most celebrated in the history of dress – was painted by Bronzino (Fig. 2).[5] It is a fine and personal interpretation of a Spanish silhouette made in lavish materials, an excellent testimony of Florentine silk production. The dress represents the pinnacle of Florentine style which developed under Eleonora. She is dressed in a rare cloth of gold, called *teletta* (tissue) which was highly fashionable and greatly prized (Boccherini 1993; Melis 1984). It was produced in Florence, the pride of the workshops, and it was greatly in demand for export, especially to France and England (Cobb 1995: 1–11; Morelli 1976: 79). In fact, in the 16th century, Henry VIII's court acquired large amounts of cloth of gold and cloth of silver directly from Florentine merchants (Sicca 2002).[6]

Eleonora's new style fashion

Skilled craftsmen in the ducal palace worked exclusively for the duchess to fashion brocaded silks with gold and silver threads, and cut velvets adorned in gold or silver and loops or bouclé wefts. Two very interesting female figures were recorded in the accounts: Madonna Francesca Donati, who lived in the palace and was the exclusive weaver of *teletta* for Eleonora, and Madonna Piera di Lorenzo who wove simpler silk cloths. Both women are examples of the highly specialised artisans to which the documents refer.[7] Only six examples of exclusive gowns in *teletta* are recorded in the Medici inventory in 1562, a key part of a noblewoman's wardrobe.[8]

Eleonora was a 'Duchess of Tuscany in history and legend' and the numerous letters of the Medici secretaries reveal her leading role and as 'a lover of power, who participated in the management of the State' (Niccoli 2005a: 18). Reading such documents, it is possible to recreate several threads of the fabric of history: the history of dress woven by the historical characters who wore it.

Eleonora personally supervised the clothing and the furnishings produced for the court. Private Medici documents from early 1540 make it possible to reconstruct Eleonora's wardrobe and those of all the ducal family (Orsi Landini and Niccoli 2005: 200–235). This is especially true of the *Giornali di entrata ed uscita* which began in 1544 and which records the clothes and other items made for Cosimo, the children, a number of courtiers and the different groups of liveried servants (Niccoli 2004a: 39–188).[9] Styles of dress were created for male and female court fashion, following the international canons. Although Eleonora modified Tuscan dress, the line of the female silhouette adopted in Florence during these years corresponds to that delineated by Spanish fashion. The duchess loved red and violet and she restricted the use of black to mourning (Fig. 3).

The correspondence of the Florentine court secretaries attests to the fact that Eleonora chose the embroidery designs for her partlets (the *gorgiera* or ruff) and she herself excelled in needlework. Female veil-makers worked in Florence to produce meshwork, needlework, smocks and hairnets exclusively for the duchess and her courtiers (Niccoli 2004a: 185–8).

Male Medici dress demonstrated a strong dependence on Spanish models, as opposed to the early years of the 16th century, when fashion was dictated by French tastes (Orsi Landini *et al.* 1993). Although some suits called *alla francese* (French style) were still listed in the inventory of apparel that Cosimo had compiled in 1553 (the *Guardaroba Medicea*, housed in the Florence State Archive), the French influence was certainly stronger during Duke Alessandro Medici's government in the 1530s or under the rule of Lorenzo the Magnificent (1449–1492) just before (Conti 1893).

For official occasions, Cosimo wore the 'French-style garment',[10] not in black which was the symbol of Spanish taste, but in the lordly crimson, grey (*bigio*) or brown (*tané*), which were his favourite colours[11] (Fig. 4). Only in Rome, faced by the pope, in 1560, did the Tuscan duke choose to dress in black: 'a long black velvet overgown with gold embroidery'.[12] His Excellency wore also a long over-gown, in the Hungarian style, called a *zimarra* as this was his wife's favourite style of over-gown.[13]

The *Guardaroba* document records the types of garments and the luxurious quality of the fabrics from which they were made, along with the hangings made of velvet, damask, gold or silver tabby, which Bronzino illustrated in several state portraits. The sumptuous materials used for male or female clothes were the same, as were the elaborate trimmings that were the Florentine answer to the rich gold and silver embroidery preferred by Spanish taste. The portrait of Eleonora in the Uffizi by Bronzino is well known and this image marks a crucial step in the development of Medici state portraits. The artist painted several portraits of the duchess and her sons as gifts to international figures or the main Tuscan towns (Langedijk 1981: 692–708).[14] For example, in *Eleonora of Toledo with her son Francesco* (Fig. 5) she wears a gown and an over-gown or *zimarra*, rich in pearls and decoration. The over-gown was left open in order to reveal the undergown.

Medici correspondence testifies that Eleonora herself provided explicit instructions regarding the clothes to be depicted by Agnolo. In another double portrait the duchess requested that Prince Francesco, the future grand duke, should wear official dress in red crimson silk with sable fur, the same as he wore at Genoa in 1548, when he was sent to greet Filippe II of Spain (Edelstein 2001: 245). Such a garment as the one depicted in the Uffizi portrait of Eleonora, in brocaded velvet, requires a considerable time to execute. Consequently, the painter was allowed to substitute the brocade with a fine decorated silk when another version of the portrait was painted.

Fashion and court life in the middle of the 16th century

In 1546, at the time of this emblematic Bronzino portrait, Cosimo issued the first decree of his government, specifically

COSTUME AT THE COURT OF COSIMO AND ELEONORA DE' MEDICI

Figure 1 A sketch of one of the stage costumes used in the *Mammalucchi*, Niccolò Tribolo, Gabinetto Disegni e Stampe, Uffizi Gallery, Florence (Plate 49 in the colour plate section).

Figure 2 Agnolo Bronzino, *Eleonora of Toledo with her son Giovanni*, c.1545, Uffizi Gallery, Florence (Plate 50 in the colour plate section).

Figure 3 Agnolo Bronzino workshop/Florentine school, *Eleonora of Toledo*, second half of the 16th century, private gallery, Rome (Plate 51 in the colour plate section).

Figure 4 *Cosimo de'Medici together with his Court Artists*, Palazzo Vecchio, Florence (Plate 52 in the colour plate section).

Figure 5 Agnolo Bronzino, *Eleanora of Toledo with her son Francesco*, 1549, Museo Nazionale di Palazzo Reale, Pisa (Plate 53 in the colour plate section).

aimed at preventing excesses in male and female dress. The legislation outlawed rich fabrics, such as cut or uncut velvets and brocaded cloths, as well as the use of pearls and gems or gold and silver embroidery to all Florentines. Only the nobility were exempt from these sumptuary restrictions; they were allowed to wear the very exclusive coloured silks produced by local manufacturers (Carnesecchi 1902). All members of the city's aristocracy took part in organising a new and graceful court life. In the mid-16th century, luxurious silk fabrics provided one of the most significant elements of the grandeur of the Florentine elite.

Public ceremonies were the main occasions for the prince and the elite to flaunt their clothes as indicators of their social status. At the baptism of Francesco I (1541–1587) in 1541, Stradano illustrates the simple lines of the women's dresses at this event, indicating the Florentine taste for soft shapes and vertical line (Niccoli 2005b: 53). In 1550 the baptism of Cosimo's son Garcia (1547–1562) was an excellent opportunity for the duke and the nobility to display themselves in all their grandeur to the people. Thus, in the traditional procession through the city streets from the Baptistery to the Medici Palace, Eleonora was radiant in silver *teletta* and her new silhouette, called 'Spanish' by the contemporaries. Undoubtedly, courtiers were eager to adapt to the tastes of their radiant sovereigns.

In fact, by that time all of Florence's aristocracy had been influenced, as documented in private papers, by international fashion. It is possible to speak of a 'diffused court' in referring to this uniformity of dress for the Italian states under Spanish hegemony (Butazzi 1995: 80–94). Over 100 aristocrats representing the state were there to welcome the little Medici boy: noblemen, each richly dressed 'in a new jerkin (sayo) and noblewomen in splendid silk and velvet fabrics, decorated with pearls and gems', as recounted in a contemporary source printed to commemorate the event (Cortesi da Prato 1893: 12).

The memory of Felipe of Spain's recent journey to Italy in 1548–49 was still very much alive in the minds of the Italians. During his stopovers in Italian cities, Don Felipe displayed the status of Habsburg power 'with great pomp'. The prince became the model for courtly male dress in the Italian city states under Spanish hegemony (Bernis 1990) (Fig. 6). The influence of Felipe's style and wardrobe throughout Europe, including England, has been widely discussed in the history of dress (Niccoli 2004b).

Bronzino portrayed the greatest names in the Tuscan aristocracy, such as the Panciatichi couple, who were very important figures in the court entourage or Lodovico Capponi (about 1550–55)[15] (Fig. 7). This young nobleman was a member of one of the oldest aristocratic families in the Tuscan capital. A historical account reports that the progenitor of the Capponi family, an excellent silk weaver, seemingly came to Florence from the nearby city of Lucca during the 14th century. During the late Middle Ages the family, whose wealth was founded on silk manufacture, belonged to the high social caste of merchants. The origins of the Capponi are therefore in part fact, in part legend: at the time Lucca was indeed the undisputed Italian capital of fine silk.

Beginning in the late 15th century, the Capponi often played influential roles in city politics under the Medici. During the Renaissance the name Capponi was associated with the history of art and a number of episodes of significant patronage in Florence. The family's eminent status is clearly documented by the great masters of Mannerism.

Lodovico the Younger, so-called to distinguish him from his father, was born in 1533. He was the last son of a very shrewd and rich textile merchant belonging to a branch of the Capponi family. His father died when he was only one year old, leaving him heir to a considerable fortune. The inventory of Lodovico the Elder's shop or *bottega* shows the basis of his renowned trade: velvets, satins and taffetas, all exceptionally rich examples of the finest quality cloths and colours produced by the local industry.[16] The Capponi, like other influential Florentine families, sold their wares in several foreign markets, including many important cities throughout Europe, most notably Lyon.[17] He was patron of the celebrated chapel in the church of Santa Felicita, whose frescoes were painted by Pontormo.[18]

But who exactly was Lodovico the Younger seen in the painting (dated about 1550–55) when he was probably 17 or 20 years old? In and of itself, his elegant, fashionable clothing has the power to tell us much. The sophisticated style of his fashionable suit lives up to his father's reputation, as does the combination of black taffetas, black velvet and white satin: a true display of fine fabric. A poem, in the chivalrous epic genre, entitled *La Capponiera*, written by the humanist Iustino Politano Muzio at the request of Lodovico, describes his life from youth to maturity and extols the values of its protagonist.[19]

Muzio's manuscript (part of the collection at the Riccardiana Library in the Medici Riccardi Palace) reveals the traditional education of aristocratic men, which was divided between

Figure 6 Titian, *Felipe II*, 1550, Palatina Gallery, Florence (Plate 54 in the colour plate section).

Figure 7 Agnolo Bronzino, *Lodovico Capponi*, Frick Collection, New York (Plate 55 in the colour plate section).

literary studies and a passion for arms. The description of Lodovico's life is intended to highlight the public role of this gentleman, an outstanding figure who took part in festivals which were among the most celebrated in Renaissance Florence. Contemporary literary sources describe a masquerade or procession through the city with Hell represented by a chariot of fire drawn by winged Furies, accompanied by many demons and the young noblemen of Florence. Among these was Lodovico Capponi as the major financer of this outstanding event, when all of Florence became a theatre.

Capponi's portrait manifestly provides an iconographic essay on Spanish male dress: the black cloak, the white trunk-hose and the black doublet with codpiece (*brachetta*) are the garments of Spanish dress. Duke Cosimo himself wears a codpiece under his suit of armour in the propagandistic state portrait by Bronzino in the Palazzo Vecchio Medici, an image of political power (Fig. 8). A codpiece belonging to the duke was taken from his tomb and is now at the Florence Costume Gallery (Orsi Landini *et al.* 1993: 70).

Lodovico the Younger is represented as a dignitary wearing the colours of his family coat of arms: black and white. Capponi's private papers attest that Lodovico the Elder's wardrobe favoured black, their family symbol, for all types of cloths. In fact, during a journey to Rome, Lodovico showed the local aristocracy some black Florentine velvet. Muzio's account describes a handsome knight, one of the main exponents of the Florentine Nation in the Eternal City, *à la page*, with a black and silver *teletta* jerkin and a black velvet hat with white feather. On several occasions Lodovico took part in the Florentine delegations and faced the spectacular papal court.

Maddalena, a member of the very rich Vettori family, was part of the Medici court. The love affair between Maddalena and Lodovico – well known at the time – was very troubled, though it had a happy ending. Lodovico and Maddalena's personal registers record their payments to silk merchants, tailors and jewellers beginning in 1558, the year of their marriage.[20] They reveal, first, that for her dresses Maddalena favoured *rosato* velvet and veils, embroidered with gold and pearls, as in a Bronzino portrait. At court, Maddalena wears a fine decorated gown in vogue at the time. Just before her marriage she spent some time in Palazzo Vecchio in Florence where she was a lady-in-waiting, in particular for Princess Maria.

The Capponi played prominent roles in the duke's entourage during two major journeys: for the wedding of Cosimo's daughter, Lucrezia, in Ferrara in 1558 and the trip of the duke and duchess to Rome in 1560. Personal Capponi documents reveal the high quality of the clothes made in Florence and the Parisian jewellery that they bought for their ceremonial wardrobes. The duchess's tastes clearly influenced the sophisticated

Figure 8 Agnolo Bronzino, *Cosimo de'Medici*, Palazzo Vecchio, Florence (Plate 56 in the colour plate section).

Figure 9 Petticoat with sleeves, *c.*1560, Museo Nazionale di Palazzo Reale, Pisa (Plate 57 in the colour plate section).

gown worn by Lodovico's wife in a very interesting double portrait, rightly attributed by Beatrice Paolozzi Strozzi to Agnolo Bronzino and his workshop (Paolozzi Strozzi 2001: 505–12).[21] Historically, the individual portraits may have been executed in two different periods (as deduced by the payments made to the artist): the young wife first, in 1559, and then her husband in 1573, when he was 40.

Surviving Medici clothes

A typical example of such Spanish male dress is Don Garcia Medici's red satin and velvet court suit, taken from the Medici tombs and now part of the collection of the Florence Costume Gallery (Arnold 1993: 49–63). The suit, which belonged to Cosimo's son, Garcia, who died in 1562, is very similar to that worn by Lodovico: the doublet fastened with buttons and was worn with paned trunk-hose. The fabrics of choice for Renaissance Medici costumes were velvet and satin embellished with slashes, embroidery, ribbons and trimmings (*Maria Medici* and *Prince Garcia*, Bronzino, Uffizi). Applied decorative bands characterise the clothing of all the ducal family and they were permitted by Cosimo's sumptuary laws for the lower classes too.

Like Garcia, Eleonora died in 1562, and her white satin and velvet funeral gown (at the Costume Gallery in Florence) is embroidered with gold in vertical bands on the skirt and bodice. It was described in the documents as a petticoat in white satin and was made up in the summer of 1562 (Orsi Landini and Niccoli 2005: 72–3 and 201–35). Another sumptuous female garment in Eleonora's style is fine crimson cut velvet embroidered with gold trimmings and red satin ribbons. This gown now forms an exceptional part of the collection at the Museum of the Medici Royal Palace in Pisa (Fig. 9). It is a fashionable gown in Eleonora's style, made for one of her ladies-in-waiting, part of the schenografic effect of the court (Niccoli 2000).

The kinds of fashions recorded in the Medici inventory of 1562 testified to the common style of Eleonora and Cosimo, which was inspired by moderation, as Monsignor Della Casa advised in the famous treatise, *Galateo*, published in Florence in 1560: 'Everybody must go well dressed according to their own status and age; otherwise they seem to scorn people.'[22]

Notes

1. See Archivio di stato di Firenze, Florence State Archive (hereafter ASF), Mediceo Avanti il Principato, 1169, c.121, Letter of Pier Francesco Riccio, 18 May 1539.
2. Niccolò Tribolo, Uffizi's Gabinetto Disegni e Stampe, Florence.
3. ASF, *Guardaroba Medicea* (G.M.),7, c.26 r, c.26.
4. ASF G.M., 7, *Inventario della roba del Duca Cosimo*, c.26 r:
   Abiti da maschera
   - vi abiti di cremisino e raso verde trinciati et foderati di tocha doro co rosati doro filato n°6
   - vi fornimenti da cavallo simili alli sopradetti n°6
   - ii habiti alantica di velluto pauonazzo e raso co due berretti divelluto cremisino alatica n°2
   - ii giboni allatica di raso cremisino n°2
   - ii Para di calze alatica di panno rosato n°2
   - ii cinture di velluto verde forniti di raso alatica n°2
   - ii Habiti ala fiamminga di teleta dargento e seta nera co maniche e habigliatura dicapo co due bordi di raso cremesino fornito doro filato n°2
   - ii habiti alla venetiana di perpignano pauonazzo co berrete del medesimo
   - vi habiti alindiana di panno accotonato nero trinciato foderati di tafeta verde co lor fornimenti da cavallo del medesimo
   - xi casache di taffeta verde alla turchesca n° xi
   - viiii casache di tafeta bianco alla turchesca n°9
   - xi girelli da cavallo di taffeta verde n°xi
   - viiii girelli da cavallo di tafeta bianco
   - xi targhe coperte di tafeta verde n°xi
   - viiii targhe di taffeta bianco con coperte n° 9
   - iiii capelli ala tedesca due coperti di damasco bianco e iiii di cordomano nero n°4

   Le xi casacche bianche et le 9 verde si consegnarono per farne a ciascuna appresso i gigliozzi et i 9 giupponi di taffeta simile et 18 pettorali per farne a ciascuna.
5. Jane Ashelford reports Eleonora had been buried wearing this dress, but the opening of the tomb belies this information (Ashelford 1983: 57).
6. B. Niccoli and C.M. Sicca, 'Luxury consumption at the court of Henry VIII Hans Holbein the Younger, his sitters and their Florentine providers of fashionable textiles', in Van Loo Colloquium, Rouen 14–15 March 2002 (in progress).
7. ASF G.M., 34 Giornale della Guardaroba di Sua Eccellenza,c.137 r:
   M D L viii
   Addì xv di giugno
   - Lxvi braccia di di teletta doro co opera in seta messa nella metà di un cortinaggio di 14 cortine toranletto sopra cielo e coperta lunga […]
   - Lii braccia di di teletta doro in seta verde a nodi di guardaroba tessuta da nostra francesca messa nel altra metà di detto cortinaggio e nel cielo […]
   - Lii braccia di teletta piana in seta rossa messa nella metà di uno letto cioè cortinaggio […]
   - XLix braccia di di teletta doro arricciata in seta paonazza di guardaroba messa nel altra metà di detto cortinaggio ,,,
8. ASF, G.M., 55, c.8, c.9, c.10.
9. In my PhD dissertation I called the 'paper gowns of Medici' the wardrobes of Cosimo and Eleonora recorded in the documents.
10. ASF, G.M.,15, c.35 r, c.43 v, c.97 v.
11. ASF, G.M.,34, c.18 r., c.18 v., c.101 r, G.M.15, c.78, c.85 r, p.57
12. ASF, 'La solenne entrata dell' Illustrissimo e Ecc. Signore il Signor Duca di Firenze fatta in Roma alli VI del presente mese di Novembre 1560' (Bologna: Antonio Giaccarello, & compagni 1560), p. 3.
13. ASF, G.M.34, c.58 r; G.M., 15, c.29 r and c. 39 r:
    M.D. L.V.
    - **Addì xxi di marzo**
    - Da maggiordomo Alessandro ritorno questo dì tutte le vesti di Sua Eccellenza
    - Una veste corta di lupi cervieri
    - Una veste corta d'ermesino tanè fodera di lupi cervieri
    - Una veste d'ermesino nero foderat di fianchi co paia di 12 punte
    - Una veste corta di grossa grana foderata di zibellini co 9 ½ paia di punte
    - Una veste d'ermesino tanè lunga fodera di zibellini
    - Due paia di stivali di cordovano bianco co fodera di dossi laltro di zibellini
    - Una veste di lontra co' sua fibbie d'argento
    - Ii paia di stivali fodera luno di dossi laltro di zibellini ambo di cordomano
    - Una veste di velluto nero foderata di bassetti co dieci paia di punte
    - Uno colletto dermisino nero foderato di dossi
    - Uno colletto tanè simile

- Una veste lunga d'ermesino bigio foderata di dossi
- Una veste lunga simile foderata di lupi
- Dodici paia di punte doro smaltate et disse haver messo à una veste di velluto nero
- Cinque punte doro simile et disse Sua Eccellenza l'haveva perse

14. ASF, Medicео Avanti il Principato, 1169, c.1176, Letter of Lorenzo Pagni, 20 January 1550.
15. Florence, Uffizi Gallery, *c.*1540, Bartolomeo Panciatichi, ambassador at the French court and his wife, Lucrezia, who wears a crimson satin gown in the Florentine style of the years before Eleonora. The square neckline is trimmed with gold veil pleats, the blue-violet silk sleeves are slashed and the wings on the shoulders are called *baragoni*. Lodovico Capponi at the Frick Collection (dated about 1550–55), New York.
16. Florence, Capponi alle Rovinate Private Archive, *Documents of Lodovico Capponi Senior* (1533–36); *Inventory of Lodovico the Elder's Shop* in 1534:
    Nella bottega
    - Braccia 129 di raso rosso di chermesi spagnolo a pagamento
    - Braccia 80 di raso simile a pagamento
    - Braccia 95 di raso simile a pagamento
    - Braccia 69 di raso simile a pagamento
    - Braccia 55 di raso incarnato di chermisi
    - Braccia 50 di raso simile a pagamento
    - Braccia 50 di raso tanè
    - Braccia 62 di raso nero
    - [...]
    - Braccia 53 di raso verde
    - Braccia 66 di raso simile a pagamento
    - Braccia 61 di raso simile a pagamento
    - [...]
    - Braccia 35 di velluto incarnato di chermisi
    - Braccia 30 di velluto pagonazzo di chermisi
    - Braccia 36 di velluto simile
    - Braccia 59 di taffettà nero
17. ASF, *Carte Gondi*, 10, c.15: 'telette chol fondo d'argento tirato e chol fondo d'oro tirato'; ASF, *Carte Strozziane*, Serie V, 100, *Giornale di Filippo Strozzi e Compagni Battilori di Lyon*, c.37 r, c.42 r, c. 87 r: 'teletta piana d'oro tirato, telette nere d'oro tirato, paghonazze', c.129 r, 'telette con e senza opera'.
18. Florence, Church of Santa Felicita, 1525–28 *The Lamentation* by Pontormo, who was Bronzino's master, is also considered the originator of Mannerist-style portraits.
19. Biblioteca Riccardiana, Manoscritti, 2139, Iustino Politano Muzio, *La Capponiera*.
20. ASF, Riccardi, 532, *Giornali di Ricordi*, 1499–1552:
    - f.86 w.
    - 1552 spese di vestire per la Maddalena nostra
    - [...]
    - uno velo dargento e doro venuto di Francia
    - f.123 l.
    - [...]
    - uno paio di pianelle di Vinezia turchine
    - 30 paternostri d'ambra per una cintola
    - una pettinatura di libbre 44 di lino di Napoli
    - [...]
    - a Francesco orafo 2 anelli per mettere agli orecchi smaltati e grandi et altri 2 anelli per mettere agli orecchi con pietra verde
    - [...]
    - f.135 w.
    - [...]
    - braccia 5 per fattura di una zimarra di seta verde di Napoli fornita di bande di velluto verde
    - braccio 1 per fattura un busto di camuiarro cangiante fornito di frange di seta bianca
    - braccio 1 di tela rossa e braccio 1 di tela saldata
    - braccia 17 di nastro seta verde da mettere a 50 paia di punte doro per la veste lucchesina
    - rifacitura di 1 veste limonata fornita di 1 stampa di velluto verde, 1 paio di punte oro per far mettere nastri di raso a dette punte
    - [...]
21. As pointed out by Beatrice Paolozzi Strozzi the portrait is similar to the double portrait of the dukes also painted by the Florentine artist housed at Erlinger collection, USA.
22. 'Ben vestito deve andar ciascuno secondo sua conditione, secondo sua età; perciochè altrimenti facendo pare che egli sprezzi la gente.' See for the inventory ASF, G.M., 55, cc.8–14. *Il Galateo* di Messer Giovanni Della Casa (Milan: Giovan Antonio degli Astoni, 1559; editor Giuliano Tanturli, Florence: Edizioni Polistampa, 2003) p. 8 v.

References

Arnold, J. (1993) 'Cut and construction', in *Moda alla corte dei Medici: Gli abiti restaurati di Cosimo, Eleonora e don Garzia*, catalogue of the exhibition at the Pitti Palace, 49–73. Florence: Centro Di.

Ashelford, J. (1983) *A Visual History of Costume: The Sixteenth Century*. London: Batsford.

Baia, A. (1907) *Leonora di Toledo duchessa di Firenze e di Siena*. Todi: Tipografia Z.Foglietti.

Bernis, C. (1990) 'La moda en la Espana de Felipe II a través del retrato de corte', in *Alonso Sanchez Coello*, 66–111. Madrid: Prado Museum Press.

Boccherini, T. (1993) 'La produzione dei tessuti di seta a Firenze. Diffusione e caratteristiche tecniche e tipologiche', in '*Sopra ogni sorte di drapperia ...' Tipologie decorative e tecniche tessili nella produzione fiorentina del Cinquecento e Seicento*, D. Liscia Bemporand (ed.), 23–31. Florence: Maria Cristina de Montemayor Editore.

Brock, M. (2002) *Bronzino*. Paris: Flammarion.

Butazzi, G.I. (1995) 'Il modello spagnolo nella moda europea', in *Le Trame della moda*, a cura di Anna Giulia Lavagna, e Grazietta Butazzi. Rome: Bulzoni Editore.

Carnesecchi, C. (1902) *Cosimo I e la sua legge suntuaria del 1562*. Florence: Pellas.

Cobb, H.S. (1995) 'Textile imports in the fifteenth century: the evidence of the Customs' Accounts', *Costume* 29: 1–11.

Conti, C. (1893) 'La Prima Reggia di Cosimo Primo de' Medici nel Palazzo già della Signoria di Firenze descritta ed illustrata con l'appoggio di un inventario inedito del 1553 e coll' aggiunta di molti altri documenti'. Florence: Giuseppe Pellas editor, 1893.

Cortesi da Prato, J. (1893) *Il Battesimo di Don Garzia de' Medici*. Florence/Rome: Tipografia Fratelli Bencini.

Edelstein, B. (2001)'Bronzino in the service of Eleonora di Toledo and Cosimo de Medici', in *Beyond Isabella: Secular Women Patrons of Art in Renaissance Italy*, S. Reiss and D. Wilkins (eds), 225–61. Missouri: Kirksville.

Giambullari, P.F. (1539) *Apparato e feste nelle nozze dello Illustrissimo signor duca di Firenze, et de la duchessa sua consorte, con le Sue stanze, madrigali, comedia, et intermedi, in quella recitati*, Copia di una lettera di M. Pier Francesco Giambullari al molto Magnifico M. Giovanni Bandini. Florence: Giunta

Kaufmann, H.W. (1970) 'Art for the wedding of Cosimo de'Medici and Eleonora Toledo (1539)', *Paragone* XXI(243): 52–67.

Langedijk, K. (1981) *The Portraits of Medici XVth–XVIIIth Centuries*, 3 vols, vol. 1. Florence: SPES.

Melis, F. (1984) *L'economia fiorentina del Rinascimento*. Florence: Le Monnier.

Morelli, R. (1976) *La seta fiorentina del cinquecento*. Milan: Giuffré.

Niccoli, B. (2000) 'Il costume nelle cerimonie medicee. Note di moda a Pisa alla corte di Cosimo ed Eleonora', in *L'abito della Granduchessa*, M. Giulia Burrosi (ed.), 14–27. Pontedera: Bandecchi e Vivaldi.

Niccoli, B. (2004a) *Florence and the Costume in the Renaissance Court System*. PhD dissertation, University of Pisa.

Niccoli, B. (2004b) 'Official dress and courtly fashion in Genoese entries in festivals in Genoa in the sixteenth and seventeenth century', in *Europa Triumphas*, R. Mulryne (ed.), 261–75. London: Ashgate.

Niccoli, B. (2005a) 'Eleonora di Toledo Duchess of Tuscany, in history and legend', in *Moda a Firenze 1540–1580. Lo stile di Eleonora di Toledo e la sua influenza*, R. Orsi Landini and B. Niccoli (eds), 15–20. Florence: Pagliai Polistampa.

Niccoli, B. (2005b) 'Costume in the Medici ceremonies', in *Moda a Firenze 1540–1580. Lo stile di Eleonora di Toledo e la sua influenza*, R. Orsi Landini and B. Niccoli (eds), 47. Florence: Pagliai Polistampa.

Orsi Landini, R. and Niccoli, B. (2005) 'The wardrobe of Eleonora di Toledo', in *Moda a Firenze 1540–1580. Lo stile di Eleonora di Toledo e la sua influenza*, R. Orsi Landini and B. Niccoli (eds). Florence: Pagliai Polistampa.

Orsi Landini, R., Ricci, S. and Westerman Bulgarella, M. (1993) *Moda alla corte dei Medici: Gli abiti restaurati di Cosimo, Eleonora e don Garzia*, catalogue of the exhibition at the Pitti Palace. Florence: Centro Di.

Paolozzi Strozzi, B. (2001) 'Gli sposi del museo di Strasburgo. Un'appendice al catalogo di Bronzino', in *Opere e giorni. Studi su mille anni di arte europea dedicati a Max Seidel*, K. Bergdolt and G. Bassanti (eds), 505–12. Venice: Marsilio.

Sicca, C.M. (2002) 'Consumption and trade of art between Italy and England in the first half of the sixteenth century: the London house of the Bardi and Cavalcanti company', *Renaissance Studies* XVI(2): 163–200.

The author

Bruna Niccoli lectures in the history of dress and stage costume at the University of Pisa. She is the author of a number of essays on the history of dress in the modern age and is currently engaged (since 2005), in collaboration with the University of Pisa, in cataloguing the important collection of stage costumes of the Cerratelli Foundation (San Guiliano Terme, Pisa).

Address

Bruna Niccoli, Via Santa Marta 42, 56127 Pisa, Italy (b.niccoli@arte.unipi.it)

Bought, stolen, bequeathed, preserved: sources for the study of 18th-century petticoats

Clare Rose

ABSTRACT Retailers' publicity documents are texts that stand in a particular relationship to material goods. Produced by retailers and read by consumers, they need to strike a fine balance between aggrandisement and realism if they are to create and sustain sales. Historic examples of merchants' cards and lists have been used as evidence of trade practices, and surviving collections of textiles have been interpreted and 'read' using material culture methodology. Both these interpretative exercises, however, need to acknowledge the problems of sampling and representation inherent in the survival of fragile textiles and paper ephemera over 200 years. Focusing on 18th-century quilted petticoats, which were widely advertised, widely consumed and survive in large numbers, allows us to analyse textiles and texts separately to identify the interpretative problems posed by each. The criminal trial records in the Old Bailey papers provide a source of data on the ownership and valuation of goods that can be analysed quantitatively. This quantitative analysis provides a framework within which we can place the qualitative data derived from surviving texts and textiles. Both quantitative and qualitative data can be framed by Pierre Bourdieu's theory of 'distinction'.

Keywords: methodology, consumption, material culture, trade cards, quilted petticoats

Introduction

This paper is presented as an exploration of the methodological issues raised by textiles and texts in the study of 18th-century practices of retailing and consumption. This relationship, which was complicated by misstatement on both sides, is analysed. The focus is on the sale and consumption of women's quilted petticoats, which were universally worn and widely sold as one of the first ready-to-wear garments traded throughout Britain and even to the colonies (Lemire 1994, 1997). Their simple construction, adjustable sizing and lack of seasonal variation meant that they could be made for stock in different fabrics and at different prices. Consumers could choose different colours and fabrics to wear as a main garment with a short jacket, or as a support garment under a full-skirted gown. The existence, however, of different varieties and prices was also problematic as retailers' documents used terminology that elided changes in manufacturing processes and places of origin. Thus the texts could only be interpreted by readers who already knew the textiles. The ways in which consumers understood and valued textiles is examined through a survey of wills, inventories and accounts of thefts. These can be used to verify and correct the information deduced from surviving textiles and from merchants' texts.

In order to interpret findings about 18th-century consumption, it is necessary to have a model of the ways that consumption creates meaning. The multiple variants of quilted petticoats make them appropriate vehicles for the demonstration of Pierre Bourdieu's concept of social meanings based on 'distinction'. The range of situations in which they were used allows us to examine the issue raised by Colin Campbell (1997) as to how meaning is constituted in clothing and whether it is inherent, situational or dependent on the intentions of the wearer. Evidence for these different types of meaning will be examined in the different sets of texts and in the textiles.

Literature on 18th-century consumption, texts and textiles

Much invaluable work has been done on production and consumption networks in 18th-century England using wills, invoices, probate inventories and other textual sources. McKendrick *et al.* (1982) have opened up the 18th-century 'world of goods' for our inspection and demonstrated its importance for the history of consumption. Maxine Berg has shown how changes in consumption practice encouraged a redefinition of the concept of 'luxury' as both a political and a philosophical term (Berg and Eger 2003), and Marcia Pointon (1997) examined the ways in which material possessions were used to create and uphold women's social networks, using wills and portraits as evidence. Beverley Lemire's research into the origins of the ready-to-wear clothing trade has been particularly important for her innovative use of source materials. She has identified the records of trials for theft at the Old Bailey Court as an important source of information about consumer goods and the values placed on them by their owners. She has also investigated a collection of surviving garments to validate her findings from texts (Lemire 1994, 1997).

Historic trade cards and commercial documents have themselves been the subject of study, notably by Rickards and Twyman (2000). Catalogues of ephemera such as that of the Bodleian Library (2001) are useful sources of information on the practices of historic retailers. These publications do not, however, address the criteria by which documents intended to be ephemeral have been selected for survival: whether this is based on their appearance, their content or both.

There are many object-centred historians (often working in museums) who have used textiles as a primary source of evidence. Two outstanding examples are Anne Buck (1979) and Florence Montgomery (1984), each of whom has integrated evidence from textiles and documents to investigate 18th-century practices of trade and consumption in breadth and in depth. Both object-based and text-based historians have also made case studies of documents from a particular source, contextualised in terms of wider 18th-century practice (Ehrman 2006; Llewellyn 1997; Rose 1995; Staniland 1990; Vickery 1993). The paradigmatic document for this approach is the clothing journal of Barbara Johnson, which includes fabric swatches and details of costs (Rothstein 1987).

Methodologies for interpreting textiles and texts

One of the most commonly applied models for linking the interpretation of modern clothing and texts is semiotics, drawn from linguistic theory. This theory relies on a separation between the meaning or 'signified' and its physical embodiment, the 'signifier'. The problem of semiotic analysis has been summarised by the ethnographer Daniel Miller as 'subordinating the object qualities of things to their word-like qualities' (1987: 95), ignoring the ways that textiles create meaning through their embodiment of financial, aesthetic and haptic values. Miller instead sees objects as 'type-tokens ... both an individual form and an example of a larger category to which it must be related' (1987: 127). He sidesteps the problems of selecting individual examples as 'type-tokens' by focusing on the process of consumption, which he sees as 'key to an understanding of contemporary society and of culture itself' (1987: 76).

Colin Campbell (1997; see also Brewer and Porter 1993) has also expressed reservations about the use of a language-based model to explain consumer behaviour, highlighting the degree to which the ability of clothing to convey meaning is limited both by the resources of the wearer and by the understanding of the viewer. The variety of texts referencing quilted petticoats allows us to examine the ways in they were viewed by consumers and to assess how and when they conveyed meaning.

A framework for understanding consumption practices is provided by Pierre Bourdieu, whose 1984 study revealed the extent to which consumption is guided by consumers' sense of what is appropriate for their social position. These findings led him to the concept of the *habitus*, which 'tends to generate all the "reasonable", "common-sense" behaviours ... which are likely to be positively sanctioned [and] to exclude all "extravagances" (not for the likes of us), that is, all the behaviours that would be negatively sanctioned' (Bourdieu 1990: 55–6). Two particular advantages of *habitus* as an analytical framework are its emphasis on learned practices and its equal applicability to all social groups. The relationship between groups is expressed not by 'emulation' but by 'distinction', from those with higher, lower or alternative social status (Bourdieu 1984: 57). Knowledge of the behaviour and consumption patterns proper to a particular social group at a particular time is defined by Bourdieu as 'cultural capital' (Bourdieu 1977).

In order to apply this model to 18th-century consumption practices we need first to establish the *habitus* within which consumers acted. This is done by referring to textiles surviving in museum collections and mentioned in texts such as inventories to establish the variety and quantity of textiles consumed by individuals. Merchants' trade cards are also used to show the workings of 'distinction' in the varieties of standard garments such as petticoats. The following sections examine separately evidence from different types of texts and from surviving textiles in order to evaluate how each source can be used in the study of 18th-century consumption practices. Evidence from different sources will be compared in order to highlight the problems inherent in each. There will then be an evaluation of the validity of Bourdieu and Campbell's methodology for this area of study.

Methods for studying textiles

Dress historians such as Lou Taylor have seen the study of surviving garments as fundamental to their practice: 'Surviving clothing provides researchers and collectors with a powerful tool for historical and contemporary socio-cultural investigation' (1998: 338). Taylor's practice is based on the methods of material culture studies as developed by E. McClung Fleming (1974) and Jules Prown (1993: 1–19) and applied to dress history by Severa and Horswill (1989) and Valerie Steele (1998). Prown summarised his aims as 'the study of material to understand culture, to discover the beliefs – the values, ideas, attitudes and assumptions – of a particular community or society at a given time' (1993: 1).

There is, however, a danger inherent in object-centred methodologies in that they may be restricted by too close a focus on aesthetic or physical considerations. Nancy Rexford identified these limited views as those of the Connoisseur, and the Antiquarian; only the Historian looks beyond the object to consider wider issues (1988: 69). A further methodological problem raised by material culture studies is how to extrapolate from the study of individual examples all garments of a similar category. This could be done in several ways: one is to select a typical garment as a case study (Steele 1998). Another is to study a selected group of garments in detail and establish significant variations and similarities (Severa and Horswill 1989). A third way is to study all examples of a particular type and to apply quantitative analysis, as suggested by Prown (1982).

The first two methods raise questions of how to select the 'type' examples without recourse to subjective judgements. Quantitative analysis of the whole dataset avoids the problems of subjectivity and enables the researcher to establish the totality of clothing practices. A cursory review of any museum collection, however, shows that the sample of surviving garments is far from representative. Items in museums may have been selected for preservation by their original users, either positively (better-made examples were kept) or negatively (poorly made examples wore out). Items may also have been deliberately selected by curators, who may see the acquisition of particular items as necessary to 'complete' their collections (Baumgarten 2002: 9, fig. 16). This implies a curatorial understanding of past practice, but the basis for this understanding is rarely addressed. The only way to address the asymmetries inherent in the presentation of evidence in textiles and in texts is through a separate analysis of the information presented by each, followed by a comparison of each set of data to see where the discrepancies and inaccuracies lie.

Reading petticoats

The evidence in this section is based on the collections of the National Trust at Snowshill Manor, the Museum of London, Colonial Williamsburg, the Victoria and Albert Museum (V&A) and the Royal Ontario Museum (ROM) (unpublished catalogue information provided by curators, and personal investigation of textiles). These collections contain numerous examples of 18th-century quilted petticoats: although established at different times and with different intentions they show a remarkable degree of consistency. Catalogue information was available for 85 18th-century petticoats: 38 from the V&A, 14 from the ROM, 20 from Williamsburg and 13 from Snowshill. Of these, 71 are faced with silk, eight with cotton or linen, and four with wool (filling and lining materials are usually wool). This sample should be large enough to provide some information about the ways in which these garments varied and expressed 'distinction' in terms of cost or exclusivity.

The most obvious factor creating 'distinction' is the fabrics used; silk was generally more costly than wool, and wool more costly than undyed linen or cotton. The wool fabric used for surviving petticoats has a glazed finish which brings it closer to silk both in appearance and in cost than unglazed woollens (Buck 1979: 187). There was also considerable range in the qualities and prices of silk fabrics used for petticoats, with heavy brocades at the top and lightweight plain silks at the bottom (Rothstein 1987: 30). Many of the surviving quilted petticoats are made from satin (Fig. 1), which was suited to quilting because it was softer and easier to stitch than stiffer taffeta. The fine threads of satins were also fragile, however, and the resultant wear is evident on some surviving petticoats (Lemire 1994: fig. 7).

The colour palette of the surviving silk petticoats shows a predominance of pale tones, with 29 described as white, cream or fawn, 13 as pale blue and 14 as pink. There could be several reasons for this palette, which is much narrower than that found in 18th-century gowns (Rothstein 1987). The first is that pale or neutral-coloured petticoats could be worn with a variety of dress fabrics, making them more attractive to the manufacturer and to the consumer. The second consideration is that pale-coloured satin would show up elaborate quilting patterns more effectively. There was, however, an associated disadvantage in that pale, single-coloured garments would also show up any stains or wear. Thus a cream satin petticoat might be more attractive but less durable than one in a darker coloured, heavier silk or silk mix.

The second variable creating 'distinction' within the group of silk petticoats is the quality of the workmanship and the degree of patterning, both of which would affect the time taken for stitching and hence the cost. As Lemire noted, many of them are hastily executed, pointing to their status as mass-produced garments (1997: 67–9). Some are quilted in a plain grid of diamonds, the minimum required to hold the wadding in place between face fabric and lining (Fig. 2); others have conventional flowers arranged in swags or within large diamonds at the hem. A few exceptional examples have additional embellishments, such as embroidery worked over the quilting (Lemire 1994: fig. 8).

More interesting is a group of six surviving petticoats whose pattern and technique are so distinctive that they have been convincingly attributed to a single designer or workshop located in London (Staniland 1990: 50). These garments have elaborate flowers at the hem, with petals and leaves filled in with corded quilting, a much more time-consuming technique than wadded quilting. Moreover, two of the petticoats in this group survive with matching quilted dresses (Fig. 1), and a third example survives with a quilted jacket probably made

Figure 1 An indoor gown and petticoat of cream silk satin, c.1750, quilted in elaborate patterns in a complex technique. This represents the peak of commercially available quilting (Museum of London 1989.56).

from a dress (Staniland 1990: 49). In each of these ensembles the quilting patterns are distributed over the garments, carefully fitted to the shape of the bodice, sleeve and cuff pieces.

These surviving quilted ensembles can be identified as high-quality products of professional workshops. The way in which the petticoats reflect the design motifs of the associated gowns suggests that they were made for wearing together. Purchasing a quilted set would evidently be more costly than purchasing a petticoat on its own, leaving aside the additional costs imposed by the more detailed stitching on these examples. Yet the plain satin fabric and quilted technique identify these gowns as informal wear for use at home in winter (Buck 1979: 47). Their presence in a wardrobe would imply the possession of other gowns for formal occasions, for wearing outside, and in summer.

Another group of highly decorated petticoats shows the workings of 'distinction' in a particular social group. These are examples made in the American colonies at a time when most clothing fabrics were imported from Europe at inflated prices (Baumgarten 1986: fig. 24; 2002: figs 125, 197). Each of them is worked in the standard techniques of wadded quilting, but with unusually detailed patterns. They have distinctive motifs that are likely to have been the choice of the wearer, and two of them are signed in the quilting. These signatures confirm that the petticoats were made to special order and probably by the wearer herself. They are visibly different from the standardised designs found on other petticoats, including the London group, which, while more elaborate than the others, share motifs and compositional features.

The final group of quilted petticoats are united not by pattern or material but by technique. Although they are made with a face fabric, filling and backing, worked with patterns, this effect is produced not with quilting stitches but a form of double-cloth weaving with supplementary filler wefts (Montgomery 1984: 291). This group includes two petticoats with a cotton face and one with a silk face.[1] The technique of woven quilting was perfected in Britain during the 1760s, encouraged by substantial premiums awarded by the Royal Society for the Encouragement of Arts, Manufactures, and Commerce (Rose 1999: 109). The design quality of this woven imitation was in no way inferior to the hand-stitched originals, as can be seen from the surviving pocket with woven patterns carefully placed to provide border, reinforced upper edge, and decoration (Fig. 3). In addition, garments patterned by weaving were likely to be more durable and more washable than hand-stitched versions.

Figure 2 A quilted petticoat in green shot silk, with plain diamond quilting, c.1740–50, to be worn with a contrasting gown or jacket. This represents the mid-range of commercial quilting (Victoria and Albert Museum T.306-1982) (Plate 58 in the colour plate section).

Problems with interpreting textiles

The overview of a sample of surviving quilted petticoats indicates that these were typically faced with lightweight, glossy silk fabrics in pale colours. Most of them had patterns worked in the quilting, ranging from the schematic to the one-off. Most appear to have been made by workshops for general sale, although a few more elaborate examples (the group attributed to London) may have been made for special orders; in the American colonies petticoats were made to individual designs that sometimes incorporated the names of the wearers. The

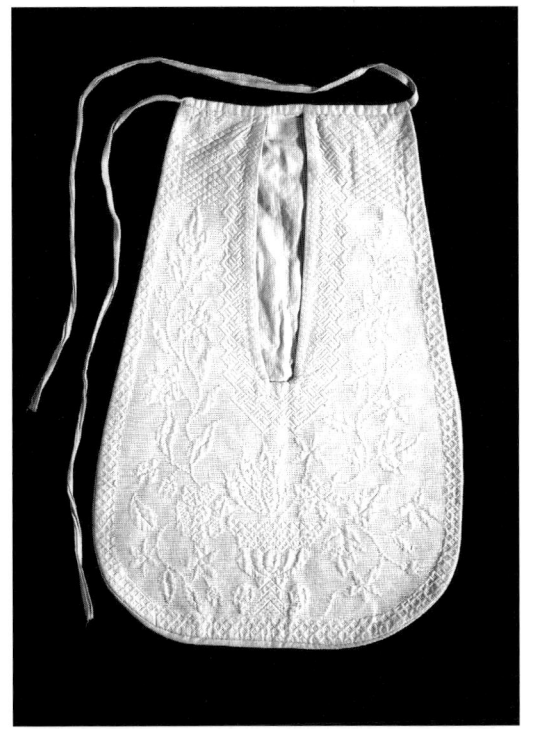

Figure 3 A cotton pocket woven in an imitation of quilting known as 'marcella', c.1760–80. The woven motifs imitate those on stitched versions (Victoria and Albert Museum T.150-1970) (Plate 59 in the colour plate section).

relative homogeneity of the surviving garments, however, might be a cause for concern. The paucity of petticoats in glazed wool is surprising as we might expect these to be more widely used than silk versions.

The pale colours of the silk petticoats are also of concern when viewed in the context of 18th-century wardrobes, in which intense colours such as saffron yellow were common. The V&A has a saffron yellow quilted silk waistcoat with matching pockets (T87.1978); one wonders whether there was originally a matching petticoat also.

The existence of quilted dress ensembles (Fig. 1) reminds us that petticoats were only part of the range of quilted goods available commercially. These included complete layette sets (Rose 1995: 78), support garments (waistcoats), accessories (pockets) and furnishings. Consumers would be able to practise 'distinction' within their own wardrobes, selecting different qualities of quilted goods for different occasions, and distinguishing between those that created a harmonious or fashionable ensemble over those that were purely functional. Shifts in colours and quilting patterns might have created a fashion cycle within the parameters of the standard garment. The lack of secure dating for surviving examples makes it hard to map this retrospectively.

Evidence from texts

The textual sources used for the study of 18th-century garments fall into two main categories: retailer-oriented and consumer-oriented. The first category consists mainly of advertising material and invoices (Heal 1925; Rickards and Twyman 2000). Invoices also provide evidence of consumer behaviour, but both their format and the information they contain are mediated by the perceptions of retailers. More direct expressions of consumers' perceptions of garments are found in letters and account books. Probate inventories and records of thefts in the Old Bailey records deal with both merchants and private individuals.

The main type of retailer-oriented texts is the trade card, and these survive in large numbers in the Guildhall, British Museum[2] and Museum of London archives. These are printed with the name and address of the business and a list (brief or complete) of the goods and services offered. They are usually undated, and without pricelists, but this information is sometimes supplied by associated invoices. Out of the 1,500 such documents that were examined, there were 150 references to quilted textiles. The most frequently mentioned items (68 references) were women's quilted petticoats, stocked by traders describing themselves as mercers, linen-drapers, haberdashers, or milliners. The petticoats were offered in different fabrics (and presumably colours and designs), with traders stocking five or more varieties at one time (Fig. 4). Some trade cards stressed the design quality of the goods, others the quality of workmanship; and still others low prices (Lemire 1997: 67–9). This is interesting in itself as it implies that different retailers were aiming at different market levels. One specialist market was for sets of 'childbed linen' which included: 'Quilted Gowns & Bed Gowns Wastcoats and Holland half Shifts, Sattin & Callicoe quilted Bed Quilts, Toilots for Tables ... India & French Quilting ... Quilted Pettycoats'.[3]

Problems with retailers' texts

The first problem with the surviving retailers' texts is determining the basis on which they have been selected. The three main archives are each based on personal collections[4] which are biased towards aesthetically satisfying, curious and early documents.[5] Furthermore, trade cards were not objective documents, but constituted a claim about the quality and value of the goods on offer, replicating the sense of copiousness, order and visual pleasure to be found in the well-stocked shop. This was done implicitly through the ordering and presentation of the goods, often within a decorative framework. It was also done explicitly through the addition of phrases such as 'Made upon the Genteelest taste and newest Fashion and Sold at the most Reasonable Rates'.[6]

The invoices were also designed as claims rather than statements of value. This was necessary because most 18th-century prices were not predetermined, but the result of extensive negotiation between merchant and consumer. Businesses selling at fixed prices for 'ready money only' highlighted this unusual policy in their publicity documents.[7] The common practice of selling on credit made the relationship between the price stated on the invoice and the value of the goods even more questionable. There was often a delay of weeks or months before the account was settled (Buck 1979: 178), and clients might return unpaid goods, even if made to special order (Lemire 1991: 69). Retailers would be tempted to include an element of 'interest' in their calculations when dealing with high-risk clients.

Figure 4 A trade card from Paulins & Coates, Haberdashers, 1767, offering ready-made quilted petticoats in 'satin, sarsnet and Persian' (silk), 'all sorts of stuff' (wool) and 'callico' (cotton). Different qualities of fabrics would command different prices (Guildhall Library, City of London).

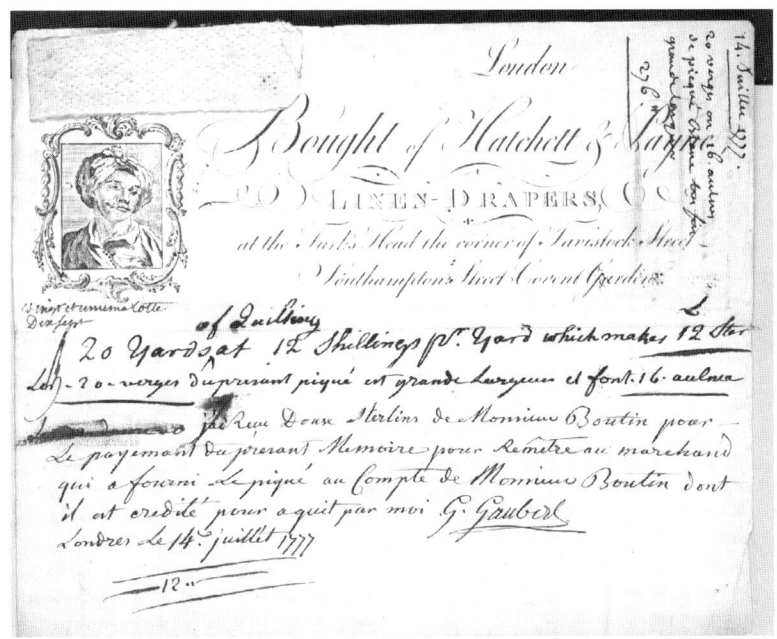

Figure 5 An invoice from Hatchett & Payne, 1777, for 20 yards of 'quilting'. This term implies hand-stitching but here refers to loom-patterned goods ('marcella') as can be seen from the attached sample of fabric (Heal 80.102, British Museum).

A further problem in interpreting the retailers' texts arises from their carefully calculated use of terminology. The term 'French' quilting in the trade card quoted above implies an imported cotton textile made in the region around Marseilles. These goods were also being made in London, however, as is shown by the existence of trade cards offering patterns and threads for 'French' quilting, and invoices for working 'French' quilted goods (Rose 1999: 107). A further layer of ambiguity was added with the introduction of woven 'quilting' in the 1760s. Some merchants identified this as 'loom quilting' (Rose 1999: 109). More often, however, it was described simply as 'quilting' or as 'marcella', a variant on Marseilles (Fig. 5). For consumers, knowing the difference between 'marcella' and 'Marseilles' was a form of 'cultural capital'.

Comparing textiles and texts

In order to understand fully the relationship between quilted petticoats and merchants' cards, we need to compare them and to look at other forms of evidence that might bridge the gaps identified above. This can help us to evaluate the surviving garments in terms of 18th-century practice and to clarify the ambiguities identified in the trade cards. Quilted petticoats are also mentioned in household accounts, inventories, wills and depositions in trials for theft. Each of these types of texts has particular advantages and limitations.

Household accounts give direct evidence of the prices paid for garments and the context in which they were purchased and used. For example in 1717–18, at the time of her daughter's marriage, Lady Grisell Baillie purchased two ready-made quilted silk petticoats for £2 15s and £1 15s; eight yards of 'Indian quilting' for petticoats at 5s 6d; and made a payment of £1 10s for 'quilting a goun' (Scott-Moncrieff 1911: 214–15). This account shows quilted garments as part of a wedding trousseau and also gives evidence of a consumer selecting and commissioning goods from merchants in order to suit their specifications. Less wealthy consumers were more likely to have generic ready-made petticoats for everyday wear: Martha Dodson, a member of the gentry, purchased several brown wool petticoats around 1760 (Ehrman 2006: 31–3), while a maid called Susan Smith had an outfit including a 'black stuff [petti]coat 7/6d' paid for by her employer in 1791.[8]

Wills and inventories do not usually give the monetary value of garments, but may indicate their relative importance in terms of the owner's total possessions. In the 90 wills selected by Marcia Pointon, quilted petticoats are mentioned only three times. The will of Margaret Mugge (1742) distinguished between unquilted petticoats that matched the gown, non-matching petticoats in quilted silk, and cotton underpetticoats (Pointon 1997: 42). Dame Cecilia Garrard (1753) used clothing bequests to articulate the status of the servants in her household: her personal maid received three patterned gowns and £25, the cook received £5, a plain gown and a black wool quilted petticoat, and the other maids a plain gown and petticoat with no money (Pointon 1997: 380).

The placement of garments within wills and inventories also indicated hierarchies of value. The inventory of the wardrobe of the duchess of Montague in 1747 noted two 'upper Pettycoats Mazzollo [Marseilles] Quilting' with the nightclothes, and two 'petticoats Sticht with yellow – which her Grace wears with her [riding] habits' (Llewellyn 1997: 64–6). These were distinguished from the silk petticoats worn with formal gowns both in location and in usage.

Further information about the way that garments were purchased, worn and valued by a wide range of consumers can be found in the Old Bailey trial records (Lemire 1997: 121–45), which include the value of the goods stolen, the occupation of plaintiff and accused, and much contextual information.[9] Searching for 'quilted petticoat' gave 250 cases between 1688 and 1805. The materials were not always mentioned, but 20

Figure 6 A panel of yellow silk embroidery over flat quilting on a linen ground, probably from a petticoat, c.1720–40. Produced in Europe, but with a colour scheme and motifs referring to textiles made in Bengal, this was probably sold as 'Indian' quilting (Meg Andrews Textiles).

were described as 'callimanco', 15 as 'stuff' and 13 as 'russel', three different grades of wool fabrics; the most frequently mentioned colour was black. The value of the stolen wool petticoats ranged from 3d for one worn by the wife of a blacksmith up to 40s for a new example taken from a shop.

These three sets of documents allow us to locate quilted petticoats in pastel silk in terms of 'distinction'. The trade cards, inventories and wills show that they were positioned in the clothing hierarchy below silk petticoats made to match a gown, but above versions in dark wool. Further distinctions based on the types of silk and the quality of the stitched patterning can be deduced from trade cards and from material culture analysis. Finally, the Old Bailey records remind us that individual garments changed in value as they aged and passed from one owner to another.

The wills show the ability of garments such as petticoats to carry multiple meanings, as Campbell (1997) postulated. They were intended by testators to embody both a personal relationship and a social hierarchy, as is seen in Margaret Mugge's careful distinctions between maid and cook. They may have been perceived differently by the recipients, however, perhaps in terms of their financial value. In the Old Bailey records, the meanings of garments are primarily financial, but they also present evidence of criminal acts, when stripped off the body of the plaintiff and found in the possession of the accused.

Conclusion

This parallel analysis of both textiles and texts shows that while textiles themselves are a key source, they cannot be 'read' in isolation, but need to be situated in a historiographic model built up from all the available sources, including different types of texts. Moreover, the limitations of each type of source need to be acknowledged openly. The analysis of collections of quilted petticoats in five major museums showed that most surviving examples are in a narrow range of fabrics (smooth silk and linen) and colours (pastels and cream). Of the four that are made of wool, three are in North American collections (Metropolitan and Royal Ontario Museums), which may indicate a regional difference either in use or in preservation. It is not clear whether the selection of garments for preservation was made by the original owners, by the persons offering items to the museum, or by the curators who accepted them, and further research in this area is needed.

The analysis of retailers' texts showed that these had a dual aim: to demonstrate the wide variety of fabrics (and colours), techniques and qualities available to consumers, but at the same time to obscure the actual origins of the goods. Quilted textiles described as 'Indian' may have been stitched in northern Europe (Fig. 6), and those sold as 'Marseilles' may have been loom-woven in Britain. This made an ability to read through trade cards a part of the 'cultural capital' of 18th-century consumers.

An understanding of the ways in which clothing expressed social distinctions both within the household and within the owner's wardrobe can be seen in inventories and wills. In these the quilted petticoat occupies a hinge position, worn informally or as an undergarment by aristocratic women, but as a main garment by their maids. The Old Bailey trial depositions allow us to track the shifting valuation of a standard garment such as a quilted petticoat as it moved from outworker to merchant to customer to thief. A quantitative analysis of the types, valuations and ownership of goods across the hundreds of examples in this source would give a more nuanced understanding of the variations in 18th-century consumption practice and allow us to reconcile the disjunctures between the evidence from garments and that from retailers' documents.

The specificity of the act of consumption to the consumer is insisted upon, for different reasons, by both Bourdieu (1977, 1984, 1990) and Campbell (1997). For Bourdieu, consumption provides an opportunity to demonstrate ownership of both financial and cultural capital, by reading through retailers' documents to identify the goods that suit their needs, their social position and their budget. For Campbell, the impossibility of applying a unitary 'meaning' to a particular garment is well demonstrated by the shifting meanings of quilted petticoats: from a merchant's livelihood to a mark of social status in a household, to defence against cold, to a source of illicit income, to evidence of a crime.

Acknowledgements

The author would like to thank all the archivists and museum curators who have assisted this research over a number of years by providing access to collections and catalogue information, and particularly: Linda Baumgarten (Colonial Williamsburg), Clare Browne and Susan North (Victoria and Albert Museum), Edwina Ehrman (Museum of London), Anthea Jarvis and Miles Lambert (Manchester Museums), Alexandra Palmer (Royal Ontario Museum).

Notes

1. Manchester 1947.4016; Williamsburg 1986.46; Montgomery 1984: fig. D69.
2. Heal and Banks collections.
3. Heal Collection 70.94, British Museum.
4. Heal, Banks and Johnson.
5. Heal, *passim*.
6. Guildhall: Hermans and Broady, 1769.
7. Guildhall: Jefferson, 1792.
8. Guildhall Collection: Petch, Haberdasher.
9. http://www.oldbaileyonline.org.

References

Baumgarten, L. (1986) *Eighteenth Century Clothing at Williamsburg*. Williamsburg, VA: Colonial Williamsburg Foundation.

Baumgarten, L. (2002) *What Clothes Reveal. The Language of Clothing in Colonial and Federal America: The Colonial Williamsburg Collection*. Williamsburg, VA: Colonial Williamsburg Foundation.

Berg, M. and Eger, E. (2003) *Luxury in the Eighteenth Century: Debates, Desires and Delectable Goods*. Basingstoke: Palgrave.

Bodleian Library (2001) *A Nation of Shopkeepers: Trade Ephemera from 1654 to the 1860s in the John Johnson Collection*. Oxford: Bodleian Library.

Bourdieu, P. (1977) *Outline of a Theory of Practice*. Cambridge: Cambridge University Press.

Bourdieu, P. (1984) *Distinction: A Social Critique of the Judgement of Taste*. London: Routledge & Kegan Paul.

Bourdieu, P. (1990) *The Logic of Practice*. Cambridge: Polity Press.

Brewer, J. and Porter, R. (1993) *Consumption and the World of Goods*. London: Routledge.

Buck, A. (1979) *Dress in Eighteenth Century England*. London: Batsford.

Campbell, C. (1997) 'When the meaning is not a message: a critique of the consumption as communication thesis', in *Buy this Book: Studies in Advertising and Consumption*, M. Nava (ed.), 340–51. London: Routledge.

Ehrman, E. (2006) 'Dressing well in old age: the clothing accounts of Martha Dodson, 1746–1765', *Costume* 40: 28–38.

Fleming, E. (1974) 'Artifact study: a proposed model', in *Winterthur Portfolio 9*, A. Quimby (ed.), 153–73. Charlottesville, VA: University of Virginia Press.

Heal, A. (1925) *London Tradesmen's Cards of the XVIII Century: An Account of their Origin and Use*. London: Batsford.

Lemire, B. (1991) *Fashion's Favourite: The Cotton Trade and the Consumer in Britain, 1660–1800*. London: Macmillan.

Lemire, B. (1994) 'Redressing the history of the clothing trade in England: ready-made clothing, guilds, and women workers, 1650–1800', *Dress* 21: 62–74.

Lemire, B. (1997) *Dress, Culture and Commerce: The Clothing Trades and English Society 1660–1800*. London: Macmillan.

Llewellyn, S. (1997) '"Inventory of her Grace's Things, 1747": the dress inventory of Mary Churchill, 2nd Duchess of Montague', *Costume* 31: 49–67.

McKendrick, N., Brewer, J. and Plumb. J. (1982) *The Birth of a Consumer Society: The Commercialization of Eighteenth Century England*. London: Europa.

Miller, D. (1987) *Material Culture and Mass Consumption*. Oxford: Basil Blackwell.

Montgomery, F. (1984) *Textiles in America, 1650–1870*. New York: W. W. Norton & Co.

Pointon, M. (1997) *Strategies for Showing: Women, Possession, and Representation in English Visual Culture 1665–1800*. Oxford: Oxford University Press.

Prown, J. (1982) 'Mind in matter: an introduction to material culture theory and method', *Winterthur Portfolio* 17(2): 1–17.

Prown, J. (1993) 'The truth of material culture: history or fiction?', in *History from Things: Essays on Material Culture*, S. Lubar and W. Kingery (eds), 1–19. Washington, DC: Smithsonian Institution Press.

Rexford, N. (1988) 'Studying garments for their own sake: mapping the world of costume scholarship', *Dress* 14: 68–75.

Rickards, M. and Twyman, M. (2000) *The Encyclopedia of Ephemera: A Guide to the Fragmentary Documents of Everyday Life for the Collector, Curator, and Historian*. London: British Library.

Rose, C. (1995) 'A group of embroidered eighteenth-century bedgowns', *Costume* 30: 70–84.

Rose, C. (1999) 'The manufacture and sale of "Marseilles" quilting in eighteenth-century London', *Bulletin du CIETA* 76: 104–11.

Rothstein, N. (1987) *A Lady of Fashion: Barbara Johnson's Album of Styles and Fabrics*. London: Thames & Hudson.

Scott-Moncrieff, R. (1911) *The Household Book of Lady Grisell Baillie, 1692–1733*. Edinburgh: Scottish History Society.

Severa, J. and Horswill, M. (1989) 'Costume as material culture', *Dress* 15: 53.

Staniland, K. (1990) 'An eighteenth-century quilted dress', *Costume* 24: 43–54.

Steele, V. (1998) 'A museum of fashion is more than a clothes-bag', *Fashion Theory* 2(4): 327–36.

Taylor, L. (1998) 'Doing the laundry? A reassessment of object-based dress history', *Fashion Theory* 2(4): 337-58.

Taylor, L. (2002) *The Study of Dress History*. Manchester: Manchester University Press.

Vickery, A. (1993) 'Women and the world of goods: a Lancashire consumer and her possessions, 1751–81', in *Consumption and the World of Goods*, J. Brewer and R. Porter (eds), 274–301. London: Routledge.

The author

Clare Rose teaches history of textiles at Chelsea College of Art and Design. She developed skills in material culture analysis working as a museum curator. For her doctoral thesis *Boyswear and the Formation of Gender and Class Identity in Urban England, 1840–1900* (University of Brighton, 2006), she developed a methodology for quantifying and comparing evidence for textiles and texts which has been applied to the 18th-century sources in this paper.

Address

Clare Rose, 147 Greenhill Road, Winchester SO22 5DU, UK (clare@brook-hart.fsnet.co.uk)

Analysing patents and objects: a preliminary investigation into the crinolines of W.S. Thomson

Katy May

ABSTRACT This paper presents research into the company W.S. Thomson and Co., who produced crinolines. Evidence from the patents and applications for patents lodged by the company is compared to evidence acquired by studying extant garments. It is argued that using both sources in conjunction builds a deeper understanding of the company and the crinolines it produced.

Keywords: crinoline, patent, W.S. Thomson and Co, Empress A, Crown Perfumery, C. Amet

Introduction

The term 'crinoline' (derived from the French word 'crin' for horsehair and 'lin', a contraction of linen thread), refers to a stiffened petticoat made of horsehair and linen. The term was also applied to the metal cage or hooped petticoat, however, sometimes called the artificial cage crinoline, which made its appearance in the mid-1850s. Advances in technology led to the introduction of sprung steel and the use of this new material allowed crinolines to be light but strong. These petticoats were able to support the ever-widening skirts and they replaced the need to wear layers of petticoats or other types of stiffened petticoat. By the 1860s the crinoline was such a dominating feature of women's fashions that the term is synonymous with the period.

This paper focuses on one manufacturer of crinolines, W.S. Thomson and Co. The research began with one crinoline (Fig. 1a,b). Analysis of this object revealed that as well as being clearly marked with the maker's name, Thomson's crinolines have specific material properties and design features that distinguish them from other makers' crinolines. This highlights why the study of objects is at the heart of this research. To date, 31 crinolines have been examined: 18 are Thomson's products; two (which are unmarked) are similar to known Thomson's designs but differ in the materials used and may be cheaper copies; the remaining 11 were either made by other manufacturers or are unlabelled. Further information about Thomson's has been uncovered in published literature at Companies' House, in trademark journals and from patent applications. This paper seeks to introduce and summarise the research so far. It focuses on the contribution of the patents in expanding what is known of the company and the first three patents connected to the company will be looked at in detail.

W.S. Thomson and Co.: the company

There is little information about the crinoline in texts on dress history and even less about their manufacture. Most references to Thomson and Co. in published sources relate to images of Thomson's products in costume collections (Bradfield 1997; Byrde and Garnett nd; Fukai 2002). There are a few tantalising references, however, for example:

> The largest firm of crinoline manufacturers was that of Thomson's in London, which had branches in New York, Paris, and Brussels, as well as others in Saxony and Bohemia. The London factory alone employed over a thousand women and turned out between three and four thousand crinolines daily. The number of hooks and eyes required amounted to a quarter of a million a day. In twelve years the branch in Saxony alone manufactured 9,597,600 crinolines. The quantities of materials required for such an enormous output may be gathered from the fact that the steel wire for the frames of all these skirts amounted to many times the circumference of the earth (Waugh 1954: 166)

According to Cunnington and Willet (1992: 166) 'those [crinolines] bearing the name of Thomson were considered superior to all others of English make', while Alison Adbugham describes Thomson's as one of 'the leading manufacturers of the Crinoline' (Adbugham 1964: 93). William Sparks Thomson, an American, is widely acknowledged as being the W.S. Thomson. As well as W.S. Thomson and Co., the company is often referred to as 'Thomson's and Co. of New York' (Lord 1993: 204). From advertisements, it is clear that Thomson's sold a range of structured undergarments and related products. In addition to the crinoline, one of its most famous products was the glove-fitting corset (Tarrant 1994: 78).

W. S. Thomson and Co. was a market leader in what became an important area of manufacturing. Madeline Ginsburg sees the manufacture of the crinoline and the innovations in steel production connected to it as being second in importance only to the sewing machine. Intriguingly she goes on to state 'When they (Thomson's) diversified to make bustles, corsets and then ready to wear clothes and even gloves they did much to standardize the appearance of the later nineteenth century woman' (Ginsburg 1996: 38–9). As yet, little evidence has been found to confirm that the company did diversify into women's ready-to wear clothing.

Where the company originated is unknown. An internet search for William Sparks Thomson came up with information on the Crown Perfumery (Basenotes 2003). The Crown Perfumery had its premises at 40 The Strand, an address that also features in Thomson's patent applications. There is a clear similarity between Thomson's trademark of a crown (Fig. 1b) and that of the Crown Perfumery. The trademark journals confirm this link with both trademarks being lodged for W.S. Thomson. Information about the Crown Perfumery claims that William Sparks was originally a corset manufacturer who produced corsets for Queen Victoria, however this is yet to be confirmed.

A search by Companies' House[1] revealed that the company was registered in 1887 and it existed as W.S. Thomson and Co. Ltd until 1972 when the name was changed to F.C. Savage (Foundations) Ltd, before finally being dissolved in 1992. In spite of the prestige of its crinolines and glove-fitting corsets, the company is almost completely absent from the written record. It could be that the records for the company are in the United States or France or they might no longer exist.

The study of extant garments

This research started with a detailed examination of an 'Empress A' crinoline. The results of this enquiry are presented in Figure 1 (a and b). The project was expanded to study 17 objects classified as 'structured undergarments worn below the waist dating from the second half of the nineteenth century' in the collections of Horsham, Worthing and Brighton museums. Seven of these were Thomson's products and the remaining ten were either left unlabelled by the manufacturer or they were homemade. Since then, a further ten Thomson's crinolines have been examined, along with two made by other and unspecified manufacturers. This brings the number of garments examined to date to 31.

This study of objects revealed that Thomson's produced a range of crinolines and 'crinolettes'[2] in a variety of designs between the 1850s and the 1880s. They were made using a number of components and construction methods which were specific to their products. Thomson's crinolines were marked with the maker's name and trademark, they had a product name, for example 'Empress', and some had an additional classification mark, for example 'A' (Fig. 1a,b). All crinolines marked as Thomson's were at least partially skeletal in structure, which is linked to Thomson being the patentee of the skeleton petticoat GB1729/1856.[3] All marked products were either red or white and there was a level of uniformity to the textile components used.

The textile components of the crinolines consist of varying combinations of wool flannel, plain weave cotton, white dimity cotton and cotton twill tape. Although the number of steels and the way they are distributed differs with each model, the steels used are 1 × 3 mm, or occasionally 1 × 1 mm, and are covered with a loosely woven tape in the same way as on the 'Empress A' in Figure 1 (a and b). The tape needs further analysis to determine its exact nature, but from observation it seems that the majority of the steels are covered with cotton rather than the wool used to cover the steels of the 'Empress A'.

Thomson's crinolines have three distinct types of vertical tapes: (1) double woven of the same design as used in the construction of the 'Empress A', which are found in two widths: 6.5 cm and 3 cm; (2) a simple cotton twill tape approximately 3 cm wide; and (3) fully lined panels of fabric, which are wider at the hem than the waistband. In addition, the steel hoops are attached to the vertical tapes using two methods: (1) threaded through self-woven casings and (2) held in place with eyelets that fold around the steels.

What the patents reveal about W.S. Thomson and Co.

Thomson's connection with patents is obvious from looking at the extant garments because some are marked with 'Her Majesty's Royal Letters Patent'. Nineteen patent applications linked to the company were found and the name that connects all of the patents and the applications for patents is that of William Sparks Thomson. These were found by looking through the *Index to the Patentees and Applicants* for the years 1856 to 1896. The date of 1856 was chosen because it is commonly believed to be the year that the metal cage crinoline was introduced (Gersheim 1963: 45; Levitt 1986: 36) when C. Amet patented the skeleton petticoat (GB1729/1856). Thomson's is connected to the first patented crinoline by an announcement made by their solicitors, which states their intention to prosecute anyone who infringed their patent rights to 'Amet's patent'. This patent is not, however, connected to the company within the patent records. The year 1856 also marks the introduction of sprung steel by Henry Bessemer, the key component of metal cage crinolines (Cunnington and Willet 1992: 163–6; Ginsburg 1996: 38; Levitt 1986: 36). W.S. Thomson applied for his last patent in 1890 and by this time, crinolines are considered to have been out of fashion for quite some time.

The patent specifications contain the names, occupations and addresses of those connected to the application. The records give the names of seven associates and/or employees of William Sparks Thomson, along with their addresses in London, New York and Paris. The patents make it clear that the majority of the inventions were communicated from abroad and that they were not the ideas of W.S. Thomson. Of the 19 patents and applications for patents applied for by the company, only the first three relate directly to the manufacture of crinolines (discussed below). The other 16 applications are not connected to a specific product, focusing instead on issues relating to production including spinning technology, dress fastenings and the heating and annealing of furnaces.

In the patents, William Sparks's occupation is defined as manufacturer. There is a possibility, however, that he may have

Figure 1 a and b Detailed analysis of 'Empress A' crinoline belonging to Barbara Burman (Plate 60 in the colour plate section).

ANALYSING PATENTS AND OBJECTS

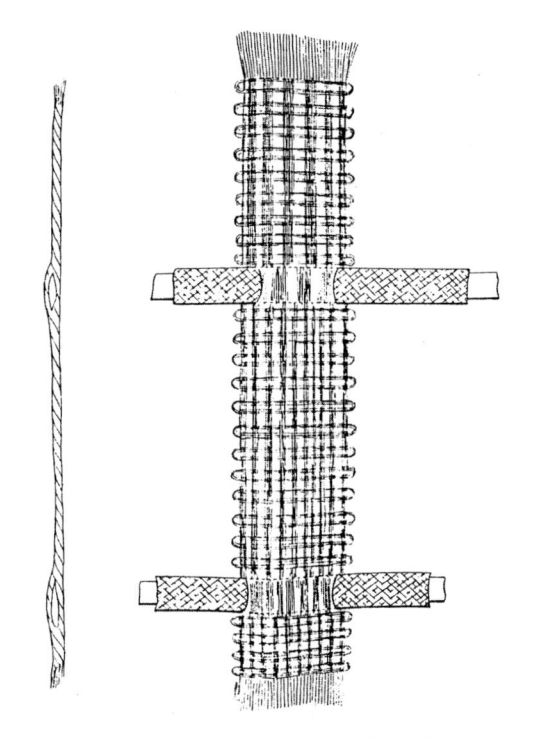

Figure 2 Image from GB1204/1859 showing detail of specification drawing for double woven tapes with casings for hoops to pass through.

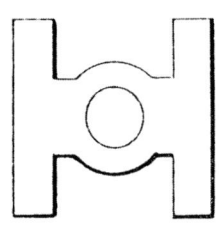

Figure 3 Image from GB1204/1859 showing detail of specification drawings of eyelet.

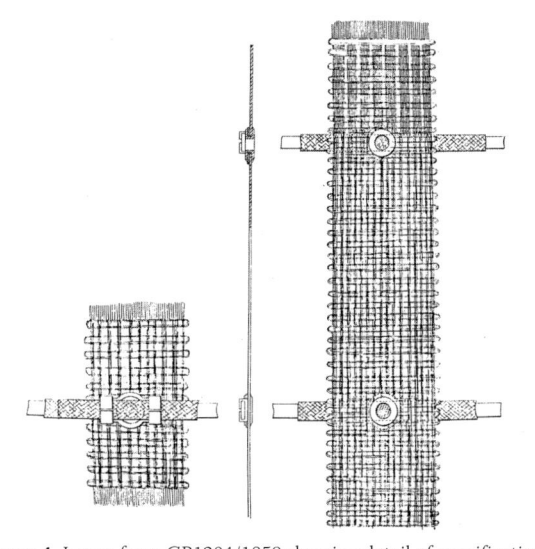

Figure 4 Image from GB1204/1859 showing detail of specification drawings of eyelets holding hoops in place.

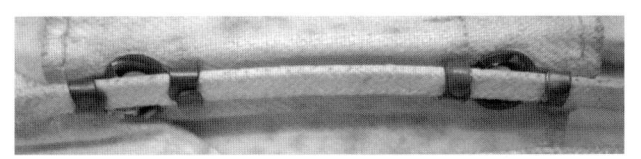

Figure 5 Image showing the back of eyelet holding hoops in place (Paris Prize No: 375. 1964/536. Worthing Museum and Art Gallery). (Plate 61 in the colour plate section)

been involved in funding innovations rather than developing them for a specific purpose. The evidence for this is the diverse range of patents applied for in his name, and the number of people linked to these inventions. The announcement made by Thomson's solicitors declaring their right to Amet's patent not only gives the solicitor's name and address but also specifies four manufacturers in London and one in Sheffield who were licensed to manufacture Thomson's products. This adds credibility to the statement made by Levitt in her book *Victorians Unbuttoned* (1986: 36) that Thomson marketed rather than manufactured crinolines. All of this supports the image of Thomson as an entrepreneur rather than a manufacturer. A more detailed picture of the company is starting to emerge, although many questions remain to be answered.

What the patents add to the study of Thomson's crinolines

Much of the information relating to the construction of Thomson's crinolines, which was gathered by looking at the extant garments, can be clarified by reading the company's patents. Patents have their limitations, however, one of the most obvious being that it is unclear from the patents if, or to what extent, an invention was actually used. For example, the first patent applied for by the company (GB1204/1859) concerns two aspects of the construction of crinolines and specifies various ways of implementing the innovations.[4]

The initial discussion presents three methods for connecting the hoops and vertical tapes: (1) 'I weave loops in the tapes at given distances apart, through which the steel ribs are to be passed' (Fig. 2); (2) 'I apply to the tapes ... a metal fastening by means of an eyelet attachment, and these ... clasp the steel ribs or hoops' (Figs 3, 4 and 5); and (3) 'when narrow tapes are used, I prefer to use a fastening ... the form of the letter I, the projections of which lap round the steel rib or hoop, while the parallel edges bend over the edge of the steel, and hold the tape firmly'.

When comparing the construction of the 'Empress A' crinoline (Fig. 1a,b) and other Thomson's products with the patent specification, it is clear that the crinolines have been constructed using two of the methods of connecting the hoops to the vertical tapes listed above. Examining the diagrams that form part of the patent alongside the existing crinolines is the best way to see how the inventions were translated into physical reality. The two methods used are the double-woven tapes with self-woven casings to take the hoops (Figs 1a,b and 2) and the specially designed eyelet (Figs 3–5) used to secure the hoops. No examples of the third method, detailed above, have been found. As yet, the reason for this is uncertain.

The second aspect of GB1204/1859 details two methods of fastening the lengths of metal into hoops: (1) 'I use a metal clip, which, being lapped over the ends by pressure, will bind them securely together' and (2) 'When, however, the hoops are required to be adjustable in diameter I attach ... a metal cap which is fitted with a tongue or wedge piece, and over the lapping ends I bend two sliding clips ... when pushed inwards or towards each other ... allow of the hoops being diminished or enlarged in diameter'. All of the hoops on Thomson's crinolines examined are joined in the same way as the 'Empress A' (Fig. 1a,b) with each end being bound with a T-shape and two rectangular pieces of brass folded around the overlapping steels (Fig. 1a). The use of brass as the material and shape of the pieces was deduced from observations of existing garments. That this method of forming the hoops made them adjustable was not clear from looking at the crinolines alone. This detail is one of the contributions made by the patent specifications. It also explains the uniform overlaps of the hoops on some crinolines and the irregular overlap on others of the same design that was found when looking at the garments.

The simple binding of the steels to hold the ends securely, which is the first method specified, is not seen in any of the examples. This could indicate that those crinolines which were not adjustable were of a lower quality and cheaper and so less likely to have survived, or that adjustable hoops were such a popular feature that more examples were produced and therefore more have survived. Alternatively, it may simply be that this method was not actually used.

The patent specification GB2045/1859 gives us an interesting insight into Thomson's manufacturing process. One of the features described is 'the pattern frame', a wooden three-dimensional template on which to construct the crinolines:

> The pattern frame, shaped in profile to correspond to the pattern skirt desired to be made, is used as a base upon which to build up the skirt. For this purpose the tapes which are to support the hoops, having been secured together at the waistband, are drawn down over the ribs of the frame, and the steel strips or bands are lapped round the frame at proper distances apart, and secured to the tapes by any of the known means of attachment, and their ends are then connected together by metal clasps or otherwise, in order to form them into hoops. By thus building up the skirts upon a rigid frame to the shape of the skirt to be made, it will be readily understood that the relative adjustment of the hoops to secure a good 'set' of skirt will be effectually secured at the time of effecting their attachment to the tapes (GB2045/1859).

These details of the pattern frame and the information from GB1204/1859 about how the steels were formed into hoops and how they were connected to the vertical tapes, provides a detailed insight into the construction of Thomson's crinolines. An image of crinolines being made, which is likely to be of French origin (Perrot 1994: 73; Saint-Laurent 1986: 111) shows a factory full of frames similar to that detailed in GB2045/1859.[5] The description of the pattern frame from the patent and the accompanying drawings suggest that this might be an image of one of Thomson's factories.

The details recorded within the patents reveal how they can illuminate the evidence preserved by the extant garments. On occasion, however, the patents can raise challenging questions, as indicated by a study of GB2044/1859. The success of the metal cage crinoline was based on it being light yet strong enough to hold out the wearer's skirts. The steels were therefore an essential element of the crinoline. One specific problem related to the use of steel hoops, however, was pointed out in patent GB2044/1859: 'for hoops formed of light bands are very liable to get out of shape and when made of thicker bands are liable to snap if subjected to undue pressure'. It went on to state that 'This invention relates to a mode of imparting the requisite elasticity to steel and other metal strips or bands (which are intended to be used in the manufacture of hooped skirts) with the employment of less weight of metal than heretofore' (GB2044/1859).

The patent sought to corrugate the metal in order to make it lighter and more flexible, while retaining as much of the strength as possible. It is not clear from the information gained from examining the crinolines if this technique was actually used. It would be difficult to establish without closer, intrusive analysis, especially for those crinolines in good condition. In addition, GB2044/1859 also proposes a way of using iron and brass as substitutes for steel. This brings into question the assumption that crinoline hoops were always made of steel. While it is unlikely that iron and brass were used, the possibility warrants further investigation.

Conclusion

The popularity of crinoline reached its height in the 1860s but this garment was still being worn despite later fashion changes. This research has established that Thomson's continued to produce crinolines in a wide range of shapes, sizes and qualities well into the 1880s. As fashions evolved and the silhouette altered, the crinoline altered accordingly. Assessing the patents and patent applications helps to widen our knowledge of the company and the crinolines that bear its name. The study of extant garments and the patents shows that not all of the innovations proposed by the manufacturers were translated into reality. The two sources complement each other: both contribute to our understanding, while raising many new questions.

It is still unclear if Thomson's was set up in England or if the company expanded into this country from the United States. The survival to this day of the company's reputation as one of the leading firms of crinoline manufactures is evidence of its importance. The question must be asked, however: why did this large, international company virtually disappear? Moreover, why is so little known about its history? The research undertaken so far has only scratched the surface. One area in need of further research is the relationship between crinoline manufacture and the steel industry. There are many leads still to be followed, areas to be explored and details to be clarified.

Acknowledgements

The author would like to thank Barbara Burman, Maria Hayward and the staff at the Museum of London, the V&A, and Horsham, Worthing and Brighton Museums.

Notes

1. Miss Rhian Bennet, Customer Services Assistant, Companies House, pers. comm., 19 December 2005 and 5 January 2006.

2. The term 'crinolette' is used to describe a cage that sits behind the body to hold out the bustle of a skirt. There is evidence that the term is one of Thomson's trademarks.
3. This announcement by Thomson's solicitors was found on permanent display at Worthing Museum.
4. GB1204/1859 was amended on 14 December 1863. The changes removed much of the detailed information on the proposed innovations. Information taken from the original specification has been used here.
5. This image is attributed to Bach 1865 in Perrot 1994, p. 73 but it is not credited in Saint-Laurent 1986, p. 111.

References

Adburgham, A. (1964) *Shops and Shopping 1800–1914*. London: George Allen and Unwin.

Basenotes, Doctor (2003) *Ask Doctor Basenotes – The History of the Crown Perfumery* [online] basenotes. Available from: http://www.basenotes.net/columnists/drbasenotes-apr03.html [accessed 19 January 2006].

Bradfield, N. (1997) *Costume in Detail 1730–1930*. Orpington: Eric Dobby Publishing.

Byrde, P. and Garnett, O. (nd) *The Museum of Costume & Assembly Rooms Bath*. Bath & Northeast Somerset Council in association with the Museum of Costume and the National Trust.

Cunnington, P. and Willet, C. (1992) *The History of Underclothes*. New York: Dover (reprint).

Fukai, A. (2002) *Fashion: A History from the 18th to the 20th Century – The Collection of the Kyoto Costume Institute*. Kyoto: Taschen.

Gernsheim, A. (1963) *Victorian and Edwardian Fashion: A Photographic Survey*. New York: Dover.

Ginsburg, M. (1996) 'Women's dress before 1900', in *Four Hundred Years of Fashion*, N. Rothstein (ed.), 74–100. London: Victoria and Albert Museum.

Levitt, S. (1986) *Victorians Unbuttoned*. London: George Allen and Unwin.

Lord, Sir W. (1993) *Freaks of Fashion: The Corset and The Crinoline 1868*. Mendonico: R.L. Shep.

Perrot, P. (1994) *Fashioning the Bourgeoisie: A History of Clothing in the Nineteenth Century*. Princeton, NJ: Princeton University Press.

Saint-Laurent, C. (1986) *A History of Women's Underwear*. London: Academy Editions.

Tarrant, N. (1994) *The Development of Costume*. London: Routledge.

Waugh, N. (1954) [2004] *Corsets and Crinolines*. London: Routledge.

Patents and patent applications

- Clothide Amet, 1856-16-12. *Ladies Petticoats*. GB1729/1856.
- William Sparks Thomson, 1859-13-05. *Manufacture of Hooped Skirts*. GB1204/1859.
- William Sparks Thomson, 1864-02-01. *Manufacture of Hooped Skirts*. GB1204/1859 Amended.
- Alfred Vincent Newton, 1859-07-09. *Manufacture of Metallic Strips or Bands for Skirts*. GB2044/1859.
- Alfred Vincent Newton, 1859-07-09. *Manufacture of Hooped Skirts*. GB2055/1859.
- Lemuel Dow Owen, 1861-05-01. *Bustles or Skirt Supporters*. GB34/1861.
- George Washington Belding, 1861-05-02. *Skeleton Petticoats*. GB295/1861.
- George Washington Belding, 1861-22-04. *Sewing Machines*. GB996/1861.
- George Washington Belding, 1861-22-04. *Making Pointed Tape Trimming*. GB997/1861.
- William Sparks Thomson, 1865-02-03. *Covering Crinoline Steel*. GB588/1865.
- William Sparks Thomson, 1868-11-11. *Corsets, Jackets, Mantels, &c*. GB3424/1868.
- Edward Drucker, 1866-17-06. *Dress Fastenings*. GB1860/1866.
- Edward Drucker, 1866-16-11. *Punching and Eyelet Machine*. GB3004/1866.
- Henry Alexander Lyman, 1867-28-06. *Skirts*. GB1893/1867.
- William Sparks Thomson, 1867-17-06. *Heating and Annealing Furnaces*. GB1784/1867.
- Alexander Horace Brandon, 1868-26-06. *Spinning*. GB2064/1868.
- William Sparks Thomson, 1868-19-12. *Skirts*. GB3872/1868.
- Alexander Horace Brandon, 1870-06-04. *Strap Fastener*. GB1008/1870.
- Alexander Horace Brandon, 1870-30-09. *Spinning Machinery*. GB2603/1870.
- Charles Ernest Thomson, 1886-15-11. *Improvements in Bustles or Dress-improvers*. GB14816/1886.
- William Sparks Thomson, 1888-23-04. *An Improved Bustle or Dress Improver*. GB6042/1888.
- Charles Ernest Thomson, 1890-22-02. *Improvements in and Relating to the Manufacture of Ribbed Undergarments and Similar Knitted Articles*. GB2903/1890.

The author

Katy May is a part-time MA student in the history of textiles and dress at the Winchester School of Art, University of Southampton. A BA in costume design from Wimbledon School of Art was followed by working as a wardrobe assistant with the BBC and as a costumier for the costume hire company Angels.

Address

Katy May, Waitiuna, Park Street Lane, Slinfold, West Sussex RH13 0RB, UK (may_katy@hotmail.com)

Patents as a source of information about synthetic textile dyes

Rosemary M. Baker

ABSTRACT Patents are a fruitful source of information about the 19th-century textile dyes that developed following the breakthrough synthesis of 'mauveine' by Perkin in 1856. They provide a date before which the dye is most unlikely to be found although they do not indicate how popular a dye was or for how long it continued to be used. This information, in conjunction with a dye identification method, can be used to date textiles. The patents also provide information about the level of commercial activity in the field of textile dyeing and about collaborations and rivalries between manufacturers. This paper deals with UK patents although information about other European and US patents is also available.

Keywords: textile dyes, synthetic, British patents, 19th century, commercial information

Introduction

Identification of textile dyes has been used extensively for providing information about the textile, such as dating and place of manufacture, and for informing conservation decisions. Much research has been carried out on dyes of plant and animal origin, generally referred to as natural dyes. The synthetic dyes introduced after the discovery of 'mauveine' by Perkin in 1856, however, have been less studied to date. They were synthesised from the by-products of the manufacture of coal gas for artificial lighting and therefore are generally purer than extracts from natural sources. For this reason it was hoped that they might generate a spectrum with a single peak which could be used to identify the dye, and the application of reflected visible light as a method of identifying these synthetic dyes was examined (Baker 2005).

For the dye identification to be useful for dating, the date of first manufacture of each dye is required as well as, preferably, some indication of how long each was in use. These dyes were manufactured by very specific, novel processes which the emerging field of organic chemistry was able to describe and therefore they could be patented. Thus, patents are a potential useful source of information about these dyes.

Patents have previously been used as a source of information about other materials such as semisynthetic plastics (Fernandez-Villa and Moya 2005). In this case, patent numbers stamped onto objects can be traced to provide information about the composition of the plastic as well as the date and country of origin. The present study analyses UK patents for synthetic dyes and relevant mordants between 1858 and 1863.

Patents as a documentary source

Patents were accessed through the British Library Intellectual Property and Business Section. Electronic databases such as Esp@cenet are useful for 20th-century patents and are multinational. For 19th-century patents, however, the data are only available in paper form and the main volumes of UK patents are bound sequentially in order by patent number. A shortened form is also available bound chronologically but with patents relating to similar inventions referred to as 'classes' grouped together. Class 14 is titled 'Abridgements of specifications relating to bleaching, dyeing and printing calico and other fabrics, and yarns; including the preparation of drugs and other processes' and this provides a much quicker way of identifying relevant patents than the sequential volumes. The 19th-century UK patents were numbered sequentially but the sequence was started again from 1 at the beginning of each year so that each patent has to be identified by a number and the year.

Information deriving from patents: possibilities and limitations

Patents provide a date before which a dye is most unlikely to have been used commercially although there is a possibility that a chemist or dyer could have used a compound before it was patented by himself or another inventor. Occasionally there are examples of two inventors producing the same dye almost simultaneously such as malachite green in 1877 (Cooksey and Dronsfield 2003). The commercial protection afforded by the patent system, however, was probably enough of an incentive to ensure that new compounds were patented on invention.

The patenting of a dye did not mean that it was immediately used for dyeing textiles – indeed it may never have been used commercially if it was too expensive or not fast enough on the required fabric. Indigo was first synthesised by von Bayer in 1880 but it took more than 20 years for a synthetic method that was commercially cost-effective to be developed (Delamare and Guineau 2000: 105). Furthermore, in some cases a superior alternative giving the same colour may have been developed which was substituted and patents do not give any information on the length of time for which a dye was used. Therefore, the data obtained from patents could be usefully supplemented by commercial information about dye manufacture.

The information supplied in the abridgements of the patents lists the person to whom the patent was assigned, the claims of the patent and also, in some cases, an overseas contact who has supplied the patented information. In the full patent the address and often the occupation of the patent assignee is given but only the city of residence of the overseas informant. The patent claim, where the information which is being protected is given, also sometimes includes an explanation of the advantages of this new dye over previous versions, giving some background about the preoccupations and priorities of the chemists.

The fashionable colours

In total, 86 relevant patents were found. Plate 62 (in the colour plate section) shows the UK patents lodged in each year of the period examined. The total number increased fairly rapidly and the colours covered by the patents changed over time. Purples, reds and violets were patented fairly consistently but blue appears more frequently at the end of the period, perhaps reflecting the search for a satisfactory true blue as indicated by Schlumberger in 1863 (Patent No. 117): 'a true blue from aniline has not been achieved – so far all have a reddish, purplish or violet tinge by artificial light'. This may also highlight the requirements of the fashions which the chemists were trying to satisfy.

The related colours yellow and brown first appear in 1860 and become frequent by 1863. This is consistent with the fashionable colours of this period. In his summary extracted from 19th-century fashion magazines, Cunnington (1937) lists 'Havannah' (a brown) as newly fashionable in 1860 and 'Cuir' (also brown) as a new colour in 1862. Both 'Havanne' and 'Cuirs' are mentioned in a patent of 1863 (Monteith and Monteith, Patent No. 660). It is possible that either the fashions were following the newly invented dye colours or that the chemists were trying to produce colours demanded by the fashionable world, but it is not possible to distinguish between these two alternatives on the basis of the information from the fashion magazines and the patents.

Collaborations

The names of the persons lodging the patent and the suppliers of the information are given in the patent abridgements but the full patent must be consulted to find any further information such as their addresses and, in the case of the patentee, their occupation. This is quite a time-consuming process since each patent is in a separate volume but it reveals additional information about the collaborations between the parties supplying the information and the parties lodging the patents. Table 1 shows some of the information gathered so far.

When analysing these data the assumption has been made that the information supplied is given willingly as otherwise there seems little point in crediting the source. Additionally, there are cases where patents are sometimes lodged jointly by two parties who, on other occasions, lodge patents based on information supplied by one or the other, for example in the case of Gratrix and Paraf Javal,[1] cited below. In many of these cases the patent assignee is a patent agent who, presumably, would not have a professional interest in exploiting the patent himself but is protecting the invention on behalf of his client.

The patterns of interaction seen between the patent holders and others are complex. Sometimes the overseas suppliers of information used a UK patent agent to lodge the patent, as in the case of the Renard brothers from Lyons. This was obviously a satisfactory arrangement as the same process was repeated three times in 1859. In 1862 the same agent (R.A. Brooman) lodged a patent on behalf of another French client, Pierre Chalamel. He did not confine his interests purely to clients in the textile trade as he also lodged a patent for a poultry wagon (1859, No. 2693) on behalf of another client from Paris. It may be that some agents maintained particular expertise in acting for clients from one country; William Gilbee (1862, No. 1939) states that he is of the firm of L. de Fontainmoreau and Gilbee so may have specific connections with France.

In other cases, however, patents seem to be lodged as collaborations between textile manufacturers. For example, Robert Gratrix, a dyer and printer from Salford, lodged a patent based on information from Mathias Paraf of Thann in France (1860, No. 2794). In a separate patent, lodged jointly with Robert Gratrix (1860, No. 2205), Mathias Paraf Javal is described as a calico printer so these two individuals clearly had common business interests. This example also illustrates how information from more than one patent can be combined to give a more complete picture of the contribution of each party to the process.

In several cases the individual lodging the UK patent did not list their occupation but gave an address, which implies that they may have been in the legal profession or a patent agent. For example, Alfred Newton lodged a patent (1863, No. 1972) on behalf of Meister Lucius and Co. based in Hoescht-am-Main. He listed his address as the Office for Patents. In another case, Astley Price, who lodged a patent (1862, No. 3312) based on information supplied by Augustus Eisenlohr from Heidelberg simply described himself as a gentleman and gave his address as 47 Lincoln's Inn Fields. Perhaps because of expertise gained in patenting in their professional field, some of the agents were engineers, for example, William Clark (1862, No. 2446), engineer and patent agent, and William Newton (1863, No. 821), simply described as a civil engineer.

Textile manufacturers did lodge patents but chemists were more numerous, with five individuals describing themselves in this way, to which it is possible to confidently add William

Table 1 Details of patents showing international collaborations (from Commissioners of Patents for Inventions 1877).

Date	Patent Number (s)	Assignee Name	Occupation	Address	Information supplied by
1859	921, 2461, 2694	BROOMAN, Richard Archibald	Patent agent	166 Fleet Street, London, EC	MM. Renard Frères of Lyons, France
1862	3423	BROOMAN, Richard Archibald	Patent agent	166 Fleet Street, London, EC	Pierre Chalamel, Puteaux, France
1862	2446	CLARK, William	Engineer and patent agent	53 Chancery Lane, Middx	Charles Philipe Collin, 29 Boulevard St. Martin, Paris, Merchant.
1860	2401	COWPER,[1] Charles	Patent agent	20 Southampton Buildings, Chancery Lane, Middx	Joseph Marie Albert Battelier, Avignon, France
1860	1300	DE LAIRE, Georges GIRARD, Charles	Chemists of the Imperial Mint, Paris		Witnessed by F. Tolhausen, 35 Boulevard Bonne Nouvelle
1860	2794	GRATRIX, Robert Hodgson	Dyer and printer	Salford, County of Lancaster	Matthias Paraf, Thann, France[2]
1862	1939	GILBEE, William Amand	Patent agent	Of the firm of L. de Fontainemoreau and Gilbee, 4 South Street, Finsbury	Prosper Monnet and Henry Dury, Chemical Manufacturers of Lyons, France
1859	1155	KAY, Richard Dugdale	Manufacturer of patent fabrics		Dollfus, Mieg and Cie., Mulhouse, France.
1863	1972	NEWTON, Alfred Vincent	None given	The Office for Patents, 66 Chancery Lane, Middx	Meister Lucius and co., Hoechst-am-Main, Duchy of Nassau, Germany.
1863	821	NEWTON, William Edward	Civil engineer	The Office for Patents, 66 Chancery Lane, Middx	David Clovis Knab, Colmar, France
1862	2107	PERKIN, William Henry	None given	Seymour Villa, Sudbury, Middx	Alexandre Schultz residing at 11 Rue St Fiacre, Paris
1862	3312	PRICE, Astley Paston	Consulting chemist	Lincoln's Inn Fields, Middx	Augustus Eisenlohr, Doctor of Philosophy from Heidelberg, the Grand Duchy of Baden
1863	117	SCHLUMBERGER, Jules Albert	Manufacturing chemist	Basle, Switzerland	Jean Jacques Muller, Basle, Switzerland
1859	2746	SMITH, Charles Lavers	Manufacturing chemist	Highbury Crescent, Middx	Albert Schlumberger, Mulhouse
1862	2130	SPENCE, William	Patent agent	50 Chancery Lane, Middx	Nicolas Philibert Guinon, Jean Aimé Mamas & François Bonnet, Manufacturers of Lyons, France

[1] Charles Cowper died on 23 December 1860 and the patent filing procedure was completed by his executors.

[2] In a joint patent (1860, No. 2205), Mathias Paraf Javal is described as a calico printer.

Henry Perkin, who gave no occupation. There is some variation in the precise description of the type of chemist including Georges De Laire and Charles Girard who described themselves as 'Chemists of the Imperial Mint, Paris' (1860, No. 1300). This illustrates the evolution of the trade from the art and craft of dyeing into a science and simultaneously the change in how its practitioners perceived themselves.

It seems likely that UK patents had to be lodged in the UK but that it was not necessary to travel to the Patent Office in London as demonstrated by Richard Kay who lodged Patent No. 115 in 1859. He described himself as a manufacturer of patent fabrics from Accrington, Lancashire and lodged the patent (based on information supplied by a firm from Mulhouse) with J. Hargreaves Kay, a solicitor and patent agent in Blackburn, Lancashire.

Conclusion

Nineteenth-century UK patents are less easy to access than later ones but the existence of volumes listed by patent subject makes manual searching viable. It is difficult to be certain about the significance of each individual record as the act of patenting an invention does not automatically imply that it will be commercially exploited and the patent, although valid for a specific timespan, does not give any clue about the length of time the dye was used. It could have been quickly overtaken by a superior compound or it could have been so successful that it continued to be used long after the patent had expired. The fact that the inventor was prepared to pay to patent his dye, however, shows that he hoped to gain some commercial advantage from the chemical. Equally, the number of patents and the types of compound patented give a good indication of both the capabilities of the chemists and the compounds they considered to be most marketable. Thus, it can be seen from contemporary records that the fashionable colours and the dye compounds developed in tandem, although whether the demand for a particular colour was driving the dye development or the new colours were creating new fashions is hard to determine. Certainly, the first synthetic dyes were adopted very quickly by the world of fashion and there was a huge amount of national prestige involved as well.

Assuming that the dyes were patented before any commercial use, the date provides an absolute time point before which the dye will not be found and thus this information could be used to date any textile on which that dye compound can be identified. There remains only the complication that the dye could have been used in a later repair to an earlier textile but this should be obvious on close inspection of the item.

The amount of information which can be extracted from the patents filed is not limited to the date, however. The number of patents in total and those relating to particular colours can give some indication of the level of economic activity in the field. The extent of information exchange between various parties, such as chemists and textile manufacturers, can give a picture of the collaborations which were developed and it is evidence of a mixture of international cooperation and rivalry. Some non-British manufacturers formed alliances with their British counterparts to obtain patents while others used patent agents.

A large number of relevant patents have been identified from the six-year period studied and the number lodged may be even greater later in the 19th century as the field expanded. This number is greater than the new colours developed so obviously not all of the patents resulted in commercial dyes. Interpretation on this point could be aided by other archival investigations such as manufacturers' sample books, dye manuals and contemporary fashion information. In addition, object-based research could be used to provide confirmation that particular colours or chemicals were in common use at a given date.

This study shows the range of information available from UK patents. Similar data can also be found for patents from other European countries and the USA, but these are less easy to search as these patents are more likely to be recorded only chronologically and not by patent topic group as in the UK patent system. In addition the UK patents are more easily accessed within the UK and electronic versions of 19th-century patents, which would facilitate remote searching, have not been found. It is possible in principle, however, to extend this study to other records and identify dye patents in the same way.

This type of data is valuable for textile conservators and curators as it can provide dating evidence for the use of certain dyes. This will be particularly applicable if particular dyes can be identified in textiles and then related to the date when they were first used. Nevertheless it is possible now to exclude the possibility that the dye is one of the known natural colours and then to identify its synthetic dye class and relate this to the date of introduction of this class of dyes. As well as dating whole pieces, this information can also be used to identify later additions to earlier textiles and thereby inform decisions over conservation treatment. Some dyes are particularly susceptible to fading and thus the dye identification can be used to make decisions on display conditions.

For the textile curator and historian, these sources can provide information on economic collaborations, rivalries and the flow of ideas within the international textile industry. They can also provide some indications of the motivations and aspirations of the inventors, including the pressures exerted from the manufacturers to supply new and improved colours.

Note

1. The names Mathias Paraf and Mathias Paraf Javal appear in different documents. They may refer to the same person or to closely related individuals but there is nothing in the records to indicate whether this is the case.

References

Baker, R.M. (2005) *The Use of Reflected Visible Light Spectra to Analyse Dyed Fabrics*. Unpublished dissertation submitted in part fulfilment of the requirements for MA Textile Conservation, University of Southampton.

Commissioners of Patents for Inventions (1877) *Abridgements of UK patents for inventions, Class 14. Abridgements of specifications relating to bleaching, dyeing, and printing calico and other fabrics and yarns; including the preparation of drugs and other processes. Part II AD 1858–1866*. London: Office of the Commissioners of Patents for Inventions.

Cooksey, C.J. and Dronsfield, A.T. (2003) 'Fischer, Doebner and the search for green', *Education in Chemistry* 40(3): 46–52.

Cunnington, C.W. (1937) *English Women's Clothing in the Nineteenth Century*. London: Faber and Faber Ltd.

Delamare, F. and Guineau, B. (2000) *Colour: Making and Using Dyes and Pigments*. London: Thames and Hudson Ltd.

Fernandez-Villa, S.G. and Moya, M.S.A. (2005) 'Original patents as an aid to the study of the history and composition of semisynthetic plastics', *Journal of the American Institute for Conservation* 44: 95–102.

The author

Rosie Baker worked as a protein chemist for the UK National Health Service developing protein purification methods. During this time she took an active interest in textiles, particularly costume, and in 2005 she graduated from the MA Textile Conservation course at the Textile Conservation Centre, University of Southampton, UK. She is now pursuing research interests in conservation science and textile dyes.

Address

Rosie Baker, AHRC Research Centre for Textile Conservation and Textile Studies, Winchester School of Art, University of Southampton, Park Avenue, Winchester SO23 8DL, UK (rmb1@soton.ac.uk)

The interaction between East and West

A paradise of pretty girls: the kimono and perceptions of Japan

Elizabeth Kramer

ABSTRACT This paper uses both objects and archives from the collection of Scottish painter E.A. Hornel (1864–1933) at Broughton House, Kirkcudbright to demonstrate the difficulties presented in examining objects that have moved across cultures and the cultural bias present not only in written texts but also in informing object acquisition. To facilitate these considerations, the paper looks specifically at Hornel's special interest in Japanese kimono[1] and textiles, which will be discussed in relation to his two journeys to Japan in 1894 and 1921, his paintings of the country, and perceptions of Japan widely held in Britain at these times.

The kimono will be demonstrated to be instrumental in maintaining stereotypes about Japan. Hornel's Japan paintings rarely deviate from idyllic imagery of beautiful Japanese women in kimono, and brightly coloured and patterned textiles dominate his compositions. The fixity of Hornel's paintings carries through to his writing, which conjures up an image of the country as 'a paradise of babies and pretty girls' (Hornel 1895). The vibrant colours employed by Hornel in depicting kimono in his paintings proved popular with the purchasing public, and he was praised for his truthful depiction of Japan in reviews of his 1895 exhibition.

However, while these repetitive images of brightly costumed women offer images of Japan to be enjoyed aesthetically and serve to reinforce ideas of Japan as a timeless and exotic land, they do not indicate 20 years of rapid modernisation and social changes instituted by the Meiji government. They further deviate from travel literature of the time, which laments the lack of such sights in the day-to-day wear of the Japanese.

Keywords: gender, Great Britain, Hornel, Japan, kimono, 19th century, stereotype, 20th century

Introduction

In 1895, Scottish painter, Edward Atkinson Hornel, held a one-man exhibition at the gallery, La Societé des Beaux-Arts, in Glasgow. This exhibition featured 40 paintings inspired by Hornel's journey to Japan in 1894, which depict Japanese girls singing, dancing, playing battledore and shuttlecock, inspecting silks in the marketplace, strolling through gardens and likewise engaged in other amusements (*Evening Citizen* 25 April 1895 in Hornel Trust 1980) (Fig. 1).[2] These images were displayed without titles or an accompanying catalogue in simple ivory frames, which must have accentuated the brilliant colour in which they were painted. The press highly praised the exhibition, one review promising that audiences would find themselves 'revelling in the grand variety of heightened colours peculiar to life and nature in the land of the Mikado, which [Hornel] alone has up to the present fully appreciated and illustrated' (*Glasgow Echo* 4 May 1895 in Hornel Trust 1980). Another review concurred: 'The rich brilliant colours of Japan, the blinding sunlight and its deep, dark shadows, Mr Hornel reproduced with virile, and even amazing strength and success' (*The Bailie* 1 May 1895 in Hornel Trust 1980). Two themes emerge from examining these paintings and the reviews of the exhibition. First, the Victorians drew a distinct correlation between the topographic colour of Japan and the colour employed by the artist in his pictures of the country.

Secondly, the image of the kimono was central to establishing this correspondence. Just as kimono dominate Hornel's paintings, descriptions of the exhibition again and again describe 'charming figures cladden in silken drapery' or 'the busy mart, with their masses of silken draperies' (Untitled February 1895 and *Dumfries Courier & Herald* 24 November 1894 in Hornel Trust 1980).

There is further evidence to suggest the importance of Japanese textiles, particularly kimono, not only in informing the artist's depictions of Japan, but also relating to wider Victorian perceptions of the country. This evidence includes both objects and archival information resulting from Hornel's two journeys to Japan, the first in 1894 and the second in 1921, including two kimono which can be found at the artist's home, Broughton House, in Kirkcudbright, Galloway, Scotland (Figs 2 and 3). Both kimono are constructed of richly coloured silk decorated in appliqué and embroidered in gold and polychromatic thread. As it was Hornel's wish that Broughton House be left to the people of and visitors to Kirkcudbright as a public art gallery and library (Thomson 2005: 5), the collection contains a number of Japanese objects that Hornel acquired over his lifetime, which include two further textiles: a padded length of material embroidered in golden thread with floral motifs and used as an *obi* with one of the kimono, and a blue brocade fabric richly patterned with dragon and swirling cloud motifs. A number of kimono pattern books from the first quarter of the 20th century also belong to the collection in addition to books on the topics of Japanese art, travel, customs and gardening, including both Japanese and English editions. In addition, approximately 350 tourist photographs can be found in the collection (Ono 1999: 12). The study of this material record is further enriched by the artist's paintings, a volume of newspaper clippings relating to Hornel's artistic career between 1890 and 1900, his 1895 lecture on Japan and letters written during both journeys to the country.

Through consideration of the textiles and texts comprising the Hornel collection, this paper will demonstrate how textiles that have moved across cultures are encoded with new meaning as well as consider the desires and fears informing these changes. The personal significance of the kimono, textiles and books acquired by Hornel is discussed and then expanded upon when taking into account the relationship between Hornel's desires and fears and those expressed by the wider British public.

Hornel's early career

A brief discussion of Hornel's background is helpful in understanding the artist's interest in Japanese textiles. He belonged to a loose affiliation of artists known as the Glasgow Boys, who came together to challenge the authority of the Royal Scottish Academy (based in Edinburgh). They admired the works of the French Barbizon painters, who depicted the peasant classes in the countryside. Likewise, the Glasgow Boys sought out quiet, isolated places, such as Kirkcudbright, where they could observe and paint rural life in a similar manner.

Hornel's Japan paintings and the desires that they express can be linked to his earlier works executed in the rural surroundings of Kirkcudbright in which the artist depicts young girls at play and in repose.[3] These idyllic images equate youth and nature with a sense of timelessness and were extremely popular among the picture-buying public in the 19th and early 20th century. Such romanticised images could offer comfort in the face of the rapid changes brought on by modernisation and industrialisation. Hornel's decision to set up his studio and live in Kirkcudbright as opposed to the thriving industrial city of Glasgow reveals an anti-industrial spirit in the artist, and his works featuring girls in the rolling hills of Galloway offer a sharp contrast to images of modern industrial centres of the time. Indeed, Hornel's contemporary, A.S. Hartrick stated that, 'It is impossible to think of Hornel apart from Kirkcudbright, as he lived there nearly all his life and bought up much of the town in the days of his prosperity, in the hopeless attempt to save it from change' (Hartrick 1939: 58). As Ysanne Holt (2004) has pointed out, in the 20th century Hornel increasingly focused his attention on the past by expanding his collection of local literature and folklore and filling his garden with the exotic plants accumulated during his travels as well as objects of local or historical interest, such as curling stones and querns. Hornel's paintings depicting Japanese women dressed in kimono in the Japanese landscape can be closely related to his paintings of Gallaway as they reveal none of the changes brought on by Japan's opening to the West in 1854 after approximately 200 years of self-imposed isolation nor those instigated by the Meiji government established in 1868.

From the late 1880s, Hornel's paintings became increasingly brightly coloured and decorative. This stylistic change can be understood in relation to wider developments in the artistic community based in Glasgow, which were characterised by a shift of focus away from subject matter to more painterly and decorative effects. This shift was sparked not only by an interest in the work of the French Impressionists, but also in the Aesthetic Movement championed by James Abbott McNeil Whistler (1834–1903), who argued that painting should be for painting's sake alone. Because of his artistic ideals, Whistler became a hero among the Glasgow Boys, and in 1891 the Glasgow Art Club petitioned for the purchase of the artist's painting *Arrangement in Grey and Black No. 2: Thomas Carlyle* (1872–73) for the Glasgow Art Gallery (Billcliffe 1985: 289–91).

Figure 1 E.A. Hornel, *A Music Party*, 1894 (Aberdeen Art Gallery & Museums Collections).

Figure 2 Kimono, undated and uncatalogued (Hornel Library/The National Trust for Scotland) (Plate 63 in the colour plate section).

Figure 3 Kimono, undated and uncatalogued (Hornel Library/The National Trust for Scotland) (Plate 64 in the colour plate section).

The paintings of French artist Adolphe Monticelli (1824–1886) also clearly influenced Hornel's work, the former's paintings described as exhibiting a 'marvellously luxuriant fantasia of colours, a most decorative command of effect' (Muther 1895–96, 3: 666). Following the display of Monticelli's works at the International Exhibitions of 1886 and 1888 held respectively in Edinburgh and Glasgow, his paintings could be viewed annually at the Glasgow Institute (Smith 1997: 41–3). The Celtic Revival of the 1890s was another factor, and its influence can be seen clearly in *The Druids: Bringing in the Mistletoe* (1890), which Hornel painted with fellow artist George Henry, and for which the artists further designed a frame embellished with Celtic motifs.[4]

In the 1890s, Hornel began to incorporate Japanese elements into the dress of the girls depicted in his paintings. Japanese art was widely visible in Glasgow during the last quarter of the 19th century. An exhibition of Asian art including many Japanese objects was held at Glasgow's Corporation Art Galleries in 1882, and Frank Dillon exhibited paintings that he had made during his 1876 visit to Japan at the Glasgow Institute in 1883. Alexander Reid's gallery, La Societé des Beaux-Arts, where Hornel exhibited his Japan pictures in 1895, opened in 1889 with an exhibition of Japanese prints. Reid himself was known as an avid collector of Japanese prints, and partially funded Hornel and Henry's travels to Japan. The Glasgow Boys collected Japanese prints, and Grosvenor Thomas even dealt in Japanese curios and presented prints to the art club in 1894 (Smith 1997: 89; Billcliffe 1985: 256). In addition to their presence in museums and galleries, Japanese art wares were widely available throughout the city in curio shops, warehouses and department stores. Although Hornel's incorporation of Japanese elements may seem out of place in late 19th-century rural Scottish dress, it demonstrates a close and perhaps indiscriminate link between the use of dress based on exotic or traditional examples to achieve idealised images. For example, in *Summer* (1891), the pattern of the standing girl's blouse strongly evokes Japanese design through its use of motifs reminiscent of Japanese woodblock prints or the *mon* (heraldic crests) found on kimono.[5] The press immediately perceived such allusions to Japan in these paintings. One review of *Summer* stated that the 'colour in the figure of the girl in the foreground is distinctly Japanese' (*Liverpool* [*Daily Evening Press?*] September 1892 in Hornel Trust 1980). The critics drew further comparisons between Hornel's style of painting and Japanese textiles. A scathing review of *Summer* argued that while it was commonplace to admire Japanese blue and white ceramics, lacquerware or kimono, one could not equate 'paint with stuff' (*The Porcupine* 10 September 1892 in Hornel Trust 1980).

Hornel increasingly extended the vibrant colour and surface patterns of dress to the rest of the canvas to achieve a uniform decorative effect in his paintings from 1891. Whether in criticism or praise, his style has been viewed as distinctive, and his contemporaries noted its affinity time and again with the decorative arts, including tapestries and Oriental rugs (Pinnington 1900: 172; Hardie 1968: 28), or less praiseworthy, an 'old woman's patchwork quilt' or 'Japanese tea-caddy' (*Liverpool Echo* 5 September 1892, *The Porcupine* 24 September 1892 in Hornel Trust 1980). Contrary to traditional art-historical accounts drawing a distinct hierarchy between the so-called fine and decorative arts, and emphasising the influence of *ukiyo-e* prints on Western painters, many painters have found inspiration in the decorative arts, including textiles, and the influence and inspiration of Japanese textiles on Hornel's work should not be viewed as out of the ordinary. A letter written in 1868 by Whistler addresses the subject of colour in painting:

> The colours should be so to speak *embroidered* on [the canvas] – in other words the same colour reappearing continually here and there like the same thread in an embroidery ... the whole forming in this way an harmonious *pattern*. Look how the Japanese understand this! (Whistler 1994: 35).

The inspiration of Japanese textiles is increasingly apparent in Hornel's paintings and the artist's interest in this medium is further demonstrated by the kimono, textiles and related books that he acquired during his travels.

Hornel in Japan

In 1893, Hornel travelled to Japan in the company of fellow painter, George Henry. Of this first trip, very little object or archival evidence remains. The artists did return with a number of photographs, which proved particularly important to them as they used them in developing paintings (Ono 1999).[6] Figure 4 depicts one of these photographs, which is speckled with paint and marred with pinpricks, indicating its presence at the easel. Most of these photographs do not depict views of famous streets or landmarks, rather images of Japanese women in kimono as shown in this example.

It is believed that the kimono now in the collection at Broughton House were acquired during Hornel's first trip. In an 1895 letter to Hornel, Henry discussed a lecture on Japan that he had delivered to the Glasgow Art Club, in which he mentioned that the dresses arrived too late for a demonstration of dancing to be given (Henry 1893–95: 18 March 1895). Whether or not this refers to the kimono is impossible to know, and no further mention of them has been discovered in the archives at Broughton House to date. Certainly they could have been acquired on either trip or even from antique shops or warehouses specialising in Japanese curios in Glasgow.

Whatever their origin, the rich colour of the kimono acquired by Hornel corresponds with his paintings in which vibrantly coloured and patterned textiles dominate compositions rarely deviating from idyllic imagery of Japanese women and girls in kimono. During his second visit to Japan in 1921, a letter written by the artist (dated 5 March 1921) to his book dealer, Thomas Fraser, demonstrates the association that Hornel drew between kimono, vivid colour and the value that the former held for him as a painter.

> I went on the hunt one day with a Jap [*sic*] dealer for a book on Designs for Dresses, Kimonos, etc., and after visiting several shops buying some modern second hand volumes on the subject we dropped into a big silk manufactures place and there saw a volume of reproductions of 100 old and beautiful Designs taken from old costumes, magnificently done in colour. I at once bought a copy and now feel very secure on that point. They really suggest pictures in themselves ... It is a most useful volume and will be useful in more ways than one.

This letter demonstrates not only an interest in textiles but also an artist actively seeking out the most vibrantly coloured examples to inspire his work. That Hornel suggested that the illustrations, each reproduced from a sleeve of an intricately decorated *furisode* (Fig. 5), could serve as pictures in themselves reveals how strongly he felt about their artistic merit.

How representative were these kimono acquired by the artist or represented in his paintings in comparison to the Japanese dress that the artist encountered on a daily basis during his travels? Following Hornel and Henry's return to Scotland in 1894, Henry admitted in an interview:

> if you take your impressions of Japanese life from the prints you see here, you are all wrong. In Tokio [*sic*] and Yokohama, and throughout the north generally, it is not good taste to dress in colours. Dark blue, unrelieved by any variety, is the ordinary walking dress of the native ladies, and women in lower stations adopt the custom (*Kirkcudbrightshire Adviser* 20 July 1894 in Hornel Trust 1980).

Similarly, other artists credited with a special knowledge of Japan following their travels there were aware of discrepancies between their personal collections of Japanese textiles and the textiles and dress seen during their journeys. Industrial designer Christopher Dresser noted in a somewhat perplexed manner that the Japanese dress and textiles that he saw during his 1876 visit did not generally compare with the colourful examples from his own collection (Dresser 1882: 440).[7] This selective vision is further demonstrated in Hornel's 1895 lecture, which was presented at venues throughout Scotland and England, in which he suggested that one should overlook the crowded and dirty streets of Japan, treating the buildings:

> merely as a background to the colour in the shop windows, and the gay costumes of the busy crowds ... Perhaps the most interesting streets are those in which silk-merchants ... congregate, with their brilliant display of silk kimonos and rich brocades.[8]

These statements relate closely to his painting *A Japanese Silk Shop* (1896), in which brightly coloured and patterned textiles dominate the composition.[9] Jude Burkhauser argues that 'Life in the Orient was viewed as a "life of colour"' (1990: 233). Hornel's depiction of a richly coloured, romanticised vision of Japan on canvas inspired an excited response among the picture-buying public. As one 19th-century critic voiced, while the works of other artists who had recently visited Japan tended to be 'topographical and dull, or pretty in an Anglo-Japanese way', Hornel had captured the true Japan, authenticated by his rich use of colour (*Glasgow Evening [License?]* 22 April 1895 in Hornel Trust 1980).

These romanticised pictures were further authenticated by the women donning kimono. While earlier British paintings

Figure 4 Photograph, undated and uncatalogued (Hornel Library/The National Trust for Scotland) (Plate 65 in the colour plate section).

Figure 5 Illustration of a *furisode* sleeve from *A Catalogue of 100 Furisode Sleeves* (Japan 1919) (Hornel Library/The National Trust for Scotland) (Plate 66 in the colour plate section).

depicted kimono as artistic drapery worn by Western models or draped over furniture as part of an artistic interior, Hornel depicted Japanese women and girls in kimono. Japanese females are inseparable from the kimono that they wear in Hornel's work, and are portrayed as exotic and childlike. Burkhauser states that, 'In looking at ... images of the exotic, it is valuable to draw on the correspondence between women as objects and the objectification of the Orient ... where the female or Orient can be read as exotic, sensual, childlike and decorative' (1990: 233). This is clearly demonstrated in *A Japanese Silk Shop*, in which Japanese women in kimono blend seamlessly among the luxurious bolts and swags offered for sale. Allusions to the childlike nature of Japanese women are made in Hornel's lecture, in which he described 'The Geisha Quarter' as being 'composed of streets of dainty dollhouses' (Hornel 1895). He further detailed one visit to the quarter:

> by the patter of tiny feet upon the stairs, you become aware of the arrival of your favourites, then appear before you 'Miss Pine', 'Miss Butterfly', and others as quaint and beautiful ephemera, fall upon their hands and knees, and bowing their heads to the ground, pay you all manner of undeserved compliments and offer you apologies for their own short-comings, as uncalled for as they are comical and absurd and ridiculous.

While Japanese guests would have expected the greeting described by Hornel, ignorance of cultural practices is expressed in his description of these working women and girls as dainty and silly, which also reinforces a childlike stereotype. Other Victorian travellers to Japan likewise embraced this stereotype. A female traveller wrote of the 'geisha' that, 'The girls, who were pretty, wore peculiar dresses to indicate their calling ... all looked cheery, light-hearted, simple creatures, and appeared to enjoy immensely the little childish games they played' (Brassey 1878: 312). These images correspond with Hornel's early paintings of girls in repose and play in the rolling hills of Galloway, however the females depicted here are not often at play, rather they are hard at work providing entertainment.

Although nearly 30 years passed between Hornel's first and second journeys to Japan, his paintings, as well as the commercially produced photographs that he acquired during both trips, offer images of an unchanged Japan. This suggests the continued interest of the British picture-buying public in quaint, romanticised images of the country and the fundamen-

Figure 6 Photograph, undated and uncatalogued (Hornel Library/The National Trust for Scotland).

tal role of women in kimono to achieve such images. A series of letters written by Hornel to Fraser demonstrates the savvy with which Japanese commercial photography studios recreated idealised images of Japan for foreign tourists. In these letters, he described hiring two Japanese girls to be photographed at a nearby studio. These girls featured in a travelling troupe that appeared at his hotel and performed 'the old Dances I knew so well in the old Japan days' (letter dated 16 May 1921). He later wrote of his disappointment with the results of the photography session, blaming the girls' inability to achieve the dance poses that he desired and to avoid looking at the camera (letter dated 19 May 1921). The studio attendant assured him that better models could be secured for photography, and Hornel consented (letter dated 25 May 1921). Of these girls, Hornel wrote satisfactorily, 'He certainly procured two very handsome and magnificently clothed females, who posed excellently' (letter dated 25 May 1921) (Fig. 6).

Both the photographs acquired by Hornel and his paintings portray a Japan unaffected by decades of change, and notably both rely on kimono to achieve such results. As Deborah Cherry writes of French Orientalist paintings, 'The images ... portray a land before or after colonisation, rather than a society caught up in and traumatised by its chaotic intervention' (2000: 87). Although absent from his paintings, Hornel's anxieties regarding changes in Japan do surface in his letters to Fraser. Following a day trip in 1921 to Tokyo, where he had resided during his first visit, he wrote of his shock in not 'recognis[ing] a single street' and described the appearance of skyscrapers in the city as 'dreadful'. He further confessed his relief that he was staying in Kyoto, which he described as 'a beautiful dream' after the horrors of Tokyo (letter dated 21 July 1921). Upon his arrival in Kyoto, he had referred to the city as 'the old Capital ... very much untouched by modern ideas ... still very paintable' (letter dated 10 February 1921). Despite the idyllic setting that Hornel suggested that Kyoto offered, interspersed among the quaint details of his trip, such as photographic sessions with Japanese dancers or tales of sites visited with his sister and companion Elizabeth, are brief comments about the 'swelled head' that Japan had developed from its economic, militaristic and political advances and the belief that the country should be put in its place by one of the Western powers (letters dated 16 May and 19 May 1921).

More widely commented upon with regard to change in Japan was the adoption of European clothing by the Japanese. This criticism applied both to Japanese visitors and workers abroad as well as within Japan, and was made known to the British public through both journalism and travel accounts. An article from 1889 demonstrates the importance placed upon Japanese dress in maintaining an idealised image of Japan:

> All travellers, whether of European or American nationality cordially agree on one point, and that is in their appreciation and admiration of the national dress [of Japan]; praising it as being at once dignified, picturesque, and charmingly graceful ... mainly from the standpoint of its happy agreement with the national culture, temper, and particular environment of this exclusive people (Reed 1889: 558).

This statement shows the inextricable connection between kimono, national identity and the landscape of Japan.

An interview with Henry in 1895 reveals a marked difference between this image and experience. The press asked if the artists had seen the emperor during their visit, to which Henry replied:

> We got a glimpse of him one day, and he struck us as being the ugliest person it had ever been our privilege to clap eyes on. He wore a sort of European uniform, and indeed the Court and Society have adopted European ideas to the extent of making our store clothes take the place of their own beautiful and artistic costumes (*Kirkcudbrightshire Advisor* 20 July 1894 in Hornel Trust 1980).

Henry goes on to describe the artists' shock in seeing one woman wearing her corset on the outside of her gowns at a garden party at the mikado's palace (*Kirkcudbrightshire Advisor* 20 July 1894 in Hornel Trust 1980). Combining elements of Western and Japanese dress was much criticised and satirised in the popular press throughout the last four decades of the 19th century.[10] To the Europeans and Americans, the abandonment of traditional Japanese dress could be viewed as a point of crisis; it was felt that adopting Western dress would irrevocably affect the art and culture so admired in the West. One article claimed that:

> it would take years for Japanese ladies to adapt to themselves and wear with equal grace a costume to which

they are entirely unaccustomed ... Foreign carpets, chairs, and tables must be added to foreign dress and shoes, and Japanese household interiors now held up to the world as models of grace, simplicity, and harmony, will have to be entirely remodelled (Rational Dress Association 1888: 7–8).

Conclusion

Hornel's Japan paintings and the objects and archives at Broughton House pertaining to his travels demonstrate the formal inspiration that the artist derived from Japanese textiles and kimono, as well as reveal how these objects were encoded with Victorian desires and anxieties relating to Japan. His depiction of Japanese women and his emphasis on the colour and pattern of their kimono perpetuate an image of a decorative, beautiful, unchanging and exotic land. These types of images were fundamental to maintaining an idealised view of Japan as the country continued to modernise. As one article raved about the paintings in Hornel's 1895 exhibition, 'Here is Japan, sure enough, as true in its atmosphere as Piere Loti's "Madame Chrysantheme"'(*Glasgow Evening License* 22 April 1895 in Hornel Trust 1980). While Hornel's Japan paintings revelled in heightened colour, however, these quaint images, like Loti's novel, were works of fiction, projecting a view of a romanticised Japan rather than an insight into what the country had become. Hornel's paintings as well as the kimono, Japanese textiles and books on textiles acquired by the artist evidence an appreciation of the luxurious and sensual as opposed to the everyday. The texts recounting Hornel's travels, in accordance with other literature of the time, demonstrate a contrasting image and desperation in trying to preserve something of the old Japan, or rather, an idealised Orient.

Acknowledgements

Special thanks are extended to the Pasold Research Fund, which made possible a trip to study the collection and archives at Broughton House. The author would also like to thank Jim Allen and Sally Eastgate at Broughton House, Kirkcudbright for their assistance and kindness during her visit. Further thanks must be extended to Osamu Maeda for his assistance with translations of the Japanese books from the Hornel Library. Finally, thanks are given to Ysanne Holt for her helpful comments with regard to this paper.

Notes

1. Kimono is used in Japanese, regardless of whether it is singular or plural, as the context determines the number.
2. The Hornel Trust assembled *The EA Hornel Newscutting Book 1890–1900* (2 volumes) in 1980, in which 207 cuttings from 96 international newspapers and journals feature. Although this source is noteworthy in its comprehensive nature, occasionally a title, source or date from an article has not been included or is illegibly written, causing some difficulty in referencing.
3. For examples of Hornel's early work, see Smith 1997 and Billcliffe 1985.
4. *The Druids: Bringing in the Mistletoe* (1890) can be found at the Glasgow Museums: Art Gallery & Museum, Kelvingrove. It is reproduced in Smith 1997, p. 61.
5. *Summer* (1891) can be found at the Walker Art Gallery Liverpool. It is reproduced in Billcliffe 1985, p. 243.
6. These images bear telltale signs that they were used by the artists while painting: grid marks, paint splatters and pin marks. The photographs acquired during Hornel's second journey to Japan show similar signs of use.
7. I discuss Dresser's journey to Japan and engagement with the textile culture of Japan in Kramer 2006.
8. The lecture was presented at the Town Hall, Kirkcudbright; Kelvingrove Museum and Corporation Galleries of Art, Glasgow; Corporation Galleries in Sauchiehall Street, Edinburgh; Walker Art Gallery, Liverpool and the Bury Literary and Scientific Society, Bury. Hornel personally delivered his lecture only in Kirkcudbright. Hornel Trust 1980 contains notices for the lectures.
9. *A Japanese Silk Shop* (1896) belongs to a private collection. It is reproduced in Billcliffe 1985, p. 246.
10. Examples can be seen in Dalby 2001.

References

Billcliffe, R. (1985) *The Glasgow Boys: The Glasgow School of Painting 1875–1895.* London: John Murray.

Brassey, L. (1878) *A Voyage in the 'Sunbeam': Our Home on the Ocean for Eleven Months.* London: Century Publishing (reprint 1984) (orig. pub. London: Longmans, Green and Co.).

Burkhauser, J. (ed.) (1990) *Glasgow Girls: Women in Art and Design 1880–1920.* Edinburgh: Canongate.

Cherry, D. (2000) *Beyond the Frame: Feminism and Visual Culture, Britain 1850–1900.* London: New York: Routledge.

Dalby, L. (2001) *Kimono: Fashioning Culture.* London: Vintage.

Dresser, C. (1882) *Japan: Its Architecture, Art and Art Manufacture.* London: Longmans, Green.

Hardie, W.R. (1968) 'E. A. Hornel reconsidered' (Part 1 and 2), *Scottish Art Review* 11(3): 19–21, 27, 28; 11 (4): 22–6.

Hartrick, A.S. (1939) *A Painter's Pilgrimage through Fifty Years.* Cambridge: Cambridge University Press.

Henry, G. (1893–95) Transcripts of unpublished letters written to E.A. Hornel. Hornel Library/The National Trust of Scotland.

Holt, Y. (2004) 'The Veriest Poem of Art in Nature': E.A. Hornel's Japanese garden in the Scottish Borders', *Tate Papers* Autumn 2004. http://www.tate.org.uk/research/tateresearch/tatepapers/artist.jsp.

Hornel, E.A. (1895) 'Japan'. Lecture delivered in the Corporation Art Galleries, Glasgow. Hornel Library/The National Trust for Scotland.

Hornel, E.A. (1921) Transcripts of unpublished letters written to Thomas Fraser. Hornel Library/The National Trust for Scotland.

Hornel Trust (1980) *E.A. Hornel Newscuttings Book, 1890–1900*, 2 vols. Hornel Library/National Trust for Scotland.

Kramer, E. (2006) 'Master or market? The Anglo-Japanese textile designs of Christopher Dresser', *Journal of Design History* 19(3): 197–214.

Muther, R. (1895–96) *The History of Modern Painting*, vol. 3. London: Henry.

Ono, A. (1999) 'George Henry and E.A. Hornel's visit to Japan and *Yokohama Shashin*: the influence of Japanese photography', *Apollo* 453: 11–18.

Pinnington, E. (1900) 'Mr E.A. Hornel', *The Scots Pictorial* 15 June: 171–3.

Rational Dress Association (1888) 'The dress of Japanese ladies', *Journal of the Rational Dress Association*. In 1978 *Catalogue of Exhibits* and *Gazette*, 7–8. London: Garland.

Reed, M. (1889) 'A chat about Japanese dress', *Woman's World* 2: 558.

Smith, B. (1997) *Hornel: The Life and Work of Edward Atkinson Hornel.* Edinburgh: Atelier Books.

Thomson, K. (2005) *Broughton House: New Beginnings.* Edinburgh: National Trust for Scotland.

Whistler, J.M. (1994) *Whistler on Art*, N. Thorp (ed.). Washington, DC: Smithsonian Institution Press.

The author

Elizabeth Kramer was Research Fellow in material culture – textiles at the AHRC Research Centre for Textile Conservation and Textile Studies and was based at the University of Manchester, where she earned her PhD degree in art history in 2004. Through a discussion of textile culture, her thesis examined Anglo-Japanese artistic exchange in the late 19th century and the political, social and cultural issues underpinning this interaction. During her AHRC Fellowship she investigated the Japan mania in Britain (1875–1900). Currently she is a Leverhulme Early Career Research Fellow based in historical studies at Newcastle University and is engaged on a project entitled 'The material culture of mania'. Her research interests include Victorian textiles, material culture, postcolonial theory, and histories and theories of consumption and collecting.

Address

Elizabeth Kramer (elizabeth_a_kramer@hotmail.com)

Dragon robes and prairie ladies: the incongruity between archives and artefacts

Julia Petrov

ABSTRACT In 1915, a concerned landlady wrote on behalf of her tenants to her local authorities to complain about her neighbours. The crime, it seemed, was that their manner of dress was too Chinese, although their food, language, customs and physical characteristics did not seem to cause any offence. The letter and its reply have been preserved and are displayed in the museum of the Calgary Chinese Cultural Centre, along with other materials relating to the development of the local Chinese community. Yet, despite the obvious significance of such a record of contemporary attitudes, the museum's artefact exhibits focus on presenting an accepted, even stereotyped, view of 'Chineseness'. The contrast between the messages offered by these two sources of historical knowledge illustrates that in a century, perceptions of Chinese clothing (and therefore culture) have simply moved from one limiting stereotype to another. It is a museum's responsibility to illustrate and mediate a more accurate and relevant history. It is vital, therefore, to examine the assumptions contained within both modes of historical analysis – archival and physical – and to bring them back into a discourse which will do justice to the stories they contain.

Keywords: material culture, archival evidence, ethnic dress, Chinese dress, trousers, Calgary

Introduction

While archival sources are commonly used by curators to complement and contextualise artefacts in museums, the pairing of these two resources to aid such a narrative is not always intuitive or obvious. As this paper demonstrates, archival sources can also challenge accepted exhibition norms. A series of letters communicating racial discrimination in the early settlement of western Canada draws attention by its content to the lack of attention hitherto paid by Western museums to displays of Eastern dress as worn within a Western context. Although the letters are set and displayed within the Chinese community of Calgary, Canada, the debates about race, class and gender that they evoke have relevance for the international museum community.

Museums and text

The Calgary Chinese Cultural Centre is located in the heart of historic downtown Calgary, Canada, where it presides over a thriving Chinatown district. Situated in an imposing temple-like structure taking up an entire city block, it has been open since 1992, and houses a Chinese library, small museum, gift shop and community hall, as well as providing facilities for language and martial arts classes. The centre's museum is housed in the basement and features artefacts of Chinese culture, including paintings, furniture, ceramics and other decorative arts, traditional dress and accessories, and other similar items.

Figure 1 The entrance to 'Our Chosen Land', Calgary Chinese Cultural Centre (Plate 67 in the colour plate section).

In a gallery off the main museum space is housed a separate exhibit, entitled 'Our Chosen Land', which explores Chinese immigration to Canada with particular emphasis on settlement in Calgary (Fig. 1). This exhibit takes a chronological and thematic approach (concentrating first on the history of Chinese immigrants to Canada and proceeding to the evolution of the Chinese community in Calgary) using photographs and archival sources, with complementary artefactual vignettes set in glassed-off displays in corners. The narrative does not shy away from discussing the shameful parts of Canada's history, including the discrimination and racism faced by Chinese people in the 19th and 20th centuries. This particular theme is illustrated with case studies, including a series of three letters around a Calgary landlady's complaint to the city authorities about her tenants' Chinese neighbours.[1] The complaint is of a curious nature, and it and the official response are telling. The following are transcriptions of the original documents:

709 – 2nd Avenue
Sunnyside
Aug 19th 1915

To Mayor Costello

Dear Sir
Knowing how willing you are to lend your influence in any matter for individual good, I take the liberty of writing to you on my own behalf. I own a piece of property at 117-2nd Ave W which I have rented to the same party for four and a half years, now they are complaining of a family of Chinese who rent the house to the west of them saying their habit of dress is very annoying to their young people (consisting of five grown up sons who of course have lady friends visiting them occasionally) – now – if said tenants were to leave it takes away the only income I have, consequently the only way of paying my taxes, which are over one hundred dollars per year, and I know other tenants would have the same objection – now it seems to me, that foreigners living in this country should be willing to dress in the same manner as our own people, if we were to masquerade in men's clothes as they do, we should soon be marked by the police and treated accordingly – cannot something be done? I am sure you will use your authority in bringing about an investigation which will ensure a change in the dress of the Chinese women, which may be a nuisance to surrounding citizens, and also help an old lady who has paid taxes in Calgary for ten years, but now rents are so cut down it will be a hard matter to do so this year but am trying to do my best. Will you kindly attend to this and do your best for me. Thanking you in anticipation of good results –

I beg to remain
Yours obediently
Mrs Sarah Vesey

Six days later, Mrs Vesey received a reply from the mayor, who wrote:

August 25th
Dear Mrs Vesey: -
I beg to acknowledge receipt of your letter of August 19th, stating the trouble you are having in retaining your tenants in Sunnyside on account of the manner of dress of the Chinese women. I have referred your communication to the Chief of Police for report, and attached you will find copy of a letter I have received from him dealing with your grievance.
Trusting that the suggestions of the Chief of Police has offered will be the means of removing the trouble you complain of.
Yours truly,
Mayor

Indeed, the chief of police had reported to the mayor:

25th August 1915
His Worship the Mayor of Calgary
City Hall

Sir:
In returning the enclosed letter from Mrs Sarah Vesey, 709-2nd Ave., Sunnyside, complaining of the habit of dress of certain Chinese women, I beg to advise you that I interviewed one of the leading Chinamen in Calgary, who has promised me that he will see the family complained of and instruct them to dress in a proper manner.
Yours respectully,
Chief Constable (Alfred Cuddy)

Apart from illustrating the manner in which the police operated in the early 20th century, the letters are also valuable to the dress historian. It is striking that what Mrs Vesey found most offensive about her Chinese neighbours was not their physical appearance, their food, their language, their customs and manners, nor even their religion; what most struck her (and by extension her tenants, as well) was their clothing.

It has not been possible to find out more about Mrs Sarah Vesey, nor is there any indication whether the 'leading Chinaman' actually reprimanded the family in question on their manner of dress. In spite of this lack of further historical context, the letters illuminate a discrepancy between the stories artefacts aspire to tell and those that are available in archival sources.

Museums and textiles

Although the Cultural Centre's museum does have a display of replica Chinese court costume (Fig. 2), as well as a display of the contents of a trunk of clothing brought to Calgary by early Chinese settlers (Fig. 3), the letters are not exhibited in a way as to directly link their clothing references to any surviving artefacts. This, in the context of the exhibition's aim, is perfectly reasonable – they are deployed in order to demonstrate problems of assimilation, not to illustrate costume history.

Figure 2 Display of traditional Chinese dragon robes and court dress, Calgary Chinese Cultural Centre (Plate 68 in the colour plate section).

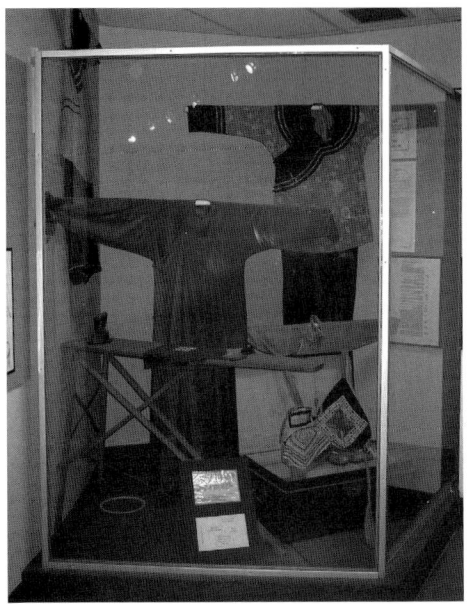

Figure 3 Display of traditional clothing brought to Calgary by early Chinese settlers, Calgary Chinese Cultural Centre (Plate 69 in the colour plate section).

It is the central contention of this paper, however, that the unwillingness of costume history to scrutinise issues of social integration represents a missed opportunity. Anthropologists, as David Howes demonstrated in his book on cross-cultural consumption (1996), have bravely re-examined notions of authenticity in cultural artefacts, and have grappled with the problems of differing definitions of goods across social and geographic boundaries. The purpose of this paper, therefore, is to serve as a meditation on how Chinese dress is presented in Western museums, and to question whether the stories of cultural and ethnic identity that archival material can tell are being effectively supported by artefactual collections. The intent is to offer some very tentative questions about what constitutes the Western vision of ethnic dress, particularly within a diaspora context. This paper, therefore, is a meditation that aims to pose questions for further investigation.

Historical background

It is important to begin with some historical context for the particular time and place in which the letters are set. Calgary was founded in 1884 as an outpost of the Northwest Mounted Police, and the coming of the railway encouraged the migration and settlement of large numbers of people. Although the population was primarily of UK origin in the early part of the 20th century, there were minority groups, such as the Native (First Nations) population, and also a core group of Chinese settlers. These Chinese settlers were not, for the most part, railway workers, as had been the case further west. They emigrated because of China's rural crisis and overpopulation, and operated restaurants and laundries, sometimes also becoming domestic servants. Although they paid tax and could be conscripted, the civil and employment rights of immigrant Chinese workers, called 'sojourners,' were severely restricted by law – they were not allowed to vote, or otherwise participate in government, and hindered by strict employment and immigration laws, they eked out a marginal existence.

As a result of the Canadian government's immigration policies, this population was overwhelmingly male, and a minority. Restrictions included the notorious head tax, instituted in 1885 to deter further immigration after the completion of the railroads. Chinese immigrants had to pay the government a large sum in order to enter the country. Though at first the tax was $50, it rose to $100 in 1900, and only three years later quintupled to $500, enough to purchase two houses[2] (which, incidentally, is how many Mrs Vesey owned). By 1923, Chinese immigration was altogether forbidden by the Exclusion Act. The Canadian government only officially apologised for these two measures in June 2006, and voluntarily began paying out reparations to survivors on 20 October 2006.[3]

The head tax ensured that the Chinese formed only 1.9% of total immigration to Canada in the period between 1911 and 1915. In 1911 (the year of the national census) the Chinese formed only 0.38% of the total Canadian population, of whom less than 1000 were female. Their total population in 1911 was 27,774 (Tan and Roy 1985: 9). Yet Calgary was a major centre: according to Richard Thomas Wright, a historian of early Chinese immigration to Canada, in this period there were over 1700 Chinese in Calgary, residing in and around Chinatown, the 'centre of their transplanted culture' (Wright 1988: 12).

By 1915, Chinatown was in its third and present location in the downtown core, and was served by a significant number of community services. The Chinese mission, a Presbyterian organisation, was located down the street from the address Mrs Vesey gave for her tenants, and the present Chinese Cultural Centre also stands on the same block as her rented house.[4] She and her tenants should not have been surprised at manifestations of Chinese culture in such a location, therefore. According to the exhibition, *Builders and Patriots: Portraits of Chinese Canadians*,[5] the Chinese Mission had been founded in 1901 by Calgary's previous mayor, Thomas Underwood, and with civic sanction became a central gathering place for the Calgary Chinese community.

Clothing and nationalism

Despite this, it is possible to interpret Mrs Vesey's complaint about the clothes of her neighbours as thinly veiled racism. To quibble about clothing might have seemed a convenient way to address an underlying discomfort with the Chinese presence in Calgary. Clothing was a blatantly obvious visual signifier of difference and represented a whole spectrum of cultural differences that were a focus for racial hatred in this period. In his book, *Selling Style*, Schorman devotes a chapter to the turn-of-the-century equation of American national identity with clothing, describing the effect of clothing on immigrant identity. He contends that:

> clothing much more than food involves the public presentation of the self. Clothing is the interface between the individual and the social world, and if citizenship involves participation or membership in civic or community enterprise, then clothing can help mediate that relationship in a way that food can not (Schorman 2003: 118).

It is important to note that the Chinese women to whom Mrs Vesey referred would have sewn their own clothing, as their ethnic clothing needs were not fulfilled by department stores or mail order catalogues. Their active rejection of the clothing norms of their host culture as perpetuated by advertising, as well as actual worn clothing by their neighbours and clients,[6] may well have been perceived as a hostile act of resistance.

Kim Fung, curatorial assistant for the Museum and Collections Services at the University of Alberta, suggests that what Mrs Vesey referred to as 'trousers' was practical working attire for Chinese women.[7] The daily necessity of working for survival would not have afforded them the luxury of silk robes. Chinese work practices were heavily criticised in this period because they were perceived as threatening to the livelihoods of the white majority; their willingness to undertake, often for significantly lower pay, jobs that whites were unwilling to do, was taken advantage of at the very same time as it was berated. Additionally, as mentioned above, women were effectively restricted from immigrating to Canada in the first place by the onerous head tax – their husbands have to have been economically successful indeed to bring them over. Undoubtedly, once in Canada, they would have worked to supplement the family income and justify the expense incurred for their immigration. Their trousers served as an unpleasant reminder that not only were the Chinese women there despite white society's best efforts, but furthermore, they were also actively threatening the moral and economic fabric of Canadian society with their customs. Mrs Vesey certainly perceived them in this way, hinting to the mayor that her income (and therefore tax-paying status) was jeopardised by their continued presence.

At the turn of the 20th century, Chinese dress was, at best, only given positive attention by scholars of costume and even then, usually for fancy-dress purposes. In the 1906 book, *Costume: Fanciful, Historical, and Theatrical*, E. Aria devotes five pages to Chinese dress, but her account is sensationalistic, focusing on the salacious (to Western eyes) customs of the Chinese imperial court. Her boredom with the prosaic realities of peasant life is almost palpable, and she skips glibly over it in her transition to a description of Japanese costume. It should be noted that at no point does she clarify which – fanciful, historical or theatrical – her description of Chinese dress actually is, but since the introduction states clearly that her book is aimed towards actors in professional and amateur productions, one can easily assume that the historical has taken a back seat to fancy dress, theatrical or masquerade purposes.

But Mrs Vesey was not interested in dressing up; it irked her that Chinese people should wear strange and exotic costumes within her quotidian reality, and their flaunting their difference, instead of disappearing into the background by assuming Western dress, was frustrating to her. She called this a 'nuisance', and stated, 'it seems to me that foreigners living in this country should be willing to dress in the same manner as our own people'. In fact, a note of moral disapproval crept in, as she interpreted the trousered traditional costume as 'masquerading in men's clothes', something that would and did invoke censure.

Chinese clothing and the meeting of cultures

Mrs Vesey may well have objected equally to the Chinese women's transgression of gendered clothing norms, as much as to the ethnic origin of their trousers. Rob Schorman writes that, 'clothing not only evokes but enacts gender; fashion not only communicates but constitutes gender identity' (2003: 84) but gender identity and fashion are culturally specific constructs. Naomi Tarrant points out that loose trousers had been worn as work-safe garments by women since the mid-19th century, even by European women, especially in factories during the First World War (2003: 82), although wearing trousers in public mixed company as fashionable wear was still frowned upon in this period. Aileen Ribeiro contends that even Paul Poiret's 1910 Turkish-inspired 'harem' costume 'never quite took off as a fashion in spite of its impeccably exotic credentials' (2003: 150). The letters, therefore, do not evoke a story of the glamorous, exoticised 'other' – instead, they present the ugly reality of racism and intolerance. Heavily embroidered silk imperial robes as worn by Europeans may have been acceptable within certain fancy-dress or haute-couture contexts; disembodied and treated as mere textiles when hung on a gallery wall, they could be admired as examples of high skill in craft. But real Chinese clothing actually worn by Chinese people outside of China intruded uncomfortably on white territory.

The second decade of the 20th century is a particularly key moment, as Chinese dress was undergoing a period of redefinition. In 1911, the Qing dynasty[8] came to a close and the establishment of the Republic in 1912 meant the end of Manchu sartorial legislation, formal and informal, and new ways for China to define itself in a larger global context. In their book *China Chic: East Meets West*, Valerie Steele and John S. Major complicate the history of Chinese dress and its perception in the Western world. Essays in the book claim that 'far from being a bulwark of social stability and hierarchy, dress in traditional China was always a contested realm of behaviour' (Steele and Major 1999: 19), and that foreign influences crept in over the years despite sumptuary legislation that attempted to delineate and distinguish 'Chineseness' from the outside world. Not only was this a period of change politically, but also sartorially, and it would be unfair to dismiss the distinctions, as they would help to tell a story of China's engagement with the Western world in terms of dress and customs – something vital for a story of emigration, which takes the struggle between tradition and innovation to a new territory, where the philosophical issues take on a very physical reality. To look modern, yet not to compromise cultural identity as expressed through dress was a dilemma which faced Chinese communities on both sides of the Pacific.

Cross-cultural curation

However, while this narrative may have been examined in books, museums have not tackled the issue in any significant way,[9] marrying archives and artefacts together into exhibitions that might reflect underlying social tensions as expressed by objects. Personal experience, as well as the suggestions of colleagues, produced a list of recent examples of exhibitions of Chinese dress, which examined only either chinoiserie or imperial robes, or sometimes both. A concentration on traditional Chinese dress might be seen as a rehabilitation of the value of that culture, a celebration of the 'authentically ethnic' – but it ignores the diaspora context, which would include not only the native values, but also the mingling and interaction of East and West. Mrs Vesey's letter is an evocative example of this mongrel material culture, which is situated neither 'here' nor 'there'. Ignoring this narrative by disembodying and decontextualising ethnic dress might be classed as a kind of cultural vandalism, closing as that does the opportunity for cross-cultural dialogue. While the display of dragon robes as unique examples of Chinese clothing does not represent a failure on the part of curators to present history through objects, it does suggest a need for more creative exploration of other aspects of Chinese material culture and its relation to societies in Asia and abroad.

In museums, the preoccupation of collectors with the spectacular dragon robes of the imperial court, though undoubtedly important in reflecting the sociopolitical reality of China for nearly 300 years, has led to an unfortunate eclipsing of the possibility for more nuanced discussion of reality for non-courtly attire, both in China and beyond; this has implications for the way both Westerners and Chinese natives view their history. Museum curators are often at the mercy of the tastes of previous generations; their collections are far more likely to contain dragon robes than the clothing of working-class Chinese immigrants, and the prevalence of these objects often dictates the types of displays curators are able to develop. The lack of provenance or archival evidence for these artefacts presents an additional challenge to curators who may be interested in engaging the public in debates about clothing and social integration. Perhaps increased awareness of this gap in representation may lead to a change in museums' collecting and acquisition policies.

That textiles and dress have further realities than their mere material existence, and that they represent difficult problems of identity and culture, have become accepted truths. This paper has attempted to demonstrate that Mrs Vesey chose the clothing of her Chinese neighbours to complain about because the clothing was a useful symbol of her larger social discontent. Additionally, Chinese dress in general may not be as homogenous as sometimes presented. The further question being posed is whether museums are communicating such realities and problems effectively by utilising the available sources and by telling ignored or inconvenient stories. It may be difficult to do, but museums cannot refuse to deal with the diffuse, downtrodden, diasporic reality of Chinese culture in the West.

Part of the solution lies in who tells these stories and what resources they have to draw upon. Most of the literature currently available on cross-cultural curation deals with either native voices speaking for themselves, or museums rehabilitating artefacts collected from so-called primitive societies in a colonial ethic. There are things to be learned here and applied to deal with uncomfortable truths. An example of a museum allowing the source culture to narrate an exhibition of colonially collected artefacts is also in Calgary, at the Glenbow Museum. One of the permanent galleries, called 'Our Way of Life', is told through first-person Blackfoot narration and includes not only traditional artefacts, but also those of disenfranchisement, such as photographs of Blackfoot children in residential schools where they were forced to assimilate. The exhibit is also available to view online.[10]

To some extent, 'Our Chosen Land' at the Chinese Cultural Centre also does this; but it does not necessarily make the connections between history and artefacts, particularly clothing. An example of an exhibition that told the story of immigration through dress as one of the ways in which national symbols are disseminated was *Becoming American Women: Clothing and the Jewish Immigrant Experience, 1880–1920*, which was held in 1994 by the Jewish Historical Society of Chicago. An excellent book was subsequently published by Barbara Schreier (1994), who examined the problem of how clothes define assimilation or differentiation.[11] Admittedly, the Jewish experience is different from that of the Chinese, but the example does provide a good methodological paradigm: the union of objects with archival and oral histories can open up new narrative possibilities within museum collections and their social contexts.

Conclusion

As anyone with an experience of immigration will know, desires and fears inform the changing meanings of the intercultural object. With the increasingly global nature of Western society, there is an opportunity to present this in museums, because the available archival and artefactual collections warrant and support the narratives of migration and integration. If museums are reflections of a society's past and present, debates about ethnic dress can serve as useful synecdoches for wider examinations of cross-cultural communication. For example, the present European debates about Muslim womens' dress in France[12] and the UK[13] could be seen as modern parallels to the 1915 example of Chinese dress in western Canada presented in this paper. If even the clarity afforded by hindsight has not caused earlier occurrences to be examined in this way, there is a danger that curators will also shy away from approaching contemporary politically sensitive topics. Will the debate about religious dress be eventually represented in Western museums, despite the uncomfortable way this might reflect on contemporary social realities? Or will Muslim dress, like Chinese dress, be represented as glamorous and unchanging, a relic from some exotic past or mythical location?

It is true that neither Mrs Vesey's letter, nor the responses from Mayor Costello and Police Chief Cuddy say anything detailed about Chinese dress, or even Western dress. The correspondence cited above does not illustrate anything about the physical reality of how Chinese dress in 1915 was worn or constructed. But perhaps more valuably than that, the letters do speak of prevailing cultural attitudes, illuminating a gap in the stories artefacts of Chinese dress have been allowed to tell in Western museums. These archival sources may lead to a more reflective perception of the artefacts to which they refer. In addition, they may serve to stimulate discussion of how traditional clothing may be effectively displayed in a museum context, drawing upon narratives of immigration, integration, assimilation and cross-cultural communication.

Acknowledgements

The author is grateful to Janice Brum, archivist, the City of Calgary, and Kim Fung, curatorial assistant, Museum and Collections Services, the University of Alberta, for their suggestions and assistance in the preparation of this paper. She would also like to thank the attendees of the AHRC conference, Dr Elizabeth Kramer, and the anonymous referee for their feedback.

Notes

1. The originals of all three letters are contained in the Board of Commissioners records, series I, box 59, Commissioners General City Correspondence, O–Z, July–Oct. 1915, Archives, Administration Services Division, City Clerk's Office, The City of Calgary.
2. *Reflections: Images of Chinese Women in Canada* exhibition (curated by the Multicultural History Society of Ontario). Alternative calculations suggest this was the equivalent of two years' wages, and that about 82,000 Chinese paid the fee.
3. 'Chinese get head tax payouts', *Calgary Herald*, 21 October 2006, A15.
4. Chinese mission: 120-2nd Ave SW. Chinese cultural centre: 197-1st Street SW.
5. *Builders & Patriots: Portraits of Chinese Canadians* consisted of *Reflections: Images of Chinese Women in Canada: A Historical Photo Exhibit*, curated by the Multicultural History Society of Ontario (MHSO), and the *Southern Alberta Chinese Photo Exhibit* curated by the Sien Lok Society. It ran at the Calgary Chinese Cultural Centre from 18 September to 16 October 2005.
6. As mentioned above, many Chinese immigrants in this period operated laundries, an example of which is displayed at the Chinese Cultural Centre museum. This employment would have offered them additional experience of Western clothing convention.
7. Pers. comm., 28 June 2006.
8. The Qing, or Ching dynasty ruled China from 1644 to 1911.
9. An important exception was the exhibition *China Chic: East Meets West*, which ran at the Museum at the Fashion Institute of Technology in New York City.
10. See: *Niitsitapiisini: Our Way of Life* http://www.glenbow.org/blackfoot/.
11. *Becoming American Women: Clothing and the Jewish Immigrant Experience, 1880–1920* first ran at the Chicago Historical Society from 6 March 1994 to 2 January 1995, and travelled to various venues throughout the USA. The exhibition, consisting of 600 artefacts of clothing and personal objects, photographs, archival documents and oral histories, was accompanied by the catalogue (Schreier 1994).
12. See 'France votes for hijab ban' by C. Bremner, *The Times*, 11 February 2004, 16.
13. In late 2006, the UK government moved away from a policy of multiculturalism towards efforts to better integrate the Muslim community in Britain. Debate centred on the veiling of Muslim women, called a barrier to effective communication by Jack Straw and Tony Blair. See 'The Muslim veil is a sign of separation, says Blair' by P. Webster, *The Times*, 18 October 2006, 35.

References

Aria, E. (1906) *Costume: Fanciful, Historical, and Theatrical*. London: MacMillan and Co., Limited.

Howes, D. (ed.) (1996) *Cross-Cultural Consumption: Global Markets, Local Realities*. London: Routledge.

Ribeiro, A. (2003) *Dress and Morality*. New York: Berg.

Schorman, R. (2003) *Selling Style: Clothing and Social Change at the Turn of the Century*. Philadelphia: University of Pennsylvania Press.

Schreier, B.A. (1994) *Becoming American Women: Clothing and the Jewish Immigrant Experience, 1880–1920*. Chicago: Chicago Historical Society.

Steele, V. and Major, J.S. (1999) *China Chic: East Meets West*. London: Yale University Press.

Tan, J. and Roy, P.E. (1985) *Canada's Ethnic Groups: The Chinese in Canada*. Booklet No. 9. Ottawa: Canadian Historical Association.

Tarrant, N. (2003) *The Development of Costume*. London: Routledge.

Wright, R.T. (1988) *In a Strange Land: A Pictorial Record of the Chinese in Canada 1788–1923*. Saskatoon: Western Producer Prairie Books.

The author

Julia Petrov completed her MA in the history of design and material culture at the University of Brighton in 2006. She is immediate past president of the Postgraduate Design History Society. Her research interests are the history of dress and the history of collections. An immigrant herself, she resides in Calgary, Canada.

Address

Julia Petrov, 214 Sierra Morena Court S.W., Calgary AB T3H 2X8, Canada (petrov.julia@googlemail.com)

Chasing the dragon: researching Chinese textiles in early 20th-century domestic interiors

Sarah Cheang

ABSTRACT This paper considers how the cultural meaning of Chinese textiles in British domestic spaces can be understood through the interrelation of textiles, archives and texts, to open up important questions around the reading of imperial archives and domestic collections of textiles. Two contrasting examples are explored. The first concerns 25 panels of Chinese embroidery that are fixed to the walls of an Oriental drawing room at Quex House, Kent. Archival evidence around their acquisition and display is scant, and the extent to which diaries can be used in general to furnish a greater understanding of the embroideries' cultural significance is brought under scrutiny. The second example investigates the use of Chinese embroidery by Queen Mary between 1911 and 1925, where the queen's husbandry of Chinese artefacts doubled for Britain's semi-colonial relationship with China at that time. Both examples can be considered as part of British imperial histories in which the material culture of domestic spaces played a crucial role in the constant circulation of meaning between metropolis and colony.

Keywords: imperialism, Chinese embroideries, gendered collecting, archives, Queen Mary, British domestic interiors

Introduction

This paper considers the role that the archive has played in my research into two early 20th-century domestic displays of Chinese embroidery. The first display – a series of 25 embroidery panels at Quex House in Kent – presents Chinese embroidered motifs that have been cut from Chinese garments and hangings and then recombined into new arrangements on panels of plain French silk (now replaced by linen). The panels are framed by carved Kashmiri walnut that fixes them to the walls, so that the effect is of a highly decorative wooden dado around the drawing room punctuated by panels of embroidery. This is an unusually architectural use for embroidery pieces that would more ordinarily have been sewn onto clothing and curtains as decoration, or used to create small and mobile domestic objects such as table centres and antimacassars (Cheang 2003: 23–31). Fortunately, the creator of the scheme, Major Percy Powell-Cotton, had also left his diaries for future researchers, offering supporting archival evidence of a highly personal nature.

By contrast, the second study is entirely focused on texts, examining the role that Chinese embroideries played in the public persona of Queen Mary, consort of George V, through the evidence of printed sources such as royal memorabilia, biographies, magazines and newspapers. Queen Mary was known as an avid collector and keen connoisseur of furniture and small art objects, including an extensive collection of Chinese jades. On taking possession of Buckingham Palace in 1911, she enhanced and created many Chinese interiors that often included the manipulation and display of embroideries.

The two collections considered in this paper are thus almost contemporary, but differ considerably in terms of their accessibility and cultural status. The private and domestic forms of evidence at Quex House – a drawing room full of embroideries that are still *in situ*, a collection of images of the home, and the Powell-Cotton's diaries – are personal souvenirs of family life. Queen Mary's embroideries, on the other hand, have not been available for study in their physical form, neither have royal diaries nor photograph albums been consulted. In a sense, they are objects of study that have only existed as text – as images mediated by the press and by official biographers – belonging to communal, national memory. The element that unites both these collections, however, is the position of China within a British imperial world-view. My previous engagement with these collections has focused on the articulation of class, gender and empire. This paper will reflect upon the role that archival material played in that analysis, to ask how the textual evidence of these collections intersected with an archive of empire, and indeed, whether the collected embroideries themselves can be considered as part of an archive of British knowledge about China.

China in the imperial archive

Thomas Richards's (1993) work on the imperial archive and James Hevia's (1998; 2003: 74–118) development of those ideas specifically in connection with China explore an understanding of texts and objects as vital in producing and maintaining narratives of empire. Collections, whether textual or material, produced knowledge about empire and added to an imperial archive that was a visible and tangible sign that the British nation might successfully govern a growing empire. In addition, as approaches to colonial histories generated by the Subaltern Studies scholars (Guha 1992; Spivak 1985, 1988) have made clear, imperial archives, the recording of imperial knowledge and colonial voices can take many forms and have many sources, and work developed since the 1990s by Anne Stoler (2002), Anne McClintock (1995) and others (Chaudhuri 1992) should leave us in no doubt that domestic objects such as textiles were not only within the reach of the imperial project, but formed an essential if sometimes problematic part of it.

A form of Western colonisation of China began with a mid-19th-century armed conflict under the rubric of free trade. In the Opium Wars of 1839–42 and 1856–60, China was defeated and forced to sign treaties with Britain, France, the United States and Russia. These treaties granted the Western powers ever-increasing trading rights and produced a kind of semi-colonial situation at key mercantile and military sites around the Chinese coastline. In the closing stages of the Opium Wars, Anglo-French forces stormed the Chinese emperor's summer palace and looted or destroyed its contents before burning the building to the ground. The spoils of the emperor's palace, including textiles, were auctioned off in France and Britain, and articles that related directly to the emperor's person took on a special significance as symbols of conquest and domination (Hevia 2003: 74–90).

China continued to be an arena for colonial war through to the beginning of the 20th century, and in 1911, the Qing dynasty fell and was replaced by a more Westernised republic. Court dress and Chinese imperial ceremony were now subjects of a colonial nostalgia that sought to preserve China in a pre-Westernised and more properly exotic state, so that in Britain, dragon robes (court attire decorated with dragons) became symbolic of China as an ordered and static empire at a time when Chinese emperors and their court etiquette were being replaced by a republic (Wilson 1999).

Dragon robes therefore gave substance to a now mythical China and also enabled a highly nostalgic recollection of China's past that can be connected to the process of Western imperial expansion (Bongie 1991; Hevia 2003: 203–8; Cheang 2006). British possession of a dragon robe thus involved a collecting of China's past that enabled nostalgic fantasies of China's present, an archiving and preserving of knowledge of Chinese customs and an expression of the power to obtain and control that colonial location through an appropriation of its textiles.

The embroideries of Quex House

Powell-Cotton's drawing room at Quex House contains eight such totemic gold embroidered dragons. It is now part of the Powell-Cotton Museum of Zoology and Ethnography that was founded by Powell-Cotton (1866–1940) in 1896 and built adjacent to his home. Powell-Cotton travelled widely in Africa and Asia between 1887 and 1939, his main interest being the animals that he hunted, studied, killed and then displayed in large dioramas in his private museum. However, he also collected the material culture of the peoples he encountered, who worked with him in the field as trackers, hunters and porters. Powell-Cotton's drawing room was designed by him in an Oriental style between 1894 and 1909, with the ornately carved Kashmiri walnut panelling, Indian and Chinese carved-wood furniture, Japanese and Chinese lacquered furniture, and an Islamic ceiling.

Powell-Cotton died in 1940, but his museum continues as a charitable trust. The drawing room was restored and opened to the public as an added attraction in the mid-1970s, when the embroideries were cleaned and remounted onto French linen. When I began my research into these embroideries, it was generally assumed that they had originated from the dragon robes of the old imperial Chinese court, and yet it was not known where they had really come from, precisely who had created the displays, and why. My own interest in the embroideries had begun a few years earlier when I overheard a member of museum staff telling a visitor that the embroideries looked Chinese but had actually been made by Kentish nuns.[1]

In terms of attribution, Chinese embroideries such as these can present some very real problems. First, they need not have been acquired directly from China, as Chinese embroidered textiles were widely available across Britain from department stores, draper's shops, and even missionary fundraising sales (Cheang 2003: 16–78). Secondly, such embroideries could be genuine antiques, worn by, or at least produced for, court officials, or for use in Chinese interiors, but they could also be products of a large and thriving export market that supplied copies of traditional Chinese needlework for the West (Wilson 2005: 35–6, 79). Lastly, many motifs and techniques were shared across East Asian embroidery, so that once pieces are cut from any distinctively shaped garments, they could be from China, Japan, Korea or Vietnam (Chung 2005).[2] Furthermore, the dismembering of Chinese garments to provide samples of embroidery for reuse around the home was viewed as a woman's occupation, and certainly not one that might interest a naturalist and military man. Thus, archival evidence is crucial in establishing an understanding of the Quex House embroideries.

Looking at his diaries, it emerged that it was almost certainly Powell-Cotton himself who both collected and executed the Quex House display of embroideries. While on a two-year 'world trip', he had devoted three weeks in China in 1891 to a hectic schedule of sightseeing and shopping, buying pictures, fans, lacquerware, ceramics, cloisonné work, wood and ivory carving, brass and silver work, as well as embroideries (Powell-Cotton 1891: 184–94). He visited Canton (Guangzhou), Shanghai, Tientsin (Tianjin), and Peking (Beijing) on a constant hunt for curios, and recorded going from shop to shop. He bought three second-hand 'capes', a 'coat', a 'petticoat', and a robe, all embroidered with gold. He also looked at new embroideries and bought some embroidery circles and a *portière*. His next port of call was Japan where he continued to purchase ceramics, lacquer, cloisonné work, silks and embroideries. Thus, the diaries provide the circumstantial evidence that Powell-Cotton bought a range of embroidered pieces in East Asia, even down to the exact details of place and price.

Powell-Cotton's diaries also secured the proof that he did indeed create the scheme himself and revealed the processes involved. In October 1907 he began unpicking and cutting the embroidered motifs from their original Chinese settings,

Figure 1 Panel of Chinese embroideries, Quex House (image courtesy of the Powell-Cotton Museum).

making patterns of the spaces in the dado and arranging the embroidered pieces in new designs. The new designs were then gummed onto plain French silk, which was tacked to frames and ultimately fixed onto the dado panelling (Fig. 1). He gradually worked his way around the room and finally completed the scheme in July 1919 (Powell-Cotton 1907: 23, 41–3; 1908: 38–42; 1909: 1, 3–4, 6, 8, 12, 42, 44; 1911: 22, 29, 32, 38–40, 44–5; 1919: 16–19, 22–3, 25–7). Throughout this time, he did not record any comments in his diaries on the actual content of the panels with the notable exception of the cutting out and gumming of some dragons in 1909, as befitted the cultural significance of the dragon robe in Britain at that time. The distinctively striped bottom edge of a dragon robe was also prominently used in three panels. The filling of the dado spaces with embroideries by degrees during this period is corroborated by photographs taken in 1913, the dating of the photographs being corroborated in turn by the diaries.

Powell-Cotton was an active member of the Royal Geographical Association and the Zoological Society, and his entire adult life was devoted to the accumulation of natural history and ethnographic specimens in the field, accompanied by detailed diary entries to provide a good record of acquisition. This habit was extended to the time spent in England between travels, so that he also documented the shopping trips to London involved in the furnishing of Quex House, and it seems highly unlikely that he would have acquired the embroideries in Britain without including that evidence in his diary. He even recorded the times he rearranged the drawing room furniture, a task for which he sometimes drew diagrams (Powell-Cotton 1909: 49). Therefore, it is safe to speculate that the embroideries used were products of his world trip, especially if we consider that the carved dado panelling was also designed by him and personally commissioned in Kashmir. Powell-Cotton's drawing room, like his museum, was a carefully constructed site of exhibition, entirely reserved for show. It was a space in which he displayed his trophies of empire, emblems of his cultural standing through connoisseurship and learning, and souvenirs of his personal experiences abroad.

Museum collecting has been analysed as an exercise in cultural definition (Belk 1995; Pearce 1995), and similarly, it is a social purpose of the drawing room to define its inhabitants to the wider world. In the drawing room, 'correct' social behaviour is exhibited to visitors, in contrast to the living room or lounge that conceptually is supposed to reflect the 'true' personality of its occupants rather than a projected identity held apart from the 'true' self (Halttunen 1989). The Chinese embroideries at Quex House were therefore part of Powell-Cotton's very conscious definition of self, as an expert in the non-Western and the exotic, and as a learned member of the English gentry. It should also be pointed out that while his Oriental room was always termed a drawing room from its inception, it does not seem to have been used for this purpose. Thus, in terms of an analysis, the diaries do little more than provide proof of what had always been assumed – that the embroideries and the drawing room were a part of Powell-Cotton's wider project, and had not been, for example, the work of his wife or daughters. In a sense, the text has merely confirmed the evidence of the textiles, reinforcing the significance of the dragon as an appropriated symbol of ancient Chinese rule, and the positioning of China within a generalised Orient that was both an object of knowledge and location of colonial pleasures for the privileged.

In his museum, Powell-Cotton arranged the natural and ethnographic specimens gathered from across Africa and Asia into huge dioramas and displays, to create a more personalised yet comprehensive examination of Eastern fauna. Similarly, the Chinese embroideries were subjected to a form of taxidermy, in which the original garments were removed from the bodies of their former owners and dismembered, and then the motifs were remounted within a domestic diorama of the Orient, realised through the decorative arts.

When showing visitors his museum, Powell-Cotton would sometimes also include his drawing room in the tour, an intersection of museum and domestic space that merely became formalised in the 1970s when parts of the house were opened to the public. The space of the drawing room was thus never quite private, a problematic idea in any case, and neither were the contents of his diaries. When in the field, his diaries acted as a scientific record of his expeditions, and when at home the entries were extremely brief, confined mainly to an account of the day's activities in a sort of shorthand. Thus, the position of the embroideries and the diaries within the archive of empire reflects the indeterminate boundaries of public and private spaces and public and private collecting in the gathering of imperial information.

Queen Mary and her Chinese embroideries

The case of Queen Mary's embroideries might seem to present a less ambiguous situation, as a study of a public figure and the representation of textiles within texts. Mary did not have any direct contact with China during the 1910s and 1920s, and appears to have acquired her embroideries by simply rummaging through the palace storerooms. Her biographers assert that the 'mandarin robes' collected and stored away by George IV and Queen Victoria were rediscovered by Mary in the course of her famously thorough and systematic reorganisation of the royal households (Pope-Hennessy 1959: 137, 410, 412, 434; Healey 1997: 212; Colville 1963: 124–5; Sitwell 1974: 24). She then used these old robes within new schemes for the royal residences, including Buckingham Palace.

From its inception, the palace had been a site of 'Chinese' interiors with large collections of 18th-century chinoiseries, furniture and decorations from George IV's 'Chinese' drawing room at Carlton House, as well as much of the 'Chinese' furniture, fixtures and fittings that were taken from the Royal Pavilion at Brighton in 1845. Generally, therefore, we can say that Mary enhanced the 'Chineseness' of existing Georgian and Victorian chinoiserie interiors. For example, the Green Room, which was a personal space located next to Mary's boudoir, was enhanced with additional Chinese ceiling decoration, Chinese textiles and lacquer (Healey 1997: 229; Nash 1980: 70). In Mary's Chinese Chippendale Room, panels of wallpaper were printed from an old piece of chinoiserie silk, and this pattern was also reproduced for the curtains and some of the upholstery (Smith 1931: 71–9). Furniture was covered with pieces of embroidered 'mandarin robes' that had come from the Brighton Royal Pavilion.

It is in her 'Chinese' treatments of some state and semi-state rooms of the palace that we begin to see the extent to which 'Chineseness' could be part of the official face of the British monarchy. The Centre Room was one of the first rooms Mary decorated in 1911, and she turned her attentions to it again in 1923. The Centre Room lies immediately below the palace's flagstaff, the central focus of the east front, and the Centre Room balcony is where the royal family show themselves to the public at moments of national importance. Under Mary's direction, the room was made emphatically 'Chinese'. Six panels of yellow embroidered Chinese silk were hung from new gilt wooden poles carved with dragons and bordered by Chinese fretwork (Healey 1997: 232; Smith 1931: 228). 'Chinese' ceiling decoration was added to match the silks, and new curtains were decorated with panels of old Chinese embroideries cut from the textiles found in the stores. Embroideries were also applied to the silk upholstery of the chairs. In common with the panels at Quex House, the bottom edge of a dragon robe was prominently utilised, creating a striped effect on a seat cushion cover (Fig. 2). This appropriation of imperial insignia within the palace played upon several centuries of Sino-British relations, in which pre-colonial 18th-century Chinese textiles came to the fore during a new era of semi-colonial relationships with China. The British royal household could now, symbolically, sit upon China's imperial past, giving the emblems of the once great Chinese Empire the potential to articulate modern British imperial subjectivities.

Whether or not Mary played any practical role in the dismembering, redesigning and sewing of the Chinese robes, their use by her was held up as an example of her modern and intelligent femininity. Katherine Woodward (c.1927: 160), discussing yet another of Mary's Chinese interiors at Windsor, claimed: 'Her mind is flexible; so too are her fingers ... She ... was the first to see ... the possibilities of the mandarin cloaks presented by some Oriental potentate to Queen Victoria, that had long mouldered in dusty obscurity and now do excellent service in the Chinese Room as hangings and settee covers.'

Of course, Mary was not doing anything particularly original, and was following the late 19th-century trend for the decoration of soft furnishings with Chinese embroideries that was a common enough feminine practice in any case with many types of embroideries. Her Chinese interiors also resonate with the early 20th-century revival of 18th-century styles, including chinoiserie, while in the 1920s there was a new fashion for Chinese styles whose vibrant colours, bold patterns and exotic associations fitted well with avant-garde and popular modern design, so much so that the use of Chinese dragon motifs in the drawing room could be synonymous with fashionable excess, superficiality and female gullibility (Cheang 2003: 97–113).

However, a photograph exists which shows that Mary not only dressed her rooms in Chinese textiles, but also her body. The image shows the king and queen attending a cinema performance in London in November 1924. Mary is wearing a full-length Chinese gown, similar in pattern to the chair cushions in the Centre Room but converted into an evening coat by the addition of a large fur collar and cuffs.

The image of Mary in her Chinese coat seems at first sight to be highly unusual, especially as she was known for extremely conservative dressing (Gore 1941: 368, 415–16; Pope-Hennessy 1959: 517; Rose 1983: 80). Mary's Chinese coat, however, being made from a richly coloured and lavishly embroidered luxury textile, and tailored in a conservative style, was a garment fit for a queen. In addition, Chinese robes were symbolic of the ruling classes, and Mary's coat was very likely to have been fashioned from robes that were in the palace stores and hence bore a double sign of royal accession. Her coat was, to a certain extent, a family heirloom, a forgotten treasure rediscovered in the palace stores, which was

Figure 2 Armchair in the Centre Room, Buckingham Palace, upholstered with Chinese embroidery (Smith 1931: pl. 287) (Country Life Picture Library).

being publicly paraded. Beyond colonial nostalgia, here was an active mobilisation of the signs of monarchism in order to reassure that, in the face of Communist revolution in Russia and possibly in China, and following the social upheaval of the First World War, imperial control still lived on in the hands of the British monarchy, who valued the old ways and wore old court robes. The relationships between fashion, court dress, masquerade and cross-cultural appropriation come sharply to the fore, and also a sense of Mary's personal motivations for wearing this coat, but these questions are beyond the remit of this short paper.

It is clear, however, in these interactions with Chinese textiles (as cushions, as needlework projects and as clothing), that the body of the queen formed a powerful site for the articulation of a British, feminine imperial identity, and a queenship that included the manipulation of a range of Chinese textiles. Here, one standard and widely discussed aspect of Mary's character stands out as particularly relevant. All writing about her stresses an almost pathological urge to catalogue and to add to the royal collections – she was seen as a natural curator. As queen consort, she was understood to be collecting and cataloguing for the nation, and her uses of Chinese textiles therefore cannot be separated from her participation in a royal archive with an imperial reach.

Conclusion

Since the 1980s, the self-reflexivity of the new museology, and indeed of the humanities and social sciences in general, has created a desire for objects to come furnished with full social documentation – photographs, receipts, oral histories, diaries and so on, enabling object interpretation to place an emphasis on the cultures of collecting or consuming as well as the cultures of production. Where British collections of non-Western objects are concerned, part of this self-reflexivity has its basis in post-colonial debates requiring institutions to consider the colonial histories, and possible illegalities, of their collections, and the way in which museum displays create cultural definitions of former colonies. For example, Partha Mitter's assessment of the 19th-century collections of the Victoria and Albert Museum as 'a perfect tool for constructing cultural difference and reinforcing racial hierarchy' (1997: 222) was produced as part of the museum's own examination of its history. If, as Richards (1993: 29) has suggested, Victorian museums were a crystallisation of the imperial archive – British institutions that provided a symbolic unity to the empire and an imperial identity for Britain – it is interesting how these early 20th-century displays of Chinese embroidery were invested so heavily in a nostalgic preservation of imperial China and a mindful presentation of self, either as individual or as national figurehead. In the constitution of these colonial subjectivities, the collections of textiles formed part of narratives of memory and self-definition within an archive of texts and of textiles.

Acknowledgements

Thanks are due to Malcolm Harman for his help with the archives and collections at Quex House, and Craig Clunas for his advice and support on the subject of Queen Mary.

Notes

1. This occurred during a visit I made to the museum in July 2004, and indicates the way in which museums can act as anchors for the multivalency of objects, with varying levels of historical accuracy and authority.
2. Thanks are due to Anna Jackson, Victoria and Albert Museum, for her comments on this subject.

References

Belk, R.W. (1995) *Collecting in a Consumer Society*. London: Routledge.

Bongie, C. (1991) *Exotic Memories: Literature, Colonialism and the Fin de Siècle*. Stanford, CA: Stanford University Press.

Chaudhuri, N. (1992) 'Shawls, jewelry, curry and rice in Victorian England', in *Western Women and Imperialism: Complicity and Resistance*, N. Chaudhuri and M. Strobel (eds), Bloomington, IN: Indiana University Press.

Cheang, S. (2003) *The Ownership and Collection of Chinese Material Culture by Women in Britain, c. 1890–c. 1935*, DPhil thesis, University of Sussex.

Cheang, S. (2006) 'Women, pets, and imperialism: the British Pekingese dog and nostalgia for old China', *Journal of British Studies* 45: 359–87.

Chung, Y.Y. (2005) *Silken Threads: A History of Embroidery in China, Korea, Japan, and Vietnam*. New York: Harry N. Abrams.

Colville, C. (1963) *Crowded Life: The Autobiography of Lady Cynthia Colville*. London: Evans.

Gore, J. (1941) *King George V: A Personal Memoir*. London: Murray.

Guha, R. (1992) 'Discipline and mobilize', in *Subaltern Studies VII: Writings on South Asian History and Society*, P. Chatterjee and G. Pandey (eds), 69–120. Delhi: Oxford University Press.

Halttunen, K. (1989) 'From parlor to living room: domestic space, interior designing and the culture of personality', in *Consuming Visions: Accumulation and Display of Goods in America: 1880–1920*, S.J. Bronner (ed.), 157–89. Winterthur, DE: Winterthur Museum.

Healey, E. (1997) *The Queen's House: A Social History of Buckingham Palace*. London: Joseph/Royal Collection.

Hevia, J.L. (1998) 'The archive state and the fear of pollution: from Opium Wars to Fu-Manchu', *Cultural Studies* 12(2): 234–64.

Hevia, J.L. (2003) *English Lessons: The Pedagogy of Imperialism in Nineteenth-Century China*. Durham, NC: Duke University Press.

McClintock, A. (1995) *Imperial Leather: Race, Gender and Sexuality in the Colonial Contest*. New York: Routledge.

Mitter, P. (1997) 'The imperial collections: Indian art', in *A Grand Design: The Art of the Victoria and Albert Museum*, M. Baker and B. Richardson (eds), 222–9. London: Victoria and Albert Museum.

Nash, R. (1980) *Buckingham Palace: The Place and the People*. London: MacDonald.

Pearce, S. (1995) *On Collecting: An Investigation into Collecting in the European Tradition*. London: Routledge.

Pope-Hennessy, J. (1959) *Queen Mary: 1867–1953*. London: Allen.

Powell-Cotton, P. (1891) Diary. Powell-Cotton Museum archive. P.H.G.P-C Diary 2 (transcribed).

Powell-Cotton, P. (1907) Diary. Powell-Cotton Museum archive.

P.H.G.P-C Diary 40, book 6 (transcribed).
Powell-Cotton, P. (1908) Diary. Powell-Cotton Museum archive. P.H.G.P-C Diary 41, book 7 (transcribed).
Powell-Cotton, P. (1909) Diary. Powell-Cotton Museum archive. P.H.G.P-C Diary 42, book 8 (transcribed).
Powell-Cotton, P. (1911) Diary. Powell-Cotton Museum archive. P.H.G.P-C Diary 45, book 1 (transcribed).
Powell-Cotton, P. (1919) Diary. Powell-Cotton Museum archive. P.H.G.P-C Diary 54, book 4 (transcribed).
Richards, T. (1993) *The Imperial Archive: Knowledge and the Fantasy of Empire*. London: Verso.
Rose, K. (1983) *King George V*. London: Weidenfeld.
Sitwell, O. (1974) *Queen Mary and Others*. London: Joseph.
Smith, H.C. (1931) *Buckingham Palace: Its Furniture, Decoration and History: By Harold Clifford Smith*. London: Country Life.
Spivak, G.C. (1985) 'The Rani of Sirmur: an essay in reading the archives', *History and Theory* 24: 247–72.
Spivak, G.C. (1988) 'Can the subaltern speak?', in *Marxism and the Interpretation of Culture*, C. Nelson and L. Grossberg (eds), 271–313. London: MacMillan.
Stoler, A. (2002) *Carnal Knowledge and Imperial Power: Race and the Intimate in Colonial Rule*. Berkeley, CA: University of California Press.
Wilson, V. (1999) 'Studio and soirée: Chinese textiles in Europe and America, 1850 to the present', in *Unpacking Culture: Art and Commodity in Colonial and Postcolonial Worlds*, R. Phillips and C. Steiner (eds), 234–9. Berkeley, CA: University of California Press.
Wilson, V. (2005) *Chinese Textiles*. London: Victoria and Albert Museum.
Woodward, K. (*c*.1927) *Queen Mary: A Life and Intimate Study*. London: Hutchinson.

The author

Sarah Cheang is Senior Lecturer in cultural and historical studies at London College of Fashion, University of the Arts London. Her doctoral thesis examined the history of Chinese material culture in the expression of British femininities (University of Sussex, 2003). She is currently editing a collection of essays examining the cultural meanings of hair, to be published by Berg.

Address

Sarah Cheang, Cultural and Historical Studies, London College of Fashion, 65 Davies Street, London W1K 5DA, UK (S.Cheang@fashion.arts.ac.uk)

Domesticity and gender
explored and challenged

'A Linnen Pockett a prayer Book and five keys': approaches to a history of women's tie-on pockets

Barbara Burman

ABSTRACT This paper introduces the AHRC-funded 'Pockets of History' study of the production and consumption of women's tie-on pockets in Britain from *c.*1690 to 1914. It outlines the range of material, visual and textual sources used in the study and its findings from the large group of extant pockets it documented. Two contrasting texts are then used to extend understanding of the usage and social life of this pocket form and link these textual sources with the material evidence. First, examples of 18th-century records of criminal court proceedings are used to demonstrate their role in uncovering the kind of small possessions carried by women in their pockets. Secondly, 19th-century stitched and inked marks on surviving pockets are situated within the practices of household economy and management. While these texts show how pockets were used and reveal aspects of their social significance, the paper also questions to what degree these sources can reveal the subjective experience of the users.

Keywords: 'Pockets of History', women's tie-on pockets, contents of pockets, laundry marks

Introduction

On 30 September 1716 Elizabeth Horn, a spinster from Southwark, emerged briefly from obscurity into the historical record because she went to court. There she told how her linen pocket, along with the prayer book and keys it contained, was stolen from her as she came along Tooley Street and she accused a man called John Steel.[1] Many women had their pockets picked, cut or snatched so, as Elizabeth Horn may have known only too well, her story exemplified a common experience of crime at that time. The paper's title borrows words from the simple record of her testimony to evoke this commonplace historical event as well as the details and miscellany of a woman's pocket that such records preserve for us.

This paper shows how AHRC-funded 'Pockets of History' has aligned textual records, such as this 18th-century court record of the theft of a pocket, with surviving examples of women's tie-on pockets in order to extend an understanding of these otherwise rather obscure though formerly ubiquitous objects.[2] Following an overview of the study and its use of sources, the paper identifies the kinds of material evidence offered by the extant pockets themselves. It then moves on to examine two very different kinds of textual sources: formal court proceedings and informal marks made on pockets by their makers. These examples have been selected to show how the material and textual illuminate and reinforce each other.

The 'Pockets of History' project

The study of women's tie-on pockets was designed to bring them into the academic fields of dress and social history and also to restore them to wider popular attention. This sort of pocket is remarkable for the fact it was worn by all classes of girls and women and its particular physical form remained constant for well over 200 years, despite substantial stylistic and structural changes to the garments it accompanied. The project's chief objectives were twofold. First, the project centred on the photography and documentation of extant pockets in museums and other collections across the UK, an estimated 300 in the time available. The completed project now provides an overview of over 300 pockets but is not a comprehensive record of tie-on pockets that may be extant in the UK.[3] Secondly, this body of material evidence was positioned and interpreted within a social and symbolic framework. Reinstating the pockets in this way was done by drawing together a diverse range of primary sources from the mid-17th to the later 20th century, most heavily concentrated on the period 1690 to 1900. Material from the 20th century, though less common, was an important element in mapping the 'afterlife' or 'evolution' of the tie-on pocket form.

Three hundred pockets make a critical mass of things, enough to give the individual collections to which they belong a context for their own pockets and to form a basis for wider frameworks of interpretation. It is a large enough sample to enable a substantial chronological perspective, and because its size lends some authority to the material evidence within it, there is scope for the development of a typology as well as the opportunity for comparative study and a more confident juxtaposition with other kinds of visual and textual sources.

The sample also offers a rich index and exposition of what tie-on pockets were like (Fig. 1). For instance, it reveals that there was variation of form within a kind of template structure and that a variety of materials was employed over time in pocket construction, mirroring changes in textile production brought about by the industrial revolution. It also shows specific practices and processes entailed in production and embellishment, such as embroidery, patchwork, knitting and recycling. Close examination of staining, structural stress, wear, tear and repair helps an understanding of use (Fig. 2). Existing documentation gives provenance to a small but valuable minority. There is an important subgroup of 19 cotton pockets with ready-made fronts woven in imitation of Marseilles quilted work.

The leading questions for the project's research were organised into three overlapping clusters: the material life of the pockets (how were these things made, and of what materials?), the social life of the pockets (who made and used them and how?) and the symbolic life of the pockets (what did they embody, signify or mean, and to whom?). To address these questions, the range of sources utilised by

Figure 1 This 18th-century pair of attached linen pockets echoes a common shape and construction: with bound or double-seamed edges, reinforced vertical openings and tape used to bind the top and form the waist ties. The embroidered decoration follows a customary pattern of free-flowing stems, leaves and flowers with a prominent feature directly below the opening. At 36 cm long, their size is typical too (BATMC 2004.468, by permission of the Museum of Costume, Bath and North East Somerset Council) (Plate 70 in the colour plate section).

Figure 2 Close examination of pockets provides clues to effects and patterns of use. In this case, the back reveals stains and other signs of wear, including a large internal patch placed over a neatened hole, a common method of mending at this period (BATMC 2004.468, by permission of the Museum of Costume, Bath and North East Somerset Council) (Plate 71 in the colour plate section).

'Pockets of History' included paintings and popular prints, fiction, poetry, ballads, essays, letters and diaries, newspapers and periodicals, inventories and court records as well as the extant pockets themselves. Thus, from the outset, the project has interwoven and compared textiles, texts and visual imagery, mindful of the different treatment and interpretation they each require. The project's three clusters of questions aim to embed the pockets back where they came from: daily life in Britain from the 17th to the 20th century. A dress and textile history exiled from the history of people's lives and a social history that does not embrace material culture would be a particularly barren prospect. In some respects the study echoes Henry Glassie's position on the study of material culture: 'The job is, in essence, to connect formal properties in the object with cultural data from beyond, allowing each to explain the other, in order to understand the act that left us an artifact' (Glassie 1999: 65).

Textual sources and the use of tie-on pockets

Turning to the usage and social life of the pockets, uncovering what women carried in them is itself a valuable stage in establishing why such pockets were so enduring and common. In this respect, the material evidence within the extant pockets themselves is limited. Although the project turned up four pockets with things still inside them and many pockets reveal clear physical signs of use, to gain a clearer perspective of what was kept inside pockets requires the use of other textual and visual sources (Fig. 3). In cases of pick-pocketing and theft from the person, the records of criminal court proceedings provide remarkable detail of what women carried in their pockets, due partly to the fact that punishment was scaled to the value of goods taken. Although subject to numerous caveats, these records offer a sustained, readily accessible source and 'Pockets of History' has concentrated particularly on the 18th century in London with other jurisdictions selected for comparison. Not only was the nature of what was kept in women's pockets revealed as their personal possessions were enumerated and described to the courts, but also the circumstances of the pockets' use were often reported, allowing for the recovery of a more expansive sense of the social life of pockets.

Elizabeth Horn's story of 1716 is a brief individual story, but it is a valuable example of this kind of source. As well as describing the pocket's contents, it is informative about the material used to make the pocket, the owner's status as a spinster and also her whereabouts. By referring to a sizeable sample of other court cases, an individual case like this can be contextualised and compared. For example, focusing on the pocket's contents and the prayer book in particular, there is evidence from other theft cases to show that prayer books were often carried in the pockets of men and women in public places. Indeed, just a couple of months before Elizabeth Horn was robbed, a calico pocket containing a prayer book, a silk purse, a thimble and a quantity of coins was snatched from a woman by a 'notorious' rogue in London.[4] In another remarkably similar case two years later in 1718, a woman's pocket that contained her prayer book, a handkerchief and 11 pence was pulled from her in the street in the evening.[5] Such crimes

Figure 3 Dressed dolls of various kinds often provide useful information about how pockets were worn, although care is required in dating separate elements. This mid-18th-century doll has a 'husswif' in her pocket. In her set of clothes there is also a yellow silk damask single pocket containing a pin cushion (MCAG.1955.21, by permission of the Gallery of Costume, Platt Hall, Manchester Art Galleries) (Plate 72 in the colour plate section).

could involve brute force. In 1717 in London, for example, it was claimed that a woman's 'Pocket was with great Violence pull'd off by a Boy, which tearing down her Petticoat in doing it, she was oblig'd to take it up, and so could not follow him, and so he got off'.[6] In the cases cited above, the calico pocket itself was valued at 3d and the other two at 1d, substantially less than the individual items they contained.

The court records can be suggestive and evocative as well as informative. They reveal how women's efforts to secure their small but meaningful personal possessions were often thwarted. In this respect they can be linked with records of other common crimes such as burglary and housebreaking, in which pockets often went missing from storage along with other personal and household linen. The severe sentences for those convicted, for example transportation or the death penalty (though not always carried out in full), indicate the level of risk taken wittingly or unwittingly by the perpetrators, itself a reflection of how some public spaces may have been perceived as dangerous by law-abiding women. Among the surviving pockets in the study, over 20 have buttonholes, most in addition to tapes for the waist, indicating they may have been buttoned to stays or corsets, an option also suggested as late as 1840 by *The Workwoman's Guide* (A Lady 1840: 73). Perhaps these buttoning pockets show us the extra precautions taken by women who knew, as the court records reveal, that a determined thief could make off with a pocket relatively easily.

The prayer book and the keys described by Elizabeth Horn come together to put the pocket at the heart of women's domestic and social roles at this time. Despite the brevity of the official record, the conjunction of these items has a special potency. The prayer book was part of a large and popular market for printed matter of all kinds, and it indicates literacy as well as a devotional life with a claim to membership of a church and its public observances. It was a book carried privately about Elizabeth Horn's person yet in a public place. In this case the pocket worked as a kind of bridge between the inner private and the outer public worlds. The keys speak of the numerous domestic and other responsibilities women had sometimes as employers of servants or as trusted servants themselves, or as traders in their own right. Books, keys and pockets were symbolic as well as practical at a time when women were subordinate in theory and practice and when private space or personal property were limited privileges rather than rights.

The testimonies preserved in the court records investigated by 'Pockets of History' also suggest other lines of enquiry about pocket usage beyond the nature and value of contents. For example, there are cases around the country in which women had their pockets stolen from under their pillows, either taken as they slept at home or in lodging houses or inns. This suggests that there was extra security perceived in the way this pocket form could be removed from the body and hidden away. It also points to the place of pockets in a world in which women could have geographical mobility and social interaction and the records show that this practice continued into the 19th century. Thus, it is possible to identify some of the kinds of places and circumstances in which women's pockets were taken. The court records also show, in early 19th-century London at least, a reduction in thefts of tie-on pockets and an increase in the number of thefts of bags and reticules. By 1858, when a determined widow from Yorkshire went to court in London after her tie-on pocket was picked on an omnibus, the pocket was described as 'old-fashioned'.[7]

It can be argued that the contents and usage of tie-on pockets represent a moral economy, prudent femininity and skilful, self-sufficient housewifery, but a further point emerges from court records that complicates this perspective. It is abundantly clear from them that many women also knew the practical value of pockets when they went thieving for themselves. For instance, in 1777 Jane Griffiths was brought before Quarter Sessions in Worcestershire accused by Thomas Wainwright of stealing two live ducks. She had tried to hide them in her pockets and escape across the fields but he caught her, spurred on perhaps by the fact she was a woman known locally for 'having a bad character'.[8] The sweeping range of stolen goods reportedly concealed in women's pockets, such as cheese, meat, soap, shawls, lengths of cloth, gloves, ribbons, lace, needles, glass tumblers, silver plate, purses, buckles and buttons, reflects both opportunistic and planned theft as well as the variety of circumstances in which women lived and worked. Popular knowledge of deep and hidden tie-on pockets in turn reinforces the material evidence that they were often long and capacious, and resonates with popular prints and fiction where a bulging pocket was frequently used to signify greed, profligacy or licentiousness. Repeated questions were asked in court in 1794 to ascertain if a woman could actually know when something was being stolen from her pocket. 'Ladies pockets are generally pretty full, they say there is no bottom to them?'[9]

While records of court proceedings can illuminate how and where pockets were used, and even, to some extent, how they were perceived, there are also limitations. For instance, in the case of Elizabeth Horn, offences and sentencing at this period were linked to the value of the items stolen, and it may be that as she walked along Tooley Street she had other things in her pocket that were given no monetary value and therefore not recorded. For example, letters or other papers were undoubtedly of significant personal value to women but having no perceived monetary value, unlike pocket books or bank and promissory notes, court records are silent on them. To discover more about the use of pockets within the household and other social spaces and practices, as well as to determine what, if any, subjective significance the pockets held in relation to new notions of personal privacy that developed as the 18th century went on, it is necessary to turn to other sources, most notably fiction, letters and diaries. These often move the story out of the populace as recorded in the courts into more elite social spaces, reinforcing our overall findings that these pockets were in use right across the social spectrum. From these texts a picture emerges of the usage of pockets as a significant concomitant to the burgeoning letter and journal writing culture of the 18th century. For example, in 1768, at the age of 16, Fanny Burney described the role her pocket played in keeping her privacy.

> I always have the last sheet of my Journal in my pocket, and when I have wrote it half full I join it to the rest, and

Figure 4 A close-up view of a Fanny Jarvis mark on a pocket shows how neatly the ink was applied over the ribbed weave of the cotton dimity, possibly aided by sizing of the area first (MCAG.1947.1252, by permission of the Gallery of Costume, Platt Hall, Manchester City Galleries) (Plate 73 in the colour plate section).

take another sheet – and so on. Now I happen'd unluckily to take the last sheet out of my pocket with my letter – and laid it on the piano forte, and there, negligent fool! – I left it ... Well, as ill fortune would have it, papa went into the room – took my poor Journal – read, and pocketted it (Ellis 1889: 17).

The pocket as a hiding place for the written word evokes a response to a world in which women had very little scope for the safekeeping of any records made of their private feelings and thoughts in journals or shared and received by them in letters.

Textual sources and the deliberate marking of pockets

The deliberate marks made on the surviving possessions of Fanny Jarvis provide yet another kind of text studied in the project. Fanny Jarvis is known by name only through a group of over 30 items of clothing including caps, collars, chemises and four large tie-on pockets, at the Gallery of Costume, Platt Hall, Manchester City Galleries. They are all marked in ink with her name or initials, numbers and dates (Fig. 4).[10] The marks are among the smallest and briefest of the texts included in the study, and quite literally they merge textiles and text. In contrast to the formal records of court proceedings, they are informal and personal, but how can we categorise and interpret these objects/texts? The Jarvis items are composed of different weights and weaves of fine linen and cotton but share the characteristics of the inked marks, a snowy whiteness, careful construction and the finest possible stitching. When they are compared with other garments of this period, the Jarvis marked items can be understood as part of the common practice of using systems of marking for day, night and underclothing for men and women.[11] In the context of the 300 pockets surveyed, Fanny's pockets fit within a substantial group of over 70 deliberately marked or inscribed pockets. Of these, about half are marked with ink in a style similar to Fanny's and half are marked in cross stitch (Fig. 5). The marks include initials, names, dates and what seems to be numbering systems. Most of these marked items belong to the 19th century.

Although instructive about the methods and types of marks used, the material evidence within this group of marked pockets is not sufficient to clarify the exact meaning of the numbering employed either by Fanny Jarvis or others. It is likely that the numbers offered some type of rotation system. This problem of interpretation is echoed even in the case of Queen Victoria's underwear: 'The Queen's cypher was always worked on each garment; the numbering system associated with the cyphers is not understood today but it is likely that the garments were ordered in quantities and then worn in rotation' (Staniland 1997: 166). Although the precise systems used probably differed between households and over time (requiring further research to explain them at face value), the marks themselves stand as a kind of text, in ink and stitch, to be illuminated in a general sense by means of more conventional textual sources. For example, some numbers may indicate that the items were part of a set, such as Fanny Jarvis's chemise marked '9/1825',

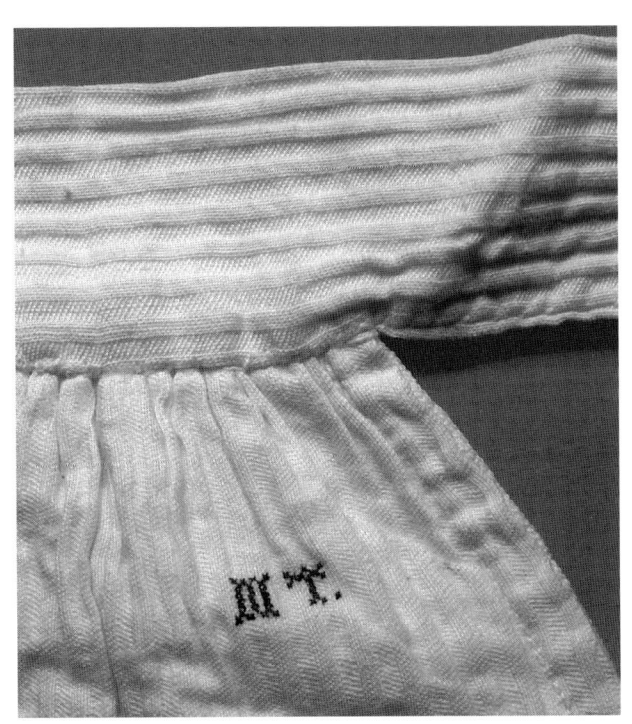

Figure 5 Typical of the cross-stitched small marks used in the 19th century, these initials are on the ribbed cotton dimity back of a pocket (CRH.1973.16, by permission of Hampshire County Museums and Archives Service) (Plate 74 in the colour plate section).

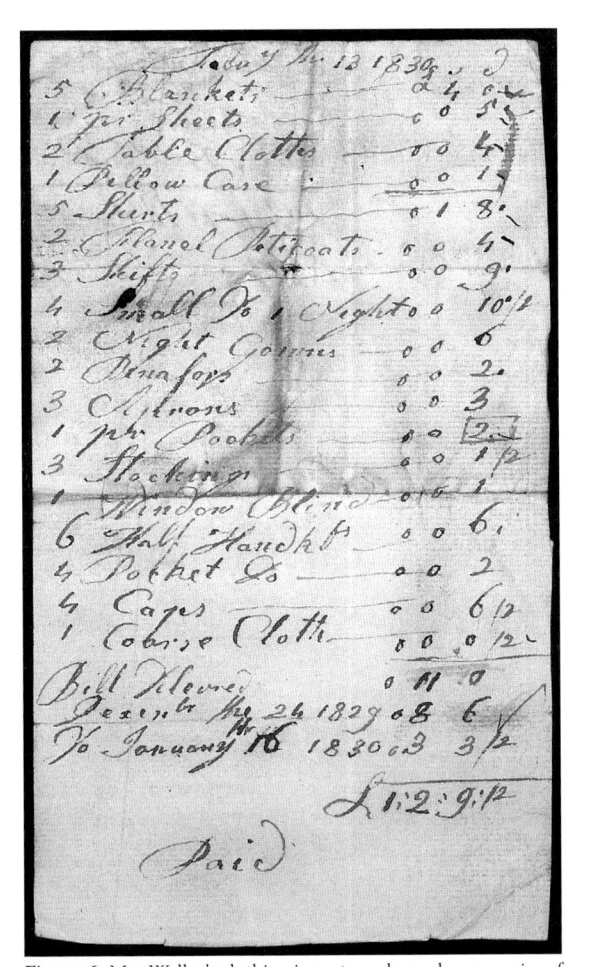

Figure 6 Mrs Waller's clothing inventory showed seven pairs of pockets in her possession at her death in 1831. This bill was presented to Mrs Waller in 1830 by her laundress/seamstress. It indicates the range of items sent and shows she paid 2d to have a pair of pockets washed (29M67/43, by permission of the Hampshire Record Office).

her nightgown marked '14/1825' or the pockets themselves marked '9/1821', '2_', '1/1824' and a near identical but separate pocket also marked '1/1824'.[12] There are other kinds of texts that indicate that ownership of multiple sets of clothing was common at this date. For example, an inventory taken in 1835 after her death in 1831 shows that Mrs Waller, a Hampshire widow of moderate means, owned seven pairs of pockets. They were among several other types of clothing in substantial sets, such as 17 each of caps and frills, 10 white petticoats and eight white aprons.[13] These are large quantities for an individual to maintain.

Keeping track of everything could be complex in households considering the substantial amount of clothing generated by girls and women, both family and residential servants, as well as men's clothing and household linen. The laundering might be done by servants at home, by visiting laundresses or sent out (Fig. 6). Marking individual items was itself labour-intensive but necessary as an aid to keep sufficient items circulating in regular use and to check against pilfering and damage. It may also have helped with returning finished articles to their correct storage place. *The Workwoman's Guide* even suggested using a variety of patterned linens for household use to help differentiate them because 'servants frequently forget to look at the marks' (A Lady 1840: 187). 'Receipts' were provided for marking ink, including a liquid pounce to size the cloth beforehand (1840: 217). The same book advised that the best economies were achieved by washing 'by the year, or by the quarter, in places where it can be done, and by the score or dozen in preference to the piece. A calculation may easily be made so as to be quite fair both to the washerwoman and her employer' (1840: 188). Under that kind of arrangement, large numbers of each class of household or personal linen would be necessary. At a time when everything was made by hand using labour-intensive methods, marks also had a special importance in helping identify and retrieve lost and stolen goods. Clothing was a favourite target for thieves and the processes and locations of laundry work presented them with many opportunities. Washerwomen took clothes away to their own homes, increasing the risk of theft; in 1782 Mary Rowland, a washerwoman in lodgings in Covent Garden, London, took a nap in the afternoon and awoke to find several items stolen including a pair of dimity pockets.[14] There was much theft of clothing put out to dry on lines or hedges. It is not uncommon to find cases in which the laundry or washhouses of private homes were broken into. In 1804, four pairs of pockets were among a large quantity of wet clothing stolen from a house in Hampstead Road, London when its outside laundry door was forced at midnight. The clothing was retrieved the next day and identified by the owner's mark.[15]

Underscoring this aspect of household management and the potential scale of laundry work, Mrs Waller's inventory recalls the popularity of high-maintenance white personal linen at this time. Of her 118 items, even the most cautious calculation is that at least half were white and, given how commonly frills or caps were white, white items may have made up as much as three-quarters of her inventoried wardrobe. The need for economy and hygiene are recurrent features of the huge household management literature of the period. By linking the inked and stitched marks found on the extant pockets to such sources, it is possible to reconstruct the circumstances that gave them purpose and meaning. But, like the records of court proceedings, these sources help us understand the social life of the marks but not uncover the feelings or subjective experience of their makers and users. The marking of household and personal linen was common yet it carried considerable significance. It indicated ownership and facilitated efficient housekeeping, but for women at the start of their marriages, the marking of their linen was also an indicator of their change of surname and status. There is more research needed on trousseaux and other practices linking marriage and linen in Britain at this time.

George Eliot gives a glimpse of the emotive and commemorative power of women's marks in her 1860 novel *The Mill on the Floss*, a story set in the early 1800s. Bewildered Mrs Tulliver, trying to grasp the implications of Mr Tulliver's intemperate business dealings that will result in a public auction of the contents of their house, is faced with the loss of the linen she had woven before her marriage. She weeps 'over the mark "Elizabeth Dodson" on the corner of some table cloths she held in her lap' (Eliot 1985: 281). Mourning the fact that the linen will not be passed on to her children, she tells them: 'And the pattern as I chose myself – and bleached so beautiful – and I marked 'em so as nobody ever saw such marking – they must cut the cloth to get it out, for it's a particular stitch. And they're all to be sold – and go into strange people's houses' (Eliot 1985: 282). Although fiction is sometimes regarded as a difficult source for dress and textile history, it can alert and sensitise us to the intricate links between the outer material world and the inner world of human feelings that is often invisible in other sources (Hughes 2006; Taylor 2002: 90–114). The marks inked and stitched on extant pockets in the study testify to a widespread practice over a long period of time and to those women who did not want their marks or their identities to be separated from the pockets, in a physical, a social or a symbolic sense.

Conclusion

In conclusion, the study of the contents of pockets and the deliberate marks made on them has added a further dimension to understanding the function and sociality of a specific pocket form. It also shows that the pocket serves as a particularly telling junction between the private and the public worlds, specifically between the body and social space, and it maps a link between the material, social and symbolic spheres. This aspect of the pocket's work reveals gender-specific practicalities and concerns of everyday life at the time. In turn, it points to issues that help explain why the tie-on pocket formed a common part of women's wardrobes for so long. Examination of court records detailing pick-pocketing and pocket theft cases has further demonstrated the value of these records as historically specific sources. The study as a whole uses them in conjunction with other documents: the far less numerous but informative advertisements taken out by people who lost their pockets accidentally, or letters, diaries, essays and novels in which the writer gave an account of a pocket's role within a personal or fictional narrative. This mix of sources does not tell a neatly coherent story. Its richness lies as much in the contrasts and nuances as the generalities it uncovers. Linking texts and textiles in this study returns to Glassie's idea of understanding an artefact by 'looping composition and association – text and context, form and meaning, structure and function – together' (Glassie 1999: 65–6).

Acknowledgements

The author owes special thanks to Dr Seth Denbo and Dr Jonathan White for their expertise and collaboration on the 'Pockets of History' project. She is also indebted to Alison Carter and Sue Washington of Hampshire County Museums and Archives Service and the many other generous curators and archivists who aided and enriched the work of the project throughout. Thanks are also due to the AHRC, the University of Southampton and particularly to colleagues at the Textile Conservation Centre for their support.

Notes

1. 'Elizabeth Horn of this parish of St Olave Southwark in the county of Surry Spinster saith on oath that as she was coming along Tooley Street in Southwark this Evening a Linnen Pockett a prayer Book and five keys were privately stolen from her person and that she does verily believe that John Steel the prisoner present did Steal the same for that she caused him to be apprehended imediately after the same was taken from her and then saw him Dropp the said pocket with the said prayer Book and keys in it.' 'Jurat 30th Die Septembrio 1716'. Surrey History Centre. QS2/6/1716/Mic/31. Although Southwark was a suburb of London, serious crimes committed there were dealt with by the Surrey assizes.
2. This paper draws on research funded by the Arts and Humanities Research Council (AHRC) and the University of Southampton between 2003 and 2006. In 2006–07, it resulted in an exhibition *Pockets of History* at the Museum of Costume, Bath, England with a catalogue of the same name and a website www.vads.ahds.ac.uk/collections/pocketsofhistory.html. See also Burman and White 2007. The study began in earlier work (Burman 2002).
3. The tie-on pockets in the study are from 30 collections in England, Scotland and Wales.
4. *Old Bailey Proceedings Online* (www.oldbaileyonline.org. 25 January 2006), September 1716, trial of Samuel West (t17160906 – 20).
5. *Old Bailey Proceedings Online* (www.oldbaileyonline.org. 25 January 2006), October 1718, trial of Thomas Wiggans (t17181015 – 17).
6. *Old Bailey Proceedings Online* (www.oldbaileyonline.org. 25 January 2006), December 1717, trial of William Carlisle (t17171204 – 24).
7. *The Times*, 4 March 1858.
8. Worcestershire Record Office. Quarter Sessions Rolls 1/1/470, Michaelmas 1777.
9. *Old Bailey Proceedings Online* (www.oldbaileyonline.org. 25 January 2006) February 1794, trial of John Mitchell (t17940219 – 74).
10. The four large tie-on pockets are dated 1821 and 1824. The last year represented in this group is 1833. Two caps and a bum pad marked Fanny Jarvis Snr indicate there may have been two women of this name.
11. For example, laundry marks found on caps of this period marked 'Mary Muir 19/ 24' and '13 / 24' (CRH 1960.36, Hampshire County Museums and Archives Service), and stockings marked 'F B 6' and 'B.A.Bridson.1.1862' (52/3/7 and 52/3/2, the Montse Stanley Knitting Collection, University of Southampton), illustrate the continuation of the practice through the century.
12. Fanny Jarvis inventory numbers: chemise '9/1825', MCAG 1947.1130; nightgown '14/1825', MCAG 1947.1189; pockets '9/1821', MCAG 1947.1252; '2_', MCAG 1947.1254; '1/1824', MCAG 1947.1253 B and its near identical companion '1/1824', MCAG 1947.1253 A.
13. 'An Inventory of the late Mrs Waller's apparel'. Hampshire Record Office. 29M67/57.
14. *Old Bailey Proceedings Online* (www.oldbaileyonline.org. 25 January 2006), July 1782, trial of Susannah Stewart (t17820703 – 38).
15. *Old Bailey Proceedings Online* (www.oldbaileyonline.org. 25 January 2006), December 1804, trial of Thomas alias William Williams (t18041205 – 41).

References

A Lady (1840) *The Workwoman's Guide: Containing Instructions to the Inexperienced in Cutting Out and Completing …* 2nd Edition. London: Simpkin, Marshall and Co.

Burman, B. (2002) 'Pocketing the difference: gender and pockets in nineteenth-century Britain', *Gender and History* 14(3): 447–69.

Burman, B. and White, J. (2007) 'Fanny's pockets: cotton, consumption and domestic economy, 1780–1850', in *Women and Material Culture 1650–1830*, J. Batchelor and C. Kaplan (eds). Basingstoke: Palgrave Macmillan.

Eliot, G. (1985) *The Mill on the Floss* London: Penguin Classics.

Ellis, A.R. (ed.) (1889) *The Early Diary of Fanny Burney, 1768–1778, with a selection from her correspondence and from the journals of her sisters Susan and Charlotte Burney*, vol.1. London: G. Bell & Son.

Glassie, H. (1999) *Material Culture*. Bloomington, IN: Indiana University Press.

Hughes, C. (2006) *Dressed in Fiction*. Oxford: Berg.

Staniland, K. (1997) *In Royal Fashion: The Clothes of Princess Charlotte of Wales and Queen Victoria 1796–1901*. London: Museum of London.

Taylor, L. (2002) *The Study of Dress History*. Manchester: Manchester University Press.

The author

Barbara Burman is a visiting Research Fellow at the Centre for the History of Textiles and Dress, University of Southampton. Her research interests are in the production and consumption of clothing from the 18th to the early 20th century. She is currently working on 19th-century domestic knitting and an exhibition of highlights from the Montse Stanley knitting collection.

Address

Barbara Burman, 7 Hocroft Avenue, London NW2 2EJ, UK (blburman@aol.com)

The antimacassar in fact and fiction: how textual resources reveal a domestic textile

Alice McEwan

ABSTRACT This paper concerns the relationship, both literal and metaphorical, between a textile and texts and the construction of gender. The antimacassar originated in the 1830s as a practical covering for chairbacks to protect them from being soiled by the macassar oil men used in their hair but it increasingly assumed a purely ornamental role in the home. By 1900 the antimacassar had become a trope for a feminised, over-decorated interior, signifying a stale domesticity where the 'feminine' and the 'decorative' were seen as not only contemptible, but also rather menacing and disingenuous. The verb 'antimacassared' was invented as a derogatory term for the Victorian period itself. Employing the methods of design history and cultural studies, this paper explores a range of archival and bibliographic resources including inventories, autobiographies, advice literature, ladies' periodicals, newspapers and novels in an attempt to understand why this particular textile generated such negative responses among those writing at the turn of the century. Textual material whether defined as factual or fictive, empirical or poetical, has the power to function at the level of representation, embodying narrative elements and imaginative qualities. As such, texts have a role in constructing their subject, thus the ways in which the antimacassar and its image have been formed to fortify certain sociocultural values and ideological positions are investigated. Nevertheless, individuals asserted their identity through this textile, challenging widespread assumptions about its use that were reliant upon gendered distinctions.

Keywords: gendered identities, domestic decoration, embodiment, literary construction, text/textuality, metaphor/metonymy

Introduction

The origins of this paper lie in a review of a staging of Ibsens's play *Hedda Gabler* in 2005. Eve Best's interpretation, Michael Billington informs us, is commendable because it 'takes the *antimacassared* heaviness out of Ibsen' (*Guardian* 2005). Such textual abuse of the antimacassar automatically mapped the object onto the 'feminine' pejoratively, while reworking the familiar trope of the feminine and textile as 'masquerade': a perceived ability to cover or adorn, conceal, disguise or shroud (Jefferies 1995: 164). Textual analysis of this review reveals the language of textiles engendering what feminist Nancy K. Miller has described as 'a metaphorics of femininity deeply marked by Freud's account of women and weaving' (Miller 1988: 80). What it also shows is the postmodern propensity for the text as textile that came to the fore in Barthes' writing, particularly *The Pleasure of the Text* (Barthes 1976). Given the linguistic play within textuality, the noun 'antimacassar' could thus become a verb.

Probing into the facts and fictions of the past however, demonstrates that both aspects of this discourse, which enacts a kind of double displacement, have historical precedents. An article on women from *The Times* in 1914, for example, spoke dismissively of 'the antimacassared ease of early Victorian times'. Similarly a novel by Edward Booth, *The Tree of the Garden*, constructed a metaphor around the antimacassar as a verb to enhance the fear of entrapment. Caught up within Mrs Suddaby's parlour like a spider's web 'everything appeared to be antimacassared – the portly Bible on the polished loo table, all the chairs, the pictures, and even the fireplaces' (Booth 1922: 64).

At the forefront of this paper therefore is the relationship, both literal and metaphorical, between textiles and text and the construction of gender. The semiotic richness of one particular textile, the antimacassar, is examined: how it is revealed by texts in archives today, but also how this object generated bibliographic material historically in the wider cultural sphere. Arguably what is constructed around the antimacassar forms a meta-language, which serves to highlight the ways in which textiles and text are often interwoven through a linguistic system that plays on gendered subjectivities.[1] Metaphors that denigrate textiles and the materials and techniques associated with textile practice on the assumption that they are innately feminine, have been in usage in English texts for centuries. Think of 'weaving' meaning to fabricate, concoct or contrive; or 'to embroider' which means elaborating the truth (Wilkinson 1993: 21, 31). Historically woven disparagingly into the very tissue of everyday language, it is all too easy for textiles, and therefore 'woman', to become the subject of condemnation and derision.

A range of textual material, both factual and fictive, is utilised to demonstrate how the metaphorics of femininity have been mapped onto the antimacassar, forming an indexical relationship that penetrates to the heart of the patriarchal order within Victorian and Edwardian society. But how might these dominant historical and popular perceptions of the antimacassar be subverted and replaced? This paper reveals how the various texts that are woven into this textile blur the boundaries between material that is often maintained in discrete categories as fact or fiction.

From useful to ornamental artefact

Macassar oil was marketed by the firm of Rowlands in London from 1800 as a product to strengthen and add shine to the hair. Initially used to smooth men's whiskers, it was later applied to head hair. The fashion for oiled hair became so pervasive that by the 1830s the backs of chairs began to be covered with washable textiles as a means of preventing the upholstery fabric from becoming soiled. An autobiography detailing life in the Victorian period described the need for such an artefact: 'the antimacassar, as its name implies, was designed to protect chairs and couches from the disfiguring stains of macassar oil, then liberally used in the adornment of the hair' (Tatlow 1920: 20). A protective cloth covering the back of a large armchair appears in a watercolour of the family home by Elizabeth Shelley, the sister of the Romantic poet. The antimacassar seems to have had literary associations from the start, especially given that Lord Byron famously used macassar oil and even mentioned it in a poem.[2]

A change in furniture design around 1830 prompted the need for a textile that would counter the effects of this sticky hair grease. In 1828 the first patent had been taken out on springs for sofas and armchairs, permitting a greater degree of corpulence and comfort. This encouraged new postures for the body, previously not tolerated in society, and the verb 'to lounge' acquired its current meaning. If one's body were allowed to assume a position of rest in a chair, then inevitably the fabric would come into contact with one's hair. An auctioneer's inventory detailing the goods belonging to a gentleman in 1848, for example, mentions an 'anti-macassar' in its description of the sofa in the comfortable, informal breakfast room.[3] It is during the 1840s that the term 'anti-macassar' is first applied.

By this date, antimacassars were becoming a popular feature of the middle-class home and like many other textiles produced during the Victorian era, were created by affluent women as hand-crafted objects. Surviving textual material such as instruction manuals and periodicals testifies to this popularity. Mrs Beal's *The Antimacassar Crochet Book* of 1848, for example, contained patterns designed for consumers to create their own artefact. These show that antimacassars were usually rectangular in shape, often with tassels. Many other pattern books survive from the 1860s and 70s, such as Riego de la Branchardière's *The Crochet Book of Emblem Antimacassars* (1874), indicating continuing widespread use and currency.[4] Designs for antimacassars featured regularly in ladies' periodicals, notably *The Lady's Newspaper and Pictorial Times* and *The English Woman's Domestic Magazine*; while *The Royal Magazine of Knitting, Netting, Crochet and Fancy Needlework* from the 1840s came complete with drawings that indicated the potential for use on different types of furniture (Fig. 1).[5] The earlier issues also reminded the reader of the functional origins of the antimacassar, placing advertisements for macassar oil close to antimacassar patterns. These often mentioned the availability of 'family bottles' suggesting that women, too, were consumers.[6]

Yet invariably the need for the antimacassar to act as a practical object to protect furniture from the unwanted effects of hair grease was tempered by the desire for display. What is evident from these texts and from examination of actual textiles in archives is their role as ornamental artefacts.[7] The

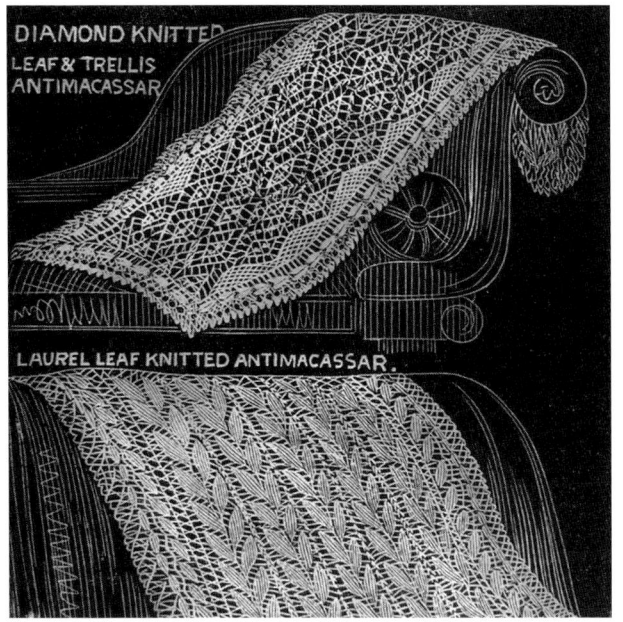

Figure 1 Illustration from *The Royal Magazine of Knitting, Netting, Crochet and Fancy Needlework*, 1850 (V&A Images) (Plate 75 in the colour plate section).

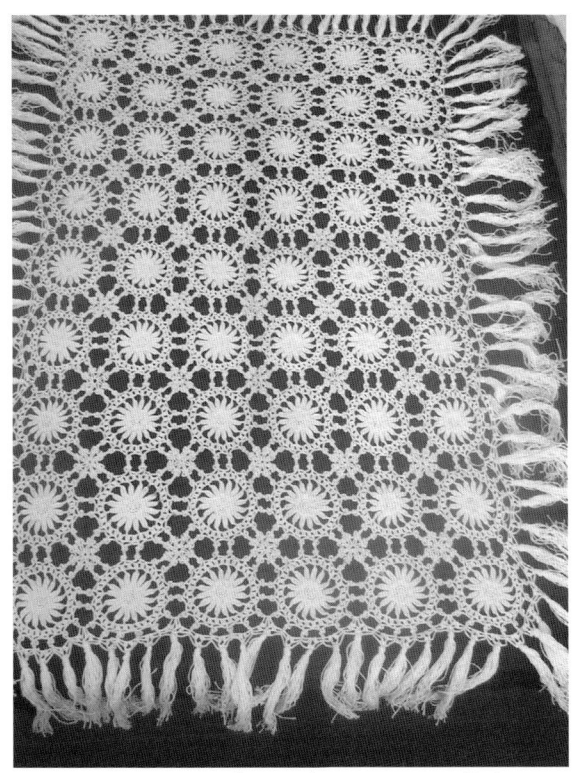

Figure 2 Antimacassar, white crochet cotton, c.1870 (Reference no. 1900–226, Nottingham City Museums and Galleries: Costume and Textile Collections).

backs of chairs were an ideal surface upon which to display a range of needlework techniques, including various forms of crochet, knitting, lacework and embroidery. Even those that occupied a more ambivalent status, such as the antimacassars in white crocheted cotton or lace that could be washed repeatedly and were hence functional in this respect, nevertheless allowed the seepage of oil through the many holes that formed part of their decorative surface (Fig. 2).

The painting *James Wyatt and His Granddaughter Mary Wyatt* by John Everett Millais (1849) reveals a lace antimacassar for example that would have done little to protect the damask wingchair it covers (Fig. 3).

Instead as a decorative object, its role lay in making laudable the leisure activities of the female producer (wife or daughter) and her ability to beautify the home. Furthermore as an article of amateur rather than commercial production, it operated as a marker of taste and distinction, given the elevated status of handmade lace at the time.[8]

The word 'antimacassar' itself then – implying something that would counter and control hair oil – became something of a misnomer almost as soon as it was created, which inevitably compounded the discourse already in place that viewed textile-making and use as acts of concealment and deception. An instruction manual from 1848, *The Colored Anti-Macasssar Book* by the appropriately named Charles Hairs, demonstrates the contradiction in terms. It contains designs for the home production of brightly coloured antimacassars using Berlin wool and crochet cotton. Owing to the strong dyes used, Berlin wool could never be washed, therefore it was impossible for such fragile textiles to be placed anywhere near oily substances. Significantly, the hyphen that typically divided the words 'anti' and 'macassar', as seen in this early text, soon disappears altogether.

As one word, 'antimacassar' no longer embodied any particular function. Dislodged in this way from its original masculine referent that supposedly gave it a purpose, the object came to be perceived as ornamental and exclusively feminine. Remembering the antimacassar as one of the principal features of his mother's parlour during the late 19th century, Walter Southgate wrote: 'chairbacks and the sofa had to be covered with antimacassars which were more ornamental than protection against the macassar hair oil, which some men used' (Southgate 1982: 67). The familiar narratives that engendered the notion of textiles as having symbolic connections with femininity were thus in place, helping to maintain normative domestic ideals. In a similar way, Victorian narrative paintings operated as texts, encompassing the idea of sewing and needlework as accomplishments essential to the woman as a female. This is made clear in a painting *The Only Daughter* (1875) by James Hayllar, where these feminine skills are reinforced by the presence of the decorative, home-made antimacassar and the sewing machine in the centre of the painting (Fig. 4). What this work also inscribes is the binary opposition that links the feminine body and textiles, and the masculine mind with the supposedly loftier text. The anonymous author of a manual of advice put forward a similar argument: 'nothing can be more pitiable than to see a female unable to ply her needle, her case being somewhat similar to that of a male who does not know how to read' (*The Mother's Home Book* 1879: 220).

A disruptive corporeality

The sanitised image that linked textiles and the female seamstress to enforce the ideal of domesticity that we see in the Hayllar painting had a darker side however. The discourse that conflated the female body and textiles allowed the antimacassar to literally embody 'woman', thereby posing a threat to bourgeois stability and identity through a disruptive corporeality. The power of the text to construct a pejorative image of woman through the antimacassar was in evidence as early as 1876, as an entry in the periodical *Notes and Queries* demonstrates. The contributor had evidently seen an antimacassar embroidered with a poem about the duchess of Devonshire, placed on a chair beneath a painting of her. Here we are presented with the negative metaphorics of femininity that would later engender Freud's discourse on women and weaving, characterised by a lack (Freud 1932: 132). This is the reconstruction of woman as antimacassar, the last two lines reading: 'How changed now her fate, to the purchaser's cost! Her charms are cut out, and her canvas is lost' (*Notes and Queries* 26 August 1876, vi: 166). The stitched text plays on the bodily disfigurement of the duchess, who according to popular reports ruined her appearance by living a life of debauchery. Her perceived deficiency is mirrored through the material qualities of the antimacassar and its making, which inevitably leaves gaps or holes in the process of crocheting or knitting. The subtext is that 'the feminine' equals absence, which in turn equates to the ineffectual and worthless. It is hardly surprising therefore to later find a journalist scathingly describing old ladies, who in his opinion had very little to contribute to society, as 'antimacassar people' (*The English Review* 1913, xiii: 482).

More than just signalling the ornamental and the feminine, the antimacassar as the embodiment of woman became something of a floating signifier. Satirists, novelists and critics alike recreated the antimacassar textually as a symbol or trope upon which various ideological concerns could be mapped. At the heart of such cultural appropriation lies anxiety – fear and loathing even – about the female body and its transgressive potential. That a domestic textile should come to signify in this way as the threatening 'other' can be accounted for by the antimacassar's particular proximity to the body. With everyday use, textiles soak up bodily fluids and smells and are left with the traces of human touch and the imprint of the body. Ornament and functionality were not mutually exclusive categories in the Victorian home, so the fact that antimacassars were often delicate and not very easy to wash did not necessarily mean that they were no longer in intimate contact with the body, male or female. In the cultural imagination, however, this intimacy was gendered as feminine, and the antimacassar retained its original connections to the body, but to an exclusively female one.

One example of the ways in which the antimacassar was presented to the public as an object of transgression was through the murdered body of a respectable middle-class lady. Harriet Novelli was strangled by her brother-in-law in Manchester in 1850, and the scopophilic newspaper reportage of the time scrutinised the domestic sphere, as the murder had taken place in her dining room (D'Cruze 2005: 181–4). Constructing a scene that might easily have been found in the pages of a novel by Wilkie Collins or Mary Braddon, the papers

Figure 3 John Everett Millais, *James Wyatt and His Granddaughter Mary Wyatt*, 1849 (Collection Lord Lloyd-Webber) (Plate 76 in the colour plate section).

Figure 4 James Hayllar, *The Only Daughter*, 1875 (Christie's Images Ltd) (Plate 77 in the colour plate section).

focused on certain objects to elaborate the central incident, one of which was an antimacassar. The *Lancaster Guardian* reported that:

> She was laying down with her legs stretched out, in a comparatively easy position, as if she had fallen from the chair, and an antimacassar which was usually placed on the chair, had fallen down with her. She lay reclining on the left side, and the antimacassar was under her (*Lancaster Guardian* 1850: 3).

Caught up with Mrs Novelli's body in this way, the antimacassar is emotionally charged and directly implicated in the crime, serving to underscore and destabilise societal expectations of the gendered body. The yoking of romance and realism in such accounts enabled the popular press to construct a

167

particular image of domestic textiles, especially those that covered chairs, as 'instruments of torture'.[9] Significantly, the antimacassar becomes one of the key fictional devices that articulate cultural concerns about the feminine in novels and plays of the later Victorian and Edwardian periods. In this role, it assumes many of the characteristics of the Novelli murder that threatened the sanctity of middle-class existence, with a perceived ability to violate and contaminate.

The gendered object

Physical violence involving antimacassars, where the object acts as a weapon or is abused, appears on several occasions. In *The Club of Queer Trades* by G.K. Chesterton, for example, the protagonist wrestles with an intruder, who is finally restrained by being tied up with several antimacassars (Chesterton 1905: 143). In W.W. Jacob's *The Lady of the Barge*, the maligned Mrs White chases her son round the table 'armed with an antimacassar' (Jacobs 1908: 21). But this violence and aggression is nowhere made more apparent than in the play by Sidney Grundy, *The New Woman* of 1894. The play opens in Gerald Cazenove's sitting room, 'somewhat effeminately decorated', where there are 'several antimacassars' (Grundy 1894: 5). The Colonel, his uncle, abuses these antimacassars to express his anger about Gerald's apparent lack of masculinity, flinging them about the room: 'throw that thing away!' he exclaims (1894: 7).

Many of these novels and plays of course have a comic element, and the fictional antimacassar features as an object of mirth and ridicule, but the use is always pejorative. Men had been concerned since the 1870s about the legal and educational advances made by women, coupled with their demand for a political voice that culminated in the Suffragette movement. There was also a surplus of women of marriageable age (one million by 1901). Grundy's satirical play sought to contain the threat posed by this so-called 'New Woman' and the accompanying feminisation of society and culture, hence the way the characters treat the antimacassar. The surface humour therefore conceals real concerns about marriage and reproduction that were seen to be under attack by this unruly figure who was automatically linked in the cultural psyche to decadence and homosexual men.

As Showalter has shown in *Sexual Anarchy, Gender and Culture at the Fin de Siècle*, gender turmoil characterised the culture of the turn of the century (Showalter 1991). The antimacassars in this play – and indeed in much of the literature and critical writing of the whole period – embody the perceived challenge to patriarchy as the uncontainable and excessive 'feminine' that has the power to disrupt and transgress certain sociocultural boundaries, including gender identities, sexuality, family norms and domestic ideals. At the centre of Grundy's play is anxiety about gender transgression and the imagined links to social decline and degeneracy, mapped onto Gerald's feminine taste in furnishings. The Colonel exclaims: 'these people are a sex of their own ... They have invented a new gender. And to think my nephew's one of them!' With that, we are told, he 'strides up and down, seizes another antimacassar and flings it into another corner' (Grundy 1894: 9). Gerald's masculinity and masculine probity, as defined by Victorian middle-class gender codes, are thus felt to be directly compromised by the feminising influences of the antimacassar.

Yet during the final decades of the 19th century, decadence and aestheticism were equally guilty of participating in misogynistic discourse. Oscar Wilde himself was often dismissive of women's decorative culture, and in his reviews satirised the popular furniture shops of the day such as Maple and Company of Tottenham Court Road, where 'pictorial print struggles through the meshes of the antimacassar' (Wilde 1888). The textual play here with meshes and struggles evokes the language of entrapment and the familiar emblem antimacassar that ensnares with its net or web. And in another review concerning a critic's preference for women's domestic ornament, Wilde wrote with typical sarcasm: 'how cultivated the mind that thus raises literature to the position of upholstery and puts thought on a level with the antimacassar!' (Wilde 1886).[10] Here we have again the coupling of women and textiles, and the coding of both as cheap, vapid and worthless. Wilde mocks women's culture with his surface wit, yet underneath is the fear that the lofty world of the (masculine) mind and ideas might be contaminated by the lowly bodily domain that the (feminine) antimacassar represents.

An instrument of torture

These dual themes of contamination and entrapment feature prominently in other male writers' work that attempts a codification of the feminine at the turn of the century. Several novelists, notably Arnold Bennett, H.G. Wells and Joseph Conrad wrote about the New Woman, and it is no coincidence that all those writers utilise the antimacassar as a trope through which to demonise, ridicule or disempower women. Bennett's novel of 1908, *The Old Wives' Tale* employs the antimacassar to symbolise a scheming, duplicitous, menacing sense of 'woman'. The two sisters Constance and Sophia bring Mr Povey, who has toothache, to the parlour. 'There were two rocking-chairs with fluted backs covered by antimacassars, one on either side of the hearth' (Bennett 1908: 52). Mr Povey:

> felt something light on his shoulders. Constance had taken the antimacassar from the back of the chair, and protected him with it from the draughts. He did not instantly rebel, and therefore was permanently barred from rebellion. He was entrapped by the antimacassar. It formally constituted him an invalid, and Constance and Sophia his nurses (Bennett 1908: 52–3).

The antimacassar appears as an object of value only when it assumes a negative role as a weapon, which reinforces Bennett's conceptualisation of the two sisters as phallicised *femmes fatales*. The classic binary opposition within patriarchal culture of madonna/whore, the maternal figure versus the predatory, seducing enchantress who weaves her web is engendered. Sophia, we are reminded 'presented a marvellous imitation of saintly innocence' (Bennett 1908: 53). This brings into play the image of the Victorian young ladies who sold craftwork such as antimacassars at the philanthropic level in bazaars; a ritual similarly viewed as a means of 'entrapping' men. Here we have the dialectic of the role of women and textiles as protector and nurturer versus their perceived ability to control, imprison, assault and deceive – the act of covering itself embodying the idea of comforting, yet shrouding and smothering.

The antimacassar as abject

Owing to the antimacassar's special relationship to the body, it engendered the dangerous realm of touch and with it the fear of contagion through abject matter that evokes death: disease, dirt and dust. In *The Anatomy of Disgust*, William Miller speaks of touch and its counterpart smell as the senses of Hell because they get closer to our core and are the senses of our bodily vulnerability, conjuring up the domain of the 'dark, the dank, the primitive and bestial' (Miller 1997: 75). Not all antimacassars were easy to wash, thus they became an easy target for satire. Conrad's novel *The Shadow-Line* brings forth the abject as feminine through a description of an interior where there are 'grimy antimacassars' (Conrad 1917: 48) and similarly H.G. Wells in *The Food of the Gods* draws our attention to 'a grubby antimacassar' that had remained in the Skinner's sitting room 'for many years' in the house that is now contaminated by giant vermin (Wells 1904: 432). Other novelists of the period utilise it as part of the same discourse: in Booth's *The Tree of the Garden* 'a profusion of antimacassars denied the sun' make the front parlour smell stagnant (Booth 1922: 64) while Miss Abbott, in E.M. Forster's *Where Angels Fear to Tread* is afraid to sit down 'because the antimacassars might harbour fleas' (Forster 1905: 100). Once the notion was in place that it acted as a repository for parasites, it was only a small step away from becoming one. And so we have Arnold Bennett taking this image of the antimacassar to its logical conclusion. A few pages later Mr Povey, we are told, 'still wore one of the antimacassars. It must have stuck to his shoulders when he sprang up from the sofa, woollen antimacassars being notoriously parasitic things' (Bennett 1908: 59).

Initially conceived as a device for controlling men and male illicit bodily fluids, stains and secretions, the antimacassar could automatically tap into the realm of the disgusting, but only if it was re-gendered as feminine; or rather, only if what needed controlling was the feminine itself. Antimacassars are amusingly satirised in Henry James's novel *The Spoils of Poynton* as 'grease-catchers', but the real object of his mockery is the 'vulgar old woman' who purchases a lady's magazine: 'a horrible thing with patterns for antimacassars' (James 1897: 28, 22). Kristeva tells us in *Powers of Horror: An Essay on Abjection* that the dominant order has historically condemned the feminine as filthy (1982). Thus the antimacassar in the cultural imagination attracts the female body, while literally repelling that of the male. Edith Wharton's character Mr Rosedale in *The House of Mirth*, for example, is almost driven off his seat by the 'starched antimacassar which scraped unpleasantly against the pink fold of skin above his collar' (Wharton 1905: 232). And the social philosopher Herbert Spencer in *The Principles of Ethics* (1892) found antimacassars disgusting on the level of aesthetics, but equally repellent because of the injuries they inflicted, disrupting his bodily health. In a manner that evokes the fictionalised responses of the time he wrote:

> some discomfort at the back of your head draws your attention to a modern antimacassar, made of string which is hardened by starch: the beauty of its pattern being supposed to serve you as compensation for the irritation of your scalp (Spencer 1892: 403)

In other novels of the period, such as Mrs Oliphant's *The Railway Man and his Children*, it is the antimacassar's decorative qualities alone that succeed in repelling the body. There is a chair in Mrs Brown's parlour where her nephew 'was always forbidden to sit lest he should discompose the antimacassar extended on its back' (Oliphant 1891: 176).

What Kristeva's work also explains are the ways in which the abject occurs at sites where the boundaries of both the body and culture are violated. In the late Victorian period, the discourses on home decoration and sanitation had become interrelated, thereby enabling critics and authors of home-decoration guides as well as novelists to condemn the antimacassar as the abject. With the advent of germ theories in the 1870s and the campaign for the elimination of decorative dust traps, here was real proof that the object was a health hazard, a genuine 'instrument of torture'. Contaminating agents such as antimacassars with their dirt and dust would lead to the unsanitary house, just as they would engender the unhealthy body. Architect Robert Edis in his *Decoration and Furniture of Town Houses* of 1881, rallied against feminine ornament, especially domestic textiles, that were 'arranged merely for show', and 'can collect and hold dust' focusing his attention on 'fluffy wool mats and antimacassars of lace' (Edis 1881: 193). Such discourse was directed towards women as the homemaker, thereby attempting to control their taste. The critic and designer Walter Crane, for example, expanded the idea of sanitary reform to incorporate design reform, stressing good workmanship and social justice, typified by Arts and Crafts furnishings. Recalling the novelists' tropes of the day he spoke out against domestic interiors 'where the antimacassar is made to cover a multitude of sins' (Crane 1911: 52).

The discourses played out by Edis and Crane embody not only aesthetic issues but also social and moral concerns. Aestheticism, with its feminising agency that allowed men to colonise interior decorating for the purposes of securing a male identity based on antiquarianism and connoisseurship, legitimised valuable collectibles – but not women's homemade craft items such as antimacassars. And for Crane and William Morris the object epitomised the poor design and workmanship to be found in contemporary 'Home Arts'; 'craft' for them meant the Middle Ages, not something procured from the pages of a cheap fashion magazine.

Uncovering the lived reality

Yet ironically the antimacassar became a symbol of their anti-commodity ideology, a marker of domestic production that existed largely outside of commodification and commercial exchange. And although placed firmly in the 'category of

Figure 5 Parlour, Markhouse Road, Walthamstow, *c.*1906 (Vestry House Museum, London Borough of Waltham Forest).

transient fashions' by the likes of male designers such as Crane or Charles Eastlake, the antimacassar lived on in ordinary people's lives as a sign of great personal affection, without monetary value (Schaffer 2000: 81). Such objects were cherished, entering the realm of sentiment and memory, of the souvenir or memento, signifying 'a woman's affection for her home and her family' (Schaffer 2000: 77; Stewart 1993: 139).

In reality even people who were directly associated with the Arts and Crafts, or who lived in Aesthetic interiors, individualised their homes to include antimacassars, as various contemporary photographs show.[11] And men not only used antimacassars – they actively chose them as decorative objects for their interiors according to surviving paintings. A group of watercolours, for example, that depict rooms belonging to men at Oxford University during the 1860s record the presence of lace antimacassars, which perhaps helped to evoke fond memories of mother and home.[12] Furthermore, the Warner Archive at Vestry House Museum, Walthamstow, London (*c.*1906) provides valuable photographic proof of the continuing use of the antimacassar in the domestic interior even beyond the Victorian period, despite the campaigns of the design reformers and others who sought to influence popular taste (Fig. 5).[13] Reading paintings and photographs of the period as texts we begin to understand how the dominant perceptions of this textile, created as a product of discourse, can be problematised through their lived materiality. Significantly, the antimacassar in use was clearly not gender-specific. Neither was the antimacassar as the embodiment of the material existence of people's lives – whether women or men – particularly affected by the controlling, propagandist advice literature, periodicals, newspapers and novels that mocked its use and aimed at its permanent removal.

Other surviving archival and textual material equally indicates problems with the gendered, partisan images of this textile formed through literary construction. Far from a menacing object that inflicted pain and torture, the antimacassar in reality was valued and cherished as a familial memento and thereby invested with memories and meaning. One working-class family used 'an antimacassar of crochet work' to protect a precious mahogany chest of drawers (Collet and Robertson 1896: 64). And in his autobiography, Joseph Tatlow chose the term 'veneration' to describe the way in which it was regarded (Tatlow 1920: 20). Archival documents suggesting this more intimate history include a gentleman's will where an antimacassar is itemised as a specific bequest, and a museum catalogue record that tells the story of how one particularly treasured antimacassar travelled the world with its owner.[14]

Conclusion

These details of the minutiae of people's lives recover a more positive viewpoint of the antimacassar: one that elucidates the active dimension to gender, rather than viewing it as a static category through binary opposition that permits the reconstruction of such textiles as representation, as a 'text' upon which can be inscribed various narratives. Yet the very method that subverts the dominant image and creates room for agency is counter-productive because of the masculine conception of the detail as intrinsically negative, as Schor has outlined. The detail, like the antimacassar, is forced to participate in what she calls 'a larger semantic network, bounded on the one side by the ornamental ... and on the other by the everyday' (Schor

1987: 4). As such, neither is able to move beyond the frame conceptualised through sexual difference.

Is it possible to move outside of this stereotype, this negative space that the antimacassar occupies? Perhaps it is productive to think instead in terms of a feminine recuperation of the masculine, utilising the symbolisation that men have forged through this textile to create new meanings. Subverting the nature/culture divide under patriarchy which views men as the creators of lasting symbols, while women reproduce perishable bodies, we need to reconceptualise the antimacassar as an emblem of culture that empowers women. Madame Riego de la Branchardière's instruction manual of 1874 therefore, is not solely concerned with ornament, but with the creation of a lasting symbolic device as her title *The Crochet Book of Emblem Antimacassars* suggests. The antimacassar as this pervasive trope testifies to the enduring power of women's culture, continuing well into the 20th century and even inspiring an entire novel. Guy McCrone's *Antimacassar City* of 1940 is totally dependent upon this textile to textually recreate the Glaswegian metropolis. Assuming the authority historically attached to the masculine, the antimacassar as omnipotent feminine emblem not only metaphorically rewrites Glasgow, it frames the Victorian city in the cultural imagination, evident from the front cover of the first edition (Fig. 6).

To close, it is necessary to return to the Victorian period itself, to a textual configuration of the antimacassar which brings us back to the pleasure of the text as textile; Barthes' idea that the 'text is made, is worked out in a perpetual interweaving' (Barthes 1976: 64). In J.M. Barrie's novel of 1889 *When a Man's Single: A Tale of Literary Life*, the central character Simms is a journalist, and in one particular scene outlines the prerequisites for successful writing, the most important being the possession of an antimacassar. He explains its significance: 'you pluck the thread with which to sew your copy together out of the antimacassar. When my antimacassars are at the wash I have to take a holiday' (Barrie 1889: 144). The metaphorical device of the antimacassar as text here brings into play the discourse of the male weaver. But this is no postmodern masculine appropriation of the feminine that erases the subject and forecloses agency. Rather it embodies in the text a dependency on, and appreciation of, women's culture through the particularity of the antimacassar as a socialised object. This privileging of the metonymical aspect of the antimacassar, as against the metaphorical that merely focuses on generality, allows space for individualisation. Through metonymy, J.M. Barrie stages the notion of the antimacassar as feminine and empowering, but without the threat to masculinity. Simms openly acknowledges his dependence, revealing that the source of his potency as a writer and hence his identity, lies in the feminine. Without his antimacassars, his animating force, he cannot create the texts.

Acknowledgements

The author would particularly like to thank Jeremy Farrell, Keeper of the Museum of Costume and Textiles, Nottingham, for the hours he spent going through the collection with her, and to textile artist Michelle Holden for introducing her to the writings of Janis Jefferies. Thanks also to her editor Dr Elizabeth Kramer and to the anonymous peer reviewer for the useful comments. The following individuals/institutions kindly gave their permission to reproduce the images: V&A Museum, Christies Images, Lord Lloyd-Webber, Vestry House Museum and Nottingham Castle Museums and Galleries.

Notes

1. See Janis Jefferies' 'Text and textiles', where she discusses Nancy K. Miller's work and Freud's essay 'Femininity', pp. 169–70.
2. Byron's poem from 1818 *Don Juan* has the following lines: 'Nothing earthly could surpass her, Save thine incomparable oil, Macassar'.
3. Shropshire Record Office, Shrewsbury, 6000/12839/3.
4. Riego de la Branchardière was an expert needlewoman who helped popularise the crafts of lacemaking, embroidery, tatting and crochet during the 1850s and 60s. She had a 'fancy warehouse' in Cavendish Square, London, from where she published books of instructions and sold patterns and materials (Wardle 1968: 163).
5. For examples see *The Lady's Newspaper and Pictorial Times*, May 1853, p. 292; *The English Woman's Domestic Magazine*, January–June 1868, p. 181.
6. *The Royal Magazine of Knitting, Netting, Crochet, and Fancy Needlework*, September 1848, back page.
7. The most comprehensive collection of Victorian antimacassars survives in Nottingham Museum of Costume and Textiles. Other important collections may be found at Carrow House, Norwich, although many of these are 20th-century artefacts.
8. See the opening chapters of *Victorian Lace* by Wardle (1968).
9. The following review of Boutillier's earlier books of crochet patterns was bizarrely included among other press opinions at the close of her '*Eugènie' Crochet Book*: 'full of ingenious directions for the guidance of that misapplied industry which usually manifests itself in the production of chair covers and other instruments of torture' (*City Press*, 30 October 1870).
10. Wilde's review is an attack on Harry Quilter's *First Principles of Art for Painters and Picture Lovers*.
11. An antimacassar may be seen in contemporary photographs of William Morris's drawing room at Kelmscott House (William Morris Gallery, Walthamstow). A similar antimacassar was on

Figure 6 Guy McCrone, *Antimacassar City*, 1940 (author's collection) (Plate 78 in the colour plate section).

view in the reception room of Great Tangley Manor, Surrey, an Arts and Crafts house belonging to Wickham Flower, rebuilt by Philip Webb and furnished by Morris & Company (Cooper 1987: 173). These antimacassars may have been handmade using natural materials or acquired as part of a politicised endeavour to support rural industries such as Langdale linen or Ruskin lace. Nevertheless, their use in these contexts was somewhat contradictory given the Arts and Crafts ethos that opposed covering things, in favour of openness and 'honesty'.

12. Attributed to George Pyne, V&A Museum and private collection. Illustrated in Gere 1989: 298–9.
13. Three interiors from the Warner album show numerous antimacassars: N7889; N7899; N7890. Figure 5 (N7899), c.1906, shows the front parlour of a house in Markhouse Road, London E17.
14. Probate of the will (9 February 1920) of William Hatten: 'sofa with cushions and antimacassar to Mrs Nason'. DR469/199. Shakespeare Birthplace Trust Archive, Stratford. Nottingham Museum of Costumes and Textiles has a curtain lace antimacassar, c.1875, which was purchased in Birmingham and 'then taken to Massachusetts, USA, and then to New Zealand' (1990-175/1-3).

References

Barrie, J.M. (1889) [1929] *When a Man's Single: A Tale of Literary Life*. London: Hodder & Stoughton.
Barthes, R. (1976) *The Pleasure of the Text*. London: Jonathan Cape.
Beal, Mrs (1848) *The Antimacassar Crochet Book*. London: B.L. Green.
Bennett, A. (1908) [1990] *The Old Wives' Tale*. London: Penguin.
Booth, E. (1922) [1956] *The Tree of the Garden*. London: Holdeness.
Boutillier, Mesdames (1873) *The 'Eugènie' Crochet Book for Antimacassars*. London: Simpkin, Marshall & Co.
Branchardière, R. de la (1874) *The Crochet Book of Emblem Antimacassars*. London: Simpkin, Marshall & Co.
Chesterton, G.K. (1905) [1987] *The Club of Queer Trades*. London: Greenhill Books.
Collet, E. and Robertson, M. (1896) *Family Budgets: Being the Income and Expenses of Twenty-eight British Households 1891–1894*. London: Economic Club.
Conrad, J. (1917) [1986] *The Shadow-Line*. London: Penguin.
Cooper, J. (1987) *Victorian and Edwardian Interiors*. London: Thames and Hudson.
Crane, W. (1911) *William Morris to Whistler*. London: George Bell & Sons.
D'Cruze, S. (2005) 'The eloquent corpse: gender, probity, and bodily integrity in Victorian domestic murder', in *Criminal Conversations: Victorian Crimes, Social Panic and Moral Outrage*, J. Rowbotham and K. Stevenson (eds), 181–97. Columbus, OH: Ohio State University Press.
Edis, R. (1881) *Decoration and Furniture of Town Houses*. London: Macmillan
Forster, E.M. (1905) [1975] *Where Angels Fear to Tread*. London: Edward Arnold.
Freud, S. (1932) [1964] 'Femininity', in *The Complete Psychological Works of Sigmund Freud*, vol. XXII, J. Strachey (ed.), 112–35. London: Hogarth Press.
Gere, C. (1989) *Nineteenth-century Decoration*. London: Weidenfeld & Nicholson.
Grundy, S. (1894) *The New Woman*. London: Chiswick Press.
Guardian (2005) 'Saving Ibsen from the po-faced moralists', 17 March 2005: 5.
Hairs, C. (1848) *The Colored Anti-Macassar Book*. London: Simpkin, Marshall & Co.
Jacobs, W.W. (1908) *The Lady of the Barge*. London: Methuen & Co.
James, H. (1897) [1967] *The Spoils of Poynton*. London: Penguin.
Jefferies, J. (1995) 'Text and textiles: weaving across the borderlines', in *New Feminist Art Criticism: Critical Strategies*, K. Deepwell (ed.), 164–73. Manchester: Manchester University Press.
Kristeva, J. (1982) *Powers of Horror: An Essay on Abjection*. New York: Columbia.
Lancaster Guardian (1850) 'Murder and suicide at Manchester', 26 January 1850: 3.
McCrone, G. (1940) *Antimacassar City*. London: Constable and Company.
Miller, N.K. (1988) 'Arachnologies: the woman, the text, and the critic', in *Subject to Change: Reading Feminist Writing*, 77–101. New York: Columbia.
Miller, W.I. (1997) *The Anatomy of Disgust*. Cambridge, MA: Harvard University Press.
The Mother's Home-Book (1879) London: Ward & Lock.
Oliphant, Mrs (1891) *The Railway Man and his Children*, vol. III. London: Macmillan & Co.
Schaffer, T. (2000) '"Not at all unakin to that homespun cult": the domestic craftswoman and the aesthetic connoisseur', in *The Forgotten Female Aesthetes: Literary Culture in Late Victorian England*. Charlottesville, VI: University Press of Virginia.
Schor, N. (1987) *Reading in Detail: Aesthetics and the Feminine*. New York: Methuen.
Showalter, E. (1991) *Sexual Anarchy, Gender and Culture at the Fin de Siècle*. London: Bloomsbury.
Southgate, W. 1982. *That's the Way it was: A Working-class Autobiography 1890–1950*. London: New Clarion Press.
Spencer, H. (1892) *The Principles of Ethics*, vol. II. London: Appleton & Co.
Stewart, S. (1993) *On Longing: Narratives of the Miniature, the Gigantic, the Souvenir, the Collection*. Durham and London: Duke University Press.
Tatlow, J. (1920) *Fifty Years of Railway Life*. London: The Railway Gazette.
The Times (1914) 'The athletic girl', 13 May 1914: 11.
Wardle, P. (1968) *Victorian Lace*. London: Herbert Jenkins.
Wells, H.G. (1904) [1977] *The Food of the Gods*. London: Heinemann.
Wharton, E. (1905) *The House of Mirth*. New York: Scriber & Sons.
Wilde, O. (1886) 'A jolly art critic', *Pall Mall Gazette* 18 November 1886: 6.
Wilde, O. (1888) 'The close of the Arts and Crafts', *Pall Mall Gazette* 30 November 1888: 3.
Wilkinson. P.R. (1993) *Thesaurus of Traditional English Metaphors*. London: Routledge.

The author

Alice McEwan obtained an MA in the history of design and material culture from the Royal College of Art/Victoria and Albert Museum in 2003. Fascinated by the territory of the overlooked and the academically uncharted, her research interests lie with everyday things, particularly domestic objects and the nature of the relationship between lived reality and constructed image.

Address

Alice McEwan (alice.mcewan@btopenworld.com)

'Inoffensively feminine': First World War military concert parties, female impersonators and their costumes

Sarah Norris

ABSTRACT This study began with the intention of analysing surviving examples of First World War military concert party costumes, particularly those of the female impersonators who were an essential feature of these troupes. None were found in any British military museums or dress collections, however, a revealing demonstration of the low priority such garments were given by those responsible for assembling and curating surviving wartime artefacts. Despite this lack of physical evidence, a large number of photographs, programmes, articles and reviews were discovered, and these sources have been used to excavate the styles, modes of femininity and fashionability of the female impersonators who performed in the numerous frontline theatres and makeshift venues throughout the areas of conflict.

This paper gives an account of the various means of acquiring or producing the costumes and examines the styles of femininity portrayed by military female impersonators, their 'realism,' and their function as performers. Their costumes are considered in the context of contemporary fashions and modernity, conceptions of gender and the idealised feminine image. The archival evidence developed a vivid picture of the absent costumes and their function within the context of military concert parties during the Great War.

Keywords: dress history, stage costume, female impersonation, popular culture, First World War, military concert party

Introduction

Concert party entertainments were an integral aspect of army life for every Allied soldier during the First World War. By late 1917, nearly every unit of the British Expeditionary Force (BEF) had its own concert party playing to packed houses every night (Fuller 1991: 96). Enquiries made to 125 British military museums and collections, however, yielded no surviving concert party costumes. Clearly, those responsible for collecting artefacts related to the Great War did not consider such relics of contemporary popular culture worth preserving.

The absence of what was intended to be the focus of this study meant that purely archival and textual evidence had to be relied on alone, and fortunately there was a great wealth of photographs, newspaper cuttings, memoirs, troop journals, concert party programmes and related ephemera to draw upon. This paper investigates the female impersonators who were so essential a feature of the overseas military concert parties, considering their role and function within these troupes and for their audiences; the kinds of femininity they portrayed; issues of sexuality and representation; their costumes, fashionability and modernity, and the sources of these costumes.

Female impersonators

One virtually universal feature of overseas concert parties was the female impersonator. Nearly always a matter of expediency, one or more members of a troupe would be assigned a female role since most British women near the front were Voluntary Aid Detachment (VAD) nurses who had no extended periods of rest or training to allow time to participate. Furthermore, nurses could not be seen to fraternise with the largely non-commissioned ranks that constituted concert parties (Collins 2004: 133).

The vast majority of accounts of concert party female impersonators emphasise realism as their most distinctive quality. This was not the coarse burlesque of femininity associated with 'drag,' although this tradition persisted in some troupes, but an earnest attempt at representing an ideal. In such a class-suffused environment as the army, even concert parties were ranked by prestige. Broadly speaking, larger units' troupes such as those of divisions were 'held to a standard of propriety' whereas the brigade and battalion troupes were much less regulated (Fuller 1991: 107), and their shows correspondingly coarser in content and tone. Thus, divisional troupes' female impersonators were more decorous and feminine, and smaller units' 'ladies' sometimes (but not always) much less so. A review of The Tanks, noted: '"Miss" Woodin is to be warmly congratulated on "her" excellent and realistic make-up and truly feminine voice and mannerisms' (*Middlesex*

Yeomanry Magazine 1917). Les Rouges et Noirs, on the first of many successful UK tours, attracted this comment from the *Daily Express*:

> They do not ape the ladies – they imitate them faithfully. Voice, manner, gait, expression – are all charmingly and inoffensively feminine. They sing, dance, and act as sweetly, daintily, and cleverly as most musical comedy actresses. They were called in France the Beauties of Bethune, and the description does not belie them (5 August 1919).

The guarded compliment 'inoffensively feminine' suggests an unspoken awareness of the 'deviant' readings possible in the spectacle of cross-dressing, principally its association with male homosexuality. Since the late 19th century, homosexuality had a growing presence in contemporary discourse, helped along by national scandals such as that of Cleveland Street and Oscar Wilde's trial. Such awareness was patchy and often related to class, given the fact that, according to Steve Humphries: 'Schoolboy homosexuality had long been institutionalized in British boarding schools' (1988: 199). In the context of the music hall, however, female impersonation was a perfectly legitimate, and very popular, form of performance. Famous stage cross-dressers, such as Bert Errol and Herbert Clifton, garnered much respect for their craft, and their imperious 'grande dame' stage personas, often punctured with deflating humour, were received unproblematically by contemporary audiences. Crucially, Errol and Clifton used strategies to reveal their masculinity; by lifting skirts to reveal a pair of trousers or descending suddenly from ringing soprano to booming bass mid-song. The 'realistic' military female impersonators who emerged from this study, in contrast, appear to have carefully maintained their illusion throughout their act.

This illusion was appreciated by the troops, who responded as if these were real women. E.N. Gladden's report of a revue by the A.B.C.s provides a valuable account of a typical response from a military audience:

> the females of the troupe were so essentially feminine and had such dulcet voices that any idea of impersonation seemed out of the question ... It was a delightful entertainment which long before the conclusion had the entire audience in an ecstasy of collective emotion. No doubt a much less competent show would have had its failings masked by that upsurge of amorous feeling (1967: 160–61).

It is apparent that there was a heartfelt need to see glamorous representations of women. Many men on the Western Front were disappointed with the French women they encountered who failed to live up to the delicate and elegant Parisienne of popular imagination, most being practically dressed peasant girls and workers in estaminets (cafés) and shops (Fuller 1991: 106). Female impersonators consequently took great care with their appearance, even their underwear, suggesting an understanding of the iconic nature of their role. Fuller claims that they would have lingerie sent out, or 'go on special leave to London or Paris to select the items themselves' (1991: 106). After a sudden rainstorm had flooded the hollow where the What Nots had just performed an open-air concert, a fatigue party was sent to retrieve their costumes and:

> when the sun shone next morning, [they] hung the sodden garments out to dry on a long wire line. Quite a crowd gathered round two pairs of silk stockings, a satin petticoat, three dresses and a pair of corsets. They were strange sights in that Eve-less horrible place (Lambert 1930: 177).

As much as they serve as metonymic indicators of the absent female body, the evident attraction of these feminine undergarments also supports Fuller's assertion that 'The trappings of elegance and luxury were the negation of war and squalor and, as such, a potent fetish of peace' (1991: 106). By substituting the word 'woman' with 'Eve', Lambert further suggests the longing for an 'original' archetype of femininity, unchanged by the turmoil of war.

Such a response to female undergarments was quite typical. Robb (2002: 54) explains that 'Given the sexual reticence of Edwardian society, and the sexual isolation of most soldiers, it took very little to awaken desire.' The high society magazine *The Tatler* was 'devoured' by the troops, eager to see its 'fashion reports and underwear advertisements depicting women in camisoles and nightgowns'. It is possible that female impersonators used this as a readily available source of fashion information.

Given this fervid atmosphere of sexual frustration, and the hair-trigger libido of the troops, it is not surprising that female impersonators 'generated a great deal of sexual excitement among soldiers' (Robb 2002: 54). Private Webster, who starred as 'L'Alouette' in The Goods, was reported as having 'taken the hearts of susceptible Tommies by storm'. His appearance was so convincing that '"she" receives love-letters by the score, that bouquets are "hers" wherever flowers – artificial or otherwise – are obtainable, and that the stage-door is nightly besieged by would-be suitors.'[1]

Despite efforts to rationalise concert party female impersonation as a matter of expediency undertaken by irreproachably heterosexual soldiers, some evidence suggests otherwise. A soldier in an embarkation camp in Salonika excitedly relayed gossip concerning female impersonators in their concert party:

> You see there was a captain who came here with his batman who was one of the female impersonators and it seems as if this officer is very jealous of anybody mixing up with this chap and so he got round the C.O. to let him have a tent all to himself. Then another girl or rather boy came and he was put in with him. He that is to say the batmen were in the officers lines in the next tent to this capt and he had us shifted because we made too much noise. If we had been girlies like his man perhaps we should not have got the boot but we used to sing etc so that done it. Oh we didn't half curse him I can tell you.[2]

These female impersonators obviously enjoyed the protection of the captain, who chose to put them in a tent next to his in the officers' lines. In the rigidly class-segregated atmosphere of the army this may not have been customary practice. Batmen were personal servants to the officers, a relationship providing an invaluable pretext for intimacy (Bourke 1996: 133).

This is not to suggest that all female impersonators (or batmen) were homosexual by any means. But being a female impersonator, paradoxically, provided an ideal 'cover'; it must be noted that homosexuality was a punishable offence in the British armed forces. Chauncey points out that 'Female impersonation was an unexceptional part of [US] navy culture during the World War I years ... The ubiquity of such drag shows and the fact that numerous "straight"-identified men took part in them sometimes served to protect gay female impersonators from suspicion' (1990: 297). A similar situation is likely to have pertained in the British forces. Furthermore, concert party performers were often exempted from all but the least onerous duties, becoming, in effect, full-time performers (Fuller 1991: 95). As the conspicuous stars of the troupe, glamorous female impersonators such as Private Webster received the adulation of, and gift tributes from, soldiers, and privileges such as the Salonika batmen enjoyed from their officer patron may not have been unusual.

Class seems to have played a part in the selection of female impersonators. The vast majority were either working-class privates or corporals. Officers may have feared that to don ladies wear would undermine their authority. Another more prosaic reason may be the clear physical differences between officers and their undernourished charges. The enlistment forms of working-class men showed that many of them were around five foot tall and very slim – a 30-inch chest was not unusual.[3] Even after a spell of army training with improved nutrition, which added on average an inch to the height and a stone in weight (Bourke 1996: 174), these men were unlikely to gain on the advantage of middle- and upper-class officers.

The sourcing of costumes

British military concert parties employed various strategies in order to obtain costumes, dependent on the size of the unit, its location, the enthusiasm of the officers, the skills available within the unit or locally, and the resourcefulness of the troupes themselves.

Thomas Brookbank, the 'girl' of the Crank Handles concert party in occupied Germany, demonstrated some initiative in his efforts to make himself presentable:

> I made a mop cap into which I stitched hundreds of long hairs pulled from the tails of our transport horses and it looked quite effective. My dresses I also made, with the assistance of helpful fraus who had sewing machines, from material my mother would buy and send out to me with such large ladies shoes as I needed (Brookbank 1993: 34).

Performers, therefore, may have called upon the help of their wives and female relatives, and amenable local women, in supplying and making costumes. Collins observes that because VAD nurses were barred from participating in troop entertainments, their 'contribution was ... confined to running up dresses for the female impersonators', indicating that concert parties near camp hospitals would have had no shortage of assistance in the construction of costumes (2004: 132).

The 7th Northamptons, stationed in Tournai, Belgium, were equally adept at improvising their own costumes, as a newspaper report relates:

> several of the boys showed how attractively they could be made up as 'girls'. The star of the piece was Sergt. Major F. Hitch ... his skirt trousers being formed of four small curtains and the remainder of the dress of odds and ends sewn together, and all dyed in common washing blue' (*Northampton Independent* 1 March 1919).

The accompanying photograph belies this evocation of a rather ramshackle set of costumes. Some of the costumes appear to be creditable versions of Chinese robes fashioned from European furnishing fabrics. Either the 7th Northamptons harboured a talented costume designer and maker in their ranks, or, as was the case with Brookbank, they may have had help from local women.

Occasionally, costume credits are given in concert party programmes, suggesting that some soldiers were capable of turning out costumes for themselves. The Bow Bells' New Year show programme of 1917 provides a typical example: 'Every costume worn in this production is designed and made by Rfn. Con. Oram.'[4]

In the case of the 85th Field Ambulance's 1917 production of *Aladdin in Macedonia*, staged in the remote village of Kopriva in Salonika, costumes were both made by staff and acquired locally. The souvenir book relates that: 'Behind the scenes invaluable service was rendered by Corporal W.H. Drury ... whose skilled hand in the art of making-up put the finishing touches as it were to the costumes so tastefully designed by Privates Jaques and Harris and executed by Private Haynes' (Kenchington 1917: xi). One officer showed admirable resourcefulness: 'Costumes and make-up ... had to be obtained. Lieutenant Horne obtained them. Some of the materials were purchased in Salonika, while a number of native costumes were procured from a village just captured from the Bulgars' (Kenchington 1917: viii). The company worked from an original book, tailored to their location, by Private Kenchington and the genuine regional dress must have added an impeccable authenticity to the staging. Such was their commitment to 'a more elaborate and ambitious undertaking' two soldiers were responsible for the wigs and one made the shoes.

It is not implausible that soldiers were capable of making costumes since it is likely that some of them had been tailors or outworkers in their civilian life, not to mention cobblers and wigmakers. Even men without previous sewing experience were often obliged to learn in the special conditions of war. Bourke points out that soldiers had to be self-sufficient, acquiring skills that were customarily identified as feminine: 'gender roles were rendered more fluid in wartime as men were required to carry out many tasks that had formerly been the preserve of the opposite sex. They sat down together to darn their clothes. They washed their dirty trousers' (1996: 133).

Sometimes, however, there was no need to make costumes. The men of the A Squadron Ninth Queen's Royal Lancers, billeted in Albert, France, were fortunate enough to stumble across theirs:

> Confined to billets ... the men of the Ninth had little diversion to pass the time, and the lucky personnel of 'A' Squadron, who found a chest of theatrical costumes in their abandoned billet and were able to put on an impromptu performance, were much envied (Sheppard 1939: 261).

In these instances, words such as 'found' and 'rescued' have a euphemistic air about them. Fuller notes that:

> many men stole property from the army, from civilians, and even ... from other soldiers. The euphemisms which disguised the nature of this act were legion, and its prevalence, 'by men who, before the War would not have dreamed of taking anything to which they were not legally entitled', was a joke to the troop journals (1991: 155).

It seems probable that some concert parties resorted to 'requisitioning' some of their stage wear, especially if they were not fortunate enough to simply discover it by chance.

There were of course other, more legitimate, means of acquiring costumes. The Tanks concert party of the Middlesex Yeomanry called upon the generosity of their audience: 'A collection which was made during the performance for the purpose of providing "The Tanks" with new costumes for their Cairo tour exceeded £32' (*Middlesex Yeomanry Magazine* 1918: 23).

Even concert parties in remote areas could acquire costumes from the nearest town or city. George Ward Price, an official correspondent with the Allied Forces in the Balkans, explained how the female impersonators of an unspecified divisional concert party maintained their stage wardrobe:

> Kitty and the Beauty Chorus which supported her were dressed regardlessly, to the full extent of the resources of the dressmakers and lingerie merchants of Salonica, and somewhere in the archives of the Salonica Army there is a telegram sent down from the front to an officer of the division who was on three days' leave in town, in approximately these terms: 'Urgent. Bring back with you without fail to-night the following: Three pairs silk stockings size seven and one lace-embroidered camisole for Kitty, five yards pink satin for Abanazar's second wife and a black stuff dress for Mrs. Twankey' (Price 1917).

Not everyone appreciated the urgency of this request since Price added: 'scrawled across the telegram is the indignant endorsement: "G.H.Q. demands an immediate explanation of this idiotic rubbish passing over Army wires"'.

Concert parties which included stage professionals exploited show business connections to obtain donations from performers, theatre management and theatrical suppliers in Britain. This happened most frequently in the divisional concert parties. Others, lacking such contacts, placed advertisements in *The Stage* and other theatrical magazines requesting donations of costumes, props and script material (Collins 2004: 86, 109). The Crumps' divisional concert party must have been particularly well connected since their programme thanks 'the many leading members of the theatrical profession for costumes, wigs etc.,' going on to provide an impressive list of donors.[5] Given the fervent mood of patriotism and eagerness to do one's best for the war effort, these concert parties were successful in appealing to the conscience of the theatre world.

It seems that for some concert parties, access to the capital required for obtaining costumes and other necessities was less of a problem. According to Fuller, divisional funds were allocated, or 'sums subscribed by the officers' (1991: 95). Once divisional theatres were built, typically providing between 400 to 800 seats, they were able to charge for entry to shows which were immensely popular, often turning men away at the door (Fuller 1991: 98; Collins 2004: 117). This generated considerable income, enough to pay for the running of the theatre and the costs of future productions, including costumes (Collins 2004: 117).

The sourcing of costumes was, it is evident, dependent on several factors. Larger units had greater funds and support, and troupes on the Western Front had access to suppliers and benefactors in Britain. Units based at more distant fronts such as Macedonia or Egypt sought local suppliers, or turned authentic regional dress to good use. Some concert parties included skilled costume designers and makers of their own, and others prevailed upon local women or VAD nurses. The more ad hoc or unofficial troupes had their own methods of preparing for the stage, some rather ramshackle and shabby, and some less than legitimate. But the soldiers' determination to entertain, and be entertained, meant that at all levels and on all fronts there were regular shows, costumed to the best of their ability and means.

The types of female impersonators and their costumes

Female impersonators were keenly attuned to the kinds of femininity that would play well with the troops. They seem to fall into types, the most obvious being the music hall or musical comedy performer. Private Purkiss of The Crumps was photographed in a knee-length sequinned dress which was appropriate for a chorus girl, but too short to be fashionable, or acceptable, for offstage wear at the time. The two 'girls' of the 2nd Battalion King's Own Royal Lancaster Regiment concert party (Fig. 1) sported dresses designed to complement the Pierrot outfits of the troupe. Their long plaits, headbands (which may have featured bows at the back), and short flared skirts were signature features of the pre-war flapper – then a term indicating a 'fun-filled, tomboyish adolescent' rather than its later incarnation, 'the drinking, dancing, sexually sophisticated' young woman of the 1920s (Rolley and Aish 1992: 115).

Although it appears that the major impulse in military female impersonation was towards a romantic and glamorous ideal, there were instances of women being portrayed in a much less reverent manner. The female impersonator in Figure 2 is presented in an overblown, blowsy fashion suggestive of the stage cocotte. His blonde curly wig is piled high with artificial flowers and his skirt is drawn up over his knees. Furthermore, he allows the 'policeman' standing behind him to rest his hand on his breast. Both the outfit and the gesture suggest that the entertainment offered by this troupe is of a more salacious nature.

For many female impersonators, fashion was an important element in their evocation of a modern young woman. Private Purkiss is shown in Figure 3 in a pale suit trimmed with white fur, accessorised with a large dark fur muff and a close-fitting

Figure 1 The 2nd Battalion King's Own Royal Lancaster Regiment concert party in Salonika (undated photograph). The 'girls' wear flapper style Pierrot costumes (The King's Own Royal Lancaster Regiment Museum, KO0860/01).

Figure 2 An unknown army concert party *c*.1918, featuring a blowsy cocotte (from the collection of Major A. C. E. Boweby, RFC 1917, The Museum of Army Flying, 087/84 Box 43A).

hat. These items were fashionable around 1916–17. The souvenir booklet of The Crumps in which this photograph featured is undated but was produced in wartime so it is fair to claim that Private Purkiss kept his wardrobe up to date.

Fashionability, or otherwise, could be used to convey character. The cast of the pantomime *Aladdin*, staged in February 1918, had two intriguing female impersonators (Fig. 4) presenting incarnations of pre- and post-war femininity; one, a dignified matron, wears a high-necked dress and piled-up hair similar to styles current in 1912, while a sharp-featured youth is a vivid precursor of the 1920s flapper in a tubular-bodiced, high-waisted dress with shoulder straps, short hair and a bandeau. Both offer 'authentic' (within the obvious limitations of pantomime) portrayals of types of women: one a mature and dignified matron, the other a youthful, modern, liberated woman.

Following the Armistice, many soldiers remained abroad far longer than they expected since demobilisation took until 1920

Figure 3 *The Crumps Divisional Concert Party.* Private Purkiss wears a fashionable fur-trimmed suit for 1916. From *The Crumps Play Pictorial Souvenir of the Divisional Concert Party, Vol. 1, No. 1* (Imperial War Museum: Collection of R.G. Plint 80/19/1).

Figure 4 Cast of the pantomime *Aladdin*, performed as part of a commemoration dinner for the 52nd Infantry Brigade held at Airaines, France, 22 February 1918. The female impersonator seated third from the right resembles a dignified matron in pre-war dress. His companion on the right is a precursor of the 1920s flapper (Imperial War Museum, MISC 207/ITEM 3002).

to complete. Concert parties were kept busy entertaining the increasingly fractious troops, and it appears that a new note of realism was introduced by at least some female impersonators. In 1919, the 1st Battalion Wiltshire Regiment concert party staged their revue *Hello Peace Time* (Fig. 5) featuring eight female impersonators, most of whom are rather dowdy in appearance. One 'lady' stands out, however; a startlingly modern-looking female impersonator sits with his hands in his jacket pockets. The reintroduction of pockets into women's clothing in 1913 after more than a century's absence 'caused some comment and the casual stance they encouraged was clearly seen as a masculine prerogative' (Rolley and Aish 1992:

110). Here, a female impersonator is mirroring contemporary female postures as dictated by recent innovations in women's wear. His outfit, 'the remarkably minimal "tailor-made" suit' was, according to Buckley, one 'which epitomised the young working woman in a man's world' (2002: 531). This company, with their practically and modestly dressed female impersonators, seems to herald a changing perception of femininity, one that more accurately reflects how ordinary women dressed at the time rather than a wishful representation of an ideal.

The First Army's concert party, Les Rouges et Noirs, took this post-war mood towards a more objective realism, with clear reservations, one step further. A photograph of one of

Figure 5 1st Battalion Wiltshire Regiment concert party advertising their revue *Hello Peace Time* in 1919. The 'tailor-made' suit is worn by the female impersonator seated second right (The Redcoats in the Wardrobe; The Royal Gloucestershire, Berkshire and Wiltshire Regiment (Salisbury) Museum: 10975).

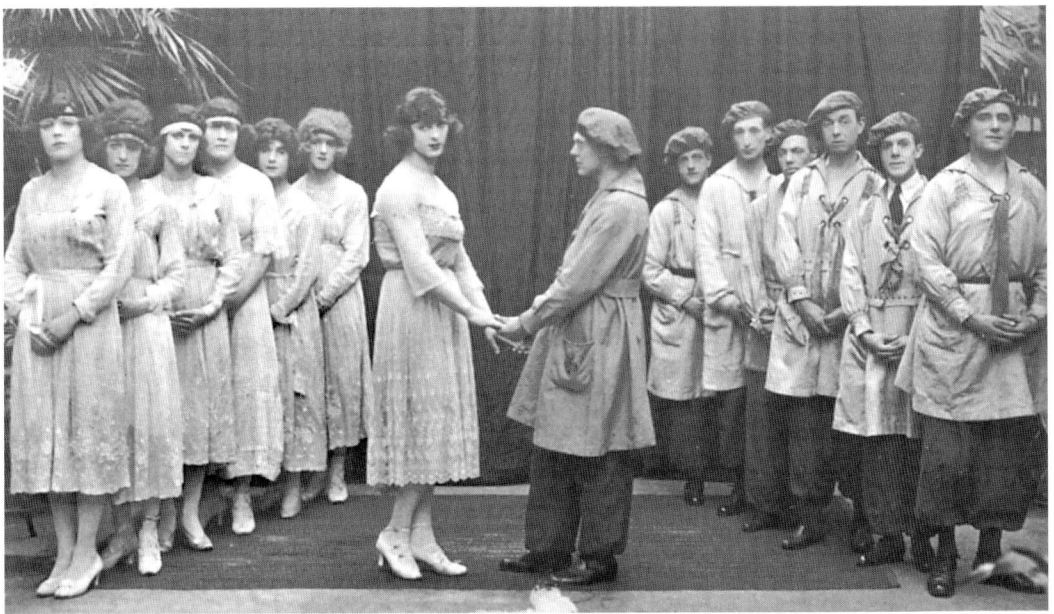

Figure 6 Les Rouges et Noirs, the First Army's concert party, perform their revue *Splinters* at the Savoy Theatre, 1919. On the left are girlish pre-war flappers, on the right are what appear to be female munitions workers (Mander and Mitchenson 1971: 74).

their items in the revue *Splinters*, performed at the Savoy Theatre in London in 1919, appears to depict an amicable confrontation between pre-war flappers and wartime female munitions workers (Fig. 6), the only example of the latter's portrayal by military concert parties uncovered by this study. Significantly, this occurred in front of a civilian audience which included women, some of whom may have worked in munitions factories themselves. The concert party's ambivalence towards working women is reflected in their unmade-up faces, visually implying that munitions workers were masculinised by their work. Buckley observes that 'There was a great deal of concern at the time that war was making women more "masculine" as they took on modes of behaviour more typical of men by becoming independent and self-reliant, working outside the home, and managing their own finances' (2002: 526).

Although this cannot claim to be a comprehensive survey of female impersonators' costumes, some tentative conclusions can be drawn from the evidence examined. There is clearly an influence garnered from stage performers. Pierrot shows, music hall and musical comedy actresses all set clear precedents for military female impersonators, as might be expected since these entertainments influenced the format and content of troupe shows. Film stars with strongly identifiable images, however, such as Theda Bara, Lilian Gish and Mary Pickford seem to have had little impact on them, judging by the evidence examined here.

Stock characters such as the dowdy old lady or the cocotte are more broadly drawn, and may have been favoured by those who wished to maintain some distance from the unspoken implications of their performance by resorting to exaggeration. Such characters may also have been dictated by the type of material the concert party was purveying, and by the physical attributes of the performers themselves – they may not have been 'pretty' enough to essay a comely young maiden!

It is the comely young maiden who figures as the most popular type of femininity for the military female impersonator, one who may be stylish but not necessarily chic, pretty but not imposingly beautiful; an accessible and recognisable 'girl next door'. Possibly the style of these modest young 'ladies' may have had some correlation with the rank of the female impersonators themselves – mostly other ranks – reflecting the kinds of women they were familiar with rather than the *bon ton*. This could, however, also simply reflect the kinds and quality of clothing that these performers were able to obtain. The appearance of the 'tailor-made' suit in an immediately post-war concert party might indicate a new responsiveness to contemporary working women and their customary practical daywear but this would require a much broader survey to corroborate.

The function of female impersonation in military concert parties

It is clear that military concert party female impersonators were concerned with a qualified and specific realism, determined by the desires of the troops. Young women, of varying degrees of fashionableness, appear to be the most favoured, with some even veering towards the winsome adolescent. This may not be as dubious as it seems to modern eyes since many soldiers were barely out of adolescence themselves. Many soldiers wanted to see evocations of the women they had left behind, reminders of the tenderness of a loving relationship and the comforts of home. Joanna Bourke notes that: 'In all-male environments, men reflected in their diaries that their girlfriends were their "only pleasure[s] in life now", their "mainstays". They gazed with longing at photographs of their wives' (1996: 168).

Female impersonators, therefore, may have served as illusory surrogates for the troops' absent womenfolk, and not just as provocative sexual stimuli. The troops had a specific notion of the kind of femininity they wished to see, one that reminded them of the pre-war gender conventions, the reassuring certainties of the 'separate spheres' which were being challenged by the activities of the women they had left behind. This ideal was often highly sentimentalised and deeply conventional. By enacting this ideal to the satisfaction of their weary and troubled audiences, they reinscribed gender roles in an emphatic manner and may thus have allayed some of the anxieties the troops felt about their own roles as men. Judith Butler declares that 'there is no necessary relation between drag and subversion ... drag may well be used in the service of both the denaturalization and reidealization of hyperbolic heterosexual norms' (1993: 125).

Conclusion

As the photographs in this study indicate, many of these concert parties were costumed to a very high standard. The soldiers demonstrated considerable resourcefulness in their determination to put on a good show, and, as a result, the female impersonators were often surprisingly convincing.

Long established as a popular turn in the music hall, female impersonation was respectable enough to afford a paradoxical 'cover' for homosexual men. Sufficient ambiguity remained for officers to avoid stage cross-dressing lest it undermine their authority; the vast majority of female impersonators were other ranks. This study suggests, in addition, that working-class recruits were better suited for feminine roles owing to their smaller stature on average.

A qualified 'realism' was the goal of most female impersonators. War had deprived the troops of female company, often for months at a time, and men with wives and girlfriends at home felt their absence keenly. This absence, not to mention the imminent likelihood of death or mutilation, added a significant imperative to the performances of the female impersonators, distinguishing them from peacetime and/or civilian equivalents, and they were consequently painstakingly thorough in their creation of an illusion of femininity. A pre-war ideal seems to have prevailed, one that took no account of the changes wrought by war on women's roles. As much as they offered sexual titillation, female impersonators also offered a consoling vision of a romantic, sentimentalised and vulnerable femininity which assuaged their anxieties that women were usurping their roles as men on the home front while they were trapped and powerless in the trenches. The practical tailor-made suit, which many working women wore, did not appear on the military stage until after the war.

This military prototype of glamour female impersonation proved to be a great attraction for civilian audiences following the war. Many military performers, having honed their skills during wartime, went on to pursue successful careers on the stage and there was a significant rise in the number of female impersonators in the post-war period (Baker 1994: 188). The new 'realism' and glamour they introduced to the form, which so delighted the *Daily Express*'s critic, suggests that the tribute 'charming and inoffensively feminine' might not just refer obliquely to the subcultural origins of female impersonation, but also to a preferred image of femininity equally appealing to the (presumably) male critic as it had been to the troops, one that was decorative and unthreatening; a pre-war belle for the post-war reconstruction.

Acknowledgements

This study would not have been possible without the kind assistance of: Professor Lou Taylor; Dr Paul Jobling; Lt. Col. (retd.) Derek Armitage (The Museum of Army Flying); Tony Bentley (The Kent and Sharpshooters Yeomanry Regimental Museum Trust); Jon-Paul Carr (Northamptonshire Regiment Association and the Royal Anglian Regiment Association (Northamptonshire Branch)); Rachel Cornes (Cheshire Military Museum); Peter Donnelly (The King's Own Royal Lancaster Regiment Museum, www.kingsownmuseum.plus.com); Jackie Dryden (The Redcoats in the Wardrobe; The Royal Gloucestershire, Berkshire and Wiltshire Regiment, Salisbury Museum); Ian Hook (Essex Regiment Museum); Department of Documents at the Imperial War Museum; Richard Jeffs (Honourable Artillery Company Museum); Richard Mangan (administrator, Mander and Mitchenson Theatre Collection) and Vivienne Rudd (Derby Museum and Art Gallery).

Every effort has been made to trace copyright holders and the author and the Imperial War Museum would be grateful for any information which might help to trace those whose identities or addresses are not currently known.

The author would like to thank Elizabeth Kramer and the anonymous referee.

Notes

1. *Souvenir of the "Goods" Divisional Concert Party*. Souvenir booklet. Imperial War Museum (henceforth IWM), 44 (41) 01.
2. April 6th The Staff Embarkation Camp, Salonica. Letter held at the Department of Documents, IWM, MISC ITEM 3358.
3. Public Record Office: various files containing First World War enlistment forms in WO 363 and WO 364.
4. *Bow Bells 56th London Divisional Concert Party 1916–1917*. Programme. Cheshire Military Museum.
5. *Divisional Concert Party 'The Crumps' Programme*. IWM, the papers of R.G. Plint 80/19/1.

References

Baker, R. (1994) *Drag*. London: Cassell.
Bourke, J. (1996) *Dismembering the Male: Men's Bodies, Britain and the Great War*. London: Reaktion.
Brookbank, T. (1993) *Recollections of the Machine Gun Corps*. J.A. Brookbank. Imperial War Museum: 99/13/1.
Buckley, C. (2002) '"De-humanised females and Amazons": British wartime fashion and its representation in *Home Chat*, 1914–1918', *Gender & History* 14(3): 516–36.
Butler, J. (1993) *Bodies That Matter: On the Discursive Limits of Sex*. London: Routledge.
Chauncey Jnr, G. (1990) 'Christian brotherhood or sexual perversion? Homosexual identities and the construction of sexual boundaries in the World War I era', in *Hidden From History: Reclaiming the Gay and Lesbian Past*, M. Duberman, M. Vicinus and G. Chauncey Jnr (eds), 294–317. New York: Meridian.
Collins, L.J. (2004) *Theatre at War 1914–18*. Oldham: Jade.
Fuller, J.G. (1991) *Troop Morale and Popular Culture in the British and Dominion Armies*. Oxford: Oxford University Press.
Gladden, E.N. (1967) *Ypres 1917: A Personal Account*. London: William Kimber.
Humphries, S. (1988) *A Secret World of Sex: Forbidden Fruit. The British Experience 1900–1950*. London: Sidgwick and Jackson.
Kenchington, F. (1917) *Aladdin in Macedonia: A Pantomime by Members of the 85th Field Ambulance 1917*. London: Andrew Melrose.
Lambert, A. (1930) *Over the Top: A P.B.I. in the H.A.C.* London: John Long.
Mander, R. and Mitchenson, J. (1971) *Revue: A Story in Pictures*. London: Peter Davies.
Middlesex Yeomanry Magazine (1917) David 'Entertainments', 1(2): 21.
Middlesex Yeomanry Magazine (1918) Reporter 'Entertainments', 1(4): 23.
Northampton Independent (1 March 1919) 'With the 7th Northamptons, memorable treat to Belgian soldiers' children: our boys as "girls"'.
Price, G.W. (1917) 'Chapter XVII: People, places and things in Macedonia', in *The Story of the Salonica Army* [online]. London: Hodder & Stoughton [cited 23 August 2004]. Available from http://www.gwpda.org/memoir/Salonica/salon6.htm: Great War Primary Documents Archive, Inc. Jane Plotke (content editor). Last updated 23 June 2006.
Robb, G. (2002) *British Culture and the First World War*. Basingstoke: Palgrave.
Rolley, K. and Aish, C. (1992) *Fashion in Photographs, 1900–1920*. London: Batsford.
Sheppard, E.W. (1939) *The Ninth Queen's Royal Lancers 1715–1936*. Aldershot: Gale & Polden.

The author

Sarah Norris is a research student at Manchester Metropolitan University. Her main interests are 20th-century dress, design history, material culture, popular culture, consumption and issues of class, gender and age.

Address

Sarah Norris, 33 Shaw Road, Heaton Moor, Stockport, Cheshire SK4 4AG, UK (s.norris@mmu.ac.uk)

Inspiring textile collections: textiles and text combined in Winchester School of Art Library and in the Special Collections, Hartley Library, University of Southampton Libraries

Linda Newington

ABSTRACT This paper focuses on three special collections at Winchester School of Art and the Special Collections, Hartley Library, University of Southampton, which combine holdings of textiles and text. The collections belonged to Janet Arnold, Montse Stanley and Richard Rutt and they contain a fascinating selection of material relating to the history of textiles and dress and the history of knitting. After providing an overview of the collections, the paper considers how they might be used for research, teaching and to inspire textile practice in the future and how cataloguing will make the collections more accessible.

Keywords: knitting, Winchester School of Art Library, Janet Arnold, Montse Stanley, Richard Rutt, knitting patterns, Jane Waller

Introduction

Three specific collections that are based, in part, at Winchester School of Art (WSA) Library form the focus of this paper: the collections of Janet Arnold, Montse Stanley and Richard Rutt. These collections were chosen because they include textiles and text and they provide three contrasting examples of how these materials can interact to create stimulating research collections. Indeed, these collections have resulted in a printed guide that was produced in 2006, *Textile Collections: Winchester School of Art Library, Special Collections, Hartley Library* (University of Southampton). The aim of the guide was to promote these resources not only to the internal audience at WSA and the Textile Conservation Centre (TCC) but also to the wider academic community across the University of Southampton, so drawing in related disciplines. In addition, it was intended for the national and international networks of textile researchers and makers, to encourage further study by as wide an audience as possible.

Winchester School of Art is an international centre of excellence for teaching and research offering a unique and broad range of programmes in fine art, fashion, textiles, textile art, graphic design, advertising design, photography and digital media, history of dress and textiles, museum studies and textile conservation. WSA's Textile Conservation Centre is one of the major conservation facilities in the field. Originally founded more than 130 years ago, WSA joined the University of Southampton in 1996, so gaining access to the resources of one of the UK's leading research universities. The WSA Library, one of six site libraries comprising the university's libraries, is a specialist art and design library which supports learning, teaching and research. One of the library's strengths is its focus on textiles, dress history and fashion. The permanent collections have recently been enhanced by the addition of three acquisitions of note from renowned scholars in the field of dress and textile history. These new additions are of national importance and significantly enrich the current holdings. In addition, the librarians are in the process of establishing a national knitting pattern collection.

The collections: Janet Arnold, Montse Stanley and Richard Rutt

The first collection belonged to the late Janet Arnold who is highly regarded as a dress historian and a scholar. The collection includes her drawings, library and papers. Her library, located at WSA, has particular strengths in costume history and the construction of dress. Janet Arnold is especially regarded for her study of costume in the time of Queen Elizabeth I entitled *Queen Elizabeth's Wardrobe Unlock'd* (1988). This scholarly piece of historical research provides the background for her well-known series *Patterns of Fashion* (for example, 1985) and numerous other articles (for example, 1975, 1978, 1993). Her drawings and papers relating to dress and fashion are held by Special Collections at the Hartley Library, University of Southampton.

The collection of her original drawings is complemented by her papers. Taken together they provide a unique resource that may inform us of her working practice in relation to her published work. The drawings take many forms ranging from quick pencil sketches made on small pieces of paper to larger detailed drawings including layouts for actual dress patterns (Figs 1 and 2). They also include some distinctive fashion drawings executed in pencil or pen and ink with watercolour washes, which are reminiscent of the fashion drawings in *Vogue* from the 1940s and 50s (Figs 3 and 4). These drawings, which are accurately observed, fresh and stylish, will be of interest to fashion and dress history students today and in the future.

The second collection under consideration here belonged to Montse Stanley, who was a collector, knitter and historian. She set up the Knitting Reference Library as a private collection comprising knitted clothing and objects, knitting tools, ephemera, her working papers and an extensive library on knitting including books, journals, magazines and patterns. She is best known for her indispensable book on hand knitting *The Handknitter's Handbook* first published in 1986, which has been reprinted many times and in a variety of languages.

Her library is located at the WSA Library and her knitting collection of objects, tools, ephemera including photographs and postcards plus her working papers are located in Special Collections at the Hartley Library. The collection of knitted objects is impressive in both range and richness, offering an interesting and varied picture of the many potential aspects of knitting thus providing researchers a resource from which to make a selection for further study (Figs 5 and 6). The collection demonstrates the high level of skill that can be found in knitting and the objects themselves illustrate the persistence of knitting as an activity which is able to find inventive ways of maintaining a tradition while also discovering new forms and applications. Her Spanish origins are reflected in the collection by the Spanish and Hispanic publications and the knitted objects.

The third collection was formed by Richard Rutt, a knitting historian and knitter, who is widely known for his classic

Figure 1 Marriage à la Ville, Janet Arnold drawing, MS 327 Special Collections, Hartley Library, University of Southampton.

Figure 2 Janet Arnold drawing, MS 327 Special Collections, Hartley Library, University of Southampton.

Figure 3 Dupion Shantung, Janet Arnold drawing, MS327 Special Collections, Hartley Library, University of Southampton (Plate 79 in the colour plate section).

Figure 4 Green antique taffeta dinner and evening dress with black and white peppermint stripe taffeta, Janet Arnold drawing, MS 327 Special Collections, Hartley Library, University of Southampton (Plate 80 in the colour plate section).

Figure 5 Babar and Celeste, Montse Stanley Collection, MS 332 Special Collections, Hartley Library, University of Southampton (Plate 81 in the colour plate section).

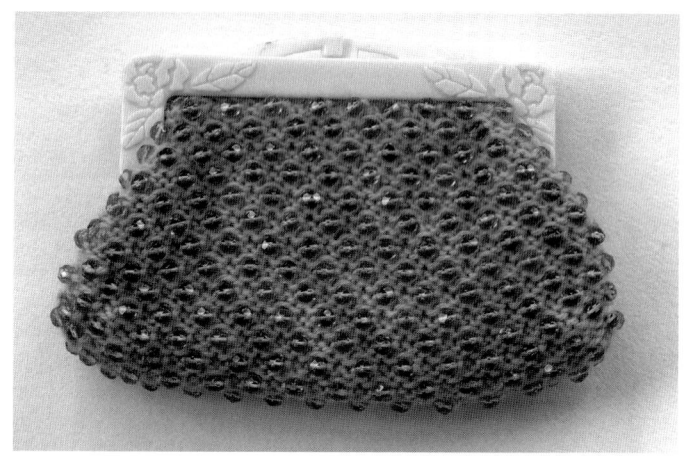

Figure 6 Beaded, knitted bag, Montse Stanley Collection, MS 332 Special Collections, Hartley Library, University of Southampton (Plate 82 in the colour plate section).

book *A History of Hand Knitting* (1987). Richard Rutt's library of books, journals, magazines, patterns and cuttings specifically on knitting is held at the WSA. A particular strength of his collection is the 19th-century ladies' manuals on hand knitting which start in the 1840s. They may be seen as a precursor of both the contemporary knitting pattern and instructional books on how-to-knit; they are still being published over 180 years later and are in demand today. In addition his library includes a comprehensive run of the knitting magazine *Stitchcraft* dating from the 1930s to the 1980s, which richly illustrates the changing graphic image and layout of knitting patterns through the decades of the 20th century. He also has interests in Scandinavian and Korean knitting which are reflected in his collection.

The Montse Stanley and Richard Rutt collections provide a rich and unique range of resources covering many aspects of the history and practice of knitting. Combined, these two libraries uniquely delineate the strong print culture of hand knitting from the mid-19th century through to the late 1990s. The book collection, for example, reflects the persistence of a traditional handcraft, the various methods applied to teaching knitting from the 19th century to the 1990s, the distinctive styles of knitting from around the world and most importantly, a range of approaches to writing and thinking about knitting.

The knitting pattern collection

This collection comprises over 12,000 knitting patterns acquired through donation and purchase. It also includes the patterns from the Montse Stanley and Richard Rutt libraries. In addition, the WSA Library has acquired further collections most notably the collection of Jane Waller, who is best known for her series of books on vintage knitting patterns from the 1920s, 30s and 40s including *A Man's Book: Fashion in the Man's World in the 20s and 30s*, which includes knitted clothing for men (1977). Overall, the collection includes patterns from the late 19th century to the current day. It covers a range of topics such as knitted clothing for men, women and children; knitting patterns for the services from the First and Second World Wars; knitting for the home; knitted toys and novelties.

The collections policy supports the aim of keeping this collection alive by updating it on a regular basis with a bi-annual selection of patterns bought from knitting shops. This policy will ensure that the collection reflects the current revival of hand knitting and the range of objects that may be knitted today. There are many themes that illustrate the continuing popularity of particular types of knitted clothing and items for the home. It is therefore possible to trace the persistence of types of knitting from their early inception in widely available published patterns to their contemporary counterparts, for example, Fair Isle jumpers, novelties and toys, hats, gloves and scarves and sportswear (e.g. the cricket jumper).

Knitted together: a new pattern for the future at Winchester School of Art Library

These three collections have notably enriched resources for academics, researchers and students both at WSA and the TCC and also for the wider academic community within the University of Southampton (Newington 2006). These resources have the potential to contribute to educational programmes and research projects and as interdisciplinary sources for related areas, for example, anthropology, engineering and sports history. In addition external users, whether researcher or makers, are encouraged to engage with these collections to support their interests and research covering the many facets of textile history and making.

Complementary to these collections is a rich and varied collection of books, exhibition catalogues, journals and audio-visual resources on dress, fashion and textiles that has supported both undergraduate and postgraduate programmes in these subject areas over a significant period of time at the WSA Library. This bibliographic material covers many aspects of these subjects including ethnic textiles, contemporary fashion and fashion theory, textile art, dress and textile history. These collections also include electronic resources such as databases and indexes, electronic journals and digital image banks. They range over a wide spectrum of subject areas in art and design including textiles, and provide access to further and different types of materials, for example, journal and newspaper articles, conference proceedings and exhibition catalogues. These secondary resources work alongside the primary sources previously described to form distinctive, focused, in-depth collections that we continue to develop to support WSA, the TCC and the wider textile community both at a national and international level.

Conclusion: access to the collections

The libraries of Janet Arnold, Montse Stanley and Richard Rutt are in the process of being catalogued, classified and indexed. Completion of this process will ensure that their collections become increasingly accessible on WebCat, the online library catalogue of the University of Southampton. The Janet Arnold Library is already available on WebCat.[1] It is likely that the cataloguing of the Montse Stanley and Richard Rutt library collections will take a further two years to complete. Work is also in hand to organise the knitting pattern collection, so improving access.

During this period the Knitting Reference Library will be developed and updated in order to fill some of the gaps. This will help to ensure that the collections meet the needs of researchers and students and that they encourage different approaches to the material. The longer term aim is to establish a comprehensive bibliographic and knitting pattern collection of national standing. This will be made possible by the rich foundation provided by Montse Stanley and Richard Rutt.

Note

1. www.soton.ac.uk/library/infoskills/webcat.

References

Arnold, J. (1975) 'Decorative features: pinking, snipping and slashing', *Costume* 9: 22–6.
Arnold, J. (1978) 'The coronation portrait of Queen Elizabeth I', *Burlington Magazine* 120: 727–41.
Arnold, J. (1985) *Patterns of Fashion: The Cut and Construction of Clothes for Men and Women c. 1560–1620*. London: Macmillan.
Arnold, J. (1988) *Queen Elizabeth's Wardrobe Unlock'd*. Leeds: Maney.
Arnold, J. (1993) 'Costumes for masques and other entertainments c. 1500–1640', *Historical Dance* 3(2): 3–20.
Newington, L. (2006) *Knitting a New Pattern for the Future*. Unpublished MA dissertation, University of Southampton.
Rutt, R. (1987) *A History of Hand Knitting*. London: Batsford
Stanley, M. (1986) *The Handknitter's Handbook: A Comprehensive Guide to the Principles and Techniques of Handknitting*. Newton Abbot: David & Charles.
Waller, J. (ed.) (1977) *A Man's Book: Fashion in the Man's World in the 20s and 30s*. London: Duckworth.

The author

Linda Newington is currently Head Librarian at Winchester School of Art. She continues to practise as a painter and has shown new paintings most recently at Bettles Gallery in Ringwood. In 2007 she completed the MA in the history of textiles and dress, her dissertation focusing on the image and status of knitting. She has responsibility for Special Collections located in the library at the Winchester School of Art that include the Janet Arnold Library, the Knitting Reference Library and the Artists' Books collection.

Contact details

To use the collections based at Winchester School of Art Library please contact us by email, telephone or in writing. The use of the Special Collections based at the Hartley Library is by prior appointment and initial appointments should be made in writing. Details can be found at the Special Collections website (www.soton.ac.uk/library).
- Winchester School of Art Library, Park Avenue, Winchester, SO23 8DL UK. Tel: +44 (0)23 80598531. Email: wsaenqs@soton.ac.uk
- Special Collections, Hartley Library, University of Southampton, Highfield, Southampton SO17 1BJ. Tel: +44 (0)23 8059 2180. E-mail: archives@soton.ac.uk

Collaborative approaches: curators, conservators and dress historians

Thistles and Thrissels: Scottish Covenanting flags of the 17th and early 18th century

George Dalgleish and Lynn McClean

ABSTRACT The National Museums of Scotland owns an important collection of flags relating to the 17th-century Scottish Covenanting movement. This paper explores the opportunity these historic textiles present for combining curatorial documentary research with object-based analysis and investigation. The Covenanters were originally the supporters of the National Covenant of 1638 and the Solemn League and Covenant of 1643. These documents were drawn up to consolidate opposition to the religious and political policies of King Charles I. The written word was of great importance to the Covenanters. They saw themselves as 'People of the Book and the Word'. The flags carried by Covenanting regiments in the wars of the 1640s–50s and 1670s–80s were characterised by the widespread use of written mottoes and religious motifs. It is possible to argue that some of these motifs and texts can be traced back to a seminal original: the 'Thrissels banner', a Covenanting propaganda document of 1640. The links between the 'Thrissels banner' and the other flags in the collection will be explored.

A programme of conservation of the Covenanting flags for display has stimulated this current research. A vital part of the conservation treatment is the importance of retaining the quality of the motifs, and the issue of their 'enhancement' to enable better interpretation by the visitor. Two examples, the Garscube flag and the Avendale flag, will be used to illustrate the importance of combining curatorial research, conservation methods and ethics to ensure the preservation and enhance the interpretation of these exceptional historic textiles.

Keywords: Covenanters, flags, conservation, symbolism, Garscube flag, Avendale flag

Introduction

The National Museums of Scotland owns an important collection of flags relating to the 17th-century Scottish Covenanting movement. These historic flags, which literally combine text with textiles, present an exceptional opportunity for combining curatorial documentary research with object-based analysis and investigation

Some 20 or more flags, or colours, associated with the various periods of Scottish Covenanting activity are known. The largest single group within the corpus are the eight held by the National Museums of Scotland (NMS). With one exception, they all feature text as a prominent part of their design, and the mottoes, motifs and symbolism of these early regimental flags provide an eloquent commentary on a profoundly fascinating but complex period of Scotland's history. A further dozen or so Covenanting flags have been recorded, most of which are in Scottish local museums, mainly in the west of the country which was the traditional heartland of Covenanting activity.

The requirement to display three of the flags in the Museum of Scotland in 1998 led to a programme of documentation of previous treatments, conservation treatment and mounting for display. A plan was also developed for rotation of the flags.[1] It is this work that has prompted current research into Covenanting flags throughout Scotland.

The Covenanting movement

The Covenanters were originally the supporters of the National Covenant of 1638 and the more radical Solemn League and Covenant of 1643. For Scots Presbyterians, they formed the manifestos which guided their opposition to the king in the civil wars and the basis of their continued opposition to Stewart religious policies after the Restoration of 1660. The National Covenant was first drawn up and signed in Edinburgh in 1638.[2] A remarkable if conservative document, it summarised the Presbyterian faction's opposition to the ecclesiastical and political changes being forced on the Scottish church and state by King Charles (Lynch 1992: 264). These were principally concerned with issues of religious observation, church government and state interference in the running of the Church.

The Covenanters held that Christ alone was the head of the Church and that Presbyterianism was the only acceptable form of church government as sanctified by scripture.[3] King Charles embraced and extended his father James VI and I's policies to bring the Scottish church into line with the English church, with its episcopal structure and a more orderly acceptance of royal prerogative and divine right. The Solemn League and Covenant of 1643 was a more radical document, the principal aim of which was to extend Presbyterian church government to the whole of the British Isles. This was to be accomplished by military means if necessary, and ultimately saw several Scottish armies invading England and Ireland. The stage was set for conflict.

The first phase of military activity by the Scottish Covenanters lasted from 1639 to 1651, with the early outbreak of the so-called Bishops Wars in 1639–40 through to the disastrous (for the Scots) campaigns of 1650–51, which culminated with total subjugation of Scotland by Oliver Cromwell. Scotland's opposition to Charles I's religious policies effectively precipitated the so-called English Civil War, now more accurately referred to as the Wars of the Three Kingdoms.

During this period, the Covenanting faction formed the de facto government of Scotland[4] and as such they raised numerous armies to counter Royalist opposition. These armies were legally constituted and consisted of well-structured regiments based on burgh and shire levies (Furgol 1990: 4–5). The regiments were commanded by local leaders of society, and officered to a large degree by the many Scots professional soldiers who had recently fought in the various continental wars. Their regular structure was emphasised by their use of regimental flags or colours, based primarily on the Scottish national flag, the saltire, a white St Andrew's cross on a blue background. What distinguished such flags, however, was the widespread use of painted mottoes. Several different armies were raised throughout this period, such as the Army of the Solemn League and Covenant, the Engager Army and the Army of the Covenants. Extensive documentary research by Edward Furgol for his book *A Regimental History of the Covenanting Armies* has shown conclusively that the colours of the regiments within these armies were distinguished by a variety of differing mottoes, such as 'For Religion, the Covenant and the Countrie'; 'For Christ's Croun and Covenant'; 'Covenant For Relligion, Crowne and Country'; 'Covenant for Religion Crowne and Kingdomes' and 'Covenant for Religion, King and Kingdoms' (Furgol 1990: 11–12).

The very use of the term 'covenant' is highly significant, as it clearly represented the view of many Scots Presbyterians that their cause could be traced back to God's covenant with Moses. One recent scholar of the period commented that '[the Covenant] drew on a deep-rooted tradition of biblical literalism' and the Scots undoubtedly had a sense of themselves as God's 'Chosen People' (Lynch 2001: 436). It is therefore no coincidence that so many of the surviving Covenanting flags have the word 'Covenant' painted on them.

The Covenanters and literacy

A concern with literacy was a common feature of many 16th and early 17th-century protestant groups, but especially those whose theology drew heavily on the work of John Calvin in Geneva. In Scotland, Calvinism provided the fundamental tenets of belief for reformers such as John Knox and Andrew Melville. In the church and society they helped create, great stress was laid on literacy as the only true and sure access to the scriptures. The Scots Reformers set out to achieve this by an ambitious programme of school provision, which, although it was never as complete as they wished, did set the foundations for a remarkable education system, and more practically produced a comparatively literate populace. It is not unusual therefore that the flags and colours under which their successors, the Covenanters, fought were replete with significant and frequently lengthy statements. Put quite simply, many of the rank and file of the armies could and did read and understand these complex exhortations, rather than rallying round simple visual symbols that were the norm in battle flags of the period.

Early Covenanting flags

The NMS has three flags which can now be ascribed to regiments of this early period: the Garscube; the Bothwell Brig and the Dunbar saltire.[5]

The Garscube flag

The first, known as the Garscube flag, was acquired by the museum in 1869, with the attendant information that it was said to have been carried by Stewart of Garscube at the Battle of Worcester in 1651 and thereafter at the Battle of Bothwell Bridge in 1679[6] (Fig. 1). The silk flag, measuring 1300 × 1900 mm, is a white saltire on a pink and blue quartered background with a linen pole sleeve. The central thistle is in red and green paint and the motto 'COVENANTS / FOR RELIGION / CROWNE AND /KINGDOMS' is in white.

The fine silk is in very poor condition, being weak and fragmentary with much loss. Overall the motif and painted white lettering are very faint, but there appears to have been some restoration of the red of the thistle and some letters. The legibility of the lettering was further diminished by the impact of a bright green silk support fabric, evident in the numerous areas of loss of original silk. The flag had been adhered to this green fabric in the late 19th century as were six others in the collection (Foskett and McClean: 1997).[7]

It was proposed that the original silk flag be removed from the green support to facilitate an adhesive treatment with a support fabric in a sympathetic colour. The very poor condition of the silk and its fragmentary nature meant this was not possible and the 19th-century support fabric, which was now also very fragile, had to be considered and treated as part of

Figure 1 The Garscube flag, after conservation
(© The Trustees of the National Museums of Scotland)
(Plate 83 in the colour plate section).

the object. The adhesive treatment[8] made the flag safe for mounting for display. The issue arose about the importance of the motif and motto to the context of the flag, and the fact that the exposed areas of green silk drew the eye from them and reduced their impact and legibility. This was particularly true of the white motto.

It was decided to try to reduce the impact of the green silk without affecting the conservation treatment or the flag itself. Silk crepeline had been used successfully to complete the lettering on the Avendale flag (see below), so it was considered again. In this instance, however, it was used in the opposite way: to reduce an old treatment in order to enhance the motifs. Consideration was given to covering each section of the flag completely with dyed silk crepeline but this would not only be difficult to remove from the very fragile silk, therefore not achieving the conservation aim of being as reversible as possible, but would also have the effect of making the imagery less visible.

The outlines of exposed areas of green silk were carefully traced and cut out of adhesive-coated silk crepeline[9] dyed to match the original silk surrounding the missing area. The shaped silk crepeline was heat set to the green silk on the front of the flag. Naturally the very poor condition of the existing silk was taken into consideration when tracing the shape onto Melinex (polyester film) and carrying out the treatment. Attempts were made to prevent the silk crepeline being adhered over the original silk, but this did happen in a few areas due to the difficulty of tracing awkward and irregular shapes. Covering the green silk in this way reduced its brightness, which made the white motto stand out more.

This treatment improved the legibility of the motto and in turn has confirmed some earlier evidence in the form of a coloured drawing done by James Drummond RSA, a renowned 19th-century Scottish artist and antiquarian. Drummond drew a group of Covenanting flags for publication as lithographs in an article in the *Proceedings of the Society of Antiquaries of Scotland* (Drummond 1859). It had been assumed that a degree of artistic licence was evident in Drummond's depiction of the flag, which he clearly shows in a much better state of preservation than is currently the case. The combination of recent conservation/documentation work and Drummond's historic evidence, however, indicates the motto to be COVENANTS / FOR RELIGION / CROWNE AND /KINGDOMS.

It is now known that this motto was first used on the regimental colours of units commanded by General Alexander Leslie, Earl of Leven, as part of his Army of the Solemn League and Covenant (Furgol 1990: 11). The word 'Kingdoms' in the plural is highly significant, as the Army of the Solemn League and Covenant invaded England at the request of some groups of English parliamentarians and with the express intention (of the Scots at least) of imposing Presbyterianism in the two kingdoms of England and Scotland. This combination of documentary research and conservation treatment indicates that the dating of the flag should be re-evaluated, perhaps to as early as 1644, making it by far the earliest extant Covenanting flag.

The significance of the Thrissels banner

The other significant element of this flag is of course the thistle. This may simply be another example of the use of the plant as a national symbol of Scotland, which can be traced at least as far back as the mid-15th century. It may, however, be the result of a more immediate and direct inspiration from the so-called 'Thrissels banner'[10] (Fig. 2). This fascinating object is not a banner at all, but is rather a piece of Covenanting propaganda, more in the nature of a printed broadside. This did not prevent a late 19th-century commentator, who had clearly never seen one, remarking that the banner was 'A national standard which was borne by the Covenanters when with a gallant army they marched into England ... and took possession of Newcastle' (Courthorpe 1928: viii).

These gallant Covenanters must have had excellent eyesight to follow this flag as it measures only some 420 × 290 mm. It depicts a flag or banner consisting of a St Andrew's and St George's cross, completely covered with religious mottoes and quotations, suspended from a sword which in turn rests upon a bible and is surmounted by a crowned thistle. It was created and published in 1640 by Thomas Cunningham who 'caused ingrave the Banner in copper and print of it 200 upon white satin and 1800 upon paper' (Courthorpe 1928: 5). One of the silk satin prints is on display in the Museum of Scotland.[11]

Cunningham was a staunch Presbyterian who served the Covenanting government as the Conservator of the Scottish Staple at Campvere, a post that oversaw and controlled the important trade between Scotland and the Low Countries. Cunningham was effectively a propagandist for the

Figure 2 The Thrissels banner (© The Trustees of the National Museums of Scotland).

Covenanting movement on the Continent, and helped publicise its cause through the distribution of the Thrissels banner. He also published an accompanying 'explication' which carefully and extensively detailed the meanings of the symbols and the text on the banner, with copious scriptural references and justifications (Courthorpe 1928: 11–25). Most of these symbols and some of the texts appear on virtually all of the surviving Covenanting flags, and one could argue that if the Thrissels banner was not the prototype of all other Covenanting flags, then its content was at least highly influential in their design and meaning.

Cunningham cogently sums up the importance of the symbols he used: 'The Book signifyeth the Bible and consequently the Word of God which ought to be the foundation and ground ... the only infallible rule whereby all ... actions of man should be squared ... The Sword signifyeth authority, and standing on the Bible signifyeth that al authority is of God ... [while] ... the Thrissel Crouwned signifyeth the Kingdom of Scotland ... and the mutual band betwixt King and Subects' (Courthorpe 1928: 11). He goes on to give a very eloquent description of the contractual theory of monarchy which the Covenanters saw as an essential foundation of the kingdom, where in return for their loyalty, the king ought to maintain and defend his subjects. If the king broke this contract, or covenant, then the subjects had the right and duty to persuade him to return to his covenant with them and God.

While the thistle is a central motif of the Garscube flag, the very structure of the flag itself (which is unique in the group), made up of different coloured quarters surmounted by a saltire, is highly reminiscent of the Thrissels banner outline. There can be little doubt that the Thrissels banner was a form of visual blueprint for the Garscube flag.

The Bothwell Brig flag

The second flag in this important early group, the Bothwell Brig, was given to the museum in 1796 (Fig. 3). The blue silk flag with a white saltire has a central motif of five painted red roses and a painted and gilded motto.[12] It measures 1340 × 1630 mm and has a plain weave linen pole sleeve.[13] It was accompanied by the information that it was carried at the Battle of Bothwell Bridge in 1679, and then again by a regiment raised from a group of Presbyterian Seceders in Edinburgh to counter the threat of invasion of the capital by Prince Charles Edward Stewart's Jacobite Army in 1745. The radical elements of the Presbyterian church in the 18th century saw themselves as the natural successors to the Covenanters of the preceding century, and were vehement in their defence of the Presbyterian form of church government established in 1690 after James VII and II had been deposed. They were obviously opposed to the attempts to restore the Stewart monarchy through the various Jacobite Rebellions of the 18th century, and several old Covenanting flags were reused to rally this opposition.

The wording on this flag now reads 'COVENANTS,/ FOR RELIGION / KING,/AND KINGDOMES', and again documentary references might suggest this was a form of words used originally on the flags of the regiments of the Engager Army, raised in 1648 (Furgol 1990: 11). The Engagers were a more moderate group of Covenanters who wished an accommodation with the king, who by now had been captured by Cromwell. The Scots army invaded England in 1648 in an attempt to rescue the king, but met with complete failure and were routed at the Battle of Preston. A recently discovered letter in the NMS archives has cast some doubt on this interpretation and has helped explain some analytical results for the paint. Written in December 1796 by Christopher Moubray, the original donor of the flag, or 'stand of colours', it states:

> In the year 1745, when the Burgesses of Edinburgh were associated as Volunteers, my father belonged to a corps under the command of the late Lord Kennet, as Colonel. An old lady had the colours in her possession and made a present of them to my father, adding 'That they had been handed through her family since Bothwell Bridge, where they were displayed by the "Covenanters"'. The motto upon them was 'For Religion Covenant King and Kingdom'. The letters at that time being much defaced; but my father got them gilded anew; and as the corps with which he was associated were burger Seceeders they added the letter 'S' to the words Covenant and Kingdom, as it now stands. Their reason for this was to include the Solemn League and Covenant with the National Covenant, and to comprehend the three Kingdoms.

The re-gilding mentioned in the letter supports the results of paint analysis carried out on a part of the lettering, which suggests that the wording was originally painted with orpiment pigment later gilded with a pure gold foil.[14]

It is clear that the original motto on the flag was 'For Religion, Covenant, King and Kingdom', but this does not exactly match any of the recorded mottoes for the various armies as described by Furgol (1990: 11–12). The closest match is to the wording employed by the Army of the Covenant which used the variation 'For Covenant, Religion, King and Kingdom'. This relatively small army was raised in late 1648 for service in Scotland. One unique and perplexing feature of this flag is the presence of roses in the centre of the saltire. It is still

Figure 3 The Bothwell Brig flag, after conservation
(© The Trustees of the National Museums of Scotland)
(Plate 84 in the colour plate section).

possible that the flag does relate to the Engager Army and that this was an attempt to rally anti-Cromwellian English support for the army on its mission to rescue the king. Whatever the meaning of this symbolism, the reinterpretation of the text on the flag suggests we have to re-evaluate its original date from 1679 back to 1648.

The Dunbar saltire

The third flag in this early group, the Dunbar saltire, is the one aberration in the NMS's collection, being a simple silk saltire with no obvious motto or other symbolism[15] (Fig. 4). The flag measures 1335 × 1475 mm and has no pole sleeve. It was donated to the museum in 1864, and came with the additional information that it was the 'standard of Col. Scott's regiment and carried at the battle of Dunbar in 1650'. Dating and securing a provenance would obviously have been helped if the flag had contained a motto. No such wording was discovered when the flag was last conserved. The original silk is very fragmentary and fragile, and the random pattern in which it had been adhered to the green silk support[16] in the late 19th century makes it difficult to be certain that there was not originally a painted motto. The Battle of Dunbar resulted in a massive defeat for the Scots Covenanters and heralded the imposition of the Cromwellian Union (Donnachie and Hewitt 1989: 61). Cromwell's effective annexation of Scotland into his Godly Commonwealth put paid to Covenanting resistance.

Later Covenanting flags

The next phase of Covenanting activity for which flags exist is the period of Scottish history known dramatically and with only partial accuracy as 'the Killing Times'. After the Restoration of the Stewart monarchy, episcopacy was reintroduced into Scotland, as was state control of the Church and official rejection of the Covenants. Many Presbyterian ministers were deprived of their parishes, but continued to hold illegal services, often in the open air, known as conventicles, for their loyal and frequently large flocks. Conventicles and Presbyterian dissent were particularly prevalent in the southwest of Scotland, and heavy-handed attempts at government suppression set the scene for a series of armed uprisings by the increasingly desperate Covenanters.[17] One conventicle held in the Irongray Parish of Dumfriesshire had over 14,000 participants (Cowan 1976: 92-3).

These gatherings were regularly attended by armed and mounted men, and quickly took on the guise of armies. Unlike the earlier period of Covenanter activity, this resistance to royal authority was more locally based, with the regiments much less official and regular than a generation earlier. They were often raised by minor local landholders, or lairds, who had been traditionally sympathetic to the Presbyterian cause. The local nature of this resistance can be seen on many flags of this period, as they now include names of the parishes they represented, as well as more elaborate lines of text.

A skirmish by one such armed group with a small detachment of Royalist forces in early June 1679 at Drumclog in Ayrshire resulted in a defeat for the Royalists who retreated to regroup. The conventiclers failed to follow up this success. This allowed the government army time to reinforce and by the time they met again at Bothwell Bridge on 21 June 1679, the Royalists were much stronger and routed and scattered the covenanters. This effectively brought to an end large-scale uprisings and heralded a period of intense persecution and repression – the Killing Times (Cowan 1976: 98–9). The events of Bothwell Bridge and Drumclog played a significant part in the history of the movement and in its subsequent mythology, and it is no surprise that there should be many relics of these conflicts. Many of the surviving Covenanting flags are said to have been carried at either or both of these battles.

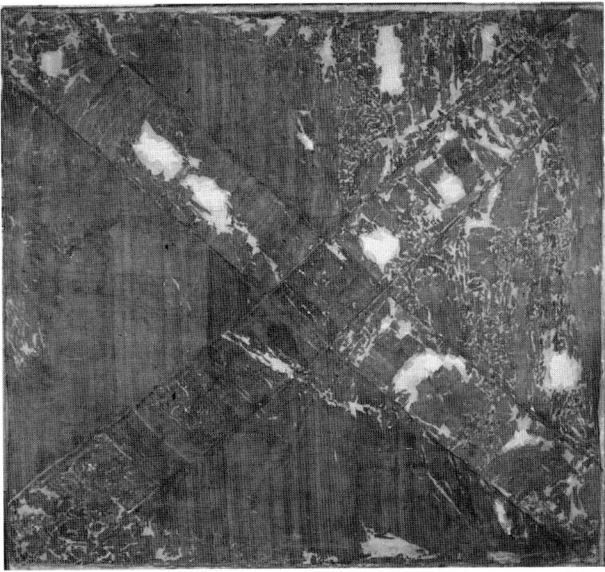

Figure 4 The Dunbar saltire, after conservation (© The Trustees of the National Museums of Scotland) (Plate 85 in the colour plate section).

The Avendale flag

Avendale[18] in Lanarkshire was a centre of dissent, and two flags from this parish have survived. The NMS example, the Avendale flag, is one of the most impressive of all Covenanting flags, replete with symbolism and no less than four separate lines of text (Fig. 5). Made of three widths of fine cream plain weave silk, it is painted with a thistle, an open book and the motto 'AVENDAILL FOR REFORMATION/ IN CHURCH AND STATE/ACCORDING TO THE WORD /OF GOD AND OUR COUENANTS'.[19] The thistle and book motifs can be traced back to the Thrissels banner, and the actual lettering bears a striking resemblance to that used on the early Covenanting propaganda document. The Avendale flag was said to have been carried by one Matthew Craig, the laird of Plewlands, at the Battle of Drumclog. The second Avendale flag is displayed in the John Hastie Museum in Strathaven, Lanarkshire.

The Avendale flag, which measures 1750 × 2120 mm, had undergone previous repair treatments (McClean and Haldane 2003) which were successfully reversed and the flag then supported onto dyed cream silk crepeline for display.[20] It presented a different issue to the Garscube flag in terms of viewing and interpreting the motto and motifs. The painted red[21] motto

Figure 5 The Avendale flag, after conservation (© The Trustees of the National Museums of Scotland) (Plate 86 in the colour plate section).

on the Avendale was clearly legible, but much of the bible and parts of the thistle were missing. Consideration was therefore given to the possibility of 'completing' these motifs to aid interpretation by the viewer.

The thistle will be used as an example. Three options were considered: (1) to complete the image using fabric in a solid colour with the suggestion of outlines; (2) to complete the image using semi-transparent fabrics to give a suggestion of the colour and outline; and (3) to use no infills other than the new cream support fabric.

Neither conservator nor curator felt it was acceptable to try to restore what was missing, as there was no evidence, historic or existing, of how the missing parts of the thistle would have appeared. Option 1 was disregarded for this reason. The use of digital imaging was employed as a tool for discussion of the remaining options with the curator. Option 3, which involved no infilling of the missing areas, was felt to detract significantly from the motifs, much in the way that the 1891 green silk support had done for the Garscube flag. It was finally decided to use semi-transparent fabric, silk crepeline, dyed simply to correspond with the dominant colour of each motif and to create the outline of the missing motif. The dyed fabric was coated with adhesive and adhered to the cream silk crepeline support fabric on the reverse of the object (McClean and Haldane 2003). This had a very subtle effect, enabling the outline of the motif to be completed and therefore more readily understood by the viewer, without attempting to recreate what no longer exists.

'The Bluidy banner'

Several other surviving flags are said to have been carried at Bothwell Bridge, including one now on display in Hamilton Museum known as the 'Bluidy banner'.[22] This is perhaps the most contentious of the surviving flags because of the nature of its painted text, part of which reads 'FOR CHRIST & HIS TRUTHS / NO QUARTERS FOR Ye ACTIVE ENIMIES OF Ye COVENANT'. This has been used to emphasise the bloodthirsty nature of the conflict and to justify the harsh repressive measures meted out to the defeated Covenanters by the government forces. This paper is not the forum to discuss this still controversial issue, but the flag does have a further piece of text which is relevant to this discussion. The top line reads 'Jehovah Nissi' in Hebrew characters. This can be literally translated as 'The Lord is my Banner' and is a direct reference to scripture: 'And Moses built an Altar and called the nature of it Jehovah – Nissi' (Exodus 17:15), ensuring victory of Moses and the Children of Israel over their enemies. This again emphasises the Covenanters' identification with the Israelites as the 'Chosen People' and the 'People of the Word and Book'.

The Jehovah Nissi flags

The phrase 'Jehovah Nissi' also appears on two final flags from the group, one now on display in the Museum of Scotland (Fig. 6) and the second in the Douglas Heritage Museum, Lanarkshire. Both have marked similarities: they are of cream linen, edged on three sides with blue silk and a yellow silk fringe. They are painted with a 'wavy' sword, a thistle and the motto 'JEHOVAH NISSI/ For God and / the Covenanted Work of Religion'. The Douglas one alone has the date 1745. It is clear, however, that they were painted by different hands. The Jehovah Nissi flag in the NMS collection[23] appears to be older, as the lettering in particular shares features with some of the earlier flags already mentioned, while the lettering on the Douglas flag looks far closer to a mid-18th-century date. The general depiction of the motifs, particularly the somewhat bizarre representation of the sword, would suggest, however, that they were both inspired by a common original, again probably the Thrissels banner of 1640. The sword on that is entwined with a ribbon, or garter, which could be mistakenly copied as the 'wavy' swords of these banners. The representation of the long-leafed thistles is also similar to the depiction of the plant on the Thrissels banner.

The flag in Douglas Heritage Museum is thought to have been made for a meeting in 1745 at Auchensaugh, near Douglas. This was the site of a series of meetings started in 1712, by a group of staunch local Presbyterians to reaffirm the

Figure 6 The Jehovah Nissi flag, after conservation (© The Trustees of the National Museums of Scotland) (Plate 87 in the colour plate section).

articles of the Covenants against what they saw as the apostasy of the times. These meetings became great annual religious festivals. Contemporary records indicate that the Douglas flag was made for the latter meeting (Hutchison 1940). It is probable that the NMS flag was made for one of the earlier, if not the earliest, meeting in 1712. It can be argued that the Presbyterian groups responsible for these local revivals of Covenanting ideology in the early 18th century would look back to Covenanting propaganda of the period of the National Covenant almost 100 years before for inspiration for their flags. The Thrissels banner would certainly have provided this.

Conclusion

Curators and conservators working closely together on this project generated a dialogue and a series of questions which required new ways of thinking. The painstaking and detailed inspection of the flags for conservation provided invaluable clues on their original construction and on subsequent repair and repainting which aided curatorial investigation and interpretation. It also made possible detailed comparisons between flags, suggesting groupings and sequences which in turn allowed crucial re-evaluation of dates and suggested new avenues for documentary research.

For both the Garscube and Avendale flags, great importance was placed on the ease with which the viewer could interpret the motifs and mottoes given that they were of such significance to the Covenanters. This was an essential part of explaining the complex historical storyline in this section of the Museum of Scotland. There was much discussion between curator and conservator about the methods and extent to which the motifs could or should be 'enhanced' to achieve this. It was felt that it was important to enhance the images that existed and that any treatment could be easily reversible, but that no attempt should be made to interpret what was not there.

This is very much a statement of work in progress and considerably more investigation needs to be done on the other flags, which will undoubtedly lead to a further revision of possible dating. It is clear, however, that such an interdisciplinary approach has made possible advances in understanding, interpretation and display that would otherwise have been impossible.

Acknowledgements

The authors would like to thank colleagues in the departments of Conservation and Analytical Research, and Scotland and Europe for all their help and encouragement with this project.

Notes

1. The policy recommended the flags be rotated every four years. This was based on their condition, the display environment and the existence of a rotation flag.
2. First signed on 28 February 1638 in Greyfriars Churchyard, the National Covenant was essentially a 'round robin' letter, somewhat in the nature of a petition, copies of which were circulated throughout the kingdom. An extraordinary number of people subscribed to it, from all levels of society, indicating the depth of feeling against Charles I's policies.
3. The Presbyterian form of church government vested power in an assembly of ministers, officers and elders, chosen from the church's members. The word 'Presbyterian' comes from the Greek *presbteros*, an older man, and refers to the dominant role of the church's senior members. The word 'episcopacy' also derives from the Greek for bishop, and in this system, the bishops were at the head of a complex hierarchy and wielded near absolute power in their sees.
4. Despite the Union of the Crowns of 1603, which saw James VI of Scotland accede to the throne of England as well, the two countries remained separate, sovereign kingdoms.
5. Saltire: a St Andrew's cross.
6. NMS Registration No. H.LF 3. Purchased from the sale of the collection of W.B. Johnstone Esq, RSA, 12 April 1869 (*Proceedings of the Society of Antiquaries of Scotland* 8 (1868–70), 115).
7. During the conservation of the Bothwell Brig flag an inscription discovered on the wooden stretcher dated the treatment to August 1891. The adhesive has been identified as starch.
8. The flag was given a full support of dyed silk crepeline coated with Lascaux 360HV and Lascaux 498 HV acrylic adhesive (thermoplastic copolymer butyl-methacrylate dispersion) in a ratio of 1:2, 15% solution with water.
9. Lascaux 360HV and Lascaux 498 HV acrylic adhesive in ratio of 1:2, 10% solution with water.
10. Thrissel is simply an early Scots spelling and pronunciation of thistle.
11. NMS Registration No. A. 1943.346. Donated by Mr E.H.M. Cox, Glendoig, Perthshire; exhibited at the Glasgow International Exhibition 1901.
12. The original silk was adhered to a brown linen fabric at an unknown date and that in turn to the green silk in 1891. In this case the green silk was removed as part of the conservation treatment.
13. NMS Registration No. H.LF 2. Donated to the Museum of the Society of Antiquaries by Mr Christopher Mowbray, 1796 (*Archaeologia Scotica* 3 (1831), Appendix II List of Donations Dec 27 1796).
14. The layer of orpiment (As_2S_3) has been applied to the silk. This was followed by a substrate of lead pigment with calcium carbonate and ochre in an oil binding media to which has been applied a pure gold foil. The sample was analysed using scanning electron microscopy with energy-dispersive X-rays (SEM–EDX). Internal NMS Report AR 06/27, Lore Troalen, inorganic chemist.
15. NMS Registration No. H.LF 5; given in 1864 by Sir Archibald Edmonstone of Duntreath, Bart; 'The flag was the standard of Colonel Scott's regiment of horse, engaged in the Battle of Dunbar in the year 1650, where Colonel Scott was killed' (*Proceedings of the Society of Antiquaries of Scotland* 5 (1862–4), 343).
16. This flag is one of the seven adhered to green silk in 1891.
17. For a masterly summary of this period see Cowan 1976, chs 2 and 3.
18. Avondale was spelled in a variety of different ways in the 17th and 18th centuries, but the NMS flag is known as the Avendale.
19. NMS Registration No. H.LF 8. Given to the Museum of Antiquities in 1897 by Miss Martha Brown, Waterhaughts, Ayrshire, along with two swords said to have belonged to noted Covenanters in Avondale (*Proceedings of the Society of Antiquaries of Scotland* 32 (1898–9), 178–9).
20. The flag was given a full support of dyed silk crepeline coated with a mixture of Lascaux 360 HV and Lascaux 498 HV acrylic adhesive (thermoplastic copolymer butyl-methacrylate dispersion) in a ratio of 1:2 mixed 1:10 w/v with water and heat set in place.
21. The red paint was identified as alizarin and purpurin, the major components of red dye plants from the madder family. Internal NMS Report AR 03/04, by Dr Anita Quye, organic chemist.
22. 'The Bluidie banner' was first given this name in the 19th century,

but has a well-documented provenance which maintains that it was carried by William Clelland at Drumclog and Bothwell Bridge. Clelland, who was a young man at the time, escaped to Holland in 1680, but returned to become colonel of the newly formed Cameronian Regiment in 1689, which fought for King William of Orange at Dunkeld against the Jacobite army. He won the battle but was killed in action. The banner descended in the family until presented in 1946 to the Cameronians (Scottish Rifles) and then later to the Hamilton Museum (Mein 1949).

23. NMS Registration No. H.LF 19 Given by Lord Clyde, 1935, who had it by descent from a Nathanial Cowan, son of the 'original standard bearer', who died May 1768 (original correspondence with donor in NMS files).

References

Courthorpe, E.J. (ed.) (1928) *The Journal of Thomas Cunningham of Campvere 1640–54*. Scottish History Society, 3rd series, vol. 11. Edinburgh: Scottish History Society.

Cowan, I.B. (1976) *The Scottish Covenanters, 1660–88*. London: Gollancz.

Donnachie, I. and Hewitt, G. (1989) *A Companion to Scottish History*. London: Batsford.

Drummond, J. (1859) 'Notice of "The Bluidy Banner" of Drumclog and Bothwell Brig, preserved at Dunbar' in *Proceedings of the Society of Antiquaries of Scotland* V3: 253–8.

Foskett, S. and McClean, L. (1997) 'A review of adhesive and stitched banner treatments in the National Museums of Scotland', in *Adhesive Treatments Revisited*, J. Lewis (ed.), 61–6. London: UKIC Textile Section.

Furgol, E. (1990) *A Regimental History of the Covenanting Armies, 1639–1651*. Edinburgh: John Donald.

Hutchison, J.D. (1940) *Douglasdale: Its History and Traditions*. Edinburgh: Blackie.

Lynch, M. (1992) *Scotland: A New History*. London: Pimlico.

Lynch, M. (ed.) (2001) *The Oxford Companion to Scottish History*. Oxford: Oxford University Press.

McClean, L. and Haldane, E.A. (2003) 'Avendale for reformation: conservation of a 17th century covenanting banner', in *Tales in the Textile: The Conservation of Flags and Other Symbolic Textiles*, J. Vuori (ed.), 143–54. North American Textile Conservation Conference, 23–25 October, Albany, NY.

Mein, E M. (1949) 'Note on the Bluidy Banner or Haughhead Banner', *Proceedings of the Society of Antiquaries of Scotland* 81: 134–8.

The authors

- George Dalgleish graduated from Edinburgh University and joined the staff of the National Museum of Antiquities of Scotland in 1980. He is now Principal Curator of Scottish History in the Scotland and Europe Department of the National Museums of Scotland.

- Lynn McClean graduated from the Textile Conservation Centre in 1993, after which she completed a one-year internship at the National Trust's Textile Conservation Studio. She took up post in the Department of Conservation and Analytical Research at the National Museums of Scotland in 1994, and has been Head of Paper and Textile Conservation since 2001.

Address

Corresponding author: George R. Dalgleish, National Museums of Scotland, Chambers Street, Edinburgh EH1 1JD, UK (g.dalgleish@nms.ac.uk)

Dye analysis, textiles and text: unravelling the puzzle of Queen Charlotte's state bed

Maria Jordan and Mika Takami

ABSTRACT Queen Charlotte's state bed (1772–78), a magnificent canopied bed of exquisite silk embroidery, underwent a change of colour scheme from the original cream and yellow to cream and purple. This change, which still physically exists, has always been regarded as Victorian. As it has degraded, the 'Victorian' purple silk satin has been replaced with the yellow silk satin where necessary. During the most recent conservation treatment, to conserve the last remaining purple silk satin, an inscription was discovered which cast new light on the story of the bed. This paper discusses the challenge this inscription has presented. To date, no written documentation has been found to explain the reason for the colour change. This puzzle challenges curators and conservators both in its interpretation as well as the appropriate treatment strategy. Through the use of dye analysis, careful inspection and reversing previous treatments, the object has offered clues to its history. Research is continuing to re-establish a link between the object's voice and the archival records.

Keywords: state bed, silk embroidery, valances, Victorian, 18th century, synthetic dyes, mordant, HPLC–PDA, conservation ethics, archival materials

Introduction

The aim of this paper is to investigate the puzzle presented by the different archival descriptions of Queen Charlotte's state bed and to establish their validity with regard to the physical evidence. Using object-based research and scientific analysis, conservators have tried to unravel the puzzle, chiefly focusing on when and why the bed hangings were changed from yellow to purple and with a view to establishing why purple was chosen.

The bed

Queen Charlotte, George III's wife, commissioned a state bed for her state bedchamber at Windsor between 1772 and 1778. It was a magnificent canopied bed, richly carved and gilded and the textile components were exquisitely embroidered (Fig. 1). The bed measures 2.39 m (L) × 2.24 m (W) × 3.96 m (H) and is comprised of 55 pieces including four original mattresses. The textile elements are embroidered with floral motifs, the design and composition of which not only reflect the aesthetic trends of the second half of the 18th century but also the queen's personal taste.

Queen Charlotte was interested in all things botanical. She commissioned Mary Moser to design the floral motifs for the bed as well as a room at Frogmore House. Designs were drawn up for the tester, the backcloth, four curtains, the three outer upper valances, three base valances, four inner valances and the counterpane. The designs are flowing, incorporating 4,200

Figure 1 Queen Charlotte's state bed 1772–78 (© HM Queen Elizabeth II) (Plate 88 in the colour plate section).

flowers including roses and lilies, all exquisitely worked in two-ply silk. The work was undertaken by Nancy Pawsey and Phoebe Wright.

The bed was taken off display at Hampton Court Palace in 1992 due to concerns over the bed structure. It remained fully erected, protected by a Tyvek covering. The environmental conditions of both the room and the interior of the Tyvek cover were regularly monitored and the bed was re-examined in 2003 after an exhibition of state beds was proposed at Hampton Court Palace.

Condition of the bed

The bed has been at Hampton Court Palace since the early 19th century and was on open display for much of the period since the palace was opened to the public by Queen Victoria in 1837 (Law 1897). It has therefore been subjected to light, dust, environmental changes, pests, handling and the visiting public. Overall the condition of the bed was stable though there were concerns about the structure. Parts of the giltwood carving were loose or lost and some areas of the gilding needed consolidation.

The condition of the textile elements varied from stable to very poor. The upper outer valances were the most fragile. These are the last remaining part of a purple colour scheme, never remounted onto the new gold silk ground. The purple satin ground was weak with much of the warp having been lost, exposing long loose weft threads. The loss of the warp had resulted in a weakening of the weave structure and of the repair work that had been carried out in black cotton thread to secure the loose wefts in the form of brick stitches (running stitching) worked through all layers, including the lining. This stitching had caused creasing and uneven tensions, accelerating the degradation. The trimmings, a gimp along the upper edge and a heavy bullion fringe along the bottom edge, were also fragile. As the silk powdered, it exposed the core and weakened the structure. In addition, the weight of the lower bullion fringe was causing stress to the degrading valances.

The combination of the vulnerable giltwood areas and the particularly weak textile elements led to the complete dismantling of the bed in November 2005. Fortunately, the concerns over the condition of the bed structure turned out to be unfounded. After the dismantling, it was decided to review all the information available in order to establish the history of the object. It would be a collaboration of curatorial and object-based research.

Archival research

Annabel Westman was commissioned by Historic Royal Palaces to undertake the archival research. The research revealed, through guidebooks, articles and correspondence, the movement of the bed between rooms at Windsor Castle, its removal to Hampton Court Palace and then its relocation between various rooms in the palace (Westman 2003). In addition, these guidebooks also provided a confusing array of descriptions of the outer hangings of the bed, variously described as pea green, blue, lilac and gold. This implied that the embroidery might have been remounted several times on different ground fabrics. The archival research had also identified a period, between 1795 and 1879, when there was no mention of the colour of the bed. By 1879 (Summerly 1879) it was described as lilac and this is corroborated by a watercolour of the king's state bedchamber at Hampton Court Palace, dated c.1890, showing Queen Charlotte's state bed hung in purple, with a cream interior.

Black and white photographs from the beginning of the 20th century provide evidence of the movement of the bed between different rooms at Hampton Court Palace. They also document the curtains and outer valances belonging to the bed, showing the deteriorating condition of the curtains. The documentation for the second half of the century is more substantial, with correspondence, estimates for materials, conservation reports and newspaper articles. These detail the transfer of the embroidery from the degraded purple satin onto the gold satin.

Object-based research

In 2005, the textiles were removed from the bed and carefully documented. This process focused on five key points: evidence

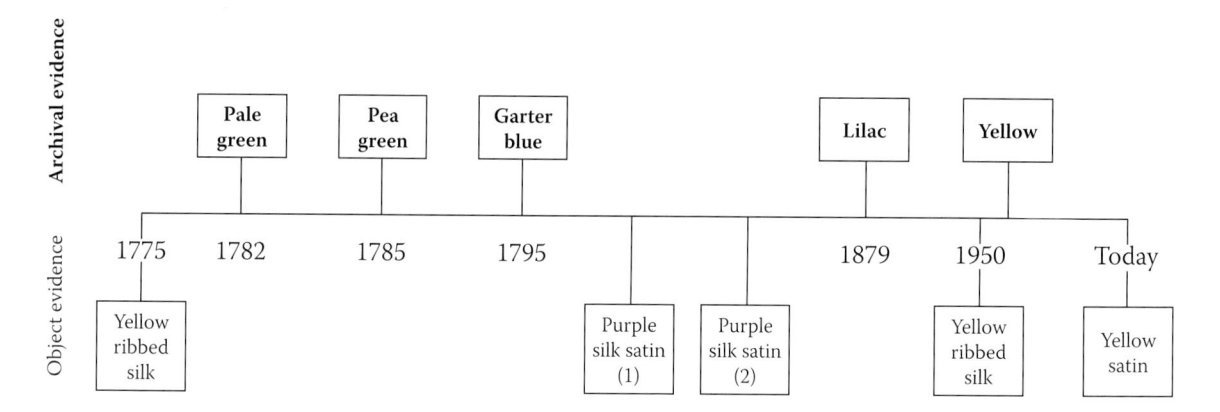

Table 1 Time line for colour changes.

Archival evidence	Pale green (1775)	Pea green (1782)	Garter blue (1785)		Lilac (1879)	Yellow (1950)	
Object evidence	Yellow ribbed silk (1775)			Purple silk satin (1) (1795)	Purple silk satin (2)	Yellow ribbed silk	Yellow satin (Today)

relating to the original silk ground onto which the embroidery had been worked, including its colour and weave; the colour and weave of any subsequent materials used for the remounting of the embroidery; any additions to the design, including the type and colour of the threads; the method of remounting the embroidery onto a new ground which might indicate who had carried out this work; and the type and design of the trimmings.

Original silk ground

A ribbed silk was discovered under the embroidery, on the upper outer valances, in areas where the silk embroidery threads were worn, lost or degraded. This silk appears to be the ground referred to in 1782 as 'a pale green' (Anon. 1782) and more fully in 1785 as 'the curtains and valances are of rich pea-green corded tabby' (Anon. 1785). This ribbed silk ground (Fig. 2) appeared cream or yellow but the exact colour was difficult to identify. When placed against a green, the ribbed silk appeared to be a very light green but against a yellow, it appeared yellow.

Subsequent silk ground fabrics

By 1795, the guidebook (Anon. 1795) refers to 'the green tabby being very much faded' and that it was to be replaced with a garter blue satin. No evidence of blue silk satin could be found on any of the elements of the bed however. Could it be that the reference to blue was in fact purple but when viewed in certain light it appeared blue? It is possible that the blue period did occur but that 'It would ... have been necessary to remove as much of the blue layer as possible when the embroidery was re-stitched onto the new purple silk, and any evidence would be difficult to identify given the extensive embroidery added' (Westman 2006). The blue period remains a source of debate.

The next reference to the colour of the bed is from 1879, almost 100 years later, when it is described as having 'lilac satin draperies' (Summerly 1879). No documentation has been found to explain the change and, in its absence, there has been a belief that it was a Victorian alteration, possibly responding to the development of the new aniline dye, Perkin's mauve of 1856.

There remain three upper outer valances and one curtain (with the embroidery removed) on the 'lilac' ground. But the colour of this silk satin is hardly lilac – it is richer and very much more purple. The purple silk satin is a shot silk, with a purple warp and salmon pink weft. As the purple silk satin has degraded, the purple warp has been lost and the salmon pink weft has become more dominant. During close examination, two different purple silks were found on the upper outer foot valance which would have received most exposure to light. The first purple silk (Purple 1) had degraded so severely that a second purple silk (Purple 2) was added on top (Fig. 3). The second purple silk satin has also degraded significantly, exposing the salmon pink weft. Faded purple silk, blended with salmon pink, may explain the 'lilac' description.

The final colour scheme was implemented in the second half of the 20th century when the bed was hung in gold satin. Every exterior textile element of the bed, other than the three purple satin upper outer valances, has been remounted onto this gold silk satin.

Changes in design, threads or colours of embroidery silks

When the embroidery was applied to the new silk ground, some areas were overworked with new silks. Some new floral sprays were added, possibly because the original embroidery was so fragile that not all of it could be transferred (see Fig. 4). This is most evident on the upper outer valances but also features on the purple satin curtain. From a conservator's viewpoint, the style of the needlework indicates several hands. This is particularly apparent on the foot valance where the needlework is of varying quality and it is worked not only in silk but also in wool and cotton.

In comparing the sophisticated design and delicate colouring of the original floral embroidery on the inside of the tester dome with the upper outer valances, it is clear that black shading was added after the embroidery was applied to the purple silk ground. It appears heavy and unnecessary but may provide a clue as to the date when the embroidery was reapplied. In addition, the workmanship of those stitching the embroidery to the new silk ground is variable. On some elements, the work is highly skilled and carefully colour-matched threads of an appropriate weight of silk threads were used to execute the embroidery additions. In other areas, the work is less impressive, indicating that this was not the work of professional embroiderers.

Figure 2 Original ribbed silk ground visible under the embroidery (© Historic Royal Palaces) (Plate 89 in the colour plate section).

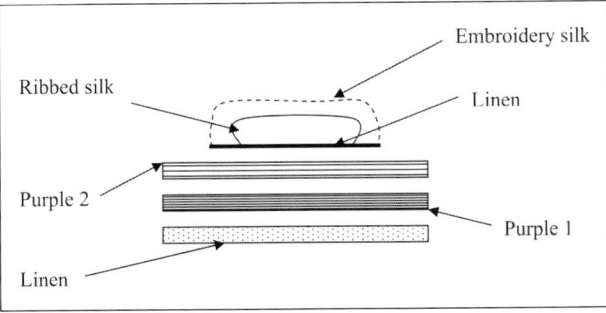

Figure 3 Cross-section of the layers on upper outer foot valance.

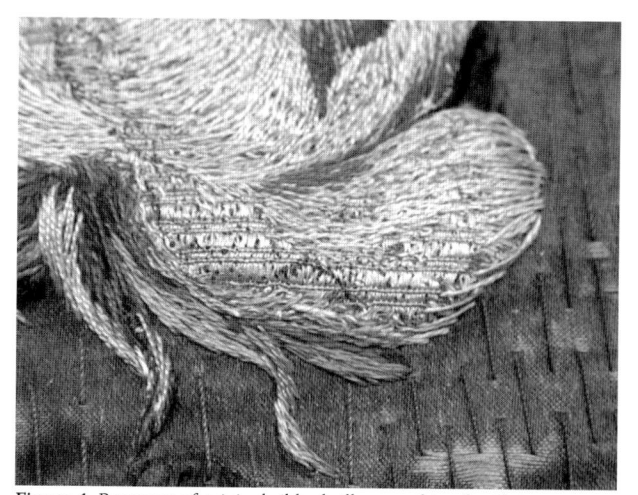

Figure 4 Remnant of original ribbed silk ground too fragile to move (© Historic Royal Palaces) (Plate 90 in the colour plate section).

Figure 5 Bullion fringe from the upper valances (© Historic Royal Palaces) (Plate 91 in the colour plate section).

Style and design of the trimmings

It is not certain when the current trimmings were applied to the valances but the style and design are compatible with the purple satin, which dates from the second half of the 19th century (Fig. 5). The elaborate design of the thick bullion fringe in green and purple, with alternate twist and ball hangers in cream/gold silk, indicates that it would have been expensive. The purple bullion reflects the purple exterior elements, while the cream/gold silk gimps and hangers echo the interior colours. During the 1950s, this heavy fringe was removed from the upper inner valances as their weight was causing physical stress to the weakening valances. It was, however, kept on the upper outer valances.

Treatment dilemma

Developing a treatment strategy for the bed was a challenge because the needs of the object, as perceived by the conservators and by the curators, were subtly different. Both wanted to preserve this beautiful, complex object and to conserve it so that it could be displayed. Central to this discussion was the level of importance attached to the purple period of the bed.

For the conservators, it was important to keep the purple satin, accepting it as a significant part of the bed's history and thereby preserving its integrity. In addition, it was necessary to preserve the object as it is now, to ensure its survival for future generations and to understand the display environment to which it was to be returned. Whereas for the curators, it was essential to undertake further research on the bed in order to make the bed intelligible to the public. With this thought in mind, presenting the bed hangings using a single colour scheme had merit. Undoubtedly the Royal Collection, curators and conservators were in agreement about the importance of the textiles and their long-term survival but how to achieve this and satisfy all parties was less clear.

The key to the debate was the level of significance attached to the purple satin which was believed to be Victorian. Should these purple elements remain, thereby contradicting the overall colour scheme and the treatment strategy set out in the 1950s? Or should they be discarded, thereby going against current ethics in conservation? The debate was further complicated by the condition of the purple silk. This silk was the most severely degraded textile on the bed and its treatment would form the major part of the conservation.

A compromise treatment of placing a dyed semi-transparent material over the purple satin was suggested, in order to make the upper outer valances appear gold from a distance. This was rejected as all the suitable fabrics, such as nylon net, silk crepeline or polyester crepeline would have a different sheen from the silk. Alternatively, a silk satin overlay was considered but the additional weight and the enormous amount of work it would require militated against this option.

Conservation and curatorial ethics and thinking have developed greatly in the last 50 years. There is now an emphasis on preserving the integrity of the object, embracing alterations made by each generation. This change in thinking influenced the final decision which was to keep the purple silk, regardless of how degraded it was, how it might distract from the object's appearance and how complicated it would be to explain to the public. The purple silk would be conserved, the upper outer valances would be returned to display and the object would be interpreted accordingly.

Scientific research

Dye analysis[1] was undertaken on samples of the various silk fabrics from the bed in order to establish their dyestuffs and therefore their original colour. It was hoped that this analysis would shed light on to how to proceed with the treatment and when to date the various colour schemes of the bed. Two sets of dye analysis were undertaken, one investigating organic dyestuffs (at the Royal Institute for Cultural Heritage, Brussels) in 2005[2] and the other focusing on early synthetic dyes and any associated mordants (at the Netherlands Institute for Cultural Heritage (ICN)) in 2006.

Organic dye analysis

Samples of the original ribbed silk and of the purple warp from the first purple silk (Purple 1 in Fig. 3) were taken from the curtain.

The results of the initial organic dye analysis in 2005 (Vanden Berghe 2005) showed that the original ribbed silk ground was dyed with old fustic and Purple 1 with indigoid dye sources. The result for Purple 1 was interesting. It indicated that this fabric, long believed to be Victorian and therefore to contain an early synthetic dye, might not have been dyed with an aniline dye but a combination of other dyestuffs including indigo. Identification of the source of the indigo is difficult as it is not possible to distinguish between natural indigo (*Indigofera tinctoria* L.) and the synthetic variety as they both contain indigotin and indirubin. Therefore the remounting onto the purple could not be specifically dated to the second half of the 19th century.

Treatment

The final treatment proposal for the purple silk was to reverse the previous treatment, removing the trimmings, separating the layers and giving a full support to the purple silk. When reassembling the valances, new lighter (in weight) trimmings would be attached and the valances returned to the bed on open display. Meanwhile, more archival and analytical research would be undertaken.

The upper outer valances were removed from bed. This was a reasonably difficult task as many of the tacks securing the valances to the tester were embedded in the fragile gimp along the upper edge. The three valances had to be taken down simultaneously as the lower bullion fringe was one continuous length, stitched along the lower edge of each valance. The process required 12 conservators and three sets of scaffold towers. Once back in the workroom, the gimp and lower bullion fringe were removed, documented and packed for long-term storage. In doing this, the bullion fringe was compared to the fringe removed from the upper inner valances during the 1950s. The latter was in much better condition, though soiled, and clearly showed the two-toned colouring of green and purple.

Detailed tracings were undertaken of each valance using Melinex overlays to record their condition. The condition of the valance linings was particularly poor, with several significant areas of loss. The previous repair stitching was contributing to the linings' degradation. In order to preserve the remaining purple silk satin, the valances were dismantled by removing the previous repair stitching and each element was conserved separately. The brick stitching was removed working initially from the reverse face. Once all the stitching had been removed, the very fragile silk linings were pinned onto lens tissue, labelled and rolled up for long-term storage.

In removing the linen interlining, the embroidery linen (the layer directly behind the purple silk through which the embroidery is worked) was gradually revealed – and the object spoke! Written in ink, in a cursive hand was an inscription (Fig. 6) giving a date, 17th janvier 1820, a name, Delui or Dellar and

Table 2 Results of organic dye analysis.

Sample	Visual colour	Dye source
Original ribbed silk	Described as pea green or pale green in archive but appears yellow	Old fustic
Purple silk	Described as lilac in archive but appears purple	Indigotin was detected, possibly an indigoid source

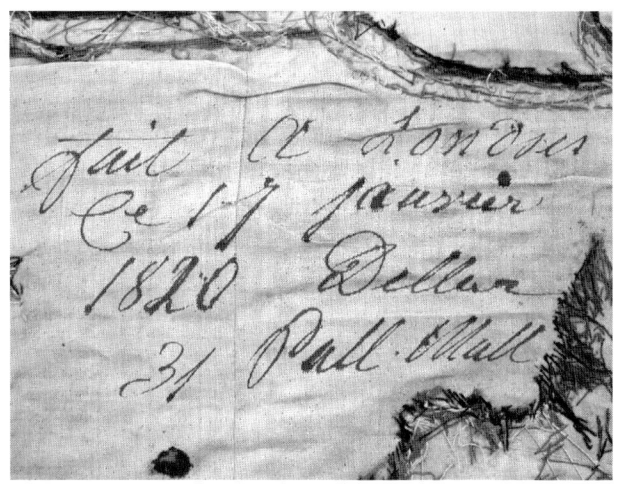

Figure 6 Inscription found on the inside linen of the viewing right upper outer valance (© Historic Royal Palaces) (Plate 92 in the colour plate section).

an address, 31 Pall Mall. The results of the organic dye analysis on the lilac silk (Purple 1) fitted with this date.

Second dye analysis and mordant analysis

It was during the dismantling process that the fabric known as Purple 2 was found on the foot valance. Having discovered this second purple layer, further dye analysis was undertaken on Purple 1 (the first 1820 purple silk) and Purple 2 (applied to replace Purple 1) as well as a purple binding ribbon, also found on the upper foot valance. It was hoped that the latter two might contain an aniline dye and so help to date this part of the treatment.

The three purples had all degraded significantly and it was suspected that the mordant might have contributed to this process. This was especially true for the binding ribbon which exhibited signs of tin weighting, therefore analysis of the mordants was also undertaken on the three purples as well as the original ribbed silk. Although initial testing indicated that the original ribbed silk had been dyed with old fustic, and therefore yellow in colour, the hue might have been changed with a mordant, such as copper, which could explain the archival description of 'pale green' (Westman 2006).

The results were unexpected: all the purple samples contained synthetic dyes. Two synthetic dyestuffs were present in Purple 1: fuchsine which was developed in 1856 and methyl violet which was discovered in 1861, although it was not available commercially until 1866. Purple 2 contained the components very similar to patent blue V which was developed in

Table 3 Results of second dye analysis and mordant analysis.

Sample	Visual colour	Dye source	Mordant
Purple silk satin with 1820 inscription (Purple 1)	Described as *lilac* in archive but appears purple	Fuchsine; methyl violet; indigo	No mordant found
Second purple silk satin (Purple 2)	Brownish purple	Patent blue equivalents; unknown blue/violet dyestuffs of synthetic origin; unknown yellow dyestuffs of synthetic origin	No mordant found
Purple silk binding ribbon	Purple	Rhodamine B; unknown acid violet dyestuff; unknown acid red and/or orange dyestuffs	No mordant found but tin and silicon were found, indicative of tin silicate as a weighting agent
Original ribbed silk	Described as *pea green* or *pale green* in archive but appears yellow	Old fustic	Alum

1888. In the purple binding ribbon, rhodamine B, developed in 1887, was present as well as an unidentified violet dye which has a similar spectrum to azo fuchsine 6B developed in 1902 (van Bommel 2006). The analysis also confirmed that the original ribbed silk was dyed with old fustic and treated with an alum mordant. The presence of alum mordant suggests that Queen Charlotte's state bed was originally hung in a yellow or gold colour. The mordant analysis also proved that the purple binding ribbon was weighted in tin.

Textiles and text

The information gleaned from the archival research, the object and the scientific analysis is, at present, confusing. The discovery of the 1820 inscription in November 2005 instigated further archival research. The address of 31 Pall Mall was the main lead. France and Banting, Upholders to the King, were found to have occupied these premises at this date. Research at the National Archive, Kew,[3] did not record any work undertaken on this bed in 1819 or 1820, although the firm was employed on several other projects for Windsor and St James' Palace during this period. A search through the accounts of the Privy Purse and the Lord Chamberlain's papers for 1819–20 was also unfruitful.[4] The results of the dye analysis undertaken at ICN contradict the 1820 inscription, however, dating Purple 1 to after 1866. So what is the relevance of 1820? It is possible that only minor alterations had occurred in that year, or that the linen, containing the inscription, had been reused from an earlier project.

Conclusion

As yet there are no answers to the conundrum: when, why and by whom was the purple scheme instigated for Queen Charlotte's state bed? Close examination of the object has yielded crucial evidence to bridge the 100-year gap in the archival material however. This information could so easily have been lost or not uncovered. By continuing to question treatments, as laid out in our professional code of ethics, the object had 'voiced' information not found in any archive to date. The analytical work carried out on the dyes, used in the various materials of the bed, has added more pieces to the puzzle. In the conservation of a composite object, the link between the biography of the object and the analytical studies is indispensable. These new pieces of information will offer fresh leads for the archival research.

Perhaps it is wrong to hope for a specific answer to 'why' and 'when'. After all, state beds were objects of status and fashion and for a bed to be hung in worn, even tattered, textiles would have been unimaginable. Therefore changing the colour of the hangings might not need an explanation, as it would be accepted as part of the evolution of the bed to fit with the style of the period. Therefore a concrete answer to 'why' may never be forthcoming but answers to when and by whom may well be revealed with more research.

Acknowledgements

The authors express their thanks to Historic Royal Palaces for supporting the work on this paper and to the Royal Collection for allowing us to publish. This has been a long project involving many conservators and curators over many years. They would particularly like to thank Sir Hugh Roberts for his encouragement and research; Annabel Westman for her comprehensive reports; Sebastian Edwards for his continuing support; Anita Quye, Ina Vanden Berghe and Maarten van Bommel for their scientific analysis; and finally Kate Frame, Kathryn Hallett and their colleagues in Conservation and Collection Care.

Notes

1. All dyestuffs analysis was performed with high performance liquid chromatography coupled with photodiode array detection (HPLC–PDA). To determine the mordants and possible weighting agents used, detection using scanning electron microscopy with an energy-dispersive X-ray spectrometer system (SEM–EDX) was performed.
2. The samples from Queen Charlotte's state bed were sent with samples from other objects in the collection. All the other objects were from the 18th century or earlier and therefore the samples were sent to an organic dye specialist.

3. K. Orfeur and A. Lucas, pers. comm., October 2005.
4. H. Roberts, pers. comm., 22 December 2005

References

Anon. (1782) *Les Delices de Windsore; or a Pocket Companion to Windsor Castle and the Country Adjacent.* J. Pote.

Anon. (1785) *Les Delices des Chateaux Royaux: or a Pocket Companion to the Royal Palaces of Windsor, Kensington, Kew and Hampton Court.*

Anon. (1795) *The Windsor Guide.* Windsor: C. Knight.

Law, E. (1897) *Guidebook Hampton Court.* Conservation and Collection Care Library, Historic Royal Palaces, Hampton Court.

Summerly, F. (1879) *A Complete Hand-Book to Hampton Court.* London: George Bell & Sons.

Van Bommel, M. (2006) *Dyestuff Analysis and Mordant/Weighting Identification of Silk from an 18th Century State Bed.* Unpublished report. Conservation and Collection Care Library, Historic Royal Palaces, Hampton Court.

Vanden Berghe, I. (2005) *Report of Organic Dye Analysis of the Four Sate Beds.* Unpublished report, Conservation and Collection Care Library, Historic Royal Palaces, Hampton Court.

Westman, A. (2003) *Queen Charlotte's Bed, Hampton Court Palace.* Unpublished report. Conservation and Collection Care Library, Historic Royal Palaces, Hampton Court.

Westman, A. (2006) *Queen Charlotte's Bed, Hampton Court Palace.* Report Update. Unpublished report, Conservation and Collection Care Library, Historic Royal Palaces, Hampton Court.

The authors

- Maria Jordan received her postgraduate diploma in textile conservation at the Textile Conservation Centre in 2000. For the last six years she has worked at Historic Royal Palaces based at Hampton Court Palace. Since 2004 she has been the Treatment Supervisor for the Furnishings Section, Conservation and Collection Care, overseeing the conservation of Queen Charlotte's state bed.
- After having worked for four years with ethnographic materials in the collections of National Museum of Ethnology, Osaka in Japan, Mika Takami completed a postgraduate diploma in textile conservation at the Textile Conservation Centre in 2000. She was a postgraduate Mellon Fellow at the Metropolitan Museum of Art, New York in 2000–01 and at the National Museum of the American Indian/Smithsonian Institution, Washington DC in 2001–02 and is currently the Senior Textile Conservator for the Furnishings Section, Historic Royal Palaces.

Address

Corresponding author: Maria Jordan, Conservation and Collections Care, Historic Royal Palaces, Apartment 59, Hampton Court Palace, East Molesey, Surrey KT9 8AU, UK (Maria.Jordan@hrp.org.uk)

Joining forces: the intersection of two replica garments

Hilary Davidson and Anna Hodson

ABSTRACT In 2004 a textile conservator made a toile of an early 17th-century blackwork jacket. This pattern was taken from the original, an extremely fragile and rare garment. At the same time a dress historian reconstructed a late 16th-century underbodice based on textual and visual research. When the two independently created 'replicas' were brought together, a different understanding of the function and shape of the original garments was formed by the way the replicas related physically. The fields of textile conservation and the history of dress are complementary, interdependent, while sometimes remaining distinct yet parallel. This case study demonstrates how the intersection between extant garments and bibliographic sources can raise questions for both fields about the value of using replicas as a research tool, and how the work of conservators and makers of replica garments benefits from greater mutual interaction.

Keywords: garment, replica, reconstruction, blackwork, toile, interdisciplinary

Introduction

This paper discusses two replica[1] garments, one made by a textile conservator and the other by a dress historian during the completion of their respective MA degrees at the Winchester School of Art, University of Southampton in 2004. Hodson worked on a conservation treatment for a fragile and degraded early 17th-century blackwork jacket in the collection of the Gallery of Costume, Manchester that involved making a toile of the jacket to handle while constructing the mounts and support. Davidson began from a textual source to bring to life flat patterns in an early Spanish tailor's book (Alcega 1999). Although these were two different starting points for construction, with different research aims, it was found that where the two replicas physically interacted, the results were more interesting and useful than either maker could have foreseen. After explaining the development of the individual projects, the discussion moves to exploring observations made about the garments when they came together, questions and issues these results raised and then considers the benefits of closer collaboration between the disciplines.

The jacket

The embroidered blackwork jacket that formed the basis of the textile conservator's replica has been on loan to the Gallery of Costume, Platt Hall (part of Manchester Art Galleries) since 1965 (Fig. 1). It is part of the Filmer Collection, once owned and worn by Sir Edward and Lady Elizabeth Filmer, who died in 1629 and 1638 respectively. Their memorial brass in Otterden, Kent, also depicts their nine sons and nine daughters. Ownership of the collection was transferred to the Gallery of Costume in 2003 by a descendant of the original Filmer family in lieu of tax. The collection is important because it has over 50 items dated between 1600 and 1640 including rare survivals such as plain linen ancillary items as well as some very fine pieces like the blackwork jacket.[2]

'Blackwork' is a term used to describe a style of embroidery fashionable in England in the 16th and early 17th century. This style employed a counted thread embroidery technique worked in black silk on a white linen ground to create intricate monochrome, geometric and naturalistic patterns. The jacket's design of regular diagonals and rows of repeating carnations, pomegranate, Tudor rose and honeysuckle, can be seen in Figure 1. The jacket came to the Textile Conservation Centre (TCC) in Winchester for treatment and the conservation brief was to make the jacket safe for storage, while making it accessible as part of a study collection.

Condition assessment and conservation strategy

The blackwork jacket is in poor condition because the silk embroidery is extremely degraded and friable. The silk fibres are structurally weak and any movement or manipulation of the jacket causes the fibres to break, leading to loss in the form of black powder. In some areas the embroidery has been lost completely, for example, on the shoulders, the top of the shoulder guards, the top folded area of the collar and down the front of the garment. This loss of silk is consistent with the fall of light from above and is likely to be the result of exposure to light while the jacket was on display. It is thought that the jacket was loaned to the Grosvenor Gallery, London, during

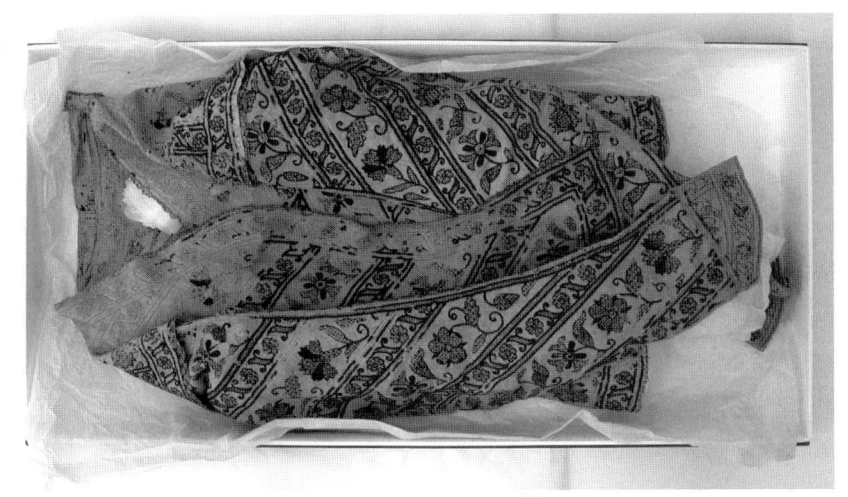

Figure 1 Blackwork jacket before conservation intervention (photo © Textile Conservation Centre) (Plate 93 in the colour plate section).

the late 19th century for an exhibition of English embroidery. No evidence has been uncovered to confirm its display and any further information would greatly contribute to the record for the garment. Due to the extreme fragility of the black silk the jacket had not been made available for use by researchers. Exceptions to this rule were made on the merit of the researcher; dress historian Janet Arnold, for example, came to study it and took a pattern from the jacket.[3]

The deterioration of the black silk fibres could have been caused by light exposure; however, as the powdering of the fibres is uniform across the jacket, another cause is suggested. The dyeing process for black dyes in the 16th and 17th centuries used tannins with an iron mordant (Finch 1996: 57). Tannins are acidic and their presence causes primary degradative chemical changes to silk (Timar-Balaszy and Eastop 1998: 95). The presence of metal ions, such as the iron mordant, accelerates deterioration and explains the uniformity of the degradation. Photo-oxidation caused by exposure to light also accelerates in the presence of acidity and metal ions, reinforcing the likelihood that the significant areas of loss resulted from this cause (Timar-Balaszy and Eastop 1998: 95). The black silk element of the jacket is degraded to the point where nothing can be done to stabilise it structurally or chemically. The loss of the black thread inherently compromises the pattern and the process will continue, resulting eventually in the disappearance of the embroidery, as has occurred on other examples of this technique. In her book on blackwork, Joan Edwards (1980: 2) refers to a hood in the collection of the Embroiderers' Guild, Hampton Court Palace. This hood is only recognisable as an example of blackwork because a few tufts of black silk can be found in the needle holes and the pattern can only be interpreted by the viewer 'joining the dots'.

The jacket arrived at the TCC in its conservation-grade storage box (Fig. 1). The box was too small to accommodate the garment without folding, so the jacket had been stored with its sleeves folded inwards and on top of its torso. This allowed the sleeves, which retained the majority of the remaining embroidery, to be studied without handling. This method of storage, however, made the cut and construction of the jacket less accessible. Consequently, a preventive conservation strategy was adopted with the following objectives: to bring together all existing documentation relating to the jacket, including locating Janet Arnold's notes and pattern; to maximise visual access through the way that the jacket is housed in its box while reducing the necessity for handling; to document the jacket thoroughly to provide information for researchers on the cut, construction and embroidery of the jacket, sourced from Arnold's notes and the conservator's observations; and to construct a toile to assist in the fabrication of an internal support and padded base upon which the jacket would sit for storage and study.

Process

The retrieval and use of Janet Arnold's research was part of the conservation intervention. No evidence of her notes or pattern draft (the sketch made of the shape and pieces for a clothing pattern) were found in her personal archive, however, which was bequeathed to the TCC in 2002 and is held at the University of Southampton.[4] The importance of having a pattern of the jacket's cut was seen as central to the conservation strategy, so it was decided that in the absence of evidence from Arnold's earlier work a new draft of the shape should be made, employing a method outlined in *A Guide to Accurate Measuring* by J. Wood (2001: 18). Threads were laid along the grain of the linen at measured intervals and the length of these lines drafted onto graph paper to make the pattern. A toile[5] was then constructed from the pattern using a cotton downproof fabric. This material was chosen for its tightly woven structure and resultant stability, making it less likely to distort through handling than a textile more similar to that of the jacket's original linen. No attempt was made to replicate historic construction techniques and so machine stitching was used to make the toile. The intention was not to make a replica but to create a toile for use as a tool to construct an internal support. The toile can also function as a surrogate for the delicate original, however, as it replicates its proportions and dimensions (Fig. 2).

The conservation intervention was considered successful. Increased visual access was achieved, the fragile structure received more support and more information can now be

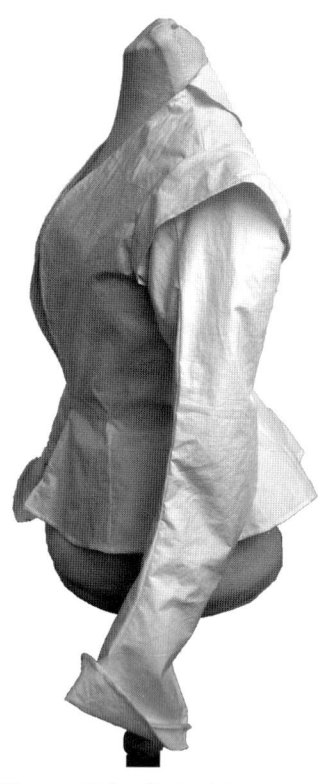

Figure 2 Toile of jacket (photo © Textile Conservation Centre).

Figure 3 Jacket after the conservation intervention (photo © Textile Conservation Centre) (Plate 94 in the colour plate section).

retrieved from the jacket without handling it. This is facilitated by storing the garment with the documentation and notes compiled during the intervention, the new pattern, and the manipulatable toile.

The bodice

In 2004, the Pasold Research Fund (UK) generously funded the recreation of two late 16th-century Spanish garments, a farthingale and a pair of bodys. The word 'bodice' which derives from the term will be used throughout this paper for clarity. The results of the project were displayed at the conference *Textile Cultures: Spain and England from 1500* held in Winchester in 2004 as part of the celebrations of the 450th anniversary of the marriage of Mary Tudor and the future Philip II of Spain. The replica formed one part of the recreator's continuing research into dress during the long reign of this king.

Spain shares the dearth of extant Early Modern clothing that makes the Filmer jacket so valuable. Visual sources record how the influence of the Hapsburg Empire in the mid-16th century made the Spanish fashions of the time widely emulated elsewhere, especially in England with its royal links to Spain through Katharine of Aragon, then her daughter Mary's marriage (Arnold 1988: 123). The resources on which to base reconstructions of Philipian Spanish clothing would be minimal if not for the existence of the master tailor Juan de Alcega's *Tailor's Pattern Book*, which was first published in Madrid in 1580 and revised in 1589. The Victoria and Albert Museum holds an original copy of this later edition. A facsimile with translations was first published in 1979 and remains in print (Alcega 1999). The book is a guide not to style but to the economical layout of patterns on fabrics of different widths for a range of clothing and textiles. The patterns in the layouts are marked with measurements according to the local Castilian system and cannot be considered exact due to the scale of the book and its intention mainly for a readership of professional tailors (Alcega 1999: 15).

Among limited sources, Alcega's work provides an understanding of the structures behind Spanish clothing of the period, and, by extension, most contemporary fashionable western European attire. His text shows some of the layers of clothing invisible in formal portraits, balancing the difficulties presented by object- and art-historical based research to this period. There is a particular value in Alcega's information on undergarments. Both Spanish and English portraits show the cone shape of women's dress given by the farthingale (a hooped

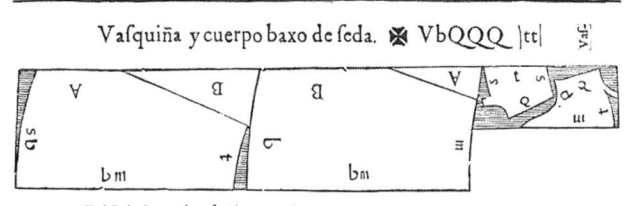

Figure 4 Alcega's pattern page (reproduced by kind permission of Ruth Bean Publishers).

underskirt) but Alcega provides the only known pattern for this mostly concealed garment.

While the replica displayed at the 2004 conference included such a skirt, this paper is concerned with the accompanying bodice. Figure 4 shows one of four pages in which Alcega lays out a *vasquiña*, or underskirt, and a *cuerpo baxo de seda*, or low bodice made of silk. The garment seems to be an evolution from the sleeveless kirtles of the early 16th century.[6] Although the replica garment was made as what is later termed a corset, subsequent research suggests this could be incorrect, and that the bodice combined the functions of two garments: a boned undersupport and the undergown or kirtle worn over it. The low-necked bodice is seen as an outer garment in portraits of the mid-16th century, such as Moro's 1551 portrait of Philip II's sister, Maria of Austria. By Alcega's time, it is replaced in portraits of the king's wives and daughters by the high-necked *cuerpo alta* with a tall collar supporting the ruff, and the *cuerpo baxo* became an undergarment again.

Construction

In her *Patterns of Fashion: The Cut and Construction of Clothes for Men and Women c1560–1620*, Janet Arnold gives the details for a surviving corset of the Pfalzgräfin Dorothea von Neuberg c.1598 (1985: 46). It has stitched boning channels visible on the outside of the garment, tabs on the lower back edge, and space for a wooden busk to create the distinct lower central point. Great Wardrobe accounts for Mary Tudor and Elizabeth I record 'paire[s] of bodys' in coloured velvets and brocades; the use of a rich fabric follows similar materials used for earlier kirtles (Arnold 1988). The English information fills in for the absence of similar Spanish sources. Arnold also records a 17th-century stomacher in the Rocamora Collection, Barcelona that is stiffened with bents, a kind of thin reed, although the Pfalzgräfin appears to have used whalebone support (Arnold 1988: 46). The reproduction bodice shown finished in Figure 5 therefore uses small bundles of bents (whalebone being impractical), following the boning pattern of the Pfalzgräfin item, a carved wooden busk and lower-edge tabs. The outer fabric is crimson velvet, lined and interlined with linen.

Unlike the toile of the blackwork jacket, the use of historic construction techniques was a primary concern. The recreation bodice is entirely hand-stitched with linen and silk threads using back stitch, stab stitch and whip stitch, and then edged in buff suede following Wardrobe accounts of leather bindings. The back and side laces were hand-woven on an inkle loom, finished with aiglets of rolled brass, and are threaded through pierced eyelets overstitched with silk according to the placing of the Pfalzgräfin corset.

Findings

The first point of interest derived from the recreation was the strength of the bents as a structural support. They were light and flexible, reducing the weight of the bodice, and gave as much stiffness and body-moulding as modern boning substitutes (such as spring steel). Putting the 1–3 mm diameter reeds into bundles of approximately 5–10 gave them greater strength once inserted down the 6 mm boning channels. The reeds did not break and moulded with the body's warmth, like whalebone.

This research finding came from reproducing the material parameters of the garment. The first significant value of the textual basis for this replica was shown through a detail of the cut of the pattern (Fig. 4). The particular curved shape of the front shoulder strap piece did not make immediate sense while drafting the pattern and seemed counter-intuitive. Accuracy, however, required following the period pattern. When the bodice was complete and tried on the cut became clear. A straight strap holds close to the body, cutting into the flesh. The external curve, when appearing to be straightened by its connection with the back strap section, sits proud of the arm joint giving it a greater range of movement than such a wide neckline would otherwise permit (Fig. 5). By turning the two dimensions into three, the skill of the cut becomes clear and illuminates the international reputations of Spanish tailors. Conversely, having this information caused revised considerations of the construction of other 16th-century dress, particularly the very narrow straps seen at the edge of the bodices in portraits of Tudor women. This small yet useful detail may not have been discovered independently during construction without using a period pattern because a straight strap resembles what can be seen in the pictures.

Another aspect of the garment's functioning revealed by researching the bodice in three-dimensional form is its creation of an illusion. Unlike later corseting garments of the 18th and 19th centuries, the objective is not so much waist reduction as torso-shaping and stiffening. The narrow waist is largely a visual trick created by an extended point and an

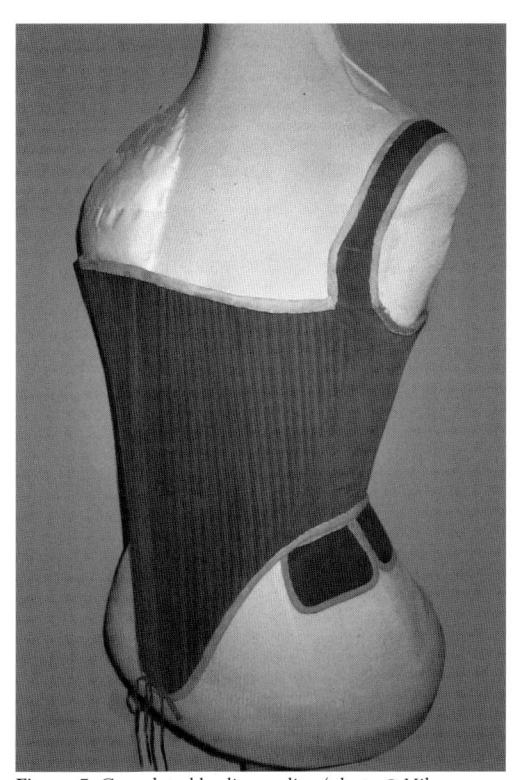

Figure 5 Completed bodice replica (photo © Hilary Davidson) (Plate 95 in the colour plate section).

artificial waistline higher than the natural waist (Fig. 5). The natural waist is relatively free, although the ribs are more restricted. The bodice fits, rather than constricts, and so the wearer is not trying to anchor herself against the garment when the back laces are tightened. It is possible, with a mirror and dexterity, for the wearer to do them up. Some effort is needed, but the length of the laces facilitates this. A portrait of Elizabeth Vernon, Countess of Southampton c.1600 (Arnold 1988: fig. 164) is rare in its depiction of undergarments, and shows a front-lacing pair of bodies, which would be easier for the wearer to fasten. In the absence of more informal portraits, Alcega's documentary source formed an effective alternative starting point for practical research into 16th-century clothing. It was discovered that a stiffened bodice, a garment emblematic of bodily restriction, allowed its wearer a greater range of movement than its rigid appearance would suggest, and could potentially have been fastened without the help of another person.

The jacket and the bodice together: the process of intersection

After being carried out in parallel and completed independently, these two projects came together unintentionally. The bodice was taken to the TCC to be mounted on a form for display at the conference. The mannequin and mounting materials were in the same room in which the jacket was being conserved. At this point, the proximity in era of the two garments was realised – c.1590 and 1620 respectively – and the toile was arranged over the mounted bodice because it looked like they could sit well together. It was the experiment of a moment without prior design.

Putting the garments together made both makers consider things that neither would have considered separately, and raised questions and discussions that only appeared with the interrelationship of the garments. It is not only what was learnt but also the fact that it was learnt from this conjunction that highlights where assumptions lie and how they can be challenged.

The intersection of the two garments resulted in the following practical observations. First, the length of the jacket back had seemed disproportionately short to the rest of the garment when seen in the toile alone; putting it with the bodice made sense of the shape of the outer garment. The top point of the godet (a triangular insert giving fullness) on the back of the jacket matches the bottom edge of the bodice, flaring out where the undergarment's tightness ends (even though the originals were made 20 to 40 years apart). The short back of the bodice could be an effect of changes in body size over four centuries. It supports the illusory waist reduction mentioned above, however, and exactly reflects the proportionate back-waist lengths shown in sculptures.

Secondly, observations of other extant garments, patterns (Waugh 1968; Arnold 1985) and jackets in paintings, revealed many round or V-shaped necklines. The Filmer jacket has an unusual shape of neckline which appears to have no comparison. The neckline curves smoothly from the centre front line to the collar. Unlike the other jackets, there is no clear point

Figure 6 Toile and bodice together on model (photo © Hilary Davidson).

at which the closure of the garment begins (Fig. 6). From the beginning of the conservation intervention, this obvious difference was fascinating, especially as no indication remains of how the garment fastened, whether by ribbons, hooks, pins or other means. It was when the jacket toile was put over the bodice that the ingenuity of the neckline's cut was revealed. The top edge of the bodice threw into relief the natural meeting point of the two curved front sections. This was not evident when the jacket lay flat or when tried on a mannequin or model without a period undergarment. The apex of the curve matches the top of the bodice, after which the two front sections meet smoothly down the centre front.

Thirdly, this observation is strengthened by the fact that the bodice, of a certain shape and size, has also demonstrated a surprising adaptability of fit. It has so far been worn by four women, and a mannequin, of different heights and proportions. Providing the back edges were laced fully closed, the bodice consistently achieved the required cone shape, as it gives structure independent of the natural shape of the body underneath. The busk creates a straight line from the waist to the bust that disregards the body's curves. This refashioning provides a basic uniformity of shape and structure that can be exploited by external garments, like the jacket. On the same range of wearers, tested after realising this material relationship, the toile alone was ill-fitting and shapeless by comparison with the universal fit it achieved when relying on the bodice's body-regulating framework.

The congruencies between the two garments may be coincidental and the information they apparently impart may be of little real value but the considerations the contact stimulated have furthered the scope of each maker's research, which has benefited both projects and identified new areas for study. The meeting of these two replicas emphasises the value of appropriate foundations for displaying historic garments and reiterates issues of how this affects the interpretation of dress. It also highlights considerable gaps in information about how this kind of jacket was worn. Furthermore, the evidence of this toile, over this replica bodice, has helped the makers reconsider the way each looks at similar extant garments and their representations.

However, the first point of reference for developing the bodice was a document, not extant objects, although these were used as further references. The resulting recreated garment has been as valuable, but in a different way, as one based primarily on material evidence, like the jacket. Turning to documents and taking print into three dimensions can lead to the creation of a new object when extant objects are lacking, expanding research values through subsequent interrelationships. This may seem self-evident, but presents a new mode for study. Making up and using an 18th-century laundry ink recipe, for example, provides a 'discourse' between the written recipe and domestic textiles with laundry markings that enhances the understanding of both text and object. Other textile-centred researchers employing recreation in their studies note the frequent and often surprising new insights this practice can bring. One example is Beverly Gordon's 'The hand of the maker: the importance of understanding textiles from the "inside out"' (2002).

In turn, recreation tests and validates the document's worth through the correspondence with material evidence. The contexts behind the cut of the bodice became immediately apparent when the pattern was used according to its original purpose, and the document-based replica garment supported knowledge about dress of the period gained from visual and material sources. Informed, academic, experimental research can re-evaluate well-mined sources. Carefully researched replicas can form a useful adjunct to more traditional methodologies yielding much worthy data, especially during the medieval and Early Modern periods, with comparatively few surviving pieces.

These garments represent two ends of a recreation spectrum. The bodice is entirely hand-stitched with hand-woven lacings and period fabrics. Every detail of it has been researched to present the most informed version of an historic garment in the time available (a crucial factor in reproduction). The jacket toile, on the other hand, presents a version of the original that in no way attempts to replicate it. The textile is deliberately dissimilar in weight, weave count and fibre; it is sewn by machine and has not even a rough sketch of the surface decoration. The main goal of its construction was to assist in creating an internal support for the jacket. Even with these limitations, its secondary unconsidered use as a wearable garment made the toile very useful and interesting.

Experimenting with the toile made the conservator consider the historic object in a different way. The conservation of objects can often be approached in a detached manner especially if, like the blackwork jacket, the object is particularly vulnerable. The toile provided a starting point to explore suppositions about the garment and integrate it in contexts outside the necessities of the conservation intervention. The intersection of the two garments greatly extended the potential of the toile beyond its intended use as a tool for mount-making. Now that it is stored with the original in the gallery's collection, the toile that resulted from a conservation intervention has also reinvigorated the object's value as a source through the toile's ability to stand in for the delicate original. It can be handled and explored while the jacket cannot. This widens access and participation by visitors, scholarly and otherwise, to the gallery's collection.

The dress historian benefited from a conservator's treatment choices and systematic insight into construction to consider the jacket's use as a garment and as a representative of early 17th-century clothing culture, beyond its first clarification of the functions of the bodice. The detailed examination made during the conservation intervention can provide immediate answers to questions about the jacket relating to clothing culture, such as did it ever contain a lining and was it made as a jacket or altered from another garment, without engaging in damaging investigation or frustrated speculation.

Particularly in museum collections, the contribution made by all of the users and stewards is enriching. The information gathered by the conservator has been left with the original object, so preserving the research of one investigator for the benefit of those who follow. Whether later findings confirm or disagree, it builds an archive around the object documenting who has looked at it and for what purpose. For something like the jacket, which is on an unpreventable path of deterioration, archival evidence will eventually be all that is left of the object. A replica or toile is a practice-based piece of research that simultaneously creates an object and forms a physical archive of information, a new textile resource.

Conclusion

The conclusions encompass a number of points. First, it was established that documentary sources can be evaluated through physical testing to assess their value at providing information that may be missing materially to support extant object-based evidence. It was found that the function of the toile as a conservation tool can be extended beyond its primary purpose to supplement research into the original object, by fulfilling an aspect of the object that the original no longer can. The possibility of trying on a replica returns the function of wear to a fragile historic piece of clothing. Since this is the main purpose of most garments, good replicas can be complementary, not secondary, in study value to the original items they reproduce. Additionally, a toile can initiate speculative discussion. This has implications for similar conservation tools that can add to the original object for future research. It will also be of interest in the future to compare the jacket patterns made by Arnold and by Hodson and evaluate any differences in the interpretation of a single object.

Replicas can present new kinds of material research. The function of recreated items of dress, which are used increasingly by museums, can be as part of a handling collection, to complete an outfit or provide correct underpinnings. In these situations the replica supports an historic garment and its own value is secondary. What the jacket–bodice intersection demonstrates is that two replica items coming together can be of primary value. Comparing the research results embodied by two carefully made replicas can be the physical equivalent of comparing published scholarship within an article. The lack of handling restrictions on a replica allows the testing of theories and a different kind of investigation into the original garment. Museums can therefore view the making of replica garments as a research opportunity that extends their collections' potential.

The results of this accidental exchange caused by two students working in the same building brought home empirically the value of working together during the research or conservation intervention process and how effectively a lateral insight into the same subject can change perceptions. We graduated with a heightened awareness of the benefits of joining forces and have taken this attitude with us. Although coming from different approaches, the intersection of two replica garments was enlightening and beneficial to the sometimes disparate research purposes of textile conservation and dress history. Understanding of both objects developed in ways that were unforeseen and may not have arisen without the meeting of the two garments. This happy accident has broadened each maker's considerations of future research methodologies and the benefits of cross-disciplinary collaboration.

Notes

1. The term 'replica' is used throughout to mean the reproduction or recreation of an original historic garment in some form.
2. Information gathered from the Gallery of Costume object records, some of which can also be found on the website: www.manchestergalleries.org/our-other-venues/platt-hall-gallery-of-costume/the-collection/.
3. Verbal communication with Anthea Jarvis, Principal Curator of Costume (retired), the Gallery of Costume, Platt Hall Manchester.
4. Arnold's pattern for the jacket and accompanying notes made in November 1986 were located among personal papers in late 2006 by her literary executor. Pers. comm. to Anna Hodson, 6 February 2007.
5. A toile is the dressmaking term for a garment made up in plain fabric to test a pattern's fit.
6. See Mikhaila and Malcolm-Davies (2006) for a discussion of this garment, based on replica work.

Acknowledgements

The authors would like to thank Anthea Jarvis and Dr Miles Lambert, Gallery of Costume, Platt Hall, Manchester City Galleries; Dr Lesley Ellis Miller; the Pasold Research Fund; and the AHRC Research Centre for Textile Conservation and Textile Studies, especially Dr Maria Hayward, Frances Lennard and Mike Halliwell.

References

Alcega, de J. (1999) *Tailor's Pattern Book, 1589: Libro De Geometria, Pratica Y Traca*, J.L. Nevinson (ed.), J. Pain and J. Bainton (trans.). Carlton: Ruth Bean Publishers [facsimile edition with translations, first published 1979].

Arnold, J. (1985) *Patterns of Fashion: The Cut and Construction of Clothes for Men and Women c1560–1620*. London: Macmillan.

Arnold, J. (1988) *Queen Elizabeth's Wardrobe Unlock'd*. Leeds: Maney.

Edwards, J. (1980) *The Second of Joan Edwards' Small Books on the History of Embroidery: Black Work*. Dorking: Bayford Books.

Finch, K. (1996) 'The ICOM Costume Committee in Stavanger, 1995', *Conservation News* 60: 57.

Gordon, B. (2002) 'The hand of the maker: the importance of understanding textiles from the "inside out"', in *Silk Roads, Other Roads*. Proceedings of Textile Society of America Symposium [electronic PDF format post-print].

Mikhaila, N. and Malcolm-Davies, J. (2006) *The Tudor Tailor: Reconstructing 16th Century Dress*. London: Batsford.

Timar-Balaszy, A. and Eastop, D. (1998) 'Role of tannins in the deterioration of fibres', in *Chemical Principles of Textile Conservation*, 95–6. Oxford: Butterworth-Heinemann.

Waugh, N. (1968) *The Cut of Women's Clothes 1600–1930*. New York: Theatre Art Books/Methuen.

Wood, J. (2001) *A Guide to Accurate Measuring*. London: Historic Royal Palaces.

The authors

- Hilary Davidson is currently Curator of Fashion and Decorative Arts at the Museum of London and Network Facilitator for the AHRC Early Modern Dress and Textiles Research Network. Since graduating from the MA History of Textiles and Dress at Winchester School of Art, University of Southampton in 2004, she worked as a freelance dress historian making replica historic clothing for museums and educational centres within the Hampshire County Museums and Archives Service, drawing on previous professional experience. Hilary was also Visiting Lecturer in the History of Art and Design, and Textiles, Fibre and Fashion at Winchester until 2007.
- Anna Hodson is currently an Andrew W. Mellon Fellow in Textile Conservation at the National Museum of the American Indian, Smithsonian Institution, Washington, DC, USA. She completed an MA in textile conservation at the Textile Conservation Centre, University of Southampton in 2004, and was awarded the Worshipful Company of Woolmen's prize for achievement in 2005. After graduating, Anna undertook a Historic Scotland Internship at the National Museums of Scotland, Edinburgh, and the Marischal Museum, Aberdeen, Scotland.

Addresses

- Hilary Davidson, Curator of Fashion and Decorative Arts, Museum of London, 150 London Wall, London EC2Y 5HN, UK (hdavidson@museumoflondon.org)
- Anna Hodson, Andrew W. Mellon Fellow in Textile Conservation, The National Museum of the American Indian, Smithsonian Institution, 4220 Silver Hill Road, Suitland, MD 20746, USA (hodsona@si.edu)

Information uncovered by conservation

Understanding the full story: acknowledging intimate interactions of textiles and text as both help and hindrance for preservation

Cordelia Rogerson

ABSTRACT Frequently texts or words make up documentary evidence accompanying textiles as labels, letters and documents. It is expected that conservators take written components into account during treatment because they embody context or significance and form part of the integrity of objects. Professional codes of practice for conservators dictate that integrity, however it is fashioned, must always be retained. Moreover, the existence of text with textile can, in some cases, present difficult decisions since embracing the 'text' can limit treatment choices for the textile. This paper argues that in endeavouring to adhere as closely as possible to codes of practice, conservators may fall into the trap of conventional wisdom, thereby preventing the most realistic solution being used. Treatment decisions may be well meaning but the outcome may have other less favourable implications. To ensure solutions are practical as well as sensitive, more adaptable ethics and a wider acknowledgement of the role of judgement are advocated. Case studies of a prayer flag, a silk-covered book and a painted scutcheon are analysed. The paper is intended to provoke thinking in conservators, custodians and textile historians alike to encourage pragmatic preservation choices in the future.

Keywords: preserving integrity, conventional wisdom, adaptive ethics, compromise, codes of practice

Introduction

Frequently texts or words make up the documentary evidence associated with historic textile artefacts in the form of labels, letters and documents. These texts may be functional, they may be part of the original object or they may represent significant later additions. The text component may consist of textile materials or, more commonly, non-textile elements such as paper. Conservators routinely take into account the written components as well as the textiles when developing treatment strategies because they embody the history, context or significance that contributes to the value of the textile. Their aim is to preserve the so-called integrity or wholeness of an object and this concept is a key objective and a fundamental constituent of best practice for conservation.

This paper examines the paradox that the existence of text or words on historic textiles, when they are intimately linked, can both help and hinder their conservation and their long-term preservation. While the existence of text with textiles may be enriching, they may also adversely affect each other by limiting interventive conservation treatment options or preventing full interpretation of either component. Perhaps more importantly, where textiles and text interact with some complexity, the prevailing ideal of 'preserving the integrity' can be applied during treatment without realistic reflection on long-term outcomes. Critical reflection on the results of treatments where textiles and text are found together allows insights into the implications of attempting to adhere to established rules of conduct.

The paper is intended to address conservators, custodians and textile historians alike to offer debate on the nature and outcome of contemporary preservation practices on our textile heritage. In highlighting possible conflicts between textiles and text components, I have deliberately assumed the role of devil's advocate in order to provoke readers into thinking. Moreover, by addressing the challenging process of decision-making in conservation, I intend to encourage pragmatic, informed yet sensitive preservation treatments and to generate realistic expectations of conservation endeavours. Three case studies are used to develop the argument: a Tibetan prayer flag, a silk-covered book and a painted scutcheon produced for Oliver Cromwell's funeral. The opinion expressed within the paper is mine and it is founded on personal experience and some questions and dilemmas that have been encountered during a 10-year career as a practising textile conservator and tutor.

Preserving the integrity of objects

The concept of preserving the integrity of objects is fundamentally ideological because it represents an ideal or a perfect circumstance that should be aimed for. The mantra of preserving the integrity of artefacts is stipulated in professional codes of practice. *ECCO Professional Guidelines* (European Confederation of Conservator-Restorers Organisations), the document adopted as the code of practice by the recently formed Institute of Conservation (ICON) in the UK, reports 'the conservator-restorer shall respect the aesthetic, historic and spiritual significance and the physical integrity of the cultural heritage entrusted to his/her care' (ECCO 2002). Similarly the American Institute for Conservation of Historic and Artistic Works (AIC) informs its members in the paper *Defining the Conservator: Essential Competencies* that they must 'preserve cultural heritage in a way that retains the integrity of the object ... including its historical significance, context, and aesthetic or visual aspects' (AIC 2003). By my understanding of this official language, conservators are being informed that they should aim to treat an object without changing it or leaving it sullied or corrupted by the treatment it has undergone. Its significance and the evidence it holds, from whatever source, should remain intact. But as the highly experienced conservator Miriam Clavir has pointed out, the concept of integrity is actually not closely defined by these descriptions and the conservator is left to interpret what can be a very broad term (Clavir 2002).

Even though the formal statements seem to be all-encompassing, no mention is made of the judgements a conservator faces on a daily basis and that are an essential part of their decision-making when it comes to retaining the object's significances. Every artefact encountered differs in meaning and the so-called integrity of each is distinct. For example, is electrical insulation tape across the face of a torn painted banner a significant addition or an unsightly rudimentary repair? Will removing the tape destroy evidence or ultimately improve interpretation and enable effective conservation treatment? The conservator is left to grapple with the often incomplete provenance of the object and their conscience on such matters.

Past Chairman of the International Institute for Conservation (IIC), Andrew Oddy, maintains that 'numerous attempts have been made to codify these rules, but all are doomed to failure because the approach to conservation can never be generalised' (Oddy 1992). Presumably Oddy has witnessed this in practice given his decades of experience. A professional code, by nature, necessarily draws together common practices that encompass an almost infinite number of variations of objects and circumstances and is potentially problematic as a result. The conservator is forced to become an arbitrator between the ideal presented in the codes of practice and the unique object they are faced with in the conservation laboratory.

Tibetan prayer flag

A block-printed cotton prayer flag exemplifies that in some cases preserving the integrity of an artefact that has both textile and textual components is apposite, straightforward and it unquestionably allows us to gain more knowledge and understanding of the artefact and its history (Fig. 1). In this case the codes of practice can be directly and appropriately applied. The flag belongs to the Economic Botany Collection of the Royal Botanic Gardens, Kew, which is a collection that illustrates human use of plants around the world. All of the artefacts at Kew are made from plant fibre and this cotton prayer flag illustrates how plants support religious practice. It was collected by Sir Joseph Dalton Hooker, a 19th-century botanist on an expedition to the Himalayas between 1848 and 1850. In 1865 Hooker was appointed Director of Kew, a role previously held by his father.[1]

The flag resonates within the collection today, not just because it illustrates the use of cotton fibre but because it was acquired by a member of staff who holds a key place in the evolution of the gardens. This is demonstrated by the handwritten and printed labels which now accompany the flag (Fig. 2). Some of these were written by Hooker while others illustrate various interpretations of the flag over time. Accordingly the text, or labels, is seen as a significant part of the object and when interventive treatment was devised, in order to stabilise the flag long term, the labels received as much attention as the flag itself. Cleaning and a safe storage method were formulated so allowing the labels to be stored and displayed with the flag (Figs 1 and 2) (Textile Conservation Centre 2006).

The labels represent the life that the flag accumulated after it was collected. Moreover, preserving the labels preserved the integrity of the object by acknowledging their contribution to the history of the flag. Although the labels are not attached to the flag, they can be displayed side by side to demonstrate that they belong together. Conservator Dinah Eastop believes that objects do not represent merely a single history but have multiple and competing histories that are open to a dynamic process of varied and changing interpretations (Eastop 2000). Fitting Eastop's analysis flawlessly, the flag does have two distinct histories but in this case they do not so much compete as sit comfortably side by side, physically and intellectually. The

Figure 1 Prayer flag mounted for storage and display, after conservation treatment (Plate 96 in the colour plate section).

Figure 2 Labels associated with the prayer flag, mounted for storage and display (Plate 97 in the colour plate section).

labels can be displayed alongside the flag or, if appropriate, the flag can be exhibited alone.

Eastop also advocates that conservators need to consider the relationship between an object's current and future social meaning, as well as its physical condition, because both of these can change in the future (Eastop 2006). In the case of the prayer flag, tracking its life history from its origins, to the moment of collection, to its presence within the collection illustrates changing functions and the different historical significances associated with these, as well as explicating why they are deemed important now. The conservation of the labels alongside the flag allows room for current interpretations and future variations. Few would argue that the approach taken was not apt for the object but seldom are cases as clear-cut as this. More complex situations that involve the integration of textile and text can result in less satisfying solutions.

Conventional wisdom

Precisely because the idea of preserving the integrity of an object is so well known and used as a justification for treatment choices, it can fall into the category of 'conventional wisdom'. The phrase was popularised by the Harvard economist John Kenneth Galbraith in his book *The Affluent Society*, published in 1958, which examined the state and shape of American society after the Second World War (Galbraith 1999). Conventional wisdom was not designed as a complementary condition but it was used to describe ideas or explanations that are habitually accepted to be true. Furthermore, it is often seen as an obstacle for introducing new theories and explanations and it is said to have a property analogous to inertia.

Conventional wisdom can be either true or false. When applied to the present context, that the integrity of objects should be preserved, I believe it is true. That is, conservators should endeavour to leave the significance of objects unharmed during treatment. Acquiescence and familiarity with this concept, however, can lead to application of the idea without realistic reflection of the long-term consequences of this action. Acceptance of the term within conservation can prove an obstacle for being pragmatic in treatment choices because conservators can be preoccupied with preserving the integrity.

Of course a conservator must strive for the ideal but, because of the many possible variants, ideals have to be adapted in real life. Conservators have to be very sure of their ground when applying these models and be comfortable acknowledging that these high standards cannot always be achieved due to the constraints of the object itself, the surrounding circumstances, such as resources and so forth. Here, conventional wisdom may set in. By allowing the mantra of preserving the integrity to prevail without realistic reflection on the long-term implications of their treatment choices, conservators may think they are doing the correct thing while actually compromising the object's future role or stability.

Analysis of two case studies where textile and paper-based text are closely integrated demonstrates the point. In both cases the paper elements enriched the textile elements, so enhancing the object, while also constraining the outcomes of treatment, so proving a hindrance. Despite these constraints, the conservators adhered to the ideal of preserving the integrity as much as they were able but arguably conventional wisdom was also at work.

Silk fabric-covered book

This book is an 1895 copy of *Koh-i-nur Diamond: Its Romance and History* by Edwin Streeter, a well-known English jeweller and writer of the time. As one of the most famous diamonds in existence the Koh-i-Nur has a long, mysterious history. It has passed violently through the hands of Mogul Indian rulers into those of imperialist Britain, finally coming to rest in a crown made in 1937 for Queen Elizabeth, the Queen Mother. What is important about the text is that Streeter questions the provenance and identification of the diamond. Furthermore, within his various writings Streeter contradicts himself, so leading to ambiguity (Thompson 2004). Streeter's work is well known within jewellery history; it is cited repeatedly and today the book belongs to a well-established corporation within the jewellery field.

The exterior of the book is covered with cream silk fabric and over time this has degraded due to the chemical deteriora-

Figure 3 Silk fabric-covered book, before undergoing conservation treatment (Plate 98 in the colour plate section).

Figure 4 Silk fabric-covered book, as presented after conservation treatment (Plate 99 in the colour plate section).

tion of the silk and the mechanical action and strain of opening and closing the book (Fig. 3). When presented for conservation, the silk was in a poor state and it underwent an adhesive support treatment for stabilisation. Conversely the paper constituents were still in a sound condition. On completion of conservation, the book was prepared for storage including instructions that the still fragile silk should be touched, and the book opened, as little as possible. A bespoke mount was constructed that held the book flat and shut and it was enclosed in an archival-quality box (Fig. 4) (Textile Conservation Centre 2005).

Possibly the silk covering on the book was originally applied to invoke a sensation of luxury when handled and read but today its presence and preservation concerns prevent the book being easily studied. Opening the book will cause further damage to the now preserved silk because it remains vulnerable and any mechanical action from handling and opening would place a strain upon it. Preserving the silk for the future means not opening the book and not viewing the text. While the book can in theory be opened, the conservator has created a physiological and physical barrier to deter such action. In essence, the conservator's concern for the silk covering outstripped the importance of the text within.

In an admirable attempt to preserve the integrity of the object with all its components intact, its significance has been reinterpreted. The textile and text were considered to be equally important components as dictated by the codes of practice and they were treated as such for maximum stabilisation. Moreover, the ultimate outcome of preserving both textiles and text equally has resulted in the textile taking precedence. Unlike the prayer flag, the textile and text of this book cannot be literally laid side by side but remain joined and in conflict with each other.

Can much enjoyment or benefit be gained from the book now it is presented in a manner that discourages any handling and observation of the important text? By accepting the conventional wisdom of preserving the integrity, the function of the book is now restricted and its usefulness reduced. As it stands, the physical integrity of the book is preserved but the integrity is not since the historically significant text is not easily accessible. The book cannot easily fulfil its future role because reading the text is discouraged. In the short term the whole book is preserved and its rate of deterioration slowed, but when evaluating the outcome of treatment in the long term it is possible to conclude that the book no longer has much point in existing.

In this case alternative treatment options are limited. Not preserving the silk will make the book appear aesthetically displeasing and unwieldy to handle and is not really an option. Of the two major components, can a judgement be made as to which element should take precedence and therefore sway treatment choices? That is, perhaps the silk should be sacrificed to ensure the text is accessible. My immediate response to this question is 'no' because as a conservator that judgement is beyond one's professional remit. It really would be a bold conservator who concluded that the textile should remain untreated to ensure the book can still be read. But then again is conventional wisdom being obeyed by saying this? If the concept of preserving the integrity was interpreted as meaning the book should function as it was intended, perhaps that judgement should be made in collaboration with the client. Realistically the text still has resonance without the textile in this case. By adhering to the idea of preserving the integrity in a conventional manner the object is altered. Not every case can be as easily resolved as the prayer flag and revisiting familiar ground in the face of complex decisions has perhaps, as Galbraith predicted, proved an obstacle for progressive thinking.

Perhaps what was missing in this situation was a completely clear indication of the book's future use and role. Other textile book bindings treated recently were done so with the knowledge, as dictated by the custodians, that the textile component would remain secondary to the function of the book.[2] Although possibly detrimental to the textile in the long term, all stakeholders were clear as to the outcome and the conservator treating the textile components did not have to second guess how to apply conservation ethics. Furthermore, ECCO ethical guidelines decree that the primary aim of a conservator is *not* maintaining objects in a functional sense, thereby reinforcing the view that Streeter's volume was conserved adhering strictly to guidelines while the other textile book bindings have actually been embraced by more pragmatic decision-making, thus applying the diktat more loosely.

The issue of maintaining an object's working function via conservation is prone to cyclical arguments because in practice a range of possibilities is evident, despite ECCO's attempts. For decades debates have raged concerning the conservation of musical instruments and historic vehicles (Karp 1979; Mann 1994; Montagu 1987; Museums and Galleries Commission 1995; Newey and Meehan 1999; Thornton 1982). Respectively hailed as beautiful works of art and monuments of innovative engineering as well as objects that are best appreciated if played or driven, preserving physical integrity versus maintaining the function depends on personal opinion (judgement) as well as circumstance. In essence, if the physical integrity is maintained then the operating function is generally forfeited while the opposite is true if a functioning object is enabled. Obviously there will be degrees between these two poles but as with book bindings, one of these standpoints has to take precedence. What is certain is that if conservators unerringly adhere to the ethical guidelines then no historic instrument or vehicle in a collection would ever be heard or seen moving again. Some would rejoice, others would weep, but what is certain is that Oddy's premonition of doomed codes of ethics becomes all too relevant.

Book conservator Edward Cheese recently levelled personal criticism at ECCO's words because he feels it negates what book conservators fundamentally set out to do; stabilise books so they can be used (Cheese 2006). On the other hand, Cheese's remarks can be interpreted as equally intransigent because he only sees books as functioning objects and does not acknowledge that a particularly rare bookbinding could, in theory, take precedence over a text block. Nevertheless, with the current interpretation of conservation codes of practice for Streeter's volume with the text and textile as theoretical equals, they will actually remain a hindrance to each other. This cycle of conflict cannot be easily resolved because the textile has become an obstacle to the text. Judgement and interpretation of guidelines therefore becomes a critical feature for all stakeholders involved with the book but remains an element sidestepped by ECCO and AIC codes of practice.

Majesty scutcheon

The final case study was treated (by me) about six years ago. The textile and text elements within it were again treated as equals and this decision is now under question.

The Majesty scutcheon is a rectangular piece of silk painted in oils depicting a heraldic hatchment surmounted by a crown (Fig. 5). Dating from 1658, the scutcheon forms part of the ephemera created for Oliver Cromwell's state funeral. In all probability it hung, with a number of other scutcheons and banners, in Westminster Abbey as Cromwell's body lay in state. Given that he and his followers deposed and executed Charles I, the use of the crown suggests Cromwell, Lord Protector of the Commonwealth of England, was more regal in attitude and aspiration than he claimed. Furthermore his funeral was modelled on that of James I, the last monarch to be provided with a state funeral and the scutcheon offers material evidence that Cromwell was king in all but name (Sherwood 1997).

Like the prayer flag discussed above, the scutcheon has a second history. Robert Uvedale, a king's scholar from Westminster School, disgusted at the regal nature of Cromwell's funeral is reputed to have looted the scutcheon from Westminster Abbey (Verney 1894: 424). King's scholars at Westminster School owe their education to funding from the royal purse, a tradition that still continues today, and gave Uvedale a good reason to be loyal. His education served him well as he became a renowned horticulturalist who is credited with introducing the sweet pea to England. Meanwhile the scutcheon passed through many generations of Uvedale's family until, in the 1960s, it was donated to Westminster School.[3] By this point it was mounted, framed and had a letter and image adhered to the reverse that outlined its origins and long history. All of these elements represent the second history of the scutcheon and a glass back to the frame allows the text to be read (Fig. 6).

When presented for conservation, the painted silk was shattering in places with some areas of loss. In addition, it had been mounted onto a stretcher and the silk and linen beneath it had sagged in the centre because they were unsupported. By acknowledging the multiple fascinating histories within the object, it was easy to conclude that each component present is significant and must be preserved in order to keep the integrity of the object intact. A strategy was devised to ensure this and it was agreed by the client after discussion.

Surface cleaning and minor consolidation of vulnerable painted regions were undertaken. Weak areas of the silk were supported using adhesive patches as stitching would shatter it further. The frame and glass were treated by a specialist in this field (Textile Conservation Centre 2000). What was not addressed was the sagging central area. The silk was too fragile to be taken off its stretcher and thus it had to be treated *in situ* with patches applied to the front. Any support from the reverse, such as a light padding, would cover the text on the back of the textile and so was deemed inappropriate, since this would compromise the integrity. Options such as a Perspex insert and semi-transparent materials were briefly considered as alternatives to padding but they were discounted on the grounds that these could damage the silk or prevent access to the important text. Instead it was left to droop gently.

At the time I truly believed the correct thing was being proposed and with great sensitivity. Both histories were, after

Figure 5 Front view of the Majesty scutcheon, as presented for conservation (Plate 100 in the colour plate section).

Figure 6 Reverse view of the Majesty scutcheon, showing documents secured to the reverse and the wooden stretcher (Plate 101 in the colour plate section).

all, being presented side by side, or on the front and back, and this was important for the integrity for the object. Even then it was acknowledged that the interaction of textile and text meant that the stability of the textile was compromised in the long term as the silk would continue to shatter along the lines of the stretcher over time. The text was indeed both help and hindrance to the important textile.

Conventional wisdom played a strong role in the judgements made, however, and too great an emphasis was given to the integrity issue. The scutcheon is now displayed in a case to ensure it is handled infrequently and the images on the reverse cannot actually be seen. In the intervening years, continuing evaluation and personal reflection have revealed that if some removable padding had been placed under the silk, but covering the images, this would not have compromised the object at all – in fact the long-term stability of the object would have increased dramatically. The images would not be physically altered and would remain in place and, when necessary, the glass could be removed and padding lifted to view them. While this may require effort, the images cannot be seen on a daily basis anyway and nor are they required to be. The solution being proposed here is merely a gentle adaptation of the conservation principle that was so strongly believed in and adhered to. In this way the text would not be so much of a hindrance to the textile after all. It may seem minor but if this solution had been requested at the time it would have been opposed strongly.

If objects have a dynamic social function, as Eastop argues, then the original treatment of the scutcheon did not acknowledge this. Permitting the text to restrict the effectiveness of conservation treatment and the long-term stability of the silk does not encourage future interpretations. The present solution does not sanction the development of future histories because the silk may not survive long enough for this to occur and the future role for the object cannot be completely predicted however much foresight is applied. Currently, the textile and text are equally important constituents of the scutcheon but with the text influencing the long-term outcomes. Without the textile, however, the text would have little value, so preserving the textile should perhaps have had an edge over reading the text. Much as the silk book binding overtook the information within book, the text on the scutcheon has overtaken the textile. In the case of the latter there is a satisfactory answer. Adding padding to the reverse would protect the silk, redress the balance and allow both textile and text to exist with greater parity.

A continually evolving profession

Salvador Munoz Vinas in his recent book *Contemporary Theory of Conservation* (2004) has recognised a revolution of common sense in conservation and campaigns for the idea of adaptive ethics. Like others he realises that principles cannot be held rigidly but need sensible adjustment on an individual basis, just as the silk-covered book and scutcheon and the cyclical arguments made for books, musical instruments and vehicles demonstrate. Interpretation of Eastop's theories also alludes to this idea. If objects have a dynamic and varied meaning, then their sensitive preservation becomes more difficult through strict adherence to rules. Approaches to treatment may need to be as sinuous as the ongoing interpretations in order to capture and embrace them. Of course conservators must continue to work within an ideological framework, but perhaps a slightly different positioning within that structure is sometimes needed. Judgement is again the key and this is a conservator's most sophisticated tool. There is room for pragmatic decision-making in conservation with simultaneous acknowledgment that decision-making is complex and subject to constant evaluation.

Fortunately some revisiting of the treatment of the scutcheon is straightforward and this highlights the point that selecting treatments that can be reworked later is essential where possible. Re-treatability is an alternative word suggested for another familiar and problematic conservation legend, reversibility. Proposed replacements for this hotly debated term further demonstrate how the profession is as dynamic and varied as the objects we treat and the circumstances in which we treat them.

Chicago University-based economist Steven D. Levitt argues that various actions we undertake in life are ruled by fear. By engaging with our emotions, of which fear is the most potent, an authority on virtually any subject can induce enough fear that we buy into their theory and turn their ideas into our conventional wisdom. He cites the surfeit of conflicting parenting literature to substantiate his argument (Levitt 2005). It may be going too far to argue that professional codes of practice by highly influential and international conservation bodies generate fear in their members. What is suggested, however, is that conservators become anxious to do the right thing in the face of conservation principles, which can allow conventional wisdom to tiptoe in – freedom to think clearly is lost or diminished because conservators are so anxious to do good. It is doubtful whether a conservator who would willingly do the wrong thing exists. Collective feeling and beliefs that have developed within the profession over decades are reflected in, rather than generated by, the written guidelines, so ICON and AIC cannot be blamed for their members acting in predictable human behaviour patterns in the light of their documents.

Finally it is worth distinguishing the widely accepted phenomenon of common sense from judgement. While common sense may seem a prerequisite for a conservator when proposing treatment strategies that are practical as well as sensitive, well-founded judgement is actually more reliable. Common sense is based upon empirical knowledge reported as, 'an endowment of natural intelligence possessed by rational beings' (*Oxford English Dictionary*).[4] Arguably, however, common sense is not actually that common, otherwise a phrase to define and identify those astounding moments of clarity would not be needed. To apply judgement successfully in conservation, on the other hand, requires not just intelligence but a combination of aptitude, learning and experience of a highly specialised subject area. Consequently, conservation is generally taught at postgraduate level and even then full maturity in the subject takes some years. Learning and reflection are ongoing. In order to accurately reflect the routine existence of a conservator, rules of conduct need to acknowledge and include the role of judgement. Perhaps greater freedom to adapt and apply principles will then resonate throughout the profession.

Conclusion

This paper has demonstrated that the interactions of textile and text can be both a great benefit and a danger for historic textiles. They conflict, contradict, assist, enlighten and elucidate the preservation of textiles and their interpretation. The prayer flag was an exemplary case that is surprisingly rare, the silk book binding struggles to find a satisfactory conclusion while the scutcheon demanded greater thought than was available at the time. Both textiles and text should be considered in treatment strategies; preserving the integrity of an object is important but solutions need to be both pragmatic and sensitive. Beware and be aware of conventional wisdom. Sometimes it is right to obey widely held beliefs but on occasion we need to think beyond them. Conservators must be mature enough to admit that the ideal cannot always be achieved and that it is the objects, not the conservator, which must dictate this.

Acknowledgements

The author would like to thank the custodians of the objects discussed for their permission to publish and colleagues at the Textile Conservation Centre for their support and encouragement, particularly Dr Maria Hayward. Also thanks to Jeremy Wakeham for introducing me to the work of Stephen D. Levitt and Kenneth Galbraith.

Notes

1. Julia Steele, Curator Economic Botany Collection, personal interview with Cordelia Rogerson, 17 February 2005.
2. Dr Maria Hayward, Reader, Textile Conservation Centre, University of Southampton, personal interview with Cordelia Rogerson, May 2006.
3. Helen Lloyd, letter to the archivist at Westminster School dated January 1974.
4. *Oxford English Dictionary* [on line] available at http://www.oed.com/ 5 July 2006.

References

AIC (2006) *Defining the Conservator: Essential Competencies* 2003 [online]. Available: http://aic.stanford.edu/about/coredocs/competencies.pdf [4th July 2006].

Cheese, E. (2006) 'A compromising profession? Professional "ethics" and contemporary conservation', *ICON News* 7: 56.

Clavir, M. (2002) *Preserving What is Valued*. Vancouver: University of British Colombia Press.

Eastop, D. (2000) 'Textiles as multiple and competing histories', in *Textiles Revealed: Object Lessons in Historic Textile and Costume Research*, M.M. Brooks (ed.), 17–28. London: Archetype Publications.

Eastop, D. (2006) 'Conservation as social and material', *ICON News* 5: 56.

ECCO (2002) *ECCO Professional Guidelines* 2002 [online]. Available: http://www.icon.org.uk/index.php?option=com_content&task=view&id=121&Itemid= [4 July 2006].

Galbraith, J.K. (1999) *The Affluent Society*. London: Hamish Hamilton.

Karp, C. (1979) 'Restoration, conservation, repair and maintenance', *Early Music* 7(1): 79–84.

Levitt, S.D. (2005) *Freakanomics*. London: Penguin Books.

Mann, P. (1994) 'The restoration for vehicles for use in research, exhibition and demonstration', in *Restoration: Is it Acceptable?*, W.A. Oddy (ed.), 131–8. British Museum Occasional Paper 99. London: British Museum.

Montagu, J. (1987) *The Availability of Instruments in Museums*. Florence: Leo S. Olschki.

Museums and Galleries Commission (1995) *Standards in the Care of Musical Instruments*. London: Museums and Galleries Commission.

Newey, H. and Meehan, P. (1991) 'The conservation of an 1895 Panhard et Levassor and a 1922 prototype Austin Seven motor car: new approaches in the preservation of vehicles', *The Conservator* 23: 11–21.

Oddy, A. (ed.) (1992) *The Art of the Conservator*. Washington, DC: Smithsonian Institution Press.

Sherwood, R. (1997) *Oliver Cromwell: King in All but Name*. Stroud: Sutton Publishing.

Textile Conservation Centre (2000) *Treatment Report on Majesty Scutcheon, TCC 2546*. Unpublished conservation report, Textile Conservation Centre, University of Southampton.

Textile Conservation Centre (2005) *Conservation Report on Silk Covered Book, TCC 2865*. Unpublished conservation report, Textile Conservation Centre, University of Southampton.

Textile Conservation Centre (2006) *Treatment Report on Cotton Cloth with Bhottia Inscription, TCC 2994.1*. Unpublished conservation report, Textile Conservation Centre, University of Southampton.

Thompson, R. (2004) *The Koh-I-Noor Diamond* [online]. Available: http://famousdiamonds.tripod.com/koh-i-noordiamond.html [15 June 2006]

Thornton, P. (1982) *Musical Instruments as Works of Art*. London: Victoria and Albert Museum.

Verney, M.V. (1894) *Memoirs of the Verney Family during the Commonwealth 1650–1660*, vol. III. London: Longman.

Vinas, S.M. (2004) *Contemporary Theory of Conservation*. Saint Louis, MO: Butterworth-Heinemann.

The author

Since graduating from the Textile Conservation Centre in 1997, winning the Woolmens' Prize, Cordelia Rogerson has worked variously as a practising textile conservator and tutor. Currently she is a part-time lecturer at the Textile Conservation Centre and part-time PhD candidate at the Royal College of Art/ Victoria and Albert Conservation.

Address

Cordelia E. Rogerson, The British Library, St Pancras, 96 Euston Road, London NW1 2DB, UK.

The interaction of textile and text: the conservation of a mid-16th-century chemise binding

Maria Hayward

ABSTRACT This paper considers how the velvet chemise binding on a mid-16th-century royal indenture has been damaged as a result of the manuscript being used and stored (TNA E36/277). In addition, it assesses the significance of the various components and describes how these influenced the conservation treatment that was carried out to stabilise the binding, so ensuring continued access to the text.

Keywords: chemise binding, Elizabeth I, illuminated miniature, velvet, laid thread couching, dean and canons of the Free Chapel of St George, Windsor Castle

Introduction

Books and manuscripts with textile bindings bring together a range of materials including paper, parchment, pigments, leather, thread, wood, metal or bone book furniture and fabric. On one level, all the component parts of a book are of equal value. On another, however, it is the text and any accompanying illustrations that give a manuscript its particular importance: they are the reason that the document was created and they are the reason why the manuscript has been kept. The role of the textile is to protect the text and to make the manuscript aesthetically pleasing to its owner. These bindings are vulnerable to mechanical damage caused by use and storage, as well as the effects of environmental factors such as light, humidity and insect activity. In the case of a chemise binding, where the cover extends beyond the boards of the book, the textile component is especially susceptible at the junction between textile and text. This can raise questions as to whether the chemise is original or a later replacement (Hofenk de Graaff 2004: 67). The ways in which one original textile binding has suffered inadvertently at the hands of the manuscript's readers are explored below from the point of view of a textile conservator in the context of the treatment of the tawny velvet chemise on a 16th-century bipartite indenture dated 30 August 1559.

Figure 1 Folio 3 of the indenture with illuminated borders consisting of arabesques, a crown, fleur-de-lis and a cartouche with E R. (National Archive, E36/277 © Textile Conservation Centre, University of Southampton).

The manuscript

The indenture, so named because the top edges of the folios and boards are cut or indented, was drawn up between Elizabeth I (1533–1603) and the dean and canons of the Free Chapel of St George, Windsor Castle (TNA E36/277; Auerbach 1951; Bearman 1996: 183). This manuscript represents a binding agreement between two parties and it consists of a single quire with 15 bifolia, one separate or inserted bifolia and two bifolia making up the endleaves forming a small book measuring 280 × 210 mm. The bifolia or folded sheets are sewn through the fold of each quire (and thus through the combined folds of all bifolia) and then sewn onto six alum-tawed supports which are then laced onto the boards (Craft 2004). The text is written in English, in secretary hand, in black ink, and it is embellished with an illuminated or historiated initial, the royal arms and the arms of St George. In addition, the early folios have illuminated floral panel borders (Fig. 1). Finally there is a narrow white silk ribbon, which passes through the entire text block, with a tail section 232 mm long to which a seal would originally have attached.

The chemise is unlined and made from a square of light to mid-brown silk velvet with cut pile which has a black silk warp, a pale brown silk weft and a pale brown supplementary silk warp. It covers the boards making up the front and back covers of the indenture and extends beyond the margins of the text (extends beyond the boards) on all four sides, from 30 to 170 mm. This means that part of the velvet is held rigid against the text block (against the boards) and part is unsupported. The point where the velvet is not supported by the text (boards) is vulnerable to damage (Fig. 2).

The front and back boards of the book are inserted into alum-tawed pockets stained or dyed red that have been stitched in turn to the velvet chemise. The cut edges of the velvet which project beyond the boards are finished with a narrow plaited cord made from five metal-wrapped threads and five red silk threads. The single-wrapped metal threads consist of thin silver-gilt strips wrapped in an S twist around a silk core. It is hard to determine whether the core is undyed or whether it was originally white or pale yellow. The red silk threads are two-ply, S twist. The threads have been combined to form a striped cord using a technique such as needle weaving or tablet weaving. In each corner of the binding there is a small tassel, also made of silver-gilt metal-wrapped threads and red silk threads. This use of passementerie to trim textiles was common in the 16th century and high-quality book bindings were no exception. Producing trimmings of this type was part of the repertoire of the silk women who plied a lucrative trade in London. There is little evidence, however, as to whether they included book binding in their repertoire or if they provided trimmings for tailors to work with.

Figure 2 Overall view of the outer face of the chemise binding showing the main areas of damage along the central fold and around the edges of the boards (National Archive, E36/277 © Textile Conservation Centre, University of Southampton).

A chemise binding of this type was luxurious, highly impractical and consequently they were often used for religious texts as a symbol of piety (Bearman 1996). When, in the late 1430s, Rogier van der Weyden painted Mary Magdalen reading, he chose to depict her holding a book with a chemise binding.[1] Textile and alum-tawed chemise bindings were also used for select secular documents at the Tudor court to indicate the political, religious or financial significance of the manuscript (Anon. 1999; Bearman 1996: 183–7; Storm van Leeuwen 1989). The choice of expensive materials, an opulent style of binding and a court artist to carry out the illumination all point to this manuscript having been produced to a very high standard as would suit the queen's own copy of an indenture.

How the interaction between textile and text has resulted in damage

The changing role of the document, moving from a private indenture between the monarch and the dean and canons of St George's Chapel, Windsor, to a manuscript belonging to the National Archive at Kew, has inevitably resulted in the document receiving an increased amount of handling. While the indenture was originally consulted to clarify specific details about the agreement between the queen and the dean, the document is now of interest to a wider range of readers, but there are three principal reasons for an individual to consult the document. One relates to the textile component. The manuscript is unusual because it is covered with one of the few surviving examples of English chemise bindings that were produced between c.1460 and 1610. A finer and better known example of this binding style is provided by the septipartite indentures drawn up on 16 July 1504 between Henry VII and John Islip, Abbot of Westminster, establishing Henry VII's chantry chapel at Westminster Abbey (TNA E33/1; Marks and Williamson 2003: 168). This set of indentures is bound in crimson silk velvet lined with yellow damask, edged with green and gold cord and with green silk tassels at each corner. Tassels and other passementerie were often used to finish a chemise binding.

The other two reasons to consult the manuscript focus on the text, which describes the re-establishment of the Order of Poor Knights at Windsor. The Order had been founded in 1348 but by Henry VIII's reign the knights were no longer appointed. The king left an instruction in his will for the Order to be re-formed, however, and Elizabeth I honoured his wish in 1559. The indenture records the duties and responsibilities of the knights and provides an insight into one small facet of ceremonial at the Elizabethan court. More importantly, on folio 4, the text begins with an initial E containing a portrait of the young queen in her parliament robes, seated on her throne (Fig. 3). For students of Elizabethan portraiture, this image is of great interest as it is one of the earliest images of the queen, it being painted in the year of her coronation (Strong 1983). Elizabeth is well known for the management and manipulation of her image but this portrait is of the type developed for legal and official documents (Auerbach 1954). The artist has been identified as Lavinia Teerlinc. Teerlinc painted a number of portraits of the queen between 1559 and 1576 including a

Figure 3 A detail from folio 4 showing the historiated initial E is of Elizabeth enthroned (National Archive, E36/277 © Textile Conservation Centre, University of Southampton) (Plate 102 in the colour plate section).

miniature of the Maundy ceremony with Elizabeth I dressed in blue c.1560 (Doran 2003: 74, 110).[2]

The textile chemise is quite fragile, while the bound manuscript is in very good condition. In part this reflects the interaction of the two materials. The textile forming the outermost layer is far more vulnerable than the parchment leaves which are protected by the binding. Much of the damage to the velvet and the silk bookmark has resulted from the use that the manuscript has received and as such it provides a record of the document's history. The velvet is soft and supple but the pile has been abraded in line with the indented edges of the boards. In addition there are several specific areas of damage: along the spine, along the margin where the velvet is stitched to the leather on the reverse of the boards and at the corners. Stitched repairs have been carried out in the damaged areas in an attempt to continue the functional life of the chemise binding.

The velvet is quite clean and the colour is fairly even, although there is some evidence of fading and discoloration associated with handling around the edges. There is also slight rippling in the velvet because of the way it has been stitched to the covers of the book. This is not causing a problem and there does not appear to be any damage or abrasion associated with this. The edging cord is in quite good condition. Some of the tassels are a little squashed and hang loose of the main binding because of loss of velvet from the corners causing the velvet to curl slightly along the top and bottom edges.

Treating the textile to make the text accessible

The conservation brief required the binding to be made safe to allow for occasional handling by a reader consulting the manuscript and for long-term storage in the archive. This meant that a sympathetic but quite robust support method was needed to ensure the textile could be handled, so allowing a reader to safely open the volume or a textile specialist to examine the velvet and trimmings. As both sides of the support patches will be visible when the manuscript is in use, or on display, the support fabric needed to be colour matched to the different shades of the inner and outer face of the velvet.

Most of the repair stitching was removed from the velvet and the damaged areas of the binding were realigned. It became apparent that the edges of the velvet binding were curling because of the uneven tensions caused by the repairs and the areas of loss. Once these areas were supported, the velvet lay flat. Consequently, the velvet was not humidified as this level of intervention was not deemed necessary. The weak and damaged areas of the binding were given a stitched support using specially dyed conservation-grade fabrics. In order to provide a support fabric with an appropriate appearance and weight, both from the front and the reverse, patches were made from cotton poplin and silk crepeline (Eagan and Hayward 2005). The most effective means of support was to have one large patch supporting the reverse of the lower

Figure 4 Overall views of the outer (a) and inner (b) faces of the chemise binding after conservation. The support fabric had to be colour matched with both sides of the velvet as it is visible on the inner face to a reader consulting the manuscript (National Archive, E36/277 © Textile Conservation Centre, University of Southampton).

section of the binding and a smaller patch covering the reverse of the upper section. Using this method, the reverse of the velvet is still visible in two areas, so providing access for those wishing to examine it in the future (Fig. 4a,b). The weak areas of the velvet were couched to the patches using threads pulled from dark brown polyester Stabiltex. Additional stitching was carried out using running stitch and stab stitch worked using Skala, a heavier weight polyester thread. The edges of the patches were secured using herringbone stitch. Where necessary, the edging cord was reattached to the binding.

The white silk pendant seal ribbon was left untreated, partly because the ribbon, while quite fragile, is in a stable condition and partly because of the way the ribbon is secured to the manuscript, it is only possible to provide support to part of the ribbon. This could create a line of weakness that might be more damaging to the ribbon than leaving it untreated.

Some time prior to the conservation of the chemise binding, a linen-covered, portfolio-style, bespoke mount was made of conservation-grade materials to house the manuscript. The mount was intended to protect the document prior to and after conservation and it has a recess for the document to sit in. The aim was to support the chemise binding and tassels which are particularly vulnerable in a conventional storage box, while also providing the reader with a purpose-made support from which to read the manuscript or examine the binding. The challenge with such a mount is to provide support without constraining the object, especially if there is a possibility that the object's dimensions might change after conservation. Readers will be provided with instructions on how to open to the mount and how to keep handling to a minimum in order to protect the fragile edges of the chemise.

Interventive conservation has ensured the long-term preservation of the chemise binding. It has made the binding fully functional once again, so allowing it to fulfil its purpose of protecting and adorning the manuscript. The text and the image of the young queen are more accessible and the conserved textile completes the object, so allowing it to be appreciated in its original form.

Acknowledgements

Grateful thanks are recorded to Nancy Bell of the National Archive, Kew, for permission to present the conservation of the chemise binding (E36/277) and to Nell Hoare of the Textile Conservation Centre, University of Southampton for permission to publish material from the conservation report for TCC no. 2855 (Hayward 2004). The author would also like to thank Angela Craft, formerly of the National Archive and now at Senate House Library, for access to her report on the binding and Jane Eagan for her invaluable advice. Finally, she would like to acknowledge the support of the AHRC's Research Centre for Textile Conservation and Textile Studies.

Notes

1. National Portrait Gallery, London.
2. Trustees of the late Countess Beauchamp.

References

Anon. (1999) *Book Bindings at the Public Record Office*. Kew: Public Record Office.

Auerbach, E. (1951) 'An Elizabethan illuminated indenture', *Burlington Magazine* 112: 319–23.

Auerbach, E. (1954) *Tudor Artists: A Study of Painters in the Royal Service and of Portraiture on Illuminated Documents from the Accession of Henry VIII to the Death of Elizabeth*. London: Athlone.

Bearman, F. (1996) 'The origins and significance of two late medieval textile chemise bookbindings in the Walters Art Gallery', *Journal of the Walters Art Gallery*, Essays in Honor of Lilian M. V. Randall, 56: 163–87.

Craft, A. (2004) *Condition Report and Technical Description of E36/277*. Unpublished report, National Archive.

Doran, S. (ed.) (2003) *Elizabeth: The Exhibition at the National Maritime Museum*. London: Chatto & Windus.

Eagan, J. and Hayward, M.A. (2005) 'A textile binding once in the library of Henry VIII: technical examination and conservation', in *Care and Conservation of Manuscripts 8*, 123–39. Copenhagen: Museum Tusculanum Press.

Hayward, M.A. (2004) *Report on the Conservation of a Chemise Binding, TCC 2855*. Unpublished report, Textile Conservation Centre, University of Southampton.

Hofenk de Graaff, J.H. (2004) *The Colourful Past: Origins, Chemistry and Identification of Natural Dyestuffs*. Riggisberg and London: Abegg-Stiftung and Archetype Publications.

Marks, R. and Williamson, P. (eds) (2003) *Gothic: Art for England 1400–1547*. London: Victoria and Albert Museum.

Storm van Leeuwen, J. (1989) 'The well-shirted bookbinding: on chemise bindings and Hülleneinbände', in *Theatrum Orbis Liborum: Liber Amicorum Presented to Nico Israel on the Occasion of His Seventieth Birthday*, T. Croiset van Uchelen *et al.* (eds). Utrecht: HES.

Strong, R. (1983) *Artists of the Tudor Court: The Portrait Miniature Rediscovered 1520–1620* with contributions from V.J. Murrell. London: Victoria and Albert Museum.

The author

Having graduated with a history degree, Maria Hayward completed the postgraduate diploma in textile conservation at the Textile Conservation Centre, Hampton Court Palace (TCC). After working as a conservator and completing a PhD, she is currently a Reader and Head of Studies and Research at the TCC, University of Southampton and the Director of the AHRC Research Centre for Textile Conservation and Textile Studies (2004–07). In 2004 she was elected as a Fellow of the Society of Antiquaries and joined the editorial board of *Studies in Conservation*. She is also Assistant Editor of *Costume*.

Address

Maria Hayward, AHRC Research Centre for Textile Conservation and Textile Studies, Winchester School of Art, University of Southampton, Park Avenue, Winchester SO23 8DL, UK (mh11@soton.ac.uk)

Plate 63 Kimono, undated and uncatalogued. Hornel Library/The National Trust for Scotland (Fig. 2, p. 137).

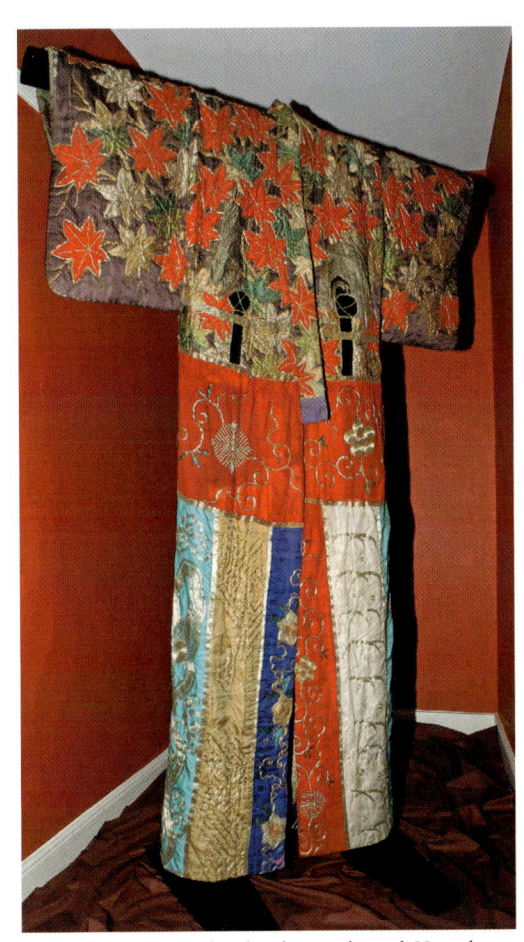

Plate 64 Kimono, undated and uncatalogued. Hornel Library/The National Trust for Scotland (Fig. 3, p. 137).

Plate 65 Photograph, undated and uncatalogued. Hornel Library/The National Trust for Scotland (Fig. 4, p. 139).

Plate 66 Illustration of a *furisode* sleeve from *A Catalogue of 100 Furisode Sleeves* (Japan 1919). Hornel Library/The National Trust for Scotland (Fig. 5, p. 139)

Plate 67 The entrance to 'Our Chosen Land', Calgary Chinese Cultural Centre (Fig. 1, p. 143).

Plate 68 Display of traditional Chinese dragon robes and court dress, Calgary Chinese Cultural Centre (Fig. 2, p. 145).

Plate 69 Display of traditional clothing brought to Calgary by early Chinese settlers, Calgary Chinese Cultural Centre (Fig. 3, p. 145).

Plate 70 This 18th-century pair of attached linen pockets echoes a common shape and construction: with bound or double-seamed edges, reinforced vertical openings and tape used to bind the top and form the waist ties. The embroidered decoration follows a customary pattern of free-flowing stems, leaves and flowers with a prominent feature directly below the opening. At 36 cm long, their size is typical too (BATMC 2004.468, by permission of the Museum of Costume, Bath and North East Somerset Council) (Fig. 1, p. 158).

Plate 71 Close examination of pockets provides clues to effects and patterns of use. In this case, the back reveals stains and other signs of wear, including a large internal patch placed over a neatened hole, a common method of mending at this period (BATMC 2004.468, by permission of the Museum of Costume, Bath and North East Somerset Council) (Fig. 2, p. 158).

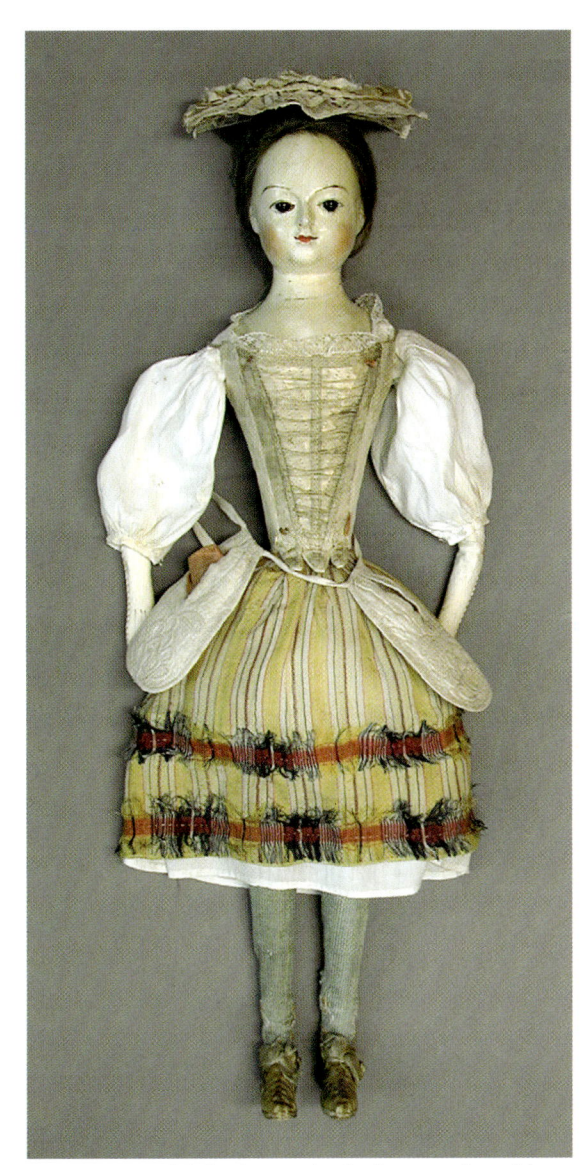

Plate 72 Dressed dolls of various kinds often provide useful information about how pockets were worn, although care is required in dating separate elements. This mid-18th-century doll has a 'husswif' in her pocket. In her set of clothes there is also a yellow silk damask single pocket containing a pin cushion (MCAG.1955.21, by permission of the Gallery of Costume, Platt Hall, Manchester Art Galleries) (Fig. 3, p. 159).

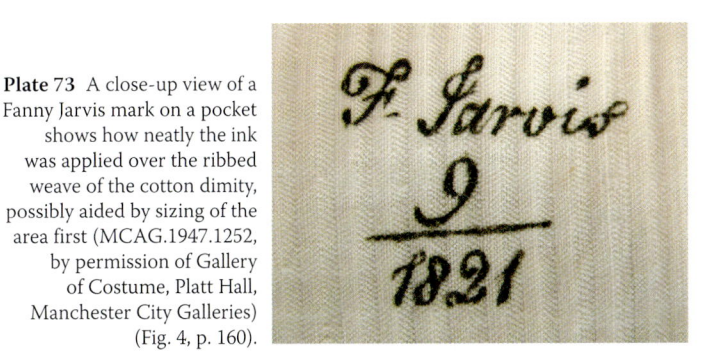

Plate 73 A close-up view of a Fanny Jarvis mark on a pocket shows how neatly the ink was applied over the ribbed weave of the cotton dimity, possibly aided by sizing of the area first (MCAG.1947.1252, by permission of Gallery of Costume, Platt Hall, Manchester City Galleries) (Fig. 4, p. 160).

Plate 74 Typical of the cross-stitched small marks used in the 19th century, these initials are on the ribbed cotton dimity back of a pocket (CRH.1973.16, by permission of Hampshire County Museums and Archives Service) (Fig. 5, p. 161).

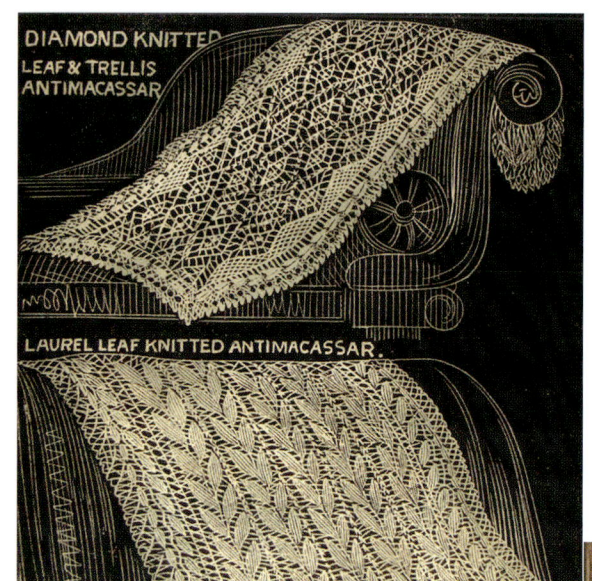

Plate 75 Illustration from *The Royal Magazine of Knitting, Netting, Crochet and Fancy Needlework*, 1850 (V&A Images) (Fig. 1, p. 165).

Plate 76 John Everett Millais, *James Wyatt and His Granddaughter Mary Wyatt*, 1849, Collection Lord Lloyd-Webber (Fig. 3, p. 167).

Plate 77 James Hayllar, *The Only Daughter*, 1875 (Christie's Images Ltd) (Fig. 4, p. 167).

Plate 78 Guy McCrone, *Antimacassar City*, 1940 (author's collection) (Fig. 6, p. 171).

Plate 79 Dupion Shantung, Janet Arnold drawing, MS327 Special Collections, Hartley Library, University of Southampton (Fig. 3, p. 183).

Plate 80 Green antique taffeta dinner and evening dress with black and white peppermint stripe taffeta, Janet Arnold drawing, MS 327 Special Collections, Hartley Library, University of Southampton (Fig. 4, p. 184).

Plate 81 Babar and Celeste, Montse Stanley Collection, MS 332 Special Collections, Hartley Library, University of Southampton (Fig. 5, p. 184).

Plate 82 Beaded, knitted bag, Montse Stanley Collection, MS 332 Special Collections, Hartley Library, University of Southampton (Fig. 6, p. 184).

Plate 83 The Garscube flag, after conservation (© The Trustees of the National Museums of Scotland) (Fig. 1, p. 190).

Plate 84 The Bothwell Brig flag, after conservation (© The Trustees of the National Museums of Scotland) (Fig. 3, p. 192).

Plate 85 The Dunbar saltire, after conservation (© The Trustees of the National Museums of Scotland) (Fig. 4, p. 193).

Plate 86 The Avendale flag, after conservation (© The Trustees of the National Museums of Scotland) (Fig. 5, p. 194).

Plate 87 The Jehovah Nissi flag, after conservation (© The Trustees of the National Museums of Scotland) (Fig. 6, p. 194).

Plate 88 Queen Charlotte's state bed 1772–78 (© HM Queen Elizabeth II) (Fig. 1, p. 197).

Plate 89 Original ribbed silk ground visible under the embroidery (© Historic Royal Palaces) (Fig. 2, p. 199).

Plate 90 Remnant of original ribbed silk ground too fragile to move (© Historic Royal Palaces) (Fig. 4, p. 200).

Plate 91 Bullion fringe from the upper valances (© Historic Royal Palaces) (Fig. 5, p. 200).

Plate 92 Inscription found on the inside linen of the viewing right upper outer valance (© Historic Royal Palaces) (Fig. 6, p. 201).

Plate 93 Blackwork jacket before conservation intervention (photo © Textile Conservation Centre) (Fig. 1, p. 205).

Plate 94 Jacket after the conservation intervention (photo © Textile Conservation Centre) (Fig. 3, p. 206).

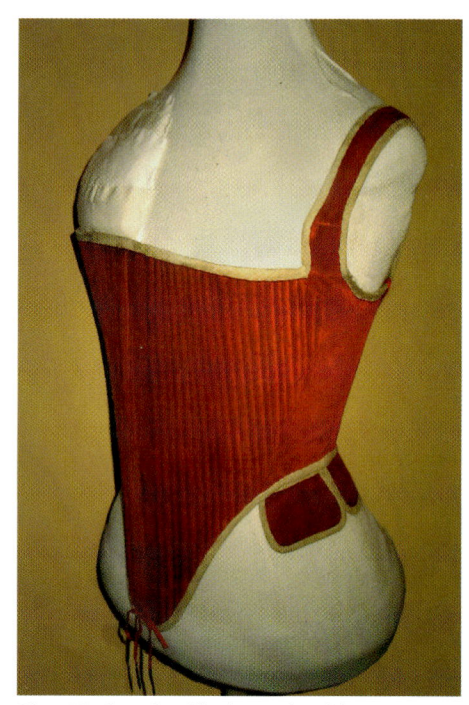

Plate 95 Completed bodice replica (photo © Hilary Davidson) (Fig. 5, p. 207).

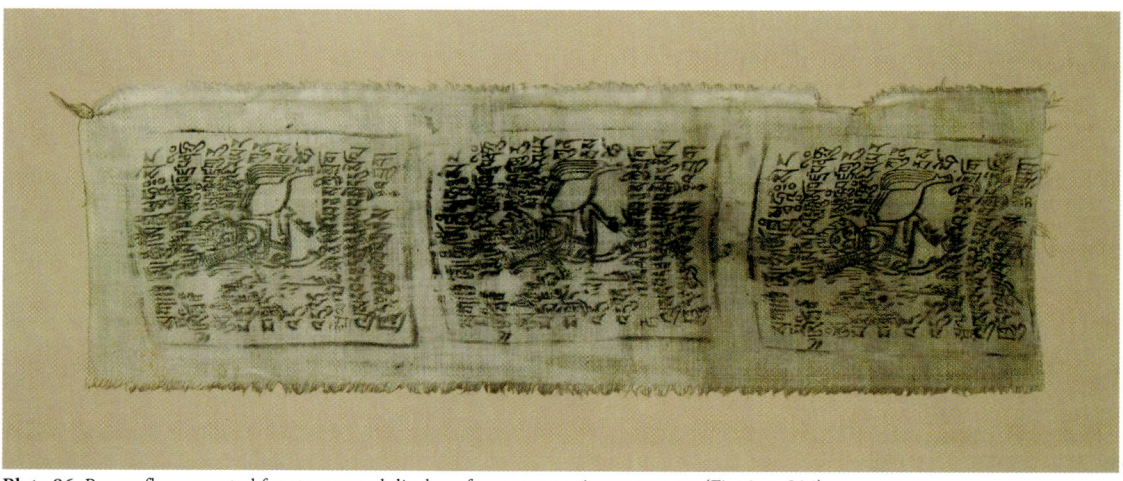

Plate 96 Prayer flag mounted for storage and display, after conservation treatment (Fig. 1, p. 214).

Plate 97 Labels associated with the prayer flag, mounted for storage and display (Fig. 2, p. 215).

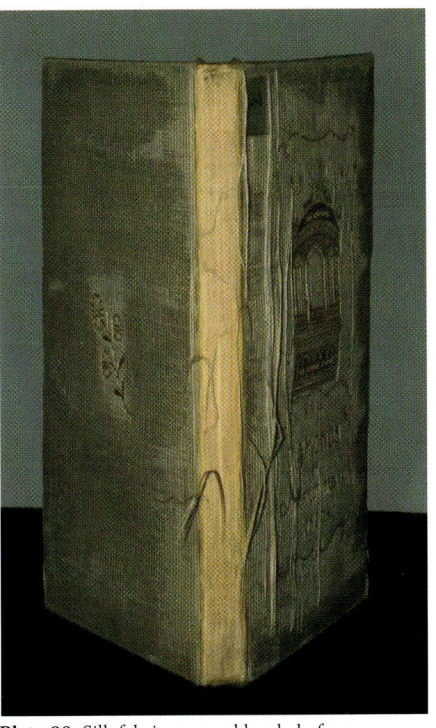

Plate 98 Silk fabric covered book, before undergoing conservation treatment (Fig. 3, p. 216).

Plate 99 Silk fabric covered book, as presented after conservation treatment (Fig. 4, p. 216).

Plate 100 Front view of the Majesty scutcheon, as presented for conservation (Fig. 5, p. 218).

Plate 101 Reverse view of the Majesty scutcheon, showing documents secured to the reverse and the wooden stretcher (Fig. 6, p. 218).

Plate 102 A detail from folio 4 showing the historiated initial E is of Elizabeth enthroned (National Archive, E36/277 © Textile Conservation Centre, University of Southampton) (Fig. 3, p. 223).

Plate 103 Obverse of table carpet (after conservation treatment) (photo Mike Halliwell © Textile Conservation Centre, University of Southampton) (Fig. 2, p. 226).

Plate 104 Reverse of table carpet (after conservation treatment) (photo Mike Halliwell © Textile Conservation Centre, University of Southampton) (Fig. 3, p. 226).

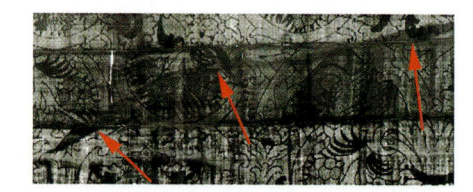

Plate 105 Concealed seam turnings of table carpet seen from obverse. Composite image formed from 15 photographs taken by Mike Halliwell using transmitted light technique. Above: Whole table carpet; white box indicates area shown in detail below. Below: Detail of table carpet; red arrows indicate shaped seam turning of blue linen fragment B3 (© Textile Conservation Centre, university of Southampton) (Fig. 6, p. 228).

Plate 106 Coverlet, 1718 (courtesy of the Quilters' Guild of the British Isles) (Fig. 1, p. 237).

Plate 107 Photography of the coverlet using transmitted light showing the unrolled section of coverlet on the bridge-shaped acrylic support, illuminated square and camera on tripod (courtesy of the Quilters' Guild of the British Isles) (Fig. 2, p. 238).

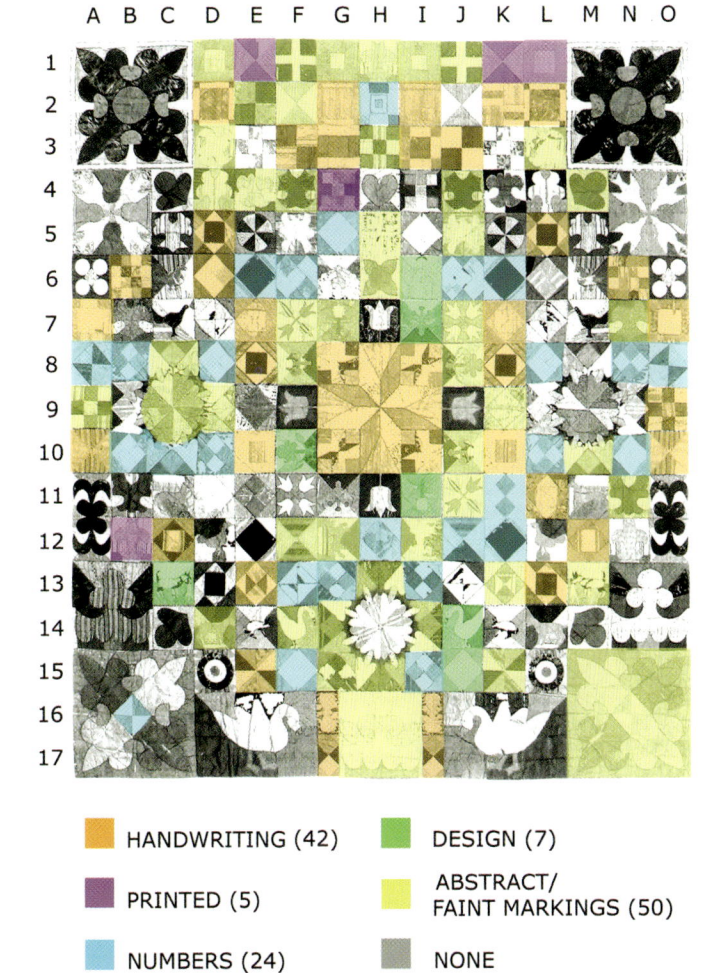

- HANDWRITING (42)
- PRINTED (5)
- NUMBERS (24)
- DESIGN (7)
- ABSTRACT/FAINT MARKINGS (50)
- NONE

Plate 108 Diagram showing the types of text found and their position on the coverlet (courtesy of the Quilters' Guild of the British Isles) (Fig. 3, p. 240).

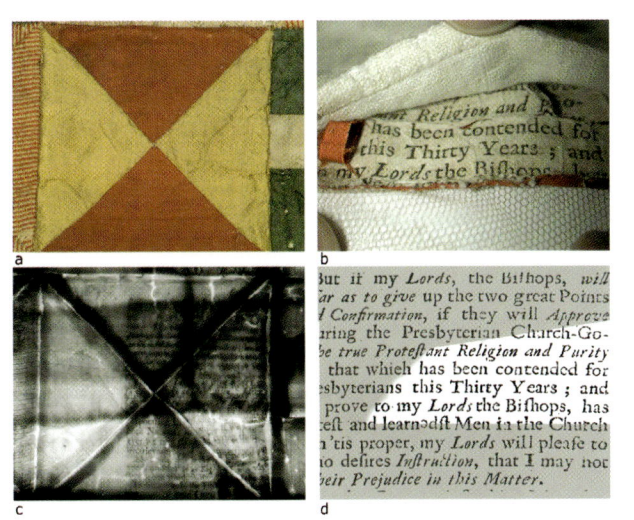

Plate 109 (a) Viewed with reflected light; (b) viewed with transmitted light; (c) paper visible through damaged seam; (d) extract from pamphlet. Note: Highlighted text corresponds to text found on papers in the coverlet (courtesy of the Quilters' Guild of the British Isles) (Fig. 5, p. 241).

Plate 110 Torah scrolls covered in mantles and silver decorations in the Torah ark (Fig. 1, p. 245).

Plate 111 Examples of flags from traditional sources, such as the federal government: (a) national colour, 10th New York Volunteer Infantry, 190.5 × 188.0 cm, pieced silk, embroidered and printed; (b) regimental colour, 159th New York Volunteer Infantry, 193.0 × 200.7 cm, silk, painted; (c) guidon, 158th New York Volunteer Infantry, 76.2 × 88.9 cm, pieced silk, painted; (d) camp colour, 20th United States Colored Troops, 47 × 59.1 cm, wool, printed (photos courtesy of New York State Military Museum and Veterans Research Center) (Fig. 1, p. 250).

(a)

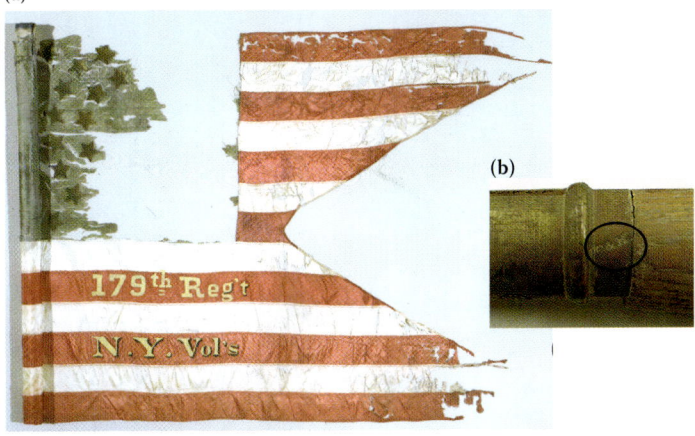

(b)

Plate 112 Guidon with maker mark by Evans and Hassall: (a) guidon, 179th New York Volunteer Infantry, 66 × 94.6 cm, pieced silk, painted; (b) maker mark 'E. & H.' stamped on the ferrule at the base of the staff (photos courtesy of New York State Military Museum and Veterans Research Center) (Fig. 2, p. 250).

(a)

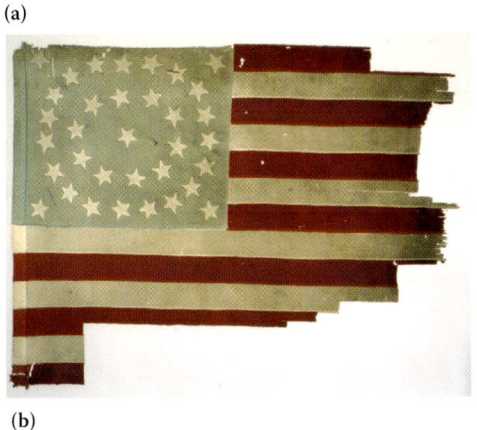

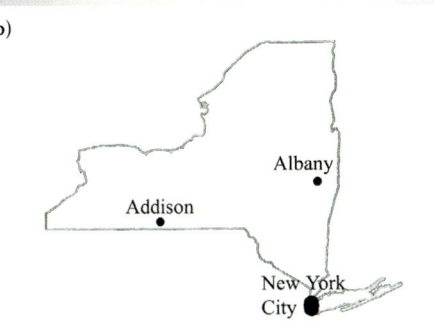

(b)

Plate 113 A flag from a non-traditional source, such as a local fundraising group: (a) national colour, 86th New York Volunteer Infantry given to the regiment by the Ladies of Addison, NY, 137.8 × 183.5 cm, pieced wool (photo courtesy of New York State Military Museum and Veterans Research Center). (b) Map of New York State showing Addison, Albany (State Capitol), and New York City (Fig. 3, p. 251).

(a)

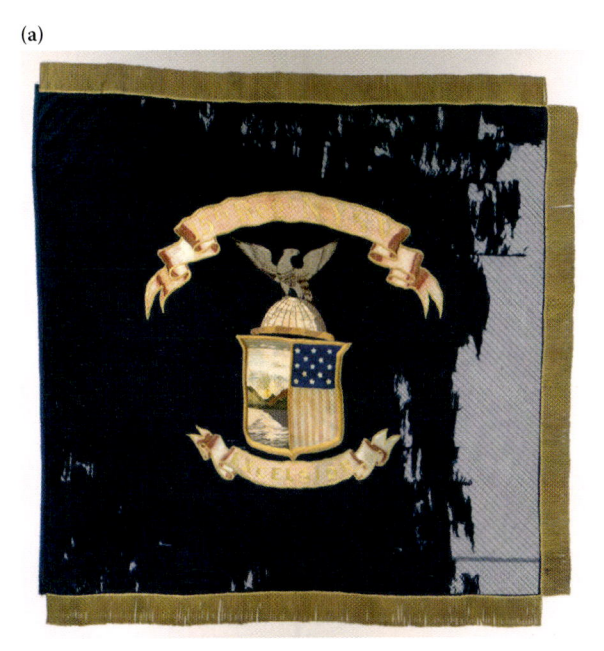

(b)

(c)

Plate 114 A series of flags from non-traditional sources. Flags of the 15th New York Engineers: (a) regimental colour made by Tiffany and Co., 194.9 × 193.6 cm, pieced silk, embroidered; (b) 1st set (earlier) of flank markers, left: 76.2 × 78.7 cm, right: 74.2 × 76.8 cm, both silk, painted; (c) 2nd set (later) of flank markers, left: 69.2 × 73.7 cm, right: 68.6 × 74.9 cm, both silk, painted ((b) and (c) given to the regiment by the New York City Common Council) (photos courtesy of New York State Military Museum and Veterans Research Center) (Fig. 4, p. 251).

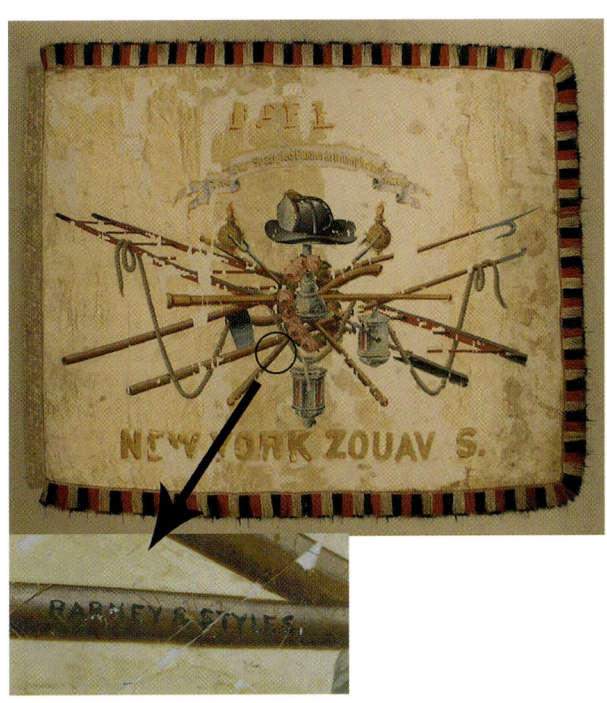

Plate 115 11th New York Volunteer Infantry regimental colour with maker mark from Barney and Styles, 40 Hudson St, New York City. The flag measures 165.1 × 194.3 cm, silk and cotton, painted (photos courtesy of New York State Military Museum and Veterans Research Center) (Fig. 6, p. 252).

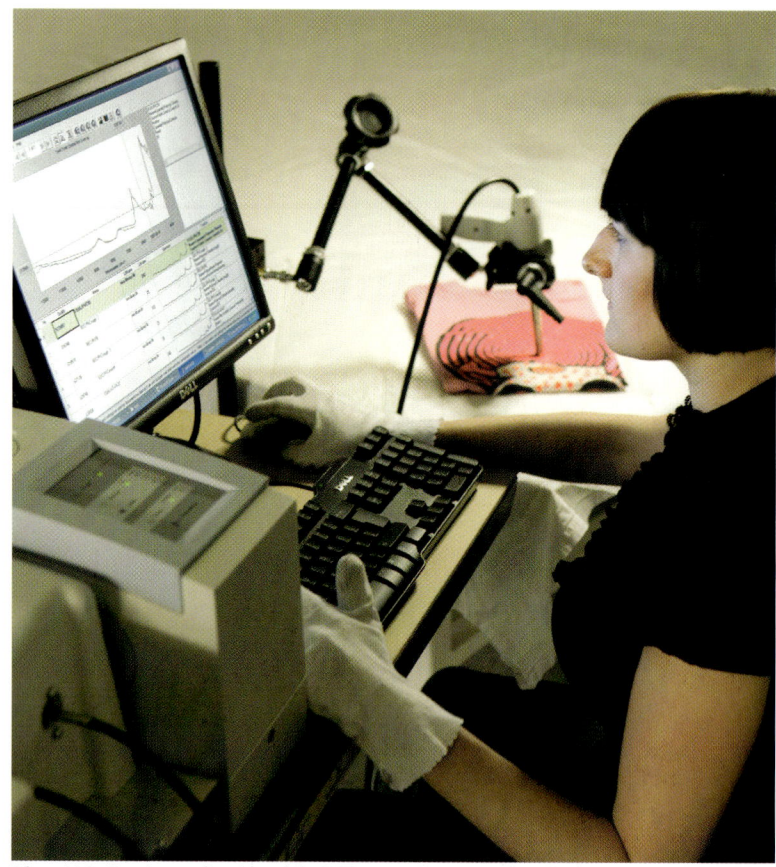

Plate 116 On-site application of the NIR spectrometer and probe (Fig. 1, p. 258).

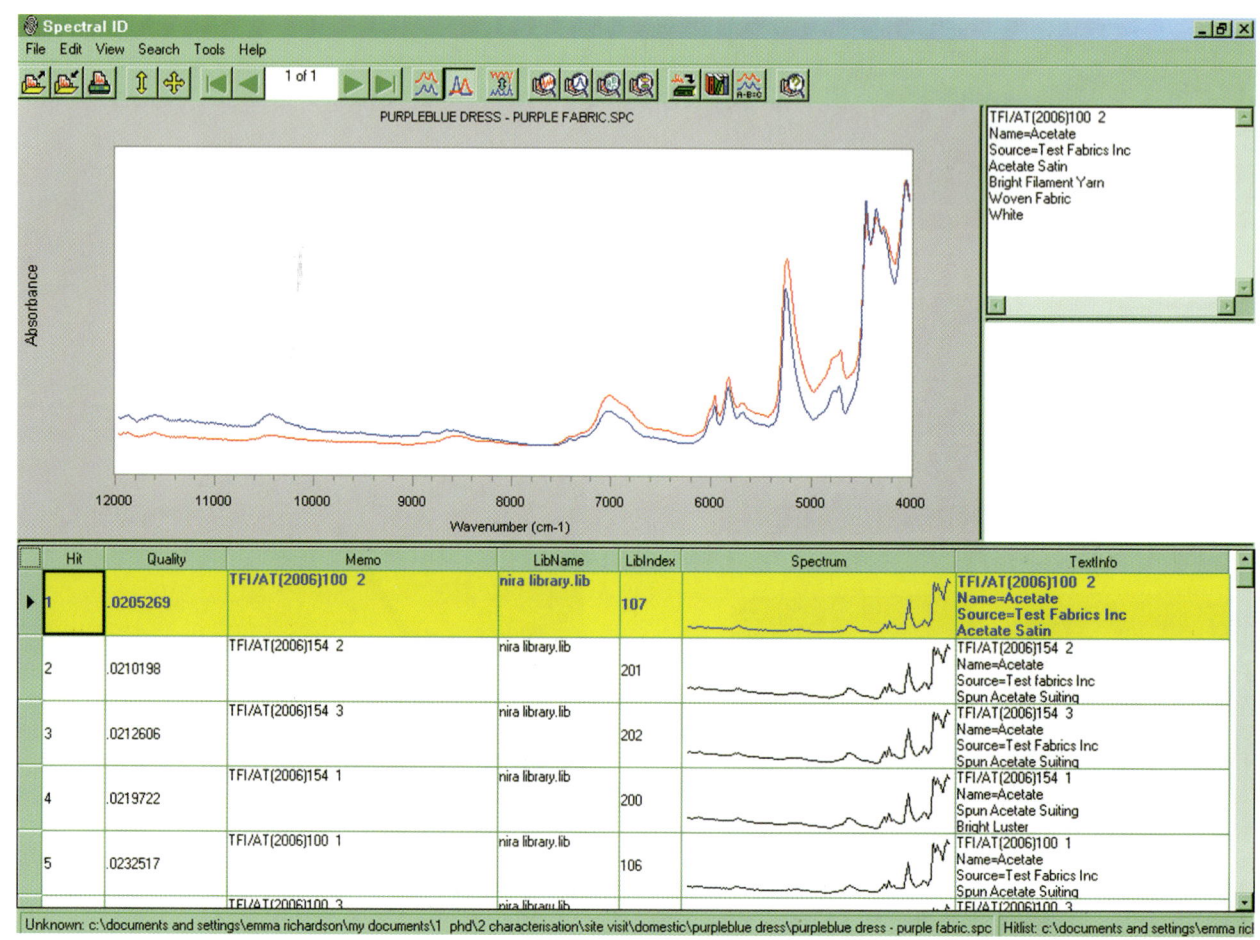

Plate 117 Thermo Galactic Spectral ID library generating a positive match of acetate for an unknown sample (see p. 259).

Plate 118 A modern handbag of mixed media, studied during an initial visit to test the on-site protocol (Fig. 2, p. 259).

Plate 119 Detail of the purple and blue 1950s dress illustrating the difficulties of sampling the lower layer of fabric (Fig. 5, p. 260).

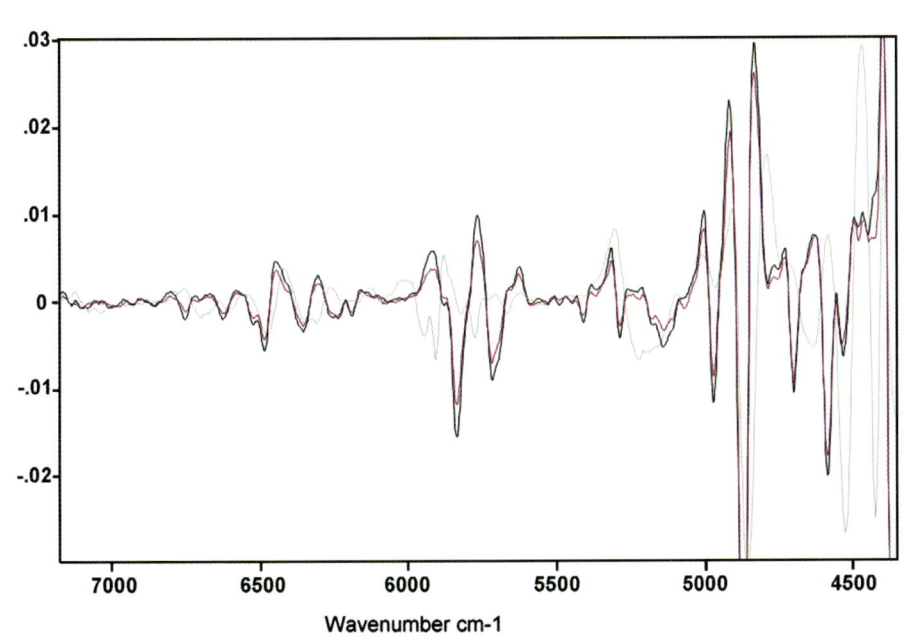

Plate 120 Second derivative NIR spectra of polyamide reference (black), silk reference (pale grey) and 'silk' slip (dark grey) (see p. 262).

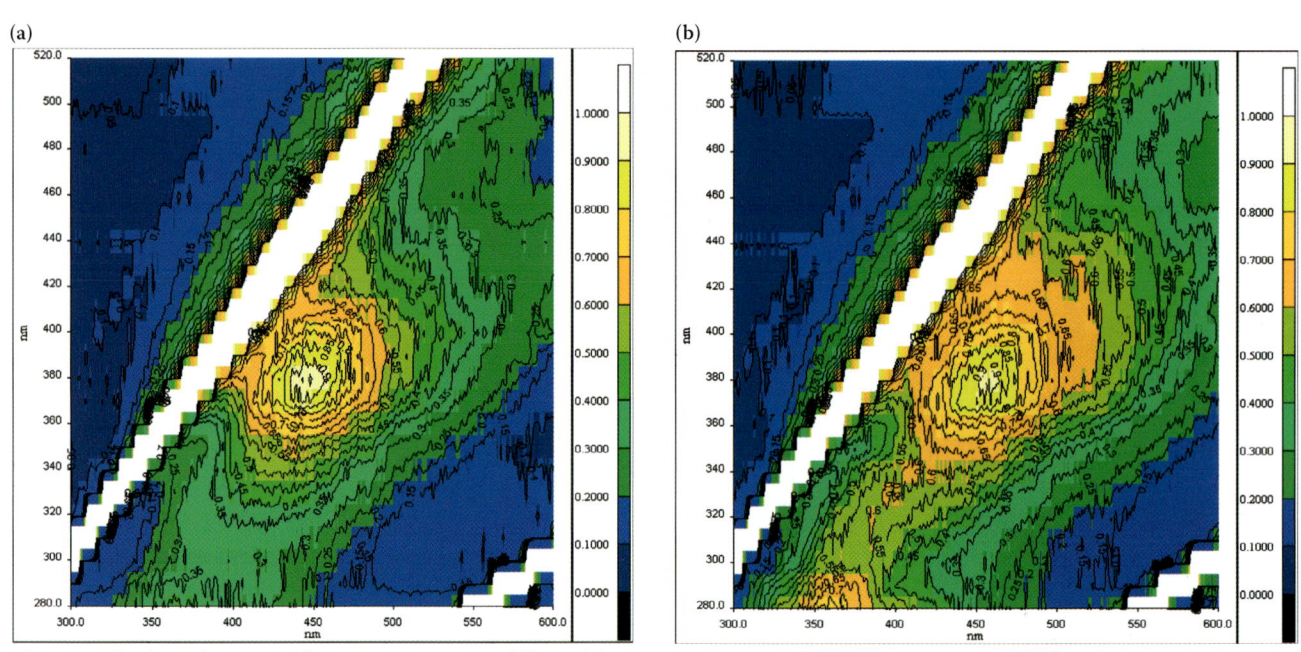

Plate 121 The three-dimensional fluorescence spectrum of fibres of the Mawaru species of *Phormium tenax* after 27 hours' irradiation with ultraviolet 'blacklight' with a spectral output maximum at 350 nm. The abscissa axis is emission wavelength and the ordinate axis is excitation wavelength in nm (see p. 265).

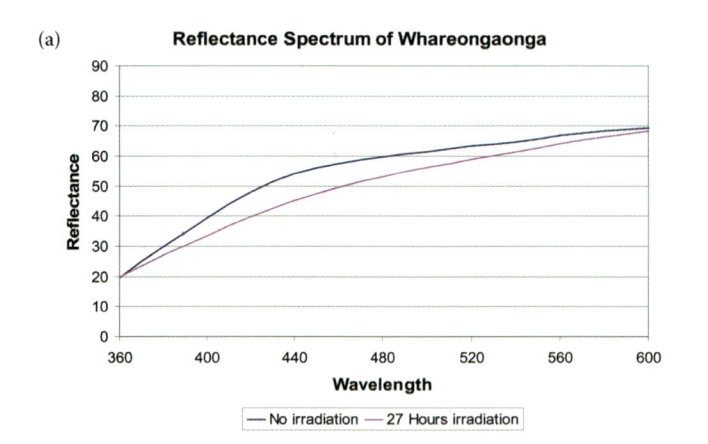

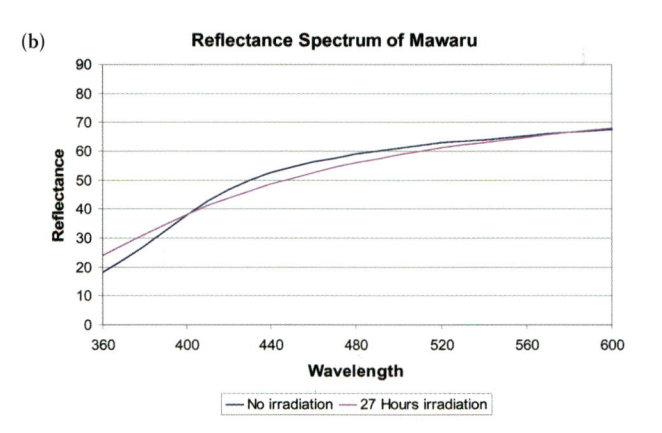

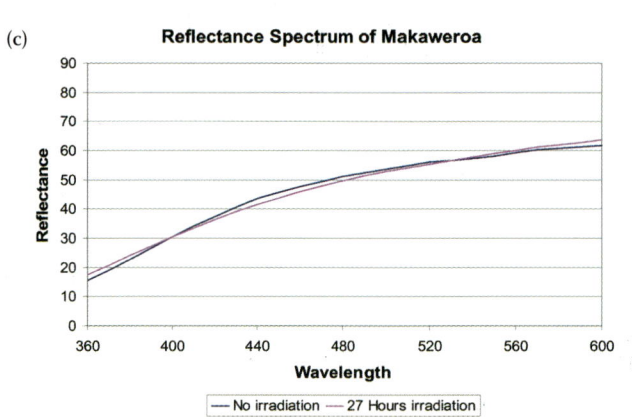

Plate 122 The three-dimensional fluorescence spectrum of fibres of the Mawaru species of *Phormium tenax*. The abscissa axis is emission wavelength and the ordinate axis is excitation wavelength in nm (see p. 265).

The investigation and documentation of a communion table carpet in Corpus Christi College, Oxford

Florence Maskell

ABSTRACT A textile belonging to Corpus Christi College, Oxford, thought to be a communion table carpet made in the late 16th or early 17th century, was investigated using the following techniques: metal thread analysis, dye analysis, weave analysis, object examination and archival research. The textile contains fragments of cloth of gold woven to order in Florence in the early 16th century to make copes for Richard Fox, Bishop of Winchester (1501–1528) and founder of Corpus Christi College (1517). The aim of the investigation was to provide new information about the attribution and history of the textile. Key findings of the technical and scientific analyses are presented here, together with an overview of the evidence found in documentary sources.

Keywords: cloth of gold, vestment, liturgical textile, metal thread analysis, dye analysis, weave analysis

Introduction

The subject of this study is a textile belonging to Corpus Christi College, Oxford. The precise function and nature of this textile are open to question, but it was almost certainly designed as a covering for an altar or communion table in the chapel of Corpus Christi College. It has been described here as a 'table carpet' as this term most accurately reflects the textile's probable function. The table carpet is roughly rectangular in shape, with maximum dimensions of 1.78 m and 1.47 m (Fig. 1). The central panel is formed from fragments of cloth of gold and it is surrounded on three sides by plain red velvet borders (Fig. 2). The table carpet is backed with a blue linen panel, also composed of fragments, that extends beyond the edge of the cloth of gold to form a fourth border (Fig. 3). For clarity of reference, each fragment or piece of the fabric components has been assigned a number (Figs 4 and 5).[1] The cloth of gold is woven with a design that features a Pelican in Piety[2] with the Latin motto EST DEO GRATIA.[3] The pelican and motto were the personal emblem of Richard Fox, Bishop of Winchester (1501–1528) and founder of Corpus Christi College, Oxford (1517).[4] Their presence must indicate that the cloth was especially commissioned by or for him.[5]

The table carpet was the focus of research undertaken for an MA dissertation (Maskell 2006), the research aims of which were as follows: (1) to create as full a record as possible of the history of the table carpet and its current state including structure, materials and condition; (2) to investigate in particular the attribution and original use of the cloth of gold, and to explore its association with Bishop Richard Fox; (3) to investigate when and why the table carpet was constructed from the cloth of gold; and (4) to suggest an appropriate strategy for conserving the table carpet, bearing in mind its history of use and reuse, and its future role. The intention here is to present an overview of the key findings of the dissertation research which involved archival investigation, object examination, weave analysis, metal thread analysis and dye analysis. Traditional and transmitted light photography were also used to explore and document the table carpet.[6]

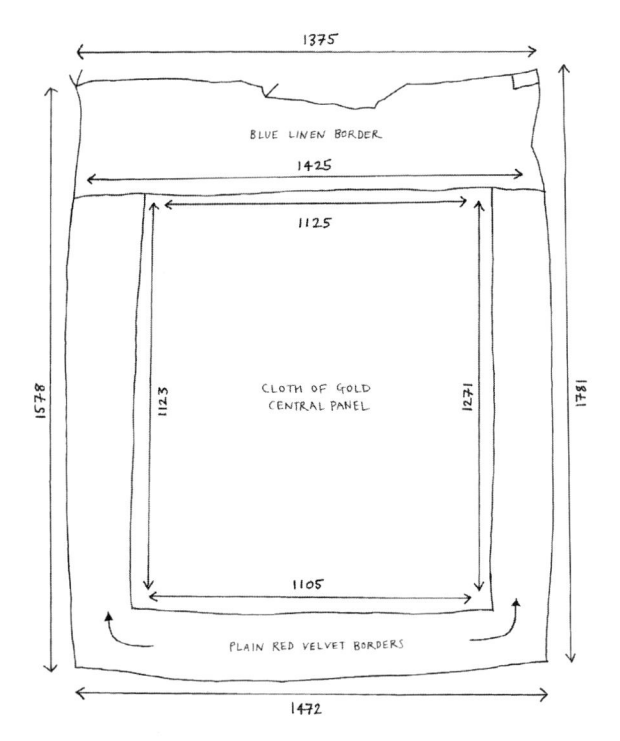

Figure 1 Obverse of table carpet: key dimensions (mm) (© Textile Conservation Centre, University of Southampton).

Figure 2 Obverse of table carpet (after conservation treatment) (photo Mike Halliwell © Textile Conservation Centre, University of Southampton) (Plate 103 in the colour plate section).

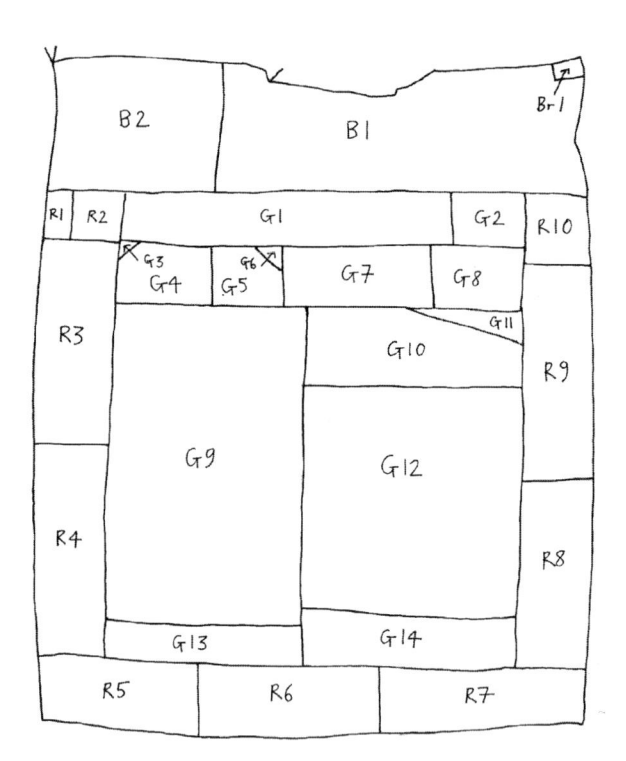

Figure 4 Obverse of table carpet: numbers assigned to fragments (© Textile Conservation Centre, University of Southampton).

Figure 3 Reverse of table carpet (after conservation treatment) (photo Mike Halliwell © Textile Conservation Centre, University of Southampton) (Plate 104 in the colour plate section).

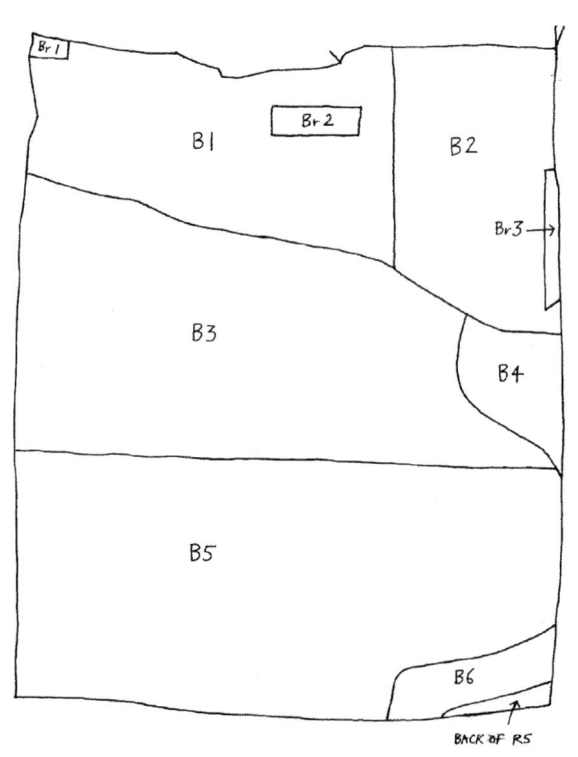

Figure 5 Reverse of table carpet: numbers assigned to fragments (© Textile Conservation Centre, University of Southampton).

The choice of analytical techniques was determined in consultation with staff at the Textile Conservation Centre (TCC),[7] with reference to available literature and in light of insights gained from previous projects at the TCC.[8] The number of samples taken for scientific analysis was limited by considerations of cost and time, and the desire to minimise destructive intervention to the object.[9] The multidisciplinary nature of this project meant that the contribution of experts was central to its successful completion. Scholars in a range of fields were most generous in providing assistance, without which such a full investigation would not have been possible. While undertaking the conservation, it was possible to examine the table carpet much more closely than would normally be possible. Privileged access such as this offers the chance to collect, record and publish information that will hopefully be of benefit to researchers in a variety of disciplines.

Documentary evidence

The establishment of a direct link between the table carpet and a prominent historical figure such as Bishop Richard Fox provided a starting point for documentary research. A number of original documents in Winchester and Oxford were examined but it was impossible to consult sources elsewhere within the timescale of the project. The archivist of Corpus Christi College, Mr Reid, identified two sources that mention the pelican cloth of gold. The first, an inventory of chapel goods in the college, dated 1566, lists 'two ... copes of purple velvet with braunches having the pellicanes of golde'.[10] The second, a history of the college written in 1893 by its then president, describes 'a cloth for a small communion table, composed of fragments of copes ornamented with pelicans wrought in gold tissue' (Fowler 1893: 114, n.1). Both these descriptions so closely match the cloth of gold fragments surviving today in the table carpet that the references can be considered as firm evidence that these fragments were originally part of one or both of the two pelican copes inventoried in 1566.[11] As yet it has not been possible to find any specific information about the circumstances of the transformation from copes to table carpet, or indeed any further direct references to these objects.

The use of copes was opposed by some Reformers in the 16th and 17th centuries (Johnstone 2002; Mayer-Thurman 1975; Mayo 1984). It is possible that copes made of the pelican cloth of gold for Richard Fox could have been cut up and reused as a response to religious reforms. On the other hand, the copes could have become worn out or damaged, in which case it is likely that every fragment would have been recycled in some way, all the more so because the cloth of gold was a luxurious fabric made by skilled workers from precious materials, and therefore would have been highly valued. The form and function of the table carpet was considered in relation to the changing usage of altars and tables at Corpus Christi College to see if this could help place the carpet within a particular historical or religious context. The history of the chapel goods at Corpus Christi was also investigated to see if it might shed light on the probable fate of pre-Reformation objects, such as the pelican copes, at times of religious reform.

During the Reformation many stone altars were replaced by wooden tables, reflecting the beliefs of Reformers who wished to move away from 'the Catholic emphasis on the sacrifice of the mass performed by the priest' towards an emphasis on 'the corporate aspect of fellowship at the Lord's Table' (Randall 1986: 183). Corpus Christi College chapel was built c.1517 as a place of traditional Catholic worship, complete with stone altar (and almost certainly side altars). The Chapel Accounts[12] suggest that the altar was abandoned in favour of a table as ordered by Edward VI's Injunction of 1550, brought into use again after the accession of Mary in 1553, and finally removed after Elizabeth came to the throne in 1558.[13]

The 1559 Prayer Book decreed that the communion table should be brought forward from its customary place against a wall or screen to stand lengthwise or 'tablewise' in the main body of the church or in the chancel, with the priest on the north side and the communicants gathered around (White 2006: 808; Duffy 1992: 464). There is no direct evidence concerning this type of arrangement at Corpus Christi College, although the Chapel Accounts for 1584/5 mention 'a carpet for the communion table' implying a different form of textile from the traditional altar frontal. It is likely that such a 'carpet' would have been draped in a manner similar to a tablecloth today, covering the top of the table and possibly hanging down around the sides.[14] The textile that is the subject of this study is more similar in form to a table carpet than to a pre-Reformation frontal.

The Chapel Accounts for c.1625–35 record refurbishments which seem to denote a style of worship promoted by William Laud, Archbishop of Canterbury (from 1633). Among other things, Laud insisted on the return of the table (or altar) to its traditional position against the east wall, protected by a rail running from north to south.[15] A throwover type of altar covering was widely adopted at this period and continued in use until the mid-19th century when the Oxford Movement encouraged a return to the medieval form of altar frontal (Pocknee 1963: 48; Pocknee and Randall 1986). The pelican table carpet is not large enough to be used as a throwover cloth, and does not match the appearance of the typical 'Laudian' frontal. It is therefore unlikely to have been made specifically for the altar at Corpus Christi during this time.

As demonstrated by the discussion of altars and tables, the college chapel and its furnishings were adapted several times to meet the requirements of the Reformers. An opposing current of activity is also attested in the documentary sources. There is evidence that many of the fellows continued to practise Roman Catholic forms of worship and that strenuous efforts were made to preserve Catholic chapel goods throughout successive waves of reform. Goods were deliberately concealed on the accession of Edward VI, again when Elizabeth came to the throne, and probably for a third time during the Commonwealth. Richard Fox's pelican copes were among items hidden during Elizabeth's reign, which were discovered and inventoried on the occasion of the 1566 Visitation.[16] No written record of the subsequent fate of these items has yet come to light, but the pelican copes need not have been destroyed on religious grounds, since there was no official injunction against the use of copes at that time.[17]

Construction analysis

A detailed analysis of the construction and wear patterns of the table carpet was undertaken using visual examination and transmitted light photography.[18] The aims were to establish a sequence of repairs and alterations, to search for clues about any previous use of fabric components, to ascertain whether the cloth of gold fragments could theoretically be reassembled into cope form, and to explore whether any fragments of the blue linen could have belonged to the same vestments as the pelican cloth of gold.

Investigation of seams and stitching threads showed that at least three interventions had been made to alter or repair the carpet (for details see Maskell 2006: ch. 4, section 1). The first was a major intervention involving replacement of borders (a concealed fragmentary selvedge is almost certainly the remains of an original border) and extensive repairs to seams. The second and third interventions were on a lesser scale, involving some repairs to seams and the application of three small patches.

The cloth of gold fragments are of varying dimensions and shapes (mainly rectilinear) and their woven designs are not aligned, indicating that they were almost certainly cut from another object to form the carpet. It was hoped that transmitted light photography would reveal traces of shaping in the seam turnings that would support documentary evidence regarding the original use of the cloth of gold as cope fabric. The seam turnings were found to be narrow and relatively straight-edged, however, and could not be related to a specific previous use (Fig. 6). Insufficient information was obtained to allow theoretical placement of cloth of gold fragments within the template of a cope (or copes), or indeed any other type of vestment.[19]

The irregular curved shapes of the blue linen fragments, and a particularly striking pale arc-shaped line of wear on B3 and B5, suggested that the blue linen had been used to line one or more vestments, almost certainly including a cope (Figs 3 and 7). Transmitted light photography showed that most of the blue linen fragments had fairly narrow seam turnings that followed the visible seam lines closely. The one exception was the seam joining B1/B2 to B3/B4: this appeared to have thicker turnings at two places along its length, which correlated to the arc-shaped wear line and indicated that some shaping from a previous use had survived (Fig. 6).

The arc-shaped wear line crosses the seam joining B3 to B5 and it can therefore be assumed that B3 and B5 were assembled and used in a manner to cause the wear line prior to incorporation within the table carpet. This hypothesis is further supported by the fact that a pale brown stitching thread has been used to attach these two fragments to each other, in contrast to the blue thread used in all the other seams of the linen backing. The arc of the wear line is strongly reminiscent of a semicircular cope hem and it seems very likely that fragments B3 and B5 were indeed once the lining of a cope.[20]

Three barely discernable lines of wear can be detected near to the pale arc, all closely following the curve of the latter. These were identified as stitch lines by the presence of several fragments of off-white thread along their lengths. They probably indicate that a fabric border, perhaps trimmed with braid, was used to finish the edge of the conjectural cope lined by fragments B3 and B5. Fragments B2 and B4 could have been used to line a chasuble and cope hood respectively, but there is no conclusive evidence of this (Figs 8 and 9). It was not possible to ascertain whether any of the blue linen fragments were used to line the cope or copes made from the cloth of gold fragments. Construction analysis allowed a relative chronology for each table carpet component to be established (Maskell 2006: ch. 4, table 14) and this in turn informed the selection of samples for scientific analysis. The analyses described below

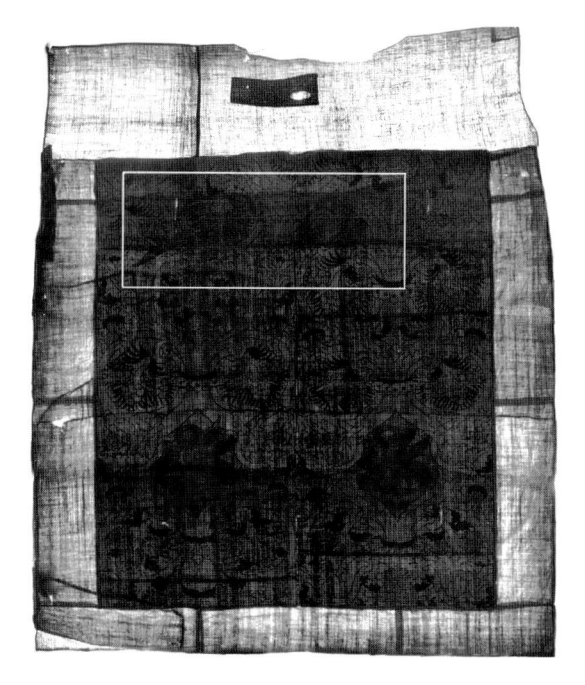

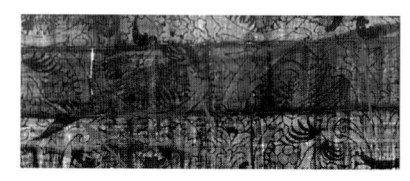

Figure 6 Concealed seam turnings of the table carpet seen from the obverse. Composite image formed from 15 photographs taken by Mike Halliwell using transmitted light technique. Above: Whole table carpet: white box indicates area shown in detail below. Below: Detail of table carpet: arrows indicate shaped seam turning of blue linen fragment B3 (© Textile Conservation Centre, University of Southampton) (Plate 105 in the colour plate section).

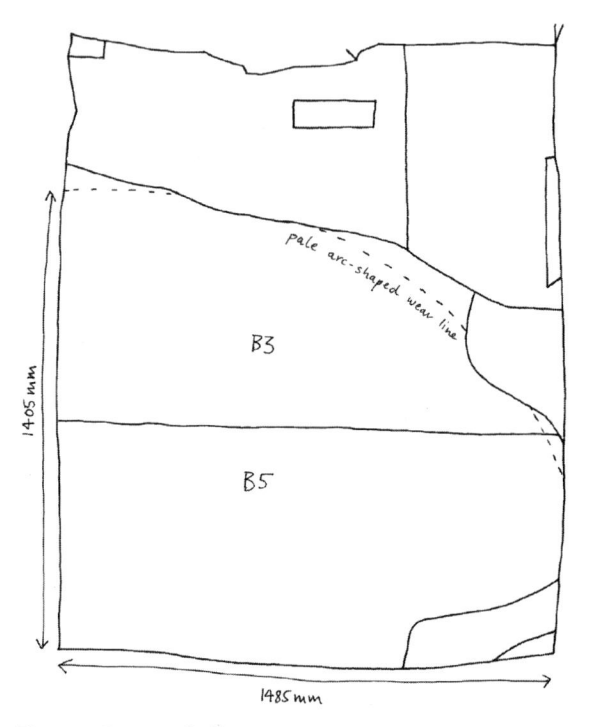

Figure 7 Reverse of table carpet: pale arc-shaped line of wear and dimensions of conjectural segment of cope lining (approximately a quarter circle) (© Textile Conservation Centre, University of Southampton).

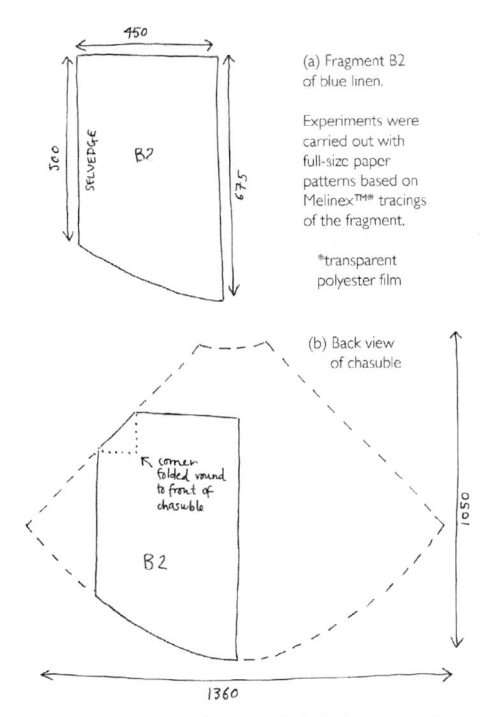

Figure 8 Conjectural placement of blue linen fragment B2 within the template of a chasuble (dimensions in mm). (Chasuble drawing based on images and descriptions in Johnstone 2002; Mayer-Thurman 1975; Mayo 1984. © Textile Conservation Centre, University of Southampton.)

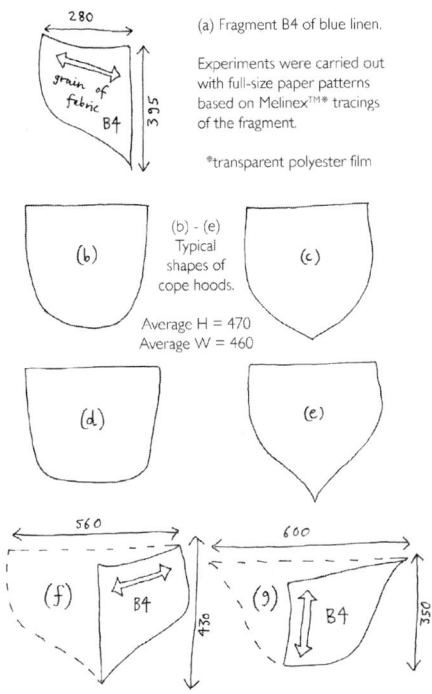

Figure 9 Conjectural placement of blue linen fragment B4 within the template of a cope hood (dimensions in mm). (Cope hood drawings based on images and descriptions in Johnstone 2002; Mayer-Thurman 1975; Mayo 1984. 'Average' dimensions as calculated in Maskell 2006: appendix I. © Textile Conservation Centre, University of Southampton.)

were undertaken in an attempt to obtain manufacture dates for individual components and thereby provide some fixed points on which to anchor the relative chronology.

Weave analysis

The primary aim of weave analysis was to determine the date and place of manufacture of the various fabric elements of the table carpet. The weave structures of the blue linen and plain red velvet were not sufficiently distinctive for any conclusions to be drawn. A detailed weave analysis of the cloth of gold was undertaken by Lisa Monnas, however, which enabled her to date the cloth to the first quarter of the 16th century and to establish that it was manufactured in Italy, probably in Florence (see appendix). Cinzia Maria Sicca has noted a particular similarity between the iconography of the table carpet fragments and that of the cloth of gold used to make a set of vestments given to Cortona Cathedral in 1526 by the Passerini family (Sicca, in this volume, pp. 93–104). Lisa Monnas, while recognising a relationship between the two designs, has pointed out some differences between the weaves of these two cloths and has judged the pelican cloth to be an example of *riccio sopra riccio* (loop over loop) fabric of the second quality.[21]

Metal thread analysis

The main aim of this analysis was to ascertain whether properties of the metal thread wefts of the cloth of gold could indicate a date for production of the fabric. Seven samples were analysed by Paul Garside using scanning electron microscopy with energy-dispersive spectroscopy (SEM–EDS). The results are summarised in Table 1. Following Garside (2002) and Wickens (2003), the findings were compared to data available in previous studies to determine whether characteristics of the table carpet metal threads matched those of other threads thought to date from the early 16th century.[22]

All table carpet samples were shown to be of similar construction, that is to say, metal strip(s) wound in a spiral around a fibre core consisting of a single-ply silk yarn (S twist). This thread type is found in textiles dating from the 15th through to the 19th century.

All samples were single wound except TC 25, which was double wound. Sample TC 22 was found to be a silver/copper alloy and the remaining samples were silver gilt. Four of the metal strips appeared to have been cut from sheets; the other four were probably produced by the 'cast, drawn and rolled' method. The latter method was known from the early 15th century but began widely to replace the former in the late 15th to early 16th century. The presence of both types of strip offers evidence for a manufacture date during this transitional period (Hacke *et al.* 2003: 3310).

Only a very few instances of double-wound metal strips are recorded in earlier studies, and these belong to textiles dating from the late 15th to early 16th century.[23] It is difficult to assess the significance of double winding because of lack of comparative data. It is thought that double-wrapped threads

Table 1 Results of SEM–EDS analysis of metal thread samples from the cloth of gold.

Sample number	Construction of thread[24]	Fibre core	Type of metal	Production method of strip[25]	Ag (Metals %*)	Cu (Metals %*)
TC 21	Single wound S	Yellow silk	Silver gilt	Probably C,D&R	86	14
TC 22	Single wound S	White silk	Silver/copper alloy	Probably C,D&R	88	12
TC 23	Single wound S	Yellow silk	Silver gilt	Possibly B&C	86	14
TC 24	Single wound S	Yellow silk	Silver gilt	Probably C,D&R	88	12
TC 25	Double wound	Yellow silk				
	Inner S		Silver gilt	Probably B&C	71	29
	Outer Z		Silver gilt	Probably B&C	94	6
TC 26	Single wound S	Yellow silk	Silver gilt	Probably B&C	82	18
TC 27	Single wound S	Yellow silk	Silver gilt	Probably C,D&R	88	12

B&C = beaten and cut; C,D&R = cast, drawn and rolled; Ag = silver; Cu = copper
*For silver-gilt threads this value refers to the composition of the silver/copper alloy substrate

may have been used to achieve particular design effects as well as creating an extremely luxurious appearance (Hacke *et al.* 2003: 3310). This does not seem to be the case, however, for the table carpet as there is no obvious correlation between double-wrapped threads and design elements. Scattered throughout the cloth of gold are short lengths (*c.*20–30 mm) of Z wound strips wrapped over the main long S wound strips. It appears that the short Z strips may have been used to cover joins between the long S strips. This presents an interesting avenue for further research as no other examples of this use of double-wound strips have apparently been recorded.[26]

In all five silver-gilt threads with single S wound strips, the Ag/Cu ratio was similar (Ag 82–88%, Cu 12–18%). The metals in the double-wound strips were present in proportions markedly different from this range, and showed a wide variation in ratio between inner (Ag 71%, Cu 29%) and outer (Ag 94%, Cu 6%) strips. The Ag/Cu ratio of the single-wound threads from the table carpet is matched in samples from a number of textiles dating from the late 15th through to the 17th century. The ratios found in the double-wound threads are matched too, but an Ag value as low as 71% is not often recorded. The Ag value in the silver alloy strip is also lower than that in most of the documented silver strips. Further investigation into the significance of these lower values is required.[27]

Dye analysis

Nine samples from the table carpet were analysed by Ina Vanden Berghe using high performance liquid chromatography with photodiode array detection (HPLC–PDA). The main aim was to ascertain if the dye sources detected could help establish a manufacture date for the various components. The findings are summarised in Table 2 (Maskell 2006: appendix H).

Woad, indigo, weld and kermes, the probable dye sources for the cloth of gold samples, all have long histories as dyestuffs and are known to have been in frequent use in Europe in the late 15th and early 16th century. Young fustic was also used at this time, though less commonly. Weld and woad/indigo continued to be important dyestuffs until the 18th and 19th centuries respectively. Their presence cannot therefore be seen as an indicator for a particular date. Kermes and young fustic were less used from the early 1500s when they were superseded by New World imports. Their presence may be suggestive of a 16th-century or earlier date, but is by no means conclusive evidence for dating.[28]

Table 2 Results of HPLC–PDA analysis of samples from various table carpet components.

Sample number	Sample description	Probable dye source
TC 10	Yellow silk warp from cloth of gold fragment G9	Young fustic, weld*
TC 11	Red silk pile warp from cloth of gold fragment G9	Kermes, weld*, tannin
TC 15	Blue silk brocading weft from cloth of gold fragment G9	Woad/indigo
TC 16	Green silk brocading weft from cloth of gold fragment G9	Weld*, woad/indigo
TC 08	Brick-red silk warp from hidden selvedge fragment (previous border?)	Madder, tannin
TC 09	Plain red silk velvet border (a) red main warp (b) dark pink pile warp (c) pale pink weft	Madder, cochineal, tannin Madder, Mexican cochineal Cochineal, redwood
TC 12	Peach silk stitching thread	Redwood, weld*, tannin
TC13	Red-brown silk stitching thread	Tannin, redwood
TC 14	Bright red linen stitching thread	Synthetic dyes: alizarin red SS (CI: mordant red 2, CI no 58260)

*The probable dye source is weld, but dyer's broom could also have been used

The particular dyestuffs chosen to colour a fabric can indicate its quality and value, as well as its possible date. Documentary sources record various dyeing regulations in Italy and other European countries, including the prohibition of certain dyestuffs in order to maintain high production standards (Brunello 1973: chs IV and V). Weave analysis showed that the pelican cloth of gold is of Italian workmanship dating to the first quarter of the 16th century. It might therefore be expected to conform to the strict standards laid down for the Italian dyeing industry at that time. The weld/young fustic and kermes/weld combinations found in samples TC 10 and TC 11 of the pelican cloth of gold were, however, forbidden by the regulations. Weld was permitted for the dyeing of yellow, while the use of young fustic was banned (Brunello 1973: 139). Kermes, the main dye source for TC 11, was an expensive red dye associated with rank (Walton 1992) and was not to be mixed with other lesser dyes (Brunello 1973: 137).

The presence of these prohibited dye mixes demonstrates that subtle gradations of quality can be found even among the most exclusive of fabrics, as has already been noted in connection with the weave structure of the cloth of gold. It may be that even the fabulously rich Bishop Fox of Winchester set some limits on his spending, and was content on occasion to purchase from the second level of the most expensive textiles. Although this might seem a surprising proposition, forbidden dye combinations including less expensive dyestuffs have also been found in textiles made for Henry VII (the Stonyhurst cope and a Hearse cloth – Wickens 2003: 64–6), and if these dyes were good enough for a king, they should certainly have been good enough for his bishop.

Samples from the concealed fragmentary selvedge, the red velvet border, and the peach and red-brown stitching threads contained various combinations of three red dyestuffs (redwood, cochineal and madder) and tannin. In the first three samples the tannin is probably evidence of mordanting (a pre-dyeing process necessary for some dyestuffs), whereas in sample TC 13 it appears to have been used as the main dye component in order to produce a dark colour (Vanden Berghe 2006).

Although the type of cochineal in samples TC 09 (a) and (c) could not be ascertained, the presence of Mexican cochineal in sample TC 09 (b) confirms a post-1550 date (i.e. after imports from the New World began) for the red velvet border. Madder and redwood have long been used for dyeing, as has tannin. A meaningful *terminus post quem* could not therefore be determined for the concealed fragmentary selvedge or for the peach and red-brown stitching threads. Cochineal, madder and redwood all fell out of use in Europe from the 1870s onwards when synthetic red dyestuffs started to become available.[29] Finally, the particular synthetic dye found in sample TC 14 indicates a post-1886 date (Vanden Berghe 2006).

Conclusion

Analysis of the construction of the table carpet enabled a relative chronology of interventions to the object to be established. The sequence of repairs and replacement of the borders implies a long history of use, and dye analysis indicates that all but one repair probably took place before c.1870. Weave analysis suggests that the cloth of gold can be dated to c.1500–25, but it is not possible to assign similarly firm dates to other components of the table carpet on the evidence of technical or scientific analyses undertaken so far. The documentary evidence plausibly suggests a more precise dating, however, and confirms the value of combining both technical and scientific analysis with historical research.

President Fowler, writing in 1893, notes that the table carpet could have been made as early as the Elizabethan period and also describes it as intended for a 'Puritan Communion Table' (Fowler 1893: 99 and 114). This implies that the carpet must have appeared well worn and of antique character by the late 19th century. It is not possible to deduce from Fowler's remarks whether the carpet was actually in use in his time. A repair made with a bright red stitching thread dated to post-1886 may indicate contemporary use, although as the thread is not closely colour matched to the fabric and the stitching is not carefully executed it could be that the repair was carried out simply to keep the carpet from falling to pieces while in storage.

In terms of general shape and form, the table carpet appears to have been designed as a covering for a free-standing communion table in the body of Corpus Christi College chapel, such as would have existed in the late 16th and early 17th century. If this is the case, we cannot be sure whether the carpet was created because of genuine conversion to the Reformed style of worship, or as an act of expediency to preserve the copes in a more acceptable and less 'Catholic' form, or simply to recycle worn-out vestments. Given the apparently Catholic tendencies of the college at this period, the first of these three hypotheses seems the least plausible.

It is unlikely that the carpet was made for the main altar in the college chapel at any time between the 1630s and the 1850s as it is not 'Laudian' in style. Equally, it cannot be an example of the medieval-style frontal revived during the Oxford Movement in the mid-19th century because of its form, and because its sequence of interventions is suggestive of a time-span longer than c.1850–70. Also, if the carpet was made around 1850 we might expect it to have appeared 'newer' to President Fowler in 1893.

The scientific and technical analyses provided data that could be used not only to support the documentary account, but also to extend understanding of the object in ways that the written word cannot. For example, the dye and weave analyses permitted a more nuanced assessment of the quality of the cloth of gold than would have been possible on the basis of a written description alone. The blue linen lining was not mentioned in the sources at all, but construction analysis yielded valuable evidence relating to its previous use. On the other hand, it may only be through a documentary reference, if one is ever found to exist, that a precise date for the table carpet's construction can be established. Overall the table carpet project has succeeded in placing on record a considerable number of findings, from both documentary evidence and technical analysis, while at the same time providing a foundation for new avenues of research.

Appendix (*by Lisa Monnas*)

Table carpet made from Bishop Fox's copes

Composed of 14 pieces of cloth of gold with applied crimson velvet borders around three sides, backed with blue, tabby-weave linen.

Cloth of gold of 'tissue'

Loom width: 57 cm within the selvedges, an incomplete selvedge measuring 0.5 cm wide visible; loom width including selvedges conjecturally over 58 cm wide (near to the Florentine *braccio* of 58.3 cm).

Weave analysis

Materials
I Warps
- Main warps: silk, yellow (faded to cream on the front, but still visible as yellow on the rear), S twist.
- Binding warps: silk, yellow (faded to cream), S twist.
- Pile warps: silk, crimson, without visible twist.
- Proportions: three main warps to one binding warp and one pile warp.
- Thread count: Main warps: 48–51 per cm; binding warps: 16–17 per cm; pile warps: 16–17 per cm (7–8 over 0.4 cm).

II Wefts
- Ground weft: silk, cream, thick, low quality thread, without visible twist.
- Accompanying weft: silk, bright yellow, without visible twist.
- Pattern weft: filé thread of silver-gilt strip wrapped in S around a core of silk, dyed bright golden yellow, S-twisted (*NB* the core thread is faded to cream in many places and, similarly, the layer of gold has worn off the silver wrapping).
- Brocading wefts
1. Filé thread of silver strip tightly wrapped in S around a core of silk, white, S- twisted.
2. Silk, blue, without visible twist.
3. Silk, green, without visible twist.
4. Silk, white, without visible twist.

Proportion
- For most of the textile: two ground + two accompanying wefts and two silver-gilt filé pattern wefts to each rod.
- In the area of the pelican:
(a) in the blue and green parts, two ground and two accompanying wefts, one silver-gilt pattern weft and one silk brocading weft.
(b) in the white part, two ground and two accompanying wefts, one white silk brocading weft and two silver filé brocading wefts.

Thread count
- Ground wefts + accompanying wefts: collectively, 24/28 per cm.
- Pattern wefts of silver-gilt filé thread: 14/16 per cm.
- Brocading wefts:
1. Silver filé, 15 per cm.
2. Silver, blue, max. 9 per cm.
3. Silk, white, 8 per cm.
- Rods: 6/7 per cm.

Weave construction

Ground weave

Main warps tie the ground wefts in extended tabby (*gros de tours*).

Pattern

There are five pattern effects:
1. Gold ground: in the silk ground weave, the main warps tie the ground wefts in *gros de tours*. The 'pattern' of the gold ground is formed by one bright yellow silk ground weft (IIA), the 'accompanying weft', tied by a main warp (M2), and by two threads of silver-gilt filé, tied in a 1:2 Z-twill by the binding warp (B). In these areas, the pile warp is voided, travelling beneath the accompanying weft (IIA) so that it is not visible on the surface (Fig. 10).
2. Pile: there is one pile warp per three main warps per dent of the reed. Where the pile forms the pattern, the pile warps tie every fourth ground weft together with the two metal pattern wefts. The pile warp passes over the first

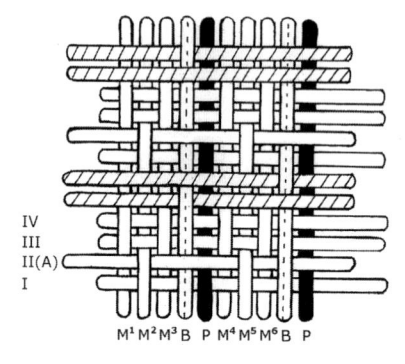

Figure 10 Pattern effect: gold ground (© Lisa Monnas).

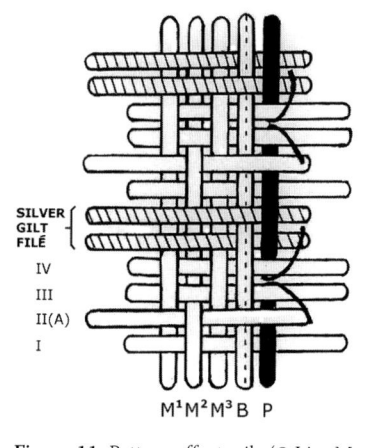

Figure 11 Pattern effect: pile (© Lisa Monnas).

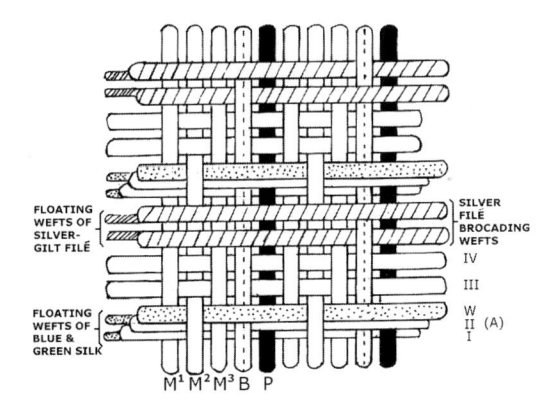

Figure 12 Pattern effect: brocaded area of white silk with silver filé (© Lisa Monnas).

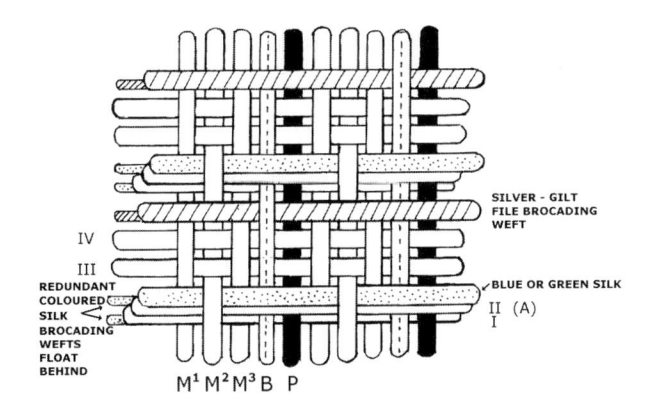

Figure 13 Pattern effect: brocaded areas of blue and green silk (© Lisa Monnas).

ground weft, passing under the accompanying weft (II A), emerging to form a velvet tuft between ground wefts III and IV, both entered in the same shed (Fig. 11).

3. Areas of bouclé metal wefts (the pelican, and details of the 'fruits' in the foliate design): these are formed by alternate silver-gilt pattern wefts. The loops occur between each binding point along alternate pattern wefts. The twill binding of these wefts automatically ensures that the loops are staggered. The loops have a distinctive profile, made from a fine thread, using a needle that was thick in relation to the width of the thread. As a result, the loops do not preserve a rounded profile but are, in many cases, twisted into a sort of figure-of-eight configuration. As far as I could make out, despite variations in their appearance, there is only one height of loop.

4. Brocaded area of white silk, with silver filé (the scroll carrying the motto): a brocading weft of white silk lies over the accompanying weft (IIA), tied by M2. A filé weft of silver on a white silk core is tied singly in 1:2 Z-twill by the binding warp. There are two silver wefts to each white silk brocading weft. In this area, the blue and green brocading wefts (see below) and the two silver-gilt pattern wefts float on the reverse of the textile. The pile warp is voided in this area (Fig. 12).

5. Brocaded areas of blue and green silk (the sky and the ground within the bishop's badge): the blue and green areas are treated identically. A blue/green silk brocading weft lies over the accompanying weft (IIA) and is tied by main warp M2, as for the white silk above. In this area, however, every second silver-gilt filé thread is carried across so that one green or blue thread alternates with a gold one. This gold thread is tied by the binding warp in a 1:2 Z-twill. The redundant alternate gold threads, and any redundant silk brocading wefts, float behind the textile. Where they have only a short distance to travel, some of the silver-gilt pattern wefts are carried across in pairs. The pile warp is voided in this area (Fig. 13).

Selvedge

Several portions of selvedge are present, but all seem to have been cut. The existing portions have main warps of green silk, then of white silk up to the outer (cut) edge. These warps tie the ground and accompanying wefts in *gros de tours* (the gold threads do not extend into the selvedges). Possibly there was another green stripe at the outer edge.

Notes

1. Numbers are prefixed as follows: 'G' for cloth of gold, 'R' for plain red velvet borders, 'B' for blue linen backing/border, 'Br' for brown linen patches.

2. According to legend the pelican feeds its young from a self-inflicted wound in its breast. The image of the pelican wounding itself was therefore adopted as a Christian symbol of redemption, sacrifice, atonement and the Resurrection, and is known as a 'Pelican in Piety' (Ware and Stafford 1974: 165).

3. Translation: 'Grace is an attribute of God' (Crook 1993: 270 and 300 n. 68).

4. Fox (b.1447/8) held high political office as lord privy seal under Henry VII and Henry VIII. He was successively appointed to the bishoprics of Exeter, Bath and Wells, Durham, and finally Winchester, but duties of state kept him from ever visiting his first two dioceses (Davies 2004). In 1517 he founded Corpus Christi College in Oxford and retired from politics the same year. Fox died in 1528 and was buried in his chantry chapel in Winchester Cathedral (Fowler 1893: 25–7). The see of Winchester was the wealthiest in England and its bishop 'had more liquid capital at his disposal than all but the king and one or two of the richest lay magnates in the country' (Dobson 2003: 234). Fox was thus able to become a lavish patron of building works, learning and the arts, and is known to have employed the best craftsmen of the day.

5. Various examples of Fox's use of the pelican motif are known, particularly in connection with the architectural works of which he was patron. The first appearance of the emblem that can definitely be associated with Fox is on carvings in Durham Castle, dating to the late 1490s during his tenure as bishop of Durham (Smith 1996: 18–19). An inventory, dated 1518, of goods in the chantry chapel built under Fox's direction (*c*.1513–18) at Winchester Cathedral attests his use of a pelican motif in connection with textiles. The list of vestments and furnishings includes the following: 'one vestment of blue velvet powdered with flowers and pelicans crossed with needlework ... one vestment of green velvet powdered with flowers and pelicans crossed with needlework ... one rich altar cloth of arras of the Nativity of our Lourde with a pelican at either end'. 'Vestment ... crossed with needlework' probably refers to a chasuble with cross-shaped orphrey. It is not clear from these descriptions whether Fox's motto EST DEO GRATIA was included with the pelican motif on any of the textiles. The inventory is attached to a schedule for the 1518 Visitation of the chantry chapel (Corpus Christi College, Oxford, A1. Cap. 2 Evid. 2).

6. The dissertation includes a detailed object record and a discussion of the conservation strategy adopted, but these cannot readily be summarised and so are omitted from this paper (see Maskell 2006, chs 2 and 5).
7. Dr Maria Hayward, Dr Paul Garside and Mr Mike Halliwell.
8. The approach used to research the table carpet was particularly inspired by Joelle Wickens's MA dissertation *Contract with Eternity: The Investigation and Documentation of a Hearse Cloth made in 1504/5 for Henry VII* (2003). She combined evidence from documentary sources with the findings of various technical analyses to construct a detailed record of the Hearse cloth and to answer questions relating to its attribution and provenance.
9. Permission was sought from Corpus Christi College to remove a total of approximately 25 samples; it was felt that this would provide a reasonable amount of data for preliminary analysis and that further removal of samples would be inappropriate until initial findings had been studied. It was hoped that a second set of analyses could be conducted, if funding could be found, but this proved impossible to arrange within the timescale of the dissertation. A list of all samples removed to date can be found in Maskell 2006, appendix B.
10. The inventory is attached to an account of the Visitation held in the chapel of Corpus Christi College by Dr Acworth in 1566 (Register of Bishop Horne of Winchester quoted by Fowler 1893: 110–15).
11. Professor Sicca argues in support of this notion (Sicca, this volume, pp. 93–104).
12. The source for the Chapel Accounts is the set of *Libri Magni* (Great Books) of Corpus Christi College that contain annual accounts of the different college departments.
13. The 1549/50 Chapel Accounts note a payment 'for a Communion table' (presumably for its purchase or construction), implying that the altar was abandoned in compliance with the 1550 Injunction. After the accession of Mary in 1553, and her attempts to restore Roman Catholic worship, the Accounts for 1553/4 show a payment for 'settynge uppe the altars and dressynge the church', and it can be assumed that the table was taken out of use at this time. According to Elizabeth's Injunction of 1559, the substitution of table for altar was optional, but the Chapel Accounts for 1559/60 show that the altar was put beyond use forever in that year, as payments are recorded for 'taking downe of the High Alter', 'covering the Aulters [side altars?]', and 'carrying the stones oute of the Churche'. The intention must have been to replace the 'High Alter' with a table and it may be that the table acquired in Edward's time was brought into use again, since we do not hear of another one until 1587/8 when a payment was made for 'a communion table bought at London'.
14. Canon 82 of the *Canons Ecclesiastical* of 1604 states that the holy table should be 'covered, in time of Divine Service, with a carpet of silk or other decent stuff'. I have not so far found any detailed descriptions of this type of textile. The concept of the communion table carpet as a drapery for the top of a table is supported by evidence from Bishop Hooper's Injunction of 1551 that forbade the 'decking or apparelling' of tables 'behind or before' as if they were altars (Duffy 1992: 472).
15. Laud, though an Anglican, was opposed to the Puritan Reformers and used his position to impose a particular style of worship (Spinks 2006). Laud's first biographer writes that by 1635 'many things had been done at Cambridge ... as beautifying their Chappels, furnishing them with Organs, advancing the Communion Table to the place of the Altar, adorning it with Plate and other Utensils for the Holy sacrament, defending it with a decent Rail from all prophanations' (Heylyn 1668: 314–15 quoted by Spinks 2006: 506). The Chapel Accounts of Corpus Christi College for *c.*1625–35 refer to hangings for the chapel walls, curtains, cushions, a pulpit cloth, new stained glass, and painting the wainscot. In 1635/6, payments are noted as follows: 'for the Rayle before the Communion table', 'for altering the Communion Table', and 'to Hall the Taylor for altering and mending the chapel cloths'. The wording of these records strongly suggests that the 'Rayle' was a single one in the north–south position prescribed by Laud, and also implies that the communion table and its cloth covering had to be adapted to this new arrangement (perhaps by lengthening). This may in turn indicate that the table had previously been in a freestanding 'forward' position. If Fox's pelican copes had been made into a table carpet by this time, the carpet shows no signs of any overall alteration in shape such as is suggested by these Chapel Accounts. However, the table carpet could have been among the cloths that are described as having been mended, since it shows evidence of several repairs.
16. In 1552, during the period of reform set in motion at the beginning of the reign of Edward VI, the president and two fellows of Corpus Christi were arrested (then imprisoned and released) for 'using upon Corpus Christi day other service than was appointed by the *Book of Service*' (Strype 1733 quoted by Fowler 1893: 97). They were presumably celebrating the feast of Corpus Christi according to the traditional liturgy. The same president was responsible for concealing chapel goods including 'Ornaments, Vessels, Copes, Cushions, Plate, Candlesticks, &c, which ... had been used for the Catholic service' to protect them from the Reformers (Wood 1786 quoted by Fowler 1893: 97). Goods were brought out of hiding on Mary's accession and hidden again on Elizabeth's accession (by the chaplain, another fellow, and the clerk of accounts). The concealment of goods was one of the matters dealt with during the 1566 Visitation (see note 10). We know that the goods found in 1566 included the pelican copes, as they are specifically described, and there is no reason to suppose that these copes were not among the goods concealed earlier, in Edward's reign. In 1666 a lawsuit was brought regarding the ownership of '60 Copes, 2 carpets and 54 pieces [of copes?]' found at Burford (Action brought at the Oxford Assizes, 1666, quoted by Fowler 1893: 245–6). These items were almost certainly the property of Corpus Christi College, but had probably been placed with the defendants for safekeeping during the Commonwealth. There is no specific reference to the pelican copes or fragments thereof among these items.
17. Although the Edwardine Prayer Book of 1552 banned the wearing of copes, the Elizabethan Prayer Book of 1559 permitted their use.
18. Transmitted light photography was carried out under the supervision of Mike Halliwell at the TCC. The carpet was laid face-up on a 6 mm sheet of colourless Perspex (acrylic resin) large enough to contain its full surface area. The carpet and Perspex were placed on low supports so that a light box could be positioned below the Perspex sheet; a camera was mounted about one metre above it. By manoeuvring both camera and light box, and progressively rolling up the table carpet, it was possible to photograph the carpet in 15 sections. The 15 images obtained were digitally joined to form one composite image of the whole carpet (Fig. 6). See Thompson and Halliwell (this volume, pp. 237–43) for another project using transmitted light photography.
19. It was particularly difficult to draw conclusions because the central panel of the table carpet contains enough cloth of gold for only about half an 'average' cope (as calculated in Maskell 2006, appendix I), and because the woven designs, of the smaller fragments in particular, do not offer any clues as to the relative position of the fragments within a cope template.
20. Not enough of the arc survives (slightly less than a 'quarter' of an imagined circle) to be sure of the hypothetical cope's dimensions. However, as shown in Figure 7, the distances 140.5 cm and 148.5 cm are both near to an 'average' cope height of 142 cm (as calculated in Maskell 2006, appendix I), and may both approximate to the original 'radius' of the semicircle of fabric.
21. Lisa Monnas has noted the following differences: Fox's cloth is not as finely woven as the Passerini cloth, and only selected details (as opposed to the whole) of the branched pomegranate design are worked in bouclé wefts; in the Passerini cloth the polychrome effects are created by means of bouclé wefts with silk cores of various colours, while in Fox's cloth the bouclé wefts all have yellow silk cores and the polychrome effects are achieved by flat brocading wefts. Her comparison of the two cloths will be included in her forthcoming book *Merchants, Princes and Painters: Silk Fabrics in Italian and Northern European Paintings 1300–1500*.

22. The investigation focused on determining characteristics that Dr Garside's experience had shown to be most likely to assist with dating: construction of the thread, method of manufacturing the metal component of thread, type/proportion of metals present (in particular the silver/copper ratio which is the most indicative evidence since it does not change over time). Apart from Garside (2002), Wickens (2003), and the literature cited by them (Darrah 1987; Montegut *et al.* 1992), it was only possible to find one other study offering comparable data on this subject: Hacke *et al.* 2003. For full details of data compiled see Maskell 2006, appendices F and G, tables 16–18.
23. Montegut *et al.* 1992: 46.109.26; Wickens 2003: 69; Hacke *et al.* 2003: 64 E6, 28 G6, 136 C6, 73 E4, 94 D6, 43 F6, 67 E6 (all quoted in Maskell 2006: appendix G, tables 16–18).
24. Metal threads incorporated into textiles can take a number of forms; for details see Garside 2002: 36–41.
25. The earliest metal strips were produced by beating metal into sheets and then cutting sheets into strips; wires could be formed by beating individual strips into shape. After about 1400 a new technique developed whereby cast metal rods were drawn through dies to form thin wires; the wires were then flattened between rollers to produce strips (Jaro 1984; Darrah 1987).
26. I am most grateful to Dr Garside for examining the table carpet and confirming my observations about the instances of short Z-wound strips. He had not seen this particular pattern of double-wound strips before and proposed that their purpose might be to cover joins between longer strips.
27. Copper was usually added to silver to make the metal harder, more durable and easier to work (Garside 2002: 41–2).
28. The following literature was consulted: Balfour-Paul 1998; Brunello 1973; Hofenk de Graaff 1969; Ponting 1980; Sandberg 1997; Storey 1978.
29. The following literature was consulted: Brunello 1973; Chenciner 2000; Hofenk de Graaff 1969; Ponting 1980; Storey 1978; Wouters 1996.

Acknowledgements

The author would like to thank the Pasold Research Fund for supporting her MA dissertation research, and the AHRC for supporting her second-year studies. She is extremely grateful to the President and Fellows of Corpus Christi College, Oxford for granting permission to investigate the table carpet, and to Mr Julian Reid, Archivist of Corpus Christi and Merton Colleges, for his invaluable assistance at every stage of the project. The author is also much indebted to the following: Lisa Monnas; Cinzia Maria Sicca (University of Pisa); Ina Vanden Berghe (Royal Institute for Cultural Heritage, Brussels); Dr Maria Hayward (Reader in Textile Conservation, Head of Studies and Research, Director of the AHRC Research Centre for Textile Conservation and Textile Studies, TCC); Frances Lennard (MA Textile Conservation Course Convenor, TCC); Mike Halliwell (Lecturer and Conservation Photographer, TCC); Dr Paul Garside (Research Fellow with the AHRC Research Centre for Textile Conservation and Textile Studies, TCC); Caroline Edwards and other staff at the Hampshire Record Office.

The table carpet was photographed by Mike Halliwell at the TCC; images are reproduced courtesy of Corpus Christi College, Oxford.

References

Balfour-Paul, J. (1998) *Indigo*. London: British Museum Press.
Brunello, F. (1973) *The Art of Dyeing in the History of Mankind* (1st American edn). Vicenza: Neri Pozza Editore.
Chenciner, R. (2000) *Madder Red: A History of Luxury and Trade*. London: Routledge Curzon.
Crook, J. (ed.) (1993) *Winchester Cathedral: Nine Hundred Years, 1093–1993*. Chichester: Phillimore.
Darrah, J.A. (1987) 'Metal threads and filaments', in *Recent Advances in the Conservation and Analysis of Artefacts*, J. Black (ed.), 211–21. London: Summer Schools Press.
Davies, C.S.L. (2004) Fox, Richard (1447/8–1528). (Online) *Oxford Dictionary of National Biography*. http://www.oxforddnb.com [accessed 27 August 2006].
Dobson, B. (2003) 'Two ecclesiastical patrons: Archbishop Henry Chichele of Canterbury and Bishop Richard Fox of Winchester', in *Gothic: Art for England 1400–1547*, R. Marks and P. Williamson (eds), 234–6. London: Victoria and Albert Museum.
Duffy, E. (1992) *The Stripping of the Altars: Traditional Religion in England c. 1400–c. 1580*. New Haven and London: Yale University Press.
Fowler, T. (1893) *The History of Corpus Christi College*. Oxford: Clarendon Press for the Oxford Historical Society.
Garside, P. (2002) *Investigations of Analytical Techniques for the Characterisation of Natural Textile Fibres towards Informed Conservation*. Unpublished PhD thesis, University of Southampton.
Hacke, A., Carr, C.M., Brown, A. and Howell, D. (2003) 'Investigation into the nature of metal threads in a Renaissance tapestry and the cleaning of tarnished silver by UV/Ozone (UVO) treatment', *Journal of Materials Science* 38: 3307–14.
Hofenk de Graaff, J.H. (1969) 'Natural dyestuffs: origin, chemical constitution, identification'. Paper presented at the ICOM Meeting, 15–19 September 1969, Amsterdam. Amsterdam: Central Research Laboratory for Objects of Art and Science.
Jaro, M. (1984) 'The technological and analytical examination of metal threads on old textiles', In *Proceedings of the Fourth International Restorer Seminar, Veszprem, Hungary, 2–10 July 1983*, 253–64. Budapest: Központi Muzeumi Igazgatóság.
Johnstone, P. (2002) *High Fashion in the Church: The Place of Church Vestments in the History of Art from the Ninth to the Nineteenth Century*. Leeds: Maney.
Maskell, F.M.L. (2006) *The Use and Re-use of Liturgical Textiles: A Communion Table Carpet in Corpus Christi College, Oxford*. Unpublished MA dissertation, University of Southampton.
Mayer-Thurman, C.C. (1975) *Raiment for the Lord's Service: A Thousand Years of Western Vestments*. Chicago: Art Institute of Chicago.
Mayo, J. (1984) *A History of Ecclesiastical Dress*. London: Batsford.
Montegut, D., Adelson, C., Koestler, R.J. and Indictor, N. (1992) 'Examination of metal threads from some XV/XVI century Italian textiles by scanning electron microscopy and energy dispersive X-ray spectrometry', in *Materials Issues in Art and Archaeology III: Symposium held 27 April–1 May 1992, San Francisco*, P. Vandiver *et al.* (eds), 309–17. Pittsburgh: Materials Research Society.
Pocknee, C.E. (1963) *The Christian Altar in History and Today*. London: Mowbray.
Pocknee, C.E. and Randall, G.D.W. (1986) 'Altar hangings', in *A New Dictionary of Liturgy and Worship*, J.G. Davies (ed.), 8–10. London: SCM Press.
Ponting, K. (1980) *A Dictionary of Dyes and Dyeing*. London: Brit/Ward.
Randall, G.D.W. (1986) 'Communion table', in *A New Dictionary of Liturgy and Worship*, J.G. Davies (ed.), 183. London: SCM Press.
Sandberg, G. (1997) *The Red Dyes: Cochineal, Madder and Murex Purple*. (Translation of original Swedish edition published in 1994 as *Purpur Koschenill Krapp* by Tidens förlag, Stockholm.) Asheville, NC: Lark Books.
Smith, A. (1996) *Roof Bosses of Winchester Cathedral*. Winchester: Winchester Cathedral.
Spinks, B.D. (2006) 'Anglicans and dissenters', in *The Oxford History of Christian Worship*, G. Wainwright and K.B. Westerfield Tucker (eds), 492–533. New York: Oxford University Press.
Storey, J. (1978) *Dyes and Fabrics*. London: Thames and Hudson.
Strype, J. (1733) *Ecclesiastical Memorials*. Oxford: Clarendon Press.

Vanden Berghe, I. (2006) 'Natural dye analysis (unpublished report, Royal Institute for Cultural Heritage, Brussels)', in *The Use and Re-use of Liturgical Textiles: A Communion Table Carpet in Corpus Christi College, Oxford*, F.M.L. Maskell, 186–94. Unpublished MA dissertation, University of Southampton,

Walton, P. (1992) 'The dyes', in *Medieval Finds from Excavations in London (4): Textiles and Clothing c. 1150–c. 1450*, E. Crowfoot, F. Pritchard and K. Staniland (eds), 199–201. London: Museum of London.

Ware, D. and Stafford, M. (1974) *An Illustrated Dictionary of Ornament*. London: Allen & Unwin.

White, J.F. (2006) 'The spatial setting', in *The Oxford History of Christian Worship*, G. Wainwright and K.B. Westerfield Tucker (eds), 793–816. New York: Oxford University Press.

Wickens, J. (2003) *Contract with Eternity: The Investigation and Documentation of a Hearse Cloth made in 1504/5 for Henry VII (b. 1455, d. 1509)*. Unpublished MA dissertation, University of Southampton.

Wood, A. (1786) *The History and Antiquities of the Colleges and Halls in the University of Oxford*. Oxford: Clarendon Press.

Wouters, J. (1996) 'Dye analysis of Florentine borders of the 14th to 16th centuries', *Dyes in History and Archaeology* 14: 48–59.

The author

Florence Maskell worked for ten years in the Ashmolean Museum as a researcher and web designer on various projects relating to classical art and archaeology. While at the Ashmolean she completed a postgraduate diploma in museum studies (University of Leicester). In 2004 she returned to full-time education as a student on the MA textile conservation course at the Textile Conservation Centre. She has recently graduated from the TCC and hopes to pursue a career in textile conservation.

Address

Florence Maskell, Textile Conservation Centre, University of Southampton, Park Avenue, Winchester SO23 8DL, UK (florence.maskell@gmail.com)

Who put the text in textiles? Deciphering text hidden within a 1718 coverlet: documentation of papers hidden within an early 18th-century coverlet using transmitted light photography

Karen N. Thompson and Michael Halliwell

ABSTRACT Transmitted light photography has been used to record papers concealed within an 18th-century coverlet. The coverlet, which is made from fabric blocks pieced over paper templates, still has the papers inside it. Glimpses of exposed papers through damaged fabrics showed that they have manuscript and printed text on them. They provide a rare source that could yield information about the makers, the people who owned it or for whom the coverlet was made. The aim of this research has been to reveal and document this hidden layer.

Keywords: coverlet, transmitted light photography, paper, patchwork

Introduction

This coverlet, which has the date 1718 worked into the design, is thought to be the earliest known dated English patchwork and has already been the subject of detailed research by the Quilters' Guild of the British Isles[1] (Fig. 1). Guild members have documented the fabrics used to make the coverlet and while they were studying the construction, it became clear that the makers left the paper templates inside the individual patches of the coverlet. So far, attempts to identify who made the coverlet and who owned or commissioned it have proved inconclusive. The papers concealed within the coverlet, however, provide a tantalising source of possible information that may shed light on these unanswered questions. Staff at the Textile Conservation Centre proposed to see whether transmitted light photography would make it possible to read any text that might be present on the papers. It is hoped that this research will not only uncover information relating to the coverlet's history but that it will supplement our limited knowledge of early British patchwork.[2]

This paper presents and evaluates the methodology used to uncover the internal features of the coverlet and considers the initial findings which serve to illustrate the potential for further research combining empirical and material history, conservation and photography. While there is considerable scope to explore some of the ideas generated by this research further, this project was undertaken with highly specific, but limited, aims. These were to record the papers in the coverlet using a specialised photographic procedure, to categorise broadly the information found on the papers and to provide a resource for future study by the Quilters' Guild.[3]

During phase 1 of this research, the feasibility of reading the hidden papers using transmitted light photography was tested. A simulation of the coverlet's construction was created to determine what factors affected the reading of the concealed text. A range of fabrics with different weave structures was placed over a printed paper template and photographed using

Figure 1 Coverlet, 1718 (courtesy of the Quilters' Guild of the British Isles) (Plate 106 in the colour plate section).

transmitted light. It was found that it was possible to read papers concealed behind many fabrics. This technique was particularly successful when trying to decipher text hidden behind simple weave fabrics made from finely spun yarn such as silk and cotton. It was concluded that the coverlet, which was composed primarily of fine weave silks, could be photographed using transmitted light and many of the papers held within it could be documented (Thompson and Halliwell 2005). This paper concentrates on the work carried out in the second phase of the project which focused on the coverlet itself.

Methodology

This section details how the laboratory-derived procedure undertaken in phase 1 was modified and applied to the coverlet. The first consideration was how to effectively scale up the process from a test target of 10 cm square to a 2 m square coverlet, ensuring that handling of the historic textile was kept to a minimum, causing minimal stress to the fabrics and keeping the light exposure as low as possible. Light exposure and inappropriate handling were both identified as risks associated with the transmitted light photography technique during phase 1. Based on the conclusions from this work, in order to minimise the effects of any light damage, a cold, UV-free light source was used to illuminate the area being photographed. In addition, to limit the amount of light exposure that the entire coverlet would receive, the light box was masked off so that it only illuminated the specific area (equivalent to 11 × 11 cm) that was to be photographed at any one time.

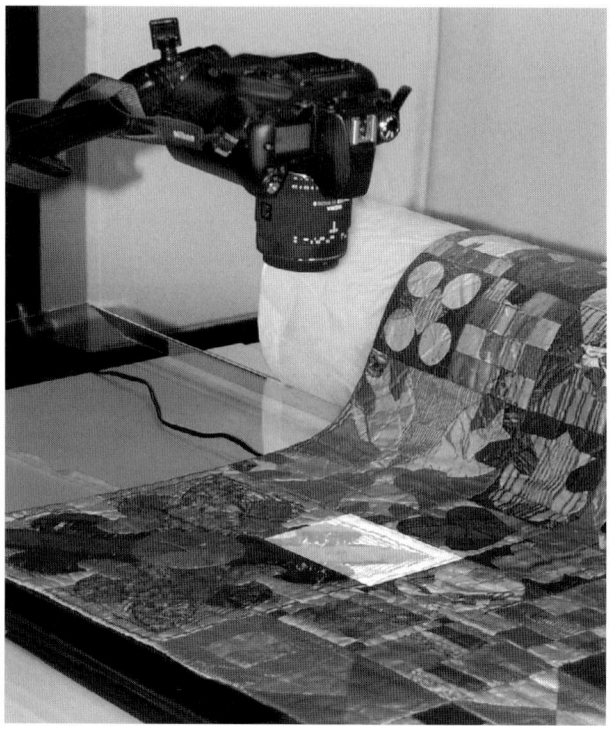

Figure 2 Photography of the coverlet using transmitted light showing the unrolled section of coverlet on the bridge-shaped acrylic support, illuminated square and camera on tripod (courtesy of the Quilters' Guild of the British Isles) (Plate 107 in the colour plate section).

The next challenge was to find a way to pass the light box under the coverlet so that each square could be photographed without causing damage and minimising handling. In addition, the camera needed to be mounted onto a tripod which limited how far it could extend over the textile. A bridge-shaped acrylic support was made that was sufficiently wide and high to allow a low profile light box to pass beneath it. This support spanned the full width of the coverlet and was deliberately made with gentle curves to prevent any chance of the textile creasing or snagging while it was passed over the acrylic bridge. Good access for photography was achieved by rolling the coverlet onto two, wide diameter rollers so that one section could be laid on the acrylic support and photographed at a time. This meant that the tripod arm and camera only had to extend over the width of the roller.

The light box was mounted on a push-pull sledge which sat beneath the bridge support and operated like a weaving shuttle. As the light box sledge was pulled or pushed, square by square beneath the textile, the tripod-mounted camera was moved in similar steps so ensuring that it was always facing down directly onto the illuminated area. Two of the tripod support legs were run along the table sides (parallel to the bridge support) in order to prevent the camera from twisting while moving between squares. Once a full row of squares had been completed, the textile was rolled on one row and the process was repeated for the return journey, in a steady left-to-right ... roll ... right-to-left ... roll fashion (Fig. 2).

The varied density of the fabrics used in the coverlet, both in terms of colour and/or weave, meant that there would not be one perfect exposure that could record all of the details present. In some cases, eight or more different exposures were made of the same square; short ones for the very lightweight silks and considerably longer ones for the dark velvets. It was decided that it was better to take more images rather than less in view of the nature of the subsequent manipulation the images would undergo and the 'costless' nature of digital imaging (as well as the minimal increase in light exposure). To repeat the set-up at a later date because of a bad exposure would have been prohibitive in terms of time and risks to the coverlet due to the additional handling and increased light exposure. Consequently, over 1000 images were taken.[4] The exposure details were recorded on an Excel spreadsheet for future reference.

Once all the images had been taken, they were processed and grouped to facilitate interpretation. Some of the images were modified using computer software to determine if an improvement in the quality could be achieved. Computer software can be of some assistance in producing enhanced images with regard to legibility. A feature of Adobe Photoshop CS2 is Higher Dynamic Range (HDR), which allows areas that are either underexposed (too dark) or overexposed (too bright) to effectively become transparent. A composite image is produced from an aligned, vertical stack of differently exposed images so allowing the correctly exposed areas to 'show through'. This results in a uniform, correctly exposed high-quality image. As is often the case, however, the software does not actually know what aspect of the image is required, so in many ways it is not ideal. It was therefore necessary to use computer manipulation selectively and employ a 'trial and error' method of finding the best image for this purpose rather than use a standard computer manipulation process.

The most significant factor with regard to legibility of the image was the proximity of the different components within the 'textile-text-textile' sandwich. This was identified in phase 1 of the project and it proved to be the case when the technique was used on the coverlet. The text becomes illegible where the separation between the top textile and paper is greater than about 1 mm. As a result of the complex construction techniques involved in patchwork, with numerous multilayered seams and overlapping fabrics, an uneven textile layer is produced. Consequently, it proved impossible to obtain a successful image of some squares without applying undue pressure to flatten the historic textile, something that could not be justified because of the risk of damage. This meant that it was not possible to achieve images as clear as was technically possible for some squares because of the need to protect the coverlet.

Interestingly, when images taken of particular squares in phases 1 and 2 were compared, the results from phase 2 were considerably less legible images than in phase 1. This emphasises the fact that multilayer textiles do not lay flat the same way twice. Potentially, on subsequent unrolling, some text may appear more legible again, however this repeated rolling-unrolling could not be justified for imaging purposes.

Most of the squares were photographed successfully. It proved impossible to take high-quality images of a few areas, notably those of very dark velvet. A combination of dark fibre colouring, high weave density and fabrics with a pile resulted in complete light absorption. There appears to be no way to photograph through this type of textile because 50% of the fibres are parallel to the imaging axis (i.e. vertical) and each seems to act as a single fibre optic light guide, channelling the light separately and resulting in very low transmission levels and complete image degradation.

After all the images were taken they were systematically examined and the best image from each batch selected. These were then documented and details of the text they contained were recorded. In some squares, the original ink used on the papers had spread and made the letters indistinct. Attempts to make this text legible met with limited success and several squares remain that may yield valuable information but at present are unreadable. This is one area where further progress could be made with future developments in computer software. Programs to find edges within an apparently featureless blur of grey are constantly being improved and the software that is normally used to increase the resolution of high-power microscopes, e.g. Image Pro Plus from Media Cybernetics, can be adapted to conventional photographic use. More user-friendly, flexible programs, such as Nikon Multimedia Sharpener Pro and CrispImage Pro Image Sharpening offer intelligent image sharpening and are being constantly improved as computer processing power increases. Once these programs are more widely available, the stock of images that were taken of the coverlet and that cannot be usefully read at present should be re-examined.

Transmitted light photography is high cost in terms of equipment[5] but these costs are minimised once the equipment is purchased as it can be reused. The cost of conservator/photographer time also needs to be taken into account. This equates approximately to 30 minutes per 11 cm^2 area[6] for large batch processing plus one day of time for set-up and handling. Nevertheless once the images have been recorded they can be accessed repeatedly at no extra cost. This results in markedly reduced handling of the fragile coverlet thus ensuring its future preservation.

A discussion of the findings

What can be learnt about the coverlet by examining its construction, fabrics and design?

The coverlet measures approximately 160 × 185 cm. It is a patchwork made from 182 blocks 'pieced over papers' which have been hand-sewn together (Fig. 1). This technique is sometimes referred to as the 'English method' (Quilters' Guild 1995: 218). The papers have been retained within the coverlet and were not removed when its construction was completed which is more common. It is not unknown, however, to find papers retained within a patchwork.[7] The patchwork is lined with a coarse linen backing which prevents access to the papers from the reverse.

The coverlet is made principally of 11 × 11 cm blocks with larger blocks around the edges and in the central area. The design is symmetrical along the central vertical axis, so similar block designs and fabrics have been used in the corresponding blocks on each side of the central axis.

Deryn O'Connor for the Quilters' Guild has carried out detailed analysis and research into the fabrics (Osler 2003: 79–93). She identified almost all of the fabrics to be recycled dress fabrics. Most of them are silk and include a combination of top fabrics and linings. The fabrics are thought to date from the 17th and 18th centuries and to represent British and European manufacture. The quality of the fabrics used in the coverlet indicates that 'the wearers were relatively high quality status ... [possibly] worn by the merchant classes, not the highest aristocracy' (Osler 2003: 79).

Tina Fenwick-Smith and Dorothy Osler (Osler 2003: 28–9) describe the coverlet as a most intricate piece of work including simple, popular geometric designs alongside complex representations of animals and flowers. Bridget Long (Osler 2003: 69) suggests the motifs as being difficult to piece and this was complicated by the detail in the background. The quality and complexity of some of the designs suggest that it was made by an accomplished needleworker or workers.[8] The representation of a man and a woman placed on either side of the date which is surmounted by a heart on this coverlet is a common representation used in patchwork to celebrate a marriage.[9] The initials may be of those for whom the coverlet was made and the date of the marriage or they may be those of the maker with the date representing when the coverlet was completed.

What do the papers reveal about the coverlet?

Over 60% of the papers within the coverlet have text on them and most of this is contained within the small blocks. The papers with text are fairly evenly distributed across the entire coverlet (Fig. 3). It appears that on the whole, recycled paper has been used for the templates. It is interesting that reused paper was incorporated permanently into an object. This use of recycled paper may have been an economic choice[10] or it may have symbolic value. The use of recycled paper in patchwork during the 18th and 19th centuries was not uncommon, however, and 'Old envelopes, or other waste writing paper ... may be used in backing up the pieces' (Fox 1994: 29). There is a clear sense that the paired/corresponding blocks on each side of the vertical axis were worked at one time because pieces of the same sheet of paper as well as the same fabrics were used to make these blocks (for example, blocks A10 and O10, and blocks E1 and K1, Fig. 3).

The papers seem to fall into five main groups and these have been illustrated by colour coding on Figure 3. These include numbering/marking systems, graphic markings (design and abstract lines), manuscript, printed texts and blank papers or those with no discernable markings. It is not possible to say categorically that the blocks with no markings are blank – it may be simply that any markings were not recorded using the transmitted light photography technique on this occasion.

The first group provided evidence of a numbering or marking system that was used on many of the blocks with geometric designs to facilitate the placing of the pieces within the block. In general, numbers were used but in several instances both numbers and symbols were employed and on one block only symbols were present (Fig. 4a). The variety of techniques used to make the geometric blocks indicates that more than one person was involved in making the coverlet. The numbering system is a simple construction technique which would have made it easy for a group of quilters to work on the project; it is a recognised technique used by many quilters today.

The second category of hidden text consists of graphic markings. Some appear to be random marks on recycled scrap paper (for the purposes of this research these have been called abstract markings) but others may be design sketches. One example was found in the block containing a swan (block F14, Fig. 3). The drawing appears to show the tail of the swan. It is interesting to note that it does not align fully with the template, possibly indicating that a skilled craftsperson has worked this block and did not need to follow the design exactly. On some papers there are lines marking out a grid, which might indicate the placement of the image in the block (Fig. 4b and block G11, Fig. 3). The block containing the figure of a woman (block I6, Fig. 3) has a rough sketch which may be an outline of the woman's shape. Equally, one geometric block (block J15, Fig. 3) has a drawing of part of a star which is a similar in shape and dimensions to the small stars found in other blocks.

The third category consists of fragments of manuscript (Fig. 4c) which were found in over 20% of the coverlet. Most of these papers appear to have been taken from pieces of personal correspondence. They are written in many different hands and they include names and dates. There is also an account ledger and a bill. The style of writing is consistent with 17th- and 18th-century hands but it is difficult to get a clear sense of what is written because only fragments of the documents remain and only odd words appear on some papers. In many cases, the writing is very small and difficult to read.

Several names were found on the papers and it was hoped that these might provide a clue to the coverlet's past. Using the research carried out so far by Mary Hewson for the Quilters' Guild (Osler 2003: 31–53) attempts have been made to determine whether there were any family connections with the names seen on the papers. The coverlet belonged to the Brown family of Aldbourne, Wiltshire, who believed it to be an heirloom but they were unsure when it was acquired and

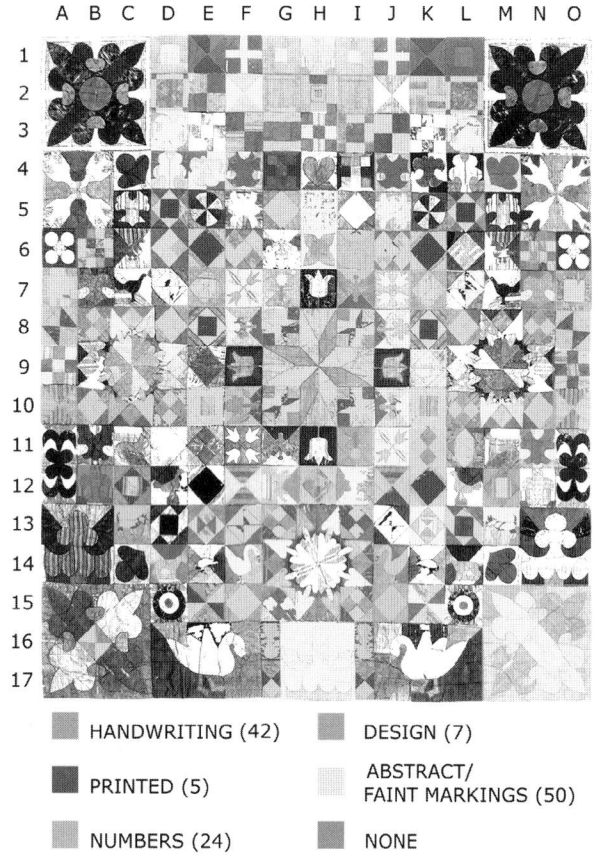

Figure 3 Diagram showing the types of text found and their position on the coverlet (courtesy of the Quilters' Guild of the British Isles) (Plate 108 in the colour plate section).

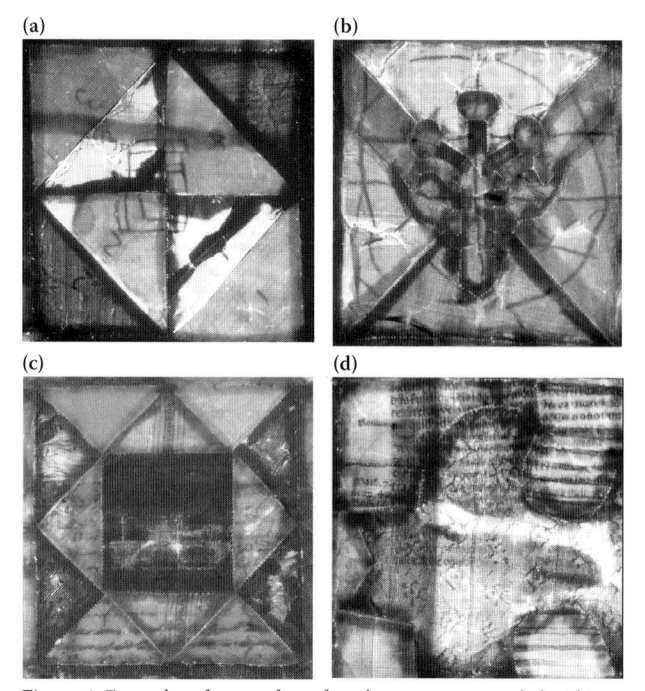

Figure 4 Examples of types of text found on papers concealed within the coverlet (courtesy of the Quilters' Guild of the British Isles).

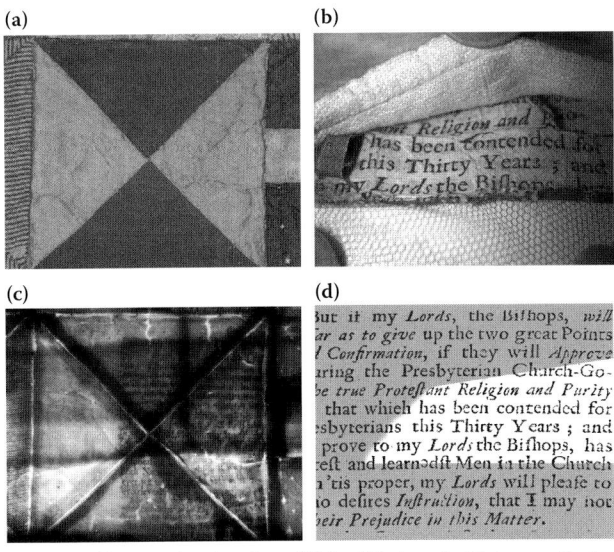

Figure 5 (a) Viewed with reflected light; (b) viewed with transmitted light; (c) paper visible through damaged seam; (d) extract from pamphlet. Note: highlighted text corresponds to text found on papers in the coverlet (courtesy of the Quilters' Guild of the British Isles) (Plate 109 in the colour plate section).

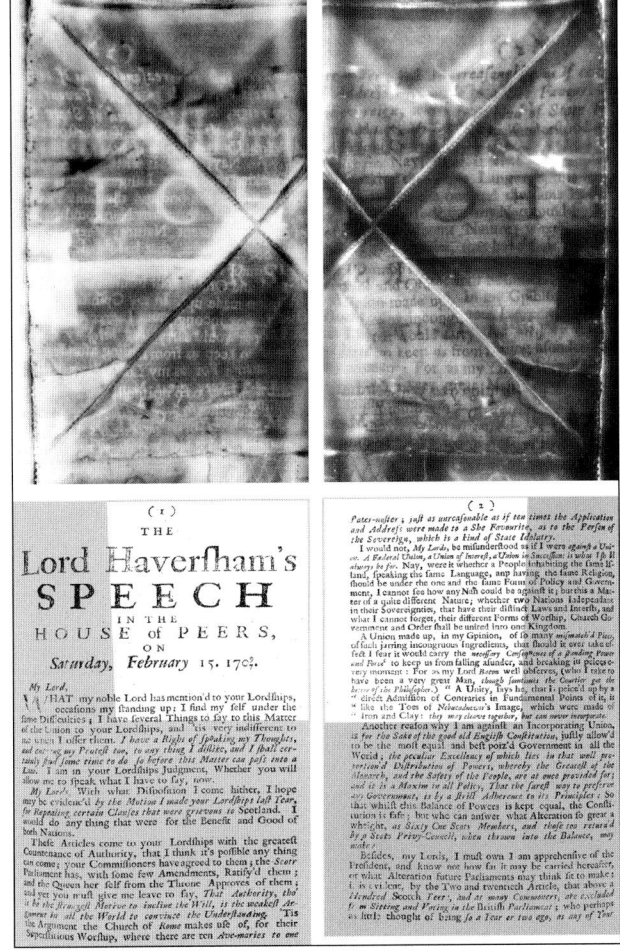

Figure 6 Top images show printed paper viewed with transmitted light; bottom images show pages 1 and 2 of pamphlet. Note: highlighted text corresponds to text found on papers in coverlet (courtesy of the Quilters' Guild of the British Isles).

whether or not it was made by one of their ancestors. The name John appears on several occasions on the papers (block F8, Fig. 3) and in the Brown family tree at the right period. Because this is such a common name, however, it does not provide any firm evidence that the 'John' referred to was from the Brown family. A complete name, with John as the given name, appears in the form of a signature (block L11, Fig. 3) but the writing is blurred so it is not possible to make more sense of the surname. Developments in computer technology may make it possible to read this in the future. The only legible complete name found so far is that of Robert Cox (block J3, Fig. 3) but from the research carried out he does not appear to be related to the Brown family. Nevertheless, the correspondence is likely to include letters sent to the maker(s) of the coverlet and it may be possible that Robert Cox is associated with the Browns. Mary Hewson of the Quilters' Guild is planning to undertake further research in this area.

The dates '1691' (block G3, Fig. 3) and 'of 168 ...' (block D2, Fig. 3) have been found on a few papers. As discussed above, the paper may have been kept for many years for reuse because of its economic value, alternatively it may have had some symbolic significance. Further study of these papers may reveal more information. It is common practice to keep scraps of fabric for many years for use in patchwork and perhaps paper was preserved in a similar manner (Quilters' Guild 1995: 218). It is not unusual for patchworks to be made over many years and the squares with these early dates could indicate that the coverlet was made over a long period of time.

The use of correspondence indicates that this coverlet was made by a person or people who were literate or part of a literate community. This adds weight to the argument that the makers were likely to be of at least moderately high status and educated people (Osler 2003: 79).

The fourth and final category with text is the printed material and this is the most intriguing. Printed texts only appear five times and they are from four different sources. Two are barely readable (block G4 and block L1, Fig. 3). Another includes what may be a page from a religious text (block B12, Fig. 3). Some of the words in the left-hand margin read 'Mar[k].7; [Acon].4; Rom.14' (Fig. 4d) and the text alongside is in Latin. This may be the Latin version of the bible also known as the Vulgate, used by Roman Catholics. If this is indeed a religious text, it is interesting to consider why such a text was used. What was the religious background of the people who had it in their possession? Another interesting feature is that the printing appears to contain two columns of text which makes the page width at least 20 cm. When open this would have been equivalent to an A3-sized book. Would such a large-sized bible be used at home or would it be more usually found in a church? It is difficult to determine much more information just by looking at the photographic representation of the square. It is possible however that a significant improvement in the legibility of the image could be achieved if this square was to be photographed in smaller segments. This was not possible within the time constraints of this project but this does not preclude further photography in the future.

The most exciting discovery to date relates to two of the printed pieces (block E1, Fig. 3, and block K1, Fig. 3 and Fig. 5a). It was possible to read both pieces of paper (four sides in total): one side was visible through an open seam (Fig. 5b) and the other three were visible with transmitted light (Fig. 5c and Fig. 6). Detailed study of the two printed pieces showed them to be from the same document (Fig. 5b,d and Fig. 6). They were taken from a speech made by Lord Haversham to parliament on the subject of the union of Scotland with England in 1707.[11] Careful comparison of the text, positioning of the font and anomalies in the printing indicate that the version found in the coverlet was printed in London in 1707. It contains a printing error in the date of the speech. The date reads 1709/7 but the correct date of that speech is in fact 1706/7 (it would appear that the '6' was inverted and so it reads '9').

Haversham was speaking out against the union and voicing his concerns, in particular, about Scotland's right to keep the Presbyterian church as the state church of Scotland and the disenfranchisement of those Scottish peers and commoners who would lose their seats in a reformed Unitarian parliament. This is a fascinating piece of social history. It shows that the people who made this coverlet must have had access to current political tracts. To date, three different print runs of this pamphlet have been identified,[12] two in London and another in Dublin. The existence of several versions of the speech suggests that it was a popular tract, so it is probable that many people may have had it in their possession. The dating of the text provides some tangible evidence that parts of the coverlet were made after 1707.

Conclusion

The use of transmitted light photography to record the papers concealed within the 1718 coverlet has proved to be very successful and some fascinating documents have been uncovered. The evidence gained from the reading the papers has shed light on the design and some of the production techniques used. Taken as a group, the hidden papers provide a rare glimpse into the social history of this object. Their nature and the subject matter provide an exciting opportunity to consider some of the wider contemporary social issues and to reflect on the people who made the coverlet. Key questions that need answering include why was a printed copy of Lord Haversham's speech used, what was the background of the people who had such papers in their possession, why did they cut up a religious text and who was Robert Cox?

There is much more to be discovered by studying the papers in close detail and the Quilters' Guild intends to undertake further research using these records in order to learn more about this fascinating piece of early English patchwork. The project has produced an invaluable archive so now the papers concealed within the coverlet can be accessed again and again without needing to expose it to excessive light and handling.

Acknowledgements

The authors would like to thank the AHRC Research Centre for Textile Conservation and Textile Studies for supporting this research; the Quilters' Guild of the British Isles (in particular Tina Fenwick-Smith, Bridget Long and Mary Hewson) for allowing them to study the coverlet and for their enthusiastic encouragement of this project; Dr Maria Hayward (Textile Conservation Centre) for support, encouragement and helping them to decipher some of the 17th- and 18th-century manuscript; and Dr Peter Jones (Birmingham University) for helping to decipher some of the 17th- and 18th-century manuscript and in particular the printed text identifying Lord Haversham's speech.

Notes

1. The Quilters' Guild undertook a two-year research project focusing on the coverlet. The research included a study of the provenance of the coverlet, a comparative study with other textiles of a similar date, a detailed study of the fabrics and a discussion of the social context within which the coverlet was made. Details of the research carried out by the Quilters' Guild were presented at its annual seminars (November 2001 and October 2002) and the papers presented are included in their publication edited by Dorothy Osler (2003).
2. There is very little published literature relating to historical evidence with reference to English patchwork with the exception of the documentation, research and publications produced by the Quilters' Guild of the British Isles.
3. A copy of all the images and the categorisation of the papers has been given to the Quilters' Guild and it intends to study the images further.
4. Camera technology is developing at such a pace that since the imaging phase of this project was completed, the range of tones that can be captured in a single 'frame' from a high-end digital SLR, has doubled. For future transmitted light projects this would mean that only half the number of images would need to be taken to record the same information and also allow some text that was previously not recordable to be imaged successfully.
5. The cost of equipment in July 2005 was as follows: camera Fuji S2 Pro £1200; lens Sigma 50mm Macro £250; light box (low profile) £250; Perspex support £125.
6. It took a conservator and photographer 2½ days each to photograph the 182 squares (approximately 11 × 11 cm) plus ½ day initial set-up time and object handling time plus a further 8 days to process the images before any analysis was carried out; this results in a total of 14 days. Therefore, the time taken to photograph and process the coverlet images is approximately 84 hours based on a six-hour working day.
7. Examples of completed patchwork quilts with the papers still inside can be seen on the Australian National Quilt Register (www.amol.org.au/nqr).
8. The skill required to make such a coverlet was borne out by the experience of the members of the Quilters' Guild, many of whom were experienced makers of patchwork. They made an exact replica of the '1718 coverlet' and found the reproduction of the complex representations of animals and flowers extremely challenging and difficult to make (Mary Hewson of the Quilters' Guild, pers. comm., September 2006).
9. Observation made by Edward Maeder, Curator of Textiles, Historic Deerfield, USA, at the AHRC Research Centre for Textile Conservation and Textile Studies, Textiles and Text: Re-establishing the Links between Archival and Object-based Research, 11–13 July 2006.
10. Duty was payable on paper from 1694 and in 1712 a tax of 1d per square yard was placed on printed, painted or stained papers. This was increased to 1½d two years later (Dr Sonia O'Connor, University of Bradford, pers. comm., March 2007). These taxes may indicate a monetary reason why paper was recycled.
11. John Thompson, Baron. *The Lord Haversham's Speech in the House of Peers, on Saturday, February 15. 1709/7* [sic]. [London]. [1707]. Based on information from *English Short Title Catalogue: Eighteenth Century Collections Online*. Gale Group. http://galenet.galegroup.com.servlet/ECCO
12. *Ibid.*

References

Fox, S. (1994) *Small Endearments: Nineteenth-Century Quilts for Children and Dolls*. Nashville, TN: Rutledge Farm.

Osler, D. (2003) *Quilt Studies* issue 4/5.

Quilters' Guild (1995) *Quilt Treasures: The Quilters' Guild Heritage Search*. London: Deirdre McDonald Books.

Thompson, K.N. and Halliwell, M. (2005) 'An initial exploration of the benefits of using transmitted visible light and infrared photography to access information concealed within multilayered textiles', in *Scientific Analysis of Ancient and Historic Textiles. AHRC Research Centre for Textile Conservation and Textile Studies, First Annual Conference 13–15 July 2004, Postprints*, R. Janaway and P. Wyeth (eds), 177–84. London: Archetype Publications.

The authors

- Karen Thompson is currently employed as a conservator at the TCC (since 1999); she previously worked as a conservator at National Museums of Scotland, Northwest Museums Service, People's History Museum and Artlab (Australia).
- Michael Halliwell is currently employed as Conservation Photographer at the TCC; he was previously employed as conservator and/or photographer at numerous archaeological sites and museums. He has undertaken major projects for the National Museum of Lebanon, Beirut; the National Museum of Sharjah, United Arab Emirates; the Dover Bronze Age Boat Project and the Buckland Anglo-Saxon Cemetery Site for the British Museum, English Heritage and Canterbury Archaeological Trust.

Addresses

- Corresponding author: Karen Thompson, Textile Conservation Centre, University of Southampton, Park Avenue, Winchester SO23 8DL, UK (thompson@soton.ac.uk)
- Michael Halliwell, Textile Conservation Centre, University of Southampton, Park Avenue, Winchester SO23 8DL, UK (mbh2@soton.ac.uk)

Jewish ceremonial textiles and the Torah: exploring conservation practices in relation to ritual textiles associated with holy texts

Bernice Morris and Mary M. Brooks

ABSTRACT Jewish texts are integral to Jewish life. The Torah (the central text of Judaism) and the vast body of rabbinical writings provide the rules by which many Jews live. These written rules extend to the correct treatment of all objects, including textiles, used in religious rituals. This work considers how these rules may impact on the actual conservation treatment of Jewish ritual textiles.

Jewish culture is rich in attractive textiles that are highly embellished and prized by their communities. In order to keep these textiles in ritual use, or to prepare them for museum display or storage, conservation measures are often necessary. Jewish texts, however, suggest that the textiles used in religious practice, such as Torah mantles, binders and ark curtains should be regarded as holy, and thus warrant special considerations for their handling, storage and display. Considerations include types of materials used, on which day and times conservation can be performed, and how any removed parts should be discarded. According to professional ethics, conservators should consider the desires of originating cultures when treating their objects, yet few conservators were aware of the commandments imposed by Judaism to preserve the textiles' holy qualities. This paper examines the conservation issues presented by Jewish ceremonial textiles in order to suggest strategies for conservators to simultaneously acknowledge the textiles' physical preservation needs as well as the rules dictated by the religious texts.

Keywords: Judaism, Torah, conservation, ceremonial textiles, ethics

Introduction

The Torah is the heart of Judaism. In its narrowest sense, the Torah is the first five books of the Old Testament, which Jews believe to be the word of God. A Torah scroll, found in all synagogues, is a scroll of parchment inscribed with these five books. It is highly prized by the community, and covered with an embellished case or textile mantle and decorated with silver ornaments (Fig. 1). In its broadest sense, the Torah is the entire body of Jewish teachings including these five books as well as the Talmud, commentaries and teachings of rabbis. These texts provide the rules by which observant Jews live.[1] The Jewish religion is intensely systemised and commandments permeate all aspects of life including diet, work, family life and, most importantly, the worship of God. These written rules extend to the correct treatment of all objects, including textiles, used in religious rituals. This paper considers how these rules may impact on the actual conservation treatment of Jewish ritual textiles.

Jewish textiles are products of the exacting commandments given in the Torah that deal with ritual worship in the synagogue and the home: Jewish law prescribes that beautiful objects are used to enhance the praise of God in order 'to glorify Him' (Exodus 15:2). The textiles used within Jewish culture are thus not only highly embellished and prized by their communities but are also intimately linked to the texts which are central to Jewish religious ceremony. In order to keep these textiles in ritual use, or to prepare them for museum display or storage, conservation measures are often necessary.

Exploring conservation practice and Jewish ritual textiles

In the last 20 years, conservators have been increasingly concerned with respecting the needs of originating communities when treating their ritual and sacred objects, and have begun to tailor conservation treatments accordingly. While much attention has been focused on the ethical conservation of the sacred objects of indigenous people, the conservation profession as yet has shown less concern about the conservation of Jewish ritual objects and, in particular, Jewish ritual textiles. This research therefore aimed to discover if there is a case for taking special measures in our conservation treatments to acknowledge the objects' holy qualities and to respect the desires of the Jewish community. Opinions were sought from a variety of interested and involved people, including rabbis, observant Jews and active members of the Jewish community, as well as conservators with experience in working with Jewish ceremonial textiles. The original texts were also consulted to understand what the Torah recommends.

Figure 1 Torah scrolls covered in mantles and silver decorations in the Torah ark (Plate 110 in the colour plate section).

Sharing holiness: linking text and textiles

An examination of Jewish texts showed that guidelines for the treatment and handling of holy material differ according to the type of object. Much has been published about the care of written material. The holy nature of the Torah scrolls has meant an entire set of detailed guidelines has emerged relating to the materials used, the style of the writing, the qualifications of a *sofer* (Torah scribe), and the procedures and guidelines for repairing or disposing of scrolls. Conversely, the requirements for the treatment of Jewish ritual and ceremonial textiles are less rigid and even ambiguous. These differences can be explained by a variety of reasons. First, an understanding of the distinctions in degrees of holiness can explain the attention given to written material: scrolls written with the word of God are extremely holy and important. Textiles, conversely, are further down in the hierarchy. The vagueness relating to textile care is mirrored by the vagueness and indifference afforded to their inception. While the *sofer* is a highly trained and pious man, ceremonial textiles were produced on a more ad hoc basis by anyone in any way they wanted, usually women at home. Indeed, certain styles and biblical motifs continuously appear on the textiles, but this unity of design relates more to convention and tradition than to any religious commandments.

This divided approach values the trained male *sofer's* God-inspired work, which will be used entirely by men in the synagogue service, over the female pastime of needlework reflects a gender division typical of much of Jewish life. As textiles were seen as a female domain, away from exacting religious commandments imposed on the more male synagogue realm, it follows that the Talmudic rabbis put less emphasis on the production of textile objects. This approach that places more value with the written scrolls seems not to be the case from a heritage perspective however. As the writing of Torah scrolls is almost completely uniform and unillustrated, they have little aesthetic or artistic value (Greene 1992: 34); ceremonial textiles, in contrast, are interesting because of their exceptional visual qualities as well as the historic information they can provide about their varied origins.

So what makes an object holy, and indeed are Jewish ceremonial textiles holy at all? In Judaism, an object's holiness is defined by its proximity to holy texts, as well as by its use in performing holy acts. There are two main categories: objects that are *tashmishey kedusha* serve holiness and are closely associated to written words containing the name of God. The textiles that come into direct contact with this text become imbued with some of its holy quality. Textiles in this category include Torah mantles, binders and the ark curtain. The less sacred category of *tashmishey mitzvah* contains objects that are essential in performing a commandment, but are not intrinsically holy themselves. Textiles in this group include challah covers, tallit and tefillin bags, Sukkah accessories, circumcision cushions and Huppah covers.

Objects that are *tashmishey kedusha* are to be treated with reverence. In every day practice within the synagogue this means placing them on a clean surface with clean hands, and handling them with care. Conservation, however, often entails more involved and intrusive treatment, some of which conflicts with other Jewish doctrine. Four areas of concern for conservators arose from this research: the use of animal products, the combination of wool and linen, work on the Sabbath and festivals, and issues of correct disposal.

Non-kosher materials

The Hebrew word 'kosher' means fit or proper. It is mainly understood in relation to food: kosher food is that which is permitted or acceptable. *Kashrut* – the system of kosher food laws – is referred to in the Torah in the books of Leviticus and Deuteronomy. Kosher foods include only certain land animals that are slaughtered in a particular way, and only certain types of fish and birds. Pigs, horses, crustaceans,

245

molluscs, insects and reptiles, among many other creatures, are not kosher.

The laws of *kashrut* become relevant to conservation when animal products are considered as materials for treatments. Types of animal products that may be used by conservators include animal and fish gelatines, thin animal membrane – also known as goldbeater's skin – and even dyes derived from insects. Gelatines in particular are used by conservators as an adhesive and to consolidate flaking paint. One popular type is isinglass, which is made from the swim bladders of sturgeons – a non-kosher fish. While it is possible to make gelatine out of kosher animals and fish, this is difficult to buy and the types of animals used in the available gelatines tend not to be specified.

However, while it is evident that non-kosher products such as gelatine are inappropriate for eating according to Jewish law, it is less clear whether these products can be used for other purposes. So, is it acceptable to use non-kosher products on Jewish ritual objects and in particular textiles? This research found that responses to these questions were varied and sometimes conflicting.

A textile conservator working in Israel thought it would be completely inappropriate and disrespectful to put non-kosher products on any type of Jewish ceremonial textile. Another conservator felt that it would be better – and indeed easy – to find an alternative if this were a controversial area.[2] The Orthodox[3] Jewish perspective was surprisingly less decided than that of the conservators. A representative of the Chasidic ultra-orthodox community said in theory there is nothing wrong with gelatine or animal glue, as long as a Jew was not involved in its production. She also said, however, that she would feel uncomfortable in applying something non-kosher to a Torah mantle or binder, though technically according to Jewish law, it is not considered sacrilegious.[4] A Reform rabbi had a more definite response: "Kosher means 'fit for', so we always have to ask 'fit for what?' – kosher in this sense means fit for eating. We are not going to eat a Torah binder, so if that is the material that you think is necessary for your work, then I don't really have a problem with that."[5]

These responses presented an interesting and unexpected situation: conservators are concerned about respecting Jewish law to the extent that they are being overly sensitive and doing more than is required in Judaism. This can be explained as a simple misinterpretation of the law: the kosher food laws are well-known elements of Judaism, and an obvious assumption could be that non-kosher products should not be purposefully applied to objects used in Jewish life. It may also suggest that emotion contributes to conservation decision-making: both conservators and the Chasidic Jew based their answer on what would feel appropriate in order to maintain a type of Jewish integrity for the object.

The conclusion would seem to be that in the case of using non-kosher materials in conjunction with ritual textiles, the emotional convictions of Jews seem to override the technical rulings. As part of the intention of the conservation profession's interest in acknowledging religious requirements is to satisfy the originating community, i.e. people, non-kosher materials are perhaps best (and easily) avoided.

Wool and linen mixture (*shatnez*)

A Shatnez garment should not cover you (Leviticus 19:19).

Do not wear Shatnez – wool and linen together (Deuteronomy 27:11).

The Torah states that it is forbidden to wear wool and linen together. No explanation is given for this commandment: it is simply considered to be the will of God, and thus obligatory. *Shatnez* in a garment occurs when wool and linen fibres are woven together, or if any stitching places the two fibres in direct proximity – essentially any lasting combination. For Orthodox Jews this is a serious concern: some will only buy clothing from a Jewish manufacturer where the precise content of the fabric is known.

A Jewish law actually dealing with textile fibres is likely to have some ramifications in textile conservation. Established practice sees textile conservators often applying new fabric elements to historic textiles for support or aesthetic reasons. Wool or linen are certainly possible candidates for appropriate supports depending on the textile being treated, and it is feasible that a support fabric applied to a Jewish ritual textile may be considered as breaking the *shatnez* commandment. Research showed that *shatnez* was a serious concern for some conservators and members of the Jewish community. A member of the Chasidic community responded that the two should never be mixed, particularly in the case of holy objects, and added that she would not even consider sitting on a chair that had linen and wool mixed in together.[6]

The Reformed Judaism approach would be expected to be dismissive of the possible issue of mixing wool and linen on Jewish textiles, as *shatnez* is thought to be a biblical law 'that has lost all meaning today and need not be maintained' (Romain 1991: 95). Indeed, this was the case, but one rabbi did try to interpret the original law to attempt to apply it to ceremonial textiles: 'This law refers to garments; that is what people wear. If textiles are decorative or functional but are not actually clothes this law does not apply.'[7]

It seems that the results of this area of research were not entirely conclusive. While it would appear that according to Jewish law *shatnez* is a commandment that must certainly apply to clothing, ambiguity surrounds its relevance to decorative or functional textiles. In light of this vagueness, it may be argued that a cautious approach should be taken: as there are always alternative fabrics to use in textile conservation, it would be better to avoid *shatnez* to remove any possibility of offence.

Shabbat

Shabbat (the Jewish Sabbath or day of rest) is thought to be the most holy festival in the Jewish calendar: it is so important that it is observed each week. Shabbat begins at twilight on Friday evening and finishes at nightfall on Saturday, during which time work is not permitted. Work, according to rabbinical literature, includes activities such as agricultural work, working with leather, construction work and working with fire. An entire section of the Talmud is dedicated to textile-related activities that are prohibited on Shabbat. It is forbidden to perform any shearing, bleaching, carding, dyeing, spinning, inserting thread into a loom, weaving, taking off a finished product from a loom, separating threads, tying a (permanent) knot, untying a knot (in order to re-tie it), sewing and tearing (Robinson 2000: 82).

For many Jews, the various categories of work forbidden in the Talmud translate into the modern day as prohibitions, for example on travelling, touching money, carrying outside of the home, using electricity and writing. But the overriding prohibition is on work; as the activity of conservation is the conservator's occupation (that engenders the earning of money), this is undoubtedly work and is not appropriate to the Sabbath.

Could it be appropriate for Jewish ritual textiles to be conserved on Shabbat? Work on the Sabbath is certainly prohibited for Jews, but in the case of Jew employing non-Jews the issue is less clear-cut. Of the many religious experts asked during this research, all showed a great preference and desire that they did not cause a Jew or non-Jew to work on the Sabbath, but realised this was not always viable and not in their control. They may ask whoever they have commissioned to refrain from work on Shabbat but it is clearly a matter of respect on the part of who is commissioned to observe these wishes. A slightly more emotional response was received from Chasidic Jews and the rabbis when asked the specific example about their feelings of *tashmishey kedusha* textiles being conserved on Shabbat: all agreed they would stipulate that no work should be done on Shabbat when commissioning a conservator.

Again there does not seem to be a definitive ruling – conserving Jewish textiles on Shabbat may cause some offence to religious Jews, but it is not actually prohibited by Jewish law. In the interests of showing respect and demonstrating integrity, however, it may be better for conservators to refrain from working on a Jewish textile on Shabbat when a religious Jew is involved. This may mean that the conservator must find out the weekly Shabbat timings and be prepared to stop work as early as 3.30 pm on a Friday afternoon in the winter.

Disuse and disposal

The disposal of holy objects is a sensitive area in Judaism. The rules of disposal originate from a passage in Deuteronomy that prohibits defacing the name of God (12: 3–4), and commentary in the *gemara* (part of the Talmud) that states 'Things used to perform commandments (*tashmishey mitzvah*) may be thrown out; things used for holiness (*tashmishey kedusha*) need to be buried.'[8] Here, an understanding of the categories of holiness is essential to determine which ritual textiles require special treatment (Table 1).

The type of burial appropriate for *tashmishey kedusha* varies from community to community, and also depends on the type of object. Sephardi (Middle Eastern and Spanish) communities tend to have a *geniza*, a type of storeroom attached to the synagogue for putting away their holy objects. Ashkenazi Jews (Jews of Eastern European origin) usually bury

Table 1 Categories of holiness and permissible burial for Jewish ceremonial textiles.

Requires burial (*tashmishey kedusha*)	Can be discarded (*tashmishey mitzvah*)
Torah mantle	Challah cover
Torah cases	Matzah cover
Torah binder	Almemor cover
Ark curtain	Tallit and tefillin bags
	Sukkah accessories
	Circumcision accessories
	Passover cushions
	Huppah covers
	Tallit and tzitzit

their holy objects: sacred written material is buried in a Jewish cemetery next to a man of great piety (Greene 1992: 34). The textile objects of the *tashmishey kedusha* category must also be buried, but as they are considered less holy this can be done anywhere (Cohen 2005). According to Jewish law the objects from the *tashmishey mitzvah* category can be discarded in any way when they are out of use, but in practice more reverence seems to be afforded to them. One rabbi stated, 'The disposal issue is about showing respect for holy and important things, especially writing. For me, this means not throwing out holy things with your household rubbish. Either bury it or put it away.'[9]

Conservators need to be aware of these concerns. The disposal issue has easily understood and quite precise biblical and Talmudic origins, and religious Jews feel strongly that proper respect should be shown to their ritual objects. While the complete disposal of historic objects is extremely rare, parts of objects, such as failing previous repairs, are sometimes removed by conservators. As the repairs have come into direct contact with *tashmishey kedusha* they have acquired a degree of holiness. In the case of textile Judaica, special measures beyond normal ethical disposal practice need to be taken. Conservators should ensure that if the removed parts are not returned to the client, that a proper burial takes place. This can be arranged by contacting a local Jewish community who can dispose of the material with their own sacred objects. If there is no local community the removed parts can be disposed of in a way that is distinct from discarding everyday rubbish, such as burial in the garden, or even placing it in its own strong bag before throwing it away. Items in the less holy category of *tashmishey mitzvah* do not technically require special disposal, but some Jews may feel their intimate links with prayer and Jewish ritual merit a careful disposal.

According to professional ethics, conservators should consider the desires of originating cultures when treating their objects. The consultation of both Jewish texts and members of the Jewish community is important to ensure effective preservation is carried out that recognises both the physical and spiritual qualities of these beautiful and fascinating textiles.

Acknowledgements

Many thanks to Judith Eisenberg, Kochavit Shiryon and Rabbi Paul Freedman.

Notes

1. The term 'observant Jews' refers to Jewish people who strictly follow the laws prescribed by their faith.
2. Personal communication (interview) with Judith Eisenberg, textile conservator in private practice, New York, 20 August 2005.
3. Orthodox Judaism is among the more religious denominations of Judaism, while Conservative (in the US) or Reform (UK) Judaism is more progressive.
4. Personal communication (interview) with a member of the Chasidic Jewish community in London who wished to remain anonymous 20 August 2005.
5. Personal communication (interview) with Rabbi Paul Freedman of Radlett Synagogue on 23 March 2005.
6. Personal communication (interview) with a Chasidic Jewish woman on 20 August 2005.
7. Personal communication (interview) with Rabbi Paul Freedman on 23 March 2005.
8. From Megila 26b in the *gemara*.
9. Personal communication (interview) with Rabbi Paul Freedman on 23 March 2005.

References

Cohen, J.M. (2005) 'The preservation of Jewish textiles'. Paper presented at the Netherlands Textile Committee symposium on the Preservation of Religious Textiles, The Hague 10 September 2002.

Greene, V. (1992) 'Accessories of holiness: defining Jewish sacred objects', *Journal of the American Institute for Conservation* 31(1): 31–9.

Robinson, G. (2000) *Essential Judaism*. New York: Pocket Books.

Romain, J. (1991) *Faith and Practice: A Guide to Reform Judaism Today*. London: Reform Synagogues of Great Britain.

The authors

- Bernice Morris gained her first degree in history of art and Italian from the University of Birmingham, and was awarded an MA in textile conservation at the Textile Conservation Centre, University of Southampton in 2005. She is currently working as the Andrew W. Mellon Fellow in Costume and Textile Conservation at the Philadelphia Museum of Art.
- Mary Brooks trained at the Textile Conservation Centre after working in the book world and management consultancy. She has worked as a conservator and curator in Europe and America. At York Castle Museum, she jointly curated 'Stop the Rot', which won the 1994 IIC Keck Award for promoting public understanding of conservation and is a member of the ICOM Conservation Committee's Task Force for raising awareness of heritage conservation. She has a special interest in the contribution that object-based research and conservation approaches can make to the wider interpretation of cultural artefacts.

Addresses

- Bernice Morris, Conservation, Philadelphia Museum of Art, P.O. Box 7646, Philadelphia PA 19101-7646, USA (BeMorris@philamuseum.org)
- Mary M. Brooks, Textile Conservation Centre, University of Southampton, Park Avenue, Winchester SO23 8DL, UK (mmb1@soton.ac.uk)

A flag's life in New York: The New York State Battle Flag Preservation Project

Sarah C. Stevens

ABSTRACT The New York State Battle Flag Preservation Project integrates extant objects (flags and staffs) with archival information and collections history on a regular basis. The flag collection started in 1863 when New York State volunteer regiments deposited their flags with the state authorities for safekeeping. This tradition continues today and the collection now numbers just over 1800 flags, with approximately half of the collection dating to the American Civil War (1861–65). This paper discusses how text and analysis of the extant object are used to confirm information about each flag, such as regiment designations and makers, as well as identifying whether damage occurred during use and/or in storage.

Keywords: flag, Civil War (American), New York State history, painted silk

Introduction

The New York State Battle Flag Preservation Project routinely integrates information from archival documents and collection records with extant flags and their staffs. The collection consists of a group of flags dating from the war of 1812 to the present, including approximately 900 from the American Civil War (1861–65). New York State started to collect these flags in 1863 in order to preserve the tangible reminders of great sacrifices. Over the last 140 years, New York State's organised militia followed the precedent established in 1863 and the collection now numbers over 1800 flags.

Two New York State agencies are partners in this project: the Division of Military and Naval Affairs, which owns the collection and administers the New York State Military Museum and Veterans Research Center; and the Office of Parks, Recreation and Historic Preservation, Bureau of Historic Sites, which hosts the conservation work at the Peebles Island Resource Center. The museum curator and the conservator from the Bureau of Historic Sites work in close collaboration to understand the flags. The curator researches regimental histories by working with sources including collections records and military regulations. The conservator documents the condition of each flag as part of its conservation treatment; to date about 400 flags have been conserved. Both have visited the various archives relating to the collection. The Flag Project website presents many of the conserved flags along with their regimental histories.[1]

Many archival records are investigated to find information about the flags. Some records are contemporary with the flags' manufacture and use such as the documents kept by the Bureau of Military Statistics, the precursor to the New York State Military Museum and Veterans Research Center. These records include annual reports to the New York State Legislature and donation ledgers noting when and by whom the flags were given to the state. Additional primary sources include federal and local government records held in the federal, state and local libraries in Washington, DC, Albany, NY and New York City. Secondary sources including published regimental histories, newspaper articles and booklets often accompany the formal deposit of the flags into the state collection.

Using information from the extant objects and archival documents, the aim is to follow the flag's life, from request to manufacture, through production, acquisition and use by the regiment, and finally to deposit into the collection, storage and its current condition. For example, during the American Civil War, regiments received flags from government agencies in the military procurement business or from private citizens, civic organisations and local governments. Civil War regiments carried and used flags while on campaign or at camp. Upon muster out, they turned over their flags, regardless of the source, to New York State for deposit in the Battle Flag Collection.

Traditional sources

For flags manufactured under United States (US) government contracts, Quartermaster depots or military supply outlets openly solicited bids to manufacture and supply flags and staffs. Figure 1 shows examples of the common types of flags procured under Quartermaster depot contracts, including (a) national colours, (b) regimental colours, (c) guidons and (d) camp colours. These flags were produced according to US Army regulations which outlined the overall size as well as the material to be used.[2]

Extant Quartermaster records from the New York City, Washington, DC, Philadelphia, St Louis, Baltimore, and

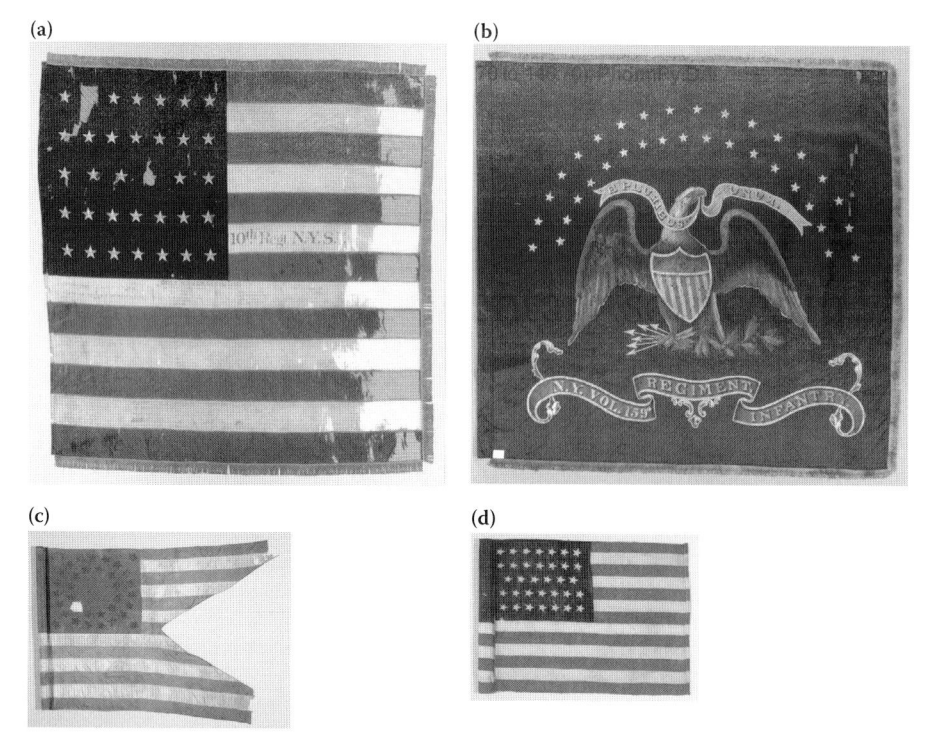

Figure 1 Examples of flags from traditional sources, such as the federal government: (a) national colour, 10th New York Volunteer Infantry, 190.5 × 188.0 cm, pieced silk, embroidered and printed; (b) regimental colour, 159th New York Volunteer Infantry, 193.0 × 200.7 cm, silk, painted; (c) guidon, 158th New York Volunteer Infantry, 76.2 × 88.9 cm, pieced silk, painted; (d) camp colour, 20th United States Colored Troops, 47.0 × 59.1 cm, wool, printed (photos courtesy of New York State Military Museum and Veterans Research Center) (Plate 111 in the colour plate section).

Cincinnati depots include the bids received from various manufacturers, product delivery information, supply orders by individual regiments for flags and details about the flags issued in response to supply orders.[3] Because New York State regiments were most likely to have received goods from the New York City depot, the initial focus was on these records. This research has revealed that the US Quartermaster records are incomplete, especially with regard to supply orders by individual regiments.[4]

As the flags are conserved, information found on the flag and staff, such as a maker's mark and/or unit designation, is compared with the archival data. So far it has not been possible to trace any flag from contract to distribution to the regiment, although it has been close. Five guidons were made by Evans and Hassall (Fig. 2a), a Philadelphia company that produced flags as well as other military goods between 1859 and 1866 (Bazelon and McGuinn 1999: 79). They stamped their mark, 'E. & H.' into the ferrule at the bottom of the staff (Fig. 2b) and/or into the finial base, found at the top of the staff.

Evans and Hassall was granted at least two contracts to make 900 guidons for the federal government through the New York City Quartermaster depot during 1863–64. Unfortunately, there is no paperwork linking the Evans and Hassall guidons in the collection to the known contracts.

Figure 2 Guidon with maker mark by Evans and Hassall: (a) guidon, 179th New York Volunteer Infantry, 66 × 94.6 cm, pieced silk, painted; (b) maker mark 'E. & H.' stamped on the ferrule at the base of the staff (photos courtesy of New York State Military Museum and Veterans Research Center) (Plate 112 in the colour plate section).

Non-traditional sources

Private citizens, civic organisations and local governments often made or purchased flags which they supplied to the regiments, often amidst great public spectacle. For example, the national colour of the 86th Infantry (Fig. 3) was 'presented to company B, by the ladies of Addison, Steuben County, N.Y.' (Doty 1865). The flag's design and construction indicate that it was probably made by them too. The flag is a twill fabric, rather than the usual plain weave bunting, with the stars in a circular pattern as opposed to rows.

In other instances, citizens or municipal government bodies raised money and paid a local firm to make the flag as in the case of five flags from the 15th Engineers (Figs 4a–c).

(a)

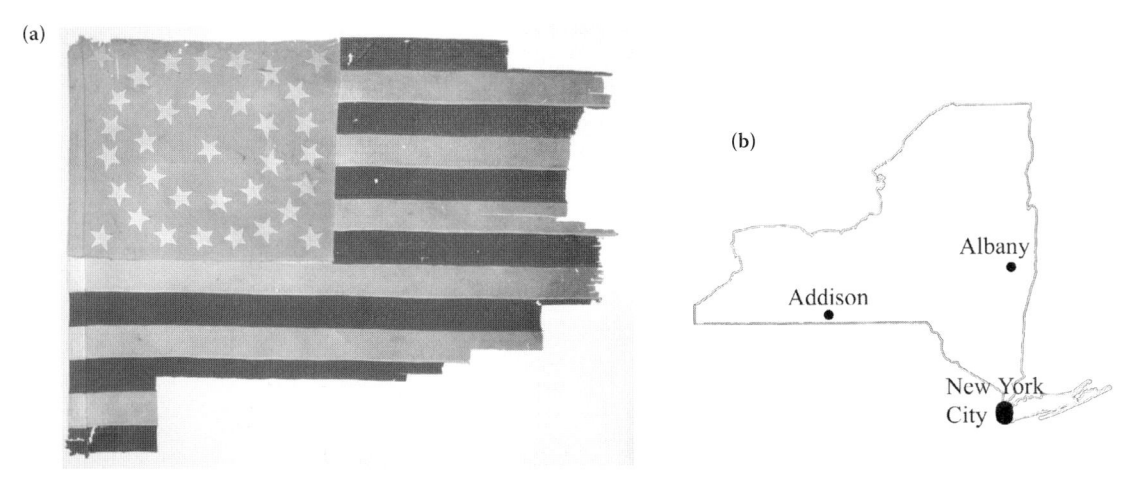

(b)

Figure 3 A flag from a non-traditional source, such as a local fundraising group: (a) national colour, 86th New York Volunteer Infantry given to the regiment by the Ladies of Addison, NY, 137.8 × 183.5 cm, pieced wool (photo courtesy of New York State Military Museum and Veterans Research Center). (b) Map of New York State showing Addison, Albany (State Capitol), and New York City (Plate 113 in the colour plate section).

(a)

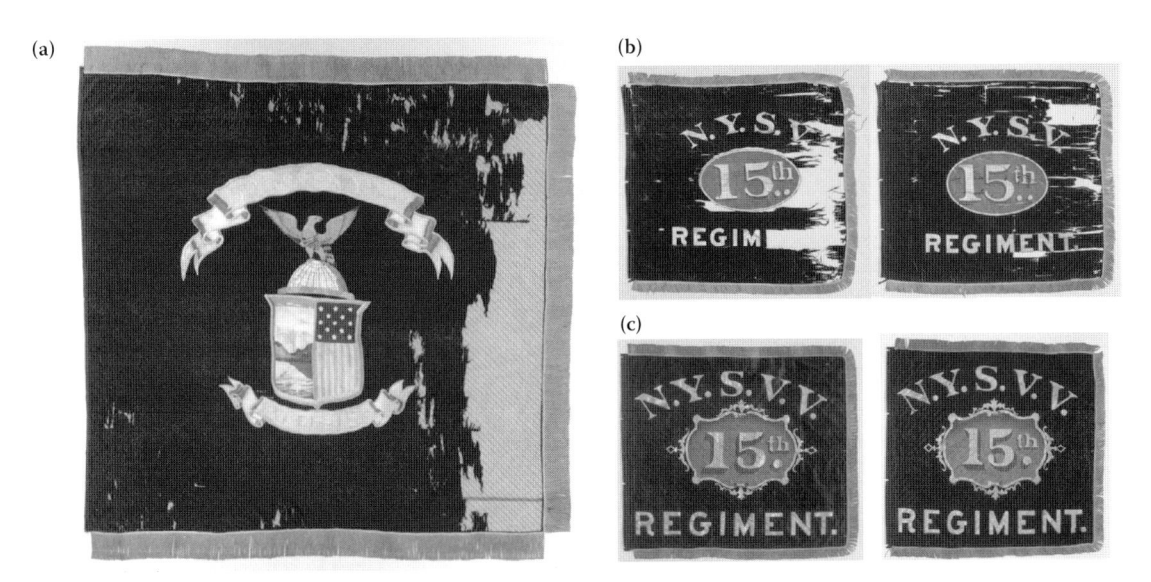

(b)

(c)

Figure 4 A series of flags from non-traditional sources. Flags of the 15th New York Engineers: (a) regimental colour made by Tiffany and Co., 194.9 × 193.6 cm, pieced silk, embroidered; (b) 1st set (earlier) of flank markers, left: 76.2 × 78.7 cm, right: 74.2 × 76.8 cm, both silk, painted; (c) 2nd set (later) of flank markers, left: 69.2 × 73.7 cm, right: 68.6 × 74.9 cm, both silk, painted ((b) and (c) given to the regiment by the New York City Common Council) (photos courtesy of New York State Military Museum and Veterans Research Center) (Plate 114 in the colour plate section).

Their regimental colour, as photographed c.1864 (Fig. 5 top), was ordered from Tiffany & Company by Colonel S.D. Bradford, Jnr. (*Frank Leslie's Illustrated Newspaper* 15 February 1862). According to a questionnaire of c.1863 (which the regiment sent to the Bureau of Military Statistics) (Fig. 5 bottom), the regimental colour was presented to the unit by Colonel Bradford's wife, while the four small flags in Figure 4b–c were given to the regiment by the Common Council of New York City, as part of the municipal government's war effort (Doty c.1863).

Newspaper accounts of flag presentations usually describe the flag in some detail, as in the case of an article in the *New York Times* on 30 April 1861 which referred to the 'Regimental Banner, white silk, painted with arms of Fire Department of the city of New York and inscribed, "1st Regiment New York Zouaves" – "The Star Spangled Banner in triumph shall wave"'. It was possible to confirm that the flag of the 11th New York Volunteer Infantry in the collection (Fig. 6) was the flag described by the *Times*. Before treatment, the flag had been stored rolled in a box and it was so damaged that the design could not be determined. During conservation of the flag, all of the elements described above were uncovered as well as the name of the company (Barney and Styles) who painted the flag because they signed their work and added their New York City address for good measure. The signature was corroborated by reference to a contemporary directory of business people in New York City (Wilson 1861; Morton 2005).

Figure 5 Archival documents of the 15th New York Engineers; these documents helped to trace the history of the regiment's flags. Top: officers of the 15th New York Engineers at camp, c.1864 (Brady Collection, 111-B-324). This photo shows the regimental flag (Fig. 4a) in use (photo courtesy of NARA). Bottom: *Historical Inquiries Relating to New-York Volunteer Regiments*: questionnaire filled out by 15th New York Engineer regiment, c.1863 (photo courtesy of New York State Military Museum and Veterans Research Center).

Figure 6 11th New York Volunteer Infantry regimental colour with maker mark from Barney and Styles, 40 Hudson St, New York City. The flag measures 165.1 × 194.3 cm, silk and cotton, painted (photos courtesy of New York State Military Museum and Veterans Research Center) (Plate 115 in the colour plate section).

Field use

Many flags in the collection show wear patterns associated with their use in the field. The fly ends of the flags are usually damaged from wind whipping over extended periods of time. Other flags show battle damage, usually in the form of bullet holes. Damage to the flags and staffs was sometimes repaired in the field, often with coarse thread and stitching (on the flags) or with leather strapping and/or nails (on the staffs). The 15th Engineers regimental colour (Fig. 4a) and a photograph of the flag from c.1864 (Fig. 5) were compared to determine when and where some of the losses had occurred. It was possible to verify that the flag in the collection was the same as the flag in the photograph because of the horizontal seams visible in both (usually regimental flags are made from one piece of silk). When the flag and photo are compared, it is clear that the fly edge had been lost before it was restored in the 1960s.

Occasionally, New York State described damage to a flag in the booklets that accompanied the flag's formal deposit into the collection.[5] In 1865, the national colour of the 86th Infantry was described in the following terms: 'The lower red, white, and part of second red stripe is gone, and also [the] ends of [the] stripes, and the flag has about twenty bullet holes in it' (Fig. 3a). During the condition assessment of the flag, the 1865 description was found to be fairly accurate, although more holes were found. Equally, the 1865 booklet identified the flag as made from 'merino' rather than the more traditional 'bunting'. The flag is not bunting, but a tighter twill weave, so the term 'merino' may have been used to indicate a finer quality of fabric and its use may corroborate the belief that this flag was homemade.

Later life

As the flags were returned to New York State for safekeeping, they were rolled on their staffs, tied in position with red twill tape (government red tape) and stored with the collection of the Bureau of Military Statistics. The flags have been in at least three known locations in Albany: the 1809 State Capitol (corner of Eagle and State streets), 219 State Street and the current Capitol (between State Street and Washington Avenue) (Waite 1993). While in the 1809 State Capitol, the flags were first stored in the Bureau of Military Statistics offices and then in a specially constructed fireproof room (Doty 1867). Sometime between 1867 and 1883, the Bureau of Military Statistics and the flags moved west, up the hill to 219 State Street and were freely accessible to the public. Many of the flags were 'so close to the visitor that the tattered remnants almost brushed the face' (*New York Times* 14 February 1881). When the flags were not in storage, they were taken out and put on display. On one noted occasion, 'scraps were left upon the floor' when the flags were put away (*New York Times* 14 February 1881). By 1883 the flags had moved into the newly built Capitol (Cleveland

1884). Some flags clearly have had sections removed as souvenirs (Fig. 1c), but determining which flags have lost pieces from non-ideal storage conditions is impossible.

The 1865 descriptive listing of flags in the collection also provides clues which correlates with flags listed in the current inventory. For example, the 1865 list includes four small flags carried by the 15th Engineers Regiment. These were usually listed as 'guidons' in the 1860s lists, but are now more correctly termed 'flank markers'. The 1865 list records one set (of two) as 'Guidons, blue silk' and another set as 'Guidons, blue silk; new'.[6] All four flags are made from blue silk with a central design, they are approximately 75 cm (2½ ft) square and have a fringe on three sides (Fig. 4b,c). Two of the flags have a 'V' in the inscription which designates a veteran regiment that existed later in the war (Stevens 2003). Those with the additional 'V' in the inscription are in better condition and so may have been considered 'new' in that respect in 1865.

Numerous flags have no documentation or maker's marks associated with them but have similar aging or condition characteristics that may help to determine where and by whom they were manufactured. Many of the painted flank markers that are similar in design to Figure 4b exhibit a white haze or bloom on the paint. Current painting conservation research has found similar problems in panel and canvas paintings from the 15th to the 20th century (Noble 2006). The white haze is an inherent defect in the paint layers caused by the formation of metal salts. These salts can migrate and cause significant damage, either by displacing the paint layers and causing cracks or by migrating to the surface and breaking through. Zucker (Zucker and Boon 2006) has found that one 19th-century banner painter added a drying agent, which most likely caused the metal salts to form. Zucker also found that canvas suppliers from New York City sometimes applied a drying agent to the ground layer before dispatching the prepared canvas. Usually 6–12 months are needed for an oil paint to dry completely but flags were needed much more quickly during the war, so a drying agent is likely to be the cause of the white haze seen on the flags.

Conclusion

As the conservation of the New York State Battle Flag Collection continues, it is possible to delve into the archival records for new information as well as for corroborating evidence to reveal the life path taken by each flag. Evidence about new manufacturers can be added to those listed in the Bazelon and McGuinn (1999) compilation, thereby adding to the historical record. Equally, as new manufacturers are discovered and their characteristic style is identified, it is possible to revisit flags without maker's marks in the collection to try to ascertain who may have made them. The 11th NYVI flag demonstrates the value of combining archival research and conservation because by comparing contemporary descriptions of the flags with the extant objects it is possible to reveal new information about the flags and make them more accessible for study (Morton 2005).

As more information is uncovered about the flags used by New York regiments, there is the possibility of applying this knowledge to flags from other states' collections. It will also be possible to compare the New York flags to state flag collections which have been conserved (Sauers 1987, 1991). The integration of new information, such as the problem with metal salts on painted flags, allows an even more detailed understanding of the history and condition of these flags.

Acknowledgements

This paper would not be possible without the extraordinary assistance and research by the Flag Project's curator, Christopher S. Morton, Assistant Curator at the New York State Military Museum and Veterans Research Center and the support of Deborah Lee Trupin, Textile Conservator, New York State Office of Parks, Recreation and Historic Preservation as well as all the technicians, interns and volunteers who have assisted in the conservation of the flags.

Notes

1. www.dmna.state.ny.us/historic/btlflags/btlflagsindex.htm.
2. Revised Regulations for the Army of the United States. 1861. Philadelphia: J.B. Lippincott & Co. pp. 475–6, para. 1436–41.
3. National Archives and Records Administration, Washington, DC. Record Group (RG) 92: Quartermaster records, including the Consolidated Correspondence File, 1794–1915, Entry 1239: Abstracts of contracts, Entry 1240: Abstracts of contracts, Entry 1003: Register of Letters, Entry 1004: Letters Received, Entry 1006: Abstracts of correspondence, Entry 1246: Contracts, Bids, Proposals by Contractor, Entry 1238: Register of Contracts, 1860-1865, Entry 1025: Records Relating to Functions, 1821–1914; Weekly and Monthly Reports of Clothing and Equipage on Hand at Depots and Posts 1860–1890, Entry 1225: Contract Books 1860–1869, Entry 1027: Orders for Camp and Garrison Equipage, 1861–1863.
4. National Archives and Records Administration, Washington, DC. RG 92: Quartermaster records, Entry 1027: Orders for Camp and Garrison Equipage, 1861–1863. The actual dates for Entry 1027 are 5 July 1861–30 March 1863; slightly less than half of the actual time of the war.
5. Chief of the Bureau of Military Records, State of New York. 1865. Presentation of the Flags of New York Volunteer Regiments and Other Organizations to His Excellency, Governor Fenton, in Accordance With a Resolution of the Legislature, July 4, 1865. Albany: Weed, Parsons and Company. Booklets are also available from 1863 and 1864.
6. Chief of the Bureau of Military Records, State of New York. 1865. Presentation of the Flags of New York Volunteer Regiments and Other Organizations to His Excellency, Governor Fenton, in Accordance With a Resolution of the Legislature, July 4, 1865. Albany: Weed, Parsons and Company. p. 216.

References

Bazelon, B.S. and McGuinn, W.F. (1999) *A Directory of American Military Goods Dealers and Makers 1785–1915*, combined edn. Manassas: Bazelon and McGuinn.

Cleveland, G. (1884) *Annual Report of the Adjutant General of the State of New York*. Albany: Weed, Parsons & Company.

Doty, L.L. (comp.) *c.*1863. *Historical Inquiries Relating to New-York Volunteer Regiments*. New York State Military Museum and Veterans Research Center, AA.2000.40.

Doty, L.L. (1865) *Second Annual Report of the Chief of the Bureau of Military Statistics*. Albany, NY: Bureau of Military Records.

Doty, L.L. (1867) *Fourth Annual Report of the Bureau of Military Statistics*. Albany, NY: Bureau of Military Records.

Morton, C.S. (2005) '"The Star Spangled Banner in triumph shall wave." The New York City Fire Department's presentation colour carried by Ellsworth's New York Zouaves, 1861', *Military Collector and Historian* 57(2): 58–60.

Noble, P. (2006) 'Binding medium defects in oil paintings (15th to 20th century)'. Paper presented at the American Institute for Conservation Annual Conference, 18 June 2006.

Sauers, R. (1987) *Advance the Colours! Pennsylvania Civil War Battle Flags*, vol. 1. Lebanon, NY: Capitol Preservation Committee.

Sauers, R. (1991) *Advance the Colours! Pennsylvania Civil War Battle Flags*, vol. 2. Lebanon, NY: Capitol Preservation Committee.

Stevens, S.C. (2003) 'Do you know where you are? Silk flank markers from the Civil War'. Paper presented at the North American Textile Conservation Conference on Symbolic Textiles, 8 November 2003.

Waite, D.S. (ed.) (1993) *Albany Architecture*. Albany, NY: Mount Ida Press.

Wilson, H. (comp.) (1861) *Wilson's New York Copartnership Directory, for 1860–61*. New York: John F. Trow.

Zucker, J. and Boon, J. (2006) 'Opaque to transparent: insights on bloom, haziness, protrusions and variable translucency from the Hudson River School and the Church Archive'. Paper presented at the American Institute for Conservation Annual Conference, 18 June 2006.

The author

Sarah C. Stevens, Associate Textile Conservator, came to the New York State Office of Parks, Recreation and Historic Preservation's Peebles Island Resource Center in 2000 specifically for the New York State Battle Flag Preservation Project. After receiving her MS in historic costume and textiles from the University of Rhode Island, she spent a year at the Metropolitan Museum of Art, NYC on a Mellon Fellowship and nine months at the Cooper-Hewitt National Design Museum, NYC as Assistant Textile Conservator.

Address

Sarah C. Stevens, Associate Textile Conservator, Peebles Island Resource Center, New York State Parks, Recreation and Historic Preservation, P.O. Box 219, Waterford NY 12188, USA (Sarah.Stevens@oprhp.state.ny.us)

Objects without documentation: the role of conservation science in revealing more about these artefacts

Collecting a near infrared spectral database of modern textiles for use of on-site characterisation

Emma Richardson, Graham Martin and Paul Wyeth

ABSTRACT Decisions regarding the long-term storage and display of artefacts within heritage collections rely on an intimate knowledge of materials and their behaviour. Over time deterioration is inevitable, but the rate at which objects deteriorate may be greatly reduced by careful control of the environment. Degradation and stabilisation vary through the material classes, however, illustrating the need for positive identification within collections, which is not always easy with limited sampling of artefacts. The *in-situ* application of near infrared (NIR) spectroscopy for the non-invasive identification and condition monitoring of synthetic textile materials would greatly assist in the long-term preservation of contemporary collections. The ability to quickly identify modern textiles would provide museum professionals with the information required for a greater understanding of their collections, enabling informed long-term action plans and more immediate remedial conservation plans to be implemented.

Keywords: non-invasive analysis, *in situ*, near infrared (NIR) spectroscopy, synthetic textiles, spectral database, spectral library

Introduction

Near infrared spectroscopy (NIR) has been used successfully within the food industry, agriculture and recycling since the 1970s, but has only received interest from the heritage sector of late as a possible means of object interrogation. A number of papers have recently been published, highlighting the potential in this area. These include the application of NIR for the characterisation of polyethylene and polypropylene (Kumagai *et al.* 2002), fibre sizing agents (Kitagawa *et al.* 1997) and carboxylated linen (Kouznetsov and Ivanov 1995). It has also been used successfully to monitor degradation and modifications in Japanese washi paper (Yonenobu *et al.* 2003) and wood (Tsuchikawa *et al.* 2003, 2005; Schwanninger *et al.* 2004). Preliminary studies carried out by Wyeth (2005) have already indicated the possibilities of NIR spectroscopy as a means of condition monitoring of textiles, through correlations between water sorption, seen in the NIR, and physical stability. In addition, Garside and Lovett (2006) have applied NIR spectroscopy to the on-site identification and condition monitoring of polyurethane foams.

Since their introduction in the 19th century, synthetic polymers have moved into almost every area of life and, hence, into a growing number of museum collections. Consequently, in recent years there has been a growing interest in synthetic materials within the museum environment, both in terms of identification and condition assessment. Of the polymeric material held within museum and heritage collections, other than biopolymers, Keneghan (2002) has identified five types of major concern regarding instability: cellulose nitrate, cellulose acetate, polyvinyl chloride (PVC), polyurethane and rubber. Deterioration of such objects is inevitable, but the rate at which they deteriorate may be reduced by careful control of the environment. The degradation and stabilisation of these polymers vary through the classes, therefore illustrating the need for positive identification within collections, which is not always easy with limited sampling of artefacts.

One area of particular interest is that related to contemporary textile collections. Manmade and synthetic polymers are used extensively for clothing. Industry exploits the ability to tune the chemical and physical properties of the polymers and further control the fabrication of the textile fibres, interlinings, paddings, surface coatings and fastenings. As with other synthetic materials, these textiles are of growing concern to conservators and curators caring for contemporary textile collections. Even simple identification of the materials within their collections is not straightforward however. Due to the origins of these objects, and the mass production methods employed for their manufacture, there is often little or no documentation pertaining to the materials of construction. Where manufacturers' labels are present, it is not always possible to have confidence in their assignments, requiring a more analytical approach to be taken. Yet, besides the sampling constraints, which are even more exacting for a new and intact textile, conventional microscopy does not readily distinguish the classes. Fibre extrusion, for example, does not convey polymer-specific morphological features.

Mid-infrared spectroscopy is currently the more popular method for modern materials identification (Cheung 2006; D'Orazio *et al.* 2001; Garside and Lovett 2006; Groom 1999; Oosten *et al.* 2006; Skals and Shashoua 2006). The spectra of the various polymer types are quite distinct. The technique, however, still requires an isolated sample in most cases. The value of a truly non-invasive means of characterisation, which could be applied on-site, is self-evident and NIR spectroscopy presents just such a methodology.

The *in-situ* application of NIR spectroscopy to the identification and condition monitoring of manmade and synthetic textile materials would greatly assist in the long-term preservation of contemporary collections. The ability to identify a particular modern textile quickly and determine its condition would provide museum professionals with the necessary information for key decision-making concerning conservation and treatments, storage and display. It is for this reason that we are investigating the application of NIR spectroscopy as a portable, non-invasive polymer characterisation technique to textiles.

Near infrared spectroscopy is a vibrational spectroscopic technique. The near infrared spectrum relates to the absorption of radiation at shorter wavelengths (780–2500 nm), and therefore higher energies, than that found in more conventional mid-infrared spectroscopy. Due to the energies involved the vibrations excited are anharmonic high frequency overtone and combinations of the fundamental modes seen in mid-infrared spectroscopy. Generally NIR spectra are dominated by bonds to hydrogen, in particular carbon–hydrogen, nitrogen–hydrogen and oxygen–hydrogen, as, due to the low atomic weight of hydrogen and the relative strength of the bonds, the associated vibrations are at relatively high frequency. This therefore makes NIR spectroscopy particularly suitable for the study of organic material, which is dominated by such bonds. One shortcoming of the technique is the lack of information available from inorganic material, as illustrated by the glass beads in Table 2 (p. 261).

Owing to the large number of overtone and combination transitions possible, the spectra produced are complex and this may be seen as a drawback as simple band assignments are precluded. The polymer spectra are still characteristic, however, and comparison with a suitable spectral reference set permits ready material identification. Derivative spectra are often employed to highlight bands that are indistinguishable to the eye. First order derivatives, and higher, are used to reduce baseline affects and to increase resolution. Derivatives reduce low frequency components while increasing signal, but also noise.

Near infrared spectroscopy is available as a reflectance technique and when coupled with a flexible fibre optic probe, this technique removes the need for sampling, ensuring a truly non-invasive method of analysis. In addition, sampling depths are 1 mm or more, allowing successful analysis of textile layers and interlinings thus removing the need for intervention. This paper introduces the work undertaken to produce a compilation of a specialist NIR spectral library for rapid characterisation of modern textiles, and illustrates its application, through two case studies, to the identification of contemporary textiles.

Experimental

Near infrared spectroscopy

Near infrared spectroscopy of all reference and unknown samples was performed using a Perkin Elmer Spectrum 1 Fourier transform near-infrared spectrometer with a quartz halogen lamp. Reference spectra were collected using an integrating sphere accessory, while all on-site analysis was carried out with an Axiom fibre optic probe attachment.

The probe has a sapphire window measuring 12 mm in diameter, set at a shallow angle to the perpendicular of the probe shaft. The optical fibre length measures 1.90 m, conveniently enabling spectral acquisition on site within collections (Fig. 1). Spectra were recorded with a wavenumber resolution of 8cm^{-1}, a scan speed of 1cm.s^{-1} over a spectral scan range of 12000–4000 cm^{-1} (830–2500 nm) and averaging over 64 scans. The background reference was Spectralon. All data were collected in absorbance. Spectral processing was carried out using Thermo Galactic Grams AI software, version 7.02.

Library and database

To ensure successful NIR spectroscopic identification, a comprehensive spectral library of well-defined materials is being acquired. At this point approximately 200 samples have been obtained from well-established textile manufactures, covering the major classes of polymers found in textiles. Ancillary data about each reference sample are collated in a Microsoft Excel spreadsheet, including the trade name, the type of fabric, the year of manufacture, the known composition, and the fabrication and finishing process. As might be expected, manufacturers are not always forthcoming with such information, so there are some gaps.

Once spectra have been recorded using a standardised protocol they are input to the spectral library. The library software is Thermo Galactic Spectral ID, which allows for creation of new search libraries with specified parameters. These can be manually input with the compound name, molecular formula, source, comments and the attachment of chemical structures in *.mol format.

Figure 1 On-site application of the near infrared spectrometer and probe (Plate 116 in the colour plate section).

Preliminary studies have been carried out to determine the possible effects to the resultant data analysis by recording the reference spectra using one sampling method and the sample spectra by another. Two sample libraries covering the major polymer classes were made for reference spectra collected via both methods. These were then compared using a validation set of analyses via the probe attachment. No significant differences were found between the two methods.

Library searching

Unknown spectra are assigned through the searching and retrieval capabilities of the Spectral ID library. The data files are opened in the library software, and with the application of matching algorithms to the reference set, the closest matches to that of the unknown are generated with a Hit Quality Index (see Plate 117 in the colour plate section), which is a measure of confidence. These range from 0 as a perfect match to 1.000 or 1.414 (depending on the searching algorithm) indicating no correlation. Due to the complicated nature of the spectra and spectral interferences caused by matrix scattering, however, the matching algorithms often give disproportionate weighting to raising baselines and noise. Therefore the application of matching algorithms must be undertaken with caution, with spectral variations and features not held in the dataset producing poor correlation and false positive results. Therefore assignments are always accompanied by visual comparisons. Through repeated application of the algorithms it has become apparent that the first derivative least squares algorithm produces the most consistent results when pre-treatment methods have not been applied. For manipulated data the correlation method is chosen.

Case studies

Synthetic materials have become commonplace in all walks of life and are therefore increasingly seen in museum and heritage collections, with textile materials being no exception. Because such material can be of concern to conservators and curators, due to the instability and offgassing of certain polymers, the ability to readily identify materials within collections is paramount.

Two trial site visits have been made in order to test our on-site protocol and highlight areas still requiring further work. The first visit was to a domestic setting to study textiles within a contemporary wardrobe, and the second to Hampshire County Council Museums and Archives Service (HCCMAS) to study a range of garments dating from the early 20th century, which had uncertain composition and was of interest to the conservation and curatorial departments.

Results and discussion

The desired aesthetics and consequent construction of a garment often demand the use of a number of textile types. These components can be pure fabrics, with different materials employed for different applications on one garment, or more complicated situations where various polymer types are present as blends, core spun yarns, ground and pile fabrics etc. It is these latter groups that can prove problematic for identification purposes. When two polymers with two distinct NIR spectra, such as cotton and polyester, are present in near equal quantities it is immediately obvious from the unprocessed spectra that these components are present. In addition, if a reference spectrum of a material of similar composition is contained within the library a match is possible. A complication arises when the second component is only present in small quantities as it may not be possible to easily recognise its presence. The problem can often be circumvented through the application of spectral subtractions, a method used in many of the cases presented here.

The unknown spectrum is first analysed using the library to identify the major component. The reference spectrum of this component is then subtracted from that of the unknown sample, the resultant residual spectrum often revealing the additional component(s).

This process also lends itself well to the identification of interlinings and paddings. In this case spectra are recorded first of the region of interest and then of the top layer alone. The latter is subtracted from the former, with the residual spectrum affording characterisation of the inaccessible material.

Case study 1: domestic wardrobe

Figure 2 shows an image of a handbag, studied during one of our site visits, made up of a number of components. A gold ground fabric was layered with a green netting onto which was applied small green sequins. The bag was further embellished with bronze sequins, black beads and a threaded tassel decoration. Through NIR analysis, all components were successfully identified (Table 1). The characterisation of the netting

Figure 2 A modern handbag of mixed media, studied during an initial visit to test the on-site protocol (Plate 118 in the colour plate section).

Table 1 Case study 1, a domestic wardrobe: an illustration of the variety of challenges within a domestic setting successfully met by on site, non-invasive NIR spectroscopic analysis.

Description	Date	Area of interest	Identification	Processing	Matching algorithm	Confidence level
Blue dress	c.1950s	Blue fabric	Silk		*	0.000026
		Dress tape	Viscose/rayon	Subtraction	#	0.525
		Blue thread	Viscose/rayon	Subtraction	*	0.0089
Purple/blue layered dress	c.1950s	Purple ground	Cellulose acetate		*	0.000023
		Blue net	Linen	Subtraction	*	0.000017
		Purple bow	Polyamide		*	0.000085
		Cream underskirt	Linen		*	0.000025
Black crepe dress	c.1970s	Black fabric	Acetate/viscose blend		*	0.000034
		Netting	Viscose/rayon		*	0.000022
		Dress tape	Polyamide		*	0.00011
		Button	Cellulose ccetate		*	0.000044
Green handbag	1996	Gold ground	Polyester		*	0.000015
		Green netting	Polyamide	Subtraction	*	0.00024
		Thread tassels	Viscose/rayon		*	0.000037
		Bronze sequins	Polyvinyl chloride		*	0.000071
		Green sequins	Polyvinyl chloride	Subtraction	*	0.00082
		Black beads	Polyester	Subtraction	*	0.000085
Green jacket	2004	Green fabric	Wool		*	0.0000093
		Lining	Cellulose acetate		*	0.000016

Key to algorithms: * first derivative least squares; # correlation

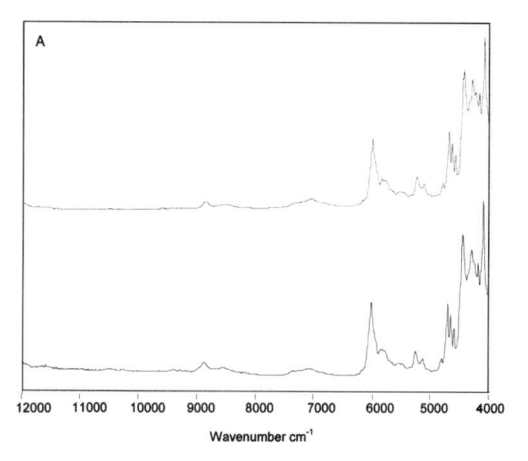

Figure 3 Near infrared spectrum of the gold ground fabric from the mixed media handbag (upper) and a reference spectrum of polyester (lower). The first derivative least squares matching algorithm giving a Quality Index of 0.0000145.

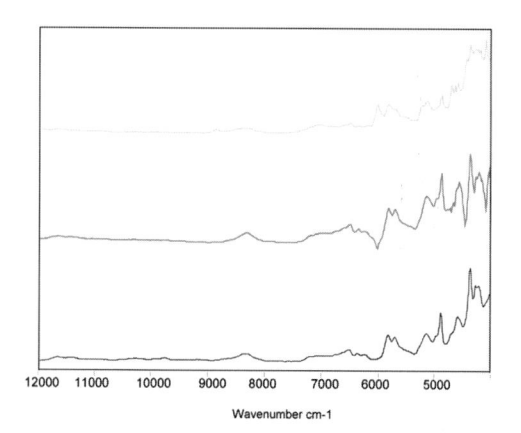

Figure 4 Near infrared spectrum of the green netting before subtraction (upper), after a spectral subtraction of a polyester reference (middle) and a reference spectrum of nylon (lower). The first derivative least squares matching algorithm giving a Quality Index of 0.000239.

required application of the spectral subtraction method described above. It was not possible to acquire a spectrum of the netting without the presence of the ground material. The ground fabric was found to be polyester, and after subtraction, the netting was positively identified as polyamide (Figs 3 and 4, respectively).

A second garment studied was a 1950s layered dress (Fig. 5). This had two major components: a ground purple fabric

Figure 5 Detail of the purple and blue 1950s dress illustrating the difficulties of sampling the lower layer of fabric (Plate 119 in the colour plate section).

with a stiffened overlayer of blue lace. The dress was decorated with a purple bow and a cream lining and underskirt. Subtractions revealed the ground as cellulose acetate and the blue overlay as cotton. The purple bow was made from polyamide and not the same fabric as the ground, which may suggest a later addition.

Case study 2: heritage collection

Table 2 shows the results from the visit to HCCMAS. The two sequin dresses were of particular interest due to the deterioration of the sequin adornments. In both cases some of the sequins had started to curl, accompanied by a dull surface and loss of lustre. After NIR analysis, all of the sequins were found to be gelatine-based, accounting for their poor condition (Fig. 6). Common at the time of manufacture of these dresses (Cheung 2006), cellulose nitrate was often present within gelatine sequins. After the subtraction of a reference gelatine sample to detect low level components, cellulose nitrate did not appear to be detectable within their composition. Cellulose nitrate is known to offgas during its degradation, releasing harmful gases such as nitric acid into the atmosphere. The ability to establish whether such unstable material is present or not will help aid informed storage and could minimise contamination in cases where it is found to be present.

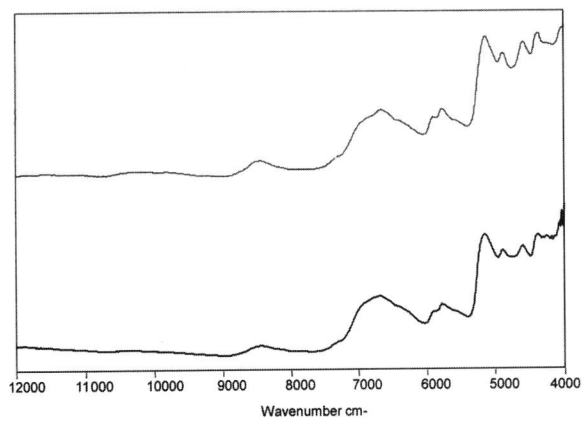

Figure 6 Near infrared spectrum of gelatine reference (upper) and an unknown sequin (lower).

During the Second World War rationing had a major effect on the availability of luxury items. Fabrics such as lace and satin were not available and it was not uncommon to adapt material from other applications. The silk from discarded or surplus parachutes was often used for wedding gowns and undergar-

Table 2 Case study 2, contemporary textiles at Hampshire County Museums and Archives Service: an illustration of the variety of challenges within a museum setting successfully met by on-site, non-invasive NIR spectroscopic analysis.

Description	Date	Area of interest	Identification	Notes	Processing	Matching algorithm	Confidence level
Blue jacket	1916/17	Blue fabric	Linen			*	0.0000084
		Lining	Linen/silk blend		Subtraction	*	0.000021
		Button	Unidentified			*	
Sequin dress	1920s	Purple sequins	Gelatine			*	0.000056
		Bronze sequins	Gelatine			☐	
		Gold sequins	Gelatine			*	0.00025
		Beige lining	Linen	Unknown treatment		*	0.00006
Black sequin dress	1920s	Black fabric	Silk			*	0.000056
		Sheer black lining	Silk			*	0.000036
		Black backing fabric	Silk			*	0.000045
		Shiny black sequins	Gelatine		Masked regions 6000–12000 cm^{-1}	*	0.00037
		Dull black sequins	Gelatine		Masked regions 6000–12000 cm^{-1}	*	0.00017
		Dull circular beads	Gelatine		Masked regions 6000–12000 cm^{-1}	*	0.0012
		Small black beads	Glass	No spectrum			
		Bugle beads	Glass	No spectrum			
Jacket and skirt	1930s	B&W fabric	Acetate/viscose blend			*	0.000035
		White lining	Acetate/viscose blend			*	0.00033
		Shoulder pads	Cotton		Subtraction	#	0.29
Stockings	1940s	Beige leg	Viscose/rayon			*	0.000014
Stockings	1940s	Navy leg	Polyamide			*	0.000073
Parachute 'silk' slip	1940s	White fabric	Polyamide			*	0.0003
Evening dress	1940/50s	Purple taffeta	Cellulose acetate			*	0.000011
		Blue gauze	Silk			*	0.0000096

Key to algorithms: * first derivative least squares; # correlation; ☐ visual comparison

ments, and the slip studied here (Table 2) was donated to the collection as such. The results from the NIR analysis and spectral library matching showed the garment to be in fact polyamide and not silk. Visually, the raw NIR spectra show similar features between polyamide and silk, due to the amide vibrations experienced in both polymers. The second derivative spectra, however, indicate clear distinctions between the silk reference sample and that of the unknown and polyamide reference (see Plate 120 in the colour plate section).

Both cases studies illustrate the benefit of rapid, non-destructive analysis, enabling informed collections care and providing curatorial staff with accurate details of construction and manufacture.

On average it took 10 minutes to analyse each object, some having multiple components. In most cases identification was unambiguous, though for one of the sequin dresses the surface treatment to the cotton lining could not be assigned. This illustrates the need for further reference material, and undoubtedly the reference library will continue to evolve.

Conclusion

Near infrared spectroscopy can be applied successfully to the identification of modern textile material. Furthermore, as a reflectance technique requiring no sample preparation, and coupled with a remote probe, NIR provides non-invasive, *in-situ* characterisation.

The textiles identified here, within a selection of garments dating back to the late 19th century, are examples of the types of materials increasingly moving into museum collections. The ability to characterise such collections quickly, on site and without the need for sampling, would offer a major advance in object-based research and the care and curation of artefacts.

Future work

To date, the raw spectral data have usually been sufficient to permit assignments, but the use of first derivate matching algorithms has allowed statistical rather than subjective identification. Second derivatives and multivariate applications are likely to assist greatly in distinguishing between polymer subclasses and blends and emphasise spectral changes relating to structure and degradation. These will be investigated in detail in due course. Further studies will also include investigating the application of NIR to the condition monitoring of modern materials.

Acknowledgements

The authors would like to thank Nell Hoare and colleagues at the Textile Conservation Centre and the Victoria and Albert Museum for their support. With particular thanks to Mike Halliwell and Peter Kellerher for the photography work and Paul Garside for his continuing assistance. We would also like to thank Hampshire County Museums and Archives Service for allowing us access to their textile collection, and in particular to Sarah Howard and Sue Washington for their interest and enthusiasm during our visit. Thanks are given to the AHRC for the Doctoral Award funding of E. Richardson (2005–08).

References

Cheung, A. (2006) 'A study of sequins on a Cantonese opera stage curtain', in *The Future of the 20th Century: Collecting, Interpreting and Conserving Modern Materials. AHRC Research Centre for Textile Conservation and Textile Studies, Second Annual Conference 26–28 July 2005, Postprints*, C. Rogerson and P. Garside (eds), 122–7. London: Archetype Publications.

D'Orazio, L. *et al.* (2001) 'Water-dispersed polymers for the conservation and restoration of cultural heritage: a molecular, thermal, structural and mechanical characterisation', *Polymer Testing* 20: 227–40.

Garside, G. and Lovett, D. 2006 'Polyurethane foam: investigating the physical and chemical consequences of degradation', in *The Future of the 20th Century: Collecting, Interpreting and Conserving Modern Materials. AHRC Research Centre for Textile Conservation and Textile Studies, Second Annual Conference 26–28 July 2005, Postprints*, C. Rogerson and P. Garside (eds), 77–83. London: Archetype Publications.

Groom, S. (1999) 'Foundry welding goggles and lenses: a case study in cellulose acetate degradation', *AICCM Bulletin* 24: 29–33.

Keneghan, B. (2002) 'A survey of synthetic plastic and rubber objects in the collections at the Victoria and Albert Museum', *Museum Management and Curatorship* 19(3): 321–31.

Kitagawa, K.S. *et al.* (1997) 'In situ analysis of sizing agents on fibre reinforcements by near infra-red light fibre optics spectroscopy', *Vibrational Spectroscopy* 15(1): 43–51.

Kouznetsov, D. and Ivanov, A. (1995) 'Near-IR spectrophotometric technique for fast identification of carboxycellulose in linen fibres', *Textile Research Journal* 65(4): 236–40.

Kumagai, M.H. *et al.* (2002) 'Discrimination of plastics using a portable near infrared spectrometer', *Journal of Near Infrared Spectroscopy* 10: 247–55.

Oosten, T.V., Joosten, I. and Megens, L. (2006) 'Man-made fibres from polypropylene to works of art', in *The Future of the 20th Century: Collecting, Interpreting and Conserving Modern Materials. AHRC Research Centre for Textile Conservation and Textile Studies, Second Annual Conference 26–28 July 2005, Postprints*, C. Rogerson and P. Garside (eds), 61–6. London: Archetype Publications.

Schwanninger, M., Hinterstoisser, B., Gradinger, C., Messner, K. and Fackler, K. (2004) 'Examination of spruce wood biodegradation by *Ceriporiopsis subvermispora* using near and mid-infrared spectroscopy', *Journal of Near Infrared Spectroscopy* 12: 397–409.

Skals, I. and Shashoua, Y.R. (2006) 'Sticky oilskins and stiffened rubber: new challenges for textile conservation', in *The Future of the 20th Century: Collecting, Interpreting and Conserving Modern Materials. AHRC Research Centre for Textile Conservation and Textile Studies, Second Annual Conference 26–28 July 2005, Postprints*, C. Rogerson and P. Garside (eds), 84–91. London: Archetype Publications.

Tsuchikawa, S.A. *et al.* (2003) 'Spectroscopic monitoring of biomass modifications by light irradiation and heat treatment', *Journal of Near Infrared Spectroscopy* 11: 401–5.

Tsuchikawa, S.A. *et al.* (2005) 'Near infrared spectroscopic observations of the aging process in archaeological wood using a deuterium exchange method', *Analyst* 130: 379–84.

Wyeth, P. (2005) 'Signatures of aging: correlations with behaviour', in *Scientific Analysis of Ancient and Historic Textiles. AHRC Research Centre for Textile Conservation and Textile Studies, First Annual Conference 13–15 July 2004, Postprints*, R. Janaway and P. Wyeth (eds), 137–42. London: Archetype Publications.

Yonenobu, S.S. *et al.* (2003) 'Non-destructive near infrared spectroscopic measurement of antique Washi calligraphic scrolls', *Journal of Near Infrared Spectroscopy* 11: 407–11.

The authors

- Emma Richardson is an Arts and Humanities Research Council doctoral award student (2005–08) who is studying for a PhD in conservation science with the Textile Conservation Centre at the University of Southampton and the Victoria and Albert Museum in London.
- Graham Martin is Head of the Science Section at the V&A. He is visiting Professor of Conservation Science at the University of Derby, a Fellow of the Royal Society of Chemistry and a member of the Institute of Conservation. His research interests are in the care and interpretation of movable cultural heritage.
- Paul Wyeth is a visiting Senior Research Fellow in the Textile Conservation Centre. He is a Fellow of the Royal Society of Chemistry and a member of the Institute of Conservation. His research interests encompass applications of microstructural and microspectroscopic analysis in conservation science, with particular emphasis on the development of instrumental methods for on-site condition monitoring of organic heritage.

Addresses

- Corresponding author: Emma Richardson, Textile Conservation Centre, University of Southampton, Winchester Campus, Park Avenue, Winchester SO23 8DL, UK (ejcr@soton.ac.uk)
- Graham Martin, Science Section, Victoria and Albert Museum, South Kensington, London, SW7 2RL
- Paul Wyeth, Textile Conservation Centre, University of Southampton, Winchester Campus, Park Avenue, Winchester SO23 8DL, UK

Photodegradation of *Phormium tenax* fibres: the role of naturally occurring coumarins

Gerald J. Smith, Raukura Chadwick, Ngaire Konese, Sue Scheele, Stephen E. Tauwhare and Roderick J. Weston

ABSTRACT Since pre-European contact, the indigenous Maori people of New Zealand have plaited the leaves of *Phormium tenax* J. R. Forst. & G. Forst. (New Zealand flax or harakeke) to make mats, cordage and containers, and extracted the ligno-cellulosic fibres to weave garments. Depending on the purpose, Maori selected particular forms of this genetically variable plant and maintained preferred varieties in cultivation. In this work the photostabilities of some of these varieties have been examined to determine whether this factor may have influenced their selection.

Like other ligno-cellulosic materials, *P. tenax* fibres are subject to photoyellowing and the relative colour photostabilities of a number of the varieties favoured by Maori weavers have been established by determining changes to their reflectance spectra in the near UV and visible regions caused by exposure to ultraviolet 'blacklight' radiation from 300 nm to 400 nm. The chemical compositions of the fibre varieties were analysed and characterised by three-dimensional fluorescence spectroscopy and gas chromatography–mass spectroscopy (GC–MS) of the fibre pyrolysates. A number of coumarins were identified in the fibres, some of which contribute to the naturally occurring fluorescence from this material. These coumarins are photodegraded by exposure to UV radiation and this can account, at least in part, to the changes in the reflectance spectra.

Keywords: coumarins, *Phormium tenax*, textile fibres, photoyellowing, lignin, fluorescence

Introduction

From pre-European contact times, the Maori people of New Zealand have been plaiting the leaves of *Phormium tenax* (commonly known as New Zealand flax or harakeke) to make mats, cordage and containers, and plying the extracted fibre into threads to finger-weave into cloaks and other textiles (Te Kanawa 1994). This plant species is a monocotyledon with a plethora of genetic forms (Scheele and Walls 1994) and it is known that the Maori weavers chose to use certain varieties in preference to others depending on the purpose.

Like other ligno-cellulosic fibres, those extracted from the leaves of *P. tenax* turn yellow when they are exposed to the UV radiation in sunlight (Newman *et al.* 2005). Although the detail of the chemistry of this photoyellowing process is not fully elucidated, light-induced reactions of the lignin component of the fibres are important (Davidson 1996). Different varieties of *P. tenax* have been reported to have a wide range of lignin compositions with respect to the constituent monomeric syringyl and guaiacyl molecular units of the lignin polymer (Newman *et al.* 2005). The photostabilities of lignins from a number of plant species appear to be related to their guaiacyl contents (Chang *et al.* 2002; Ruggiero *et al.* 2005; Sarkanen *et al.* 1967).

In this work the stabilities of a number of named varieties of *P. tenax* with respect to photoyellowing have been determined to establish whether this could have been part of the traditional knowledge of Maori weavers in preferring certain varieties for their craft. In particular, varieties of *P. tenax* with a range of different syringyl to guaiacyl contents were studied (Newman *et al.* 2005). These molecular units can produce a highly fluorescent and photochemically reactive class of molecules, i.e. the coumarins (Holt *et al.* 1976; Mattoo 1956; Sardari *et al.* 2000). The possible involvement of coumarins present in the fibres of the different varieties of *P. tenax* on the appearance (whiteness/brightness) and susceptibility to light-induced yellowing of the fibres has been investigated.

Methods

Fibre samples and preparation

Fibres from three named varieties of *P. tenax*, Whareongaonga, Makaweroa and Mawaru, whose genetics have been preserved for many years, were supplied by Landcare Research, a New Zealand Crown Research Institute (Scheele and Walls 1994). The fibres were extracted by scraping off the upper and lower epidermal layers of the leaf using the traditional method used by Maori weavers (Te Kanawa 1994) and were thoroughly washed in water to remove chlorophyll and other soluble plant matter. Portions of the fibres weighing 0.2 g were cut into short lengths, 2–3 mm long, and compressed into solid, self-adhering discs with a diameter of 8 mm using a hydraulic press.

Detection of coumarins

The semi-volatile components of loose *P. tenax* fibres were released by pyrolysis at 400 °C under a stream of nitrogen gas. The pyrolysate was condensed onto a cold finger in the gas stream and dissolved in dichloromethane and 15 μL of the pyrolysate solution was analysed by combined gas chromatography and mass spectrometry (GC–MS). The mass spectrometer was set to the single ion monitoring mode in order to selectively detect the coumarin, hydroxycoumarin and methylhydroxycoumarin molecular ions of 146, 162 and 176 respectively.

Irradiation of samples

The compressed discs of fibres were exposed to ultraviolet (UV) radiation from two 6W, Philips 'blacklight' UV fluorescent lamps for periods up to 27 hours. The emission spectrum of these lamps extends from 300 to 400 nm with a maximum at 350 nm.

Three-dimensional fluorescence spectroscopy

The discs of the fibres were placed in the solid sample holder of a Hitachi 3010 spectrometer. Three-dimensional fluorescence spectra, i.e. in excitation wavelength, emission wavelength and intensity space were recorded from 280 to 520 nm in excitation and from 300 to 600 nm in emission and displayed in the form of contour 'maps'.

Reflectance and fluorescence spectra

Combined reflectance and fluorescence spectra of the samples were recorded using a Konica-Minolta CM-2500d colour meter under D65 standard illumination from wavelengths of 370 nm to 600 nm.

Results and discussion

Naturally occurring coumarins in P. tenax

The single ion chromatograms of the molecular fragments with masses of 146, 162 and 176 are shown in Figure 1. These are derived from all products in the sample which fragment to produce an ion with those masses. In the 146 ion chromatogram, the intense peak at 19.8 minutes is very probably due to coumarin and likewise in the 162 chromatogram, those peaks at 20.8 and 22.0 minutes are probably hydroxycoumarin isomers. These compounds occur naturally in a wide range of plants. They are produced from the monomeric precursors of lignin and in some cases the biosynthesis of different sets of coumarins is stimulated by wounding of the plant tissue; in other plants some coumarins can be produced in response to microbial infestation (Kai *et al.* 2006). It is believed this process is a protective response of the plant to such stresses (Sardari *et al.* 2000). A number of coumarins can also be produced photochemically by exposure of precursor molecules to UV light (Kagan 1966).

Many hydroxycoumarins and methoxycoumarins are strongly fluorescent in the blue region of the spectrum when excited by near UV light at wavelengths from 320 to 380 nm (Mattoo 1956). Because of this behaviour they have been used as fluorescent whiteners and brighteners for textiles. They are very photochemically active, however, and have been implicated in the photodegradation of many fibres, particularly wool and silk (Holt *et al.* 1976) so their application in this role has been limited. Therefore, if occurring naturally in the plant, they could be involved in the photoyellowing of lignocellulosic fibres such as those of *P. tenax*.

Fluorescence spectra and discoloration of fibres

Samples of all three varieties of *P. tenax* studied exhibit blue fluorescence emission with a maximum at a wavelength of about 450 nm and an excitation wavelength maximum at 350 nm shown as a three-dimensional fluorescence spectrum in Plate 121 (see colour plate section) for non-irradiated (a) and irradiated (b) Mawaru. This is consistent with fluorescence originating from hydroxy- and methoxy-coumarins (Mattoo 1956). Upon irradiation with UV light with a maximum at 350 nm from the 'blacklight' lamps, the fibre fluorescence decreases in the blue region of the spectrum. The effect of this will be to make the fibres appear duller and more yellow. This light-induced bleaching of the blue fluorescence is most pronounced for the Whareongaonga variety and least apparent for the Makaweroa variety.

The combined reflectance and fluorescence emission spectra under D65 illumination for the three varieties of *P. tenax* fibres given in Plate 122 (see colour plate section) show that there is a substantial decrease in the reflectance of the Whareongaonga fibres across the entire spectrum from 360 to 600 nm, indicating the formation of products absorbing in this spectral range with a maximum absorbance about 430–460 nm as shown in Plate 122a.

The combined reflectance-fluorescence spectrum of Mawaru fibres shows the formation of similarly absorbing photoproducts (Plate 122b) but in this case the decrease in reflectance is offset by the production of fluorescent species emitting at wavelengths about 410 nm (maximally excited at 340 nm). In addition, there is another species produced that emits at approximately 350 nm (excited maximally at wavelengths of 270–290 nm). The formation of these fluorescent whiteners/brighteners has the effect of reducing the apparent yellowing of *P. tenax* fibres resulting from exposure to UV light. The photoproduct emitting at wavelengths about 410 nm is consistent with hydroxyl- and methoxy- coumarins. These have been reported to be produced *in vitro* by UV irradiation of coumaric, caffeic and ferulic acid precursors of lignin (Kagan 1966). Furthermore, the UV irradiation of the coumarin molecules is known to lead to their dimerisation and a number of these dimers absorb maximally at about 280 nm and fluoresce strongly at about 320 nm (Belfield *et al.* 2003). Therefore, the observations reported here for the Mawaru variety fibres are consistent with the UV-induced formation

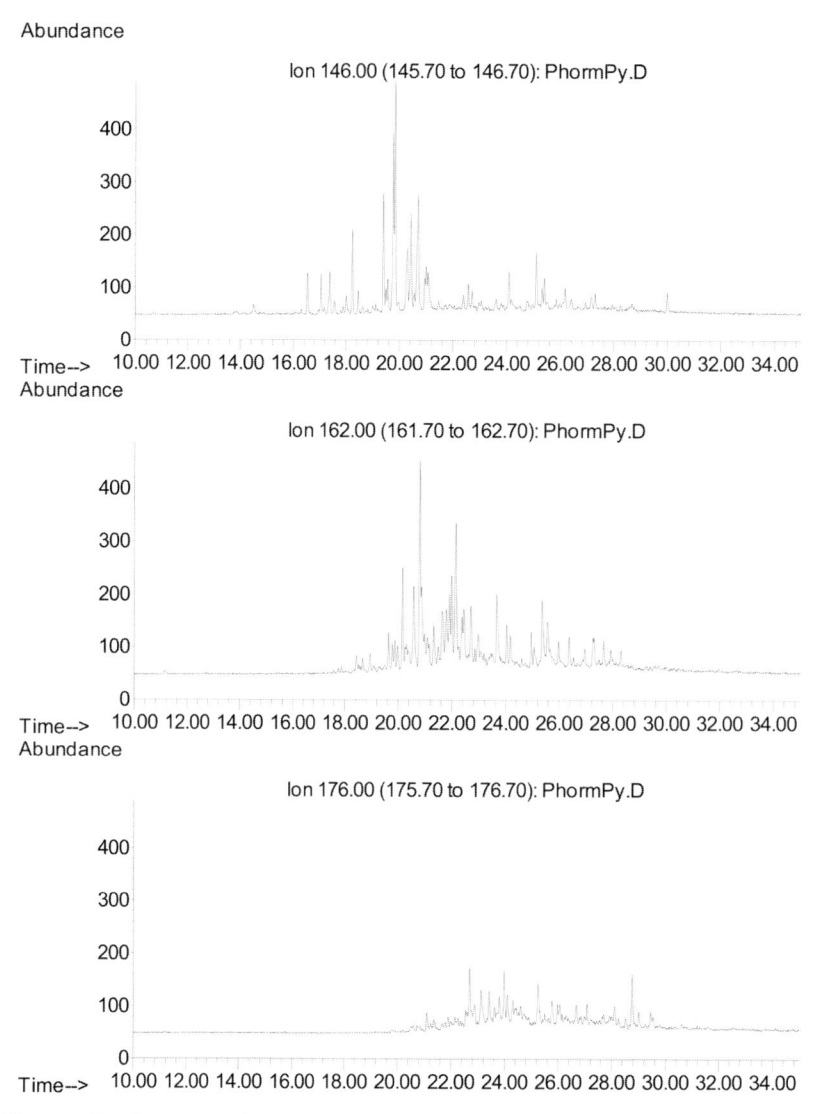

Figure 1 Gas chromatography–mass spectroscopic traces recorded for three coumarins present in the volatiles collected from the pyrolysis of *Phormium tenax* fibres. The upper panel is coumarin, the middle panel is hydroxycoumarin and the bottom panel is methylhydroxycoumarin.

of fluorescent coumarins from lignin precursors present in the fibres and their subsequent photolysis to give coumarin dimers that also fluoresce at shorter wavelengths.

The combined reflectance-fluorescence spectra of irradiated and non-irradiated Makaweroa fibres given in Plate 122c display the least changes in fluorescence and reflectance following exposure to UV light. Therefore this is the fibre that is least subject to photochemical discoloration.

Conclusion

The significant results presented in this report and the main conclusions to be drawn from them are:

- Changes in the colour and brightness of *P. tenax* fibres caused by exposure to UV radiation result in part from the coumarin-photosensitised formation of products absorbing in the blue and green regions of the spectrum and/or fluorescing in the blue.
- The greater light/colour-fastness of the Makaweroa variety on exposure to UV radiation is because there is very little photodegradation (loss) of the blue fluorescent coumarins in this variety implying that the coumarins present in this variety are relatively photostable.
- A blue fluorescing photoproduct is formed in the Mawaru variety which offsets the appearance of yellow products on exposure to UV.
- Resistance to photoyellowing may have been a factor in the choice of these varieties by Maori. Makaweroa in particular is renowned as a superb variety for weaving dress cloaks, the pinnacle of Maori traditional weaving. Mawaru has a reputation for maintaining a desirable colour in the plaiting of soft kete.

From the perspective of the museum curator and textile conservator, three-dimensional fluorescence of the fibre can be a non-invasive indicator of the variety of *P. tenax* used in the production of the woven or plaited textile. From this, the textile's susceptibility to colour change with exposure to light can be predicted.

References

Belfield, K.D., Bondar, M.V., Lui, Y. and Przhonska, O.V. (2003) 'Photophysical and photochemical properties of dimethoxycoumarin under one- and two-photon excitation', *Journal of Physical Organic Chemistry* 16: 69–78.

Chang, H.-T., Yeh, T.-F. and Chang, S.-T. (2002) Comparison of the chemical characteristic variations for photodegraded softwood and hardwood', *Polymer Degradation Stability* 77: 129–35.

Davidson, R.S. (1996) 'The photodegradation of some naturally occurring polymers', *Journal of Photochemistry and Photobiology B* 33: 3–25.

Holt, L.A., Leaver, I.H. and Milligan, B. (1976) 'Fluorescent whitening agents. Part VIII: The photochemical behaviour of coumarin and stilbene whiteners in polymer films and in surface whitened wool', *Textile Research Journal* 46: 539–44.

Kagan, J. (1966) 'The photochemical conversion of caffeic acid to esculetin: a model for the synthesis of coumarins *in vivo*', *Journal of the American Chemical Society* 88(11): 2617–18.

Kai, K., Shimizi, B., Mizutani, M., Watanabe, K. and Sakata, K. (2006) 'Accumulation of coumarins in *Arabadopsis thaliana*', *Phytochemistry* 67: 379–86.

Mattoo, B.N. (1956) 'Absorption and fluorescence spectra of coumarins', *Transactions of the Faraday Society* 52: 1184–94.

Newman, R., Tauwhare, S.E.K., Scheele, S. and Te Kanawa, R. (2005) 'Leaf-fibre lignins of *Phormium* varieties compared by solid-state NMR spectroscopy', *Holzforschung* 59: 147–52.

Ruggiero, R., Machado, A.E.H., Gardrat, C., Hoareua, W., Gelier, S., Siegmund, B. and Castellan, A. (2005) 'Photodegradation of sugar cane bagasse acidolysis lignins', *Journal of Photochemistry and Photobiology A* 173: 150–55.

Sardari, S., Nishibe, S. and Daneshtalab, M. (2000) 'Coumarins, the bioactive structures with antifungal property', *Studies in Natural Product Chemistry* 3: 335–93.

Sarkanen, K.V., Chang, H.-M. and Allen, G.G. (1967) 'Species variation in lignins III. Hardwood lignins', *Tappi* 50: 587–90.

Scheele, S. and Walls, G.Y. (1994) *Harakeke. The Rene Orchiston Collection*. Lincoln, New Zealand: Manaaki Whenua Press.

Te Kanawa, D. (1994) *Weaving a Kakahu*. Wellington: Bridget Williams Books.

The authors

- Gerald Smith is the Director of the Heritage Materials Science programme in the School of Chemical and Physical Sciences at Victoria University of Wellington. This programme is about the identification and understanding of the materials that make up objects which are part of our cultural heritage and the means to preserve them. His research speciality is the investigation of the chemistry responsible for the degradation of organic materials of cultural significance such as textiles, wood and natural dyes. A particular research interest is the dyes used to decorate *Phormium tenax* fibres used in Maori weaving that are susceptible to deterioration and fading.
- Roderick J. Weston and Stephen E. K. Tauwhare work for Industrial Research Limited, Lower Hutt, New Zealand.
- Sue Scheele is employed by Landcare Research, Lincoln, New Zealand.
- Raukura Chadwick and Ngaire Konese were research students in the School of Chemical and Physical Sciences, Victoria University of Wellington.

Address

Corresponding author: Gerald J. Smith, Victoria University of Wellington, PO Box 600, Wellington, New Zealand (Gerald.Smith@vuw.ac.uk)